Striking Through the Masks

Striking Through

MORTON MARCUS

the Masks

A Literary Memoir

CAPITOLA BOOKS
Santa Cruz, California

"Ray Carver" first appeared in a truncated form under the title "All-American Nightmares" in *Remembering Ray: A Composite Biography of Raymond Carver* (Santa Barbara, CA: Capra, 1993, pp. 53–67), edited by William L. Stull and Maureen Carroll; and in a different, almost complete form under the title "Remembering Ray: A Ramble" in *Quarry West* 31.

"Bill Everson" appeared in an earlier form under the title "Moments, Musings & the Great Calling" in *Quarry West* 32.

"Czeslaw Milosz" and "Milosz & Popa" first appeared in a slightly different form as a single article entitled "Milosz in Memory" in *METRO* newspapers (2004).

"Al Young" appeared in a slightly different form entitled "Al Young Laureate" in *METRO* newspapers (2005).

"Morton Marcus," a scattering of literary reminiscences about the literary growth of the poet, some of which appear in this book, were first published in *Contemporary Authors,* Vol. 214 (Farmington Hills, MI: Gale, 2004, pp. 52–71).

"The 1999 Santa Cruz High School Commencement Address" originally appeared in *The Santa Cruz Sentinel* (1999)

Special thanks to Gerard Malanga for graciously allowing us to use his archival photographs of Robert Bly, Andrei Codrescu, George Hitchcock, and Charles Simic. And special thanks, as always, to my daughter Jana, whose technical assistance and help in all areas, which she gave unstintingly, took endless hours from her own pursuits.

Capitola Book Company
Capitola, California
www.capitolabook.com

Design: Mark Stuart Ong, Side By Side Studios, San Francisco, California

Printed in U.S.A. by Edwards Brothers

FIRST EDITION

10 9 8 7 6 5 4 3 2 1

Books by Morton Marcus

Origins (Kayak, 1969)

Where the Oceans Cover Us (Capra, 1972)

The Santa Cruz Mountain Poems (Capra, 1972; Capitola Books, 1992)

The Armies Encamped in the Fields Beyond the Unfinished Avenues: Prose Poems (Jazz Press, 1977)

Big Winds, Glass Mornings, Shadows Cast By Stars: Poems, 1972–1980 (Jazz Press, 1980)

The Brezhnev Memo (novel; Dell/Delacorte, 1981)

Pages from a Scrapbook of Immigrants (Coffee House, 1988)

When People Could Fly: Prose Poems (Hanging Loose, 1997)

Moments Without Names: New & Selected Prose Poems (White Pine Press, 2002)

Shouting Down the Silence: Verse Poems 1988–2001 (Creative Arts Book Company, 2002)

Pursuing the Dream Bone: New Prose Poems (Quale Press, 2007)

EDITOR

In A Dybbuk's Raincoat: The Collected Poems of Bert Meyers, with Daniel Meyers (University of New Mexico Press, 2007)

for
the children

All visible objects, man, are but pasteboard masks. But in each event—in the living act, the undoubted deed—there, some unknown but still reasoning thing puts forth the mouldings of its features from behind the unreasoning mask. If man will strike, strike through the mask! How can the prisoner reach outside except by thrusting through the wall?

Herman Melville, *Moby Dick*

Whoever wishes to get rid of the violent prejudice of custom . . . let him rip off that mask, return matters to truth and reason, and—although at first he will think his judgment topsy-turvy—he will achieve a much clearer sense of things.

Michel de Montaigne, "On Custom"

Rejoice with me. I feel my face
shining behind its bones as it did
before my parents were born.
How can I describe the sensation
of sinking through one identity
after another, of endlessly falling
from one mask to the next,
my face collapsing and reappearing,
each time different yet the same.
Some faces I recognize, others
I've never seen, or have forgotten,
the one and the many, all of them
drifting off like nodes of light
among all the other nodes scattering
like fireflies throughout the universe.

Morton Marcus, *The Eight Ecstasies of Yaeko Iwasaki*

"Fear not, and do right."

Leo Hecker

Friends, I do love you, it's true.
And I hope I'm lucky enough, privileged enough,
to live on and bear witness.
Believe me, I'll only say the most
glorious things about you and our time here!
For the survivor there has to be something
to look forward to. Growing old,
losing everything and everybody.

Raymond Carver, "In 2020"

Contents

PART TWO

Outward Bound

All my life I have in one way or another attempted to strike through the whale-like masks of the anonymous, the hidden, in many cases, the unknowable. I have tried to bring to light from behind those masks what hides out of shame or stealth in the dark places of our psyches.

Most of all I have tried to strike through the masks of my own obfuscations in search of a simplicity by which I could live my life with equanimity and dignity, not only among my fellow humans, but as a speck of light glinting for an instant in the ocean of the universe.

With a pen as my harpoon, I lanced the waters of experience and dream, at times pinioning and hauling from the deep strange creatures with accusing eyes and bloody teeth. Now I set out for possibly the last time, voyaging on the waters of memory and half-remembered desires.

Prologue

Whether we admit it or not, we make of memory a picture of how we want to remember ourselves and how we want others to see us, coloring it with our vanities as well as our faulty perceptions. With those notions in mind, I have to qualify the account of my life that follows, for I do not profess my memories to be true or accurate. They merely record the way I saw things, or, more to the point, the way I remember seeing things. To lessen these imperfections, I have tried to avoid self-aggrandizement, although it may not always seem that way. There is little I can do about that: events are events, and a person's part in them should be reported as honestly as possible, even if the teller looms large in the telling.

What makes the situation even more problematic is that my attitudes and goals are products of the twentieth century. My first sixty-four years were spent in the horrors and hopes of that century, and I grew to manhood unwittingly following the notions and values of the culture that surrounded me. From radio and film I learned of my nation's professed ideals of justice, the sacredness of individuality, and my obligation to exercise social responsibility for the good of my fellow humans no matter what the consequences, none of which, I discovered as I grew to adulthood, the powers that be really wanted me or anyone else to pursue. I learned about heroic action from Captain Marvel, Superman, John Wayne, Muhammad Ali, and Jackie Robinson, and about love from Frank Sinatra, Frankie Laine, Vic Damone and Tony Martin, and later from Buddy Holly, Elvis Presley, Roy Orbison, and the Beatles. And I learned about the mysteries of the world and the enigmas of the human condition from *Classic Comics* and books in general in the heady atmosphere of art and thought that permeated every aspect of the popular culture of my youth, a popular culture that has all but disappeared.

Although I didn't realize it, that whole complex of learning how to think and behave was always changing. The acceleration of those changes toward the end of the century, with the discoveries of science and the advances in technology, has also colored and possibly distorted my memories. The behavioral psychology I learned in college, which refused to accept any but provable facts regarding the functions of the brain, has given way to a more humanistic psychology that at times borders on mysticism and "higher

modes of consciousness." The sacredness of property, the "territorial imperative" of popular midcentury Cold War anthropological theory, has given
way to notions of communal sharing and dissolved borders. Geology texts,
which taught me the concept of continental drift, where continents wandered through the seas, gave way to new books that proposed a theory of
tectonic plates overlapping or grinding against one another to explain
movements of the earth's crust, especially earthquakes. Even Einstein's theory of relativity, so hard for the layman to understand for most of the century, was undermined, as it turned out it had been since the 1930s, by quantum mechanics. And the phrase "global warming," along with the concept
that defined it, wasn't coined until I was middle-aged.

Meanwhile, the Bomb blossomed like a cancerous flower in everyone's
mind, Nazism and the Cold War haunted everyone's dreams, and when they
were gone, capitalism ran wild, ransacking the planet. Not unrelated to capitalism's supremacy, the old tribal, racial, and religious hatreds, which had
been suppressed in the main by the century's earlier conflicts, returned
more virulently than ever. So did a fierce fundamentalism in most of the
planet's evangelizing religions. Of seemingly lesser importance, film gave
way to videos and DVDs, radio gave way to television, mimeograph machines to Xeroxes, typewriters to computers. And all these changes engendered a change in values and lifestyles by the end of the century that
brought with them a different sense of justice and individual behavior.

In light of the above, how can my memories hold anything but nostalgia
for the readers of my generation and provide even a modicum of interest for
the new generation and the generations that will follow it? Such questions
have caused my pen to hover uncertainly above these pages more than once.
As they made me pause, however, I recognized that everyone has a unique
story to tell, and if there is nothing exceptional about my life, it is unique in
that it is like no one else's.

With those thoughts as guide, I formulated a structure for these memories based on incidents that gave rise to metaphysical assumptions and ethical decisions that shaped the way I have tried to live my life. At the same
time, I realized that many of the anecdotes revealed why I became a writer
as well as determined what kind of writer I would be and what I would write
about. A number of the anecdotes involved friends or acquaintances who
became famous during the latter part of the twentieth century, and since
these personages were important to my development as an individual and a
writer, I decided to include the events in which they figured as well as portraits of them I had written over the years—portraits which in many cases
show them in moments when they had set aside their public masks.

In the end, I concluded that the value these and other such memories
have is to provide a record of how one person grew and flourished in his

times and to offer another perspective on how an ordinary person understood his world and life in general.

All these different elements have been woven like ghostly figures into the tapestry of the times in which they occurred so that in many ways this volume is a personal, literary, social, and political history of the last two-thirds of the twentieth century, at least as far as I experienced it. If anyone mentioned in these pages feels slighted or abused, I can only say that such was not my intention. I only wanted to get events on paper as I was involved in them and interpreted them—as faulty and wrong-headed as my conclusions at times may have been.

What follows, then, is the story of a little boy without a father, whose mother, for all intents and purposes, abandoned him, and it integrates the writing life with the personal life, which, as far as the old man who was once that little boy is concerned, are inseparable. It is a story that begins eons ago, and I'm sure has been repeated one way or another throughout history by countless people. In this little boy's case, it begins in his imagined memories of windswept villages in western Russia and the Ukraine centuries before he was born, villages burning on hot summer nights where the roar of flames was punctuated by the screams of women and the death cries of helpless men. The man who was that boy knows this image is not part of his story and will not be included in the pages of this book. But he also knows it is the picture that hovers like a shadow behind all the book's events and is what the boy, at a young age, may only have imagined but instinctively understood he must never forget.

PART 1

We spend the first half of life looking inward . . .
—Novalis

BOOK ONE

CHILDHOOD

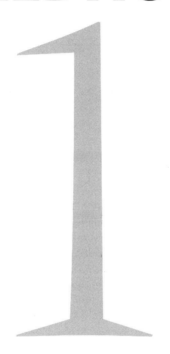

CHAPTER 1

First Memories

Awareness arrives as I run in circles in front of the apartment house on Eastern Parkway. Not a jolt or a shock. Suddenly I am *me*. That's the great revelation. I am looking down at my brown Buster Brown shoes, the pavement spinning like a carousel, and watching my knees pump up and down under my tan short pants like mallets inside a piano, although I won't know about carousels or the inside of pianos for a while yet. At this moment, I am fascinated to discover *my self* and the environment revolving around me. It is Brooklyn, autumn, 1941. I've been on the planet for five years, but I have not been conscious of that fact, conscious of myself, until this moment. In the years to come I will wonder about this instant again and again and liken it to Superman or Captain Marvel, with all their gaudy colors, sweeping into the real world in mid-flight from the cover of a comic book. Someone flipped a switch and turned on my mind and maybe the daylight, the trees, the five-story apartment building I'm running dizzily in front of, as well as the boulevard on my right and the park beyond it.

1941 was a seminal year for me in several ways, and two events in particular have remained vivid in my memory since then. The first involved my uncle Abe. He was short and pudgy and always wore dark suits and ties and gold-rimmed glasses. He was kindly and doted on me, but the most complete memory I have of him is that we would shave together every morning, he staring in the steamy bathroom mirror and me next to him, standing on a chair, with the empty razor he had bought me sliding over my cheeks through the shaving cream he had taught me how to slather on my face.

The second memory is not such a happy one. The German janitor of the apartment house in which I lived—or the "super," as we

At 7, somewhere on the east coast, 1943

4

called him—had a blond, blue-eyed, ten-year-old son. This son, and the gang of five or six kids who always followed him, stopped me one day, dragged me to the basement, undid my pants, and, pointing at my circumcised penis, yelled, "Jew, Jew, Jew," jumping on top of me and beating me bloody. Not only was this incident traumatic, but it had several far-reaching effects. It showed me that as a young boy alone, I was a natural victim. Not that I hadn't been beaten up before. I had, many times. But this beating was different. It made me aware that I was an outsider. I didn't have a father like the other boys, and my Jewishness seemed stamped on me like a hot coin searing its image into the center of my forehead. In the years to come I would redefine this otherness as having less to do with my Jewish background than with my Slavic roots. I wasn't any kind of Jew, I was an Ashkenazi Jew—a Jew from Eastern Europe—and therein, I would come to believe, lay the difference between me and other "Americans."

There is part of this incident I have not told. When the super's son first grabbed me and said, "Jew, come here," I had broken away from him and run up to my apartment on the fifth floor and through hysterical tears told my mother what was happening. She immediately turned me around and propelled me out the door, saying that a man should fight his own battles. Her reaction was certainly terrifying to me at the time, but it instilled in me the concept that I should stand up for myself; that, as she also said, "A man should never hide behind a woman's skirts."

Years later I graphically described the Eastern Parkway incident in the poem, "The New Apartment House," in my book *Pages from a Scrapbook of Immigrants*. I talk about it as a loss of innocence similar to Adam's expulsion from Eden.

The New Apartment House

There is a war somewhere, and his father is gone,
but here, now, there are the halls and stairs
of the new apartment house. The lobby floor
is a maroon and white mosaic garden, its tiles
reminiscent of his mother's Persian rug.
But the tiles are cracked and scarred,
the floor pocked with gaps. Maroon runners,
resembling forest paths, lead the boy
past urns and potted plants to an elevator
big and bronze as a bank door, but as slow
as a bent grandma lowering herself into a chair.
He watches the gilt dial limp endlessly
from right to left, as if marking the sun's progress

across the sky, and when the door rolls back,
out waddles that wart-faced witch
Mrs. Solomon muttering curses about the Evil Eye;
or, like the black hull of a pirate ship,
a baby carriage pushes its prow into the hall.
The boy prefers to climb the stairs to the apartment
where he lives with his mother and uncle,
although he spends his days near the lobby plants,
flying the airplane at the end of his arm,
marching his soldiers from cigar box forts,
or watching the German janitor limp and mutter
as he mops the hall or drags ash cans full of cinders
from the darkness beyond the basement door.
At times, the boy examines marbles from his pouch
just like a jeweler; or he lifts one to the light
as though he could see the inner workings of a world in it
if he looked close enough and held his breath.

Sometimes he prowls the halls and stairwells,
lighted only by grime gray windows on each floor,
and plays "find the treasure" or "surprise the gnome."
Or he trails the older boys, all nine and ten,
who rush past to the cellar in a loose-knit gang,
or push him in the chest and tell him, "Blow!"
One day in early summer, the janitor's blond-haired son,
with the other boys peering from behind his back,
grabs the boy's arm and says, "Jew, come here!"
The boy shakes free and runs upstairs,
where his mother, cradling his face in her palms,
tells him that "a man can't hide behind a woman's skirts,"
and holds him close before she pushes him out the door.
Wrestled to the floor, he is carried, kicking,
to the basement, where cinders crunch underfoot
and the fiery furnace god, now cool and somber,
shudders only an occasional breath
of gases and ashes, vinegar and bits of bone.
Here the boy is thrown to the floor,
unbuttoned and exposed to all those eyes
looking down at him. The janitor's son
points and kicks the breath from his chest.
"Jew!" he shouts again and again,
as he straddles the boy's ribs
and beats him in the face with his fists.

All the while, the boy's mother stands
weeping behind the apartment door.
But the boy won't learn of that for years.
When he rises and staggers from the cellar,
all he will know is the laughter behind him
as he wanders through the once-familiar halls.

Both incidents occurred after the day I experienced my sudden awakening to consciousness. Later I would remember fragments from that year and the years before it. But even that afternoon in 1941, there were glints and glimmers of other memories: Somehow I understood that the world hadn't begun with my birth; I knew the people around me as well as the apartment building and neighborhood where I lived; I knew there were reasons for things being as they were that went back years before I was born—reasons that made the uncle I shaved with every morning leave one day, taking his gold-rimmed glasses and dark brown suit with him, never to return. And there was a reason that the super's son hated me as, probably, his father did, a hatred brought like an heirloom from faraway Germany, a country whose name I would become more and more aware of as the days and years wore on. All those glimmers, and the ones that fell by the thousands around me unnoticed like sunlit dust motes, had brought me to that day on Eastern Parkway and would accompany me into the future.

CHAPTER 2

Family

Throughout history, families have fled from backgrounds of massacre and persecution. One of them was mine. My grandmother's family was from Vilna, Lithuania, then part of Russia. They dealt in oil and grain and "owned a mill on the river." If not well-to-do, they had enough money to send my grandmother to the *gymnasium*. But she married beneath her: a peasant from the Ukraine. He was a hard man, a laborer with restless energy—with that sense of dreaming, no matter how material or self-serving it may be, that inspires humans to give up all they know and either set out for a better life or journey just to see what's on the other side of the ocean.

My grandparents had five children—David, Bertha, Abe, Frankie, Rachel (my mother), and, later, when they were settled in the United States, the baby of the family, Ike, the only one before me to earn a college education.

The family's immigration was well planned, almost meticulously so. My grandfather came over to the United States in 1908 and settled in the lower east side of New York City where he worked day and night sewing knee pants and earning enough money to bring over David and Bertha three years later. Then the three of them worked together day and night until they had made passage money to bring over my mother, her two brothers, and my grandmother in 1914, a month before the outbreak of World War I.

The family settled first in the Brownsville section of Brooklyn and later in a house on Avenue B, where my grandfather had a cow, a goat, chickens, and a horse. He sold eggs and milk in the neighborhood and dabbled in real estate. David, who had been chosen to be a scholar and a rabbi in the old country, a kindly, docile man, helped my grandfather and abandoned his dreams of a scholar's life early. Bertha grew into a hefty, physically powerful woman. She—both hardheaded and single minded—fought with her father and married a man half her size to get out of the house when she was sixteen. Abe and Frankie got into mischief early and soon were involved in the gang life of Avenue B. In time, Abe became a numbers runner for, and later a friend and advisor to, the notorious Abe Reles (aka Kid Twist), who he may have known from his early years in Brownsville. When Reles joined Murder Incorporated, he supposedly "gave" my uncle Abe control of Brownsville.

Frankie, purported to have a tinderbox temper, was Abe's enforcer.

Is this true, or is it family myth? The story goes that there were only two killings in Brownsville during the eight years my uncle Abe controlled the section. Supposedly, he earned millions in the numbers racket, had two hundred runners selling tickets, paid the cops and judges in the area, and had interests in two or three restaurants. The family insists he wasn't a gangster but a gambler, while others, taking the middle road, said he was a racketeer.

What is fact is that on September 24, 1941, he was found slumped in his car with two bullets in the back of his head. His killing made headlines in several New York newspapers for a number of days and was the subject of several stories in the *New York Times*. All the stories were quick to point out that since July a subpoena had been out on him to be interviewed by the New York State Crime Commission headed by the future governor of New York, Thomas Dewey. What is also fact is that my uncle's money was never found. Frankie, realizing a contract out on Abe must have marked him as well, disappeared. The

Uncle Abe, Brooklyn, 1932

day after he left, someone called my mother and said if anyone tried to find out about or avenge Abe's murder, the whole family would be killed, "starting with the kids." The panic this caused made everyone vow to forget Abe, an undertaking that was never really accomplished and was dealt with by not mentioning his name at family gatherings or in front of the children.

It was the great family tragedy. Abe was loved by everyone and considered the head of the family after my grandfather's death in 1930, and the mention of his name would send my mother and Aunt Bertha into hysterical tears for years to come. But the newspaper headlines were also a public humiliation, and my relatives quietly changed the family name from Bebchick to Balzac a few weeks after the shooting.

Although I was only five years old when all this happened, I would never forget Uncle Abe. He haunted my dreams, and years later I wrote a moderately long poem about him, identifying him with his biblical namesake, Abraham, who God commanded to sacrifice his son. In the last section of the poem, I speculate how Abe's life might have turned out in a different time:

Who were you, Uncle? The newspapers
say one thing, the family another.
Did family tradition lead you to the rackets,
some fly speck in your chromosomes
that swarms through me? In another time
would you have followed the life of the mind
toward which your gentle eyes inclined?
Or did you pursue the same pragmatic hopes,
stripped of morality, which drove the old man
from the snows of southern Russia
to the tenements of New York?

Questions addressed to the wind
come back on the wind unanswered,
and the only words anyone remembers
you saying—"If you want something
from someone, kiss his ass.
When he wants something from you,
he'll kiss yours"—tell nothing,
provide only a momentary glimpse of you,
and, ironically, like your life and fortune
and the circumstances of your unsolved death,
by balancing both phrases, rub themselves out.

In time the family accepted your death
as a corrupted New World version
of your biblical namesake's life,
where the angel sent by God arrived too late,
and where you were son and father both—
father to your shortlived youth.
There was also the fear,
an almost palpable foreboding,
that whoever did the killing
would come back to annihilate
brother, nephew, aunt—the entire family,
one by one—like an avenging angel
whose mission no one could comprehend.
As a result, the family agreed
that no one would speak your name
or seek the ones responsible for your death,
hoping that would end it, and it did.

Now you are a picture in a scrapbook—
those brooding eyes, that relentless stare.

And when a nephew or a grandchild
comes upon your fading photograph,
you are identified as someone who died young
and left no son to intercede for him.

from "Uncle Abe"

While all this turmoil was going on, my mother had grown into an exceptionally beautiful woman, a woman with movie-star good looks. Men and women would stop her on the street and ask for her autograph. She was a willful girl, determined to make it out of Brooklyn into the glamorous life of money and fast living across the river in Manhattan. Dropping out of school in the fourth grade, she learned early that her beauty could be the magic key that would open all the doors she wanted to walk through. She never liked men, really; they were to be used: they were the means to an end—money and a good address.

By the time Abe was murdered, my mother was thirty-four years old and may have already been married three times—it's still unclear how many marriages she had—and had been separated from my father, husband number three, for two years. He was also a Russian Jewish immigrant, and he had risen to become one of the top manufacturers in the garment industry in New York. If he had given her enough heartache for her to leave him, he had also given her two of her dreams as well—the move from Brooklyn to Manhattan and an apartment in an exclusive neighborhood, first on Eighty-sixth Street near Central Park and second overlooking the park at the ritzy Century Apartments on Sixty-second Street and Central Park West.

My mother, New York,
early 1940s

But like so many immigrants, my mother's material dreams made her feel obligated to take care of the less fortunate members of the family. She was known not only to pay medical bills for her sister and brothers and their children, but to have her chauffeur drive her nephew, Leo, Bertha's son, in her cream-colored Cord to play baseball in Prospect Park. She was also known to take her jewels and furs off in her parents' old house on Avenue B and get down on her hands

2¢

DAILY NEWS

Copr. 1941 by News Syndicate, Inc. NEW YORK'S PICTURE NEWSPAPER Trade Mark Reg. U. S. Pat. Off.

2¢

Vol. 23. No. 79   New York, Thursday, September 25, 1941★   68 Main + 16 Brooklyn + 8 Queens Pages   2 Cents IN CITY LIMITS | 3 CENTS Elsewhere

MARTIAL LAW RULES PARIS, VICHY REPORT

Story on Page 3

(NEWS foto)

Bullets For Breakfast

The Mobster Died at Dawn

A detective looks over the corpse that was Abe Bebchick, crap-shooting mobster, in front of 675 Empire Boulevard, near Albany Ave., Brooklyn. Bebchick was slain at dawn yesterday by two bullets behind his left ear. Special Prosecutor Amen says Bebchick may have been murdered to forestall exposure of a tie-up between police and policy racketeers. District Attorney O'Dwyer labeled Bebchick a cheap punk who was trying to muscle in on a dice games combine. Police said Bebchick had begun to operate as Brownsville's "policy king" and suggested he may have been exterminated by rivals.

Story on page 4.

New York World-Telegram

Local Forecast: Local showers tonight and tomorrow; moderately warm tonight; cooler tomorrow night; fair with moderate temperatures Saturday.

Copyright 1941, by New York World-Telegram Corporation. All rights reserved

VOL. 74—NO. 3 — IN TWO SECTIONS—SECTION ONE   NEW YORK, THURSDAY, SEPTEMBER 25, 1941.   Entered as second class matter, Post Office, New York, N. Y.

7TH SPORTS
Final Stock Tables
Latest Racing on Page 32.

PRICE THREE CENTS

GAMBLER SLAIN TO SEAL LIPS, AMEN HINTS; PAID 20 COPS

LATEST BASEBALL RESULTS

Dodgers	1
Braves	0
Cardinals	0
Pirates	0
White and Wyatt. Butcher and Lopat.	

U. S. Drafting Profits Bill

Morgenthau Believes Big Business Will Go Along

By the United Press

WASHINGTON, Sept. 25.—Secretary of the Treasury Morgenthau, asserting that the profit motive must be eliminated from the nation's defense effort, told a press conference today that Treasury experts had started drafting a bill to carry out his plan to limit corporation profits to 6 per cent for the duration of the emergency.

Mr. Morgenthau expressed himself as not sure whether big business believes his plan is practicable or not.

Mr. Morgenthau said he saw no reason for some individuals and corporations to be allowed to make huge profits from the war when hundreds of thousands of Americans were serving in the armed forces for a day and while many other sections of the American population are making sacrifices.

He recalled that in the last war ...

Tanker and Collier in Collision

ROBERT. HO

Parallel Seen To Murder Of Rosenthal

Negotiations for Surrender Of Policy Slip Racketeer Revealed by Prosecutor

John Harlan Amen, special prosecutor investigating the possible connection of certain members of the police force with the policy slip racket, declared today there "was proof that more than a score of patrolmen had been taking protection money from the murdered Abe Bebchick."

Following "definite substantiation" of this long suspected tieup, Mr. Amen immediately convened two extraordinary grand juries and called "plainclothes men, a Brooklyn lawyer and other witnesses" to testify about the possibility of "official corruption."

The scope of the inquiry was revealed by Edwin L. Rea, administrative assistant to Mr. Amen, who admitted that 15 policemen were to testify. Among them were superiors, captains, lieutenants and sergeants, in addition to patrolmen.

Mr. Amen hinted that the killing of Bebchick might parallel the Herman Rosenthal murder, which rocked the New York underworld and other circles 29 years ago. Police Lieut. Charles Becker was sent to the chair for picking Gyp the Blood and three other gunmen on the

---

The New York Times.

"All the News That's Fit to Print."

Copyright, 1941, by The New York Times Company.

VOL. XCI...No. 30,562.   NEW YORK, SATURDAY, SEPTEMBER 27, 1941.   THREE CENTS

LATE CITY EDITION
Fair and today. Tomorrow mostly cloudy and moderate cool. Temperatures Yesterday—Max., 77; Min., 62

DEFENSE SUPPLY FACES BIG SHIFT IN NELSON PLAN

Wide Allocations of Raw Materials to Be Tried First on Farm Implements

COUNTIES BREAK DOWN

Realistic Treatment of the Cartel System, Nelson's Aide, Is Urged by SPAB Chief at Home Hearing

By the Associated Press
WASHINGTON, Sept. 26.—...

'Break' Due in 'Policy-King' Murder; Police Graft Angle Is Being Pressed

Part-Time Chauffeur of Bebchick Tells of 2 Well-Dressed Men Who Drove Off With Him—8 Policemen Questioned by Amen

MAIL BAGS LINKED TO NO-WAR GROUPS ARE INVESTIGATED

Government Agents Examine Undelivered Envelopes With...

JAPAN SAYS AXIS SEEKS NEW ORDER BUT ALSO PEACE

Foreign Minister Holds Pact Permits Freedom in Tokyo

CRIMEA LAND DRIVE BLOCKED, NAZIS POUR IN PARACHUTISTS; DRIVEN BACK AT LENINGRAD

RUSSIANS ATTACK

Smash at Germans on Perekop Isthmus and Gain at Odessa

FIERCE CLASHES IN NORTH

Reds Report 7-Mile Advance in Leningrad Area—Nazis Claim 574,000 Prisoners

By DANIEL T. BRIGHAM

'Break' Due in 'Policy-King' Murder; Police Graft Angle Is Being Pressed

Part-Time Chauffeur of Bebchick Tells of 2 Well-Dressed Men Who Drove Off With Him—8 Policemen Questioned by Amen

Abe Bebchick, Brooklyn "policy king," mysteriously slain Wednesday while being sought as the alleged payer of $3,000 a week to police for gambling protection, was met beside his parked car by two well-dressed men and drove away with them less than four hours before his body was found, according to a story related yesterday to police by Bebchick's part-time chauffeur, described only as "Zoo."

Meanwhile, Special Prosecutor John Harlan Amen, who had uncovered proof of payments to police to protect Bebchick's policy bank, which had a "take" of $8,000 a day, questioned eight policemen, including two captains and four sergeants, before his extraordinary grand juries investigating official corruption.

Mr. Amen denied that the "payoff" man for police in Bebchick's racket was in custody, but he admitted that what appeared to be an important "break" concerning the official corruption phase of the case was imminent.

It was learned that Mr. Amen had started an investigation of police assigned to his inquiry because of their report that they were unable to locate Bebchick for the last few months, although other policemen have asserted that Bebchick had been seen daily in his usual haunts.

Detectives investigating the murder questioned "Zoo" at the Empire Boulevard station in Brooklyn, a short distance from where Bebchick's body was found slumped in a coupe with two bullet wounds in the back of his head, a manner of death usually associated with underworld "ride" slayings.

The witness, said by police to have been employed by Bebchick from time to time as a chauffeur, depending on the nature of the gambler's business, allegedly told police that he worked for Bebchick on Tuesday night and that at 1:30 A. M., Wednesday, they left a Brooklyn restaurant at Utica Avenue and Eastern Parkway and went across the street to Bebchick's parked car. Two young, well-dressed men stepped up, flanked Bebchick and spoke quickly to him and then all three got into the car and drove away, "Zoo" is reported to have said.

Police have approached the murder on the theory that Bebchick was the victim of a combined hold-

Continued on Page Eighteen

HIGH ASSESSMENT DENIED BY MAYOR

Lowered by Several Millions, He Asserts—Newsography Is Lloyd Church Comment

My mother and father,
Atlantic City, 1934

and knees and scrub the floors. After my grandfather died, she and my uncle Ike—who had been born in Brooklyn in 1922—would take care of my grandmother, a gentle soul who never learned English.

THE EARLY YEARS

It was into this tumultuous milieu that I was born in 1936. I was to see my father only twice in my life, and I vaguely remember visiting his mother, my paternal grandmother, and her sister a few times. I recall that my paternal grandmother was a tall woman, rather reserved if not severe, and she and her sister were playing cards. That is a telltale memory, since my father was a compulsive gambler who lost several fortunes and his business to cards. That addiction and his constant womanizing, my mother said, were two of the reasons she left him. The third was his jealousy of me. He wanted her complete attention, and he also wanted to parade her in all her beauty in front of his friends, associates and the public in general on any number of social occasions. But even though I had an English "nanny," my mother would not stop fawning over me, the boy who was to be her only child. When she left my father, the high times came to an end. We moved to Brooklyn for a time, to another good address, on Eastern Parkway, and Abe, who was a bachelor, moved in with us (he had told my aunt Bertha, with what seems in hindsight a soothsayer's prescience, that he and Frankie would never marry because they didn't want to leave young widows behind).

In New York, 1936

My troubled youth began years before I shaved with my uncle, years before the day on Eastern Parkway when I became aware of my five-year-old self as a conscious being. My beautiful mother had a life to live, a life that promised wealth and excitement, and a little boy was a barrier to such aspirations. Therefore, by 1940 she had already put me in several boarding schools in Florida while we were there on vacations, and after Abe's death in 1941, she sent me throughout my childhood to thirteen different boarding schools for neglected or emotionally troubled children. In fact, from the time I was three years old to the time I was twenty-one, I lived at home only four autumns and winters—and every summer, with two exceptions, my mother sent me away to camp until I was a teenager.

The schools were similar to the ones immortalized by Charles Dickens in the nineteenth century, and when I first read *Oliver Twist*, I seemed to recognize many of the places I'd spent my early years. Not that I needed to read great literature; such films as *Tom Brown's School Days* and *David Copperfield* showed me my life on film, so that I accepted my lot as being the normal course of every child's experience. I'm not only talking about the beatings and other cruelties I suffered at the hands of teachers and fellow students, but also the special sadistic touches, such as the one I endured at a school my mother sent me to when I was five.

It was a month or two after my uncle was murdered, and I remember the school was near Church Avenue in Brooklyn. Of the school itself, I only remember the dining hall, a large room laid out with a number of long tables and benches. The surrounding walls were decorated with a continuous mural that depicted the Pilgrims receiving gifts of food from the Indians. The mural was painted in autumnal tones of orange and brown. My first night at the school, I sat under those images of Thanksgiving, sniffling and weeping for my mother, the new boy among forty or fifty curious children. At that time, I refused to eat. I don't know why, but I think that may have been the reason my mother decided to send me to the school. I remember her giving the teachers firm instructions to be sure I ate. I imagine the teachers tried to cajole me into eating at first, then threatened, and finally ran out of patience. But no matter what they did, I sat there, crying for my mother, thrashing my head from side to side when they tried to feed me, and clamping my jaws shut in the face of all entreaties. Then the dining room was empty. I could hear children shouting and playing in a distant part of the school, and I was alone in the big room with the mural high overhead and a teacher standing on either side of me. "You're gonna eat," one of them said, and then he grabbed me by the nose, wrenched open my jaws, and the other one force fed me the entire meal. I wriggled and fought against them and finally vomited what I had eaten onto the table. They were unfazed, handed me a soupspoon, forced me to scoop my vomit onto a tray and carry it into the kitchen. There they sat me in front of the tray and for several hours slapped my head and face and twisted my arm until I had eaten every morsel of that gruel-like mess. How long I would have had to endure such treatment, I'll never know. Within a week I contracted chicken pox, and then over the next two months, mumps and measles. Informed of all this, my mother took me out of the school when I was no longer contagious—only to send me to another boarding school several weeks later.

I may have thought such a youth was normal, but that didn't keep me from rebelling against it. I was a boy without a father, as my schoolmates were quick to remind me. And not only was my mother a divorcee, a status regarded by most Americans at the time as close to whoredom, but, it seemed clear, she had abandoned me. In retaliation, I did not obey teachers or staff, I refused to eat or learn my lessons, and I was always fighting or moping in a corner somewhere. No wonder I was expelled from one school after another. By the time I was eight I was running away from these institutions, which were not only in Brooklyn but in Westchester County, New York, and Connecticut.

Always the new boy at the schools, I was constantly beaten up by the bullies in situations similar to the traumatic incident at the apartment on Eastern Parkway. This victimization continued until, at the age of six, I had an ingenious idea. Instead of letting the bullies beat me up, I would beat them up. I quickly discovered it was an idea that was easy to put into successful action. I would observe from the lead bully and his cohorts' approach and words when they were about to attack (and, out of the corner of my eye, I would see the sneaky kid who crept up behind me and got down on all fours so the lead bully could push me over his back). At such moments, I struck, and struck first, doing things no dull-brained bully would—not pushing or wrestling (as you might suspect, I was always smaller than the ringleader), but punching not only my opponent's stomach and chin but his throat. So ferocious was my assault that I was left alone afterward.

My immediate successes at bully beating surprised me at first. I hadn't expected it would be so easy. Sometimes it wasn't, and I came away from such encounters bloody and black and blue. But I came back for more so often, and with such ferocity, that in the long run I won, if not the respect, at least the avoidance of most of the bullies and their cronies. On the other hand, my reputation may have accounted for my being left alone most of the time. As the new kid who had been expelled from one school after another for fighting and generally incorrigible behavior—information that somehow was known by the students at each new school before I arrived—I was someone to be wary of by the time I was nine.

I just wouldn't let myself be a victim. And although I didn't understand it then, I know now that my decision to fight back involved the realization that I would probably be hurt more often than not if I refused to kowtow to the bigger boys, but whatever pain I suffered would be worth it if I could find a way not be afraid all the time. Oh, yes, I was frightened more often than not after I began to strike back but not all the time. Later, much later, I realized that the roots of such a decision lay in the attitude that I didn't care whether I lived or died as long as I could live with a sense of self-worth and dignity. This may sound melodramatic, but by giving such little value to my existence, I was, in the future, able to confront situations I wouldn't have otherwise. Such an attitude, I was to realize, gave me an advantage over most of my fellow humans who valued their lives and property so much they were at a disadvantage before they undertook any action. To consider your life a trifle, I came to believe, was a decision great human beings embraced from the beginning, knowing that it not only distinguished them from the masses but allowed them to undertake important as well as personally dangerous projects, whether for good or ill. Such an attitude marked the undertakings of Jesus and Gandhi on the one hand and Hitler and Genghis Khan on the other. Mind you, I am not saying I am a great man; it is just that my standing up for myself as a child, without regard for the consequences, would reveal to me as an adult that I had stumbled on a secret as a boy that would enable me to achieve much more than just fighting bullies.

A more immediate consequence of my fighting back was possibly the most defining lesson of my life. I was not only left alone by the bullies after the first one or two skirmishes, but many times the leader offered me membership in his band. I never accepted. Having been a victim for three years until that fateful day in Sheepshead Bay when I first struck back, I knew what the cowed and victimized felt like, so instead of joining the bullies, I'd warn them to leave the other kids alone or they'd have to deal with me again. I didn't know it at the time, and certainly had not heard nor would have understood the concept that had motivated my actions, but from that day onward, I practiced putting myself in other people's places so that I was not just sensitive but empathetic to them. That is, I identified myself with others, and out of these feelings arose a sense of compassion for my fellow humans as well as for animals and plants. So pronounced was my identification with the lot of others that much of what seemed my peculiar behavior to classmates and teammates when I reached my high school years—and what was to become the roots of my writing and social activism in later years—originated with this early response to bullies. Even my sense of responsibility to animals and the land were further outgrowths of this original realization.

■ ■ ■

Many patterns were set in these early years. I was a terrible and inattentive student. Not only was I unable to read, I refused to obey the teachers' commands. I was often sent from the classroom to stand in a corner of the hall, staring at a fire extinguisher or broom, or I remained in the class, sitting in a corner, wearing a conical paper dunce cap. Left to myself, with no contact with my father and only a few visits a year from my mother, I tried to imagine with a child's natural curiosity how things worked. By the time I was ten, I had a complex cosmology in place. From popular cultural assumptions, Old Testament Bible tales, radio programs, advertisements, and comic books, I created an eccentric if not absurd universe where everything from why the stars came out at night to how can openers worked took on serious, convoluted, and, in many cases, interconnected explanations. These explanations were accompanied by a variety of daily rituals it was my responsibility to perform in order to maintain the order of the universe.

With my mother, the Hudson School, 1943

To make sure the sun rose each morning, I held open my eyes to that blazing circle in the sky the day before. If it was cloudy, I walked in circles a number of times or did not touch the floor with my feet when I got out of bed in the morning, sliding my toes into the mouths of my waiting shoes, which on behalf of the world carried my feet gently all day in their obedient jaws. These rituals were endless and most of the time were performed on behalf of the planet, if not the universe, rather than for myself. Psychiatrists might interpret these rituals as examples of self-empowerment, even early delusions of grandeur or incipient megalomania. But the truth is that they were more the honing of the imagination than the workings of a diseased mind. Out of them emerged a world of wonder and mystery that has inspired my writing and my vision of life to the present day.

As part of these rituals, I began to play a strange game that was to have far-reaching consequences. I'm sure the game arose because I couldn't draw. Even in kindergarten art periods, I created the most wretched stick figures saluting the flag or, with hands joined, setting off on a smiling family outing. To this day, my one painterly achievement is drawing the head of Dick Tracy, which I render with enough resemblance to that hard-jawed fighter of comic book crime that most people recognize him without my prompting.

This deficiency in my artistic abilities inspired me to paint word pictures instead. I started playing this word game when I was seven years old. This is how it came about: I was at the Hudson School in New Rochelle, New York, and my room was adjacent to the housemother's. She was an elderly heavy-set woman who always wore a gray, uniform-like dress with starched white collar and cuffs. She would get up at 5:30 each morning and turn on the radio, first listening to gospel music, the news of the war in Europe, and then Arthur Godfrey. That was her ritual, and it took place an hour and a half before she woke the boys and girls in her "house." But the radio woke me, and soon I was looking forward to hearing the church music and opening my eyes in the predawn dark to see the plane of light outlined at the bottom of the old woman's door.

By overhearing the news reports on her radio, my world was enlarged beyond the school grounds and New Rochelle. World War II was raging in Europe and the Pacific, and strange names like "Guadalcanal," "Bataan,"

"Midway," "Nanking," "Stalingrad," "Leningrad," and "the Urals" snaked down through my ears into my eustachian tubes to exit from my lips as I murmured their names like litanies over and over again. On one report accompanying news of the Russian front, there was a dramatization of Napoleon's march into Russia and his defeat by both the winter weather and the heroic Russian people. They attacked his supply lines and rear guard under the orders of the wily Marshall Kutusov, who became my hero for years. I pictured him (quite wrongly) as a squat peasant in furs, crouching in a tent while looking into a small fire and sipping tea, one eye closed as he muttered one brilliant order after another to his lieutenants who, one by one, hurried from the tent to carry out his wishes. That he resembled my uncle Abe in these imaginings would not occur to me until years later.

That program and other news reports of events at the Russian front led me to idealize Russia. After all, my family on both my mother and father's sides came from Russia. I was proud of my heritage. In Russia, I was convinced, I would not be an outsider. I would be a heroic fighter, loved by the world. And so began the romantic fantasies of my pre-immigrant past that would mature into the notion that I carried Slavic ways as well as Slavic blood in me, which, more than my Jewishness, explained the difference in temperament and looks between me and what I imagined was the laconic, psychologically repressed, blond, blue-eyed majority of the American populace.

These were the kinds of notions that scampered through my brain each morning as I lay undisturbed for the hour and a half before the other students woke and the day began. And as I murmured the names I heard on the radio in the other room or thought about the experiences of the previous day or the dreams from which I'd just awoken or the longings for my mother who was in such faraway places as "Frisco" or Little Rock, Arkansas, I would create pictures of those events or places. These pictures were drawn with the words I'd mouth from the piles of words I would pick through like a scavenging bird, discarding some, choosing others, until I had words that best described what I was seeing in my head.

Soon I was playing this word game throughout the day, snatching the words that would capture how the wind moved in the trees across the road or what the cruel mathematics teacher looked like when he was angry or what the sound resembled when all hundred or so boys and girls were let loose on afternoons to run wild on the athletic field in winter snow or on that same field, edged with fat green maple and walnut trees, in spring twilights.

In New York, 1942

Was this the beginning of my becoming a writer? I have no doubt it was. Did I know it at the time? Of course not. I was just a seven-year-old kid playing a lonely boy's game, a game, like the rituals, which gave me a sense of my place in the world and kept me from wondering why my mother, who called me on the phone every week or two from one faraway place or another, wouldn't visit me—or take me home.

Another reason the games didn't suggest my future as a writer was that I was an illiterate child who could neither read, write, nor do the simplest mathematical problems. Maybe stranger than this is the fact that I didn't care. Even playing the word game didn't inspire me to master the function of reading so I could bury my loneliness in books.

I remember that there were times when I was outgoing, full of joy. But they almost always occurred when my mother was near. She would ask me to entertain her friends when I came home, so by six, I was imitating Jimmy Durante, Peter Lorre, James Cagney, and Edward G. Robinson; and by ten, I was singing like Al Jolson and Eddie Cantor. The impersonations forced me to concentrate on the intricacies of language and sound, and they were a benefit to my writing endeavors in the long run. But for the most part, I was a morose, angry, violent child whose heroes were Samson and, later, Judas Maccabeus—Jews whose physical powers rocked the world. The idea of meek, cowed Jews wasn't even a part of my consciousness. My uncles and cousins were loving, jovial, and tumultuously emotional to be sure, but they were tough, unbending, even belligerent when confronted individually or as a group.

WHO THEY WERE

Leo, U.S. Army, World War II

Unlike my mother, who put on airs and had pretensions to heightened social status, the rest of the family remained working class: butchers, salesgirls, garment workers. They were down-to-earth and struggled to make ends meet from one day to the next. Their only moments of public notice were when my uncle was at the pinnacle of his gangster success or when my mother would come to visit, showing off her latest jewels and furs.

These were the people who took care of me when my mother was away, especially her older sister, my Aunt Bertha, whose two children, Carol and Leo, were my closest contacts among my relatives. When I became ill, was suspended or expelled from school, or when my mother was away during Christmas or Easter holidays, Carol would pick me up at Grand Central Station and drag me screaming and complaining through the streets of Brooklyn to Aunt Bertha's apartment in Flatbush. Leo, Carol's elder brother, had enlisted at the outbreak of World War II, and until the end of the war I would see him only when he came home on leave. He was part of the army engineers' Panther Division, whose insignia was an open-mouthed black panther with a red tongue sewn onto an orange background. I could almost hear it roaring from the sleeve of his khaki uniform.

During the war years, Carol, six years older than I, was my principal connection with my uncles and aunts. At thirteen, she was already an extension of her mother physically. Short and chubby, she was the daughter of a now single mother and was expected to run errands, help clean the house, and follow Aunt Bertha's demanding orders.

And demanding they were. Aunt Bertha, who never spoke more than broken English—her native Russian forgotten, but her Yiddish, as with the rest of the family, constantly in use—would battle her way through every day, making war on dust, corroding silverware, and worn-out furniture. The furniture and lamps in the living room of her one-bedroom apartment were covered in plastic, and, except on formal occasions, no one was allowed to sit in the room, let alone on the furniture. Except me. I was special to my aunt, and she would endlessly feed me and coo over me, allowing me anything I desired.

Needless to say, my aunt's privileged treatment of me sparked resentment in Carol, who, her hormones newly humming, went out of her way to torture me. Put in charge of me by my aunt, she would drag me around Brooklyn with her girlfriends, take me to soda shops, grocery stores, and even the movies. I was poked and prodded, teased and made fun of by my poor cousin who seemed put upon endlessly by a mother who was a fuming volcano likely to erupt at any moment for any reason.

Carol's great revenge came one Saturday afternoon when she and her friends took me to a matinee movie. I was excited. All the children around me in the theater were giggling and wrestling with each other, and Carol bought me a candy bar to accompany the film. What I didn't know, and could in no way have prepared myself for, was the film itself. It was 1945, and the film

With cousin Carol, New York, 1937

was called *The Body Snatcher*. It starred Boris Karlof and Henri Daniell and was about the famous Edinburgh grave-robbers-turned-murderers, Burke and Hare. It was filled with stormy nights and shroud-wrapped cadavers being dug out of muddy ground and delivered to the patrician doctor (Daniell) for purposes of medical experimentation. I was terrified. Not only did I find it hard to breathe, my tongue seemed to be shrieking. A quavering sound rushed from my mouth but was lost among the delighted screams of the other children. I wrestled to get out of my seat and run from the theater, but Carol had clamped her hands on my shoulders and was forcing me to stay where I was, laughing at my terror. Her laughter was almost fiendish and I'm sure geysered up from her burgeoning hormones as well as the roots of her jealousy. Strangely, it never occurred to me to close my eyes.

If Carol sounds like a monstrous teenager, I cannot remember one moment that I didn't love her, and although she teased me endlessly for being the brat I was, she also tucked me in when I went to sleep at night and calmed me when I scraped my knee or began crying for my mother—that disembodied voice floating to me over the telephone from I knew not where. I also knew instinctively that I could count on Carol being there whenever I needed her. If I lost her in a crowd or felt disoriented on the

My mother, Leo, and Aunt Bertha, the Catskills, 1950

street, as children will, I knew that all I had to do was stand still and she would find me.

She and Aunt Bertha, in fact, were the only two people I *could* count on. When I was sick, I knew I'd be taken to Bertha's apartment and cared for until I was well, although the curing process—endless bowls of hot chicken soup, glasses of tea, and dozens of enemas—may have bordered on the unendurable for any but a frightened nine- or ten-year-old child like me.

Bertha—strict, domineering, unyielding—may have loved *me*, but she resented my mother for her beauty and how she had used it, and she resented how materially successful my mother had become because of it. As the other sister in a family of four brothers, she also resented my mother lording it over the rest of the family and their seemingly delighted acceptance of my mother's dominance. And above all, she resented her for how she was raising me.

Bertha had kicked her husband out of the house after the war started. He had been a member of my uncle's illegal operations and had once served a prison sentence for him, taking his identity. Sweet but weak, he was the eternal loser. Now raising a son and daughter alone, Bertha took any minor job she could and raised her children with vigilant strictness. Her apartment alone showed the meagerness of her means. Besides the kitchen and bathroom, there was the living room where Leo slept on a roll-out couch—which was folded up into its plastic-covered frame immediately upon Leo's waking—and the bedroom where she and Carol slept.

It was her apartment, in fact, that Abe had used as a safe house to tally the day's take, receiving his dozens of runners after 3 PM with their slips of paper and other accounting documents. Leo, Carol, and Bertha were not allowed to be at the apartment during those hours. For the use of her home, Abe took care of Bertha financially, as he did the entire family, until his death, and after that my mother helped Bertha meet her bills in innumerable ways. But to a sharp-eyed nine-year-old always on the balls of his feet, ready to dart in one direction or another at the slightest sense of danger, Bertha's hostility to my mother was apparent.

I could see Aunt Bertha's side clearly. It was not so much a matter of empathy on my part as it was an absence of loyalty to my mother and father because I hardly knew them. I'm not talking about resentment here. My parents were strangers, and only Bertha and Carol, and later Leo, were there when I needed them. Such a lack of identification with my parents made me regard the world with a clear-eyed objectivity, an objectivity that allowed me to observe details of behavior in others that I later realized many people did not or were not able to do. The dynamics among friends, acquaintances, and family members revealed themselves to me with every word, change in tone of voice, shift of weight, or assumption of posture I observed in the people around me. Always on the defensive, expecting danger from every side, I could read with an almost uncanny accuracy the faces in the crowds that surrounded me. Such an ability is an essential trait in a writer, and I found that I was fascinated by the way people acted when they thought they weren't being watched as well as by the way they interacted with one another.

In the years to come, my observations would not be stimulated by a protective impulse—that is, would not revolve around whether I was about to be in a situation of jeopardy—but would be motivated by my interest in human beings in general. In fact, I would be struck by the comic nature of humanity: more and more I would see the comedy in how the species carried on, and when I reached maturity, I would come to see myself in my early and teenage years as the funniest person of all—with my glumness and black moods, my violent reactions to anyone around me. But that observation would come much later.

AFTER THE WAR

I was nine years old in 1945 when the war ended. I could not remember having seen my father, and my mother had opened a small business as a personal dress buyer in her apartment. She was living in a duplex apartment in New York City, once again in the exclusive Century apartment building on Sixty-second Street and Central Park West.

On the other side of the river in Brooklyn, my uncle Ike still lived with my widowed grandmother, Aunt Bertha continued shouting commands at Carol, and my uncle Dave, with his hardworking wife Ida, was providing for his two daughters by making an ice cream with his own secret recipe he called "coconut whip," which he sold in a small stand called Jungle Jim's on Pitkin Avenue. This stand was decorated with green crepe-paper palm fronds and football-sized coconuts. Wearing a pith helmet atop his gaunt Ukranian face, his lanky six-foot, four-inch frame towering over most of his customers, Uncle Dave welcomed all who came to the stand with a heavy, tongue-flopping Russian accent. By working eighteen to twenty hours a day, he and Ida were able to eke out enough money to support his family.

Abe and his money were gone, and Frankie, still in hiding, snuck back to Brooklyn twice. On the first occasion, in either 1943 or 1944, I was taken from school and brought to Brooklyn to see him. Like Abe, he was short and pudgy, and I would not learn until thirty years later how fearsome he was. To me, he was the kindly uncle who broke horses for the cavalry out west somewhere—a story the adults in the family had concocted to explain to the children why he was no longer around—and

Uncle Frankie,
Brooklyn, 1939

brought me a gun belt, complete with two white-handled six-shooter cap pistols, and a straw cowboy hat. After I was dressed for the part, he took me by the hand and whisked me to the pony rides in Coney Island, bestowing pink cotton candy and ice cream cones on me, his little nephew, whom he instructed to watch him canter around the dirt track with its white fence posts. "Giddyap! Giddyap! What kinda nag is dis?" he called to the teenagers who ran the concession, and they smirked as he bounced up and down like a rubber ball atop the creeping mare.

Then it was my turn, Frankie leading me around the track, ignoring the protests of the boys as he lectured me on the use of the bit, the stirrups, and the reins. I was in another world. Uncle Frankie, who I barely remembered, was every boy's dream uncle, full of stories and jokes and a swagger, all aimed at entertaining and taking care of me in a way that would make any little boy dizzy with glee.

But the evening and the next two days were soon over, and Frankie was gone once more—back to his "cowboy life." I was never to see him again. A year after the war he called Aunt Bertha from "the candy store" to tell her he was in town and would be over that evening. "The candy store? What are you doing there? It could be dangerous," she said, knowing that was one of the two places Abe's mob hung out. Frankie laughed and told her not to be such a worry wart, she told the family later. After that call, Frankie was never heard from again. But in the few days I was with him, Frankie gave me a hunger to go west that was secretly with me from then on and would become a reality in the years ahead.

LEO

The year 1945 was also memorable because my cousin Leo returned from the war, and since I lived at home that year, I was able to spend time with him. He brought a dozen Baby Ruth candy bars and a vibrant energy with him. He was a returning twenty-one-year-old warrior ready to make his mark in a world he had won for freedom. Only five foot six, he had a square face, bull neck, the torso of a six footer, and thick, short, muscular legs.

To enlist, Leo had left high school without a diploma. Now he wanted to get on with his life. Before the war, he had been an intercity champion sprinter and football player at Tilden High School in Brooklyn. Now he participated in sports only on weekends with his buddies, playing a rough touch football in the streets between rows of parked cars. I would watch him receive the ball from the quarterback behind the line of scrimmage, feint one way, dart another, do a jitterbug two-step that froze the defense, and suddenly scamper through a nonexistent hole for a touchdown at the end of the block without anyone laying a finger on him. His short legs churned out touchdown after touchdown to the delighted war whoops of his admiring friends, and his brawny arms powered him to victory on Brooklyn's asphalt handball courts.

He also transformed Aunt Bertha's apartment. When I came to visit shortly after his return, Bertha's spotless, plastic-covered, museum-exhibit living room was in disarray. Piles of books were everywhere, some strewn on the floor. The fold-out easy chair bed was open and unmade, and shoes and shirts were tossed over the plastic-covered couch. Freud's *Interpretation of Dreams*, a book called something like *Mathematics Made Simple*, a volume

With Leo, Brooklyn, 1946

on astronomy, and another on how to sing were just some of the titles and subject matter of the books that littered the floor.

Leo wanted to be a crooner and had a fine voice and a winning way with the ladies. Tough, aggressive, but always jokingly good natured, he decided to adopt me and be the big brother I never had. I idolized him as he taught me the fundamentals of baseball, football, and street fighting, took me to see the Brooklyn Dodgers at legendary Ebbets Field, taught me how to score a baseball program, and let me hang around with him and his friends when they sauntered down the street, creating innocent but jolly mayhem, or looked for girls. The rest of the guys adopted me as their mascot; with Leo as their leader, there wasn't much else they could do. But as intrigued as I was with them, so they were with me— this little kid from the other side of the river whose head they could fill with all kinds of male truths and bragging, most of which I was forbidden on pain of death to repeat to my mother or any other woman.

At other times, Leo and I would eat our way through Brooklyn. He would choose a direction in which we would walk, with the stipulation that we had to eat at least one, if not two, hot dogs and drink an egg cream in every delicatessen or hot-dog stand we passed. These walks were also times for serious talks about Leo's dreams, his difficulty in finding a good job, but most of all they were times for him to find out how I was doing and to advise me on my problems. He also explained to me what was going on between my mother and the rest of the family and the shifting relations among other family members. He instructed me on all aspects of becoming a man and was the hero of my youth. Sensitive and patient during these sessions, he was brimming with energy and humor at other times, seeming to go in several directions at once, never still, never looking backward.

But jobs were hard to find, especially for someone without a high school diploma, and Leo went from newsstand clerk to neon sign maker, burning his fingers badly. Next he found lucrative but dangerous employment as a collector for various buy-now pay-later companies, a job that ended a year after it began with several guys waiting for him in a darkened tenement in the Bronx where they beat him senseless and threw him over a second-floor banister. After he mended, he found a job installing outdoor TV antennas in all five boroughs in all kinds of weather.

Eventually, Leo married and became a butcher. In one of the many memories I have of him I see him standing behind a counter, flirting and joking with the sad-faced wives of Queens who, on seeing him, would light up like golden flowers for the few moments he bantered with them.

Leo rose to be head butcher for a small supermarket chain, but the chain closed down in the recession of the 1980s, and even though he was a union member, he was forced to take on his old job as collector at the age of sixty-three. Never complaining, always full of energy and play, he raised two girls, provided them with a college education, and bought a condominium. With the money he'd saved, he was able to indulge the dreams of his life in old age—two vigorous hours of tennis a day and a full schedule of lifelong learning classes at the community college near the condominium in Sheepshead Bay where he'd lived since the year after he was married.

My favorite memory of Leo is an incident that occurred when I moved back to New York for a time in 1964. I was visiting him at his condominium on a sunny Sunday in late September, and he challenged me to a game of handball. I was twenty-eight and he was forty-one. I wasn't in the best of shape and never played handball, but I was confident I would give him a good game. We strolled to a nearby handball court, and he proceeded to bombard me from every angle. In fifteen minutes he had beaten me in three games. I think I scored only two points. He hadn't even broken a sweat. He was a bull.

During the third game, a fat middle-aged man and his ten- or twelve-year-old son appeared, holding tennis rackets.

"How long you gonna play?" the man asked.

"We just got here," I wheezed, after diving for one of Leo's shots in vain.

"I asked, 'How long you were gonna play?'" the man said.

I stopped and turned to him. "You know the rules: we were here first."

"Yeah, but you can't hog the court."

"Look—" I said, my voice rising. I was in no mood for someone pestering me.

Leo grabbed my arm. "That's okay," he said to the man. "You and the boy can play with us"

"We'll play you for the court." The man said, swinging his racket.

"No need for that," Leo said.

"No: for the court," the man said, swinging the racket again and smiling malevolently.

The man and his son walked onto the court, the boy looking apprehensively at his father.

We began to volley, Leo and I barehanded and the man and the boy with their tennis rackets.

We had tossed the hard black handball against the fence and were playing with tennis balls. As the ball ricocheted off the wall, the man kept hitting Leo with his racket, first on the hand, then on the arm and shoulder.

"Hey," I said.

Leo said nothing.

We began the game, and again the man swatted Leo with the racket, muttering "sorry" each time he did. Leo continued to say nothing.

"You going to let him do that?" I said to Leo.

Leo remained silent and continued to play, and the man continued slapping him with the racket.

I finally turned to the man, my fists balled, "What the fuck—"

Leo grabbed my arm and whirled me around. "Play," he said softly but firmly.

"Are you going to let—"

"Play," Leo repeated.

We quickly lost two out of three games, the man slamming Leo with his racket more openly with every point. He was gloating as we left.

I turned on him enraged, but Leo grabbed me again and led me off the court.

We walked back to the condominium in silence. I was as confused as I was angry. Was this the Leo I knew, the tough guy who wouldn't let anyone get away with such blatantly abusive antics?

"What was that all about?" I finally asked him.

Leo stopped and turned me around so I was facing him. "Look, Muttle," he said in a quiet voice. "You don't humiliate a man in front of his son."

Leo has always been my idol, representative of what to me are the working-class values of pride in work and a sense of self worth. He taught me fortitude, honor, and an insistence on always maintaining one's dignity with a ribald sense of humor and, most important, a joy in life. The motto he attempted to live by and taught me in my childhood has been branded on my soul, and goes a long way to explaining who I am. "Fear not," he always told me, "and do right."

Fortitude, honor, dignity, humor, joy, an attempt to be fearless and always to do the right thing—if those traits are in any way parts of my character, it is because I learned them from him.

CHAPTER 3

Finally a Father

A year before the end of the war, my mother began dating a rich garment manufacturer named Larry. He was of average height and strongly built, but what was most noticeable about him was his flat, dark-complected face with its broken nose, small watery eyes, and neat pencil-thin black moustache. His parents were Romanian Jews. His mother was a tall, stout woman, and his father, a meek little man completely under his wife's control. When they stood next to each other, the mother towered over Larry's father like a teetering building.

I met Larry in the spring of 1944 when he drove my mother in his black, bulbous-topped Fleetwood Cadillac to visit me at school. Countless other men had performed the same service over the years and had quickly disappeared from my mother's life. Not Larry. He was soon her only escort, always friendly, full of questions, while generously taking us both out to lunch or an early dinner. When I came home on weekends, he was invited for supper. Soon he was visiting me on his own at the school and taking me for drives.

When I was expelled from school and lived at home the following year, Larry would take my mother and me

My mother and Larry,
New York, 1946

to fancy restaurants like Longchamps and Ruby Foo's or pick me up and drive me around, teaching me to read by sounding out the advertisements on billboards. He quizzed me on spelling and tutored my reading skills by making me read the daily newspapers aloud and would always take me to movies, not to first-run shows on the Broadway strip, but to theaters on seedy, smarmy, old Forty-second Street that was a jumble of hot-dog stands, pickpockets, amusement arcades, teenagers looking for trouble, and girly shows. We pushed through the crowds to movie houses like the *Laff Movie* and various other third-rate theaters, some of them showing ten-year-old films like

Gunga Din and *Lives of a Bengal Lancer*. Permeating the hustle and bustle of Forty-second Street and its slightly dangerous denizens were the muted odors of popcorn, French fries in old grease, mustard, and sizzling hot dogs. I was intrigued, as my new adult friend—what else could I call him?—guided me through this maze of intoxicating, titillating sense experiences, while I snuck glances at the pin-up photographs outside the doors to the walk-up honky-tonk dance halls.

This was the same year Leo returned from the war. He would pick me up in the city and take me on our adventures in Brooklyn. I had a more emotionally intimate relationship with him than with Larry. Maybe it was the difference in age between the two men, or the different roles they played in my mind, one as older brother, the other as prospective father. But the outings were different as well. Leo and his friends had little money and did what single working class men in their twenties did. I don't remember ever going to the movies with him. Larry was wealthy, took me and my mother to fine restaurants and loved movies as well as sports.

I'm sure that my love of film began at this point, although, before she met Larry, my mother had hustled me out of the house with sandwiches in brown paper bags and candy money to Saturday matinees on those rare weekends when I was home from school. And she herself would take me with her to neighborhood films on the spur of the moment, even on weekday school nights during the times I lived with her in the city. Film became for me, as for millions of others, an escape from my daily problems and a dark place in which to dream my dreams of adventure and romance. But unlike other people, I became obsessed with film, and that obsession pointed to my future scholarly pursuit of all things related to cinema. By the time I was twelve, I knew not only the major stars at all the Hollywood studios, but the character actors as well: Guy Kibbee, Frank Morgan, Walter Brennan, Edward Arnold, Oscar Homolka, Eve Arden, Lionel Stander, Harry Davenport, George Tobias—I could go on and on.

Larry also took me to the boxing matches at St. Nicholas Arena on Sixty-eighth Street and to Madison Square Garden, where I was mesmerized by the fighters and the crowd. So it was no wonder I jumped and clapped with joy that August when I returned from camp and my mother told me she and Larry were going to be married. She had approached me worriedly, I could see, not knowing what my reaction would be, and was delighted at my response. "This is what I've always wanted—a father for you," she said with tears in her eyes, "You'll have to go back to board school for a few months, but it will be for the last time. Just as soon as we've found a house and are settled, I'm taking you out of those schools forever."

I was delirious with happiness. Out of the schools! At home with my mother and "the best guy in the world!" Larry loved me; he had to, the way he paid attention to me and took me everywhere with him, teaching me to read and doing things with me that nine-year-olds found exciting and loved to do. I didn't even mind that I was going back to the schools for a few months.

Larry was at the apartment all the time now. He would arrive from business in suit and tie, putting his gray fedora decorously on top of the afternoon newspaper as he poured his cocktail, asking my mother, who was cooking dinner in the kitchen, about her day, slipping me at the same time a nickel or a candy bar and winking for me to keep silent as he continued his easy talk with her. All the years of paternal deprivation and emotional turmoil were gone.

In late September I went off to a new boarding school. My mother and Larry picked me up every weekend, and I'd sit in the back seat of the Cadillac as they drove through Westchester County and Connecticut, looking for the perfect house for us. There were arguments—he liked one house, she liked another—but I thought nothing of them, and my mother always turned to smile at me from the front seat, and Larry caught my eye in the rearview mirror and winked so many times it became a game. Returning from those expeditions at night, I'd stretch out on the backseat, engulfed by the scent of the Cadillac's leather. Listening to their voices, I watched the trees and sky slide by and drifted off to sleep with a sense of security I had never known before and have never known since.

My mother and Larry still hadn't found a house when, in the winter of 1946, she called me at school to tell me that she and Larry were married and were on their honeymoon in Florida. I was happy but taken aback. I had imagined I would be at the wedding, which would be a big affair, just like in the movies.

"And will you take me out of school to live with you soon?" I remember asking.

"Soon, very soon, my son," my mother answered.

But it wasn't soon. The days stretched into weeks, and the weeks into months. And Larry and my mother had stopped picking me up on weekends.

By spring, my scenario of living with my mother and new father was taking on grotesque shapes in my mind, similar to the ones in the distorting mirrors in the arcades of Forty-second Street, and the memory of my mother's voice on the phone sounded like a broken record with its "Soon, my son, soon." I had to do something to change what was happening. But what?

At that time, I was boarding thirty miles from the city at the Beechwood School in Rye, New York, just down the road from the old amusement park. I was ten years old, but very independent. When I had lived in the city the previous year I took buses and subways alone, and I came back to the city from the Beechwood School several times on my own aboard the New York Central Railroad. I knew where the Rye train station was, and I knew how to get there. I also knew my mother was calling me from the apartment in New York where she and Larry were now living. And so I began to formulate a plan. All I needed was a train schedule from Rye to Grand Central Station— and money. I had run away from other schools before, but they had been closer to home, several of them in Brooklyn—but now I was running to a new life, one I desperately wanted, and I wouldn't let it slip through my childish fingers.

THE GREAT ESCAPE AND THE GREAT SHAME

There was a boy my age at the Beechwood School who was not too bright. Everyone made fun of him, and when they insulted him to his face, he would smile dumbly back at them. It was evident by his behavior that he was not physically, intellectually or social in tune with his schoolmates. Through his clumsiness he had angered teachers and older students and was involved in several misadventures the other kids had engineered to get him in trouble, and he got into predicaments through his own escapades as well, escapades that didn't make sense. I don't remember his real name, but I do remember he had red hair and buck teeth and his mouth was always slightly open with an off-center smile. He had money, though, money his parents sent him every week as an allowance, enough money certainly to get us both to New York. Red, as I remember he was called, looked up to me. I had gotten him out of several fights and told the bullies who teased him that he was under my protection, but that didn't mean I let him hang around with me. Now, however, I sought his companionship, which he responded to eagerly, and when I told him my plan, he practically pushed the money into my hands.

We had to wait several weeks for enough of his allowance to accumulate and to go on a class trip to the railway station, where I memorized the train schedule to New York City. After that I was ready to put my plan into action.

When the day arrived, we simply walked into the woods on the school grounds at afternoon play time and nonchalantly wandered off campus. Far from being "cool customers," we were bristling with nerves. Red, in fact, was trembling. But nobody noticed we were gone, and we hitched a ride to the railroad station, telling the curious driver that our mother was sick and we were on our way to see her. At the station, the ticket seller only asked for our destination before handing us our tickets in exchange for most of Red's money. And so we waited for the 4 PM train to New York City, staring at the station clock with spiraling excitement and fear.

No one was on the platform, but about ten minutes before the train was due to arrive, Charlie, the headmistress's husband, rushed from the station house and turned toward us like an angry bull. Like his wife, he was middle-aged, but unlike her, he was short and squat with a thick neck and bullet-shaped face. Red's mouth fell open, and he couldn't move. Charlie was the school's handyman, known for punching the students in the arm or rapping them on the skull and laughing when they cried out. I took one look at his glowering face and ran in the opposite direction. It took him less than half a minute to catch me, squeezing me in a bear hug that robbed me of my breath. Then he dragged Red and me to the school's station wagon and back to the campus.

What followed was not only a night of physical torture, but one of the most shameful moments of my life. Its repercussions have affected me to this day.

Charlie swatted us in the head and smacked us on the back of our legs with a classroom yardstick while his wife called our parents. We cried and shrieked as Charlie pinched our cheeks and arms and rapped us in the head with his knuckles for what seemed hours. Night fell. We were given no supper, and after the forty or so other students went to bed, Charlie had free reign to play his sadistic games. Red and I were beyond crying by now and were whimpering and hiccupping. Charlie made us stand with our arms outstretched, and whenever we dropped them from fatigue, he'd swat the offending arm or smack us behind the legs with the yardstick. This went on into the night until Charlie, seeing how tired we were, allowed us to face the wall and lean against it with our fingertips. When this became excruciating and we fell against the wall, he would slap the yardstick against the back of our legs again.

Sometime in that endless night, the headmistress appeared. She was stern but not sadistic like her husband, who all the students feared. We stood before her, sniffling and trembling. She told us that our parents had been notified and would pick us up the next day. But for now, she wanted to know which of us had planned the runaway.

I was terrified, and without hesitating, I turned and pointed at Red. "It was him," I said, "He made me do it."

Red was too upset, too frightened to argue. He stood with his nose running, sobbing, unable to talk, and even as I pointed at him, I knew I had done something unforgivable. This not-too-bright kid, who I had taken under my protection, who looked up to me, who I had manipulated to run away with me for the sake of his money, I had now betrayed in the most cowardly manner.

Years later, I tried to find him to ask his forgiveness, but I was so ashamed of myself that I had blocked out his name and address. My mother didn't remember it either, and when as an adult I tried to find the Beechwood School, it was no longer in existence.

From that night on, however, I vowed that I would not allow anyone to take the blame for what I did, no matter what the consequences, and that I would never commit an act that would make me feel bad about myself. It is a vow that has been impossible to keep. But although I have done many things I'm not proud of since that night, I have tried to commit no act that would hurt others or damage my self-respect. A corollary to this promise to myself is that the opinions and practices of those around me mean nothing and are not to be followed if they go against my own ethical values. To help me follow these precepts, I vowed to act simply and straightforwardly in my dealings with everyone.

PARADISE GLIMPSED

I never saw Red again, but I did achieve what I'd set out to do. The next day, my mother picked me up and took me home. She was not pleased but not as angry as I imagined she would be, and I like to think she felt a little guilty about not bringing me home sooner, as she had promised.

My mother and new father had not found a house yet, so we lived in the New York apartment and continued to look for a house in the country on weekends. Larry was as friendly as ever and continued to take me to the movies on Forty-second Street and other places where I'd be amused. But it was obvious that things were not right. Larry had put locks on all the closet doors and secreted food, papers, clothes, umbrellas, and little knickknacks in the closet interiors. His flawless manners and attention at supper had ceased altogether, and he would read the newspaper, ignoring my mother, suddenly getting up from the table and throwing the food she had prepared for him across the room and then stomping from the apartment, calling her "whore" and "bitch" over his shoulder and not returning until late in the night. Some nights, he wouldn't come home at all.

And my mother and Larry argued ferociously. Every once in a while he'd grab her or slap her. It was obvious she was miserable and frightened.

The apartment was a duplex, with a kitchen, living room, and half bathroom on the first floor and a bedroom and a bathroom on the second floor. I slept on a couch in the living room downstairs, and not until the fights became loud and violent did I really understand what was happening. After most verbal eruptions that occurred during the day, Larry would come down the stairs and take me out first to eat and then to a movie. He'd be exhilarated and would devote full attention to me, partaking in my childish delights as much as I would. Everything must be all right, I thought. Shouting and doors slamming must be what marriage is all about, so I happily went along with Larry on his ice-cream-and-movie binges.

All that changed when I realized that the explosions upstairs were not just verbal. One of Larry's favorite actions was to break into the bathroom without warning when my mother was taking a bath and to start beating her. As she lay helpless in the tub, he would grab her hair, pull it, and then push her head under the soapy water.

It all became clear to me the day he broke the bathroom door down and I heard my mother scream. I rushed up the stairs to see Larry standing over her, slapping her and pulling her hair while she struggled to get away and surges of water slopped over the rim of the tub in lathery waves.

I was horrified. I stood there, not knowing what to do. Larry turned and saw me and immediately let my mother go. He left the bathroom, grabbed me by the arm, changed his wet clothes, and, smiling as if he hadn't a violent bone in his body, took me for lunch and a double feature at the *Laff Movie* on Forty-second Street.

PARADISE GAINED

At about this time, Larry and my mother found a house in the country, a five-acre estate in Westchester County. It sat in a secluded lane with five other palatial homes, each with more extensive acreage than ours. The house, a sprawling, two-story wooden structure faced with fieldstone, contained a huge living room, formal dining room, large den, and screened-in back porch on the first floor, and four bedrooms, two of colossal size, on the second floor. The house was approached by a flat half-acre lawn shaded by stately elm and maple trees. The gravel driveway led past a one-acre vegetable garden and circled to the garage in back of the house where the kitchen, pantry, and servants' quarters were to be found. The screened porch looked out on the rear of the property—a half acre of rock gardens and fish pools and a large grass field separated from the fish pools by a piled rock wall.

The house was a paradise few people would be able to resist, certainly not a little boy who had never really had a home. I'm sure that was one of the reasons the marriage lasted as long as it did. My mother wanted me to have a father and a home, it seemed, at any price, and, with this house and her upper-class neighbors, the six-year-old immigrant, who had come to America in steerage and had never gone past the fourth grade, reached the material plateau she had only seen in movies.

Larry, meanwhile, continued his bizarre if not schizophrenic behavior. He bought my mother a car, furs, jewels, put the house and property in her name, and my mother happily went about redecorating the rooms with her impeccable taste.

I was excited as never before. Each morning I went exploring in one direction or another and soon realized there were uninhabited woods all around the area.

We were one of the few Jewish families in this section of Westchester, and soon Larry and my mom met a prominent Jewish lawyer with a daughter my age with whom I was immediately infatuated but who made it clear, at twelve years old, that she was interested in older boys. More important, the lawyer gave me a puppy from the litter his dog had just birthed. It was a black, shaggy-haired French poodle. Larry took it back to our house and tied around fifty yards of laundry rope to its neck and told me that if I called it, and called it by name, and then tugged the rope, it would always run to me and obey me. The puppy had sniffed at everything, including my face, when we brought it home, and it belched continually. Larry told me that poodles were dogs of royalty, so on the spot I named the dog Nosey de el Burpo and tugged the rope. I still remember the astonished expression on Larry's face when Nosey galloped up to me, ears and coat flapping, jumped into my arms, and joyously licked my face. From that moment on, I had only to say something to Nosey and he would obey me. It certainly seemed that he understood English, and if this sounds like a ten-year-old's imaginings, adults were continually astonished at the way Nosey followed my commands. The first time I said, "Stand," Nosey stood on his two hind paws, and when I said, "Dance," he twirled around several times, a trick he performed with joyous yaps to the delight of any adults Larry or my mother brought to the house.

Nosey went everywhere with me. We explored the whole county, it seemed, ranging farther and farther from home, and at night he slept with me at the foot of my bed or snuggled and burped next to me under the covers during the winter.

We had moved to the new house in the late spring of 1946, so I had all summer to roam about the property and the countryside while my mother was preoccupied with redecorating the already elegant house. The house had been owned by a corporate lawyer for one of the big oil companies, and I think he said he and his wife wanted to spend their last years in Texas, his home state. I do know he decided to sell us the house because he wanted a family with a child to own it since his children had grown up so happily there. As it turned out, his decision would prove to be an inadvertent irony of almost Aeschylian proportions.

Summer turned into autumn, and I was registered at the public primary school. Needless to say, I was academically far behind my sixth-grade fellow students. They were mostly the town's working-class Italians, and the upper- and middle-class "Americans" who were moving into houses that had just been built on uprooted forests or into stately old homes that had been put up for sale. I mention this because there was a definite class difference, with the wealthy attempting to exercise their status over the local Italians, something I had not encountered before and felt uncomfortable with. I liked the Italians' earthiness and loudness. Our gardener was a handsome Italian from the village who not only let me work with him, but, like Leo, advised me and spent more time with me than he needed to.

So rural was this part of Westchester that it was easier for me to walk from the rear of our property through several woods to get to school two miles away than to follow the circuitous two-lane roads. By the time school began, I knew the way through the woods as if I were a native.

Wanting to make friends with my classmates, I put aside my tough-guy ways at school, and my classmates accepted me readily enough—especially since I played a passable game of baseball and other sports with them. But abandoning my belligerent attitude had other unexpected results. Not only did I find myself with a plethora of friends, I discovered a humorous side of my personality I never knew I had. I shouldn't have been surprised. My mother would come up with hilarious statements and could pull grotesque faces in knowing parody of her beauty, and Carol's quips and Leo's street humor are constant remembrances of my early childhood. Much of my humor, like Carol and Leo's, was verbal and consisted of puns and quick retorts. Now it seemed humor was nudging aside my anger, and why not? I had nothing to be angry or morose about any longer. As far as my teachers and classmates were concerned, I was a happy-go-lucky ten-year-old who liked to whistle pop tunes too loudly, play with his friends and his dog, and tell childish, bad jokes. I may have been a bit obstreperous in class and a poor student, but so were most of the boys my age.

Even though I was Jewish, I was accepted by my classmates, one in particular, an Irish insurance salesman's son named Spike. We became best friends, as did Nosey and Spike's dog, a beige cocker spaniel. Spike and I would play Monopoly and Parcheesi when it rained, baseball and cowboys-and-Indians or Nazis-versus-Americans when it was sunny, and listen to *Tennessee Jed*, *Captain Midnight*, *Jack Armstrong*, and *Sky King* on the radio just as it started to get dark. But most of the time we were outside exploring the woods or getting together with ten or so other guys to play ball. Then, as autumn wore on, there was Halloween. Six of us filled bushel-sized bags and pillow cases with candy as we went from door to door trick-or-treating, something I had never experienced before.

One of the two woods I had to cross to get to school had a running stream sliding through it. One day I came across an old log a quarter of a mile away from the spot where I crossed the stream every day. It wouldn't budge when I tried to lift or drag it, so I went home, got some clothesline, and, with Nosey barking

With Larry and my mother, New Jersey, 1947

encouragement, I tied it to the log in a slip knot a quarter of the way down and dragged it to the stream as my private bridge. I then got an axe and saw from home and chipped away here and there to give my construction its own distinctive design as well as to "secure" it in place.

Could any boy have been happier? The years of misery in the boarding schools were forgotten. I was living as children should—in a wonderful house, among new friends, my own dog, and most important, with my mother and father. Yes, my father, because within six months after Larry married my mother, he legally adopted me.

But my newfound paradise was an illusion. Larry's behavior became more and more irrational. My mother and I had realized how secretive and paranoid (I didn't know the meaning of the word then, of course) Larry was when he put locks on all the closets in the apartment in the city. It soon became apparent that he was not the generous person he had appeared to be during their courtship either, but a tight-fisted, nasty miser who wanted to know where every cent my mother spent went, and who began to cut back on her allowance, although he expected her to both maintain the house and entertain on a grand scale. Soon, overdue bills began to mount, all to my mother's confusion.

And the violence continued as well. Larry's business was in the city, and he commuted by car or train. But he sometimes would not return home for days on end, particularly after he had flown into a furor for seemingly no reason and started beating my mother, punching or dragging her by the hair, or twisting her fingers until several of them broke.

Even more peculiar were the evenings when he would behave with the same charm and attentiveness he had shown before the marriage. He would have dinner, talk to my mother romantically, and ply her with sweet liquors; then, before he took her upstairs, they would go over the bills together in the den. We didn't learn until it was too late that he was drugging her and having her sign over to him not only everything he had given her but what she had acquired from my father and possibly whatever money my uncle Abe may have entrusted to her care.

PARADISE LOST

For Christmas that first year in the country, Larry bought me a rifle and showed me how to use it. I had always wanted a Red Ryder BB gun, which was advertised in full color on the back covers of most comic books. But Larry hadn't bought me a BB gun. He presented me with a much deadlier weapon, a .22.

We had planted corn, tomatoes, and other vegetables in the one-acre garden on the garage side of the house, but the rabbits and birds ate or fouled what we tried to grow. "Those damn rabbits," Larry kept muttering.

That was all I needed to hear. With my new rifle, I became the hunter, the protector of the homestead's crops.

One morning in early January 1947, after Larry had gone to the city, I loaded the new rifle with its forty or so bullets and went into the vegetable garden, squatting near the wall, where I had a view of the entire field. I felt all-powerful, and a calm patience came over me I had never experienced before. I looked out at the field and waited.

The field, of course, was frozen. The withered corn stalks crackled like paper, and patches of snow were everywhere, tangled in weeds or glittering on the rocks beyond the garden. I heard a scuttling among the corn stalks, then saw the weeds move, took aim, held my breath, and, as Larry had taught me, slowly squeezed the trigger. The rifle kicked against my shoulder just as a rabbit flew into the air twenty yards away. He came down screeching and hobbled frantically away, rattling dead weeds and frozen corn sheaves.

I ran to where I had first seen it. There was blood on all the stalks and half a rabbit leg. I ran after the rabbit and fired at it several times. Again it was thrown into the air, hit the ground with a thud, and dragged itself away. I was more horrified than panicked and kept following the blood and shooting. Finally, I caught up with it. It was squirming on its back and sides, its eyes large and unfocused. What had I done? I shot bullet after bullet into it, but still it kept squirming. I was crying hysterically, and kept crying even after the small body, dribbling nauseating, foul-smelling innards out of dozens of bullet holes, was still.

I was trembling and sweating despite the cold. I didn't know what to do. It never occurred to me to bury the rabbit or just leave it there. Instead, I picked it up on the muzzle of the rifle and brought it home draped over the barrel, and stood with it, as if it were an offering, extended to my mother in the living room. She shrieked and yelled at me, telling me to get it out of the house and bury it, which I meekly did.

I was undone. All the exhilaration of using the new rifle was gone. I was sick at my stomach, not because of my mother's reaction but because I realized I had taken the life of one of the earth's creatures, and taken it for no reason. The effect of the experience was traumatic. As I hacked at the frozen earth to bury the rabbit, I thought about life, death, what I had done, and what I should and would do about taking lives in the future. It is not too grandiose for me to say that I was having my first philosophical meditation. My betrayal of Red had affected me at an emotional level. So did the unexpected suffering of the rabbit. But as I dug its frozen grave, the rabbit's death summoned up in me a new kind of examination—one of ideas on the level of objective contemplation. I was ten years old, but I would not look at the world the same way I had before that day. The subjects of life and death would become an obsession with me, especially my responsibilities to living beings in the various cycles of existence, whether those cycles were human, animal, vegetable, or cosmic.

That spring, as Spike and I walked the mile or so from school to the town of Harrison, Nosey was hit by a car. I never used a leash on him, and he had padded onto the street in town. The driver took us to a veterinarian and Nosey survived, but his behavior became erratic, he was easily spooked, and when my mother sent me away to camp that summer, Nosey purportedly trotted all the way into town, boarded a train for the city, got off three stops later, and was adopted by the family who found him. I never saw him again and do not know if the story of how he went out of my life is true.

Both these incidents mark the beginning of my last year in paradise.

■ ■ ■

Although things continued in apparent normalcy for the winter and spring of 1947, I knew something was wrong when my mother insisted I go to camp that summer. I protested with angry tears. She wasn't sending me away again! I was supposed to remain at home and play with my friends. Why, several times this spring I'd invited twenty kids to play baseball in the rear field, and my mother provided sandwiches, Coca-Colas, and lemonades for everyone. But, no, she was insistent I go to camp.

Even an eleven-year-old should have guessed. Larry had grown more violent in the past year, and my mother was striking back. No longer would she stand for his brutality because she thought patience and, alas, a smirk would save the marriage. She began to punch, throw punch for punch, and I saw her several times work her way in close under Larry's punches to deliver ferocious blows to his groin that crumpled him, making him writhe on the floor of the elegant living room. Soon, she moved out of the master bedroom and locked the door to the guest room where she slept. But Larry, arriving late at night from the city, sometimes broke it down and started pummeling her in bed.

During one violent argument that spring, Larry chased my mother into the kitchen where I was listening to the radio with the maid. The maid rose to help my mother, but Larry shoved her aside and kept yelling curse words and hitting and slapping my mother who was curled on the floor. I ran to the utensil drawer and grabbed a butcher's knife and charged him, but he saw me coming, deflected my arm, picked me up and threw me across the kitchen against the refrigerator. I lay on the floor, gasping for breath. Everything stopped. Then Larry ran from the room, and we heard the Cadillac start and roar away. My mother and the maid lunged for me. It was the beginning of the end. That summer I was going to camp.

■ ■ ■

This maid was to play an important role in our lives. Her name was Maddie Jackson. She was a tall, wide, black woman, around sixty years old, one of a string of black maids who I found in my mother's employ when I returned for weekends or school holidays. Maddie had been taking care of the house, the cooking, and me since my mother married Larry. When I was a baby and my mother was still married to my real father, my mother had hired a white, English "nanny" for me—my mother's pursuit of grandeur should neither be forgotten nor underestimated. But since the divorce, she had hired black women exclusively. They were all wonderful to me, caring and full of stories and snack candy, but Maddie was the best of all, a kindly, grandmotherly woman who, like the others, spent endless hours alone cleaning and cooking and must have welcomed the company of a curious little boy who listened to her stories and conversation with fascination.

When my mother took her to the country with us as a live-in maid, Maddie and I listened to the radio together, especially to the soap operas in the late afternoons. During the first summer in Westchester, I explored the woods in the morning and early afternoon and would tromp back to the house where I would always find Maddie in the kitchen looking out at the fish pools. I'd tell her my adventures, and she would tell me about her grown children before her favorite programs came on. Then we would listen to the soap operas together in comradely silence.

Maddie and I had become close. Several times before we moved from the city she had taken me to her apartment in Harlem where I'd stay the night. I never found out why—probably because my mother had nowhere to put me when she and Larry had gone off for a day or two. But the visits were memorable. I met her children and their families, went to church meetings, and observed a life very different from my own. I was constantly comparing the poverty, the clean but shabbily furnished old apartments in various states of disrepair, with my mother's apartment. The disparity between the apartments did not seem fair, even to a ten-year-old. The black people I met seemed kind and caring. Why shouldn't they have what I had?

Prejudice didn't enter the equation. I only saw the difference in skin color, nothing else. And despite the Italians' lack of wealth, and the rich "white" kids and their parents who looked down on them as inferior because of it, I saw no difference between them either. I loved Vinnie Figuerro and our gardener, who both brought long Italian sandwiches stuffed with meat and peppers for lunch, which they would share with me. Vinnie, who'd been left back twice and was big and muscular for his age, would trade me for peanut butter and jelly sandwiches at school, and, as he watched my eyes water from his hot peppers, he would pluck a pepper from the sandwich and gobble it himself so that both of us would share joyous tears together.

Larry sneered more out of jealousy than prejudice at our handsome Italian gardener, but my mother had been raised in a Jewish neighborhood surrounded by Italians and Irish and felt no prejudice. In fact, the tough Jews, like her brothers, were fist-in-glove with the Italians. It may have been for that reason that I have felt a kinship with all races and ethnic groups. I am not romanticizing here; I am just stating that from an early age I heard few prejudicial comments from my family—although occasionally even my mother would refer to an Italian or black by a derogatory name, which was never reflected in her behavior toward them.

At any rate, Maddie Jackson may have saved my mother's life. I found out how this happened when Leo drove from Brooklyn to Pennsylvania to unexpectedly pick me up from camp that summer. I packed my trunk, and we drove back to New York all afternoon and late into the night, talking and listening to the radio and especially to a new crooner Leo was intrigued with named Tony Bennett. There were also records by Frankie Laine, Tony Martin, and Vic Damone, my favorites among pop singers. But Leo didn't sing along with them as he usually did. He listened grimly, his demeanor made more grave by night shadows and oncoming headlights, as he imparted to me, as gently as possible, that my mother had left Larry. Several weeks before, Maddie had found her in bed one morning, half conscious, her face bloody and swollen, with several fingers and toes broken and a possible fractured wrist. There were teeth marks on her toes. Maddie had tossed what valuables she could find into a valise, called a local cab company, bundled my mother into a cab, and drove with her to the apartment in the city. There, my mother had been under a doctor's care and was all right now, but when Larry had found out that my mother had left, he went to the Jewish lawyer who had given me Nosey and sued for divorce, claiming my mother had beaten *him* up, broken *his* fingers, and bitten *his* toes.

It was another family crisis, and Leo was taking me to stay with Aunt Bertha where he and Carol could keep close watch over me so Larry's lawyer or other hirelings could not kidnap me or have me make unwitting statements that could be used against my mother in court. There was no worry about that. Larry and his lawyer had other plans, as soon became apparent.

I don't remember when the case came to court. I know I was twelve, and it was either that autumn or the following spring of 1948; I think the latter. By then, the New York newspapers had gotten hold of the story, and the family was once more in the public eye. It was just too titillating a tale for the tabloids to ignore, especially the *New York News* and *Daily Mirror*, which ran highlights of the proceedings with headlines and photographs on the front page and more photographs in their centerfolds. The headlines read something like

BEAUTY BITES TOES, HUSBAND CLAIMS
HUSBAND BEATEN BY BEAUTIFUL WIFE

Larry had even collected an affidavit signed by 270 men who claimed to have had sexual relations with my mother while she was married to him.

I was present at all the court proceedings, wearing a new suit. I was a silent character witness and sat in the row behind my mother and her lawyers, listening to the accusations read one after another by Larry's lawyer. I couldn't make sense of any of it, least of all the changed demeanor of Larry's lawyer who had been a guest in our home and who was always so friendly, the same man whose daughter was not only my classmate and friend but had become Spike's girlfriend. Obviously, no one was who they seemed. No one could be trusted. This twelve-year-old's litany would become an adult's belief.

Two incidents occurred at the proceedings that would have lifelong repercussions. First, I learned in one of the many accusations droned by Larry's lawyer that my mother had been married a handful of times before my father. I kept leaning forward after one revelation and another, asking, "Is that true?" only to be shushed by my mother and waved away by her lawyer. I didn't know what to think, but if there was any innocence left in my childhood, it was erased by that court case.

Second, my real father appeared as a witness on behalf of my mother. I had seen him once before when I was six years old and had wrestled myself off his knee in a taxicab on our way to some legal matter before a lawyer and a judge that had to do with custody or alimony, but I remembered nothing about where we were going except that it was on Nevins Avenue in Brooklyn. I didn't even remember what my father looked like. But here he was, walking toward my inquisitive and ever-observing twelve-year-old eyes. He strode up to my mother, her lawyer, and me in the corridor outside the courtroom, his glossy shoes snapping on the granite floor. He was dressed in an expensive navy blue double-breasted suit with a light blue tie and matching handkerchief in his jacket, his silver hair combed straight back. He looked like a movie star, although a short one. He said hello to my mother, got instructions from the lawyer, turned to me, looked me in the eye—we were the same height— as he shook my hand firmly, and said in a neutral voice, "So you're my son," and without giving me time to reply, he turned on his heel and marched into the courtroom.

He testified strongly in my mother's behalf, but he neither looked toward me nor her when he was on the witness stand, and I never saw him again. I spoke to him on the phone once after that, when I was home on leave from the air force and he happened to call my mother in order, she said, to borrow money for gambling. A year after the court proceedings, I invited him to my bar mitzvah, an invitation he never answered, and although I will not deny the hurt and anger his absence from my life has caused, he has been dead to me in an emotional sense for many years.*

*As I was preparing the final draft of this book, my daughter Jana discovered an irrefutable source of knowledge about my father. I have placed the information where I think it is most fitting—as far as time sequence and subject matter are concerned—at the end of chapter forty-six about my friend Kirby Wilkins. Those interested in finding out more about this enigmatic man will find it there.

In the end, the judge threw Larry's case out of court. The judge was enraged, I remember, and tongue-lashed Larry's lawyer. He had reached the end of his patience when my mother's lawyer revealed that the 270 names on the adultery affidavit belonged to winos from the Bowery to whom Larry had provided bottles of muscatel if they signed the paper. The judge annulled the marriage, ordered my adopted name and my mother's married name to revert to what they were before she married Larry, and ordered some sort of financial recompense in her favor.

But Larry was the winner, in the end. He had closed out all my mother's bank accounts and taken the furs, jewels, and car he'd given her and had her sign over to him when he'd drugged her and she thought she was paying bills. All she had left was the duplex apartment in New York City, from which she once more began selling dresses as a personal buyer.

Larry, however, was still not satisfied. For the next ten years he would call my mother at all hours of the day or hire someone else to call her, saying nothing when she answered. He also bought appliances and furniture in her name, and when they were delivered to the apartment, my mother had to explain the situation to the irate movers and the company from which the purchases had been made. Once Larry darted out of a crowd, grabbed my mother's hand and snapped her wrist, vanishing before anyone could grab him. Many other incidents occurred, until the Treasury Department came to my mother, asking permission to tap her phone because they were investigating Larry for tax evasion. But that's another story. Larry's role in my story was at an end.

To this day I can't judge the emotional and psychological damage I suffered during those years. For a time, I abandoned my newfound happy-go-lucky ways. I was a solitary again, once more on guard against everyone around me and as violent and morose as I had been when I was at the boarding schools. I was just a little wiser. What had happened to me was the way life was. I knew nothing else. My experience with Larry had taught me to be wary of even the friendliest adults. More than that, he had shattered my hopes of being part of a happy family and destroyed the notion that happy families existed. Such realizations may seem uncomfortable, if not shocking, to some. But, in truth, they were necessary pinpricks needed to burst the soap bubbles of childish illusions. In the long run, I was not willing, or maybe not able, to abandon my newly acquired sense of humor and the acceptance by others that came with it. I felt I was being pulled in two different directions. I may have been only twelve, but I was growing up.

BOOK TWO

YOUTH

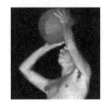

CHAPTER 4

The City

My mother did not send me back to boarding school after the divorce. I lived at home that year and the next. I had lived at home three years prior to that, when I was nine, the year before my mother married Larry. It was during these two stays in New York that the city, without my realizing it, became my model for what the ideal city should be—not a Babylon with hanging gardens festooning its sun-baked walls, nor a Paris of the nineteenth or early twentieth centuries teeming with artists and expatriates, but a raw, rough city that had developed its own distinct identity, an identity that had been achieved by the industry of the immigrants of my mother's generation who were coming to the fore of American life. Their energy had built the Chrysler and the Empire State buildings and created a skyline that would rise in my adult psyche with a nostalgia I would carry with me for the rest of my life.

As I remember, my first stay in the city occurred because I had been expelled from one school or another, and my mother, busy with her chores as a personal buyer selling knock-offs of high-fashion dresses in the upstairs bedroom, didn't have the time or wherewithal to hunt down another school in which to confine me. It was a seminal year during which, among other things, I got to know my way around the city, riding buses and subways on my own.

I also remember that first stay as being one of the happiest periods of my boyhood, the first time since I was three years old that I lived at home for any length of time. It was during the winter and spring of 1945, just before the end of the war, when my mother was seriously dating Larry, and just about everything I experienced had an aura of magic about it. To my nine-year-old eyes, the city was a place of modern wonders. Everything in it, both large and small, seemed enchanted, touched by the marvelous.

Even the building where I lived with my mother in her duplex apartment seemed magical. Her apartment was one of hundreds in the Century Apartments, a vast, twin-towered edifice thirty stories high that took up the entire block between Sixty-second and Sixty-third streets, across from Central Park. On my initial stay, I would roam the Century's halls and stairways and endlessly wander through the several basement levels, going from one floor or corridor to another as if I was exploring the tunnels of Carlsbad

Caverns, or was one of the intrepid travelers trudging endlessly downward in Jules Verne's *Journey to the Center of the Earth.*

Every day or so, I would rummage through my mother's handbags in her closet, like a pirate searching for treasure in a captured galleon. And if I was lucky enough to find a scattering of dimes and pennies, or my mother didn't have time to make me dinner because she was going off on a date to a fashionable nightclub with Larry, I would scamper down to the building's upscale drugstore on the corner of Sixty-third Street and sit at the soda fountain, talking to the countermen as I ate fat-sizzling hamburgers with either a lemon coke, a chocolate malted, or a vanilla ice cream soda with chocolate ice cream known as a "black and white," a sobriquet that was matched only by New York's notorious egg cream. An egg cream consisted of chocolate syrup and a dollop of milk deluged with gushes of soda water that bubbled the concoction into a sweet, frothy brew. Afterward, I'd lounge by the candy counter and the comic-book stand and make my way past the bottles of over-the-counter medicines to look longingly at the tall brown bottles of cod-liver oil. The bottles were shaped like upended fish and contained the most delicious orange syrup known to the human race.

Sometimes, as a treat, my mother would take me to one of the Horn & Hardart's Automats, particularly the one on Fifty-seventh Street between Sixth and Seventh Avenues. This was another building full of wonders. The inside was a large, high-ceilinged airy space with an open balcony on the second floor that overlooked fifty or so tables on the first floor, the entire interior featuring art deco design and black grille work everywhere. With a fistful of nickels exchanged from several dollars from the change lady seated in a glass booth in the center of the first floor, I would half-run to the stacked rows of chrome compartments embedded in the tan marble walls. The compartments had little glass doors that exhibited sandwiches, wedges of pie and plates of hot foods inside. I'd drop some nickels in a slot next to one of the doors, turn the knob next to it, and the door would spring open and I'd remove the sandwich or pie. My favorite dish was a chocolate-brown, elongated bowl filled with Boston Baked Beans topped with a hot dog. When all the items had been purchased, the entire row of compartments would revolve and disappear for a few moments, as if turning their backs on me, and then, like the last part of a magician's trick, they would turn back filled with fresh sandwiches and hot plates. After I removed my food, I'd trot over to a chrome lion's face protruding from another wall and put a glass underneath its mouth. When I shoved my coins in the nearby slot and pulled the lever beside it, a stream of chocolate milk would fill the glass, or I would put a cup under a chrome dolphin's jaw and get a cup of coffee for my mother.

During that first stay in the city, I went to an all-boys private school off Central Park West and Eighty-ninth Street called the Franklin School. I only remember two things about it. One was the gym where all the school's students played a ferocious game of "war," which consisted of the school population being divided into two teams with ten volley balls that were thrown indiscriminately by the players on one side at the players on the other. When someone was hit and couldn't catch the ball thrown at him, he was eliminated from the game. The game continued until only one player remained. Naturally the older boys had an advantage because of their strength. They would unmercifully target the younger boys. I gave as good as I got and delighted in aiming at the bigger boys.

But it was what I did after school hours that is most memorable. I would walk the twenty-seven blocks home from school along Central Park West because I saved my bus fare to buy raspberry ice cream pops from the Good Humor truck that was always parked on Eighty-first Street near the planetarium of the Museum of Natural History. Next I would stroll into the museum. As with most New York City museums in the 1940s, entry was free of charge, so rich and poor alike had access to these invaluable collections as if they belonged to them: the museums were there, always available, a part of every New Yorker's daily life if he or she wanted to visit them. Certainly I felt that way. My sense of ownership may have been more acute than other peoples' because I went to the museum after the groups of children on class trips were gone and I had the building more or less to myself. I even had favorite places I'd visit in the museum as I would a relative's apartment where I was certain an aunt would have a glass of milk and cookies always ready for me. The museum provided a different kind of sustenance, of course: it fed my curiosity and nourished my wonder at the planet's many kinds of animals and the diversity of its cultures. I'd wander through the Hall of African Mammals with its dusty dioramas of stuffed animals grazing in sunlit plains with painted mountain backgrounds, or I'd stop to gaze at dense green jungle scenes where monkeys and gorillas peered from the foliage. Next, in fascination and awe, I would circle the herd of elephants that dominated the center of the hall in dignified silence. And I'd always climb the stairs to see the giant four-foot wax-and-wire replica of a mosquito on the second floor, shivering in terror as I imagined it staring at me and about to break through its glass case. Then I'd run to the shadowy basement, with its cedar-lined exhibits, to view the sixty-three-foot Haida canoe manned by six or seven life-size statues of Northwest Indians whose totem poles loomed over me and whose strangely painted pots and utensils filled the glass cases in all the side aisles.

The long walk home, my visits to the museum, and the fact that I would many times play catch and bat a ball back and forth in the park with a friend I made at the school named Tito Texador, meant I wouldn't get home before dark, and my mother would be frantic. She would scold me and at times beat me with the plug end of a waffle cord, telling me not to do such things again. But I always did.

Most of the time, however, I wandered around the apartment building and drank sodas at the drugstore. When I wasn't exploring or eating, I would hang around the doormen and elevator operators who would greet the celebrities who lived in the building and afterward, in garrulous gossipy yarns, tell me about their exploits in sports and entertainment. Among these celebrities were legendary heavyweight boxing champion Jack Dempsey, stage and screen star Ethel Merman, and Ira Gershwin, who had written the lyrics for his brother George's songs before George's untimely death.

No less celebrities were Leo and Clara Lindy, who owned Lindy's, one of the two or three most famous restaurants in New York. They also lived in the Century. To all these people I was "Rae's boy" and received a pat on the head from the men and a hug from the women. But to the Lindys, who had no children, I was something special. And they were special to me, since my mother spoke about them as if they were royalty and warned me to be on my best behavior when I was with them. Their restaurants were known to New Yorkers as, "old" Lindy's and "big" Lindy's. My mother preferred old Lindy's on Fifty-first Street and Broadway. It was small and intimate, dark and narrow, pungent with the odors of dill and sauerkraut that rose from the buckets that squatted on every table, creating an atmosphere that impressed me as foreign and exotic. New, or "big," Lindy's was on Fifty-third and Broadway and had huge plate glass windows and was somewhat more American and contemporary. It was large and full of light and the hubbub of conversation. Both restaurants were famous for their cheesecake and over-stuffed sandwiches, were favorite hangouts for theater people and reporters in the 1920s, '30s, and '40s, and were immortalized as "Mindy's" in the tales of Damon Runyon.

As with all New York restaurants during the war, Lindy's was closed on Mondays, and the Lindys, who lived in a penthouse on our side of the building, would occasionally invite me to dinner, while my mother counted stock, was engaged with a customer, or had gone out with Larry for the evening. The initial invitations soon became a regular Monday night event in the large penthouse apartment that was crowded with tables full of expensive china and glass knickknacks that I was careful not to brush against. Mostly I sat and listened while Mrs. Lindy chatted warmly like a kindly queen. Mr. Lindy spoke haltingly like a distracted king, suddenly falling silent and staring blankly at the wall behind me because, my mother said, he was afflicted with narcolepsy. Among other things, the Lindys served me alcoholic beverages in tiny stemmed glasses, sweet aperitifs and good wines, which they taught me how to "nurse" so I wouldn't get drunk, lessons that stood me in good stead when I grew up.

As for companions my own age with whom I could roam through the building and Central Park across the street, it seemed that for all the hundreds of people living in the Century Apartments, only six of them were children. We stared at each other curiously in the labyrinthine lobby with its dark walnut walls and silver art deco fixtures and dimly lit sconces, but we didn't know how to approach one another. Two of the children were boys my age, and one of them, named Freddy, was as curious as I was, and soon we overcame our awkwardness and were exploring the building together and playing catch and tag in the park across the street. Like me, Freddy was given free reign in the afternoons by his mother, who had little to do with him. She rarely left their apartment, and I thought she looked much older than the mother of a nine-year-old boy should. She was a listless Texan who wandered through the rooms of her apartment in a housecoat at all hours of the day.

In contrast, Freddy's father was a ball of energy. He was a short, round, balding New York Jew who loved his son and was full of jokes and kindness. On Sundays, when my mother would usually go on an outing with Larry, he would take Freddy and me to old Lindy's for an early lunch; then we would return to our separate apartments, change clothes, and play baseball in the park, mostly hitting fungoes and ground balls to each other and getting other kids our age to play with us whenever we could.

Once a semipro ball player, Freddy's father was full of chatter and hand tricks, a wonderful man who loved kids and baseball and spent most of those Sunday afternoons patiently instructing Freddy and me, and any of the other kids who joined us, how to bat and field. I'm sure I owe my solid batting techniques to his tutelage.

Freddy's father had one other attribute. He was the nephew of Benny Leonard, the legendary lightweight boxing champion of the 1920s. Renowned more for his brains than his brawn, Leonard was revered as the quintessential representative of Yiddish culture, it seemed, by every adult male Jew in New York. He would visit Freddy's father every month or so, and I remember meeting him in Freddy's apartment that spring of 1945, a year or two before he died. Although he was only five foot six, in my memory he towered over me, dressed in an ornate black merchant marine uniform with gold piping all over the arms and shoulders. "Hello, kid," he said with a smile and twinkle in his eye when Freddie introduced me, and his hand, which seemed to swoop from the ceiling, came down to grip my own. It was one of the unforgettable moments of my early life, although when I looked back on it years later in a poem, I realized how ironic his reputation among the immigrant Jewish community was. His fellow Jews may have seen him as the prototype of the successful Jew, but he and Hank Greenberg, another legendary Jewish athlete, saw themselves as successful Americans.

■ ■ ■

Another magical memory of my stays in New York was listening to the radio and imagining all the worlds the many dramatic, comedy and adventure programs would transport me to. One show in particular, *Escape*, was my favorite, and I remember listening to it terrified one night as it presented a story full of bloodcurdling sound effects called "Three Skeleton Key." The tale, set on an islet off the Florida keys, concerned several men trapped in a lighthouse surrounded by thousands of rats who were gnawing through all the building's wooden structures to get at their human meals. My mother had gone out on a date and as usual had left me alone, but she had given me a phone number where I could reach her in case of emergency. By the end of the show, I was in a panic, gasping for breath. When I lifted the receiver to call the number, however, for some reason there was no welcoming buzz: the phone was dead. My panic turned to outright dread as I immediately assumed that someone was in the apartment downstairs and had cut the phone line. I was in my mother's bedroom upstairs, and I ran to all the doors and windows and locked them, then waited trembling under my mother's bed until she came home.

One of my favorite pursuits during those years had to do with the many premiums and items advertised on kids' radio shows. I was fairly obsessed with—maybe "addicted to" is a more accurate phrase—the items as much as the programs. They seemed to arrive from dreamlands beyond this world after I sent away for them to destinations so mysterious and remote only my imagination could comprehend them. Each item usually cost five- to twenty-five cents and a box top from a cereal carton or a label from a jar of a chocolate drink mix like Ovaltine. I usually disliked the cereals, and my mother wound up with shelves of them, which she threw out, shrieking at me for wasting money and food, when the shelves became too crowded. But her anger, even her slaps, couldn't keep me from my "habit" of mailing my nickels and dimes to exotic locations that existed somewhere in Radioland. *Sky King, Captain Midnight, Superman, Jack Armstrong, The Lone Ranger, The Shadow* and *Terry and the Pirates* were some of the shows that offered send-away rings that whistled, glowed green in the dark, and had secret compartments. The pot metal they were made of almost always turned my fingers green. My favorite item was a weather ring that had a secret compartment and was topped by what looked like a pink sliver of stone that turned blue when the weather changed. There were also badges, membership cards, code detectors and once a foot-high walky talky set that came with a plastic (or was it cardboard?) transmitter and receiver connected by a seemingly endless spool of string with which a friend and I could communicate over a distance of several yards, one of us behind a tree in Central Park or in the next room. I considered each of these items to be talismans and charms that would protect me from evil, and to this day I wear some object on my person that holds the same magic for me—but doesn't turn my skin green.

I have many other happy memories of those years—happy yet melancholy, since most of the places and experiences that marked New York in the 1940s and 50s as the metropolis of an art deco fairyland have vanished. They are memories that made the city my personal wonderland: the automat, the museum, the adventures with Larry and Leo, but also the times when Carol would come into the city with her girlfriends and take me to the first-run movie palaces on Broadway near Times Square: the Capitol Theater, the Roxy, The Times Square Paramount. Those theaters, with their ornately decorated interiors, always showed a new film, a newsreel, a short, a cartoon, and most memorable of all a stage show with a comedian, a tumbling or animal act, and a big name band.

The bands didn't play in the orchestra pit but onstage, and were an integral part of the show. Most were serious swing groups like Benny Goodman, Gene Krupa and his Orchestra, Xavier Cugat ("The Rhumba King"), Sammy Kaye, and Tex Beneke with the Glenn Miller Orchestra. Their trumpets, saxophones and trombones flashed golden splashes of sound into the darkened audience where I sat. Others were comic orchestras that provided shows all their own, like Spike Jones and His City Slickers whose consummate destruction of pop tunes and classical compositions were accompanied by the madcap antics of the band members who raced around the stage, creating mayhem everywhere. Slightly more sedate was Kay Kyser and his "Kollege of Musical Knowledge" orchestra which featured Ish Kabibble, with his bowl-shaped haircut and bangs, who recited nonsense poems at the most inappropriate times and engaged a frustrated, bespectacled Kyser in double-talk dialogues. Kyser, wearing a mortarboard, would pose as a professor to Ish Kabibble's country bumpkin dumbbell student. He would quiz Kabibble who replied to him with wrong but somehow right answers I would identify in my adult years as the utterings of an idiot savant, or wise fool, but as a nine-year-old I greeted with childish glee.

The live acts included Bert Lahr doing his woodman's routine, Chico Marx playing trick piano music, and such comedians as Jack E. Leonard and Milton Berle performing their stand up tomfoolery. And once, fresh from his movie role in *The Killers* that had made him an instant star, a young Burt Lancaster and his buddy Nick Cravat performed their acrobatic act on portable high wire equipment—and I was sure they were flying.

After the movies I would stroll with Carol and her friends down Broadway and be mesmerized by the huge Camel Cigarette billboard high on the side of the Claridge hotel on Forty-fourth Street. It featured the giant painting of a man's face, his mouth a gargantuan hole from which every few seconds perfect smoke rings floated over the heads of the crowds below. That eighth wonder of the world was joined several years later by the even taller and more stupendous fifty-foot-high Bond clothing store sign that stretched two hundred feet from Forty-fourth to Forty-fifth Street and was composed of two gigantic figures flanking a real waterfall twenty-seven feet high and one hundred twenty feet long.

But the happiest memories of my two stays in New York were the weekday evenings when my mother wasn't off on a date with Larry to such chic places as the Stork Club, the Copacabana, the 21 Club, and El Morocco, or when she was tired of counting her stock of dresses in her upstairs closets, or when she was just bored. At such times, she would come down to the kitchen and pull me from the radio where I was listening to *The Lux Radio Theater* or *Escape, The Lone Ranger, The Great Gildersleeve,* or *The Life of Riley,* and whisk me to one of any number of theaters in the neighborhood: the RKO Colonial on Broadway and Sixty-second Street, the Alden on Sixty-eighth Street or the Beacon on Seventy-fourth. Those spontaneous events became a ritual, with either my mother coming downstairs, announcing we were going to the movies, or me clomping upstairs, breathlessly suggesting a similar outing. At the theater we would stop at the candy counter where she always bought herself a box of licorice Crows or Jordan's almonds and me a Bonomo's Turkish Taffy. Bonomo's was a slab of hard candy I would smash, still unwrapped, into bite-sized pieces on the arm of my seat, and when I unfolded the red-striped white wrapper, a vanilla perfume would envelope me like church incense.

The Alden was our favorite theater because its double features could be new second runs or obscure films, some of them foreign, that were several years old. Most often, the movies were film noirs, which were at the height of their popularity. Their shadowy view of life played in my mind again and again. With my experiences at boarding school and then with my mother's marriage to Larry, I eagerly accepted their bleak view of the human condition. I watched with grim resignation as the troubled antiheroes portrayed by Glenn Ford, Alan Ladd, Dick Powell, and Robert Mitchum tried to extricate themselves from threatening situations that occurred with such inevitability that the actors at times seemed unable to cope with them. Along with Daoism and later existentialism, I have no doubt that film noir was a major contributor to my fundamental vision of life.

More important than the films, however, those evenings in the theaters allowed me to sit near my mother, turn every once in a while to look at her staring intently at the screen, and at times to rub my head on her arm, which seemed to rise of its own accord and encircle my shoulders. The dark movie houses permitted me to be closer to my mother than at any other time, and that part of the mystery of moviegoing has never left me. It is not nostalgia I experience every time the lights lower in a movie theater, but the memory of being in the intimate presence of the one person who loomed larger in my dreams than the figures on the screen—and who was usually as distant and unapproachable as they were.

■ ■ ■

By the time I lived in the city again after my mother's divorce from Larry in 1948, I was twelve years old. I went back to the Franklin School, resumed my friendship with Freddy and his father, and would exchange pleasant but brief greetings with the Lindys when I encountered them in the elevator. I was no longer invited to their apartment for Monday dinners, maybe because Mr. Lindy's condition had worsened or because I looked older than my age, no longer the little boy they could imagine for a few hours was their own. And I had changed, changed in more ways than I understood, although I wouldn't realize it until the following year after I returned home from summer camp.

The realization came in the fall of 1949, several weeks after my thirteenth birthday. My mother had enrolled me in Joan of Arc Junior High School, a New York public school on Ninety-second Street between Columbus and Amsterdam avenues, thirty blocks from where we lived. Every day I had to take a bus back and forth to the Century, or walk the mile and a half each way. The thirty blocks roughly covered the same area to the apartment from the Franklin school, but instead of ambling down Central Park West, I had to make my way through Broadway or Columbus and Amsterdam avenues, the separate territories, or "turfs," of five different teenage gangs. At first, crossing the turfs was a scary undertaking, but by the end of September the problem was solved in an unexpected way.

I was playing in a six-man touch football game on a grassy strip on Riverside Drive when six other boys challenged my five friends and me to a game. The six were tough and looking for trouble and had spotted what they thought was a group of not-too-athletic Jews. One of their number was older and twice as big as any of us, a square chunk of muscle the five others addressed as "Patsy." Soon the game turned into outright attack on their part. When they had the ball, Patsy either blocked or ran over us. My companions cowered, but I was angry. "Give me the ball," I said in the huddle, and on the next play, I zigzagged down the field, well away from Patsy, stiff-arming two of the other boys and prancing my way to a touchdown.

On the next play from scrimmage, Patsy said, "I'll take *him*," pointing at me. He had been aloof from the proceedings up to then, not bullying as his friends had.

"I'll take *him*," I echoed, pointing at Patsy. He smiled.

On the first play from scrimmage, he ran right at me, but I'd gotten so low, I up-ended him and he went over my back and fell with a grunt. I turned and helped him up, neither grinning nor saying anything sarcastic. The next time my side went on offense, I carried the ball again, this time running right at Patsy, suddenly feinting to my right, then sweeping left for another score. Everyone, including my companions, was shocked. So was I.

I knew I was practicing what Leo had taught me about getting low, as well as imitating his shifty moves as he ran, but what surprised me was my speed and the sharpness of my movements.

"Hey," called Patsy after the game was over. I walked over to him. "You're pretty good. We could use you on the Baby Saxons." His friends crowded around me, eager to know who I was. My own friends stood at the far end of the grassy strip, intimidated and not knowing what to do. They also stood in another world, I realized, one from which I was now turning away, one in which Freddy and his father also existed, who I would rarely spend time with after that day.

Patsy stuck out his hand with a smile. "Whadya say?" We shook, and I smiled back. "Great," I said. And so I joined the Baby Saxons, the lowest echelon of the most powerful gang on the west side of New York City. By wearing the reversible black and gold athletic jacket, with its bold *Saxons* printed over a shield flanked by two axes, I was allowed to cross the turfs of the other gangs undisturbed. I don't remember playing a single game for the Saxons, but at least I had their protection, which went from the center of their power in Hell's Kitchen all the way to sixty-fifth Street—where Lincoln Center now stands—and beyond to Ninety-second Street.

That football game, however, was just the beginning of the year I discovered my athletic abilities.

In the schoolyard on Ninety-second street, I watched the tough kids play punch ball, a game like baseball that mainly consisted of smacking a pink rubber ball with one's fist through a crowded concrete infield. Only the bullies played. They took over the schoolyard at recess and lunch on the first day of school. One day, a black kid pointed at me and yelled, "Hey, you, we need one more." I hesitated for a moment at the invitation, but I was curious about what I had observed of the game for the first few weeks of school. Watching how the game was played had given me ideas that had not seemed to occur to the players, so I trotted over and joined the team that was one man short. In the field, I scooped up a ground ball and threw the runner out, as I had in regular baseball games in Harrison or the previous summer at camp, but it was during my time at bat that I startled everyone. Starting well back of home plate, I ran, angling toward the third base side of the field, holding the ball in my left hand and swinging my right arm up like a pendulum, but at the last moment I pivoted toward first base and slammed the ball with my fist between first and second base. The opposing players were caught off guard, the ball sped past them, and I ran all the way to second base for a double before they could retrieve it.

What I had observed during the previous two weeks was that none of the punch-ball players feinted or in any way disguised their final moves. That was the first of many tricks I used to change the face of the game in the schoolyard.

Immediately I was accepted and befriended by the tough guys, most of whom were black and had already had minor scrapes with the law. One of them was an undersized, skinny, nervous kid, who hopped more than walked, called Cool Breeze. He was full of smiles and wisecracks and took to me immediately. He was a sort of social director and moved between all groups, even among the whites. His best friend was a brooding, muscular brother called Tennessee, who was as much Cool Breeze's bodyguard as best friend. Even though he was one of the punch-ball players who wanted me on his team, Tennessee eyed me with suspicion and jealousy because Cool Breeze kept me close everywhere in the schoolyard.

The three of us happened to be in the same ceramics class. All the tough guys were there because it was not an academic class and was run by a beautiful Puerto Rican woman. On the third or fourth day of class, I was washing the dried clay off my hands at the trough-like communal sink when suddenly I was flying sideways, landing on my back with the wind knocked out of me. The left side of my face was numb; I was gasping for breath, and I was looking up at Tennessee, who was standing over me, scowling, his hands clenched into fists.

The other students had stopped what they were doing and turned toward us, or so I imagined. The teacher either wasn't going to get involved, or she was on the other side of the room and hadn't seen what had happened.

When I got my bearings and my breath back, I stayed down. I wasn't stupid enough to rise into Tennessee's waiting fists. "What did you do that for?" I asked, not whining but obviously annoyed. There was still no sensation on the left side of my face.

"You sprayed water on my arm," Tennessee said.

The other guys had crowded around us, including Cool Breeze. What I would do or say, I knew, would determine everyone's attitude toward me from that point on. I couldn't think and was more than slightly panicked. But I knew I had to get up and show that I was not intimidated. What had he said? "You sprayed water on me"?

Before I considered my words, however, I growled back at him, "Prove it!"

Tennessee blinked, grinned, let out a loud laugh, reached down and helped me up, and put his arm around me. Cool Breeze and everyone else was smiling and, as simply as that, I was one of the guys. Was it my tone of voice? It certainly wasn't the ineptness of my retort. A long while later, I realized that Tennessee didn't really want to fight me but wanted to make his physically and socially superior status in the relationship clear to me and everyone else.

After that, he, Cool Breeze, and I were a trio. I persuaded Tennessee not to throw the namby-pamby kids' balls over the school fence, and we continued to control the recess and lunch schoolyards with our punch-ball team. We even played in the schoolyard after school before we walked the two blocks to Broadway, where I would wait outside while Cool Breeze and Tennessee stole anything they could get their hands on in the endless assortment of candy stores, drugstores and other small shops that lined both sides of the street.

My quick retorts and childish puns were barely acceptable humor with Cool Breeze, Tennessee, and the other black guys I hung around. They taught me street humor, adding a new kind of play to my repertoire of wit and wisdom by demonstrating more than instructing me in a game they called the "dozens," which consisted of insulting thrusts that almost always concluded with the refrain "your mama" at the end of every sentence. Trading insults about relatives and physical inadequacies, in fact, became an exercise in aesthetics that I quickly learned didn't make the receiver of the jibes angry but filled him with respect—that is, if the insult was clever enough and couched in original, glittering phrases. In many ways, I realized years later, the verbal jab was a nonviolent form of attack that reassured friendship and trust rather than a pretext for confrontation and mayhem.

It was less than a week after the incident in ceramics class that Cool Breeze introduced me to one of his basketball-playing friends on the schoolyard courts. I had played for years at camps and in Westchester with Spike and his friends, and I had become increasingly excited over how sharp my shooting, passing, and quick moves had become over the past year, so I wasn't surprised when it took only a single game for me to become one of the players regularly chosen during after-school pick-up games. In time, basketball became my favorite sport because it was as mental as it was physical: it joined split-second decisions and constant movement and called for a flexibility of approach, since problems on the court changed from one moment to the next.

One of the other players, a tall, thin black kid named Jimmy, became my best friend. He was no tough guy and didn't play the dozens; he was a sweet, sensitive, loyal friend, and all the other black kids looked out for him. Jimmy was a terrific basketball player for his age and an equally good baseball player. I shared my lunches with him—he never had one of his own—and even took him to a Jewish delicatessen up the street once in a while, where we would sneak illegally, since we weren't supposed to leave the schoolyard at lunch period. Jimmy was the best friend I'd ever had. Spike had been full of moods and was concerned with social status—he frowned at my hanging out with the Italians. But with Jimmy, there was none of that. I think he was happy to have a non-black friend he could talk to without fear that that friend would use his confidences to make fun of him among the other blacks.

And talk we did, about our lives and our thirteen-year-old dreams, and about our parents. Jimmy's mother was a prostitute and totally ignored him. He dressed in torn shirts and pants and seldom had money, never a lunch. I told him about the schools I'd lived in, and about Larry, and we walked the streets and talked and talked some more. After a few weeks of hanging around together, Jimmy asked me to try out for his sandlot baseball team that played in Central Park, and our afternoons were soon divided between basketball in the schoolyard and baseball in the park.

So my life was full of sports. I wouldn't get home until dusk, and during the winter months I played basketball for the school team and boxed at the Police Athletic League center on Fifty-second Street, a few blocks from the old Madison Square Garden. Boxing had fascinated me ever since Larry took me to the fights at St. Nicholas Arena and Madison Square Garden. Now, at thirteen, I was eager to try my feints and moves against an opponent and to dance out of his attack range on my quick feet. I learned the basics of boxing and found it intriguing to read my opponents' intentions and try to counter them. But after four successful matches, I fought a kid who not only knew what he was doing but had natural athletic abilities and all the requisites for being a boxer. He beat me every way one could be beaten, and despite the protective headgear, my face was a swollen mess and my nose wouldn't stop bleeding for several days. Except for a match every now and then at summer camp, that was my last prize fight, although I would spar later during my air force years. But my fascination with the physical and psychological dimensions of the sport has never left me, and boxing remains my favorite spectator sport.

Through all my sports endeavors at that time, but particularly through boxing, I worked out a philosophy of sports that fit neatly into my view of the world, although I wouldn't be able to coherently verbalize that philosophy for years to come.

From punch-ball, basketball, and boxing, as well as Monopoly, checkers, and any number of card games, I observed that all sports were divided into offense and defense, attack and defend, and, by extension, victimizer and victim, bully and bullied. In boxing, especially, I had observed and practiced the balance between offense and defense, as fighters advanced and retreated as though in a dance of give and take; and I knew that you had to develop a good defense in any sport, or whatever you were playing would become a free-for-all that would benefit the superior offensive player or team.

At the same time I understood that an opponent couldn't win if he didn't score points, and so I concentrated on attack. My deceptive moves were part of my offensive strategy and led to my masking my excitement and anxiety during play in an appearance of calm. This was another form of misdirection, which I used in all its guises, and can be looked at as flanking movements and ambushes rather than frontal attacks. Sports quickly became a matter of strategizing for me, a calculated, rational undertaking that was as much mental as physical.

However, my emotional nature, which was guided by instinct and intuition, would erupt at the most unforeseen moments to wrench my plans in startling directions. Many times these risky changes were successful because they were unexpected and broke whatever pattern the opposition thought it had detected in my game plan. In this way, the changes created shock and surprise in my opponents that worked to my advantage—and are as much a metaphor for the way I have conducted my life as they are a description of how I played sports.

All in all, 1949 was a year of enormous growth, and my discoveries about my athletic prowess determined the direction of my life for the next six years. But all was not good. My grades remained terrible and my education worse. I would daydream in class and not do my homework, and I was so far behind my grade level in English and mathematics, I hardly understood what the teachers were talking about. I still played my word-picture games and could read well enough, but books just didn't interest me.

At home, my mother was working at all hours, selling dresses in the upstairs bedroom to make ends meet, with no time for me. Maddie Jackson was in charge of my meals and my behavior and was as grandmotherly as ever. But I was seldom at the apartment.

By spring, Jimmy and I were playing basketball on the courts in Central Park near Fifth Avenue and Eightieth Street and soon advanced to the number one court—for the high school and college players. We were out of our depth, but not by much.

Jimmy and I spent less and less time at the schoolyard and more in the park, both at our baseball team and on the basketball courts. We also played hooky from school to go to Yankee Stadium or the Polo Grounds to watch the ballgames from the bleachers. I'd save up $1.30 for two tickets, and we'd have great afternoons watching the games, getting the players' autographs, and running from the truant officers, while the adults in the bleachers, usually drunk or crazy, whooped with laughter.

Jimmy and I saw less and less of Cool Breeze and Tennessee. Jimmy refused to join them when they stole from stores. He and I would stand outside and wait for them to be done, usually talking about Joe DiMaggio or Jackie Robinson and Roy Campanella, the two black Brooklyn Dodger ballplayers.

I took Jimmy home with me a number of times. At first the doormen eyed both him and his ragged clothes suspiciously and called ahead to my mother to make sure it was all right for him to come up to the apartment. It was, of course. Maddie Jackson made a fuss over him and always fed him. And my mother, although surprised at my having a black friend initially, became so concerned about the poor condition of his dress that she gave him some of my old clothes, which, of course, were too small for Jimmy who was already a thin six-footer.

But my two years in New York were as fleeting, it seemed, as the year I had lived at home when I was nine. The idyllic spring of 1950 came to a halt late one afternoon when I returned from playing basketball with Jimmy in the park to find an anguished Maddie Jackson motioning me upstairs. My mother, as usual counting her inventory of dresses, turned to me with a mournful face. Two policemen had come to see her earlier in the day, she said. They'd told her I was hanging around with the "wrong" kids, kids who would wind up in the penitentiary and were already stealing and dealing drugs. And I was playing hooky from school regularly as well. I knew about the thievery and I had seen marijuana joints knotted in Cool Breeze's hair, but I had never engaged in either of Cool Breeze or Tennessee's pursuits and told her so. But I could sense what was coming. "The policemen told me I should get you out of the city if I could, and so I've decided to send you back to boarding school."

I was stunned, but no matter how loudly I yelled or begged her, her mind was set. What I didn't know was that my mother had decided to send me to a prestige prep school with the aim of getting me into an Ivy League college. With my grades the way they were and our lack of social status, that she could get me accepted in any prep school was astonishing. In fact, it was astonishing that she even knew of such places and, further, that she could seriously have me considered as a candidate for admission.

She finally found the Irving School in Tarrytown, New York. Named after Washington Irving—the headless horseman supposedly rode over the front lawn of the school in pursuit of Ichabod Crane—the school had prepped especially to Yale for over one hundred years. I was to be on a work scholarship because, it turned out, the young, twenty-five-year-old head-master wanted to break the exclusive caste of the students, who were all white Protestants and Catholics. I was to be the school's first Jew.

I finished the school year at Joan of Arc and then was bundled off to summer camp again, where I continued to develop as a baseball and basket-ball player and boxed on boxing nights. That September my mother bought me jackets, ties, and shirts—a new wardrobe befitting a prep school student. I was ready to enter a new phase of my life. I never saw Cool Breeze, Tennessee, or Jimmy again. But my sense of equality among people, no matter what their race, religion, ethnic background, or social status had solidified into a concrete permanence.

CHAPTER 5

The Prep School Years

I had run into anti-Semitism before. There was the humiliation at the apartment house on Eastern Parkway and other incidents. Once, Spike's father had come home to find Spike and me playing in his living room and had asked his wife, thinking I was out of hearing range, "Is he still playing with that Jew?" And then there were the endless "circles" in the city over the years: five to seven older boys would surround a single young boy, and the leader would say, "Catholic or Jew?" If the boy answered "Catholic," though he was obviously Jewish, the five would let him pass, laughing as he ran off. If the boy said "Jew," the five or seven would converge on him with fists and shoes until he was bloody. I had been beaten up more than once in such situations because of my foolish pride.

Now I was to be an experiment. My first day at Irving, the headmaster called me into his office and told me that he knew my life at Irving might be difficult, but he was determined to integrate the school. He was smooth-faced, slim, dressed in Ivy League tweeds and sedate ties, and spoke without emotion in a voice that seemed to be coming through jaws that were wired shut.

It was an Indian summer day in 1950. A few hours afterward, I had my first fight. Two days later, I had my second fight. I don't remember what sparks set them off. But the third one, at the end of the week, remains vivid. It was in English class, and before the teacher entered the room, a tall, crew-cut kid named Charles Curtis III, who was the third in his line to attend Irving, came up to me, pushed me backward, and with his face close to mine began mimicking me in a whining Jewish accent, saying, "Neusbaum, Neusbaum, where's your mom," probably referring to the Mrs. Neusbaum character on Fred Allen's popular radio show.

I responded by punching him squarely in the nose, following it with a left to the side of his head. He staggered backward, blood all over his face. But I leapt at him, carrying him to the floor, and kept punching. The other kids were yelling and trying to pull me away just as the teacher entered the room. "What's going on!" he said, slamming his book down on the desk in front of the blackboard. Everyone scuttled to his seat. Mine was near the window across the room, but before I reached it, an outraged shout made me turn to see Charles charging with arms outstretched. Without time to think, I hunched down to avoid his attack just as he reached me, then I straightened and turned my body to the side. The effect was to lift Charles off his feet and, his momentum still carrying him forward, launch him through the window near my desk. The window and its wood panels shattered, and my stunned opponent found himself out on the veranda in a shower of glass shards. Luckily, he only had minor cuts.

The headmaster smiled when the teacher sent me to his office, and said nothing.

The sound of Charles Curtis III's body exploding through the window brought the whole school running, students and teachers. The story circulated through the entire school by noon. At lunch, several older students came up to me and nodded or sympathetically said, "Forget it: Charlie's an imbecile." It was my last fight at Irving.

I already knew several of the upperclassmen who had nodded to me and seemed to be assuring me that everything was going to work out. I had gotten into several half-court basketball games with them at lunch time and free play following afternoon classes, and my roommate had told me that word was getting around that I could play ball.

It was a curious time in East Coast prep school history. In order to entice alumni back to campuses and have them provide ever-needed endowment money, the prep schools were offering all state ballplayers, from the eastern seaboard all the way to Illinois, free postgraduate status so they could attend college. It turned out that many of the ballplayers' grades were not good enough to get them into the college of their choice or a college that wanted them. I soon learned that college coaches and administrators were negotiating deals with the schools. The result was that most prep schools fielded what amounted to college ball clubs. The scores of the games were carried in the sports section of the *New York Times*, and alumni from all the prep schools flocked to the games and endowed and endowed and endowed.

The football coach asked me to try out for football. I was speedy and occasionally ran back kicks, and my feints and shifts, modeled after Leo's, were generally effective since I was terrified of being tackled. But when my nose and a rib were broken and I was knocked unconscious playing linebacker against the best team in Westchester County (we were the winless worst), I retired from the game forever.

Not so with basketball and, later, baseball. Although minor anti-Semitic events occurred, the headmaster had been told of my prowess and was grooming me for a four-year career at the school, not a one-year postgraduate season. Our basketball coach was Ken Slattery, a broken-nosed, flat-faced chunk of granite who stood only slightly taller than Leo but was unstoppable as playmaker, passer, and shooter and had played with some of the legendary early professional teams in the 1920s and '30s.

Slattery took me in hand, broke my bad habits, and drilled me in the fundamentals of the game. He even had the team go to NBA games at the old

Madison Square Garden and analyze what the players were doing,
and he had us scout the teams we
were to play.

Slattery was my most important
coach and, above all else, showed me
that basketball was a mental as well
as a physical game that called for
split-second mental and physical
coordination. I started several varsity games that year and was a frequently used substitute. I was a play-
making guard who set up the
offensive plays on the court. By the
end of the season, I could also shoot
with either hand and had perfected a
deadly two-handed set shot and
stop-on-a-dime jump shot. Unfortunately, Slattery didn't return the next
year, but the team, second in the
league the first year, was even better
the next.

When spring came, I was a starting left fielder on the baseball team

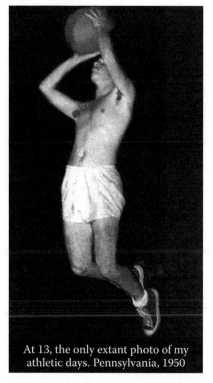

At 13, the only extant photo of my
athletic days. Pennsylvania, 1950

and batted over .400 on the freshman squad and .298 on the varsity team. I
also fell in love for the first time. She was a local girl, and I would sneak off
campus before dinner and after lights-out to meet her, and we would go
swimming in one if the ponds on the vast Rockefeller estate down the road.
We would sneak onto the property in the late afternoon or evening and
frolic until it got dark and she had to go home. It was delirious young love. I
would put my arm around her as we walked, and every once in a while we
would stop and awkwardly kiss. I realized that a girl's love was what I had
longed for with a desperation I'd never acknowledged in those early years at
the boarding schools. All in all, I was happy. Jimmy, Cool Breeze, and Tennessee were soon forgotten.

Then everything came apart. The previous headmaster's wife, who lived
with her retired husband on campus, saw me meeting my girlfriend at the
edge of the school grounds and reported it to the present headmaster. He
called me into his office and casually informed me that "Irving boys don't
consort with town girls. We're making a gentleman of you, Morton, and
you'll learn you are of a higher class. You will not see the young lady again."

I was furious. It turned out that he had gotten in touch with the girl's
father. She came from a strict Irish Catholic family and never spoke to me

again and would run away in tears when she saw me on the street in town. I actually contemplated suicide and became more morose and depressed than ever before. It would be more than a year before I dated another girl.

But more than the loss of my first love, I was enraged by the headmaster's assumption of class superiority. I yelled at him, calling him every name I could think of. His face reddened, but he remained calm, and, raising a hand for silence when I took a breath, he said, "We have great plans for you, and one day you will thank me for this."

"Not when my mother hears about it," I shot back.

"I've already informed her of the situation," he said.

"And she accepts it?"

He nodded.

"I don't believe you," I said and bolted from the office to call my mother. It was a decisive moment in my relations with her. She had always been the distant goddess whose love I longed for, but when she spoke on the phone that day, our relationship changed forever.

"Did you hear what's happened here?" I asked through my gulping tears.

"I know, my son. You must listen to what he says. He has your good at heart."

"But he says I'm to consider myself better than other people."

"You are."

"Mom, he's talking about you, Leo, the family. We're dirt to him."

"Listen to him and you will be a great man. He's right."

I couldn't believe what I was hearing, and I saw that my mother yearned for status so much she couldn't see that the headmaster's insult was directed at her as well as the family.

THE GREAT AWAKENING

Of all the events that befell me that first year at Irving, the most important was meeting Richard Martin. There is an old saw that each of us will meet one person who will change his life forever. The influences of Leo and Larry notwithstanding, that person was Richard Martin.

Martin was the dorm master on the freshman wing in the main house, the top floor of which contained one of the building's two dormitories. He'd been hired that year as the school's English teacher (Irving only had one hundred or so students), and he was a linguist, musician, translator, and writer. He was in his early twenties, just under average height, and exceedingly thin. He folded himself like a contortionist when he was sitting or standing, hugging his arms around his body or wrapping his legs around each other. A beaklike nose protruded from his gaunt face.

The first night of school he invited all twenty of us living on the hall into his room. We crowded inside and around the door while he played the guitar, sang folk songs in several languages, passed around a gallon jar of apple cider, and tried to get to know us.

On other nights he would play 78 rpm records of Django Reinhardt, Louis Armstrong, Bessie Smith, and Ledbelly and tell us about their lives—but that was later, when a coterie of three or four would visit his room and talk into the night about life and art. Most of the other students thought him "weird" because he came from a world they had never been exposed to and didn't want to know about—the world of art and culture.

Martin fascinated me with his stories and songs. Django and Ledbelly struck immediate responses with me, and within a month I learned by heart Martin's renditions of "Sam Hall" and "Barbara Allen," as well as a dozen other English folk songs. But that was later. At first I liked the big sound of Ledbelly's twelve-string guitar and Django's unique picking style.

"Any time anyone wants to come in and talk, or wants to borrow a book, just knock on my door," Martin said, raising his arm toward a packed bookshelf.

I took him up on his offer two days later, but in my inimitable New York street style. I knocked on his door and told him I'd like to read a book, and when he asked what kind, I answered, "Something dirty."

Without hesitating, he took down James T. Farrell's *Studs Lonigan* trilogy. "I'll give you this and any book you would like to read, but on one condition: You've got to discuss it with me after you're finished, and you must write down questions you may have while you're reading it."

And so I was introduced to the world of books with my personal tutor. Next came *Gulliver's Travels* and Rabelais, and the questions and discussions got deeper and deeper. My grades, even in English, remained deplorable, but I was reading everything I could get my hands on, transported by word pictures to other places and other times and into the lives of other people—in the case of Charles Dickens's characters, into lives similar to my own.

Finally, Martin gave me the key to the school library, which stretched in glass cases down the side of the classroom hallway in the main building. I read almost all the books in Random House's Modern Library series—histories, novels, poetry—with Martin showing me the fine points or directing me to the significance of what I was reading. Soon, I was tackling Joyce's short stories, *Portrait of the Artist as a Young Man*, and *Ulysses*, as well as Kafka's stories and Mann's *Magic Mountain* and *Buddenbrooks*.

By Christmas vacation, I'd begun to write, trying to put my word pictures on paper. But my efforts were mostly short science-fiction stories or satirical fantasy tales along the lines of Swift and Rabelais. Then, somewhere, I heard that a poet's "sensitivity" made him "attractive" to the opposite sex, so

I turned my literary endeavors to poetry—bad poetry, really bad poetry. The word pictures were somehow forgotten and replaced by a lot of abstract protestations using a lot of "thys," "oe'rs," and "ye's."

As for Martin, his strange body movements and bohemian ways made him the subject of ridicule behind his back, although if it had been expressed to his face it would have made little difference—he was no disciplinarian and in the end couldn't care less what the students thought of him.

Still, I was his defender: first verbally, then physically, and let everyone know that if they bothered Martin they would have to cross me, and now that I was one of the school jocks, a part of the "in" crowd, only a belligerent few wanted to get on my bad side. Actually—and it occurred to me even then—I was once more defending someone I considered a victim against the bullies.

All the attitudes toward Martin came to a head one Saturday when he drew weekend faculty duty and was supervising play in the gym. As usual, his girlfriend Penelope had come to visit him. She seemed twice as tall as Martin and bony, all legs and arms, but also sweet and attractive. She was a free spirit, and clapping her hands and jumping up and down, she asked if she could play basketball with several of us who were playing a three-on-three half-court game. I picked her for my side, while the other guys grumbled and cursed under their breaths. On the first play, one of them elbowed her in the breasts and she fell with a shriek, rolling over. Martin and I rushed to see if she was all right. Then I ran at the boy who stood smirking at what he'd done and punched him with all my strength in the stomach. As he writhed on the floor, I said something like, "Remember this. Anyone who touches or bothers Mr. Martin will get the same."

Penelope was fine in a few minutes, and the incident was forgotten. But my warning spread through the school, and I like to think I saved Martin some embarrassment, although the students still ridiculed him behind his back.

On other weekends, Martin had other visitors. One who came several times was the poet, fiction writer, and social theorist Paul Goodman, whose book on the growing disaffiliation of youth in America, *Growing Up Absurd*, was an important contribution to the thinking of the 1960s. Martin introduced me to him, and we met several times. He was the first "real" writer I encountered personally, and when he said he was pleased to hear I had started writing, I was encouraged to go on with my newfound life. Later that year, I read his book of short stories, *The Break-Up of Our Camp*, which had a profound influence on the direction of my work.

Regrettably, the headmaster had taken notice of Martin's unorthodox teaching methods and dismissed him at the end of the school year. But Martin's influence on me was permanent—the tough street kid, the once morose loner, was now completely absorbed in the world of literature and art. I searched for Martin on and off for years to thank him, even got in touch with Paul Goodman, but I could never find him until a strange incident happened years later, which I will discuss in its proper time and place.

■ ■ ■

In the city on holidays or during the summer before I went to camp, I became a haunter of bookstores—the used book row below Fourteenth Street and the Marboro Book Shops with their seemingly endless tables of remainder books. In addition, the headmaster had insisted I join the ballet and opera clubs, and I went with them to the city during the school year to attend performances of the New York City Ballet and the Metropolitan Opera Company. Once, in person on a bare stage and dressed in tuxedoes and an evening gown, Charles Laughton, Sir Cedric Hardwick, Charles Boyer and Agnes Moorehead, reading "Don Juan in Hell," the center section of George Bernard Shaw's *Man and Superman*, held me spellbound and made me aware of the intricacies of voice modulation, timing, nuance, and dramatic presentation in general.

On the weekends when I came home that year, and all the others during my teenage years, my mother—at the expense of her dozens of anonymous suitors, whom she would have take us to dinner at one fashionable restaurant or another and then a show of some sort—made sure I continued to attend the opera and Broadway and off-Broadway shows as well as foreign films: the Alec Guinness British comedies, the early masterpieces of Ingmar Bergman, the last Italian neorealist films of Rossellini and De Sica, and Fellini's first great works.

Although emotionally in turmoil over the loss of my first love the summer after my freshman year at Irving, I honed my basketball and baseball skills at camp, sharing my passions for books as well as my tales of love with a wonderfully compassionate and athletic counselor called Whitey, who showed me that a man could be sensitive as well as manly, another lesson I was not to forget.

For the month after camp was over and before school began, I once more played basketball every day at the Eighty-first Street courts in Central Park. Jimmy was never there, and when I went to look for him at our old haunts, he wasn't there either, and the few people I remembered said they hadn't seen him for a while. Now, however, I started playing early and leaving by 2 or 3 o'clock in the afternoon to sit or wander until closing time through the nearby Metropolitan Museum of Art. Like the Museum of Natural history years before, admission was free and the galleries were practically empty since school was out and the heat on the upper floors was stifling. I studied the paintings in one room after another, a sweaty kid in T-shirt and sneakers that the guards at first eyed with concern but after a while would smile at and nod to in greeting. I had changed. So had my picture of New York as a magical city. It now included bookstores, museums, opera houses and theaters of all kinds. What my mother and the headmaster had intended was happening. My rough edges were being smoothed.

■ ■ ■

My second year at Irving wasn't a lonely one. Although my former girlfriend refused to see me and Martin was gone, I was an accepted member of the student body and an important part of the headmaster's plan to field winning teams in all sports—or at least in basketball and baseball. Now my scholarship was clearly athletic. The Jewish experiment had worked: two more Jews were admitted to Irving at the start of my sophomore year.

Basketball and books were my obsessions that year. I read by flashlight under the bed covers after lights out or listened on my radio to Al "Jazzbo" Collins in his Purple Grotto as he played some of the best jazz of the 1950s.

During the day I spent every extra minute in the gym, many times coming late to class because I kept shooting after the bell had sounded and the other students had hurried off. The other students thought I was a bit of a flake, but they liked me, and as teammates we got along fine. In fact, my flakiness had come into fashion earlier that year with the publication of J. D. Salinger's *Catcher in the Rye*. To many of my classmates, I was Holden Caulfield personified: moody, disaffected, but (unlike Holden) a jock and most of the time lots of fun. The humor I had discovered in myself several years before stood me in good stead, and my punning and quick retorts, though they elicited groans as well as grins, made me of interest to the more studious students. They appreciated my knowledge of books as well, which, along with my quips, inspired intelligent discussions spiced with repartee. All in all, as comic, tough guy, jock, and budding member of the literati, I was one of the more popular students.

Ken Slattery did not return as basketball coach, but the math teacher and football coach had taken over, and under his direction we were 10 and 0 by mid-February of 1952. I was the starting left guard. My responsibilities were to set up plays, stay back when we were on offense, and lead the fast break down the middle of the court when our tall center and forwards hauled down the rebounds on the defensive boards.

The fast break became our specialty. The rebounder, the center or a forward, would come off the boards with the ball, fire an "outlet pass" to a guard or one of the other forwards on one of the two sides of the court. They, in turn, would pass the ball to me and speed down the sidelines toward the opponents' basket. We would then converge on the lone defender at the other end of the court. I woud be in the middle, passing at the last moment to one of the other two as they cut to the basket from the right and left sidelines or I would take the shot mysel, a simple lay-up.

With three postgraduate all-state players and several of us who had played together the year before, we seemed unstoppable. Then, in early February, we ran into Milford Military Academy on their home court.

Milford had a good record but not nearly as good as ours. When we took the floor to the howling and shouting of the uniformed cadets in the stands, we weren't intimidated. But we were alarmed to see that the Milford coach had hired only one referee to "call" the game. That meant that only one end of the court at a time could be overseen. Our coach protested immediately, but if we didn't play, we would have had to forfeit the game.

It quickly became apparent what was going on. With the referee still down at the other end of the court as I led the fast break, the lone Milford defender would bang into me before I could pass the ball to one of my two cutting teammates. Sometimes he would grab my jersey or knee me as I came toward him.

We lost point after point. The coach protested, the captain of the team protested, and I protested. Soon, we were down by ten points, then fifteen. The cadets in the stands were jeering and howling at our exasperation and making fun of our complaints. Worse than that, the player who was defending against the break was smiling at me.

The coach called off the fast break, and we began to get back into the game. But early in the third quarter, a rebound and quick outlet pass set the fast break in motion almost automatically. This time the defender moved aside as I rushed at him and pushed me from behind so that I slammed against the padded wall under the basket.

I lay on the floor, dazed. Then the defender's face appeared above me with a wicked smile. His arm leaned down and he extended a hand to help me up. I could hear the cadets in the stands yelling and laughing. I was furious. I accepted the defender's help with my left hand, putting all my weight on my right foot as I rose, my right fist swinging up from the floor and catching him flush on the jaw. He went down, and I was on top of him.

There was shouting and wrestling everywhere around me as both teams pulled me off the Milford player and went at each other. Why and how the cadets stayed in the stands was a credit to Milford's discipline, I guess. I was ejected from the game, and when I passed the Milford stands on my way to the locker room, I answered the oaths and threats they showered on me with some unmannerly words of my own.

The headmaster, who had come to the game with us, followed me into the locker room. He said nothing until after I showered and dressed, all the while slapping his legs with his leather gloves, one foot resting on a bench. Then he said, in his New England drawl, without a preamble, his voice still neutral but tighter than ever, "I think we've gone about as far with you as we can go, Morton. I'm afraid you'll never be a gentleman."

He took his foot off the bench and stood before me. "I'm sending you home on suspension. I'll let you finish the year at Irving, but you won't be coming back, and your playing days for us are over."

I could understand the headmaster's attitude. I had done the unforgivable—held the school's name up to public shame, not to mention almost causing a riot.

My mother was grief stricken. When would I stop being such a source of misery to her? I didn't feel a shred of guilt. As my teammates agreed, Milford was at fault for purposely hiring one referee and obviously "planning" the way they were going to destroy our fast break. Several of my teammates commented on the excellence of my punch, and others said they wished they had done the same thing. As for me not being a gentleman: the headmaster was right. I was proud of my peasant origins, and I took his pronouncement as a compliment.

CHAPTER 6

Nixon, Daoism, and Death in the Afternoon

After my suspension was over, I was not allowed to finish the basketball season, but I was allowed to play baseball and was starting left fielder on the team that spring. One of our games was against Storm King, a prep school in Cornwall on Hudson, New York, which was near West Point and was built on a mountainside. The baseball field was laid out with right and center outfields ending in a road and, beyond that, gently rising to a hilly pasture. But left field fell off sharply after 270 feet to a 10- or 15-foot ravine. This wouldn't have been a problem with the undeveloped batting power of most high school players, but that was the year of an extraordinary distance-hitting, Storm King postgraduate named Johnny Kovalchek, whose home-run-hitting exploits everyone on the prep school circuit had heard about.

Before the game, the umpire, our coach, and Storm King's coach pointedly warned the center fielder and me to be aware of the left-field hazard.

Kovalchek hit a home run to right field in the first inning and one to center field in the third. They were high, towering drives that seemed to take the crowd's shouts of astonishment with them over the road and into the upland pasture.

Kovalchek came up to the plate in the fifth inning and connected again, this time to left field. But he had hit the ball too high. I judged its arc immediately, turned my back to the infield, and, looking over my shoulder, charted the course of the ball's flight and raced toward where I knew it would land. I'd seen DiMaggio and young Willie Mays do the same and had perfected my judgment of fly balls for the past three years. I was elated. The great Kovalchek was about to be bagged in sensational style, and I was going to get another mention in the newspapers to go along with my toss from deep left field two weeks before that had cut down an opposing player at home plate.

I was sprinting, buoyant, still peering over my shoulder, the ball totally in my sights against the blue sky, sailing to just where I knew it would land. I could feel my cleated shoes, one after another, ripping into the grass and pushing me onward to the target area. I was controlled, rhythmic energy, like a slow motion film of a galloping racehorse.

Then, there was no grass beneath my shoes. My cheats were slicing through air, and I was falling head over heels—and everything went blank.

The next thing I saw was my coach's worried face staring down at me. "Marcus, Marcus," he was calling. When he saw my open eyes, he said, "You all right?"

I don't remember my answer, but the words I uttered promoted great glee among my teammates on the school bus as we rode back to Tarrytown after the game, despite the fact that we had been thoroughly trounced. They hit me over the head with their gloves and caps, and the coach just kept shaking his head and looking at me as if I were a freak in a carnival sideshow.

Luckily (and I'm sure purposely), Storm King had planted springy bushes at the bottom of the left field drop-off, and though I had almost broken my neck and was cut and bruised all over for a week, I was not hurt seriously—although I think I had a slight concussion because I was groggy sitting on the sidelines for the rest of the game and just grinned stupidly at my teammates' antics on the bus afterward.

What I supposedly answered the coach as he peered down at me and asked, "You all right?" was, in a serious, contemplative voice, "Coach, I just learned what death is."

And so I had, and I do not deny my teammates' reporting of the facts, which remained the point of their good-natured ribbing for the rest of the season.

What I had realized while flying through the air and falling unconscious is that death is a cessation of consciousness. In the same way I had experienced the loss of my presence within my body, I thought when we die we are suddenly no longer where we were the moment before, when our faculties were sharply, perfectly focused and in sync. A door closes like a guillotine, and the world, with all its colors and sounds, smells and tastes and ideas, is on the other side, and we are nowhere, not even in unending darkness. There is no afterlife, no purgatory or gray, cloudy atmosphere. We are nothing. Being is sensation and thought. Death is its opposite. Death is what Hemingway said life was in "A Clean, Well-Lighted Place." It is "all *nada y pues nada y nada y pues nada.*" So strongly was this impression embedded in my consciousness that I've never altered my opinion. My conception of the nothingness of death has determined the way I have faced life and made my ethical and aesthetic choices since that day.

But my newfound truth presented problems, problems I could see even as I groggily swayed from side to side on the school bus, enduring my teammates teasing and horseplay. Somewhere in the hazy recesses of my mind, I was aware that I had in some way chosen life over death that afternoon—or my body had chosen life when confronted with death. But the ramifications that came with that decision were problematic. Since there had to be a foundation of values on which a person drew to act responsibly in moral matters, where was I going to find that foundation now that I had denied life after death and the rewards for living an upright life promised by most religions? A Jew I might have been, but I was a cultural rather than a religious one, and organized religions of all kinds, to which I was exposed by school rules every Sunday by my compulsory attendance at different churches, held no appeal for me.

I may not have reasoned it out in these exact terms, but the problem of acting in an ethical manner definitely concerned me. It was also clear to me that I needed a simple foundation on which to base my actions, one in which there was no possibility I would fall prey to the rationalizations and cowardice I had experienced in my betrayal of Red, although I had no idea what that "simple foundation" might be. But I was looking, and in retrospect it is no surprise that I found part of my answer three months later.

As for the rest of the school year, my grades remained poor, but my mother managed to have me admitted for the following year to another and better prep school, Cheshire Academy, on another athletic scholarship.

I looked forward to the summer vacation as never before, still smarting from my girlfriend's rejection and her refusal to speak to me. I couldn't imagine why she had so completely removed me from her life, no matter what the school or her parents said. But the affair had been over for more than a year, I was fifteen years old, and although I didn't know it at the time, my period of mourning for my first love was over.

NIXON AND DAOISM

Psychologically, if not physically, I was too old for summer camp. I'd gone to the same camp as my friend Ronnie Rosner since I was nine years old. Ronnie and I had become such good friends over the years that we saw each other off and on when we were home in the city. He lived a half-hour subway ride away from me in Queens, and because of my stay at schools we didn't get together as often as we would have liked. But we were inseparable at camp each summer, and in the future we would hang around together and even double date well into our adult years. Ronnie was a fine all-around athlete, and we played baseball, basketball, and boxed together at camp. I admired him from the day I met him, and I was not surprised that he went on to graduate with a Masters degree from Columbia University, become an economist, teach economics at Penn State, give up his career to join a Peace Corps project in Central America, and finally settle in Wisconsin, where he earned his PhD, was president of the Wisconsin chapter of the Sierra Club, and, among other things, testified in court on behalf of the Chippewa Indians in one of their disputes with the government. We never lost touch, and our adult adventures include camping in Yosemite and taking a week-long canoeing trip in the lake-strewn Quetico Boundary Waters between Minnesota and Canada.

During our pubescent teenage years at camp, Ron and I loved to get into innocent trouble and explore the world around us. The summer after my freshman year at Irving, we had not only gone canoeing and swimming together when we were supposed to be doing other things, but we'd often left the camp grounds in the Poconos Mountains and hitchhiked all over Pennsylvania. Although it was never said, I don't think the camp directors wanted us back in the summer of 1952.

And we didn't want to go back. We wanted to work and have adventures. But we were too young. Working papers weren't issued in New York until the would-be worker was sixteen. My mother, however, knew the owner of a shady employment agency, and when Ronnie and I entered his grimy office, he scowled, took a well-chewed cigar stub out of his mouth, pointed it at us, and without so much as a "hello," instructed us to buy black pants, white shirts, and black bow ties and get down to Rehoboth Beach, Delaware, by the next afternoon to begin work as waiters at an exclusive political hideaway.

Thus began the summer of 1952, one that was to minimally affect my political attitudes and completely direct my spiritual orientations.

Ron and I bunked in a house with twenty-five other staff members of the hotel. We each earned $15 a week, but that was supplemented by hundreds of dollars in tips. The bellhop and other waiters were a wild crew of college students, most of them from Delaware and Maryland but some from as far away as New York and Canada.

Not only were there late-night drinking parties and drunken card games, but there were women everywhere, from the wives and daughters of the wealthy people we waited on at the hotel to the waitresses, local girls, and girls on vacation at Rehoboth Beach, a well-known summer resort town.

Among our fellow waiters were several basketball players from the University of Maryland and the University of West Virginia, and along with them and two of the black dishwashers, we played ball at the outdoor high school courts on the outskirts of town. It was still a time of segregation, but that didn't matter to us, although when one of the waitresses I was having an affair with found out I was playing ball with blacks, she walked up to me and, without a word, slapped my face and called me a "nigger lover." I never spoke to her again.

Around three weeks after Ron and I arrived, the hotel manager informed us that Senator Richard Nixon and his family had booked the Presidential Suite (the hideaway's name for what would normally be called a hotel's bridal suite) for a week and would take room service for breakfast and dinner during his stay. Nixon was very much in the news then because he had been selected the week before as Eisenhower's presidential running mate at the Republican Convention.

Everyone was excited about Nixon's coming to the hotel. Which of us would be his exclusive waiters for the week? The manager decided to have the waiters draw straws for the honor, and I drew a short straw along with a dental student from the University of Maryland who was convinced he could exploit his week serving Nixon and his family into a career fixing the teeth of all the congressmen that Nixon would send his way.

The night of the Nixons' arrival, we wheeled the food-laden carts to the door of the Presidential Suite and knocked, towels over our arms, tuxedos crisp and neatly in place.

"Come in," said a female voice.

We opened the door and stood transfixed. Arranged in front of a couch against the wall opposite us, as if posing for a family Christmas card photo, stood the Nixons, Pat on one side of the couch, the two little girls in the middle, and Senator Nixon on the other side. Pat was wearing a black evening gown with matching elbow-length gloves. Her hands were joined, and as we stood gazing in surprise at the scene, she said, in a queenly way, "Good evening. We are the Nixons. I'm Pat. This is Tricia. This is Julie." As she said each name, the identified girl, in lacy Sunday finery, curtsied. Then Pat nodded to the senator and intoned in a proud but joking voice, "And this is *Vice President* Nixon."

Nixon awkwardly waved and half turned away, as if he could not face us directly. Nor could he look us in the eye.

And so our week with the Nixons began.

For six days at breakfast and dinner, my partner flattered Pat and the girls and desperately tried to engage Nixon in conversation. But it was no use. Nixon was uncomfortable and unresponsive. He had no social graces. Pat directed our service and chatted easily with us while the senator, soon to be vice president, averted his eyes and let her do the talking. He reminded me of those namby-pamby kids at the schools who were the bullies' favorite targets. More than that, he had no charisma, a word I wouldn't learn or use for several years to come.

The last night of their stay, the Nixons had dinner in the large dining room. The Republican Party committees of Delaware and Maryland had reserved all the tables, and the hotel manager whisked Nixon from one table to another. Photographers' flashbulbs popped as the senator shook hands left and right and was guided into the kitchen where he met the chef and the sous-chef. Everyone applauded, more flashbulbs popped, and the suave trio, who entertained from 6 PM until midnight, struck up a dinky version of the presidential victory march, "Hail to the Chief."

Nixon's final stop was at the hostess's table, where he was introduced to her and her beautiful daughter, Nancy, on whom all the waiters had a lascivious crush. My partner and I had been given the night off (as well as a steak dinner) for a job well done and were seated at the hostess's table.

The manager finished his introductions by extending a hand toward us and saying, "And, of course, you know these two fine young men."

A sweaty Nixon looked from one of us to the other and said, "No, I don't believe I've had the pleasure."

I glanced at my partner out of the corner of my eye and saw the stricken look on his face, as if his entire dental career had come to an end before it had started.

Worse yet as far as I was concerned, the Nixons departed the following day without leaving a tip. For all our efforts, my partner and I had earned $15 each that week. It must have been a terrible lesson for my partner—he cursed the senator roundly for several days—but for me it showed that public leadership had little to do with individual personality. Authority figures—teachers, headmasters, and the like—had proven to be less-than-commendable human beings. And now, national figures had revealed themselves to be nothing more than ordinary humans who cast oversized shadows.

■ ■ ■

Two weeks later I was fired after drawing after-hours linen count on the night the kitchen icebox was robbed. I was suspected of being the inside contact man for the thieves. The accusation was absurd, and no charges were brought against me. It was more probable that my departure from the hotel was instigated by the guardians of a young heiress who took an interest in me when her family had dined at the hotel and who I began to date several days later. Whatever the reason, I was now without a job or place to stay, although I had the $700 I had already earned safely tucked in a local bank.

Over the previous weeks, I had befriended the musicians in the hotel trio, one in particular, the swarthy bassist and vocalist who called himself Hank Jerome but whose real name was Herman Goldberg. The musicians didn't live with the rest of the staff. The hotel had rented them rooms in a local boarding house, and Hank persuaded the other trio members, one of whom was the group's leader, to go to their landlady and convince her to rent me the porch of her house for $10 a week.

The musicians lived on the top floor, and the three bedrooms on the first floor were let to young waitresses from various restaurants in town. The landlady had a reputation as a high-minded Christian lady who was against the use of alcohol. In reality, she was a sweet old thing who could not think ill of anyone and had no idea of the shenanigans that were going on in the house all summer. Not only were there drinking parties after the waitresses got home after work, but there were young men in all the girls' rooms. By that hour, however, the old woman was always asleep. As for me, I got to know the waitresses quickly and didn't sleep on the porch more than five nights for the rest of the summer.

But it was Hank who was the main influence on me. He seduced middle-aged ladies at the hotel for a fee, set me up with a number of them, and became my tutor in vice and philosophy. Today, I would call Hank amoral rather than immoral. A World War II veteran, he lived by his wits and his questionable values, which were based on his questionable readings of the *Daodejing (Tao Teh Ching)*. He introduced me to the book and urged me to read his copy. Once I did, like Martin before him, he would talk to me about the various enigmatic verses.

The book intrigued me. Its insights and proclamations, often expressed in sharp, concrete imagery, thundered in my mind, sending lightning flashes through my imagination. A number of the ideas in the book I had fancifully toyed with over the years in my word-picture games. But here, the images were rigorously tied to specific ideas that in many cases called into question the linear thinking that was the customary way of looking at things in the America in which I was growing up. Daoism (Taoism) demanded leaps of the imagination—other ways of looking at the world around me. Even though I was reading Witter Bynner's extremely flawed translation (as I was to learn years later), the ideas and images were startling to an impressionable fifteen-year-old. Particularly verse number 11, which stated that the usefulness of an object depended on where the object was not, or, in other words, where the object didn't exist—thus, the walls and windows were not important in a house, but the emptiness those enclosures contained was. In the same way, a pitcher was important because of its empty interior.

In other imagery, the dichotomy of the things of this world was sharply brought into focus by such statements as

> We find one thing beautiful
> because we find another ugly.

I had never seen this dichotomy so clearly stated and now understood the necessity of opposites, which eventually would lead me to yin-yang thinking, where opposites were actually pairings that moved in and out of cosmic balance with each other.

All summer long I read the *Daodejing* over and over again and discussed with Hank the many implications of its words. At the end of the summer, I bought my own hardcover copy of the Bynner version in New York City and have it with me still, although it has been joined by eight other translations. I never take a trip without its slender volume in my knapsack or suitcase.

Reading and reflecting on the *Daodejing* (a reading that in many ways a Daoist (Taoist), I'm sure, would find as questionable as I found Hank's) not only changed my life at fifteen, but has guided my thinking as well as my writing ever since. It is the foundation for my responses to the world and, along with my notions of death, has affected all I've seen and done—as well as presented me with more problems concerning how I should conduct my life. For instance, if life is constant change, a flux of yin and yang imbalances, how can you arrange your days, not to mention your life? The paradoxes and shifts of fortune, the alternating good and bad times, leave an impression of nature's arbitrariness. And so the world can be viewed as chaotic, a collection of fragments, shattered bits of a cosmic vase that continue to scatter through the universe forever and which we cannot hope to piece together. If my notions of death had forced me to seek whatever answers I would find in life, this new concept was upsetting to say the least, especially since I was looking for a simple foundation for my universe, not one which, at the outset, would become confused and knotted with complexities. I sensed, however, that Daoism, despite the difficulties I encountered, would in the end provide me with a clear, forthright metaphysical explanation about the nature of things if I could grasp its inner design. In time I would come to see that a universe undergoing constant change was an orderly universe, just not one my adolescent, linear-thinking mind could accept, because constancy, whether of change or stasis, I would eventually understand, is a definition of order.

There was also the problem, which Hank expounded on continually, that there was no moral or ethical basis for one's actions in a world of constant change, no foundation of eternal moral values, so why bother following a code of conduct that seemed antithetical to the ways of nature? In essence, he was saying, *just go with the flow.* It would be another eight years before I found an acceptable answer to this difficult and, for me, most pressing problem.

TO BEGIN AND BEGIN AGAIN

By the time I entered Cheshire Academy that fall, I was a different person than I had been the previous spring. I continued my reading, concentrating on Kafka and Joyce, but now I was writing poetry more seriously than in previous years. For the first time, I was trying to express in verse the word pictures I had been playing with for years.

For all my concern with literature, I still wouldn't pay attention in class and spent most of my time in the gym. Since I was on an athletic scholarship, that was not surprising. I was expected to be one of the starting guards—that is, until the quarterback on the football team, an all-state Illinois athlete in football, basketball, and baseball, was ready to play in December. Cheshire "prepped" almost exclusively to Yale, and as a consequence, its athletic program was under the eyes of the university athletic department to the point that illegal collusion between both schools on recruitment policies was a definite possibility. Cheshire's entire first-string football team was composed of postgraduates, the line averaging over 240 pounds, and the basketball team had so much postgraduate depth that I was "bench security." I also quickly learned that Cheshire's athletic teams, especially the football squad, were so fearsome they weren't allowed to play most high schools but competed against college freshmen and junior varsity squads.

In the end, this information made no difference to me because I was seriously injured in the third exhibition game with what seemed a season-ending ankle injury, and Cheshire revoked my scholarship.

After Christmas break, which I celebrated by hitchhiking to Miami with a friend I'd made at Cheshire, I found myself enrolled at Blair Academy on another athletic scholarship. My indefatigable mother had succeeded in persuading another school to accept me—or had my athletic reputation preceded me? I'll never know. What I do know is that each prep school I attended was better than the previous one. Blair was one of the best and prepped specially to Princeton. Why they would have accepted me—deplorable scholastically and incapacitated athletically—is something I will never understand.

My injury proved to be only a severe strain, and by the end of January I was back in the gym. But then another mystery presented itself: Blair's basketball team didn't need me. They were 12 and 0, and again I was a substitute. I appeared in uniform for their thirteenth game and played almost a half in what proved to be the team's first loss. As far as my teammates were concerned, I was a jinx. I think the coach thought so as well, for I played irregularly the rest of the season, despite some excellent moments on the court. But I wasn't depressed by my lack of playing time because I recognized that the first string was a smooth unit, used to playing together.

I played baseball that spring and spent the days that summer playing basketball in the park in New York City and again visiting the Metropolitan Museum of Art on an almost daily basis. I also spent whole afternoons at the Museum of Modern Art, the Frick, the Whitney and the Cloisters, the last of which overlooked the Hudson river and was always relatively cool during hot spells. By night, I worked as a doorman, janitor, and incinerator cleaner in an apartment house on Second Avenue and Fifty-first Street. Off at midnight, I would walk across town to Birdland or Basin Street East on Fifty-second Street and Broadway, gaining entrance on a false I.D. card, and listen to jazz, mingling with such musicians as Lester Young, Miles Davis, Sonny Stitt, Stan Getz, Sarah Vaughan, Billy Eckstine, and any number of other jazz immortals. It was a great summer, one I've often remembered nostalgically over the years.

I returned to Blair that fall to have the coach present me with a key to the gym and an introduction to two new postgraduates. We were to be the

Blair yearbook
photo, New Jersey,
1954

mainstays of his team and were to play together every
afternoon until football season was over and other
members of the team joined us.

But my grades remained exceptionally poor, and I
was so below the level of Blair students that even if I had
wanted to, I wouldn't have been able to cope with the
schoolwork.

The coach was also the dean in charge of discipline
and a strict disciplinarian. He warned me early in the
fall term that if I couldn't keep my grades at a C level,
school rules forbade me to play on Blair athletic teams.
In January he benched me, and in February when I was
failing two classes and my average sank to a low D, he
asked me to hand in my uniform. My jovial good humor, which had made
me a popular upperclassman over the past year, disappeared. I was morose
and solitary again. Why couldn't I do my schoolwork? Why had I gotten so
far behind in my studies that it seemed I would never be able to catch up
with my classmates? Even my love of basketball was not enough to motivate
me to take action and change the situation.

I wandered about the school grounds in a permanent funk. At one point,
the assistant headmaster, who had been responsible for my admission and
had a sincere liking and respect for my mother, called me into his office. He
was an emaciated man with a gaunt face who dragged himself from one
place to another, permanently bent over. He had been gassed in World War
I and seemed to be alive through an effort of will more than anything else.

"Look at you," he began when I was seated on the opposite side of his
desk. "Your mother has done everything to get you an education, and you
mope about the campus doing nothing. What's wrong?"

I didn't answer.

"What's wrong with you? Answer me, you ungrateful brat!"

And when I didn't answer him again, he wrenched himself from his chair,
leaned over the desk, and slapped me as hard as he could across the face.

I smiled and did nothing.

"Answer me," he said, growing more and more infuriated, and proceeded
to slap me again and again. Finally, he fell back in his chair, exhausted.

"Get out," he said. Without a word, I rose and left his office.

I was miserable. I knew the old man was trying to reach me for my own
good, and my behavior had brought him to such a level of frustration that
he had lost control of himself. As for the beating, my cheek didn't even
sting. The old man was so weak, his blows felt like nothing more than buf-
fets of wind. But no matter how much I tried to swagger it off, it was the low
point of the year for me.

The one bright spot was my writing. The previous spring I had won the
school's literary award with a short story that was printed in the school's lit-

erary magazine, and this year I was voted the magazine's editor. I threw what energy I had into the assignment and produced the best issue of the literary magazine in the school's history, or so everyone said.

My relationship with the other students remained good. Many of my class-mates thought I should never have been removed from the basketball team, which wound up having a mediocre season. A number of them felt the team's record was the result of my not being allowed to play. They blamed the coach for that, however, not me. They commiserated with me, and were intrigued by my flaunting the school's rules in my dress and in my other odd behavior, which I engaged in more out of depression than rebellion. Although we had to wear jackets and ties, I had taken to wearing an old firehouse red, corduroy shirt over my white shirt and school tie, and my classmates thought such dar-ing antics deserved affection as well as respect. I also listened to their problems with interest and sensitivity and could be counted on to keep a confidence and provide good advice. They all seemed to understand the disappearance of my good humor.

At about this time I consciously made the choice to follow my own bents and not be fashionable. I would not, in other words, hide my emotional nature behind the mask of the strong, silent male my classmates prized and sought to emulate. Instead, I would be the Slavic peasant I imagined I was, guided by enthusiasm and intuition and full of a passionate intensity.

Despite those bright spots, the year ended as badly as possible. I was not allowed to graduate: I had, in effect, flunked out of high school.

Without a degree, my basketball career seemingly at an end, I moved into my mother's apartment in the city.

My mother was beside herself with anger and frustration. She cursed me from one day to the next. Her boyfriend at the time, a slickly dressed, fun-loving bruiser named Mike, persuaded her to let him take me on a ten-day trip down the East Coast to Maryland so she could calm down and I could think about my future. An executive salesman, he drove me in his Buick convertible as he checked the efforts and effectiveness of the salesmen under him. We stopped in one city after another, and wherever we went, the Army-McCarthy hearings were on television sets from morning to night. I watched them at restaurants and at the stores and places of business we vis-ited. I didn't completely understand what was happening, but I knew that the country had averted a serious attempt to curtail individual freedoms thanks to a handful of brave men who had stood up to the grasping senator when the whole nation should have. I wouldn't forget that lesson about the necessary loneliness of individual action—and the failure of the masses to accept their responsibilities to their neighbors and the nation.

Sometimes in the afternoons, Mike would take me to the nearest race-track and instruct me on how to read the racing form, judge the horses in the paddock before the race, and gamble accordingly. At night we would eat at the best and worst restaurants, then make our way to the closest racetrack again. It made no difference whether the track featured horse or trotter racing: everyone knew Mike wherever we went. I thought he was a wonderful guy and knew he loved me. As for Mike, he introduced me to his friends and acquaintances with a pride I had never seen before. I was the son he never had, and he had a lot to teach me. Unfortunately, he wasn't the kind of man who could be controlled by a woman, and my mother broke up with him a month later.

When we returned to New York, my mother was still upset. Her boy was a failure. She wasn't to be denied, however. She somehow got an appointment with Benjamin Fine, the education editor at the *New York Times*, who listened to her patiently, then personally gave me a series of diagnostic examinations. When I'd finished the tests and he'd marked them, he called my mother into his office where I was seated.

"I wanted you both to hear this at the same time," he said softly. "I looked over Morton's tests, Mrs. Marcus, and I want you to accept the fact that he is not educable. You've been trying to make him accomplish what he is not able to do. My advice is that you send him to a school for plumbers or electricians. I'm sorry."

My mother broke into tears. She was inconsolable. I sat there nonplussed, as usual. Fine didn't explain how he had reached his conclusion, but he had put into words what, in my constant state of depression, I wanted to hear. Not that I accepted his judgment. Somewhere in the recesses of my consciousness I knew that I could be successful in almost anything I undertook if I could find the wherewithal to apply myself and, I would come to realize, if I could overcome my rebelliousness and self-pity.

For the rest of the summer my mother continually nagged me to finish the courses I had failed and attempted to control my every move. I got a job as a stock boy at Lord & Taylor's department store and had my own money. But living with her in her new small apartment on Central Park South, where she continued her personal dress-buying business, was difficult if not intolerable for both of us, and I realized I had been lucky not to be raised by her. I came to see that I had achieved a sort of independence by living in the schools that she would never have allowed had she raised me herself.

Two months after the incident in Fine's office, Leo accompanied me to the Army recruiting station in Times Square, and I enlisted for a four-year term in the air force. The Korean conflict was in its fourth year and a truce had been declared, but negotiations were at a stalemate, and the country continued to be in a state of war.

In early September, at age eighteen, having lived at home less than three months since flunking out of high school, I was again going away, but I thought that even an experience that resembled boarding-school life was preferable to remaining in the tiny apartment with my mother. Besides, I was the one who had initiated this action. My life, for better or worse, was my own.

BOOK THREE

THE AIR FORCE YEARS

CHAPTER 7

You're in the Army Now

My first day in the air force was memorable. Around seventy of us were loaded into a bus and driven north. It seemed the route was purposely circuitous. I think we crossed into New Jersey several times, and I remember driving through one small town after another. The ride seemed endless, and all of us, raucous boys trying to swagger off our anxiety, had no idea where we were or where we were going.

Just before sundown, we arrived at the gates of Sampson Air Force Base on the Finger Lakes in upper New York state. At the gate, we were joined on the bus by a squat sergeant in starched fatigues who shouted that he would be our training sergeant and we were all scum as far as he was concerned. He strode up and down the aisle, yelling instructions and telling us what we were to do when we reached our barracks, pointedly ordering us to ask no questions, keep our mouths shut, and do what he said, glaring at us individually as he talked.

When we arrived at our area, we were issued sheets and blankets, and the sergeant lined us up and marched us to our barracks. He kept us lined up outside and berated us, telling us to stand there, holding our bedding in our arms for the rest of the night. The sun was going down, and although it was Indian summer, a chill breeze we'd soon get to know all too intimately was scything off the lakes.

We hadn't eaten since lunch, and we stood, hungry and shivering, with the night closing in and our arms aching, all of us probably thinking the same thing: we'd made a big mistake by enlisting. I added to that a vow that I would have to follow the rules and not get into trouble, suddenly realizing my four-year enlistment period was a long time. When we were finally allowed into the barracks, we collapsed bleary-eyed in the corridor outside the partitioned, doorless cubicles, each of which would house six of us on three double metal bunks. The sergeant strode back and forth between our seated bodies, yelling insults, epithets, and instructions, informing us that we were "lower than whale shit" and, more to the point, that we were the worst kind of recruits because we were from New York City, known incorrigibles, along with enlistees from Philadelphia and Chicago. But we were the worst, he maintained, and that was why he, one of the toughest of all drill sergeants, had been assigned to us. And, by God, he was going to make *men* out of us, make *soldiers* out of us.

He punctuated these last words by stepping on the shins of the one of the recruits who had stretched his legs out in front of him. The kid howled in pain, and the rest of us gasped. The sergeant had made his point.

It was four in the morning, and he dismissed us for two-and-a-half hours of sleep, when, he said, our life in the air force would begin.

That was my first night in the air force, and I was more determined than ever to mind my own business, control my temper, and do whatever I was told, making myself as inconspicuous as possible. The latter quickly proved impossible, since I was one of only two members of the squadron who wore glasses, which made us both immediate targets for the sergeant's wrath. The other recruit was quickly called "Specs," and I was "Four Eyes," a nickname that had never been applied to me before since I had only been wearing glasses since the previous winter.

"What's wrong, Four Eyes, you want your mama?" "You, Four Eyes, don't you know your left from your right?" "Four Eyes, come here, and show us how you do twenty pushups."

I obeyed all the sergeant's commands, and when all my hair was shaved off the next day, I must have looked and acted like an exemplary wimp, especially to the sergeant who used me as the primary butt of his insults. There were seventy-two of us in the squadron, whites, blacks, Puerto Ricans, and one or two immigrants. We marched everywhere, each assigned, according to height, a specified place in one of four lines. The fellow who marched behind me was a gangling six-footer with a bulbous forehead and green bulging fisheyes named Lazotte, and from the first day we all knew he was a little crazy. He would giggle every time the sergeant would insult someone—even him—and would ask questions even when he was told to keep quiet. His behavior was clearly abnormal. Then, three nights after we arrived, he left the barracks after lights out, returning with a tray of cakes he'd stolen from the area mess hall.

By then, a pecking order of power had been established in the squadron, shared by four cliques of muscular black kids. When Lazotte went from room to room offering his cakes, four of the blacks took him into the latrine and told him he was going to make things hard for everyone and he should "ditch" the tray. Lazotte merely giggled. The black guys took all the cakes, dividing them among their four groups, and slammed Lazotte in the head with the tray, throwing both the tray and Lazotte out of the barracks. Lazotte giggled and got rid of the tray.

Lazotte remained impervious to threats, being roughed up, or logic. He did one wacky thing after another and soon decided to follow the sergeant's example of harassing me. He didn't bait me or call me names; he merely stepped on my heels so I momentarily lost step or stumbled, a fact the sergeant always seemed to notice. "What's wrong, Four Eyes? Don't you know your left from your right?"

The second time Lazotte stepped on my heels, he giggled and I knew it was deliberate. "Watch it," I muttered.

"You talking in the ranks, Four Eyes?" the sergeant called.

"No, sir," I said.

"Fall out," he replied. "Get down and do twenty." Several of the guys in the squadron snickered, and I realized the group was being drawn into the sergeant's strategy of regarding me as the squadron fall guy. Or, to put it in the vernacular, the squadron's second fuck-up after Lazotte. Worse than that, others had seen Lazotte treading on my heels, and since the squadron as a unit regarded him as the group's major troublemaker, they now saw me as the troublemaker's victim. Dean Martin and Jerry Lewis were in their midst.

During the next break, I went over to Lazotte and whispered, "Listen to me, Lazotte: I'm trying to get through basic training with the least amount of trouble. So lay off."

He snickered and turned away.

I grabbed his arm. "I'm warning you, don't fuck with me," I said.

"Hey, what's going on over there, Four Eyes?" the sergeant called. I was beginning to think that he was staring at me every moment of the day.

Lazotte giggled and walked away. An hour later he stepped on my heels again. Soon I noticed that the other squadron members were avoiding me or turning away when I approached.

Twice more Lazotte trod on the heels of my brogans that day, throwing me out of step, and each time the sergeant was ready with a comment directed at me. Soon almost everyone in the squadron was laughing outright, as if the sergeant, Lazotte, and especially me were part of a comedy performance being presented for their amusement. Martin and Lewis had become the Three Stooges.

I warned Lazotte again, but he only giggled. That night I went into his cubicle and told him I wouldn't warn him again. He just stared at me and smirked.

The following morning, as everyone scrambled to get out of the barracks and fell into line, my resolve to remain inconspicuous and follow the rules came to an end.

We weren't allowed to wear our brogans in the corridor or in our cubicles. We had to carry our footgear and put it on in the foyer of the barracks each morning. The last person out of the barracks was ordered to do pushups or run laps and was generally made a laughing stock.

On this particular morning, someone had taken one of my brogans and tossed it far under the bed, so as everyone ran to the foyer and laced up their shoes, I was still not out of the cubicle. By the time I arrived at the foyer and plopped down to put on my boots, most of the squadron were sprinting out the door.

"Fall in! Fall in!" the sergeant kept yelling outside.

I laced up one brogan and put on the other. The last three or four squad members were rushing out the door, but Lazotte was standing against the opposite wall watching me, a smirk on his face. He was waiting for me to lace my last shoe and then he was going to race through the door and take his position in line a few steps ahead of me.

I stared at him, and he stared at me, and he began to giggle.

As I gave my laces a final tug and started to rise, Lazotte pushed himself off the wall and headed toward the screen door. I was incensed. "Come here, Lazotte," I ordered, probably louder than I intended.

"What's wrong, Four Eyes?" he said. I lunged at him, grabbed him by the shoulder, and threw him back against the wall and starting punching. I was in the same state of rage I had been at the Milford game several years before, but my attack was more savage yet more controlled.

I continued punching left and right combinations. The fight seemed endless but certainly lasted no more than half a minute. Every shot found its mark. I know I broke his nose with the first or second blow. I kept punching and hauling him to his feet every time he started to sag to the floor, and then I was punching him when he was on the floor. He was squealing in terror and pain, curled in a fetal position, and though his arms and hands were protecting his head, his face was a bloody mask.

The sergeant burst into the foyer with most of the squadron crowding behind him. "Marcus!" he yelled. "Marcus!"

I turned toward him and rose with my fists still balled. "You're next, fucker," I said.

His eyes widened and he took a step backward. I went straight at him. He backed out the screen door and used it as a barrier between us, as everyone watched. "Take it easy, son," he said. "Calm down."

He was no longer the sadistic sergeant, and I saw concern and more than a little fear in his eyes.

I opened my hands, and he said haltingly, "Now I'm coming in, so be calm."

I stepped back and he and his assistant dragged a groggy, still-squealing Lazotte to his feet, and the assistant took him to the infirmary.

There was blood on the floor and the wall and all over my hands and fatigues, and when Lazotte cowered past me, his face was covered with it. He was trembling and mumbling.

"The rest of you, take a break," the sergeant yelled out the door to the staring squadron. Then he motioned me into the latrine and shut the door. "Hell, Marcus, do you realize I can have you court-martialed for that? What do you think you're doing?" he shouted, and stopped when he saw me ball my fists again.

His shoulders slumped and he spoke in a weary paternal voice. "I know I've been hard on you, but it didn't mean anything. Lazotte's on his way out, but you've got a future—"

"I'm not your patsy," I hissed.

He lifted a hand to placate me. "No, no, I was just—"

"I know what you were doing, and it's fucked."

I was shocked at the change in the sergeant's demeanor but too exhilarated to calm down. He was wilting in front of me, and I was going to take full advantage of it.

"Get this," I said. "You'll never call me Four Eyes again!"

He didn't answer, just nodded. "Look," he said, "we can work together. I need someone like you in the squadron to keep an eye on things."

Now it was my turn to snicker. "You've got to be kidding," I said, and turned to the row of sinks. He didn't say anything as I washed the dried blood from my hands, and walked out the door.

As I stepped from the barracks into the morning light, all eyes were on me and they were looking at me in a different way. The black leaders of the four cliques were nodding. I said nothing, just took my place in line, and a few minutes later the sergeant sauntered out and, as if nothing had happened, led us in the morning's drill. Midway through the exercise, he lectured us on various moves, reviewing our marching steps, and unexpectedly called, "Marcus, fall out." I did. "On my command," he ordered, and took me through the various steps, which I executed perfectly, my fatigues still crusted with Lazotte's blood.

That evening the four black clique leaders and several of their lieutenants crowded into my cubicle. They wanted to know more about me. They had not only seen Lazotte being led away, shrieking and covered with blood; they had seen the sergeant backing out of the barracks and protectively talking to me through the screen door. They also noted, as I had, that the sergeant had abandoned the nickname he had assigned me and had addressed me by my last name for the rest of the day. Later, one of them told me that they had also seen me without my glasses (I had flung them into a corner when I attacked Lazotte) and realized I was a different person than they at first believed.

Now they stood in my cubicle, an ominous presence, saying nothing, to the alarm of my five white bunkmates. Everyone seemed to be waiting for the biggest and baddest of the group to say something. Finally, he said, "You really gonna take on the sergeant this morning?"

"Yeah," I said with a nod.

The silence enveloped us again. He stared at me, waiting, and I was suddenly reminded of my confrontation with Tennessee in the ceramics class five years before. Somehow I had become a challenge to this man's unspoken authority in the squadron. To have him maintain his reputation, and to solidify my own, I had to be deferential in my answer to him, but not servile. I smiled and said, with an edge of irony in my voice, "I know you wouldn't have let him get out the door, but I guess I'm just a wimp."

My adversary and everyone behind him broke into big smiles. The tension was broken, but before they could say anything, I continued, "He even wanted me to spy for him, but I told him what he could do with that idea."

That comment interested them and steered the conversation to another subject, one that I think may have prompted their visit to my cubicle as much as the authority issue. They were looking for a sort of liaison among the whites, someone who would help them keep order and plan various scams, and they wanted to know if I was interested. I only half listened to what they were saying. I was thinking about when I had first decided to fight back, all those years ago when I was six years old. Trying to be inconspicuous, trying to obediently "play by the rules," had clearly been as bad a strategy in the military as it had been when I was a victim of the bullies. I should have known. Never again would I take the seemingly safe way out. Never again, no matter what it cost me.

The silence in the cubicle woke me from my reverie. The biggest of the blacks was once more looking at me and frowning. "Well?" he asked.

"Count me in. But what we do, we do for everyone in the squadron," I said. "And no one's a victim."

"What?" he answered, not understanding.

"We don't pick on anyone in the unit. That's my deal."

"Deal," he said and smiled as if he understood. But I don't think he did.

I had relearned a lesson I had taught myself years before, and I wouldn't forget it again. I had all too easily become a victim through my own foolish desire to stay out of trouble. But now there was an added dimension to my learning. Before, I wouldn't let the bullies pick on the timid kids; now, I was aware of the victimization of people in social groups, like the squadron. If we did things as a unit, working together, we could overcome all obstacles. Not that my eighteen-year-old mind could define this concept and its implications with such exactitude at that time, but a rudimentary social consciousness was at the core of my saying, "What we do, we do for everyone in the squadron." It was the first formulation of my idea of community, which, years later, I was to realize had attracted me to team sports, especially basketball where the player not only had to think on the run, but always had to operate as part of a five-man unit, recognizing that individual spokes were useless until they were fastened together to make a wheel. At the root of almost all the scams I devised and was part of for the next four years, that idea was paramount.

Several days after the Lazotte incident, one of the blacks, having gone to sick call, stole a handful of twenty-four-hour-excuse-from-duty slips from the infirmary. The four cliques were going to use the slips in bunches among themselves to get out of training. They learned from the thief that the doctor carelessly left the slips on his desk, so the four cliques planned a campaign of continuous thievery and "goofing off."

I explained that their scam would be easily found out if the twenty of them were continually off duty, and I suggested that everyone in the squadron who wanted to should be a beneficiary of the doctor's careless-ness. Further, I advised them to hoard the slips and allow no more than five people per day to use them so the sergeant wouldn't get suspicious. The blacks were not happy with my advice at first, until I told them that it was in their interest to let everyone in on the deal. Such thinking was, of course, not mine, but an example I remembered from American history class: it was Benjamin Franklin's doctrine of "enlightened self-interest," his belief that in helping others, in the end you are helping yourself. It is a practice I have kept in the forefront of my dealings with people ever since, and its ini-tial use in this case proved the efficacy of it: for the three months we were basic trainees, our little game was never discovered.

As for Lazotte, two weeks after the attack he was deemed mentally unfit for military service and given a Section Eight discharge.

CHAPTER 8

Embarrassments, Skills, and Transformations

After basic training, I was assigned to the radio school at Scott Air Force Base in southern Illinois, although I'd been given a bypass specialist recommendation in journalism and a special services recommendation to play basketball.

The air force had a meticulously researched career-placement examination that took an entire day to administer. The exam measured the emotional and mental aptitude of the examinee in a number of job areas, and I was recommended for clerical work. But the air force at that time needed cooks and radio repairmen, so I was assigned to the radio school, the area in which I registered my lowest test scores.

Scott Air Force Base was the site of the best radio school in the world, but for almost eight months I struggled to pass the first six-week semester. I went to NCOs and officers at the school as well as to high-ranking administrative officers in the base's first area, where base headquarters was located, trying to convince them to reassign me to a more conducive career field. Everyone listened to me, looked at my test scores, but said they couldn't help me. My situation seemed hopeless, and I was getting more and more depressed.

It was during this time that an event occurred that was not only one of the most embarrassing of my life, but one that influenced the rest of my air force career.

I was languishing in the summer heat of my barracks one day in 1955, frustrated by my attempts to get out of radio school, when an announcement over the squawk box ordered me to dress in my class A uniform and report to the squadron orderly room. I thought one of my requests for transfer had finally come through, but when I entered the building, I found everyone in turmoil. The moment I walked through the door, everyone stopped what they were doing and stared at me. The first sergeant, obviously agitated, came toward me.

"What's going on, Marcus?" he asked.

I had no idea what he was referring to.

When I didn't answer, he nodded over his shoulder and said, "The old man's waiting for you. Get in there."

I went into the squadron commander's office and saluted. He gave me a quick acknowledging salute in reply and said, "Who are you, Marcus? I want the truth."

His vehemence left me speechless.

"Don't play dumb. Are you a provost marshal inspector?"

"Sir?" I said.

"I didn't expect you to answer." He then pointed out the window. "See that car and the flags on it? That's a two-star general's car come to pick you up and haul your ass to Air Training Command headquarters. But you probably know all about that."

I looked out the window, still not knowing what was going on.

"You've been in long enough, but do you know how to report to a general? I'll bet you do, but let's go over it anyway so you won't embarrass the squadron."

He grimly gave me instructions and sent me on my way. A master sergeant was waiting by the car and politely opened the door for me and drove me to the base's first area, where Air Training Command headquarters sat, a huge red brick building with Greek columns in front holding up a white peaked roof over a large portico.

It was a humid Midwest day with the temperature in the nineties, but inside, the headquarters building was like a refrigerator. A woman air force enlistee sat behind a round reception counter. "You're Airman Marcus, aren't you? Just go right and then up the stairs. The general's secretary will be waiting for you."

The coolness was luxuriant but no more so than the ankle-deep carpeting I trudged through on my way to the general's office, where the secretary had come to the door to greet me. "The general will be with you in a moment. Would you like coffee, tea, a Coke?"

I shook my head, still unable to speak, wondering what was going on. Everyone—from the master sergeant to the two women at headquarters—were acting as if I were no mere enlistee but someone special. I was totally undone—nervous, confused, and disoriented. I had never seen a full colonel, let alone a general, and now a two-star general, no less, had sent for me. But about what?

"You may go in now," the general's secretary said, pointing to a door on her right.

I entered an enormous, longitudinal room at the end of which, behind a mahogany desk, sat a handsome, tanned officer with a crew cut. He was framed by the tall backs of two chairs that sat facing him in front of the desk. It was either his iconic figure or the football-field size of the room that finally undid me. I stopped in the doorway, feeling as if I was sinking into the carpet, and saluted. "Sir, Airman Third Class Marcus, sir, Morton J., reporting as ordered."

"Enough of that," the general said rather sternly. "What's all this about your not writing your mother?"

I couldn't believe what I had just heard, but almost before I could register my amazement, I heard someone sniffling, and from the side of one of the tall chairs, my mother's face appeared. She was dabbing her eyes with a handkerchief.

"You fucking bitch," I said automatically.

The general slammed his desk and said, "Don't you ever speak to your mother like that. Haven't we taught you respect?"

He didn't actually shout or yell, but bit off his words in clipped phrases that were even more frightening.

My mother had risen and come toward me. "My son," she said, gulping back tears. "Look at you. You've lost so much weight." And she embraced me.

"What have you done?" I whispered to her, but it was a rhetorical question. I knew immediately what she had done. She had robbed me of my attempt to be free of her. She had tromped on my decision to join the air force and become an independent human being.

The general gave me a three-day pass, and over the weekend I learned what had happened. My mother had been in Puerto Rico for reasons I did not want to know and had managed to get herself introduced to a lobbyist who was very important to the Pentagon. He, in turn, had used his connections to get her an appointment with the general, who was very accommodating.

The lobbyist, of course, had flown out with my mother and spent the weekend with us. He was a fat slug of a man who laughed like a hyena and had saliva incessantly collecting at the sides of his mouth. Where my mother found these characters was beyond me, but when I came to visit her from prep school, they were always there, eagerly paying for meals in fancy restaurants and for tickets at first-run theaters. My mother collected these payments for the privilege of her company as if they were scalps, trophies paid to her beauty.

Like the others, the lobbyist flew away at the end of the weekend, never to be seen by me again. And before my mother left with him, she elicited a promise from me that I would write to her.

But the damage was done. My files were stamped "VIP," and never again was I regarded as just another airman. Or so I believe to this day, and that's just as damaging.

The incident had other ramifications since the general, after ordering me to his office once again on the pretext of finding out how I was getting along, invited me to lunch a number of times, and took me for rides in his Buick. He did most of the talking on those occasions. I listened, but he

At 20. Scott Air Force Base,
Illinois, 1956

would always ask me questions about how I saw this and that, and what I would do in certain situations as a nineteen-year-old, as if he was trying to understand a teenager's psyche. Our visits, although always formalized by our awareness of rank and military decorum, soon resembled a father and son relationship. His own son was rebellious to the point of defiance, I found out, and I think may have had some mental problems. I was, of course, respectful and courteous out of necessity, but I soon came to like the general and feel sorry for him. I would have been extremely insensitive not to have realized that the situation with his son—which he never directly spoke about—had hurt him greatly and had something to do with our relationship. Our friendship, if that's what it was, had grown to the point of his taking me for a flight in a training version of his jet fighter. Soon after, however, Air Training Command was ordered to transfer from Scott and another headquarters command took its place. The general was among the first to leave. He called me up to his office to say good-bye. We sat quietly as I drank a Coke. He looked at me but didn't say anything, and finally rose and shook my hand. "Good luck, Mort. I know you'll do well in life," he said.

I nodded. It was a touching moment. I could see how locked the general's jaws were. He was grinding his teeth. I knew he wanted to say more, and so did I. As formal as our dealings with each other had been, he was as close as I had come to having a father since the years I'd spent with Larry and the weeks I'd traveled with Mike. But I only said, "Thank you for everything, sir."

Then I left, and never saw him again.

■ ■ ■

Several months after meeting the general, my troubles in radio school took an unexpected turn, one that was terrifying at first: I was brought up on charges of being a slacker. I was stunned and frightened. By the time I arrived at the pre-court-martial hearing, I was in a state of panic, although somewhat relieved to see all the officers and noncommissioned personnel I had talked to about my problems over the past year seated in the court.

My relief turned to shock and then anger as each one of them testified that I was lazy, not trying, incompetent, uncooperative, and an out-and-out laggard who should be dealt with accordingly.

By the time I was called before the panel, my fear was gone. I was irate. I sat on a hard wooden chair facing the panel of five officers. The lead officer was a lieutenant colonel named White who sat in the center of the group.

"You have heard the charges and accusations, Airman Marcus. Now it's your turn to reply before we make our decision," he said in a not unkindly tone of voice.

As far as I was concerned, the case was open and shut. I had been "sold down the river," and there was nothing I could do about it except give my side of the story. At least the panel would hear that.

I launched into my defense by expressing my commitment to the air force, told how I had taken the initiative to seek out each of the men who had testified against me, and referred to my records, specifically the career tests. Colonel White looked through my file as I spoke. He couldn't help but be aware of the indignation in my voice. I didn't care.

When I finished, the other officers on the panel looked toward the colonel, and he politely asked me to wait outside the courtroom for the panel's decision.

As I sat depleted and disgusted in the anteroom, I heard the colonel's voice loud and angry through the door. Five minutes later, my accusers strode from the courtroom, their faces flushed with embarrassment and irritation. Several glared at me as they passed.

After I was recalled to the courtroom and had taken my chair in front of the panel, Colonel White smiled at me. "I'm sorry you've been put through such a difficult time, Airman Marcus. You are the kind of man the air force wants and needs, as your spirited and intelligent explanation made clear. The board recommends that your career field be changed to clerical and you attend clerical school here on base. If you need any help on this or any other matter, don't hesitate to get in touch with me personally." And he flipped my file shut and dismissed me.

I found it difficult to rise from my chair. I couldn't grasp what had happened until I was halfway back to my squadron. Then everything was clear. I had beaten the unfair pressures that can be applied by rank and privilege as well as the inanity and injustice that I had come to know all too well in my year of military life. Once more, I had refused to become a victim. More than that, I now realized that I had the brains to engage, as well as the wherewithal to bring about, change, and the power to do so through the way I used words. I could convince even the most hardened soldiers of the rightness of my cause. It was a revelation. Not only would I stand up for others and myself from then on, but I would do so with eloquence and the powers of persuasion.

CHAPTER 9

Several Adventures

I If the military taught me discipline and allowed me to discover strengths I didn't know I had, I learned them in an atmosphere of intimidation that kept me constantly on my guard, and I had to put up with small things that rankled or frustrated me on a daily basis. Of all the daily annoyances, the one that disturbed me the most was the military class system. And, yes, there is a class system in the military, with the enlisted men representing the lower classes and the officers the upper. In this connection, it's no accident that officers are promoted and "recognized" as "officers and gentlemen" by acts of Congress. I, of course, was an enlisted man and for four years was subjected to one humiliating experience after another at the hands of officers, a situation that all too often reminded me of being bullied when I was a kid. A short prose poem I wrote years later indicates how I reacted to the petty give and take of exercising personal power in the military.

When I Was Twenty

When I was twenty and a platoon leader on an air base defense team, I might have killed anyone who got in my way. I'm thinking about the colonel who didn't know the password and insisted I let his jeep go through. I actually reached for the .45 in my holster. It was dark and I was standing in the shadows, but the colonel saw the movement and ordered his driver to turn the jeep around. I felt great, all-powerful, especially since I knew the pistol wasn't loaded.

I could tell many stories about an officer dressing me down or shouting at me for no reason except that he was in a grouchy mood or, more likely, because the system gave him the right to do so. But I am more concerned with the almost comic levels of corruption and stupid behavior that seemed to go on daily. They instilled in me a street-smart cynicism concerning government agencies, big corporations, and bureaucracies in general. Several examples, I'm sure, will suffice.

I was posted to Air Training Command headquarters during my second year of duty and received a top secret clearance. The clearance accounted for so many different assignments that by my last year in the service, I hardly knew where I would be working each day. I was a squadron leader on an air-base defense team, barracks sergeant, clerk typist, special TDY courier for sensitive material, permanent member of the base rifle team (which, in turn, meant I was a permanent member of the base funeral detail), and, not least, writer on the base newspaper. The clearance also led to any number of offbeat projects and adventures.

As a sergeant with a class A pass as well as a top secret clearance, I was allowed to fly anywhere in the country on any plane that came through my base. During the last days of September in 1956, I had the opportunity to fly from Illinois to Washington DC on a C-47. There was a good chance I could get a "hop" from there to Hamilton Air Force Base in New York, which was near where my girlfriend, and future wife, Wilma, lived. But just after we landed at Andrews Air Force Base in Washington, torrential rains and snapping winds, the unexpectedly powerful end of a hurricane named "Flossy" that had roared up the East Coast from the Caribbean, caused the flight line to be closed down. I sat in the cafeteria near the runway with a dozen other stranded officers and enlisted men and with them glumly drank cup after cup of coffee. The officer on duty informed us that we would be put up in guest quarters, but that didn't make us any happier: it was evident that everyone in the cafeteria imagined their plans for the weekend were ruined. As night fell, so did our complaints, and soon we sat in a silence that emphasized the sound of the rain lashing the large windows.

Suddenly the inner door to the cafeteria was flung open, and two full colonels in class A blue uniforms rushed into the room. One was short and stocky and the other tall and thin. The short one led the way and was all bluster and irritation.

"Where's the flight line officer? Who's seen him, huh?" he said, his lips working below a thick brown moustache.

Before we could answer, the duty officer appeared from behind another door.

"You close the base down?" the little colonel asked him, his chin thrust forward.

"Yes, sir," the officer, a captain, answered.

"Well, it's not closed down for me: I've got to get to New York," he said, and with the back of his hand, he slapped the briefcase locked to his tall companion's chest. That briefcase meant urgent top secret information and that the little colonel's companion was a courier.

"I'm sorry, sir. I can't do that."

"You can, and you will, Captain," the little colonel replied.

"Only if you sign responsibility for whatever happens to you and your aircraft."

"'Course I will. And I've got my own plane. I'll sign for that too."

The captain went to get a responsibility form, which the colonel signed, then dismissed him and turned toward us. "I'm going to Hamilton in New York. I've got a Beachcraft ten seater. Anyone want to join me?"

Even though the colonel's invitation provided us with the possibility of restoring our weekend plans, everyone hesitated as the wind and rain kept slamming the cafeteria windows. Finally a WAF sergeant said, "I'll go," and six of us followed her lead.

The duty officer provided us with two jeeps, and we drove out to the plane. The jeep was enclosed by a canvas shell, but we were soaked through by the time we boarded the twin-engine Beachcraft.

When we had cinched ourselves in, the little colonel turned in the pilot's seat, and said in a grave, calm voice, "And I think you'd better put the chutes on that are under your seats."

The seven of us looked at each other, alarmed. The little colonel, who had seemed so self-assured in the cafeteria, obviously wasn't. But it was too late now. We all sat rigidly as the colonel radioed the control tower, taxied down the empty runaway, and took off into the rain and darkness, the plane literally swinging left and right

Once we were airborne, the plane bounced from one air pocket to another or unexpectedly dropped hundreds of feet, as if the earth was intent on yanking me and my stomach to destruction. At times, the engines groaned and seemed about to stall. These conditions were continuous, but I got used to them enough to observe the big colonel sitting with his head bent forward in the copilot's seat; he was obviously asleep. He hadn't said a word during the showdown in the cafeteria or on the plane, and in the aircraft's single enclosed space all of us could smell the aroma of alcohol from his breath.

Meanwhile, the little colonel was radioing control towers at checkpoints as well as operating the plane, his arms flying back and forth, his hands frantically moving from one instrument to another as he single-handedly drove the Beachcraft through the storm. Soon the seven of us were aware of what was going on and were nodding to each other with concerned expressions, all of us bolt upright in our seats.

We flew under these conditions for two hours, finally coming into radio contact with Hamilton, or rather with a control tower in New Jersey, fifty miles away from the base. He was assigned to have us land "blind," he told us, by radioing us down, or by what is better known as having us perform an instrument landing.

But there was a plane ahead of us, a C-47 transporting a number of military dependents, women and children, from Newfoundland. We listened as the New Jersey-based operator guided the C-47 into Hamilton step by step, the voice of the C-47's pilot becoming more and more tense until it rose to a shout as the plane overshot the runway and, we found out later, nosed over in the marshy muck beyond it.

"Holy shit!" said the little colonel, but that was the only sound in our plane except for the whirring engines and the storm around us and the frantic voice of the C-47 pilot yelling to anyone who would listen.

We circled the base in a wide pattern.

"You still there, flight 703?" the control tower operator finally said.

"Yeah," the colonel answered.

"Keep circling. We've had difficulties with the plane ahead of you."

"I heard, but I'm running out of fuel."

"I'll have you down soon, but ambulances and fire trucks are on the runway now."

The little colonel didn't answer, but we were all thinking the same thing.

We circled for ten minutes, the wind and rain buffeting us back and forth. Then the colonel called the control tower. "I'm almost on empty."

"Five minutes. Just five minutes," was the reply.

Finally, the control tower operator began to guide us in. I was holding my breath, more numb than frightened, and I'm sure everyone else, including the little colonel, was doing the same thing.

We descending through the darkness, the colonel following the point by point instructions. Suddenly the runway rose before us. We touched down, and, like the C-47, overshot our mark. But the Beachcraft was so small, the colonel was able to brake the aircraft and guide it to a halt before we slid past the end of the runway.

The colonel taxied the plane to the lighted buildings in the middle of the flight line, and cut the engines. We sat there in silence as the colonel expelled a huge breath and sat quietly, regaining his composure. Then he radioed the control tower. "We're down. Thanks, New Jersey," he said, and switched off the radio.

Next he slapped the tall colonel on the shoulder. "Wake up, Harry. We're there," he said.

"What? What?" said the tall colonel.

And the little colonel, as if he hadn't heard him, continued with his old bravado, "That was one for the books. But what did I tell you, huh? We made it." And he reached over, flipped open the briefcase slung across his companion's chest, reached inside and withdrew two slips of paper. "Yes, sir," he said, and held up the two slips. "Two tickets to the first game of the World Series. I told you we'd get here in time."

The seven of us sat in stunned silence, all of us, I'm sure, realizing how close our brush with death had been—and how unnecessarily foolhardy the flight had been as well. What I couldn't understand then, and can't understand now, is not only that the little colonel offered to take us with him, but what, in the first place, had compelled him to fly to New York through a killer hurricane that blustery Friday night when he knew the World Series wasn't scheduled to begin until the following Wednesday.

Such instances of stupidity were commonplace during my four years in the air force. But none was more stupid than the one that occurred the spring previous to the hurricane episode, when I was first assigned to Air Training Command. I had gotten off a full day of KP duty and had gone to bed, immediately falling into an exhausted sleep, only to be woken by shouts and other agitated noises of bodies rushing back and forth. "Up! Up! Up!" yelled several voices, and before I knew it, my bed had been tipped over and an Air Policeman was standing over me. "Get your ass up, Marcus, and over to headquarters."

"What?" I groaned, still half asleep.

"The base is flooded, and General Martinson wants everyone at headquarters. There's a truck outside."

I wrestled my way out of the overturned bedclothes, but by the time I had climbed into my fatigues and brogans, the barracks was empty and the truck had left. The base flooded? What was the joke?

I left the barracks and trudged to headquarters a quarter of a mile away. Sheets of rain were streaming out of the night. I cursed and grumbled, stepped off a curb and sank up to my waist in water.

The rain had started after I'd gone to bed, and the base, which was a drained marsh, had returned to its natural state in the unexpected downpour.

I waded and swam to headquarters, which was swarming with activity and lighted flashlights. The electricity had gone out. Over all the commotion, General Martinson, the deputy headquarters commander, was bellowing orders left and right. "Who can swim? And who has a top secret clearance?" he kept saying, as I approached. He caught sight of me. "What about you, Marcus?"

"Yes, sir," I said.

"Yes, sir, what?"

"I have a top secret clearance and can swim, sir."

"Good. Sergeant give him a .45 and a belt," he said to an air policeman. I stripped to my underwear, strapped on the webbed belt, loaded the heavy pistol, and jammed it into the holster as the General briefed me. "The basement's flooded," he said, "and I don't have to tell you the vault down there is vulnerable. This is the kind of situation the commie sympathizers have been waiting for. I want you and those three men over there to go to opposite ends of the basement and patrol the vault."

"Patrol, sir?"

"Yes, dammit, don't be so thick. I want you to tread water in front of the vault at ten minute intervals, then trade off with the airman on your side of the building."

"Sir?"

"Just do it!"

And do it I did, treading water for six chilly hours with the three others, each of us splashing about and spitting at the basement ceiling two feet above our heads, protecting whatever important documents were in the submerged room-sized vault from possible Communist infiltrators. Or worse—Russian frogmen who might make it to the middle of Illinois in a sudden spring flood, somehow knowing that the headquarters's vault was susceptible to their evil intentions.

■ ■ ■

At other times, the stupidity of military life was comical and resembled a chapter from Joseph Heller's *Catch 22*.

Two years after my experience with the colonels and the Beachcraft, a flight was announced to Florida. I put in my request to go along and was interviewed by the pilot, a beefy major. He asked me a number of irrelevant questions, obviously gauging my character, and finally agreed to take me on the flight. My girlfriend, who was now my fiancée, had moved to Florida with her family, and I wanted to visit her because her father was objecting to our impending marriage.

The plane was a VIP C-47 passenger model. Like a commercial airliner, the main cabin was outfitted with rows of upholstered seats and other luxury trappings since one of the plane's tasks was to transport senators and other political dignitaries. The flight was full, and all of us reported in class A uniforms: a collection of women's air force regulars, an assortment of lower grade officers, a few enlisted men like me who were visiting their families, and the plane's mechanic wearing fatigues. We greeted each other politely and divided into cliques. A number of the women knew the officers and murmured with them in low voices.

But when we were out of radio range of the base, the major emerged from the cockpit and said, "We're free!" and immediately the flight turned uproarious: everyone tore off their uniforms to reveal tropical vacation attire beneath their class As. Some of the women sat in their bras and began kissing the officers next to them. Bottles of whiskey emerged from beneath seats, and soon everyone was drunk and singing off-color songs like "Roll Me Over in the Clover." We enlisted men, on our way to visit families, sat quietly in the midst of the revelry.

When we arrived at Orlando Air Force Base, the major taxied the C-47 to a remote corner of the air field, and the drunken passengers disembarked in a disheveled mass and disappeared in waiting jeeps and taxis.

I spent the weekend with my fiancée's family and reported back to Orlando at the prescribed time for the flight back. The other enlisted men were there too, as well as the C-47's mechanic, but none of the officers and women had shown up. We waited for hours. I struck up a conversation with the mechanic, a master sergeant who cynically told me about the continuous parties the major conducted to one post or another throughout the

---

year. He revealed that most of the officers on board were married, and the women on the flight were their mistresses.

At about eight o'clock, jeeps and taxis arrived. Singing and laughing raucously, the officers and women piled out of the cars and staggered onto the plane, the men making several trips to the cars to haul sacks of oranges and grapefruits onboard, which the mechanic had told me they would sell back home. The major was too drunk to take off, and, without a word, the mechanic took the controls, taxied down the runway, asked the tower for permission to proceed, and took off, piloting the plane for the next several hours as the party continued in the passenger compartment.

Four hours later, the mechanic emerged from the cockpit and told the major, who was sitting with a young woman on his lap I recognized as his secretary, that the plane was approaching our base's radio range. Immediately the laughter stopped. The major, shooing his secretary away, rose and announced to no one in particular, "We're there," and headed for the cockpit. He was completely sober.

Two minutes later he was radioing our home control tower, and within the hour we landed at the base, everyone sober and dressed in their class As once more. The officers waved to their wives and hugged them at the gate, lamenting the engine trouble that had made the flight so late, as the women on the plane strolled silently past them. The sacks of fruit were nowhere in sight. I guess they were picked up the next day.

■ ■ ■

Corruption was just as troubling as stupidity in military life. The amount of wasted taxpayer's money was astonishing, and I encountered it almost daily for the four years I was on active duty. Sometimes the encounter got dangerous.

After Air Training Command headquarters was reassigned to another base and the general and most of Air Training Command's personnel had left Scott, Military Air Transport Command headquarters took their place. It was during this transition that the base commander saw an opportunity to ingratiate himself with the new command and possibly gain a much-sought-after increase in rank. To that end, he went about outfitting all family housing and single-officer quarters with new beds, stoves, refrigerators, and other furniture, and he called for all the base's squadron commanders to supply enlisted men to do the moving and hauling on a temporary duty assignment. Most squadron commanders saw the project as an opportunity to get rid of their most troublesome men. The air police even let light offenders out of the brig to take part in the operation. Between them, they mustered 150 of the base's worst misfits. My squadron commander, however, was one of the few honest officers on base, and he determined to send his best men to the job.

By then I had been assigned to base command, and my rank, which had quickly risen when I was a member of the now departed Air Training Command Headquarters, earned me an almost automatic assignment as barracks sergeant in my new squadron. Unfortunately, a barracks sergeant was needed to facilitate the base commander's new pet project. The sergeant was to oversee the 150 incorrigibles in an unused barracks in a remote area of the base that had closed several years after the end of World War II. Since I was the highest ranking unmarried enlisted man available and a barracks sergeant as well, my commander designated me for the job. At the time, I had a room to myself in my home barracks, with a radio and small stereo system. I wasn't about to give up those hard-earned comforts.

I immediately called a meeting of all personnel in the new barracks on the other side of the base. When I arrived with my duffel bag, they were all waiting in the open bay, lying on two-tier bunks or standing several deep beside them or sitting on footlockers, a crowd of over a hundred or more. They had left the center aisle of the bay clear. I dropped my gear in the room at the front of the barracks and strode into the bay. All eyes were on me, and they weren't friendly nor was anyone saying anything. They were waiting, ready, it seemed, to pounce. I walked to the end of the open aisle, saying sarcastically, "So here we are: one happy family," and turned around and walked back the other way. No one laughed or even grunted, and when I approached the center of the aisle an open pen knife sailed out of the group on my right and with a clatter rolled over the floorboards several feet away from me. My nerves were a shower of needles all over my body, but I didn't let it show. I continued walking, picked up the knife, folded the blade, and calmly said, "Someone drop this?" A squirrelly man in his thirties darted out of the group, snatched the knife from my hand and darted back into the thicket of bodies. But the tension had relaxed. I seem to have passed a test of some sort—the first part of one, anyway.

I stopped and stood with my hands on my belt. "So you don't want to be here, and I don't want to be here either. What are we going to do about it?"

"Get drunk," someone muttered, and several people chuckled.

I ignored them, and went on. "I'll tell you what we're going to do. We're going to do just what we want to. You all have class A passes, right? How many of you have girlfriends in town or places to head for after work?"

Several dozen hands went up.

"Well, you're going to be seeing a lot of them," I said and paused for a moment. "I've got a plan."

I thought everyone leaned forward.

"Let's be straight," I said, "You guys are fuck-ups. That's why you're here. I'm not, and I've got a cushy room over at my squadron, and I want to keep it."

"How you gonna do that, with having to stand reveille at five every morning?" someone called.

"Easy," I said. It was the question I had been waiting for. No one stood reveille in the air force, and the base commander had instituted the practice specially for this group to insure that they would be on the job by 8 AM.

Everyone was quiet, waiting for my answer. "You can stay with your girl-friends, drink with your buddies till dawn without a worry. No one's going to stand reveille," I said. They seemed to lean closer. No one was wisecrack-ing now. "But there's a catch. We're going to beat the brass at their own game. And to do that you're going to have to follow the rules for once."

Everyone groaned and shifted their weight. "No, listen. I will put a detail chart on the bulletin board, assigning five guys each day to report reveille count to the squad room, clean the latrine, sweep the bays, and dust the shoes. The rest of you can do whatever you want, but you have to be at the warehouse at eight sharp. You get what's happening?"

Several guys shook their heads.

"Okay, here it is. The five guys—that is five different guys each day—will be responsible for making it seem that we've all spent the night here and were at reveille, and if there's an inspection, the place will be spit-polish clean. Five each day, and with 150 of you that means your turn will come around every thirty days, and this detail isn't going to take more than two months."

"What if one of the five guys doesn't show up for his assignment?" some-one asked.

"Yeah, that's the hitch," I said. "That's where you guys have to earn this bit of freedom. Because here's part two of my little plan. Any guy who fails to do his barracks' assignment or doesn't get to the work area by 8 AM is going to fuck the whole thing up. For everyone. So I propose that you guys beat the shit out of anyone who fucks this sweet deal up."

There was an audible sucking in of breath. They hadn't expected that.

I waited, and finally said, "What do you say?"

Grins appeared everywhere, and everyone chimed in their acceptance and crowded around me. Even the squirrelly knife thrower come over, introduced himself as Tex, and shook my hand.

Then the miracle occurred. For the next six weeks, this group of misfits were model soldiers. The officers and NCOs in charge couldn't believe it. Everyone was accounted for at reveille, the barracks was clean, and, most important, no one was late for work. What was my magic? they asked. I smiled and said, "They're good men, that's all."

But when I arrived at the warehouse in the middle of the seventh week, I immediately knew that things had gone wrong. Several NCOs turned away from me, four or five guys from the barracks nodded gravely and shook their heads, and I was told to report to the captain's office where the captain and two lieutenants were waiting for me. The captain was furious, one of the lieu-tenants looked at me with disdain, and the other stared at me with the curious expression you see on people's faces when they stare at monkeys in a zoo.

It turned out that a truckload of weapons and ammunition had been stolen from the base ammunition dump, and figuring that one or all the culprits were assigned to the moving and hauling detail, the air police had raided the barracks in force at four in the morning to find only five men there. My little scheme was quickly uncovered. "You're a disgrace, sergeant," the captain concluded. "And I'm placing you under arrest. Unfortunately, I can't bring charges against you since you're here on a temporary duty assignment, but your commander is waiting for you and I'm sure has the court martial paperwork already done."

With that he nodded to two air policemen I'd seen standing on either side of the door as I entered the office, and they escorted me back to the orderly room of my home squadron. I knew one of them, a guy I'd gone drinking with several times, but he wouldn't look at me.

At my orderly room, the first sergeant shook his head and led me to the commander's office. The commander stared up at me from his desk as I saluted and reported in. He looked more hurt than angry, and before I could finish reciting my serial number, he sat forward, waved away my salute and said, "Why, why, why? You are one of my best men."

Until that moment, I hadn't said anything for over an hour. As far as I was concerned, I had gambled and lost and deserved whatever punishment I received. But when the commander, a man I respected, asked me why I had engaged in my scheme, I knew I had to explain myself. "Major, with all due respect, I have to tell you that you were the only squadron commander who took the base CO's request for men seriously. All the others sent their fuck-ups, and the provost even let some guys out of the brig for the detail. I know I did wrong, but for the past six weeks, those men were doing their jobs as they never had before. I'm sorry. You're a good man, but if I had to do it again, I'd do the same thing."

I stood back and waited. The commander sighed and tore up the court-martial paperwork, but he took away my stripes and made me do clean-up detail and KP for the next thirty days. Somehow he forgot to take away my room and continued to let me serve as barracks sergeant. I figured that he knew the assignment was a shuck. Everyone else did, and a number of people, NCOs and officers, couldn't believe the money the base commander was shelling out for furniture and decorations for the family houses. No one, of course, said a word about the money any more than they acknowledged what happened to a shipment of two thousand pairs of fur-lined arctic boots that arrived unannounced at the quartermaster's warehouse one day the year before. The boots had been making the rounds of one base after another. No one knew what to do with them. And when the quartermaster had his men bury them on the flight line one night, no one said a word about that either.

■ ■ ■

There is another military story I need to tell. It also happened when I was barracks sergeant at base command, but it provides a necessary counterpoint to the half-comic tales of stupidity and corruption I have just related. It is a story that has little to do with human folly and everything to do with what is emerging as one of the major themes of these memories. I'm talking about racism, which I have discovered not only permeates American life but the life of every country I have visited and is responsible for more brutality and viciousness than any stupidity and corruption I encountered in the air force.

Like much of the country, the military was segregated until after World War II. In the summer of 1948—one year after Jackie Robinson broke the color barrier of major league baseball—President Truman issued Executive Order 9987, which called for a committee to oversee the integration of the armed forces as quickly as possible. By 1950, that integration was complete.

There had been turmoil in the ranks over the desegregation decision, much of it quiet and subtle, but some of it involved rioting and individual acts of violence, almost all of which was kept from the public. One of the hushed-up riots had occurred in the abandoned section of the base where I had been sent on the ill-fated TDY assignment. Rumor had it that several black airmen had been killed and a barracks burned down, which, said the rumormongers, was why the area had been closed.

By the time I enlisted four years later, whites, blacks, browns, and yellows were living in grudging acceptance of each other, and there were few outward signs of racism, nor did the majority of recent enlistees think much about the subject since we were all enduring the same hardships together, which, as any veteran will tell you, brings men closer emotionally than any other experience. This was the atmosphere in which the following tale occurred.

It was 1957, and there were ten or twelve blacks among the hundred or so enlisted men living in the barracks under my supervision. One of them was a light-skinned, twenty-two-year-old named Steve, who worked in the embryonic and little-understood computer field. He avoided the other blacks, and they, in turn, avoided him. No one seemed to know why the separation had occurred or why it continued. The situation was noticeable not only because Steve kept to himself but because the rest of the blacks were always together, joking, jive-talking, trading phonograph records, and generally showing a solidarity that made Steve's exclusion more apparent than if he had been white.

I had bunked next to Steve before I was assigned my barracks sergeant's room at the end of the open bay, and although I tried to be friendly and engage him in conversation, he would only nod or murmur in response and otherwise ignore me. The other white guys in the barracks were leery of Steve for other reasons, although he did nothing to outrightly offend anyone. Two of his habits in particular riled them.

The first was certainly strange and occurred every night just before lights out. Steve would climb into bed and tuck the sheets and blankets tightly around him on both sides, so he seemed to have strapped himself to the mattress as if he feared he might fall out of bed while he was sleeping. This habit, which was more like a ritual, proved to be a dangerous practice one night when I was alerted to a commotion in the bay outside my room.

"Sarge! Sarge!" several voices called. I had already heard shouts and the sounds of scuffling and rushed from the room in my undershirt and boxer shorts to see Steve, helplessly lashed beneath the covers, with a big black airman kneeling on top of him and punching him in the face. Several black barracks' members stood around the bed, cheering the attacker on.

I rushed toward them, yelling, "Hey, cut it!" or something like that.

A white friend grabbed my arm and hissed in my ear, "Don't get involved," but I yanked my arm away and descended on the attacker, grabbing his raised right arm and pulling it back.

He turned to me, eyes blazing, and spat, "Let go my arm, motherfucker. Let go, you white —"

"Harley, it's the Sarge," yelled one of the blacks around the bed, and the attacker, who was not a barracks' member, hesitated, his arm and shoulder rigid in my grip.

We were nose to nose. "Get your ass out of here, you hear me," I rasped.

He stared into my eyes, wavering between one decision and another.

"Get the fuck out of here before I write you up!" I shouted, still looking him in the eye.

Reluctantly, he dismounted and was led away by the group around the bed.

When I tried to examine Steve, he turned away. I turned his head toward me. There was a lot of blood leaking from his nose and several abrasions but nothing serious. I loosed the blankets and Steve rolled over.

"You okay?" I asked.

"Leave me be," he said.

"I'm asking you if you're okay. You want to go to the infirmary?"

"Just leave me be."

And that was how it ended. The next day, I asked him if he wanted to prefer charges, but he ignored my question and walked away. The other black barracks' members told me that the attacker, "Harley," was drunk but an "okay guy," and he came to me contritely, and told me, as the others had, that Steve was "no good." I reported the incident to the squadron top sergeant, but without Steve's statement, nothing could be done. Steve was a man alone, and nothing I or anyone else could do would pierce his stony exterior.

The white barracks' members found Steve's second quirky habit more difficult to accept because it affected them directly. In the end, it explained all the questions Steve's antisocial behavior had raised.

Every morning, Steve would get up half an hour before everyone else and shower. These showers were so lengthy that by the time he was finished he had used the barracks' entire supply of hot water. Several airmen, both black and white, asked him to make his shower time shorter, and when that failed, they asked me to officially direct him to "cease and desist" his overly long bathing practices. I talked to him, he nodded as usual, walked away, and continued taking his overlong, hot-water-depleting showers.

The blacks grumbled and glared at him, but the whites were furious and resolved to surprise him while he was showering and force him to stand under a blast of cold water so he could experience what everyone else went through because of him. Several of the white guys asked their black barracks mates to join them, but the blacks turned away, mumbling something or other which was loosely interpreted as protestations that they wanted nothing to do with whatever happened. But it seemed to those who approached them that the blacks knew something they weren't saying.

I was apprised of all this afterward by the same white airman who had grabbed my arm and told me not to get involved in Steve's beating. He told me that he and twenty other white barracks' members had waited until Steve was in the shower and then had crept down to the latrine as quietly as possible with the intention of grabbing him unawares and holding him in place as they turned off the hot water and opened the cold water spigot full force. The shower water was so hot, he said, that the latrine was blanketed in a steamy fog when they entered. He and several others were in the lead, and, he said, he would never forget what he saw: "Steve was standing under one of the last showers in the shower room, his back toward us, scrubbing himself all over. At first we couldn't make out any more than that. Then it was clear he wasn't scrubbing himself with his hand but with a stiff brush of some sort. I didn't get what was going on at first, but Norm and Karabedies did, and they turned and pushed their way out of the crowd. 'Christ,' muttered Norm as he passed, and then I understood. Steve was trying to scrape the color off his skin, I swear it. I felt sick and turned away with the others, and by the time I was out of the latrine a handful of guys were following me. No one made a sound. Everyone just looked, understood, and got out of there without saying a word. Then I guess Steve turned around and yelled something when he saw the guys who were left. But they just turned around and exited with the rest of us. It was creepy. What's going on with that guy?"

That was a rhetorical question, and the teller knew the answer as well as I and everyone else did. As for the ten or twelve black guys in the barracks, they didn't want to hear anything about the incident and for a few days wouldn't look any of us in the eye. Nor did they approach Steve with sympathy. Instead, they glared at him with tightened lips and expressions that can only be described as contempt. They had known what he was doing all along, and, as far as I was concerned, that explained their ostracizing him. Steve was a casualty of racism in America whose wound was visible to them daily. It was a wound they didn't want to see or acknowledge because it was deep and festering and they feared they carried pieces of it like shrapnel somewhere in themselves.

CHAPTER 10

Taking the Man Out of the Boy

During my last two years in the air force, two incidents occurred that radically changed my life. One was an ending, in many ways a good-bye to youth, and the other was a beginning, a greeting to adulthood.

The first incident concerned my athletic career. As an addendum to Colonel White's decision at the pre-court-martial in 1955, I was sent to clerk typist school, and on completing the course, I was transferred to Air Training Command Headquarters on the base. In deference to my recommendation for journalism, I was then assigned to *Air Training Magazine*, a slick, *New Yorker*-like monthly magazine that was distributed throughout the Air Training Command's forty-two bases.

Whether a phone call from the general at Air Training Command was the reason Colonel White turned the pre-court-martial hearing in my favor in 1955, I will never know—and prefer not to think about. White was assigned to the base, not Air Training Command headquarters, which happened to occupy several buildings in the first area, so my concerns may be groundless. On the other hand, I'm sure the general, who may have gotten me assigned to Air Training Command headquarters after I completed clerical school, must have pulled strings to get me assigned to *Air Training* magazine.

At any rate, now that I had a career field and permanent assignment, I tried out for the base basketball team and easily made the squad, and my job allowed me to play basketball unabated. For the next year I enjoyed military life and learned a lot about journalism and the inner workings of the air force. But the magazine didn't really need me, and when Air Training Command headquarters was transferred to Texas, I was left behind, reassigned to base command as a clerk typist and reporter on the base newspaper. It was then my troubles returned.

Basketball practice was at night, which didn't interfere with my clerical duties, but the away games took me from work for days at a time. One day the coach took me aside when I came for practice. He handed me an order and said, "Sorry, Marcus, there's nothing I can do about this." The order stated that my career field was clerk typist, and as such it had precedence over any extracurricular activities.

I returned to the orderly room and argued my case. But now my eloquence went unheeded. My career field was not special services, and that was that, said the first sergeant. He needed me where I was assigned. I liked old Joe, the top sergeant, and knew he was right, but giving up basketball for the next two years seemed unendurable. It also seemed final. Before I joined the base team, I had gone without playing serious, organized basketball since I had joined the air force. I didn't want that to happen again, knowing that if it did, my playing days would probably be over. I argued with the top sergeant to no avail for another week, and then I let it go and entered a depression I couldn't shake. I had defined myself as a basketball player for six years, and I couldn't imagine my life without it.

All this occurred at a time when Wilma had temporarily broken up with me and was between the incidents concerning the flights to New York and Florida I related in the last section. I'm sure the breakup added to my depression. I began to drink and, with a friend named Fred, began to hit the bars around the base and generally live a dissolute existence. Fred had a car, and soon we were driving to St. Louis every night after work. That is, we were playing a game in which we would drive toward the city every night by a different route but stop at every bar along the way. We almost never reached the city.

The days unfolded and crisscrossed each other, the nights were a jumble of different women's faces and waking up in strange bedrooms or by the side of roads, sometimes with a black eye, scraped knuckles, and dried blood on my shirt. Fred and I only went to the barracks to change clothes, shower, and dust the shoes lined up for inspection under our beds. This period in my life is recalled in the poem "Waking," which I wrote many years later.

Waking

Once I woke on a picnic table
by the side of a highway in Illinois,
next to a girl whose name I couldn't remember.
Her odor was all over me
and mine all over her.

I was twenty, and still drunk,
and what had wakened me was the dawn,
a bloodshot eye emerging from layers of mist
like the anger of God rising in my face.
I snickered. "The hell you say," I said aloud to the sky,

knowing how the mind makes of the world
whatever it wants to. I didn't even wake the girl.

The days go over my head like dusty herds,
but that dawn rises in my brain again and again.
The stop was in a clump of trees I'd pass
driving to and from the base,
and for the next year I'd think of her.
I've never been back: it was just a roadside stop—
tables, benches, two garbage cans—
memorable for nothing, except that dawn.

At twenty I expected so much from the days
that came at me as I went face forward into them:
I wanted to be a man and hoped someone,
tall and proud, would happen along
and show me how it was done,
and somehow I'd know,
somehow I'd walk differently
and be a person I could be proud of.

She was twenty-three. We never said goodbye.
And I never took her number.
Not that it would have made a difference.

Once it was "the hell you say"
and squirting spit between my teeth,
while voices spoke from the other side of thunder
and I refused to listen. Now it is these words
that have nothing more to tell me.

                              As for the girl,
she went away into the afternoon,
other nights, other dawns, other men,
until, I'd like to think, she found someone
who would wake her, or who she would wake,
when either of them heard the other
muttering in the dark.

I'm not exaggerating when I say that I was drunk for six months. How long the situation would have lasted, or my body could stand the punishment, I have no way of knowing. I do know it ended when, in a moment of clarity, I woke on a dance floor in an East St. Louis honky-tonk to find myself mauling my female partner. When I pushed her away to look at her, she turned out to be the smiling sixty-eight-year-old grandmother of the girl Fred had currently been romancing. The shock of what I was doing was further exacerbated when Fred gleefully told me I had been shacked up with the old woman for two days.

Fred thought the situation was hilarious and voiced it all around the barracks. I was not only humiliated; I thought I had sunk as far as I could. Worse yet, I had gained thirty pounds from the drinking, which I would never be able to take off. My playing days were definitely over now; I had made sure of that. Or had I? During those six months, I came to realize, I had mourned an athletic career that had never really happened and with it a false identity that had sustained me for six years.

The day after the incident in East St. Louis, I called up my mother and asked her to send whatever textbooks of mine she could find. One life was ending and another one beginning.

■ ■ ■

I had been writing with increased seriousness and devotion since I'd arrived at Scott in January 1955. My troubling situation at radio school and the realization that by the time my tour of duty was over I would have spent almost one-fourth of my twenty-one years in the military and more than half my life living in dormitories, increased my need to write for both solace and self-understanding. This need started during a pass from boot camp in November 1954 and has continued unabated ever since. During the pass, I bought three books by Kenneth Patchen at a Syracuse, New York, bookstore and read them to pieces during the next three years, as if they were biblical utterances that would sustain my sanity. At Scott, I began studying and copying poetic techniques, especially closed forms and varied diction. My models were the poems of Richard Wilbur, Karl Shapiro, Theodore Roethke, Elizabeth Bishop, Muriel Rukeyser, and the young Adrienne Rich. I found many of those poets in the Twayne *Mid-Century American Poets* anthology that I had also bought in Syracuse. I was especially intrigued with evoking spoken American through closed forms and marveled at how Robert Frost projected a New England voice through blank verse and rhymed, metered quatrains and sonnets. I also learned the lifelong lesson that even the smallest and most innocent library *could*, and probably *did*, carry literary gems and oddities. At Scott's library I found David Ignatow's *The Gentle Weightlifter* in the poetry section and renewed it again and again. Ignatow's plain, spoken language intrigued me.

I also discovered the main library in downtown St. Louis and began dating one of the librarians. She introduced me not only to her wholesome Midwest family but to the small St. Louis literary world and had me send my poems to the library's annual contest, in which I took third place. At the awards ceremony, I wore my uniform and read my poem. I was an anomaly—a warrior poet. On the basis of the award, I was courted by several fledgling poets my own age, and the editors of local literary journals published my early poems. I also discovered the poetry of T. S. Eliot. Eliot was de rigueur at that time, and I appreciated his work not for its endless allusions but for the subtly nuanced speech rhythms he used in "Prufrock," "Gerontion," "Marina," and "The Preludes," as well as in sections of "The Waste Land." From Eliot I went to Pound, who I never could appreciate, and then Wallace Stevens, whose elegant but spoken language, if not his themes, intrigued me. And, of course, I was drawn to the poems of William Carlos Williams, whose imagist background and concerns with American speech patterns were enormous influences.

I was also taking out library books on such subjects as history, literary criticism, and biography. André Maurois's biography of George Sand and her relationship with the great French novelist Honoré de Balzac, intrigued me since my family, wanting to avoid notoriety, had changed its name from Bebchick to Balzac after my uncle's murder.

The most instructive books were Brooks and Warren's *Understanding Fiction* and *Understanding Poetry*. I read them diligently and came away with many notions about writing.

All this literary activity was suspended during my six-month, self-pitying binge. When my mother's shipment of books arrived, I reviewed them with gusto, got my high school diploma from Blair in a complicated process led by my mother and the old assistant headmaster, and decided to go to night school at Washington University in nearby St. Louis. I seemed to be blossoming with questions like a thorny rose bush. My first two years in the air force had made me hungry to learn because I had been directly exposed to war, politics, and military folderol. A part of my reason for going to night school was to resist the temptation to drink, but learning was the overriding motivation. I wanted to know why certain things had happened in the past, how things worked, why people reacted as they did as a species and as individuals—and what the great thinkers had to say about those subjects, all of which, of course, encompassed history, the physical and social sciences, and literature.

I looked through the Washington University schedule of classes to see what might interest me. I was restricted to night classes, of course, so the choice was not extensive. But I came up with a creative writing class taught by Jarvis Thurston, a wonderful short-story writer and editor of the national literary quarterly, *Perspective*. Thurston, who was in his late fifties, was married to the poet Mona Van Dyn, who coedited *Perspective* with him. Both of them were very encouraging, and before I left the workshop, they would publish one of my poems in the magazine, a closed-verse, rhymed meditation on Goya's famous painting of Don Manuel Osorio de Zuñiga. More important than publication was the infectiousness of Thurston's excitement about literature. He taught me that a reader and writer were inseparable, that a reader should read as a writer wrote and intended, and that the act of reading was as creative in its way as the act of writing. I attended the workshop for the year and a half left of my enlistment.

Another night course that caught my eye in the schedule was "The French Revolution and the Napoleonic Era," a seminar taught by a professor named Dietrich Gerhard. My interest in French writing of the nineteenth century, particularly George Sand and Balzac, drew me to the class in order to find out how the events of the preceding era had influenced their lives and work.

At registration I strode into the university gym and boldly signed up for both classes. I must have exuded such confidence that no one questioned my choices. The people who registered me took my money, put me on the class roster, and smiled me on my way.

The first night of school, I entered the history classroom half an hour early, moving to the windows, which were at the far side of the room, separated from the door by five rows of desk chairs, ten or so chairs in each row. Soon, my classmates shuffled in. There were only fifteen of them, and to my surprise they appeared to be in their late twenties or early thirties. The men were dressed in tweed or corduroy jackets and ties, and the women in fancy blouses beneath cardigan sweaters. They spoke in subdued tones until the professor entered. He was a slightly harried older man wearing an ill fitting brown tweed jacket and a maroon bow tie. But his most noticeable features were a florid red face and eyeglasses thick as ice cubes. He introduced himself and passed out three-by-five cards, instructing us to fill them out with our names, numbered degrees, colleges attended, and thesis advisors in those colleges. I suddenly felt that something was wrong.

When the professor had collected the cards, he read the contents of each one aloud, as though they were introductions not only for him but also for the members of the class. It didn't take me long to realize that my classmates were working on their PhD theses and had been sent from universities around the country to attend this seminar, and that Dietrich Gerhard was a famous European historian who was a visiting professor at Washington University that year. I didn't know what to do. My inclination was to rise and leave the classroom, but the door was too far away, and I would have to scramble by seven people to leave my row. I was flushed with self-consciousness.

As he read each card, Professor Gerhard greeted the class member who wrote it, sending his regards to the professor who had sent the student to him. Many of those professors, it was soon clear, had sent him introductory letters about their protégés, including the protégés' theses topics.

My card was the seventh. The professor peered at it through his goggle-like spectacles and looked up. "Mr. Marcus?" he said in a thick German accent.

I raised my hand.

"You haven't filled out your card."

"No, sir."

The class turned toward me, and I felt my face flush all the more.

"What is your thesis topic, Mr. Marcus, and what college are you attending?"

I explained that I was not a PhD candidate, and when the professor asked where I had received my MA, and I answered that I didn't have a master's degree, he was clearly confused and unnerved. I, on the other hand, was humiliated, since the class remained turned in their chairs, staring at me.

"Then who recommended you to my class?" the professor asked, assuming, I gathered, that I had been urged to take the course by one of his colleagues at Washington University.

"No one, sir. Actually, this is the first college class I've ever taken."

The professor's reaction resembled a gag in a slapstick comedy. My announcement so upset his sense of order that his body twitched, and the three-by-five cards flew into the air in all directions like escaped pigeons.

He sputtered, and his face grew more florid. He couldn't speak for a few minutes, but when he retrieved his cards and regained his composure, he said, "I will see you during the break." He intoned the words with gravity and continued with the class.

After he finished going over the remaining cards, he conducted a question-and-answer review of European and French history that led up to the Revolution. "And so with the destruction of the Byzantine Empire, the way to Asia was blocked and Europe had to look west, ever west. What is the theory that expresses this idea?" he asked at one point.

As with the other questions he put to them, my classmates remained silent. I had been surprised at this, but until this question, I had been reluctant to raise my hand. I did now.

The professor saw my hand and pointed to the door. "If you have to go, just leave. There's no need to ask permission," he said dismissively. A few of the class members chortled.

"No, professor," I said, "I know the answer. It's the Pirenne Theory, which states . . ." and I went on to explain it.

The silence was profound when I finished. Either everyone was holding their breath, waiting for the professor's explosive retort, or they were in shock. But Professor Gerhard kept nodding as I spoke and, when I finished, said, "Good, good," and continued his review.

Within a minute I answered another question and then another.

So began a game of question and answer between the professor and me. The class kept turning to one and then the other of us, as if the professor and I were playing a tennis match and they were the spectators. I was more and more surprised at how little those star scholars could (or would) answer and even more intrigued by how much I knew. I realized that my reading and supposedly wasted prep school education had provided me with far more knowledge than I had imagined.

At the break, a curious Professor Gerhard led me to his office where he was going to sign a release that would refund my tuition fee. "Tell me," he said as we walked down the corridor, "why did you take this class?"

"When I saw it in the schedule, it interested me. You see, I've been reading Balzac and George Sand, and I wanted to find out what events had influenced their lives and their writing."

By the time I finished this statement, we had reached his office. His hand was on the doorknob, but he had stopped with the door half opened and had turned and was studying my face. "No one has ever taken one of my classes for such a reason," he said, and continued looking at me. "Do you still want to take the class?"

"Yes, but—"

"You have a lot of catching up to do," he said as much to himself as to me, and then, as if coming to a decision, he continued, "Here's what I will do. I will let you continue in the class for six weeks. Your money can be refunded up to that time. Meanwhile, you will have to read twenty or thirty books I will assign you. Are you willing to do that?"

Was I! My feelings of humiliation evaporated. I was honored and touched by the professor's challenge. No teacher, except Richard Martin, had provided me with such an opportunity, an opportunity that implied that I had the ability to do the work, but it was up to me to do it. It was also immediately apparent that the overwhelming reading assignments would take enormous amounts of time, time that I might otherwise be tempted to spend carousing. As I stood at the professor's door, I vowed to accept the challenge and ensure my success by volunteering to take my fellow soldiers' overnight charge-of-quarters assignments, which consisted of spending nights alone, locked in the base headquarters building, guarding files, safes, and the base communications center, and inspecting the premises every hour.

So began my life as a student and one of the most satisfying if not happy periods I can remember. I easily caught up with the class and formed a warm relationship with Professor Gerhard, one of the finest teachers I've ever had. His final examination was an oral one. He scheduled three hours for each student in his office. Sitting across the desk from his student, he produced two glasses and a bottle of brandy from a desk drawer and proceeded to outline a scenario, a scene from history that he and the student would enact. My scenario was taken from a passage in Alex de Tocqueville's *Journey to America*. On his travels, Tocqueville had been told of a fellow Frenchman who lived on an island near Detroit, but when he visited the island, he found his countryman's cabin abandoned. The professor assumed the role of the island's inhabitant, who he imagined had traveled to America before the French Revolution in 1789 and had returned to France after the Bourbon Restoration in 1815. He met me, an old friend, in a Paris café and proceeded to ask me about everything that had happened in France while he was gone. It was one of the most intriguing and difficult examinations I have ever taken—and one of the most delightful.

I met the professor's challenge successfully and received an A for the class. When I was about to leave his office after the examination, he asked me if I would like to come to Germany with him and live in his household as his protégé. He would make sure that I received a classical education that would lead to my becoming a historian.

I contemplated his offer and made one of the stupidest statements of my life. It profoundly decided the course my future would not take, and I've often wondered what my existence would have been like had I accepted his invitation. I said, with all the unthinking stupidity of youth, "I am a Jew, professor. The Nazis murdered more than 234 members of my family. And I vowed never to set foot in Germany."

The old man didn't reply at first. He looked down at his desk, and when he lifted his head, I saw that tears were slipping down his cheeks from under his glasses. "We were not all like that," he murmured.

I felt embarrassed and foolish. I really loved the professor and knew that my answer was untoward and, worse, cruel. But my decision had been made.

In the years to come, I was to visit Germany several times and grew enamored with the land and its people. I also had a chance, at least partially, to atone for my rash comment. While I was teaching high school in San Francisco in 1966, one of my students elected to go to Washington University to major in history, ten years after I had been a student there. When he visited me at school the following year, he enthusiastically told me about his classes at Washington and, in particular, one seminar conducted by an old German professor.

"What's his name?" I asked, the words almost catching in my throat.

"Dietrich Gerhard," my ex-student answered, looking quizzically at my incredulous expression. Gerhard had only been a visiting professor in 1956. He had either returned for another visiting professorship or assumed a permanent position there since I'd left.

"Tell him," I said, "tell him that your high school teacher was Morton Marcus, and tell him that I have become a teacher because of him."

When the student visited me again the next semester, he told me that the old man had beamed on hearing my message and broken into joyful tears.

Thus began my college education. I took several other classes at Washington University, and between them and the courses taught by Jarvis Thurston and Dietrich Gerhard, I embarked on a new life. My adult years had begun.

■ ■ ■

During my last year in the air force, I met the Catholic chaplain's assistant while on assignment for the base newspaper to write about his bosses, both amateur golf champions. Vic Burnett was short and thin and had a quick, endless line of patter that ingratiated him to everyone. He was in his early twenties, a devout Catholic, and was married with one child. Soon I was going to coffee with him and the two middle-aged golf-playing Jesuit priests, and then to parties and dinner. It was a jovial group, full of conversation that was always light and humorous but at the same time full of substance. Both Vic and the two priests were intrigued that I wanted to be a writer, had read so widely, was going to night school, and—not least—by my being a Jew. They never tried to convert me. On the contrary, they gently upbraided me for not following my religion more closely.

Vic had me over for dinner a number of times, and I got to know his wife Pat and their baby. Both Vic and Pat were from Iowa, where Pat's father owned a big farm. One night as we sat eating dessert, I told them about my looking for a college to attend after I was discharged.

"No problem. I've got just the place," said Vic, taking a cigarette out of his mouth. He always had a cigarette in his mouth that he held delicately clamped between his front teeth. Many times, the cigarette went unlighted.

"Where's that?"

"Iowa!" he said as if the problem was solved, and turned to Pat. She nodded. "It's famous for its writers' workshop," she said.

Vic was already hurrying to the bedroom to get me the catalog. He was to be discharged three months earlier than me and had already been accepted as a student by the university.

"Look," he said, holding out a brochure when he breathlessly returned.

He and Pat were excited, I think, as much for bringing a new member to their state as for finding me a school that they thought would perfectly suit my needs. That week in class I mentioned Iowa to Jarvis Thurston, and he smiled and told me that he and Mona had taught there and would be happy to send a letter of recommendation for me. Coincidences seemed to be pointing me in a definite direction, and I decided to let them carry me along. "Besides," Thurston smiled, "Mona and I have accepted one of your poems for *Perspective*. So you're now a nationally published writer, and Paul loves having published writers in the workshop."

And so he did. With Jarvis and Mona's letter in one hand and my high school and Washington University transcripts in the other, Paul Engle, head of the famed writers' workshop, walked my admissions form through the registrar's office at the State University of Iowa and found me a place to live in town. Vic, out of the air force, was my liaison, getting me whatever papers or other information I needed.

On a hot, humid August day in 1958, my discharge papers and college acceptance forms in hand, I drove my Volkswagen Beetle up the Missouri side of the Mississippi River, through Hannibal, Mark Twain's hometown, to Iowa and the life of a bona fide writer.

PART

... we spend the second half of life looking outward.

—Novalis

BOOK FOUR

HI DIDDLEY DEE, A WRITER'S LIFE FOR ME

CHAPTER 11

Iowa

My attendance at the State University of Iowa was much more than I expected in some ways and much less in others.

My three years there was a period of great change, not only because of my studies, but because I was married the spring I was discharged from the air force. I had met Wilma Kantrowich during the fall of my senior year at Blair Academy. She was two years younger than me and an intelligent, aspiring dancer who took the train from far away Long Beach into New York City once every week to study with some of the top choreographers in the country. She was intrigued by my knowledge of music, books, and art in general, and she had never met a boy before me who knew about dance. We corresponded and began to date when I came home from Blair during the holidays. We continued writing each other almost daily when I was in the air force and dated when I came home on leave. Wanting freedom to do as she pleased when she went to college, she ended the relationship three months before my six-month binge but then began it again my last year in the military. Her intelligence, commitment to art, and our intimate rapport led to our marriage a few months before my discharge, despite her father's disowning her and her mother's disapproval. As for my mother, after insulting Wilma on first meeting her (causing Wilma to run from the apartment in tears), she accepted Wilma in a love-hate relationship and even arranged for the marriage to be performed by a judge she knew. She also paid for our honeymoon suite in the fashionable St. Moritz Hotel and wished us good luck. I came home on a three-day pass for the marriage and Wilma came down from Bennington, where she was going to college. Her mother and aunt and my mother were in attendance in the judge's chambers. It was noon, and the judge, who had been sitting on a murder trial all morning, bustled into the office in his robes, stood behind his desk, looked at the quintet standing before him, and said, "Will the defendants step forward." It was an unexpected jest that cast an ominous shadow into the future.

After the marriage, Wilma's father refused to pay her last semester's bills at Bennington. I had several thousand dollars in bonds and gift money my mother had put away for me over the years, and with it I paid her tuition. Wilma supplemented my GI Bill income by working at various jobs around town in Iowa, the most steady in a paperback bookstore that had been started by two young New Yorkers who had come to Iowa City when we did, became close friends, and would reenter our lives years later.

The apartment Engle had secured for us in Iowa City was on the top floor of a two-story building that had once been a large garage and was now the site of ten apartments on the first floor and five on the second. We lived at the end of the second floor, overlooking the building's flat tarpaper roof, our own apartment covered with a sheet of corrugated metal. It was sweltering during the hot, humid Iowa summers but livable in winter. We shared our three-room apartment, as did everyone else in the complex, with a horde of giant cockroaches whose scuttling could be heard in the kitchen all night long. Occasionally, the cockroaches would come lumbering onto the living-room carpet, big as walnuts. By and large we tolerated them with a saintly, if uneasy, resignation. But they became triggers for trauma when we found them in our bed sheets or woke to discover them crawling over our faces.

The apartment had previously been rented by the poets Donald Finkel and Constance Urdang, who were married and had lived in it for two years. Don had been teaching in the workshop, and he and Connie were about to leave for St. Louis, where he was to be a member of the English department of Washington University for the next thirty years. Jarvis and Mona had published a good deal of his poetry in *Perspective*, and he had become one of my favorite poets because of his imagery and the conversational tone of his work. I liked Connie's poetry as well.

At Engle's suggestion, Don and Connie gave us the apartment. On their own, however, they invited us to dinner. It was a wonderful evening. Both Don and Connie were warm and full of enthusiasm for us and gave us advice in a way that made us feel like fellow artists, not just star-struck kids.

Two things that Don said that night would guide me for the rest of my literary life. The first, he and Connie said at dinner: "The workshop can be both good and bad. You have to watch out for the competition. Everyone's competing with everyone else for recognition and publication. Poetry's not about those things. You have to always keep that in mind." Don made the second statement as we stood at the door, saying good night. He leaned forward and murmured, "Connie and I liked your poem in *Perspective*. We hope you'll keep writing."

I was surprised by the remark and answered with false humility, "I will, if I'm good enough."

Don blinked and straightened. "If you're good enough? What's that got to do with it?"

Those two comments have allowed me to avoid mental and emotional pitfalls in my writing life. The first made me realize that writing is a solitary undertaking in which you cannot be in competition with anyone else since it is an individual act. The second showed me that you don't have to be a "good writer" since you can only write what you write, and goodness or badness have nothing to do with a writer's concerns. Only the necessity to pursue the act of writing is important, and to pursue it to the best of your ability.

I wouldn't see or correspond with Don for more than thirty years, but when we met, we greeted each other like old friends. During dinner, I told him how important his comments had been to me that night so long ago, especially his words about goodness having nothing to do with your pursuit of writing. He turned his gentle eyes toward me and said bashfully, "Did I say that?"

THE WORKSHOP

I entered Iowa as an undergraduate in English, but, since I was already publishing nationally, I was allowed to attend the graduate poetry workshop. In a way, it was having the best of two worlds. But if my experiences in undergraduate studies in Iowa were to be more than I expected, the writers' workshop proved to be much less stimulating.

I had come to the workshop thinking I would learn the secrets of writing I had not been able to discover on my own. I also hoped to find a camaraderie, a principle of communal sharing and encouragement, among men and women with concerns and attitudes similar to mine. Don Finkel had already warned me about the competition for recognition and honors among workshop students, and I quickly learned how territorial, solipsistic, and ungenerous a number of my fellow students, as well as many of my instructors, were. The instructors formed a private club, much like a fraternity (they were all males) and determined which of the students, all of whom vied hungrily for membership, they would select for entrance into the club's inner sanctum. Once admitted, the student would be invited to social gatherings where on certain nights the men played cutthroat poker. On other nights, they attended dinner parties where the men—some of the most renowned writers of the time—would drink and discuss various non-literary subjects. On these second occasions, the men's wives would huddle in the kitchen, talking about children, recipes, and other domestic subjects. Some nights the couples would sit on couches, arms folded, and silently kick a balloon back and forth. Membership in the club was limited to those students whose work found favor with these instructors, although students attempted to ingratiate themselves with the instructors by various means, including playing a brutal game of softball or touch football on weekends. Those games, in many cases, became settings for the unaccepted students to vent their frustrations on the privileged ones and vice versa. They resembled a grotesque version of class warfare.

Paul Engle was the director of the workshop. He had been in the first class of the university's creative writing program in the 1930s and rose to be its long-time director over the years, winning a prestigious Yale Younger Poets Award along the way. His bearing was paternal, and he prided himself on being a wit. But it wasn't Paul's personality that was a problem; it was the workshop itself that was so disappointing. I'm speaking of the workshop as it was from 1958 to 1961, and only about the poetry section, although friends told me the fiction workshops were run much the same way.

Early each week, the students would drop off work at the Quonset hut where the workshop was conducted. The instructors would usually select five to ten poems that were mimeographed on seven or eight sheets of paper, stapled together, and made available in a carton inside the Quonset hut front door on Friday. The workshop consisted of discussing the poems on the sheets the following Monday. Just to get your poems on these work sheets was a form of publication and a mark of success, which inspired spite and envy among the other students and could well determine the nature of critical comments during class.

On Monday afternoon, the twenty or so students would gather in the main Quonset hut room, which had wooden desk chairs set around the perimeter against the walls—one of which was glass—while the instructor, either Engle or Donald Justice, conducted the class from a large wooden desk situated at the edge of the circle closest to a small office. Against the wall, immediately to the right of the desk and opposite the glass wall and the hut's door, was a bench where the most favored if not the most celebrated of the students usually sat, making them appear to be the instructor's favored cohorts.

When everyone was assembled, mimeographed poetry sheets in hand, the instructor would lead the class in critiquing the poems. The poets would not read their work aloud, and it was silently agreed they would not defend their work or explain it—although there were rare occasions when such events did happen. Most of the time, the poets sat silently while the favored sons ripped their work to pieces, as if the poets were condemned criminals being flogged with the most stinging cat-o'-nine-tailed words. Rarely were the criticisms given graciously or kindly or in any way concerned with the delicateness of the writers' feelings, although the favored sons' poems were handled in a different manner, usually praised at the outset by the instructor, using such phrases as "Now here's an example of how a poem should be handled" or "I was impressed by the way the writer of this poem. . . ." The less-favored members of the workshop, particularly those who were unknown to the group or who were not yet publishing, were victims of what can best be described as vigilante violence that the sheriff (the instructor) allowed to happen right before his eyes, and which, most of the time, he led or joined.

Besides the cruelty, what was most upsetting about these sessions were the underlying assumptions of the teachers and their acolytes about what a successful poem was. Iowa had become a bastion of what was termed at the time "academic poetry"—a poetry that was founded on closed forms and was almost completely concerned with technique. Not only sonnets but especially such forms as sestinas and villanelles were held in such high regard by the powers that be that merely writing a moderately successful one ensured not only a favorable comment, but recognition from Justice and Engle and their favorite students. That I was at least approved of as deserving membership in the workshop was due to a sestina in the voice of the Prodigal Son I submitted early in my first semester. Several of the inner group came up to me with smiles and approving comments on the poem even before it appeared on the worksheets, which meant that Justice and Engle had shown it to friends in advance. Need I say that anyone experimenting with free forms was not only frowned upon but derided in class—if their poems reached the worksheets at all.

Technique wasn't the only area of the workshop's concern. There was an unspoken rule that subject matter and theme should be impersonal and non-controversial. Most of the poems, therefore, concerned scenes, characters, or stories from Greek and Roman mythology, fairy tales, and the Bible, from which the poet would make ironic and/or insightful comments. Visionary poetry or ecstatic utterances were not fit subjects for poetry—or the worksheets. Neither was social commentary. Although these dictates would loosen somewhat in the early1960s, when Anne Sexton, Robert Lowell, and W. D. Snodgrass published the first books of confessional poetry, the essential conservatism of the workshop remained in place during my tenure.

It is not surprising, therefore, that Engle, when he attended the workshop, took to beginning each class with a reading from Allen Ginsberg's *Howl and Other Poems* as a sort of blessing, except that he was reading the passages to ridicule Ginsberg's work, mocking it unmercifully. Had we ever heard anything so vulgar, so lacking in restraint and poetics? I, however, liked what I heard, and after Engle's second "blessing," I purchased *Howl* at a local bookstore and read it cover to cover again and again.

I found all these elements depressing. I was relishing my new friends and all my other classes at Iowa except the one I had come to the university to attend. My attitude toward the workshop, and in many ways the workshop instructors' attitude toward me, came to a sort of climax at the beginning of my second year.

I should preface this anecdote by saying that over the years I had covered my early morose belligerence with a jovial exterior. But like Dr. Jekyll's Mr. Hyde, I was quick to anger and subject to moodiness and depression, as if those emotional states lay in wait, hidden—as if my good humor was only skin deep.

In those days, participants were not rigorously screened before being admitted to the graduate workshop, and somehow a young man who had never written before, or at least was totally wanting in the fundamental knowledge of what poetry entailed, had signed up for the class. Justice put the young man's poem first on the semester's first work sheets, now that I think of it, possibly to instigate the situation that followed—or least the first part of it.

It was the second week of class and after the twenty of us—mostly old hands like myself, Jim Crenner, and Vern Rutsala—were assembled and clutching the first work sheets of the semester, Justice turned to Robert Mezey, the workshop's golden boy, who was the youngest poet represented in the influential anthology *New Poets of England and America*. He was the one, sitting on the bench to Justice's right, who was always called on first to comment on the worksheet poems, which he did in a solemn, rabbinical manner. He was full of himself, arrogant, and, worst of all, cruel, and the level of his comments (and those of other favored members of the workshop) can best be illustrated by his remark on a beautiful blank verse elegy by Carol Johnson, written in memory of a friend who had been killed in an accident. Mezey, as if admonishing her in his reverential baritone, exclaimed, "This would have been a great American poem if Miss Johnson had not dropped a syllable in line 35."

That was criticism of a work by a professional, well-schooled writer. Now he was being asked by Justice to pass judgment on a piece by a person who should have been taken aside by Justice and Engle and advised to sign up for an introductory writing class. Mezey launched into a chillingly calm, point-by-point destruction of the poem and its author. He went on for more than ten minutes, at the end of which everyone in the workshop sat in embarrassed silence, many of the new members of the workshop in shock, not the least of whom was the author. No one knew him, but his posture and expression clearly identified him.

I was furious. Mezey had triggered my anger because he was playing the bully, showing not the slightest bit of compassion, kindness, or understanding for the person whose work he was demolishing. His behavior had irked me before, but never like this. Before I knew what I was saying, I said in a calm but tight voice something like, "Bob, that was cruel and unnecessary. I've sat in this workshop time and again as you've done things like this to one person after another. This is the end. I want you to step outside with me right now."

If there was a shocked silence before I spoke, now it seemed all the air had been sucked out of the room. The color drained from Mezey's face; Justice spluttered. Never had such a thing happened in the workshop before. I rose from my chair, glaring at Mezey, who didn't move but swallowed and said, "Wait a minute, Mort, let's talk this over."

"There's nothing to say. Let's go," and I turned toward the door.

Mezey remained seated. I turned back to him and sneered, shaking my head, and took my seat. The session resumed and proceeded tensely. After its conclusion, Mezey came up to me and tentatively asked me to go to coffee with him. I told him we had nothing to say to each other and resumed my challenge. He walked away. It would not be the last time we clashed, and his behavior over the next ten years didn't change much, but I'll come to those incidents in their own time.

The situation in the workshop made me come to some important conclusions about what I wanted the writing of poetry to do for me. In fact, it wouldn't be too far off the mark to say that the workshop acted as a catalyst that made me confront my reasons for writing. Certainly I didn't want to write about the Greek gods or comment about biblical tales. And witty irony was no more a part of my writing than it was of my personality.

By the end of my first two months at Iowa, I decided to work in free verse, speaking in an informal, conversational American idiom. My subject matter would be taken from common everyday life, and I would elevate the ordinary to the marvelous, as if I was uncovering a glittering diamond buried in a clump of mud. I wouldn't fully understand this direction in my work for years to come, but I knew it was a grasping for the visionary over the insightful, the intuitive over the rational, and the resultant poems were rendered in nonrational imagery that welled up from I knew not where in my psyche—imagery that would be called by others "surreal," "subconscious," "deep," and heaven knows what else.

At the same time, my subjects, which arose as naturally as the imagery, were anathema, if not taboo, in the workshop. One of my first free-verse poems was in three parts, each part in the voice of a different character, all three of whom were involved in a ménage à trois. Based on a situation I had encountered while in the air force, the characters were members of a traveling carnival—a white acrobat, his striptease artist wife, and a black geek who was the wife's lover.

Justice put the poem first on the weekly worksheet. Engle had been away and had left the selection of poems to him. (In fact, Engle would have less and less to do with the workshop as he traveled around the world more and more, met the woman who would become his second wife, and set about organizing the international translation workshop at Iowa.)

Engle returned just in time to conduct the workshop with Justice and read my poem as he sat in front of the class. I watched his face as he read. It sagged from cheery animation to worried annoyance. He took off his reading glasses and looked at me as though I were a naughty boy who had transgressed the rules. What followed was a free-for-all as Justice, Engle, and their coterie disemboweled my little experiment. Not that the poem didn't deserve it. It was rhythmically and syntactically awkward and probably far too heavy-handed in its racial content. It was obvious, however, that the real problems for the work-shop powers that be lay elsewhere. Justice said he couldn't parse the lines and asked me if the poem was supposed to be in free verse, and if it was, would I tell him what free verse was, since he didn't think it existed. Engle was con-cerned with the racial and sexual subject matter, which he was unhappy to see on the workshop sheets, since they were freely distributed and, it was rumored, were looked over by wealthy farmers and state politicians from time to time.

When the discussion ended half an hour later, Engle again removed his glasses, stared at me, and said, "And I hope, Mr. Marcus, you will take our comments for what they are worth."

I replied calmly but foolishly, "To me the comments are worth nothing."

Engle's eyebrows contracted, and he stared at me for several seconds, a tired but malevolent gaze that crossed me off the list of students worthy of his help and time. Never again would I receive aid of any kind from him, although I would remain a member of the workshop for three years, cer-tainly one of the poets whose increasing national reputation made me one of the workshop's steady if lesser lights.

Engle and I remained civil to each other, and to this day I am grateful to him for getting me into Iowa. Our relationship can best be summed up, however, by an incident that took place toward the end of my last year at Iowa. It was at a party at Vance Bourjaily's farmhouse, just outside Iowa City. Vance, a well-known editor and novelist, was celebrating the publica-tion of his new novel *Confessions of a Spent Youth* and had invited every writer and writing student for miles around to join him. Hundreds of people congregated outside his house and jammed the interior. As I navigated through the crowd in the kitchen with drinks for myself and Wilma, I came face to face, nose to nose really, with Engle who was standing with his back to the kitchen refrigerator. He broke off his conversation with the person on his right and looked me in the eye. "Hello, Paul," I said, holding the drinks high above my head.

"Mort, you are stepping on my toes," he said dryly. "You are always step-ping on my toes." I smiled and moved on without a word.

The carnival poem, which I have never seen fit to include in any of my collections, took on a life of its own. It was noticed by several class members who, on the strength of it, invited me for coffee and became, in several cases, lifelong friends—such people as Vern Rutsala, Lew Turco, Jim Cren-ner, Christopher Wiseman, S. J. Marks, and, in future years, Lawson Inada and Michael Harper. Soon we would make up a group that sat together and became known as the rebels of the workshop because of the direction our poetry was taking and our outspokenness in class. After that year, Marks would leave the workshop and return to Chicago where he founded *Decem-ber* magazine and published the group's poems as well as the early stories of

Jerry Bumpus, who was another member of the group. Later, Marks would found the *American Poetry Review* with Stephen Berg, who was another member of the workshop that first year.

Somehow, more than a year later, the poem surfaced in Michael Harper's hands and served as the basis for our getting to know each other. I believe that Michael, big and truculent, was the first black poet in the history of the workshop and was finding life in all-white Iowa City disturbing. But more of that later.

With the rebels' encouragement, I continued to write raw, gritty poetry, some of it personal. There was a snarling poem about my explosive arguments with Wilma ("Poem to Wilma") and another about loneliness and impotence ("The Man Downstairs"). There were also mystical poems, like "The Whirling Dervish," that Justice selected for inclusion in an anthology of national college student poetry that appeared in *Mademoiselle* magazine.

Events in the workshop came to a head at the end of the first semester of my second year, not incidentally the same semester I challenged Mezey to "step outside." Engle made it clear to me, I thought, that I was no longer welcome in the workshop. That was fine with me; I had a lot of undergraduate work to do, especially in Chinese studies. Besides, many of the writers in the workshop had reinforced an attitude I had had before and have maintained to this day: I don't particularly like artists, nor do they particularly like me. To me they are, in the main, too self-involved, too precious, and worst of all, they conceive of themselves as better than the rest of humanity, who they think should give them financial and emotional support because of their talents. Even when I was young, I thought I was like everyone else and have worked for a living at various jobs all my life, neither seeking nor expecting special favors to succor my writing. At the same time, I have met many artists who feel the same way I do, and they are the friends and acquaintances that for the most part I write about in these pages. Still, it's ironic—to me anyway—that much of the last half of these remembrances will be about my fellow writers and will read like a literary as well as a personal memoir.

DONALD JUSTICE

Even though I was no longer in the workshop, I still hung out with my friends, which meant that I saw Justice regularly. One day he invited me to take a walk with him and asked why I hadn't signed up for the workshop that semester. I told him that Engle had subtly let me know he didn't want me there anymore because, I gathered, my comments were too confrontational and divisive.

"That's not true," Justice said. "There are no such feelings, although I'll say for myself that I think you're wasting your talent by not disciplining yourself more by using closed forms."

"Don, that's not the issue, and you know it. If I wanted to write villanelles, I would—and could. In fact, I could have two on your desk by Friday."

"Prove it."

"It's not just the forms or the poetics. My subject matter is equally offensive to you and Paul."

"I think you're trying to wriggle out of your boast."

"I'm not. It's just—"

"Then have them on my desk by Friday." And he walked away.

Donald Justice,
Pulitzer Prize
winner

By Friday I placed two new villanelles on Don's desk. Both were cityscapes that depicted violent events. One, "Wondering What It's All About," was a street scene depicting the aftermath of a murder and would appear more than twenty years later in *Kayak* magazine.

I didn't hear from Justice for several weeks, then ran into him walking across campus. "Did you get my villanelles?" I asked.

He sneered, half grunted, and kept walking. However, next semester, the beginning of my third year at Iowa, I rejoined the workshop, and the atmosphere seemed friendlier, maybe because Mezey had graduated the previous spring.

My relationship with Don Justice, who would eventually win a Pulitzer Prize for his poetry, was complex. Although it became more and more adversarial in class, outside we socialized in various activities, playing softball with the workshop team and ping-pong during the afternoons. In class, he took to what would pass for badgering me but was really forcing me to define what I was doing. When he was unable to scan the lines of a poem on the worksheets, he would look at me and say, "I find this piece impossible to parse. It must be free verse—in which case Mr. Marcus will enlighten us on how to read it." When Justice attended my first public reading in Iowa City, he walked out in disgust at my dramatic presentation, telling Vern Rutsala that poetry should be read in a monotone so the words would do all the work as they did on the page.

For my part, Justice infuriated me but also became my mentor. I adopted his rigorous, objective reading of a text as my modus operandi, and his relentless analytical questioning of every aspect of a poem became de rigueur for me, both as a writer and a teacher. As a student, I always respected Justice's intelligence without question.

Don and I clashed over method and approach. I was freewheeling, ready to tear into any subject that appealed to me, like a hungry peasant attacking a meal. I knew no boundaries in technique, treatment, or theme. Writing was a learning experience, a voyage of self-discovery, and, much of the time, a celebration. I was seeking self-knowledge, wisdom, ecstatic being, and what I would later term "heightened consciousness."

Justice had set boundaries for himself everywhere. Generally speaking, his work showed a purposeful limitation in subject matter, approach, and range of response. His award-winning first book, *The Summer Anniversaries*, which came out in 1960, was precise in its plain style and exhibited control in every aspect of its utterance.

In fact, Don's poetry was the essence of control. Not only would he return over the years to such closed forms as villanelles and sestinas, but his diction was almost always formal and his tone grave. All of these components led to a suppression of emotion in his poems, a purposeful understatement or withholding of feeling that many of his readers thought elicited a greater sense of emotional power for its being avoided directly, since the reader knows it wants to break out of the pressure it's under.

On the other hand, Don's use of closed forms can be seen as his strapping himself into an emotional straitjacket, and his formal diction as a remoteness that keeps his readers at arm's length. (Even Richard Wilbur, the most conservative of academic poets, sprinkled the formal diction of his poems with informal and vernacular words, which provided unexpected delight.)

Here is a sonnet that captures memories of childhood, a subject Don was fond of writing about. Notice that the speaker takes himself out of the poem by using the third person. This causes an emotional distancing Don would not have achieved had he written the poem in the first person. The result is a curious detachment that I have felt in a number of Don's poems. That is why I may admire Don's work but do not love it.

The Poet at Seven

And on the porch, across the upturned chair,
The boy would spread a dingy counterpane
Against the length and majesty of the rain
And on all fours crawl in it like a bear,
To lick his wounds in secret, in his lair;
And afterwards, in the windy yard again,
One hand cocked back, release his paper plane,
Frail as a mayfly to the faithless air.
And summer evenings he would spin around
Faster and faster till the drunken ground
Rose up to meet him; sometimes he would squat
Among the foul weeds of the vacant lot,
Waiting for dusk and someone dear to come
And whip him down the street, but gently, home.

What Don loses with his distancing devices is immediacy, which, along with direct emotional response, was what I was seeking to evince in my work. This difference was a constant problem between us.

At times, Don did allow himself to express joyous rapture, as in the middle section of "Ladies at their Windows":

The light in going still is golden, still
A single bird is singing in the wood,
Now one, now two, now three, and crickets start,
Bird-song and cricket-sigh; and all the small
Percussion of the grass booms as it can,
And chimes, and tinkles, too, fortissimo.

It is the lurch and slur the world makes turning.
It is the sound of turning, of a wheel
Or hand-cranked grinder turning, though more pomp
To this, more fiery particles struck off
At each revolve; and the last turn reveals
The darker side of what was light before.

Six stars shine through the dark, and half a moon!
Night birds go spiralling upwards with a flash
Of silvery underwings, silver ascendings,
The light of stars and of the moon their light,
And water lilies open to the moon,
The moon in wrinkles on the water's face.

To shine is to be surrounded by the dark,
To glimmer in the very going out,
As stars wink, sinking in the bath of dawn,
Or as a prong of moon prolongs the night—
Superfluous curve!—unused to brilliancies
Which pale her own, yet splurging all she has.

Such passages, unfortunately, are found all too seldom in his work.

The difficulty between Don and me can be explained in large part by our different personalities and upbringing. Don was a Southerner, raised in Florida, who had been sickly as a child, at times almost a shut-in. As a result, he didn't take part in the games and pranks of childhood and sought to rectify the situation as an adult. He was extremely competitive, whether he was playing softball, ping-pong, or poker, and I recall his emotional outbursts when a decision went against him. On one occasion, after an umpire called a ball instead of a strike on a pitch Don had just made, he jumped up and down on his baseball glove. Another time, he shot an angry yelp at me when a ground ball skidded through my legs. His many outbursts certainly were not the stuff of maturity. Nor was his ferocious competitiveness.

Most telling was the way he approached any game. He would analyze every move, planning his strategies a number of moves in advance. Several years later, when he was staying in San Francisco on a Rockefeller grant and we briefly chummed around, he purchased one of the first electric football games and challenged me to a contest. Knowing he would employ conventional strategy, meticulously reasoning out every play, I did everything against usual football tactics. Within ten minutes I was up by five touchdowns, 35 to 7, and Don was furious, yelling at me. Yes, it was my old athletic strategy of feinting my opponent out of position, using trickery, misdirection, and attack, but more than that, it was another illustration of the difference between Don and me.

THAT OLD GANG OF MINE

The best thing about any creative workshop is the people you meet there. They are usually your own age and are as dedicated as you are. Soon you and several classmates are meeting outside class, discussing writers and writing, trading manuscripts, and commenting on each other's work. The relationships are often the most intense, long lasting, and artistically satisfying you will ever have.

It was no different in Iowa. The group I've already mentioned would meet after Monday's class in the student union cafeteria where we would rehash what had transpired in the workshop. After several cups of coffee, we would wander downtown to Kenny's Bar where we would meet with others and talk writing and politics for the rest of the evening—although most of us went home, at least for part of the night, at dinner time.

And there was plenty of politics to discuss. Although I was the only undergraduate in the writers' workshop, most of us were Korean vets on the GI Bill. We were not naïve kids but men in our early to mid twenties, who were questioning everything about the tranquil, buttoned-down world of America in the 1950s. In 1960 the United States was in the midst of the Cold War, and I remember the reaction at Kenny's the day the Russians shot down our U2 spy plane, claiming we were provoking a crisis by invading their air space. At first, President Eisenhower angrily denied the charges, but a few days later, after the Russians paraded Francis Gary Powers, the pilot, in front of foreign journalists, he acknowledged the charge was true. We were angered at the Russians initially, although we knew firsthand what covert actions our military, directed by the government, was capable of, and that made us uneasy. But when Eisenhower admitted to our pursuing a program of spy flights, we were both angry and depressed: the Cold War had irrevocably revealed to us and the world that we, the United States, were not the "good guys" we'd always been told we were. I remember Vern Rutsala raising his head from his tenth beer, lighting a cigarette, and delivering one of his classic declarations in his typical low-keyed delivery: "Hell, I don't want to fight the Russians. They sing too well."

There were a number of graduate students at Iowa from New York doing doctorates in history, political science, and economics. Almost all of them were the first political activists of the postwar period. They turned Iowa upside down on one social or legal issue after another. We socialized with them and they with us, many times meeting for parties at one person or another's house where the beer flowed, the discussions continued, tempers flared, and young, blonde, blue-eyed Iowa coeds were endlessly seduced. Many evenings, however, Vern and I would drift over to his house from Kenny's where his wife, Joan, who usually joined us at Kenny's when she got off work at the hospital, would cook a fast but delicious pot of chili or spaghetti for the four or six of us who had unexpectedly shown up for dinner. Some nights, Joan, Vern, Wilma, and I had prearranged dinners together, and I remember one evening at my apartment when, with lights lowered, Joan enacted the final ventriloquist's scene from the film *Dead of Night* and scared all of us half to the grave.

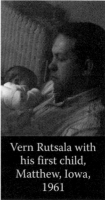

Vern Rutsala with his first child, Matthew, Iowa, 1961

A big, heavy-set man who had been a high school football star, Vern was clearly the leader of our group and was only two years away from the publication of his first book, *The Window*. His poetry defied categorizing and was praised by the inner and outer groups of the workshop for its phrasing, imagery, and control of poetics. That his subject matter was the vacuous nature of American life in the 1950s, described in trenchant, satirical terms, didn't seem to bother the workshop academics. Vern's work was too good.

During those years, Vern wrote his poems in the voice of an astute, removed observer commenting on the world around him. The poems, written in a mordant vernacular from either a third- or second-person perspective, were usually punctuated by a poignant insight. This method remained one of his favorite approaches.

Other Lives

You see them from train windows
in little towns, in those solitary lights
all across Nebraska, in the mysteries
of backyards outside cities—

a single face looking up,
blurred and still as a photograph.
They come to life quickly
in gas stations, overheard in diners,

loom and dwindle, families
from dreams like memories too
far back to hold. Driving by
you go out to all those strange

rooms, all those drawn shades,
those huddled taverns on the highway,
cars nosed-in so close they seem
to touch. And they always snap shut,

fall into the past forever, vast lives
over in an instant. You feed

on this shortness, this mystery
of nearness and regret—such lives

so brief you seem immortal;
and you feed, too, on that old hope—
dim as a half-remembered
phone number—that somewhere

people are as you were always
told they were—people who swim
in certainty, who believe, who age
with precision, growing gray like

actors in a high school play.

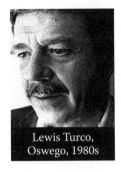

Lewis Turco,
Oswego, 1980s

In the workshop, Vern commanded everyone's respect by the intelligence of his comments and the
depths of his insights. Outside, he and Joan were an
inseparable couple, and she would almost always join us
at Kenny's. Wilma seldom did. She was too busy completing her undergraduate degree at Iowa as well as
teaching stage movement to prospective opera singers
in the university music department and giving modern
dance classes downtown.

If Vern was thoughtful and deliberate in his speech
and manner, Lewis Turco was a force field of energy,
scattering words like sparks in all directions. Short and squat, with a crew
cut, ready grin, and merry eyes, Lew was one of the most verbally facile people I ever met. He was always jabbering, it seemed, but his jabber was a fun-
filled patter of puns and jokes. He had also perfected the art of speaking
backward and would delightedly—and exasperatingly to those around him—
immediately repeat whatever you said reversed, and not just the sentences
and words reversed, but the letters. There was something innocent and boy-
ishly joyous about Lew that was still very much in evidence when I saw him
forty-six years later in 2006 when he and Vern gave a memorable reading at
Tor House and the three of us took part in a reunion reading several days
later in Santa Cruz. When Lew left the workshop after the first year, the
group was certainly more brooding and staid because of his absence.

Though he would deny it, Lew was essentially a formalist, a master of
forms and meters and all the technical trappings of poetry. Anything not
written in meters, although it might be rhymed and in lines, he did not consider poetry. It's no surprise, therefore, that he is best known for his *Book of
Forms*, which is considered by many to be "the poet's bible." In the end, he
published more than forty books of poetry, as well as several prose works on
one aspect of literature or another. His poems, even when "free," almost
always were in syllabics, as is the following, one of his most popular pieces.

Burning the News

The fire is eating
the paper. The child who drowned
is burned. Asia is in flames.
          As he signs his great
bill, a minister of state chars

          at the edge and curls
into smoke. The page rises,
glowing, over our neighbor's
          roof. In the kitchens
clocks turn, pages turn like gray wings,

          slowly, over armchairs.
Another child drowns, a bill
is signed, and the pen blackens.
          The smoke of Asia
drifts among the neighbors like mist.

It is a good day for burning.
The fire is eating the news.

Many of us were ex-high-school athletes, and besides
the workshop softball games, we would play pick-up
basketball games together. We played half-court three-
on-three basketball. On that score, Iowa wasn't a good
time for me. Carrying thirty-five extra pounds, I was
cumbersome, always falling back on my heels on
defense, and missing a depressing percentage of shots.
My athletic days were definitely over.

Lawson Inada,
Santa Cruz, 1993

Lawson Inada joined the group in 1959, my second
year at Iowa. He arrived from Fresno State University in
California where Philip Levine had been his teacher and
had recommended him to Engle. Levine had been a stu-
dent at the workshop several years before and a good friend of Peter Everwine, a marvelous poet who was not in the workshop but was pursuing a
PhD in English literature. Everwine had shown me several of Levine's
poems my first year, one a graphic, angry poem about the torture of Algeri-
ans by the French during the Algerian Revolution in the 1950s. The poem
was called "Gangrene." Although it was in closed verse, I was astonished at
the power and urgency of the voice in the poems, and I have read Levine's
poems devotedly ever since.

Lawson had been one of Levine's first students at Fresno State. He was a
Japanese American who was always sharply dressed, his outfits showing
clear affinity with black culture, jazz, and hipness in general. His voice was
soft and level although he would break into raucous laughter at the corniest
joke. He was a great companion.

Iowa was not an easy place for Lawson. Most of the population was blond and blue-eyed and looked upon anyone whose complexion was different as an anomaly. One of my Caucasian friends, who was black-haired and brown-eyed, was described by his landlady as "a foreigner." If you were black or Asian, the Iowans' submerged racism rose to the surface. The few blacks at the university were on athletic scholarship and usually hung out together, kept away, it seemed, from the general populace. But Lawson—and later, Michael Harper—were alone. When Lawson walked down the street at night, farm boys or fraternity boys in beat-up cars would drive by and yell every anti-Japanese insult they could think of. Even if several of us were strolling with him, the verbal attacks came, and continually, it seemed, we ran into the roadway, challenging the occupants of the cars to stop so we could beat them to chopped meat. The cars, of course, never stopped.

During all those episodes, Lawson acted as if he didn't hear the insults and walked on unperturbed. Even when we broke away from him and sprinted after the cars, shouting our challenges, he kept walking on the sidewalk, the picture of composure. But it was all a front: the anger and humiliation that must have boiled inside him finally erupted one night when he was alone and broke every mirror in his apartment, as he tried to destroy any reflecting surface that showed him the face that had elicited the vicious verbal abuse he experienced every day in Iowa and, I imagine, for what must have seemed an infinity of years before that in California.

Although Lawson's poems would examine many aspects of his life—such as memories of growing up in Fresno and creating a jazz poetry—one of his main stances early in his career was as a spokeman for the tribulations that Japanese Americans endured during World War II when they were imprisoned in internment camps, in one of which he spent his childhood. In "Concentration Camp Constellation," he looks at a map of the United States and sees not cities but the locations of the camps. The poem ends with the locations being transformed into a celestial constellation. The names of the camps are in italics.

> . . . *Minidoka* on the moon
> Of Idaho, then down to Utah's
> jewel of *Topaz* before finding
> yourself at northern California's
> frozen shore of *Tule Lake* . . .
>
> Now regard what sort of shape
> This constellation takes.
> It sits like a jagged scar,
> Massive, on the massive landscape.
> It lies there like the rusted wire
> Of a twisted and remembered fence.

—from "Concentration Camp Constellation"

The sequence "Looking Back at Camp" begins with a bitter memory of the Fresno fairgrounds, where he and his family and many others were rounded up before being sent off to the camps.

> To get into the fair,
> You have to pay admission.
>
> We got in for free,
> To the Fresno Family prison.

Michael Harper came to Iowa my third year, and although there was enormous antiblack feeling in town, no one bothered him: he was too big, too truculent—his angry stare and belligerent body language caused everyone to give him a wide berth. He and Lawson hung out together, and after Lawson, I guess it was, showed him my carnival poem, we were on friendly terms. But Michael didn't let any of us get close to him, probably because we were white. Who knows? Down through the years we bumped into each other several times and were always on good terms, and I spent several days with him and his family at their Minnesota house in the 1970s. When I last saw him in Rhode Island in 1998, we hadn't seen each other in twenty years. I was reading and visiting classes at Providence College and he had been teaching at Brown, a mile or two down the road, since the year I stayed with him in Minnesota. He was very busy, he said, but after we exchanged several phone calls he found time to meet me my last morning in town, take me along while he did some chores, and then drop me off at the railroad station. We didn't have much to say to one another. His years at Brown hadn't softened him: he was as truculent as ever.

Racial prejudice wasn't experienced only by people of color in Iowa. I was subjected to several instances of anti-Semitism as well. For the most part, its expression was covert, since racists rarely confront the recipients of their bigotry without a crowd to support their action. It normally showed itself in stares and such comments as the landlady's remarks about dark-haired people being foreigners. But at times it exploded to the surface. One instance in particular occurred in the barbershop where I regularly went for a haircut.

I had taken off my glasses as I entered the shop and gone directly to one of the empty barber chairs. A youngish man—I couldn't see him clearly without my glasses—was sitting against the wall opposite me, obviously a friend of the two barbers, and he was complaining. As one of the barbers spread the sheet over me and fastened the paper catchall around my neck, I realized the man was in the middle of a long diatribe about how the Jews controlled the country. He went on and on. I said nothing, getting angrier by the minute, but I wanted to see how far he would go. When he accused

the Jews of stealing Iowa's corn and pork for "their fancy tables back east,"
my curiosity came to an end.

"We ought to gas them all," I said.

There was a sudden silence in the shop, not that the barbers had said
anything to begin with. They were just listening to the man.

"Hitler was right, wasn't he?" I continued.

The man said nothing, and the barber who was cutting my hair pressed
his hands on my shoulders and whispered, "Easy now, Mr. Marcus. Harlan
was just talking."

"No, let's do something about them." I stared at the man. 'Isn't that what
you want, you stupid son of a bitch?"

The man said nothing. He didn't move.

"You're so stupid you don't even know Jews don't eat pork."

The man bowed his head.

"Hey, you. Guess what? I'm a Jew, a Jew who's going to kick the shit out of
you in thirty seconds. What do you think of that?"

The man still refused to answer and continued to sit motionless. The
barber, who had clamped his hands to my shoulders, however, was holding
me down. I had realized several minutes before that I was not in the best
position to start a fight, but I was furious.

The barber continued to press his palms on my shoulders and murmured
soothingly in my ear, "Now, now, Mr. Marcus, you don't know—"

"I damn well *do* know," I replied and leaned toward the man. "So you're a
coward as well as a bigot. Come on, make the first move," I said, and pushed
my palms against the arms of the chair, readying to launch myself at him.

But the man continued to sit motionless and say nothing.

I continued berating him for the ten minutes it took to finish my haircut.
All the while the barber kept murmuring, "Come on, Mr. Marcus. Harlan
was only talking. That's all he can do. You know that."

When I rose from the chair, I paid, called the man "stupid scum" and left.

The man may not have wanted to fight, but I couldn't understand why he
would sit there and take such a verbal beating. Whatever the reason, I was
elated. I had struck a blow against narrow-mindedness and stupidity that
the man wouldn't soon forget. Like my heroes Samson and Maccabeus, I
had stood up for my people with glorious biblical valor.

The barbershop was next door to the building where I lived, and, with
growing euphoria, I climbed the stairs to my apartment and told Wilma
what had happened. She was angered too but reminded me that I had forgotten to pick up the bread and milk I was supposed to buy after I got my
haircut.

I immediately went downstairs and reached the sidewalk in time to see
my antagonist half a block away, dragging himself down the street. With my

glasses on, I now understood the barber's remarks. The man was crippled; heavy metal braces encased both legs.

My stomach turned over. I returned to the apartment and told Wilma how pathetic my gesture had been and how bad I felt.

"Don't," she said. "He was as much a mental cripple as a physical one."

That didn't relieve my self-disgust. There was a lesson here I couldn't fathom. What kind of battle had I won? The man probably hated Jews now more than before, adding the epithet of "bully" to his list. And I? What had I gained? If I had won some sort of victory, it was a pyrrhic one. But I didn't think it was even that.

■ ■ ■

As I spent more time with my new friends, I saw less and less of Vic and Pat, the two people who had steered me toward Iowa during my last year in the air force. Vic was busy in the drama department, and we would warmly say hello when we ran into each other, and occasionally Wilma and I would go out to the farm for Sunday dinner with Pat 's parents, but our lives were going in different directions. After Iowa, Vic became a weatherman on a Peoria, Illinois, TV station, and when he and Pat came to San Francisco in 1967, we spent the day together but didn't have much to say to one another. It was "the summer of love" in San Francisco, and Vic and Pat looked askance at the new freedoms and the new manners of dress that surrounded them.

■ ■ ■

So the three years at Iowa passed—the parties, the daily discussions at Kenny's, the evenings at Vern's, the enthralling classes, the hours and hours of study, with every now and then a memorable event: Robert Frost giving a reading, Sir John Gielgud presenting a one-man show, and, on the large-screen student-union television set, an aging Ray Robinson battling Gene Fulmer for the middleweight championship, and Floyd Patterson's three historic bouts with Ingmar Johansen. None of us owned TVs at that time. We went to films three or four times a week. There was even an art movie house in town that showed the newest foreign films: Ray's *Pather Panchali*, Resnais's *Hiroshima Mon Amour*, Godard's *Breathless*, Truffaut's *The Four Hundred Blows*, Fellini's *White Sheik*, *I Vitelloni*, and *La Strada*. I was paying rent, buying food, and paying my out-of-state tuition fee of $120 a semester almost completely on my $110 monthly GI Bill check. Wilma supplemented that amount with her various part-time jobs. It was an exciting and idyllic time, to say the least. And although Wilma and I fought a lot, we were newlyweds sharing a life of adventures and new experiences.

The most memorable literary event of my three years at Iowa was a weekend of panels and readings sponsored by *Esquire* magazine, featuring Norman Mailer, Mark Harris, and Dwight McDonald. To a packed audience of hundreds in the college theater the first evening, Mailer—at that time still considered one of America's top novelists for his World War II bestseller *The Naked and the Dead*—attacked Harris's opening talk (and by inference his work) as being vacuous and not engaging the American experience. Harris, a literature professor at San Francisco State and the author of such popular novels as *Bang the Drum Slowly*, crumpled and by the end of the evening was denouncing his early work and wayward literary ways as well as paying obeisance to Mailer. An insouciant McDonald looked on, dropping witty comments here and there like olives into a martini glass.

Mailer warmed to his victory. He was the enfant terrible of American literature at the time and relished playing the street-wise tough guy. He had just published a selection of essays in a book entitled *Advertisements for Myself*. One of the essays, "The Talent in the Room," audaciously rated contemporary American novelists with whom he thought he was in competition for the title of best American fiction writer.

At the party after the first evening, Mailer entertained the eager young members of the writers' workshop with yarns and bar games. The next day was more of the same, Mailer dominating the proceedings and being followed everywhere by an entourage of adoring young writers. One of them was a fellow member of the poetry workshop I'll call Stan, a former paratrooper who enjoyed walking the narrow ledge that separated the first and second stories of the massive campus buildings. As everyone gasped, he'd stroll off the end of a ledge and land in a perfect roll on the grass beneath, after which he would amble away. Our group distrusted Stan because he wanted to belong to the inner circle so desperately that he agreed with many of their criticisms during the workshops and took part in their assaults on any and every poor soul who came under their verbal guns.

Slim and supple, with a crew cut and all-American good looks, he took to following Mailer everywhere and unabashedly sucked up to him. He and Mailer engaged in verbal jousts, and Mailer demonstrated his bar games on Stan, using him as his fall guy. They were quite a pair, clean-cut Stan in his usual slipover sweater and sports slacks and Mailer in his blue suit, white shirt, red tie, and thick black belt, which made him look like a thirteen-year-old bar mitzvah candidate.

At Saturday's late afternoon cocktail party, Mailer showed the adoring crowd surrounding him how to play "thumbsies," a bar game in which you join hands with your opponent and try to pin the thumb of the held hand to his chest while he tries to do the same to you. Proclaiming he had never lost a thumbsy match, Mailer challenged Stan to a game and easily won the first two rounds, to the cheers of the onlookers. But in the third round, Stan, having gotten the hang of the game, pinned Mailer's thumb to the lapels of his blue jacket. Mailer's response was immediate: he slammed a right-hand punch to Stan's jaw that dropped him to the carpet. Stan sat there, looking up at Mailer, both surprised and emotionally hurt that his new friend would do such a thing to him. "Why'd you do that?" he asked like a pouting child.

"You cheated, that's why," said Mailer and let Stan get up on his own.

Meanwhile, the crowd, which moments before had idolized Mailer, almost instantly turned hostile and began to mutter threateningly. Mailer faced them. "What are you gonna do, huh?" he said, looking around. "I can take all of you." Then his gaze stopped on Vern and me. We had arrived at the party a few minutes before and were standing on the outer edge of the group. "All except those two," Mailer concluded with a winning smile. "I wouldn't want to mix it up with them."

Don't ask me why he singled us out. Vern was a big guy, but we certainly weren't in a threatening posture, nor were we wearing hostile expressions, although we were displeased by his action. Whatever the reason, this smiling reference to us was an acknowledgment to the crowd that he wasn't invincible, and once more they gathered around him in fawning approbation.

When I saw Mailer at the fights in Madison Square Garden several years later, I reminded him of the incident. He didn't remember it but in a friendly gesture invited me to join him and Jose Torres, the ex-light-heavyweight champion. Since I was with a friend, I declined, but we would greet each other every fight night, his expression showing that he was trying to place where he had met me.

CHAPTER 12

Beyond My Expectations

Since I had a 4.0 average from my classes at Washington University, I was admitted to Iowa as an honor student, which, under a new policy, encouraged me to visit any professor in his office at any time for private conferences.

It was this part of my stay at Iowa that far exceeded my expectations. Every department had at least one world-renowned faculty member. In physics, it was James Van Allen, who a few years before had discovered the Van Allen Belt. He was seconded by the famous European physicist Max Dresden. I got to know Dresden at one of his monthly soirees for his protégés and their wives. He had invited Wilma, who was teaching his daughter Jana in a dance class she was conducting in town. Wilma and I liked his daughter's name so much we decided to bestow it on our first child, if it turned out to be a girl.

Dresden's soiree was interesting because he brought up the subject of art for discussion, asking his team if they were spending their free time creating or following the arts, which he told them he considered, along with science, important in fostering the development of a fully rounded human being. It turned out that he had invited Wilma and me, as representatives of the arts, to talk about the creative life. We gathered that the soirees were usually a chance for team members to informally talk about what they were writing or to report on a new theory of this or that that they had been assigned to outline for the group.

Dresden's remarks took his eight protégés and their wives by surprise. Only one of them, a Chinese fellow, volunteered that he painted in his spare time. His colleagues were shocked. Several said they had been working with him for ten years and never suspected his "secret life." As for the others, neither they nor their wives listened to music, read literature, or went to museums of any kind. It was obvious that Dresden knew this and wanted to inject a new kind of energy into the group. He introduced Wilma, who presented her ideas on a life filled with artistic endeavor, and then me. Using Alfred North Whitehead's ideas as an acknowledged guide, I spoke about the similarity of all creative acts, whether in science or art, and how one had to be open to intuitive impulses and seemingly accidental connections in both areas. C. P. Snow had already published his book, *The Two Cultures*, which bemoaned the separation of the arts and sciences, and I used it as my point of reference. When I finished my brief talk, I could see that Dresden's protégés, who had given Wilma and me a warm welcome, were clearly uncomfortable—and were gazing at us as if we were a different species of human. Even the Chinese art student now seemed to be regarded suspiciously by his compatriots. The evening ended with my becoming more aware than ever of the separation between the arts and the sciences .

I had much more to do with other renowned professors. I visited Gustav Bergmann, the famous logical positivist philosopher, in his office and immediately became embroiled in an argument with him. I have no idea what the disagreement was about but soon learned that the great man argued about almost everything. More to my liking was his wry colleague, a young Richard Popkin, the beloved skeptic and follower of Sextus Empiricus, whose renown in philosophy circles would grow with the years. Popkin would have a moment of public fame in 1964 when he wrote a long article in the *New York Review of Books* that proved with philosophical logic that there had to be two shooters in the assassination of JFK in Dallas.

Popkin was in his midthirties in 1958. He was dark complexioned and slightly overweight. When he talked of philosophic issues, his eyes danced merrily and he spoke in a tone of voice that wasn't so much sarcastic as ironic, as he slowly and carefully unspooled his ideas as if he were unrolling a turban from around his head.

I took both semesters of the history of philosophy with Popkin, and early in the first part of the course he called me into his office. He knew I was a writer in the famous workshop and asked me, as a fellow Jew, if I had read Isaac Bashevis Singer's "Gimpel the Fool." I shook my head, and he handed me a paperback book. "Read it and tell me what you think of it next week at this time."

I read the story and was moved by it and told him so when we met in his office the following week. "Moved by it? What do you mean by that? That's an emotional response. I wanted you to see the philosophical implications in the story."

I sat there dumbly.

Popkin leaned forward on his desk. "Gimpel cannot reason his way out of his difficulties, nor can he rationally explain why his difficulties befell him. Yet he is not a skeptic either. He is a believer to the end. His faith is unshakable. His faith is what the story is about."

Popkin sat back. "That story changed my life," he said. "I played the skeptic for years, until I read it. But then I couldn't deny its message. You believed, or the world was chaos."

He smiled. "So I've come back to Judaism." He had not been bar mitzvahed as a boy, so he was now learning Hebrew in a class with twelve-year-olds. He was an amazing man. Philosophy wasn't a game to him, although he brought a sense of play to his study and teaching of it; it was a life-affirming quest. One of his favorite philosophers was David Hume, whose attitude as well as taboo-breaking ideas, such as disproving the existence of cause and effect, I also found captivating. Hume seemed a bon vivant, a fun-loving, sharp-minded wit who was generous and loving to all those around him. He was a wonderful writer as well—a fact I found was not always true of other famous philosophers.

Despite Popkin's stimulating lectures and the intriguing questions the philosophers contemplated, I had difficulty understanding their abstruse logic. Their reasoning was too abstract for my image-riddled (or addled) brain and left me cold. Besides, I was looking for simplicity in my ideas and reactions to life, not complexity or endless syllogisms and word games. However, Popkin's attitude and his love of Hume and Sextus Empiricus left a skeptical streak in me that translated into my continuous questioning of everything and a refusal to accept not only commonplace ideas but also the very values of the status quo.

Popkin left Iowa for the University of California at San Diego in 1961, the year I graduated. It was rumored that his arguments with Bergmann, duels really, in which he employed the parries and thrusts of Sextus Empiricus's "rule book," drove Bergmann into apoplectic fits, and the gruff logical positivist had demanded Popkin's removal from the Philosophy Department. Popkin, for his part, refused to talk about his departure and went on to an illustrious career in the philosophy departments of the University of California and, later, believe it or not, Washington University in St. Louis.

In another philosophy course, I read *The Myth of Sisyphus* by Albert Camus, a book that profoundly influenced my thinking. Camus insisted that there were no moral values in the universe and that we existed in an absurd situation where, as humans, we tried to impose notions of order on a mindless cosmos that just kept proliferating and, in the end, killed us without malice or thought. This idea became a cornerstone of my thinking and my guide to accepting the terrifying notion of being totally free of preconceived ideas of any kind. Complementing my conception that all we as humans could be sure of was the life we lived, Camus' definition of our absurd situation simplified my ideas of the human condition and at the same time dispensed with unanswerable questions about free choice or determinism. Since ethics and morality were no longer valid concerns in a universe without values or preconceived ideas, personal decisions were the only actions a human being could make, and though Camus made clear that one is responsible for one's actions, the decision to harm or help fellow humans, as well as plants and animals, was always open. For me, the latter was a foregone decision. Ever since I was a child I had been concerned with the well-being of others, and as I grew older this notion had grown into a sense of communal responsibility. Even my poetry was conceived of as a communal action, a way both to speak to other humans and affect, if not enrich, the life of the human community with new ways of experiencing the world. Hovering in the background of these ideas, and metaphysically encompassing them, were the lessons of Daoism, which, with its concepts of dichotomies and continuous change, now took on the guise of the mindless universe in which we existed. I remember musing at one point that I may have been the first existential Daoist—or was I the first Daoist existentialist?

■ ■ ■

The professor who probably had the most influence on me at Iowa was Mei Yi-Pao, the head of the Oriental Studies Department. Actually, he was the only member of the department and had been offered the position when he was forced to flee Communist China. Mei had been president of Yenching University in Beijing and was one of the five hundred most revered Mandarins in pre-Communist China. He had led a march of 2,500 men, women, and children out of Beijing and out of harm's way during the Japanese invasion of China in World War II. That minor miracle, his assistant once told me, rankled Mao Zedong, who somehow saw it as in competition with his famous Long March. That was hard for me to believe. I think what Mao and the Communists saw as dangerous about Professor Mei was that he was a clear representative of the old ways and was revered by the people as well as by academics and scholars in the West.

Mei, who had been educated in Western university, was the world's foremost authority on the Zhou (Chou) Dynasty philosopher Mozi (Mo Tzu) and had contributed copious articles and a partial translation of the *Daodejing* to the groundbreaking *Sources of Chinese Tradition*.

I met him at his office at the start of my first semester. The old man who curtly answered my knock on his office door was thin and bald with a few wisps of black hair combed sideways across his skull. He was dressed in a tie and jacket.

The reason for my visit was that I had discovered Robert Payne's collection of Chinese poetry, *The White Pony*, in the university library when I first settled in Iowa City that summer. I was astonished by many of the poems and intrigued by the introductions to the poets, none of whom I knew. In fact, I realized I knew nothing about Asian culture, and since I now wanted to learn everything about everything, I was determined to broaden my knowledge of Asia.

I told all this to Professor Mei, who listened restlessly and, it seemed, with some vexation.

"So, sir," I ended my reason for being there, "I'd like to take your Introduction to Chinese Literature course."

"And how will that benefit you?" he asked, shuffling through some papers on his desk.

"Well, I'm a poet in the Writers' Workshop, and I'd like to learn more about Chinese poetry, so I thought that if I took the Introduction to Chinese Lit— "

"Well, I won't allow it," he said. "The only way you'll understand Chinese literature is if you know Chinese civilization. So you'll have to take Chinese language, Chinese history, and Chinese philosophy in addition to Chinese literature," he concluded dismissively and continued looking through the papers on his desk.

Thank heavens he wasn't looking at me, so he didn't see my mouth hanging open in shock. I don't know how much time went by in silence as I contemplated what was clearly a challenge. He was asking me to virtually major in Chinese civilization, and I had a lot of other courses I had to take in addition to those I wanted to take. But here was a chance to totally immerse myself in a civilization I knew nothing about, the civilization that had produced the *Daodejing*, which had been my spiritual guide since I was a teenager.

"Okay," I replied, "I'll do it."

The old man looked up, gave me the smallest of smiles, nodded, and said, "Good."

So began my three years of intensive study of Chinese civilization.

There were never more than seven or eight students in any one class in the Oriental Studies Department. Professor Mei ran the program alone, except for a good-humored Taiwanese student studying in Iowa, named Frank Pong, who was employed to lead the beginning language students in endless drills of spoken and written skills, the first for correct pronunciation, the second for checking our brush strokes, since Professor Mei was instructing us in classical Mandarin as it would have been taught when he was a boy in late nineteenth-century China. We were assigned small pamphlets with the outlines of six or eight characters on each page, which we were to fill in, memorizing not only the meaning of each character but the correct formation of each one according to a prescribed order of brush strokes. The strokes, which might include more than twenty rigid rules, were applied by "paintbrushes" and had to be followed in order or the stroke would smudge or blot out other strokes within the character. It was tedious, hard work, which usually took four to six hours a night, and after the first semester it was evident to me that I would have to drop all my other classes and major in Chinese civilization or drop the language part of my Chinese studies.

I went to Professor Mei with my dilemma. He was a strict, old fashioned schoolmaster, who had first refused to compromise his original demands. But now, after I had taken a semester's work with him, he relented, knowing I had at least gotten the hang of how the language worked. And, as it soon became clear, he didn't want to lose me as a student.

Professor Mei was a sweet man as well as a strict disciplinarian. Life certainly hadn't been easy for him. He was over sixty by the time he fled China and had to adapt to middle-class American life. That may have accounted for his occasional short-temperedness. Once there was a knock on the classroom door well before the end of the hour, and the professor's wife appeared in the doorway with a shopping bag over her arm. The professor closed his copy of the book we had been discussing and stood up, announcing with an edge of exasperation in his voice that the class would end early that day because he had to go shopping. He then walked to the door, book in hand, and was about to step into the hall, when he suddenly turned, and shouted, "In China, I had fifty houseboys!" and slammed the door behind him.

I like to think that the old man's sharing his culture with appreciative American students in some way alleviated his loss. Certainly, I was devouring all the other aspects of the program he had set up and at the end of the first semester was doing my own "versions" of Chinese poetry as well as verses from the *Daodejing*. I'm sure my rambunctiousness flabbergasted the professor. Although he had translated portions of the *Daodejing*, he was uncomfortable with poetry. He had a scholar's awe and a reader's love for its intricacies but thought he was unable to tackle the demands of translating it. By the time I undertook my versions, Professor Mei knew of my membership in the Writers' Workshop as well as my publishing record. He looked with amusement as well as interest at my forays into recasting Chinese poetry into English by using a mélange of available translations, a practice I was to follow throughout the coming years in order to write when the muse was on vacation, so to speak. I also composed a private notebook of poems from other languages, which I believed had not been translated as effectively as they could have been.

I learned that the practice of making versions was a great learning device, since I was forced—or at least forced myself—to follow the original poet's intent as strictly as I could. Therefore, I wrestled with both the intricacies of how other languages worked as well as distancing my own ego and writing practices, thereby allowing myself to study how poems in other languages were understood and to find approaches to poetry that were different from my own. In this way I enlarged my concepts of how a poem could make an impact on a reader. In addition, I began studying the history and culture of the poet whose work I was recasting so I could understand the themes, metaphors, and usage the poet employed. In this way my education has continued to the present, more than forty years after my student days.

An even more intimate association with poetry from other languages began in my second year at Iowa when I took Spanish. Halfway through the first semester I was attempting to translate Lorca and Neruda (whose work at that time was only available in several anthologies: a volume by Angel Flores from New Directions, and *Twenty Poems of Neruda and Viejo*, a small book that had appeared that year from Robert Bly's Fifties Press). Translating, I quickly found out, was twice as demanding as making versions—and twice as instructive.

It was no accident that I took Spanish. I was entranced by Bly's Neruda translations. In fact, Bly's Fifties Press, the creation of which I consider one of the most important groundbreaking literary undertakings in American poetry in the second half of the twentieth century, was pointing me in a myriad of literary directions I had never imagined existed. The poetry he published in his *Fifties* magazine and the incisive, long reviews he wrote about such poets as John Logan, Louis Simpson, James Dickey, and others, led me to kinds of poetry I had been unaware of, and it was another factor that forced me to confront why I wrote poetry and what I wanted from it.

My education at Iowa was unexpectedly rewarding in other ways. I was expected to take a number of required courses. All of them I found to be inspiring in their presentation and content. There were the English classes, of course, since I was an English major. The English department had little to do with the workshop, although such professors as Sven Armens—a gentle, friendly man—were publishing poetry in some of the nation's best literary journals. The department had set up a program for undergraduates that was thorough and outstanding. It included medieval literature and Shakespeare with a wry Curt Zimansky, Romantic literature with the young Clark Griffith, brilliant surveys of American literature with John Gerber, and comparative, that is, European, literature from an inspired and inspiring, not yet famous Ralph J. Friedman.

By the time I graduated from Iowa, I had a thorough grasp of the history of English and American literature as well as of the important movements and writers of European literature. In fact, my senior honors thesis was a study of Dostoevsky's last four novels, using *Notes from the Underground* as the basis for the paper.

THE TIMELESS MOMENT

There were other required classes that were equally inspiring. Although psychology was a disappointment because of Iowa's emphasis on behaviorism, geology was a revelation and accounted for one of the most memorable and important experiences of my life.

I was required to take two semesters of geology, and although at first I groaned at the prospect, I soon came to consider my study of geology second in importance only to my endeavors in Chinese civilization. The first semester I learned to identify rocks and land features and was given reading assignments in the history of the science and its different areas of study. I did well and was either called into the head of the department's office or went in on my own; I don't remember which. William Furnish, the head of the department, knew of my membership in the Writers' Workshop as well as my status as honor student. Soon he was talking about his love of good science writing and asked me if I had read Loren Eiseley's first book of essays, *The Immense Journey*, which had been published the previous year. It so happened that the book was a favorite of the English department and the Writers' Workshop crowd, and, because of several instructors and friends, I had already read it with delight, becoming a lifelong Eiseley fan.

The professor was happy to learn of my appreciation of Eiseley, and after discussing our favorite pieces in the book, he asked if I would like to take his field geology course in place of the second semester of Introduction to Geology. The class, he said, would be spent outdoors, digging up fossils. I didn't hesitate to say yes, and so I spent the spring term as a member of a fifteen-person field geology team.

The first day in the field was sunny, but a late winter chill was still in the air. We drove in a school bus to a farm outside Cedar Rapids. The farm was enclosed by a rusted barbed-wire fence, and a peeling metal sign on the gate proclaimed KEEP OUT—STATE PROPERTY, but, as Professor Furnish told us, the state had leased the land to a farmer.

The professor strode off to the farmhouse and returned with the farmer at his heels, the latter complaining about how stony the land was and how he had been "hoodwinked" into leasing it. The professor bobbed his head in commiseration, as if this were an often-repeated scene, until the farmer unlocked the gate. Then the professor herded the fifteen of us off the bus and onto a gravelly wagon path that hadn't been used in years. Sparse patches of grass had grown down the middle of the track, and we followed it for several hundred yards when it suddenly curved downward, below the level of the land, and descended a hundred feet or so. The path had become a flinty trail that led to an abandoned quarry with a muddy green pond at the bottom.

We trudged down the rock-strewn path, leaving the sunlight and the upper world behind us. It was shadowy and chilly, and most of us had stopped talking before we reached the quarry floor. We were surrounded on all sides by a giant wall.

"Okay," said the professor. "I want you to line up against the wall, facing me." He waited until we did. "Now this is what we've been talking about in class that many of you doubted was the truth. Ready? I want you to turn around and look at the wall."

We did as he instructed. I actually gasped and heard the same reaction from several others. I was facing a gray wall of compacted bushes and sea creatures, and the pattern of animal remains and vegetation continued from the floor of the quarry to as far up as I could see. It was like a giant ceramic sculpture in relief.

As we watched, transfixed, the professor continued to talk. "As I said in class, Iowa was once part of a tropical inland sea. What you are looking at—and standing in the middle of—is a reef from the Late Cambrian period, 500 million years old, that's crammed with fossils. A hundred years ago this was a limestone quarry that the owners had to abandon because of all these little buggers. It was a nuisance to them but a goldmine to geologists. We'll be visiting five or six more quarries like this. But now, to work. I want you to. . . ."

I was entranced, and the professor's words whirled away in the vortex of time. I recalled Loren Eiseley descending a narrow cave on the Great Plains, each footstep down taking him thousands of years back in the Earth's history. It was a mystical experience for Eiseley, and I realized that the descent into the quarry was a mystical experience for me. Suddenly time, that ungraspable dimension, was palpable. I felt claustrophobic, hemmed in by the immensity of time trapped in the wall around me. One hundred feet of wall equaled hundreds of millions of years. In many ways, I was standing nose to nose with my ancestors, creatures who would eventually crawl onto land and stand erect in the thin air. I felt like a flyspeck, less than a blink of dust in the scheme of things. My ego deflated like a punctured balloon.

I worked for the next four hours in a daze, breaking open rocks and exposing the fossils of trilobites and other ancient sea animals. Back in Iowa City late that afternoon, I burst into Kenny's Bar and told my buddies about the quarry. Immediately, a half-drunk squadron of eight poets and fiction writers was formed, and, after we bought several six-packs of beer at the state liquor store, we were off to Cedar Rapids.

We arrived, two carfuls of us, at the farmer's gate an hour before dusk. The farmer's house was some distance away, out of sight beyond a windbreak of trees, so he didn't hear us cursing and laughing as we scrambled over the barbed wire, ripping our clothes and hands, and made our way, stumbling and traipsing, arms full of six-packs, down the gravel road to the quarry. I waited until we reached the bottom. Then, as the professor had done, I lined the motley crew up against the wall in the dimming light and told them to turn around. Again, like the class earlier in the day, several of my friends gasped, then all of them stood silently and marveled. Though covered in a darkening layer of shadow, the details of the reef were clearly visible. A few of my friends went up to the wall and ran their fingers along the edges of the fossils. Soon all of them were performing the same act, as if tracing a reality they couldn't believe was possible. Then they were running their palms over the contours, almost caressing the wall as they would a woman.

Slowly the light drained from the quarry, and the silence was broken only by one or two of my friends expressing wonder. Then we were all talking at once, opening the beers, and becoming more and more boisterous as darkness enveloped the quarry and our voices echoed across the now black pond.

We continued talking, jostling each other, purposely bumping into one another and laughing, as if each of us needed to make physical contact with another human being and was trying to dispel the eerie atmosphere of the quarry and the pervasive chilliness around us. Then someone said, "Hey, look up," and we turned our gazes skyward to see a scattering of stars above the quarry's small, rounded opening. I shivered. I felt I was at the bottom of a well, looking up at eternity shooting infinitely outward above me, spreading far beyond my gaze and the limitations of my vision. Several of the guys let out wild whoops, and Jerry Bumpus, a wonderful, possessed fiction writer, began his drunken goat dance, stomping around in circles. All of us joined in, and I suddenly conceived of us as prehistoric men living in a primeval world, dancing in fear and celebration at the immensity of our ignorance in the cosmic scheme of things yet, at the same time, feeling an integral part of it.

Although the class was to visit other spectacular sites, none of them was as memorable as my two visits to the quarry in Cedar Rapids that day in the early spring of 1961. What I had learned more immediately than any book could have told me was the immense span of geologic time and humankind's infinitesimally small place in it. I came away with a view not of human, but of cosmic history, and along with notions of the absurd I'd learned from Camus, my own notions about death, and my embracing a Daoist-existential universe where I was answerable to no one but responsible for all, my vision of life became, pardon the pun, set in stone.

This vision, if I may be so bold as to call it that, would inspire the themes of my writing, the selection and treatment of my subject matter, and the very conception of my imagery and metaphors. It would become the foundation of my thinking and would allow me to comprehend the essential nature of the Dao as I never could before. Although hints of this notion can be seen throughout my work to a greater or lesser degree, it is most clearly stated in the poem "My Aloneness," which is the opening poem of my 2002 poetry collection, *Shouting Down the Silence*.

My Aloneness

Nights standing in a field
I sense that one of those points of light
is signalling me from deep space.
I know this is nothing more
than my own longing cast like fishing line
into the depths of another kind of ocean,
and that my aloneness
is reflected in whatever splinter of light
I can imagine out there,
but there's a comfort I won't deny
in the images and word groupings

I invent, no matter how outlandish
or ornate they are, or bare.
And when I realize that nothing
is going to respond to my bait,
and that I'm standing at the edge
of a bustling milky stream
packed with sparkling shards
of dumb rock, there's something
terrifying yet wonderful
about acknowledging
my complete aloneness
that only this procedure can impart,
like standing one foggy dawn
ankle-deep in a freezing brook
with no one else around
just as the sun burns through
and the trees like tattered thoughts
release the hidden circle of the sky—
endless, empty, cold, and blue

■ ■ ■

By spring semester of my third year I was getting ready to graduate. My grades put me in the top ten percent of my class, I made Phi Beta Kappa, and the professors in the English department had nominated me for a Woodrow Wilson Fellowship, which I won, breezing through the preparatory interviews.

A student could not apply for a Woodrow Wilson Fellowship but had to be nominated by his professors. Having won the award, the student received $15,000 a year for three years to do graduate work in exchange for a promise to consider going for a PhD and eventually teaching. The college at which the student chose to do these studies also received $15,000 a year for three years. There was one catch: in order to avoid corruption or nepotism on the part of the nominating professors and the institution they represented, the rules of the fellowship specified that the candidate had to do graduate work at a school other than the one from which he or she had been nominated.

This last stipulation was problematic for me since I wanted to stay at Iowa and do graduate work in Chinese studies under Professor Mei, who had promised to get me a government scholarship. As a result, I didn't apply to a college for the Wilson Fellowship. I waited all spring for Professor Mei's scholarship to come through until the Wilson people informed me that they would give my fellowship to someone else if I didn't apply to a college within two weeks. Professor Mei advised me to take the fellowship and suggested two schools where I could continue my Chinese studies under friends of his—Columbia University and the University of California at Berkeley. I immediately applied to both colleges. There was a third choice on the Wilson form, and I impulsively put Stanford University in that space. That made one college in New York and two in California. I was curious to see California, where I had never been. And San Francisco, which was near both Stanford and Berkeley, had intrigued me ever since I saw Alfred Hitchcock's film *Vertigo*.

Columbia and Berkeley never answered my letters, but Stanford sent back an airmail special delivery acceptance within a week. Ironically, I had applied there for graduate work in English literature rather than Chinese studies, and the future course of my career was decided as simply as that.

When Justice and Engle learned—I don't know how—that I was going to Stanford, they sought me out. Justice was delighted and insisted I work with Yvor Winters, whose *In Defense of Reason* he had given me to read two years before. Engle had a more politic reason for buttonholing me. Mezey had gone to Stanford the previous year on a Winters' Fellowship, had collected his money and left, having nothing to do with Winters or Stanford. Winters was furious, and Engle wanted me to "mend the fences" with Winters since there was an unofficial connection between the writing workshops at both schools.

"You want me to do what?" I said to Engle after he made his request.

"Mend the fences."

"Me?" I answered, "Your bête noir?"

He smiled, but his eyes uncharacteristically beseeched me.

"Paul, I appreciate everything you've done for me, really, but I've read Winters and I'm not going near him at Stanford. If anything, I'll enter the fiction workshop there."

That is how we took our leave. I never saw Engle again. As for Justice, our paths were to cross in the not-too-distant future.

My mother came to Iowa for my graduation. She was bubbly and joyous, and at a celebration in a local restaurant that evening we toasted Benjamin Fine and laughed at his declaration of me being "uneducable."

A month later, Wilma and I packed our little Volkswagen with our few belongings and headed for California. Although we didn't know it, Wilma was pregnant with our first child, a girl we had decided, at Max Dresden's soiree three years before, to name Jana.

BOOK FIVE

CALIFORNIA AND NEW YORK

CHAPTER 13

Stanford

If I was exhilarated by my classes at Iowa but disappointed in the workshop, I was depressed by my year at Stanford. The academic politics and traditionalist, unadventurous professors were exasperating. There *were* some good classes: Richard Scowcroft's Eighteenth-Century Novel class was one of the best I ever took, and A. E. Merritt's enthusiasm, knowledge, and humor made Old English not only bearable but enjoyable. There was also the Emerson and Whitman class.

But other than those courses, my year at Stanford, with the exception of the birth of my daughter Jana, was torturous. Twenty-five Woodrow Wilson fellows from around the country had elected to do their graduate work in the English department at Stanford. By the end of the year, twenty-three of them decided to quit school altogether. The situation was so scandalous that the Woodrow Wilson people sent a team from their headquarters at Princeton to investigate what was going on.

Typical of the despotic attitude was Harry Levin's Colonial American Literature class. One of the books he assigned was Benjamin Franklin's *Autobiography*, a pleasant enough volume but one that many of us felt did not warrant its placement with the great books of American letters. When a nun, one of the Wilson fellows, respectfully voiced this general consensus in class, Levin slammed his hand on the seminar table and shouted, "You're Stanford students now and will learn to accept the importance of the material you have been assigned to read."

Without letting anyone know I was a publishing poet, I signed up and was accepted into the prestigious graduate fiction-writing class. I wanted to keep away from the poetry workshop, which was controlled by Yvor Winters and his acolytes, because I disliked both his poetry and the doctrinaire thrust of his critical writings. Justice had been a student of his as had many other bright young poets of the time. But Winters's emphasis on reason and form, and his dictum that one should only lift one's pen when about to write a great poem, had stopped many young prize-winning poets from ever writing again. I thought of Winters as a literary dictator, a notion that was not only borne out by various stories I heard about him, but by the power his desires and utterances had on the rest of the English department, many of whom quoted him frequently. One example of both his power and narrow-mindedness was that the Emerson and Whitman class was taught in the Education building. When I asked the professor who taught the class why this was so, he replied that Winters's antipathy to the two not only great but seminal American authors was so pronounced that he had been instrumental in banishing the course and its professor from the physical confines of the English department.

Another reason I had signed up for the fiction workshop was that I had begun to write a novel in Iowa, and I was hoping to use it as the thesis for my master's degree. The novel, in a way, could be called fantastic, but in the same way as Swift's *Gulliver's Travels*. It was satiric and dreamlike and obviously written under the influence of Kafka—a symbolic rather than a surrealistic novel. But certainly it was not realistic. It was on the basis of the first three chapters that I was admitted to the graduate workshop with the unspoken stipulation that the work would, if completed, be accepted as my thesis.

Richard Scowcroft, who took over the workshop for Wallace Stegner the first semester, was the professor who admitted me to the august group, which consisted of a select eleven students, nine of whom were that year's recipients of Stegner Fellowships and already had books out. All went well the first semester, and I finished three more chapters of the book.

The second semester, Stegner returned from leave and everything fell apart, although I was unaware that things weren't going well. Stegner was a handsome, dapper, and seemingly unaffected man, easy to talk to, and eliciting good feelings and respect from anyone he dealt with. He was critically acclaimed from coast to coast as a historian of the American West and a fiction writer who wrote several bestselling novels such as *The Big Rock Candy Mountain* and *All the Pretty Little Things*. He was also an elegant stylist who prized polished, balanced language in his students' work. His writing was, in all genres, realistic.

The clash between us was so subtle I didn't realize it existed. It began the second or third week of class. Stegner had been sent a complimentary copy of Ken Kesey's just-published first novel, *One Flew Over the Cuckoo's Nest*. Kesey had been a student in the workshop the year before, and his wild exploits were talked about with both awe and disdain by the students who had known him.

Stegner read the novel's prologue to the class, tossed the book on the seminar table, and proceeded to berate the writing in much the same way Engle had ridiculed Ginsberg's poetry. Here was lack of control, rough phrasing, and absurd imagery, he said. Clearly, the prologue was being told by Big Chief, an Indian. How could the reader accept that such a character would describe the black orderlies in the asylum as having eyes like vacuum tubes?

The class laughed and shook their heads, while Stegner smirked and shook *his* head.

I was uncomfortable. I had thought the prologue was vivid and full of raw energy. Frankly, I was captivated by it.

I raised my hand and told Stegner my feelings and remarked that we should withhold judgment until we had read the rest of the book. All eyes were on me and then on Stegner, who nodded pleasantly at my comments and said, "Then how do you explain an Indian describing the orderlies as having eyes like vacuum tubes?"

I shrugged, and Stegner waited. "I don't know," I finally replied. "I haven't read the book."

"Take a guess."

"Well, Big Chief could have been a radio operator in the army," I sputtered, having been put on the spot.

Stegner broke into laughter, and the class followed suit. "The Great Explicator," he said a moment later in obvious merriment, and for the rest of the year the nickname stuck.

I felt like a fool. I don't think my reputation in the eyes of my classmates ever recovered from that sally. I had given my absurd answer only because of my aborted training in the air force as a radio operator. Once more, my emotional reaction and rash tongue had opened me to ridicule. Imagine my reaction a year later when I read the book and discovered that all the mechanical and electronic imagery Big Chief uses in the novel comes from his training as a radio operator in the army. Kesey had written One Flew Over the Cuckoo's Nest in Stegner's class, and Stegner had known the answer to his own question the day he asked it. As I read the book a year later, I wasn't as angry as I was disgusted. By then, I had seen behind Stegner's pleasant mask.

The differences in taste and interpretation between Stegner and me were evident in literature classes as well as the workshop, but I saw them as nothing more than differences that led to spirited dialogues. I should have known the truth when I took his survey of twentieth-century American literature, an upper-level undergraduate and graduate course that drew over one hundred students to a large indoor amphitheater-like classroom.

One of the assigned books was The Great Gatsby, and Stegner lectured on it for several sessions, opening the last half hour of the second session for questions and comments. No one else had anything to say, so after a few moments I raised my hand.

Stegner recognized me, and smiled, fidgeting with a rubber band over the knuckles of one hand, as he always did while lecturing. "Ah, the Great Explicator has a comment."

I said that I had and explained that my interpretation of Gatsby differed from his. I didn't agree with him that the book was Gatsby's but rather Nick's, since he told Gatsby's story and was the one who had learned the disquieting truth about Gatsby's embracing the great American dream.

"I suppose you can show proof of that?"

"Yes, sir," I answered, and proceeded to give a page-by-page illustration of my ideas.

Stegner flipped from one page to the next as I called out a page number and read the passage aloud. The class followed. The sound of riffling pages fluttered through the room.

When I had finished, all eyes were on Stegner. He was looking down at the open book, still playing with the rubber band. Finally, he looked up at me and smiled. "It's all there all right," he said, "but, Marcus, I don't trust you." And he dismissed the class.

Still, our relationship remained cordial and, I thought, respectful. I had been at his house for an evening session of the workshop when Wilma called to tell me to come home because she was in labor, and he and his wife, Mary, made a grandparents' fuss over packing me off into the night. It was a great surprise to me, therefore, that two weeks before graduation, Stegner called me into his office and informed me that he wasn't going to accept my novel as my master's thesis. I was in shock. There had been no hint of the possibility that he wouldn't accept the book as, week after week, I handed in parts of one chapter or another, nor was there any word of warning when I'd given him the completed manuscript weeks before. "How can you do this?" I asked.

He replied that he had been "uncomfortable" with the novel since he had seen its plan. He didn't understand such writing and had finally shown the manuscript to Albert Guerard, the eminent Stanford critic who had done work on Kafka and Conrad. Guerard read at least part of the book and proclaimed that "a symbolic novel could not be written that way," and that pronouncement had determined Stegner to reject the book. Or so he said. Besides, he was worried that if the English Department questioned him on the manuscript, he wouldn't be able to defend it with an unconditionally favorable response—and he wanted no trouble with the English Department.

I was as astonished as I was angry. I saw before me a scared man. He was a nationally known writer who had taught at Stanford for decades and was still frightened of the department. I had seen similar fear of the English department in Iowa. The scholars of academia looked disapprovingly on the writers of the workshops, but more than that, Stegner's handling of the situation bordered on treachery. His smiling camaraderie proved to be the expression of a false face. For the next five years he rejected every thesis proposal I presented to him, and only when Jim Houston, then a published novelist and Stegner fellow, interceded on my behalf did he relent. He did, however, refuse to accept a creative thesis from me even then, telling Jim he would only approve a critical monograph.

Stegner's decision was the final incident in my unpleasant tenure at Stanford. I was so disgusted by my experiences there, I determined to leave school forever.

■ ■ ■

We lived in Palo Alto that year, the town adjoining the Stanford campus. It was a wealthy suburban community, quiet and sedate. But to Wilma and me, it was bereft of creative energy. Kenneth Patchen, the poet whose work had meant so much to me in boot camp, lived in town, but by 1961, he was bedridden with a spinal disease that would eventually kill him. In some grotesque way, his condition was a metaphor for the town's cultural life.

Such generalizations are rarely accurate, and they're not in this case, since the happiest memory of my year at Stanford, besides the birth of Jana, was befriending Norman Thomas, a Welshman ten years my senior, who is not to be confused with the socialist leader of the same name.

Norman's wife, Alice, worked with Wilma at the Paris Theater, Palo Alto's only art movie house, and while chatting one day they discovered that both their husbands were writers. A meeting was arranged to introduce us, but it was clear the moment we arrived at the Thomases' cottage that Norman wasn't particularly happy about it. He cherished his time alone and had met some strange people through Alice, who was the kind of person who continually brought home stray cats. She was also a bit daffy.

Norman loved her, but, although he would never admit it, she exasperated him. He was continually ruffled by her non sequiturs and silly remarks and would rip the ever-present pipe from his teeth and say, "Alice, really!" before he could control himself.

Norman was a small, slim, good-looking man with a pronounced English accent and a body that like most men from the British Isles was boyish to the point of looking almost undernourished. Under the British education system, he'd been chosen to receive a nonacademic education, and so, in his early twenties, he had come to America to seek his fortune.

For a number of years before I met him, Norman had been working as a mail carrier. One of the houses on his route belonged to Kenneth and Miriam Patchen. In the course of things, as always happened with Norman, the Patchens invited him in for tea and befriended him. Eventually, Patchen sent Norman's first novel to his publisher, New Directions, at that time America's most renowned avant-garde publishing house. New Directions brought out the book under the title *Ask at the Unicorn*.

Norman Thomas, Palo Alto, 1961

It was an extraordinary novel about an expatriate Welshman who returns home to discover the mystery and spiritual underpinnings of Welsh life. Norman's style was unique and can be compared to that of John Hawkes, another New Directions author whose fiction was beautiful to read but possessed none of Norman's profundity and vision.

That the Patchens would befriend their mailman and launch his literary career says a lot about their egalitarian attitudes, but it says even more about Norman, a truly charismatic character who gathered people around him wherever he went. It was a power he despised, not only because he was humble, but because he preferred the solitary life of a backyard gardener and contemplative writer.

Luckily, Wilma and I were exceptions to his annoyance with the hordes of people Alice dragged home. He liked my poetry, and we got along famously. Both of us smoked pipes, traded tobacco regularly (since I was always trying out new blends), and spent hours together talking about life and literature. Even after Wilma and I left Palo Alto, we would regularly visit the Thomases, and the year we lived in New York (1964–1965) we spent time with them when James Laughlin, the head of New Directions, let them stay at his brownstone in Greenwich Village for a few weeks before they left for Greece.

That trip was to be seminal in their lives and in mine. A year later, they returned excited about the Greek way of life and especially about the people they had met, among them the flamboyant expatriate American poet Harold Norse. They also met a distinguished Greek surrealist poet named Nanos Valaoritis who had an international reputation and would settle in San Francisco eight years later, fleeing the rule of the fascist junta known as The Colonels who took over the country in 1967.

Norman was so enthusiastic about his year in Greece that, less than eight months after his return, he wrote a novel full of adventure and mystery set in the islands—a mystery that had to do with the gods and the secrets of the earth. I liked it better than *Ask at the Unicorn*. Unfortunately, he finished it just as John Fowles's *The Magus*, which it resembled, was published to international acclaim and record sales, and New Directions passed on Norman's book.

By then, Norman no longer cared about literature. He and Alice had difficulty re-adjusting to American life, which they saw heading down a rocky path of rampant materialism and a foreign policy, highlighted by our growing involvement in Vietnam, which in the end would change the direction of the country. Several years after their return, Norman and Alice sold their house and all their goods and left for the international community at Sri Aurobindo's ashram in Pondicherry, India, where they lived for the rest of their lives. Not surprisingly, the spiritual leader of the ashram, the woman Aurobindo proclaimed to be the Mother, tapped Norman to be one of the community's leaders, a position he held until he retired.

Before he left for India, Norman entrusted me with his Greek manuscript and the remaining copies of *Ask at the Unicorn*, and we remained in touch through traveling friends. But for all intents and purposes, Norman's life in America was behind him. It was a loss for us all but I'm sure a gain for that small population that would, if they could, make this world a better place for all of us with their spiritual practices.

I would experience repercussions of my friendship with Norman for years to come, not only from the aura of his personality, but from the people he had known. Although Patchen was too ill to meet me the year I lived in Palo Alto, I would eventually get to know his wife Miriam in the early 1970s, and I'm sure, although I have no reason to suspect it was the case, that she insisted I be part of the Patchen Memorial Reading in San Francisco in 1972. Not incidentally, again because of Norman, Harold Norse and I would have an amiable relationship when he returned to the United States. More important would be my friendship with Nanos Valaoritis and two people I met at Norman's house in Palo Alto, an eccentric young metallurgist named Ian Brown and his fiancée and later wife, Nan, both of whom would figure prominently in my life ten years later. They would become important followers of Maharishi Mahesh Yogi, a conversion that I have no doubt was inspired by Norman's emigration to India. As for Nanos Valaoritis, I would meet him when he came to San Francisco in the late 1960s, and his encouragement and my memories of Norman's stories about his stay in Greece would influence my decision to make that country my destination on my first trip abroad.

■ ■ ■

Another happy memory of that year was meeting James D. Houston. We both took Old English and Colonial American literature together and

struck up a conversation after one of the classes. Jim was six foot three, fair-haired, muscular, and handsome. He had been discharged from the air force the previous year and was determined to be a writer. When I met him he had already taken the fiction writing class twice, once under Malcolm Cowley and the second time under Frank O'Connor.

Jim and I would have intense conversations about fiction and fiction writers. His great discovery that year was Nathaniel West, whose four tightly constructed novels (none of which ran more than one hundred pages) intrigued him. I had read *Miss Lonely Hearts* and loved it, but Jim was especially taken with

James D. Houston, Santa Cruz, 1977

The Day of the Locust, West's nightmarish novel of Hollywood outsiders. I didn't know it then—and I don't think Jim did either—but that novel marked the beginning of Jim's lifelong literary quest to capture the California zeitgeist.

Jim and I would meet in the quad, at the school cafeteria, my rented duplex, or his, and talk, talk, talk, or show each other what we were working on at the time. We also met with other graduate students at one gathering or another and once or twice played full-court games of basketball. By then, my reflexes were gone, I couldn't stay on the balls of my feet, and my shots were constantly off the mark.

I met Jim's wife, Jeanne, a Japanese American who had grown up in California during World War II. Jeanne was a beautiful young Asian woman, bubbly and full of joy, but she was harboring ghosts. What neither Jim nor I were to learn for a decade was that Jeanne had spent her early years in Manzanar, a detention camp for Japanese Americans in World War II. My old friend Lawson Inada had spent his childhood in one of the camps as well—although I knew nothing about that when I was in Iowa. Like Jeanne, he never mentioned it, and I learned about it at the same time I learned of Jeanne's incarceration. But more about that later.

■ ■ ■

Wilma's job as cashier at the Paris Theater figured in another high point of my year at Stanford. The theater contained a coffeehouse of thirty tables or so, and I talked the owner, who wanted to increase his slow business at any cost, into letting me stage a poetry reading there.

Lawson was living in San Francisco at the time, and Wilma and I went up to see him every month. He was dating Jan, a pretty former member of the Iowa Workshop who had moved to San Francisco. I asked Lawson to come down and do the reading with me, and I set about publicizing the event, which, in my youthful enthusiasm, I scheduled for two shows on a Saturday at 8 and 10 PM. Not only did I go to the newspapers, but I put published poems by both Lawson and me in the outdoor theater display cases. It was my first entrepreneurial undertaking.

I grew nervous about the attendance when Lawson and Jan arrived the afternoon of the reading and he told me his parents were driving all the way from Fresno for the event. But my usual pessimism was groundless. When we arrived at 7:30, the coffeehouse was half full, and by 8 PM all the tables were taken and people were sitting on the floor and crowding both entrances. We turned dozens away, telling them to come back to the 10 o'clock show, which was as crowded as the earlier one.

The evening was a great success. The only problem occurred when the audience in the movie theater exited at the end of both screenings and found a virtual sit-in in the coffeehouse, blocking their way out.

I met Lawson's parents, who beamed at his performance and came back to the house for the party afterwards. Lawson and Jan stayed the night, and the next day, as we lay sprawled over a bed in the spare room, full of our previous evening's success, Lawson told me that he and Jan were getting married. I noted his apprehension, which I took to be uncertainty at whether his white friend would approve of his marrying a white girl. I dispelled that uncertainty in a moment, jumping up and shouting the news to Wilma. We were both delighted, and Lawson was smiling broadly with what I took to be relief.

I wouldn't see Lawson again for more than a decade. By then he had published *Before the War*, his first book and the first book of poems by an Asian American ever published by a major New York publisher. On the strength of it, he had become an unofficial spokesman for Japanese Americans, a role model for Asian American writers, and his readings would draw large audiences across the country. Many of his public appearances were concerned with the problems of minority groups in America. But when he and I got together, he was the old Lawson, friendly, ever ready to laugh at my bad jokes, and always dressed sharply and perfectly groomed. The occasions for our meetings were a number of reading tours I started doing in the Northwest in the 1970s, and Lawson, who had settled in Ashland, Oregon, and was teaching at Southern Oregon University, would arrange for me to read at the school.

In Iowa days, Lawson's poems were concise, short-lined pieces, many of them in two-beat lines. In the ensuing years, his structures and rhythms relaxed and his poems became more expansive, emulating jazz riffs composed of repetitive phrases and song-like chants. They summoned up ideas of improvised blues solos lamenting remembered injustices, specifically injustices done to Japanese Americans.

The seriousness of Lawson's poetry was enriched by humor, a joy in life, and a love of language, all of which endeared him to his wide circle of readers and especially to audiences who relished his live, often-sung performances, a number of which were accompanied by jazz musicians. His best poems and my favorites are, unfortunately, too long to quote here. Long gone were the quietly defiant poems of his youth, like "The Stand."

The Stand

I am somewhere
where I have decided to stand.

There has been long
maneuvering,

having been staked to a land,
sowing in the heat,

moving huge tools
in an absurdity of moon.

Chanting, my own
tune in the machinery,

I find the chanting soothes.
That sweet voice is ruined.

I move now,
sifting pavements through my feet,

Sweat in the eyes, a horizon.
Sun turns the wheat.

Braced to my spine,
I resume the chanting—

utterances in a sound
octaves older than my own.

Buddhism became a serious concern as he grew older, and although he
continues to write many poems about his family and the many aspects of
the life around him as both a Japanese American and a human being alive to
the wonders of life, it's fitting that I end this section with a simple, serene
later poem by him.

In a Buddhist Forest

Even if you're not Buddhist,
Even if you don't know
Anything about Buddhism,

Even if you're not interested
In its precepts and paths,
Even if you're anti-Buddhist,

Your Buddhist Self proceeds
Accordingly, in a Buddhist city,
In a Buddhist forest . . .

■ ■ ■

My decision to leave Stanford meant that I was forfeiting the two-year
stipend remaining on my Woodrow Wilson Fellowship. I began looking for
a job, hoping to find work as a ticket-counter salesman with the airlines or a
baggage handler, but all the airlines said I was too educated for such
employment. No matter where I looked, that comment rang like a cash register signaling a "no sale" sign. Only two possibilities surfaced. One was selling shoes door to door, and was a 100 percent commission job—that is, with
no salary. When I was told that my pitch would begin by my thrusting the
cutaway section of a shoe in the homeowner's face when he or she opened
the door, accompanied with the words, "Squeeze this!" I decided against
employment with the company. The other job was at first more mysterious—and in the end more sinister. It was with a shipping company, and I
had answered an ad asking for someone willing to travel. What did I think of
the shipping business? How would I handle being attacked? How had I
reacted to personally dangerous situations? When I answered the interviewer's questions, I guess satisfactorily, and he had looked over my resume,
he said he would be in touch. The next day he phoned, requesting I come in
for a second interview. When I entered his office, two rough-looking men in
suits sat quietly in the back of the office as the interviewer explained the job:
I was to be a strike breaker and muscle-man for the company, hired to put
down any trouble that might come up on their ships at sea. I would be flown

out by helicopter with other members of the team. The pay was excellent, although the danger might extend beyond shipboard to vengeance on my family by the crew members I might have roughed up, once they got back to shore. I couldn't believe what I was hearing. "I think you've got the wrong guy," I said, rising.

"I don't think so," said the interviewer, looking down at his notes. "Your profile is perfect."

"Maybe," I said, "but I'd be on the other side, with the strikers in the crew."

The interviewer flipped my file shut at those words, and the two rough guys stared through me as I passed them and left the office.

The job situation became desperate by mid-July. We had little money left and were living on rice, eggs, and Campbell's soups. I landed a job as stockman and delivery boy for a local drug store but was handed the extra work of organizing the stock room, cleaning the store, doing inventory, and resupplying the display shelves in front. The owner fired me after three weeks. "You're over-qualified for the job, that's all," he blurted, and told me my efficiency was driving him to distraction.

That was it. I could not fight what everyone was telling me. The next day I called a teachers' employment agency and asked if there were any jobs available for a man with my academic qualifications. Two weeks later I was hired by the Point Arena Elementary School District to teach primary school in a small remote town on the Northern California coast, and a week later Wilma, Jana, and I once more packed our belongings and headed for a new home.

CHAPTER 14

Point Arena

In 1962, the remote fifteen-mile coastline between Gualala and Point Arena in south Mendocino County was cut off from the outside world a good deal of the time during the winter rainy season. The coast road north and south of the area, twisting through cliffs and bluffs above the ocean, was tricky at best and treacherous between Jenner and Fort Ross, a twelve-mile stretch immediately below Gualala that was likely to wash out when the rains began. The only passable road inland was twenty miles north of Point Arena at Booneville, and that was likely to wash out in the rainy season, too. Two general stores served the area, and, the roads being what they were, they had difficulty getting supplies during the winter months and were always stocked with an overabundance of frozen foods—a situation that turned out to be immensely important when the only butcher in the area ran away with his neighbor's wife. Not that his absence greatly inconvenienced the local populace, who were used to hunting for their meat.

I quickly understood that the job was available so close to the beginning of the school year because no one wanted it. Not only was the isolated location a factor, but the pay was only $2,900 for the year.

Wilma and I found a ramshackle house situated above the ocean. We rented a four-room apartment that was actually the entire second floor of the building, which had been a coach stop in the nineteenth century. The bottom floor was occupied by a family of four, newcomers like ourselves. The husband had just been employed as a lineman for the telephone company.

The difficulties to come were signaled the day after we arrived, when our downstairs neighbors invited Wilma and me and little Jana for a dessert of homemade ice cream and wild berries they had picked that afternoon. They knew I was a teacher at the school and were delighted to have us as neighbors.

For the most part, the get-acquainted conversation was carried on energetically by the lineman's vivacious wife, while he quietly observed the scene, puffing on a pipe, and their two little boys ran in and out of the house.

At one point the wife gleefully suggested that we should go to church together the following Sunday. Wilma and I froze. Then Wilma turned to me. "I'm sorry," I said, "but Sunday isn't our Sabbath."

The wife blinked and replied with a sunny smile, "How come?"

"We're Jewish," I answered.

Flustered, she looked at her husband, then back at us, and said, "What difference does that make? We all believe in Jesus."

I cleared my throat and explained as politely as I could the fundamental difference between Christianity and Judaism.

Within three days, a petition was sent throughout the area demanding I be released from my position because the signers didn't want a Jew teaching their children. School hadn't even started, and already I was in trouble. Luckily, the school board had a sense of decency and refused to take the action demanded by the petition.

With Jana near Point Arena, 1963

We soon found out that the lineman was a member of the John Birch Society, a popular right-wing organization of the 1960s. Happily, he and his family found quarters more to their liking and moved out within a month, leaving the house completely to us.

If the area was remote, it was idyllically beautiful. We drove on all the side roads, hiked on the cliffs, and played with Jana on the beach.

When school began, Wilma stayed home with the baby. I would drive the fifteen miles to school and shop for what we needed on the way home.

My assignment was to teach fifth grade, and I was to instruct the class in all subjects. I had forty-seven students, which I later learned was the largest class in Mendocino County that year. But numbers made little difference. The students were an inspiration, raucous but eager, and I soon learned that I had a natural propensity for teaching. The kids hung on my every word and loved the crazy games I devised to fulfill the math, science, English, and social studies requirements.

The autumn of 1962 was a tumultuous one in American history, and the children brought in all sorts of questions as well as opinions they had overheard from their parents' conversations.

In September, James Meredith challenged segregation practices in the Deep South by enrolling at the University of Mississippi. Most of the Point Arena parents were angered by the racist opposition to his entrance on the campus. My students revealed their parents' attitude during show-and-tell, but there was such self-righteousness in their words, I couldn't help telling them that since there were no blacks in Point Arena, it was easy to be critical of the Southerners. I went on to say that each region of the country had its own racial and social bigotry, and, as an example, I identified the attitude of the white populace in Point Arena to the local Native Americans, who lived in poverty conditions on a reservation above Gualala. Again the parents were unhappy with me.

There was no petition this time, but a number of parents called the principal to complain and demanded disciplinary action. The principal called me into his office and, clearly perturbed, told me to avoid such incendiary comments in the future.

Barely had the Meredith incident subsided when the missile crisis was upon us. It was a scary time, the closest the nation was to come to World War III during the Cold War.

While Kennedy and Khrushchev tried to outmaneuver each other, my students brought in alarming reports during show-and-tell of their fathers' cleaning rifles and gleefully planning to go to war with the Russians. The students shared their parents' excitement and enthusiasm. I was shocked and told them what nuclear weapons do to people. I also brought in a copy of John Hersey's *Hiroshima* and read portions of it to them.

The students' enthusiasm for war instantly disappeared. In fact, I quickly realized I had gone too far and had scared them. At that time they were learning how to write form letters during English class, and I attempted to rally their spirits by suggesting that they write business letters to Khrushchev and Kennedy, telling them anything they wanted, and when they had finished they could read each other's letters and sign them if they agreed with what their classmates had written. I would change nothing in their letters, I declared, but only correct the spelling and grammar before they wrote their final drafts. All the students were more excited than they had been before: imagine, writing the president of the United States and the premier of the Soviet Union!

I congratulated myself on how quickly my plot had dispelled their fears. Kids: all you had to do was know which string to pull and when.

But my arrogant cynicism was quickly dispelled when I walked around the classroom to see what the students were writing. Almost every student, boy or girl, was appealing to the two leaders to settle the crisis peacefully so their relatives, friends, pets, or barn animals would not suffer the consequences of World War III. Some even appealed to the leaders on behalf of their neighbors' unborn children.

My condescension crumbled. For the first time in my life, I had been able to peek into the psyche of my species, and what I saw melted my anger. Here was the unselfish, compassionate impulse, which the great religious prophets had preached about so fervently, surging up spontaneously in forty-seven children.

Tears welled in my eyes and my lips were trembling as I went from one desk to another. None of the students saw my reaction; they were too intent on their letters. Oh, yes, two of them wrote that there should be no war because they didn't want to die, but forty-five of their classmates were following a different course.

At the end of the day I gathered up the signed letters, put them in two large improvised envelopes we made in class out of large sheets of drawing paper, and took them down to the post office. When I gave the assignment, I hadn't intended to mail the letters, but there was no way I wouldn't mail them now.

As I handed the envelopes to the postmaster, he looked at the addresses and said, "Kennedy and Khrushchev, huh? You're doing some mighty strange things in that class, Mr. Marcus."

Within twenty-four hours, a petition for my termination, signed by several hundred parents, was presented to the school board. The board could not ignore this petition. It was signed by the full colonel who commanded the radar installation in the hills behind Point Arena as well as by several of his troops. The depth of the colonel's involvement was clear to everyone, since his daughter was one of my students, and he presented the petition to the board himself.

A special meeting of the board was scheduled for the following night in the high school gymnasium. Several hundred adults jammed the bleachers. One by one, they accused me of being a Communist, misguiding their children, being a traitor, not following the state-prescribed lesson guide, or just being unfit for my job. Several said I must have transgressed some law by having the children write to the president and had thereby put their children at risk of arrest. The colonel was the last to speak. He was young, clean-cut, and dressed in full uniform. He didn't attack me but solemnly explained how such a letter from his daughter might prejudice his promotion by calling into question his security rating. When he had finished, the head of the board turned to me. He was the most politically and economically powerful man in the community and had disgustedly thrown out the petition that demanded I be fired because I was a Jew, but this was a different matter.

"What do you have to say about all this, Mr. Marcus?" he asked.

I was sitting in the first row of the bleachers. I rose and walked onto the basketball court, half facing both the table where the board sat on one side and the crowd in the bleachers on the other. As each person had spoken, I had felt the anger rising in me. The situation was similar to the pre-court-martial hearing I had gone through in the air force, and my indignation was the same. Once again, an inexplicable calm came over me and the words slid from my lips, gathering force and meaning.

"I've sat here listening to what each of you had to say. But not one of you asked about or said what was in those letters. You assumed the letters contained anti-American sentiments, that I had dictated what the students, your children, should write. You never asked them what they wrote, did you? The fact is that writing form letters was a class assignment and I told them to write anything they wanted to. But even if you knew that, you assumed whatever they wrote had to be insulting, traitorous, or worse. You don't even know your own children. You don't know how beautiful they are. I didn't either, until I read those letters. Let me tell you what was in them," and I proceeded to describe the contents of some of the letters. Lastly, I turned to the colonel, took a step toward him, and spoke to him in a respectful, almost intimate manner. "I'm a veteran of four years' active duty in the air force, Colonel, and I must say that your words surprised me. I thought that one reason you chose the military for your career was to protect our freedoms, one of which is to address our leaders without fear of recrimination. Your security clearance is not in jeopardy from your daughter's letter. But it is in jeopardy, all of our security is in jeopardy, if we cannot freely address our leaders."

I stepped back and looked at the crowd in the bleachers. Several women had been crying since I described the contents of the letters, and everyone was sitting in embarrassed silence.

The colonel rose before I had a chance to sit down and addressed the board. "Mr. Chairman, I want to withdraw my name from the petition," he said, "and I want to thank Mr. Marcus for reminding me of why I serve this country."

The chairman scanned the crowd, looking for someone who wanted to comment or speak. Everyone remained silent, not moving. He lifted his gavel, let it hang in the air for a moment, then brought it down hard on the table. "Petition denied," he said, "and I'm getting damn tired of these accusations against someone it seems we're pretty lucky to have teaching our kids."

Everyone hurriedly headed for the door, not looking at me, all except the colonel, who came over and shook my hand. "Stephanie talks about you all the time," he said. "Thanks," he finished, giving my hand a final tug.

I understood that he was not so much thanking me for inspiring his daughter or reminding him about freedom as he was saying he was sorry. All three were fine as far as I was concerned.

That was the last time I was harassed by the community. People would stop and say hello in the general store or on the street or wave from their cars as we drove past each other. But the damage had been done. Shortly before the missile crisis incident, I developed a peptic ulcer that would send me into spasms of agony for the next twenty years.

My enthusiasm for my class, however, remained unabated. When I found out that most of the kids didn't know the name of the ocean that slapped against the shoreline where they lived, I added geography to my lesson plan and instituted geology clubs by assigning rock- and land-formation identification problems for extra credit. Kids living in the same areas were to get together on weekends or after school and work together on the assignment.

The kids loved it, and the parents were delighted with how much their children were learning. By the end of the school year, I received dozens of phone calls from parents hoping I would stay on, and a final petition was sent around, urging me to do so. Although it would be one of the most rewarding years of teaching in my career, I didn't even consider acceding to the appeals. I wasn't bitter about my early treatment: the area was too remote, the pay barely enough on which to feed my family, and I had greater aspirations.

THE HOUSTONS VISIT

One of the memorable events of the year was a visit from Jim and Jeanne Houston, with whom Wilma and I had kept in touch by phone. Knowing we hadn't eaten fresh meat in months, they arrived shortly after the end of the rainy season with two huge pans of roast beef, which would have been welcomed at any time because Jeanne was an exceptional cook. Jim was eager to show me what he had written since we had last seen each other. The Houstons had left Palo Alto a few months before we did and had settled in Santa Cruz, a seaside town seventy miles south of San Francisco, known to Jim and his friends as a great surfing area from the time they were in high school.

Wilma and Jeanne visited. The Houston's two-year-old daughter, Cori, played with one-year-old Jana, and all of us talked about what had happened during the eight months we hadn't seen each other. I also critiqued the seven stories Jim had brought with him. I thought all of them had major problems. I remember shaking my head and telling Jim, as I had at Stanford, that I would always be honest with him and that certainly my opinions weren't to be taken as gospel. Then I proceeded to show him point by point what I thought was wrong with the stories. He was crestfallen, and my criticism put a pall on the two-day visit.

But whatever rift I feared my words had created between us soon evaporated. When we left Point Arena late that spring, we drove to Santa Cruz and stored several cartons of books and our stereo system in Jim and Jeanne's basement as well as what little furniture we had accumulated since coming from Iowa. We were heading to the East Coast for the summer to visit family and make some money. We told Jim and Jeanne we would be back to pick up our belongings that fall—or so we thought.

CHAPTER 15

New York

Our plan was to drive across country, visit my mother and her new husband in New York, and then continue to Florida, where Wilma's parents lived. Wanting to see their grandchild, both families had provided funds for the trip. But four days after our arrival in New York, our plans changed drastically.

Wilma's boss at the bookstore in Iowa City had called my mother the week before we reached Manhattan. He was looking for us and said it was important that I get in touch with him. As displaced New York Jews in Iowa, he (I'll call him Milton) and his wife had become fast friends with Wilma and me, but we had not kept in touch. When I called him the second day we were back, he told me he had sold the bookstore and returned to New York where he'd bought into a partnership in a bookshop across the street from Columbia University. His partner was the son of Simon & Schuster's president, and Milton had wrangled permission from Vance Bourjaily to restart publication of *Discovery* magazine, which had been published by Simon & Schuster.

Along with *New World Writing*, *Discovery*, under Bourjaily's editorship, had been a mass-market paperback literary journal in the 1950s. Now Simon & Schuster wanted to bring it out again. Bourjaily wanted nothing to do with the project except to make sure it would be edited competently. Milton had brought up my name, among others, and Bourjaily, who had known me in Iowa, assented. Now Milton wanted to know if I would "take the helm" of the resuscitated magazine, while he served as managing editor. There would be a good salary, entry into the New York literary establishment, and renewed friendship. It was kismet that Wilma and I had come to New York at that time, he said.

Milton's enthusiasm was infectious. I had no job waiting in California and was open to any offer—and I would be editing *Discovery*! I had been weaned on it and *New World Writing*. Of course I would take the job!

There was only one hitch, said Milton: negotiations were still being discussed, but Wilma and I could work at his new bookstore until the deal was in place.

Thus began the nightmare year of 1963–1964 in New York City. Wilma and I moved into a small but expensive two-room apartment at a good address on

With Wilma in New York City, 1964

West Seventy-ninth Street, two blocks from the Museum of Natural History, in preparation for my entry into New York's rarified literary world, and each of us worked a five-hour shift each day at the bookstore, one of us taking care of Jana while the other was at the store. The negotiations for the revival of *Discovery*, of which I was never a part, dragged on from one month to the next, while Wilma and I received minimum wage and could barely pay our bills. We did not have enough money to eat at restaurants or go to movies. We worked day in and day out, six days a week. The schedule was intolerable, and within three months Wilma developed intestinal problems and had to quit. Now I was working full-time and taking on more responsibilities at the bookshop. In fact, it soon became clear I was a name Milton could use to impress the professors at Columbia, whose book orders he wanted to wrest from the university bookstore. I was his "writer-in-residence" and was soon doing consultant's work at beggar's wages for the likes of Lionel Trilling, Kenneth Koch, and Susan Sontag.

In what free time I had, I visited my favorite places. But the city had changed. The live stage shows were gone from the Broadway movie houses, and many of the theaters, both on lower Broadway and in my old neighborhood, were either closed or no longer there. The Bond sign had vanished from Times Square, and the Camel cigarette billboard, now advertising another cigarette, had only a few years of smoke rings left. The museums were soliciting pricey "donations" to enter them and were always noisy with crowds of tourists. Although its old facade was intact, the Automat on Fifty-seventh Street had become a high-class delicatessen that resembled a supermarket more than the old family-run neighborhood stores with their mingled scents of pastrami and corned beef steaming in metal bins behind the counter, and pickles soaking to the desired sourness in wooden barrels filled with a watery concoction of brine and dill.

Closer to home, the tenements that had been the heart of Saxon territory from Sixty-fifth to Sixty-eighth Streets had been torn down and were now the site of Lincoln Center. The restaurants my mother took me to with her never-ending parade of boyfriends—Longchamps, Vorsts Century Sea Grille, to mention a few—had vanished. St. Nicholas Arena, where I went to my first boxing matches, and dozens of other landmarks, had also disappeared, and new young people were playing basketball at the old courts in Central Park. More than once, I imagined those young ballplayers wondering who the over-weight guy with the baby carriage was—the one who sat on the bench every now and then, watching them with a mournful stare. I felt out of place. New York had become the lost city of my youth. Soon I took to wheeling Jana's stroller into the basement of the Museum of Natural History and sitting for hours in front of the diorama of a California redwood forest. Jana cooed and turned to look at me as the tears rolled down my cheeks. I was homesick—but no longer for New York.

THE MOST VIVID MEMORY

My most vivid memory of that year in New York was Kennedy's assassi-nation. At that time, few if anyone outside of Washington knew of Kennedy's sexual peccadilloes and stubborn turn of mind. To the general populace, he and his wife Jackie were glamorous, energetic young people who promised a new kind of America that we wanted to believe was possi-ble, a selfless nation striving to make the world a place where everyone on the planet could live with dignity in material comfort.

I was at work, standing behind the cash register, when Milton rushed up the stairs from the offices in the basement. He was shaking. "Kennedy's been shot, shot," he said and blinked and stood looking at me with nothing more to say, as if waiting for me to respond. I stared at him, not understand-ing, and, finally, after what seemed like an hour, said, "What?"

"He's been shot. Kennedy," Milton repeated. The moment of comprehen-sion bristled around us, as if the air were suddenly charged with static elec-tricity. Then the moment ebbed, and, as if in a trance, we closed the store, Milton going home and me wandering toward the bus stop down the street.

The store was located on 116th Street and Broadway, and from there to 79th Street was a distance of roughly three miles. As I waited at the bus stop, people started to come out of the stores and apartment buildings around me, dozens of them, and no one was saying anything. The scene was oppressive. Even the noises of cars and taxis seemed to be muffled. I was numb, and, without making a conscious decision, I began to walk home.

More and more people were leaving buildings and milling around silently on the streets. They weren't congregating but moving in individual circles of confusion and disbelief, so overwhelmed with the burden of the information they had just learned that they had to get out of their stores, apartments, shadowy bars, and be on the open street.

By the time I reached Ninetieth Street, the sidewalks were packed with people who had now broken out of the shocked isolation that encircled them and were going up to strangers and engaging them in conversation, normally taboo behavior in the city. Young, old, men, women, black, white, Puerto Rican—everyone was talking to everyone else, sympathetically consoling and sharing their misery. I was stopped by people of different ages, as if they wanted me to answer some question that would determine their future, their stares vacant, uncomprehending, or their faces crumpled in grief.

I must have looked the same to them. I wandered on, realizing I was as stunned by the spontaneous display of group emotion as I was by the news of the assassination. When I arrived home, Wilma and I fell into each other's arms and stood in the middle of the tiny living room, holding each other. We sensed that a way of life had come to an abrupt end, a youthful dream of possibility from which we were waking to a new and unknown reality.

Several months later, the Beatles ushered in that new reality when they appeared on the Ed Sullivan television show. But I didn't realize the significance of their appearance then, nor the change in American life that was signaled by the hysterical crowds of teenagers who greeted them.

CIGARS

When did I have my first intimations about the mystical properties of cigars? Certainly it began that year in New York when I would browse, broke but longing, in the cigar store on Broadway and Seventy-ninth Street. It was owned by a grumpy old man who I would use several years later as the model for the speaker of a long coming-of-age sequence I called "Memories of a Cigarmaker."

My notions about cigars definitely took shape after I returned to San Francisco and sat for hours almost daily with a lonely old cigar roller named Juan. It was in an empty store I had wandered into on Irving and Twentieth Street in the Sunset District. The window display showed bundles of cigars, but only Juan, three chairs, and several refrigerators filled with cigars were inside. Juan was delighted to see a customer and offered me a sample cigar and, after we'd talked for a while, invited me back for more. And so our afternoons began. It turned out his boss was never there, and Juan spent his days alone rolling cigars that were shipped all over the country. Juan would roll us both big fat Churchills and taught me how to crack the crowns with thumb and forefinger as we talked about his life and mine and smoked and smoked. By the time the store went out of business a year later, my ideas about the holiness of cigars were fully formed.

There was something about leaves and smoke that started it: the spicy scent I remembered from childhood of crisp, multicolored leaves piled in suburban streets and burning on chilly autumn afternoons. Whirling up in the brackish smoke were the once-green leaves that I came to see as the countless dead in the bone pile of the earth beneath my feet. In time, I thought I understood the Native American reverence for the ceremonial peace pipe and, later, the Aborigines' need to inhale the smoke of corroboree fires. It was a connection with the earth, a communion with ancestors. It was taking the past into one's body and making it live again, much as in Catholic communion: the supplicant eats the body of his god so holiness will live inside him.

Pipes and cigarettes—with their processed, chemically-treated, flavored tobacco shreds—were not the same as the cigar's tobacco that even when rolled bore the unmistakable features of leaves.

I tried to show these ideas in several poems. I think I was most successful in the following prose poem.

Smoking Cigars

When I smoke a cigar, I'm part of the earth again, but a wilder earth than municipal parks and public gardens. The wrapped brown leaves, brittle as autumn, smell like rotting fish and crumbling stone.

Even in an apartment high above the city, I become an element of the earth once more, when the cigar smoke enfolds me like the air inside a tomb.

I sit at a table opposite an empty chair when I smoke, and imagine the cigar is an earthen whistle through which I summon whatever ghost will come. Most of the time it's a leathery man, his skin as brown and thin as tobacco leaves.

We sit face to face across the table, not speaking, smoking the same cigar from opposite directions, my mouth clasping the unlit end, and his the fiery cinder whose glow must resemble the burning coal that sprang from the darkness to start the world.

He blows into the cigar as if blowing on the coal, and I suck until I am filled with the life beyond this one. When I exhale, he sips my living air through the pink nipple that scorches his tongue.

In church on Sundays, some people eat and drink the body and blood of their god. I consort with those who are less sublime, the ones who built the pyramids and tombs with their hands, and who vanished without hope of being revered or even remembered.

■ ■ ■

Living on subsistence wages became more and more intolerable. Milton and his wife would have us over for dinner, and he would take me to the fights at the old Madison Square Garden every Friday night to placate me, but life was becoming unbearable. Then, in the spring, he accused me of stealing from the store, and I knew I had to leave the city one way or the other as quickly as possible. But with no money, how was I going to extricate myself from what amounted to economic bondage?

I conceived of a wild plan. Wilma would go on a TV quiz show and win enough money to transport us back to California.

"Why not you?" she said, looking at me as if I had finally reached the state of insanity she always expected I would.

"Because I've got a beard, and you're pretty and outgoing—and that's what the networks want."

We were so desperate, she accepted the plan, and to her surprise was selected to be a contestant on "Jeopardy." She was the high money winner throughout the show but got overconfident at the end and lost all but $1,800 of her winnings. It was enough. Her parents bought us a new VW, and, with curt farewells to Milton and more touching ones to my mother, who adored Jana, we set off for California at the end of June.

■ ■ ■

As I write these words, the shadow of another incident from that year falls over the page, giving the lie to those glib notions of new and old realities I wrote about several pages ago. It is an incident that reminds me that no matter how things seem to change, we live in a continuum where the problems of the past continue in the present and reach toward the future.

It happened in the spring after the Kennedy assassination, a month before I left New York. I had just left the basement office of the store, where I had been discussing one thing or another with Milton. The bookstore, remember, was on Broadway and 116th Street, opposite Columbia University and nine blocks south of 125th Street, the unofficial beginning of Harlem.

As I stepped from the basement into the morning sunlight, a taxicab swung to the curb and stopped. The driver leapt out and ran up to two policemen who were strolling on their beat, and pointed frantically to his vehicle. The driver's behavior was so agitated that a dozen or so passersby stopped to watch. So did I.

One of the policemen strode up to the cab and asked the lone passenger to step out of the car. A big, burly black man emerged. He was wearing an expensively cut light-brown suit with an unknotted maroon tie lying on the white shirt beneath the jacket.

"What's the problem?" he asked the cop, a redheaded, sallow-faced young man.

"The cabbie wants you out of his cab," said the cop.

"What? He can't just—"

"He owns the cab. Look at the shield on the hood."

"I don't care what he owns. I've got an appointment on Fifty-second Street in—"

"Sorry: he owns the cab. It's his place of business. That means if he doesn't want to serve you . . . "

While the discussion was going on—between the passenger, surprised and increasingly irritated, and the cop, in a situation that was unpleasant to him and clearly unwanted—the driver had retreated, gotten back into the cab, and suddenly drove away in a squeal of tires and a gunned engine.

The cop leaped back in surprise, but the black man reflexively stumbled forward as the cab skimmed the back of his legs. "Motherfucker!" he exclaimed.

"What did you say? " said the young cop, his voice rising.

"I said, who does that motherfucker think—"

But before he could finish the sentence, the cop had lifted his night stick and slammed it across his face. The black man toppled to the sidewalk, face first, then, dazed, rolled over on his back. The cop stood over him. "Stay down!" he commanded.

The black man, half-conscious, his nose squashed and blood burbling down his chin and over his jacket, started to rise.

"I said, 'Stay down!'" the cop repeated.

By now the dozen passersby had become a crowd of Columbia students as well as blacks, Puerto Ricans, and strolling whites.

The cop looked around in a panic. His partner was heading for the police phone box on the corner.

The black man was trying to lever himself into a sitting position with one arm.

The cop looked down at him and drew his revolver, holding it a foot from the man's face. The crowd gasped.

"I said, 'Stay down!'"

Still in a stupor, the black man stared into the barrel of the pistol and continued to lever himself up, saying, "Pull the trigger, boy. I ain't no dog: I don't lie in the street for no one."

The cop held his arm rigid and cocked the revolver. The entire crowd—blacks, whites and browns—surged forward. The cop instinctively backed away, waving the pistol at the advancing group.

At that moment, two patrol cars pulled around the corner, and the young policeman's partner came running back with a drawn revolver. Assisted by a cop from the patrol cars, the two patrolmen managed to hold the crowd back, while another cop cuffed the black man and bundled him into one of the patrol cars and drove him away.

A number of the people in the crowd angrily asked what was going to happen to the black man. Others wanted to give statements on the spot, telling how out of line the young policeman had been. But he and his partner had been put in the other patrol car, and no one had seen his badge number. The only information anyone had was the patrol car numbers and the precinct they were from. Five minutes after they arrived, the cars and cops were gone.

Many people milled around, traded phone numbers, and vowed to set right the injustice they had just witnessed, and a number of them followed through on their promise, including Milton and his partner. But everyone who called the precinct was given the same answer: there had been no incident on 116th Street that day, nor had any black man of the description given been booked in any precinct or registered in any hospital.

For three weeks people pursued the matter through their assemblymen, the district attorney and mayor's offices, and personal contacts—all with no result. No records existed anywhere. The incident, it seemed, was a mass delusion, and as far as I know the young cop and his partner were never again seen on the streets of upper Broadway.

So the old reality of racism continued, despite the promised new reality of social change that had been ushered in that January with the appearance of the Beatles on the Ed Sullivan show. I wasn't as impressed by the four young singers at the time as I was by a young, rambunctious heavyweight boxer named Cassius Clay who was fulfilling his predictions of what round he was going to knock out his opponents. But the social significance of the mop-headed four would overwhelm me within the year, as would the further exploits of the young boxer, who would do battle against the old reality of racism and expose its ugliness as few athletes had done before. All that was in the future, however. Unbeknownst to me the day I left New York, I was heading to the city where the supposed new reality, entwined with the old, was about to take shape.

BOOK SIX

SAN
FRANCISCO
IN THE 1960s

CHAPTER 16

1964–1965

We arrived in San Francisco with no prospects—no job, no housing. But within two weeks we found a six-room flat in the Mission District and I was hired to teach history and English at a yeshiva, a parochial high school for Jewish boys and girls. The salary was good, so Wilma could stay home with Jana, although within the month she was teaching modern dance classes at the downtown YWCA.

During August, we got the flat into shape with furniture from the Salvation Army and St. Vincent de Paul shops and journeyed down to Santa Cruz to pick up the odds and ends we'd left with the Houstons the year before. Jim had written several more stories and a couple of articles and showed them to me. I was amazed and delighted. In my opinion, Jim had made great strides in style and craft. He had become a stylist of the first order. One piece in particular impressed me. It was an article showing the creeping environmental destruction of the small town of Santa Cruz as seen by the author sitting high in his house, looking out at the surrounding neighborhood from his cupola.

I had been reading the stories in the dining room, and when I finished I tracked Jim down in the living room where he was listening to a jazz LP. He looked up.

"They're great," I said. "You've made it. You're a pro."

He merely smiled and nodded.

My words may not have elicited the impassioned reaction from Jim I expected, but they were a declaration of both awe and respect. They expressed admiration not only for the pieces I had just read but for the rigorous work he had done since we first met. He had willed himself to be a writer and had attained his goal by relentless persistence. Within the month, *Holiday* magazine bought the environment piece, and a few years later Dial Press brought out his first novel, *Between Battles*. Jim had hit his stride and would never look back.

After two short novels—the second one, *Gig* (1969), a tightly constructed story set in a piano bar on the Northern California coast—Jim began writing works of fiction more complicated in structure and theme. They were laid across different time periods, each moving toward present-day California, or beyond to the Hawai'ian islands. All the novels, in one way or another, deal with journeys and unobtrusively approach mythic odysseys as his characters explore themselves in their cultural environments and in the end come to profound discoveries about themselves and the world. In his later novels, he adds an underlying spiritual dimension to the mix.

Besides his fiction, Jim has written many magazine articles that grapple with the California and Pacific Rim zeitgeists, concerns that are the subjects of two of his nonfiction books, *Californians: Searching for the Golden State* (1982) and *The Ring of Fire: A Pacific Basin Journey* (1997). As the years went on, he gained national prominence, especially with his last two novels, both of which are written in parallel time sequences: *Snow Mountain Passage* (2001), a story about the ill-fated Donner Party, won notable book-award recommendations from the *Los Angeles Times* and the *Washington Post*. His latest novel, *Bird of Another Heaven* (2007), is partially set in the late nineteenth century, links Hawai'i and the West Coast through the adventurous life of a half-Hawai'ian, half-California Indian woman and her relationship with Hawai'i's last king. The story is told by her great-grandson writing a hundred years later.

Over the years Jim has been recognized as an authority on California literature and has edited several anthologies of California writing. He has also won many awards, including a commendation from the California State Assembly, a National Endowment for the Arts Award, a Carey McWilliams Award, a silver medal from the California Commonwealth Club, a Rockefeller Grant, and two American Book Awards.

My observation of Jim's lack of reaction to my praise that day in 1964 calls for a further comment on my part. Like most men I've met and talk about in this book, Jim is taciturn, self-contained—a quiet man who keeps personal information and emotional reactions to himself. In this way, he is an iconic American male, portrayed in the movies by Gary Cooper, John Wayne, and Clint Eastwood. Those actors, along with numerous other social examples, provide a cultural template for American males to follow from one generation to the next. I come from a different culture—one where talk is an imperative and emotions are always on display. The American male's reticence is met by my emotional intensity. I don't understand him, and he doesn't understand me. I distrust what is hidden as repressed; he distrusts what is exposed as aggressive and, he considers, self-serving. As for Jim in this scheme of things, he and I are writers: we both use words to bring to the surface what might be purposely or unknowingly concealed, but I always felt he distrusted the flamboyance with which I would reveal it, and therefore he distrusts me. I make him nervous, uncomfortable. My intensity wears on him. I'm not just talking about Jim. I've thought that many of the other men I've known, especially in the Midwest and West, thought the same thing. This estimate, of course, is oversimplified: the difference is not as clear-cut as

I've made it sound. But it isn't that far off the mark, either. Interestingly, this supposed difference has not interfered with my affection for Jim, nor has it diminished my respect for all he has accomplished.

THE YESHIVA INCIDENT

In September, I threw myself into work at the yeshiva. There were fifty or so students in the school, all of them intelligent and orderly. But they were also chubby, lazy, and physically inactive. I went to the rabbi who acted as principal, and asked if I could add a physical education period to the curriculum. He happily assented, and I proceeded to lower the two basketball hoops that had been lashed to the ceiling years before in the school's small theater, transforming the room into a gymnasium of sorts. During sixth period, I led all the students in calisthenics, divided them into two teams to play "war" with several volleyballs, and instructed them in the rudiments of basketball. I also had them run laps around the "gym." I would have taught them punchball, but there were too many students in too small a space.

The students livened up within a week, their skin tone changed, and their parents began calling the front office, joyfully acknowledging their children's progress, intellectually and physically. Everyone was happy with my work, including Mr. Shapiro, the three-hundred-pound fundraiser with a shriveled right arm who smiled at me with reptilian eyes from the administration office every time I passed the doorway.

There was only one problem. At the end of the first week, I was accosted by four people who were waiting for me across the street from the school. Introducing themselves as former teachers at the yeshiva, they wanted to warn me about the rabbi and Mr. Cohen, who they said had never paid them. Several of them claimed they were owed three years' back pay. They also wanted me to act as their advocate, since by court order they were not allowed to come within fifty feet of the school.

When I went to the front office and informed the rabbi and Mr. Shapiro about the group's accusations, they told me that they were troublemakers and "bad Jews," and to forget about them. I was more than happy to do so; I was enjoying the job too much and didn't want any trouble, especially from "bad Jews." When the four approached me after school the following day, I told them I didn't want to talk to them.

But on payday at the end of the month, the faculty was informed that the checks would be a few days late, and by the end of the following week the faculty still hadn't been paid. At the top of the stairs outside the classrooms I stopped three of the teachers, two women and a man, all in their seventies, who had been teaching at the yeshiva for ten years.

"Is this normal?" I asked.

"Don't make trouble," they replied.

"Are you being paid?" I asked.

They were silent.

"When were you last paid?" I asked, with rising alarm.

Grudgingly, they told me they hadn't been paid in five years. But they insisted they were not complaining. They had Social Security checks and were not teaching for the salary but to serve Judaism in their last years.

Once more I went to the office, and Mr. Shapiro answered my increasingly pointed questions with reassurances that we would be paid by the end of the week, continually smiling, his eyes glittering. But once again, pay envelopes were not forthcoming on the appointed day.

This time the rabbi was in the office to hear my complaints. I had polled the school's five other faculty members and two of them wanted me to speak on their behalf, but not the three old people who refused to be a part of any action that might be construed as opposition to the Jewish community. The rabbi told me he was one of a council of rabbis from San Francisco and Oakland who made up the yeshiva school board. They had been apprised of my work by a number of people, including him, and were so happy with all I had accomplished that they wanted to give me the title of head of secular education and a $10,000 increase in salary. Unfortunately, the school was having a cash flow problem at present, the rabbi said, so the increase in pay might not show up on my paycheck immediately.

I was completely undone, flattered by the unexpected promotion and the rabbi's reassurances. He was so concerned, so sincere—and he was, after all, a rabbi. All the paychecks, he promised, would be ready at the end of the second pay period. But instead of paychecks, two eminent rabbis from the council were on hand to pass out token payments when that second payday arrived. Wilma and I had long before gone through all the money she had won, and we had borrowed money from our parents to tide us over for the previous two months.

I respectfully told the rabbis that the situation could not continue; that the two faculty members I represented—I was careful to exclude the three old people from my words—had no money for food or rent, and if something wasn't done, I'd have to take action.

The two listened in sympathetic silence and then commiserated with me, insisting that full payment, as well as retroactive pay for the old people and those who had accosted me on the street, would be forthcoming within the month. Mr. Shapiro, who was present at the meeting and nodded in agreement, was at that moment, they said, organizing a $100-a-plate (or was it a $500-a-plate?) dinner at the Fairmont Hotel ostensibly to honor Ben Swig, the Fairmont's owner, but actually to raise money for the school.

The next month came and went in a flurry of activity. Mr. Shapiro was constantly on the phone, Wilma and I borrowed more money from our parents, and I assured the five active faculty members as well as the four former teachers—with whom I was now in touch almost daily—that the situation would soon be rectified.

The dinner at the Fairmont was a great success, and the current faculty was introduced from the dais to enthusiastic applause. I was identified as director of secular education for my introduction. But two weeks later, at the end of November, there were still no paychecks. The rabbis were again on hand to ask for patience, explaining with Mr. Shapiro that the money was still being collected and entered into the books.

At Hanukkah we were again given token checks, and I had the temerity to ask the rabbis to front the money for all faculty member checks until the accounts were "full." If not, I said, I would be forced to take legal action. The rabbis smiled, sympathized, and again assured me and the faculty that our pay was imminent, adding that, alas, they were unable to provide personal funds at that time. When there were still no checks by the end of January, I called a meeting of the other current faculty members (excluding the old people, who still did not want to participate in any grievance action) and what was now eight former faculty who had not been paid. A strike would mean nothing, I told them. I had done research, and there was a state organization called the California Labor Council that handled workplace complaints. I wanted to approach them without delay. Everyone agreed, voting me their spokesman.

I was incensed. For some time I had suspected that the council of rabbis were skimming money from the school, but I could not bring myself to believe that they would hire people in the name of the religion with no intention of paying them. Now I was positive that the profits from the dinner to aid the school were going into the rabbis' and Mr. Shapiro's bank accounts. The avarice, the blatant criminal intent, and the lack of concern for the welfare of their fellow humans outraged me. What made their actions more heinous in my eyes was that they counted on the religious fervor of their victims to shield them from any retribution. Once more the injustice of a situation had brought me to uncompromising action. But now, instead of defending myself, I was acting on behalf of others as well. I had taken a step forward into the world of political and social action.

The officials at the Labor Council were apprehensive. They didn't want to bring charges against a religious organization, especially Jews, who they thought, and I agreed, would counter any accusations with charges of anti-Semitism. But the rabbis' legal transgressions were too numerous to ignore. Shrewdly, the Labor Council assigned a Jewish agent to handle the case. He was as incensed as I was, and by the time the paperwork was completed, the school was charged with over thirty counts of labor violations. Eventually, all of the teachers were paid their full salaries from monies collected from wealthy donors. As far as I knew, the rabbis contributed nothing, and the money collected from the Fairmont dinner was never accounted for. Unfortunately, the school filed for bankruptcy soon after and closed its doors permanently.

For several months I received angry phone calls from Jews on both sides of the bay, either reviling me for showing the religion in a bad light to the gentile public, cursing me for causing the school to be closed, or just insulting me on general principles. There were also some bizarre phone calls as well. One was purportedly from "a woman in the community" who, in the weeks before the council made its charges, offered me, in transparently veiled terms, more than money if I would withdraw my complaint.

The whole experience left me more disgusted than angry. I felt no guilt for bringing to justice the people who ran the yeshiva. As far as I was concerned, they had nothing to do with the spiritiual essence of Judaism any more than corrupt officials of any other religion . But by February 1965, I found myself out of a job. Oh, yes, I finally received all the money owed me—but minus the $10,000 I was to receive as director of secular education.

DON JUSTICE IN SAN FRANCISCO

The immediate result of the yeshiva fiasco was that Wilma went to work as a saleslady at the Emporium department store, and I stayed home with Jana. I had been writing and publishing in literary journals with more and more regularity, but remaining at home gave me more time to write than I'd had since going to Iowa.

Wilma was happy to be out of the house after six months of being a housewife. Not only was she working at the Emporium, she continued to teach dance classes several nights a week at the downtown YWCA. Coming home one evening, she ran into Don Justice on the street. He and his family were staying in San Francisco for the year on a Rockefeller grant, and he was excited that we were in the city, too. He invited us to dinner and gave Wilma his phone number, telling her to have me call him.

Don and I spent one or two days a week together for the next several months. His grant was a short-lived program that put recognized novelists and poets as observers into theater groups all over the country in an attempt to stimulate interest in drama writing. Don was attached to the Actors' Workshop in San Francisco, and he took me to rehearsals and introduced me to various members of the company. I met the directors, Jules Irving and Herbert Blau, who within the year would be moving the core of the group to New York to become Lincoln Center's first theater company. One of the actors I briefly met was an imposing, booming-voiced thespian of the old school named George Hitchcock. I saw him perform in various roles over the next year and was impressed by him, but I had no idea that I would be working with him in various artistic and activist pursuits in the near future.

Don was extremely friendly the months he was in San Francisco. I think he was happy to see a familiar face, even if it was mine, in a city of strangers. Mostly we met at his house to play cards or board games and talk about poetry and Iowa. He was eager to tell me that the year after I'd left Iowa, he'd come to understand what I was attempting to do in my poetry, and he showed me the latest pieces he was working on, which were looser technically and pursued what Robert Bly had labeled the "deep image." Bly's explanation in his *Sixties* (formerly *Fifties*) magazine of nonlinear, intuitive imagery, of what he called the "deep image" as well as his concept of "leaping" or nonlogical sequencing, had helped me define what I was doing, too.

During one of our first get-togethers, Don asked me about my time at Stanford. He was sorry I had kept my distance from Yvor Winters, but he was shocked when I told him that Stegner had not accepted my novel. Now, without hesitation, he told me to come back to Iowa for a semester of residence, and he would make sure I received my MA. I thought his offer over for a day or two and then refused with a genuine thank you. I was tired of moving, and California, my body and mind told me, was home, for better or worse.

On one of my visits to Don, Bob Mezey showed up. Actually, he was there before I arrived, on his way back to Fresno where he was teaching with Philip Levine at Fresno State.

When I rang the bell, Don yelled for me to come out to the kitchen. Mezey was talking to him when I entered the room and continued talking as if I wasn't there. After several minutes of this behavior, Don literally began to twitch with discomfort and broke into Mezey's monologue, saying, "You remember Mort, don't you, Bob?" But Mezey didn't even turn to acknowledge my presence. He just continued talking. After another minute, I shook my head in disgust and said, "I think I'd better leave, Don, before something unpleasant happens," and I did, leaving Don irritated and at a loss as to how to handle the situation. He called me the next day to apologize, but I told him he had nothing to apologize for; the situation was Mezey's doing and hadn't surprised me.

CHAPTER 17

John Logan

During his year in San Francisco, Don regularly socialized with most of the academic writing community in the city, many of whom he had known before he arrived. One of the elite members of that community was John Logan, the much-honored, award-winning poet who had taught at Notre Dame for years. At the same time, Logan had directed a poetry workshop in Chicago, which had produced, under his magical touch, such poets as Dennis Schmitz, Naomi Lazard, Marvin Bell, Bill Knott, and Roger Aplon, among others. Logan was also the editor of a fine literary journal called *Choice* and had published some of my poems several years before at the urging of Marvin Bell, who came to the workshop in Iowa the last year I was there. Now Logan was living in San Francisco and teaching at San Francisco State.

That fall, Logan invited Justice to a party and told him to bring any poets Don might know in the area, and he was delighted when Don mentioned my name. He had planned the party to feature an informal reading by Gary Snyder, Robert Duncan, Justice, and himself, but when he heard I was living in town, he added me to the list. I was flattered, to say the least, and gave my first reading in San Francisco to what seemed like more than one hundred people packed into Logan's large apartment on Powell Street.

That was the beginning of my friendship with John Logan, a gentle, wonderful man who was going through the most difficult period of his life. His marriage had broken up several months before the party, and John had lost not only the stability of his home but daily contact with his nine children, who loved him as much as he loved them. Although I never asked him the reasons for the dissolution of the marriage, I thought that his drinking and homosexual proclivities had a lot to do with the break-up. Certainly from then on, his drinking and other activities got more and more out of hand, which seemed to me somehow connected with his sense of beauty. John's love of beauty was boundless. Both moments of spiritual beauty and

John Logan, 1970s

instances of physical beauty, it seemed to me, would send him into rhapsodic bursts of poetry and inflame his libido.

Before the break-up of his marriage, most of his poems had been formal
explorations of Catholic themes. But after the break-up, he wrote in an original,
musical free verse that pursued secular settings and themes and dealt mostly
with his personal experiences. His poems were composed of jagged lines,
sometimes of only two or three beats, that featured complex voice rhythms,
shifts of tone, and internal rhymes. I remember he went over one of my typically
prosaic poems, substituting one word after another until he had brought out a
scintillating music that danced on the page, a music alive with alliteration and
half-rhymes. His poem "Three Moves" illustrates his method and his content.
Read it slowly to appreciate the music and the shifts of tone. The immediacy of
the voice and its personal probing are beyond anything Justice allowed himself
to write.

Three Moves

Three moves in six months and I remain
the same.
Two homes made two friends.
The third leaves me with myself again.
I we harmly speak |
Here I am with tame ducks
and my neighbors' boats,
only this electric heat
against the April damp.
I have a friend named Frank—
The only one who ever dares to call
and ask me, "How's your soul?"
I hadn't thought about it for a while,
and was ashamed to say I didn't know.
I have no priest for now.
Who
will forgive me then. Will you?
Tame birds and my neighbors' boats.
The ducks honk about the floats . . .
They walk dead drunk onto the land and grounds,
iridescent blue and black and green and brown.
They live on swill
our aged houseboats spill.
But still they are beautiful.
Look! The duck with its unlikely beak
has stopped to pick
and pull
at the potted daffodil.
Then again they sway home
to dream
bright gardens of fish in the early night.
Oh these ducks are all right.
They will survive.

But I am sorry I do not often see them climb.
Poor sons-a-bitching ducks.
You're all fucked up.
What do you do that for?
Why don't you hover near the sun anymore?
Afraid you'll melt?
These foolish ducks lack a sense of guilt,
and so all their multi-thousand-mile range
is too short for the hope of change.

A year after the party at his apartment, John was asked to be guest editor of *Poetry Northwest* and asked me to submit some poems. He accepted several with his usual enthusiasm, passing the rest on to the journal's editor, Carolyn Kizer, who took several more for future issues.

That was a typical Logan gesture. He was always on the lookout for good poetry and promoting poems and poets whose work he liked. In the literary world, where individual backbiting and self-aggrandizement were the norm, John was a singular example of generosity and an arbiter of taste.

John was adored by his students, both past and present. He kept in contact with them, and they with him, so that to the end of his life he had a support group of what seemed dozens of first-class poets scattered throughout the country. This widely dispersed coterie became increasingly important to him during his last years because as he became more dissolute, he needed friends to take care of him. On a drinking spree, he was liable to end up anywhere, waking in any number of strange rooms or even alleys. Friends would be responsible for picking him up at airports and getting him to readings and other engagements as well as getting him fed and housed and making sure he hadn't left his manuscripts in a plane, train, or taxi. And he was so beloved that everyone took care of him gladly. In fact, the element that drew many of us together in friendship was concern for John.

During the next four years, a group of us would meet every several months in Ghirardelli Square at the Rusty Scupper, a bistro that had been built and was managed by one of John's protégés, the poet Roger Aplon. Roger, a handsome, muscular, dark-haired poet, had saved John's life when he fell off a boat in Lake Michigan and had felt responsible for John ever since. I found Roger's demeanor appealing from the start. Friendly and sensitive as well as a physically powerful presence, Roger was also generous and welcomed the gatherings at the restaurant. The group included Roger, Robert Hass, Joseph Stroud, and any other poet who might be in town. Stroud, who I will discuss later, was one of John's prized students at San Francisco State in an extraordinary class that included Stan Rice, Phil Dow, Shirley Kaufman, and Linda Gregg (who was always accompanied to class by Jack Gilbert). Circumstances would draw Joe and me together in the years to come, and we would become the best of friends.

John's reputation was greatly enhanced by an article Robert Bly wrote about him in his *Fifties* magazine. Each issue of the magazine featured an essay by Bly on a poet he considered one of the best poets over forty years of age working in America at the time. His article on John cited him as one of that group.

John's reputation continued to grow, and by the end of the 1960s he was hired as a full professor of literature, with a large salary, at the State University of New York at Buffalo, at that time one of the premier schools of literature in the country. The English department included Robert Creeley and Leslie Fiedler, and now they had John in their fold. Robert Hass, the future United States poet laureate, who had been Logan's student at St. Mary's, followed him to Buffalo, where he earned his Ph.D.

The second year he was at Buffalo, John invited me to be visiting poet for a week. I had a wonderful time and gave a bizarre reading to a large audience at the university's student union. In the adjoining auditorium, a student organization was showing Leni Riefenstahl's "Triumph of the Will," a documentary about the gigantic rally of the Nazi party in Nuremberg in 1934. Periodically my words would be buried by crowd roars and frenzied calls of "Seig Heil," and Goebbels and Hitler interrupted my tenderest verses with what sounded like angry criticism of my work, sending my audience into uncontrolled laughter that I played to with a stand-up comedian's panache.

John put me up in Jerome Mazzaro's house. Jerry was a fine poet and critic, intense and scholarly, who would write a long, appreciative article on my first four books in the *Cream City Review* several years later. I met with students at Buffalo, went to eat with John and Jerry on a number of occasions, and, best of all, attended one of John's workshops. Unlike most of his coterie, I had never been one of John's students, and the workshop gave me an opportunity to see him at work. Although I was supposed to lead the workshop, I deferred to John. He looked over each student's poem with intense concentration and started almost all his remarks to a student by saying, in a gentle, fatherly voice, "This is not your best work." This ploy always left the student with his dignity and sense of self-worth, no matter how thoroughly John might savage his poem. It was a lesson I took back to California with me, and I let it guide the way I conducted my own workshops. Logan's method was to nurture, not destroy; it was far different than the Iowa approach.

John was one of the featured poets at the Marin Writers' Conference in 1974, and I was tapped to pick him up at the airport. He was drinking more heavily than ever, and when the conference directors saw the shape he was in, they put him in my charge. That was fine with John, who didn't want to stay with the family that had offered to put him up, and he complicated my assignment by insisting I take him from restaurant to bar and finally, around midnight, to my motel. I was a bit apprehensive at the latter, and when we got to the motel, which I'd booked for one person, my uneasiness elevated to slapstick panic when I saw there was only one bed in the room. John was very drunk. I stood in the doorway, looking at the bed with John swaying beside me. "Look, John," I said, "I'm not getting into bed with you. Let's put the mattress on the floor and you can sleep on it, and I'll bed down on the bedsprings."

John was insulted and replied in obvious irritation, "You don't think I'd try anything with you, now, do you?" as if it was the most distasteful suggestion he had ever heard. Without a word, I dragged the mattress off the bed and we settled in for the night, John snoring within minutes, and me, to end the comical evening, for some reason still awake and highly insulted at the disgusted tone in John's voice at the suggestion that he might make a pass at me. Ah, vanity, it is a rose by any other name, but doesn't smell half as sweet. . . .

Several years later, John was invited to the conference again. Joe Stroud and I picked him up and were joined by Jack Gilbert, the celebrated Yale Younger Poet winner in 1965, who had just returned from living a number of years in Greece and who Joe knew from San Francisco State.

John was scheduled to give a reading with the Russian poet Yevgeny Yevtushenko, and, anticipating a large crowd, the organizers of the reading had set it up in the Marin College gym, with chairs set on the floor of the gymnasium flanked by bleacher seating on either side and a mobile stage at the end of the gym opposite the entrance.

Yevtushenko was scheduled to read at 8 PM, and John was to read at 7:00 as, I couldn't help thinking, the warm-up to the main attraction. Jack and Joe had the same thought, and all three of us were annoyed for John's sake before we set foot in the building. As for John, he was too drunk to care and obviously let us steer him wherever he had to go.

People had just started to enter the gymnasium at 7:00 when John began his reading. The audience talked and joked as John read one poem after another. Clearly, they, as most of the crowd who had not yet shown up, were coming to hear Yevtushenko. It was the middle of the Cold War, and Soviet artists—musicians, dancers, performers of all sorts—were greeted by huge audiences in the United States as if we Americans wanted to assure the Russians that we were good people who loved them and didn't want war.

By the time Logan ended his reading at 7:50, the gymnasium was almost full. But most of the several thousand in the audience had ignored him, and he received only scattered applause. He didn't seem to mind, but Joe, Jack, and I were incensed. It was one thing to welcome a foreign artist but another to dismiss one of your own great artists in the process.

At the start of John's reading, however, Jack had spotted Yevtushenko seated alone in the bleachers on the opposite side of the gym. He sat with his elbows on his knees, his chin propped on his palms, for the entire fifty minutes of John's presentation.

Joe went down and guided John back to our seats, and we listened to Yevtushenko emote. He was tall, blond, lanky, and soulfully handsome. Russian poets don't read or recite their poems; they declaim them, like melodramatic actors in old silent films, although here a booming voice joined flamboyant gestures. Yevtushenko held forth in Russian, and a British actor, who was touring with him, read the English translations. It was a grand show, which elicited wild applause at the end of every poem and a standing ovation at the conclusion of the recitation, John joining in with genuine if tipsy appreciation.

Afterward, we were invited to a soiree on a ferryboat moored at one of the piers in San Francisco. A millionaire had rented the ferry. Champagne, caviar, oysters, and other extravagant fare were served to the wealthy and cultural elite of San Francisco who jammed the boat, waiting to gawk and flatter Yevtushenko when he arrived half an hour after we did. John, Jack, Joe, and I were ignored or avoided, although the crush of people was so great, avoidance was hard to accomplish. But clearly our dress wasn't up to code, and only a few out-of-place fellow poets greeted us with nods and rolled eyes at the high-society crowd so unfamiliar to us.

When Yevtushenko arrived, the mass of bejeweled and perfumed cognoscenti leaned toward the entrance with calls of "Bravo, Bravo" and applause. Yevtushenko, who towered over the crowd, was unmoved and was craning his neck, searching the room. Within moments, his gaze alighted on us and, calling "Logan, Logan," he waded through the throng toward us. John had continued to keep pace with his drinking since arriving on the ferry and had probably not heard Yevtushenko's impassioned calling to him. Finally, the Russian stood before the four of us, looking down at John, who swayed in our midst. A crowd had followed Yevtushenko to where we stood, and people on either side of us turned our way, wondering what had so upset the Russian, causing him to battle his way to us.

Caught in a paroxysm of emotion, Yevtushenko, stood in front of John, who was too befuddled to raise his head, and blurted, "Logan, such music, beautiful music."

John looked up, continued to sway, and said nothing. The people in the crowd turned to each other, uncertain. But Jack, Joe, and I were beaming with delight. I remembered Yevtushenko seated in the bleachers across from us in the gym. Damn, he was really listening to John, I thought, and though he hardly understood any English, as a fellow poet he recognized the magnificence of John's language. It was not a gracious diplomatic move that made him wade through the crowd; it was genuine admiration for a fellow artist. The crowd turned away, embarrassed at the scene. John swayed goggle-eyed in front of Yevtushenko, and the Russian, with an understanding smile, turned toward his admirers and was gone. He had, needless to say, gone up in our estimation enormously. The next day, I asked John about the incident. He didn't remember anything about it.

John retired from New York University at Buffalo in 1985 and moved back to San Francisco. He died two years later, at the age of sixty-four, his life so much a shambles by then that it was hard for me to visit him. He was a poet who pursued and attempted to live with beauty twenty-four hours a day, and, of course, he could not. But as one of our truly orphic poets, he sang about the beauty as well as the pain, longing, and transcendence that we all seek in one way or another.

After John's death, two of his children—his son John, Jr., and his daughter Alice—and several of his former students organized an annual memorial reading in which the participants would reminisce about John, read his poems, or read something of their own about him. Roger Aplon took part, so did Dennis Schmidt, Robert Hass, Joe Stroud, and I. But we were the only ones who showed up, and after the second year, we abandoned the idea.

CHAPTER 18

1966–1967

TEACHER AND POET

While I was home with Jana and hanging around with Don Justice, I was also looking for another job. In the summer of 1965, I applied to the California School of Mechanical Arts and was hired to teach senior English and world history. The school was also known as Lick-Wilmerding High School, a title that combined the names of the two benefactors whose trust funds had originally created the all-boy school at the end of the nineteenth century. Both Jellis Wilmerding and James Lick were millionaires who had begun life as poor illiterates, and they wanted to create a school where any boy, regardless of race, religion, or creed, could acquire a first-class education free of charge in both academic and occupational courses. Prospective students had to pass a standard examination and finish with scores in the top twenty percent of those taking the test with them. The level of student ability, therefore, was exceptionally high. In addition to his academic classes, every boy was required to take wood, metal, electrical, and machine shops. There were also advanced shops in all those areas as well as in welding and plumbing. The school did not employ a maintainence crew. The students maintained the buildings.

Since the students paid no tuition, the teachers were free to design their classes and the level of instruction and were answerable only to the administration. Almost all the teachers were as exceptional as the students. Some were retired teachers; others were young teachers like myself who lacked the credentials or degrees to teach at public schools. Still others were retired military personnel who were also teachers. We were all alike in one particular area—we received low salaries. The retirees were supplementing either their military pensions or Social Security checks, but the younger of us were earning $60 a week.

One of the teachers earning that low salary was a long-time faculty member named Jack Coffey, a witty loner who taught sophomore and junior English with unrivaled panache. His annual three-week exploration of *Moby Dick* featured him standing on his desk, declaiming Ahab's bitter lines. He and I became fast friends and formed part of a riotous quartet in the faculty lounge, which included one of the math teachers, a sixty-year-old political activist named Sarah Crome, and the beautiful new French teacher, Mary Fitzmaurice. Sarah was "the mother of us all," as Jack would ironically remind us whenever she got too bossy. There were a number of instructors with interesting pasts but none more than the art teacher, who rarely entered the lounge. His name was Rolf Penn, and although he looked no more than a trim, physically well-conditioned thirty-five years old in 1965, he had been part of a crack German commando unit that had rescued Rommel from the desert during World War II. One night I met Penn and his wife leaving a World War II action film. He nodded a greeting and walked on, then turned back and strode up to me. "We were not that stupid," he said in his thick German accent and turned on his heel and sauntered away. All in all, it was a fascinating group of students being taught by a charismatic array of instructors.

Despite the poor pay, teaching at Lick was exhilarating. The boys were as rambunctious as any high school students, but I quickly had them immersed in their reading assignments and seeking answers to the questions I posed, and their level of work, both in class discussions and essays—although they didn't know it—was on a par with upper-level undergraduate college students' work.

We read short stories by Chekhov, Joyce, Sherwood Anderson, Hemingway, and Flannery O'Connor, poems by Yeats, Eliot, Donne, Ginsberg, Snyder, and others. And if Coffey's treatment of *Moby Dick* was the high point of sophomore English, my presentation of Dostoevsky's *Brothers Karamazov* was the high point of senior English. For two months, five days a week,

At Lick-Wilmerding,
San Francisco, 1967

Eloquent answer to a rambunctious
student, Lick-Wilmerding,
San Francisco, 1966

one hour a day, we read, discussed, and wrote about every idea, every character, every emotional and intellectual nuance in the book.

And so my professional life went for three years.

After the first day or two of class, discipline was never a problem. I would capture the boys' imaginations, and my humor created a rapport that leveled my position of authority but never lessened respect on either side. Homework was always done, the boys were learning, and, more important, they were thinking. If teaching the fifth grade at Point Arena was my most emotionally rewarding teaching experience, my years at Lick were intellectually exultant—and never to be repeated. My first four years of teaching, therefore, were the high points of my life as a pedagogue.

Outside the classroom, I hung out with the students, joining them in the gym during lunch period where I demonstrated my by now old-fashioned ways of shooting as they gawked in disbelief. I also counseled them individually on emotional and family problems. And one year I coached the B and C basketball teams to league championships while imparting secrets of East Coast tactics to the varsity coach, with whom I sat during the varsity games. Needless to say, my coaching methods emphasized attack and misdirection.

At about that time, my friend Fernando Mercado, who had married a fiction writer Wilma and I knew from Iowa, got me a try-out with his industrial-league basketball team. But my weight was still inflated, my reflexes were shot, and I didn't wait for the decision: I knew my playing days were over for good. (In earlier years, Fernando had been groomed as the next Elgin Baylor at Portland State University, but he gave it up to pursue painting. We lived a few blocks from each other in San Francisco and played half-court pick-up games together until he moved to Oakland. Over the years we've remained close friends, even after he moved to the New Mexico desert, where he lives alone, one of the most talented and art-addicted painters I've ever met.)

The second year I was at Lick, the senior class voted me best teacher and dedicated the yearbook to me. I reciprocated by scoring three crucial baskets in the student-faculty basketball game (which the faculty won, thanks to the new basketball coach, All-American Jim Brovelli) and by hitting a three-run homer in the bottom of the ninth inning that won the student-faculty baseball game.

■ ■ ■

But Lick wasn't occupying all my time during the three years I taught there. I was writing steadily and publishing in journals throughout the country. As my literary reputation grew in San Francisco and I met other writers, I invited them to the school to read and talk with the students. Jim Houston was one of the first who came, driving the seventy miles north from Santa Cruz. James Schevill and Sonia Sanchez came together and introduced the Poetry in the Schools program, which was just starting.

I was also giving readings of my own work around the city as well as attending readings by others. One night I heard Robert Peterson read in North Beach. I went up to him afterward, told him how impressed I was with his work, and asked him if he would visit my classes at Lick. I was reacting not only to his precise speech rhythms, but to the voice they projected, which reminded me of a contemporary American version of some Chinese poets of the Tang (T'ang) and Song (Sung) dynasties. The persona in the poems was a sort of comic Humphrey Bogart, a self-deprecating tough guy who was humorous without being witty, personal

Robert Peterson, San Francisco, 1970

without being confessional, and human without soliciting pity or any of the trappings of the cult of personality. In addition, Peterson forced the listener to pay strict attention to his poems because he cut out connections between phrases and, leaping from one subject to another, required the listener to link phrases and images and so enter the experience of the poem. Here's his laconic (and comic) description of sitting in a dentist's chair and listening to the drill do its work in his mouth:

> Hands folded like napkins in my lap
> I'm staring willfully at the future.
> Just one of the crowd, a bystander.
> It's my teeth they're after.
>
> Someone's trimming a hedge,
> the Paris Express arrives . . .
> It's the last lap at Le Mans, and the band is playing.
> What's the sound of one castanet, decaying?
>
> —from "Hands Folded Like Napkins"

Whatever I said to Bob that night wasn't half as articulate as my comments in the last paragraph, but my words or the invitation must have impressed him because he invited me to join him and his girlfriend, Dorothy, for a beer. His reading at Lick the following week was a great success as he regaled the students with such immediately appealing poems as "The Dog Is Breaking Down," which exhibited his usual humor and pitch-perfect Amercian speech patterns:

> *The Dog Is Breaking Down*
>
> The dog is breaking down.
> To and fro he runs around the clock, pissing on seedlings
> and chasing moths and butterflies
> into the house.
>
> He can't think. Sticks worry him. He'll eat
> six biscuits in a row, then bark at the box.
> His owners don't know, they think he's fearless.

But he's a loser.
Dreams of unnatural relationships,
and blinks, cow-eyed,
when sparrows perch on his nose.

Loved only by his fleas, as doomed
as we are

He's trying to keep busy.
But his nerves are shot. He'll be killed by a car.

We went out for a few beers and more talk after the reading. We met again several weeks later at one of the collating parties for *Kayak* magazine, where he asked to see some of my poems and invited me to meet him at his afternoon hang-out at the Steam Beer brewery tap room. There he introduced me to his sidekick Clemens Starck. The three of us hit it off, and the next thing I knew, Bob asked me to a party at his house in Marin county, which he shared with his girlfriend Dorothy and where he had me read some of my poems. That was where I met Leonard Gardner and Gina Berriault, who would become close friends, and in what seemed like less than a month after I met him, Bob, Clem, and I were giving readings in venues around the city.

Clemens Starck,
Dallas, Oregon,
2002

It's still a mystery to me why Bob and Clem included me in their readings. Both were minimalist poets, using as few words as possible, whereas my poems were flamboyant verbally and metaphorically. Bob's poems were rooted in his wry observations of the everyday world. Clem's poems, at that time, were composed of short cryptic pieces that reached for Zen-like utterances. Mine were full of Whitmanesque rhapsodies of the everyday world and the cosmos.

What may have united us was our public reading styles. Bob was not a strong reader. His voice was too soft, and he had a habit of clearing his throat with small coughs all the time; you really had to listen to understand what was happening when the poems began dropping their connections.

Clem, on the other hand, was an incandescent reader. His eyes blazed, his squat, muscular body and chiseled face with its wedge-shaped beard quivered with intensity as he stared at each member of the audience and recited his poems by heart. I was a dramatic reader too, so Clem and I could hold an audience and prepare them for Bob's quiet, subtle delivery.

Clem shipped out on a merchant freighter in late 1966, and I didn't see him until he emerged fifteen years later as a carpenter at the University of Oregon at Corvallis. He had abandoned poetry for a decade, he told me. But his new poems were as spare as his early ones and still showed their Zen-like influences, although the subject now was his workday, and his metaphors were drawn with subtle nuances from the lexicon of carpentry and building. His poetry won many honors.

In the Meantime

Spiritual efforts may come to nothing;
right behavior's not easy to form.
In the workshop I put my tools in order
and sweep the floor—
sawdust and shavings, three bags full.

Idly I pick up a handsaw,
inspecting the blade for true.
This saw has a life, it uses my hands
for its own purpose. Lucky,
to know your own uses!

In the meantime I stay busy.
Emery cloth and steel wool
will take the rust off metal. Linseed oil
rubbed into the handles
keeps the wood alive.

Left to right: Gary Young, Morton Marcus, Clem Starck, Joe Stroud.
Robinson Jeffers' Tor House, Carmel, Californa, 2004

Clem and I would meet whenever I came up to Oregon on a reading tour, and we arranged to read together on several occasions. One of the best times was in 2004, when Clem was contracted to do a weeklong residency at the University of California at Santa Cruz. We gave a nostalgic and explosive reading downtown, hung out with Joe Stroud and the poet Gary Young, and as a group visited Robinson Jeffers's Tor House in Carmel, where my friend, another excellent poet, Eliot Rochholz Roberts, led us on a personal tour of the estate. The only person missing to make the week perfect was Bob Peterson, who had died two years before.

Bob and Dorothy had left San Francisco in 1970. The year before he left, he spent a few months in Greece. It was during the dictatorship of The Colonels, and Bob told many stories about what Greece was like during that time. At my request he also bought me a bouzoukee and hauled it all the way home. But as far as I was concerned, the most important part of his trip was his enthusiasm at meeting the Greek poet Nanos Valaoritis, who I had first heard about from my friend Norman Thomas. A year after Bob's visit, Valaoritis would leave Greece for San Francisco. Bob, meanwhile, had settled in Taos, New Mexico. The following year, Dorothy left him. After being at loose ends and working in a bookstore in Albuquerque for the rest of the 1970s, Bob moved to Santa Cruz to be near several old friends from his school years at San Francisco State, and me. He had garnered a number of awards by then, the most prestigious, the United States Poetry Award for his book *Leaving Taos*. But Bob was lonely. He never had much luck with women until he met Joan Kloen in the early 1990s. She let him live on her property in Marin County and made the last decade of his life a happy one. He continued to write marvelous poetry and was poet in residence for two years at Reed and another year at Willamette College in Oregon, where he was reunited with Clem and read with him on a number of occasions.

CHAPTER 19

The Artists' Liberation Front

During the spring of 1966, police raids of the improvisational acting troupe called the Committee, police closures of various theater groups, and especially their harassment of the commedia dell'arte and minstrel performances of the San Francisco Mime Troupe in city parks caused a furor in the art world of the city. Finally, the mayor's formation of a committee of elite citizens to study the arts in San Francisco with the purpose of centralizing exhibitions and performances downtown, and the seemingly pointed elimination of city funds to support the mime troupe, prompted the troupe's director, Ron Davis, to call an open meeting of all interested city artists at either a warehouse on the Embarcadero or at the Howard Street studios of the troupe—I can't remember which—to counter what appeared to be a concerted effort to censor and control the arts in the city. To give the meeting an aura of respectability, the organizers asked young Willie Brown, then the city's state assembly representative and its future mayor, to chair the meeting.

I arrived at the building twenty minutes before the proceedings were to begin and found it packed: painters, sculptors, dancers, writers, poets, actors, musicians, architects, as well as doctors, lawyers, entrepreneurs, social activists, and reporters were there. So many people showed up that most of us had to stand throughout the evening. I heard that several hundred people signed up to join the group that night, although official counts later said only one hundred people were there and signed the petition.

I found myself standing next to a handsome, middle-aged woman with high cheekbones, a pointed nose, and short, brushed-back hair.

"I don't think they expected this kind of turnout," I said to her.

"No—no, but isn't it wonderful to see artists willing to support each other?" she replied with a slight stutter. We continued talking and were happy to discover we were both writers.

"I'm Mort Marcus," I said, extending my hand.

"I'm Tillie Olsen," she answered, and shook my hand. Lucky she did; I almost fell over when she so matter-of-factly stated her name. I had heard about her work from several writers at Stanford, and Wilma and I had both read *Tell Me a Riddle,* her book of short stories, in wonder and awe. When I regained my composure, I told her how much Wilma and I loved her work. She was surprised I knew her writing and was flustered at my enthusiasm for it.

Meanwhile, the meeting began with stormy outcries and incendiary statements. Everyone had something to say. Brown finally got the crowd under control, and, after three hours of focusing on the problems at hand, the formation of a permanent group was proposed and a provisional steering committee of seven individuals was chosen. The committee included Ron Davis, head of the street-performing mime troupe, Peter Berg, actor and scriptwriter for the troupe, and Bill Graham, former business manager for the troupe who had left to create the area's major rock-and-roll venue at the Fillmore Auditorium. Other committee members were the poet Carol Tinker, actor Alan Myerson from the Committee, Arthur Sheridan of City Lights Books, and musician Yuri Toporov of the Sopwith Camel rock goup. For future meetings of the group, Graham volunteered the Fillmore on Monday nights when the auditorium was closed.

After the meeting was over, Tillie asked for a ride home, and we discussed the proceedings and some of the problems we foresaw. She had been an activist since the 1930s and was well aware of the pitfalls to which such organizations were prone. But we were both enthusiastic, and by the time I dropped her off, we had become friends, a friendship that would increase over the months as we became more involved in the as-yet-nameless group—and after she had read some of my poetry.

By the end of two stormy meetings at the Fillmore Auditorium, the steering committee was reorganized to constitute representatives from all the arts, although the performing artists had a disproportionate majority of seats, with Davis, Myerson, and Graham (whose ties with the mime troupe had to be counted among the performing artists' numbers) overwhelming the other four members, which now included Tillie as the writers' representative.

Committees were formed and volunteers called for. I enlisted in the Neighborhoods Committee whose purpose was to advocate a decentralization of the arts by recognizing and encouraging artists and arts groups from the different ethnic neighborhoods of the city. George Hitchcock, who refused repeated requests to join the steering committee, was elected chair of the Neighborhoods Committee, and I was chosen to be his vice chair. Since I had seen George act with the Actors' Workshop two years before, the theater had moved to New York, and George—who in addition to acting was a playwright, poet, and social activist and had founded *Kayak* magazine when the *San Francisco Review*, of which he was poetry editor, had folded in 1964—had elected to stay in San Francisco. Now we were working together.

First, we assigned different members of the committee to seek out neighborhood arts groups and encourage them to organize and continue their work. I was living in the largely Latino Mission District and found a group of painters, musicians, and poets at the community center. I helped them organize into a Latino arts group they named the *Commission Bailes Artes*, under a Salvadorian poet named Amilcar Lobos. I enlisted some of the young lawyers who had volunteered their help to set up charters for such groups, and at the same time I organized the first neighborhood performance of the as-yet-untitled artists' organization I represented with the *Commission* at the Mission Community Center. The evening consisted of readings by Latino and Anglo poets as well as jazz music by several well-known Latino musicians and a recitation by a gaucho poet from Argentina who was living in the Mission. The poetry reading was bilingual. The members of the *Commission* translated the Anglo poets' work, and the Anglos, with the *Commission's* assistance, translated the Latino poets' work. An overflow audience cheered and applauded, laughed and cried throughout the evening. A bristling energy pervaded the auditorium as the mostly Latino audience heard their language fill the theater with impassioned oratory spiced with the words of their Anglo fellow citizens. It was an unforgettable evening. As for the *Commission Bailes Artes*, they continued to promulgate Latino arts for the next two decades.

But such evenings were a small part of what the Neighborhoods Committee was doing. Under Hitchcock's tutelage, and with the steering committee's enthusiastic backing, we planned a series of neighborhood festivals in the different ethnic and low-income areas of the city. Using architects, painters, and set designers from the organization at large, we built mobile kiosks and enclosed environments to exhibit art work, and we supplied rolls of butcher paper, crayons, and watercolors with which anyone attending the festivals could paint. At the same time, we developed collapsible stages for poetry readings, performing short excerpts from plays, and musical groups. It was the time of the "San Francisco Sound," which soon developed into psychedelic rock and roll, with such names as Janis Joplin, Jimi Hendrix, Country Joe and the Fish, the Grateful Dead, Jefferson Airplane, Big Brother and the Holding Company, Steppenwolf, and many others. Graham persuaded a number of them to perform at the festivals, which brought out not only the members of the neighborhoods, but the costumed, gaudily tie-dye-resplendent inhabitants of Haight-Ashbury as well. Thousands attended the festivals, a mélange of people of all races and ethnic groups from everywhere in the city.

One evening that summer, when Hitchcock was out of town, the city scheduled a debate with our group over the efficacies of centralized as opposed to decentralized arts. I took over for Hitchcock, passionately arguing for the grass-roots arts that arose as cultural expressions of the different ethnic groups in the neighborhoods, importuning the city representatives to encourage the diversity of culture in the city by supporting decentralized art and not, as seemed to be their plan, bring all the arts into an "official" area downtown. After the debate, two of the city's representatives came to me and said they were almost convinced of the necessity for not going ahead with their plans to centralize the city's arts. Two weeks later, one of them quit the committee.

Meanwhile, the weekly meetings of the entire organization were taking place at the Fillmore Auditorium. Unlike the neighborhood committee meetings, they were stormy sessions, full of wranglings and posturings. The possibly 200 to 300 or more who showed up for the first meeting halved in number by the third meeting and settled into a steady 75–100 by the second month. The sessions were exhausting, lasting three to five hours, crowded with individual catcalls, attempts to block power plays by one group or another, verbal attacks from one steering committee member on another, defenses of the attacked from the floor, and generally egotistical behavior all around. I remember Tillie being insulted continually by fellow steering-committee members whenever she questioned their statements or asked for clarifications, and the ensuing angry rebukes to her insulters from the writers in the chairs on the floor.

At the third meeting, fifty or so of the visual artists walked out when the organization failed to include one of their number on the steering committee. That was the first crisis. The second came several weeks later when we tried to decide on a name for the organization, and someone suggested it be called the Artists' Liberation Front. Individual voices shouted for and against the proposal. The nation was in the middle of the Vietnam conflict, and the native forces opposing U.S. intervention were called the National Liberation Front. The advocates for the name to be applied to our organization insisted that such a title would identify us as a revolutionary group opposing the establishment. But the other side, of which I was one, protested that such a name would label us as a purely political group aligned with an organization that most of the nation's populace identified as the enemy, and therefore we would alienate a number of people in the community at large who would otherwise support our goals. Tillie, with her slight stammer, spoke for the protesters and was cursed and told to shut up by several steering-committee members. The people in the audience against the name, as well as fellow writers who felt they were defending one of their own, shouted curses and insults at the offending members of the steering committee, a response that elicited jeers and cries and a number of insults from the proponents of the name. Such outbursts were typical occurrences at the meetings. They also elicited typical threats that almost came to blows. But more mayhem was averted by the steering committee's decision to delay the vote until the next meeting.

What was being expressed was the division between the politically motivated members of the arts community and the aesthetic members. Most of the latter, a number of us pointed out, opposed the war in Vietnam and as individuals had said so in print as well as had demonstrated on the streets. But we thought that as a name for the organization, the Artists' Liberation Front was a mistake.

The following week, the Fillmore was packed with people, far more than had been attending the last several meetings. Ron Davis had enjoined all the members of the mime troupe to attend and had convinced the local chapter of the Du Bois Club to come en masse to the meeting. Both groups were highly political. A number of us protested the presence of these nonmembers, especially in a voting situation. The novelist Herb Gold was eloquent, but he was shouted down. Kenneth Rexroth, or someone who looked like him, also protested and was also shouted down. The vote went forward, with the person I took to be Rexroth striding from one side of the auditorium to the other, chanting, "Bolshevik takeover! Bolshevik takeover!" as voices from the members seated around the auditorium told him to shut up and sit down. But the protests were no use. By the end of the evening, we were officially named the Artists' Liberation Front—and several dozen more artists left the organization.

As the meetings continued, they became more and more tumultuous, exhausting, and, in the end, destructive. In many ways, they reminded me of my readings about the French Revolution in Dietrich Gerhard's class at Washington University. Specifically, they resembled what I imagined the final days of the French National Assembly must have been like in the summer of 1792, shortly before the August bloodbath at the Tuileries and the September Massacres. There were the same kind of cliques, shifting alliances, opposing goals and motivations at the meetings, as well as the threat of war and revolt outside.

I am not being overdramatic. In many ways, the tensions at the meetings resembled the tensions on the street, where the exhaust fumes of paranoia permeated many of the city's neighborhoods. I recall the underlying belief among my friends and acquaintances that the entire arts and intellectual populace of the United States was about to be rounded up, packed into boxcars, and sent to concentration camps. The rumor was everywhere among us that the government had been refurbishing the old World War II Japanese internment camp at Toulee Lake and it was ready for the first trainload of political prisoners.

■ ■ ■

I met many members of the San Francisco arts community through my association with the Artists' Liberation Front. Together with two poets I met there, Laura Ulewicz and Steve Schwartz, I organized poetry readings at a small café called the I-Thou Coffee Shop, which was located on upper Haight Street near the Stanyan Street entrance to Golden Gate Park.

It was a time in which the young were in open rebellion against established ways of dressing and behaving and, more important, against the values and ideas of their parents. Vietnam had entered a period of open and intense warfare, young people were protesting the draft as well as the war, and the year before, the free speech movement had begun on the campus of the University of California at Berkeley, a town that was a fifteen-minute drive over the Bay Bridge from downtown San Francisco.

Arts of all kinds were part of this expression of freedom and rebellion, and poetry readings—the language-based art form in which ideas and attitudes are expressed with the most clarity—were, along with psychedelic rock and folk music, among the most frequently and numerously attended artistic events.

The weekly readings Laura, Steve, and I staged were a great success. The coffee shop was jammed for every performance, and I was learning more about organizing and publicizing with each event we put on. I was also being invited to give readings of my own in other venues in the Haight and in different parts of the city, and Clem Starck, Bob Peterson, and I gave a number of readings at different branches of the city library.

One of the people I met in the course of these events was a Yugoslav professor of literature named Alexander Nejgebauer who was in the United States on a Fulbright Fellowship. We struck up an acquaintance, and he and his wife came over for dinner. Eventually he asked if he could read translations at the I-Thou which he had made from the work of Yugoslavia's greatest contemporary poet, Vasko Popa. I thought it would be a novel event, different from most of the readings, and, getting Laura and Steve's approval, I accepted. Would I look over the translations and "brush them up?" Nejgebauer then asked. I shrugged in disinterested agreement, and he handed me an envelope containing a sheaf of poems. When I read the poems at home an hour later, I underwent one of those moments archaeologists must experience when they unexpectedly discover a treasure-laden tomb or a lost city. Even in their awkward English renditions, the originality and vision of Vasko Popa's poems shone with a mythic light that gripped me as the discovery of a poet's work seldom does. I felt an immediate kinship with Popa, although I recognized that we were completely different in temperament and approach.

Popa wrote sequences of short poems. The poems took their direction from riddles and, I discovered later, Serbian folktales. Poems from one sequence in particular, "Games," set me off on a three-month explosion of writing which within the year would turn out to be my first book. Like Popa's work, the poems I wrote were connected to each other, a series of sequences. From that point on, half my work has been conceived of in sequences. Popa had entered my consciousness. Several years later, he would enter my life.

Among the biggest productions Laura, Steve, and I organized were three fiestas of music, acting, and poetry to raise money for *El Corno Emplumado*, a bilingual literary journal based in Mexico City, which published Latin American and North American prose and poetry. The editors, Sergio Mondragon and his wife Margaret Randall, were to be present for the concluding fiesta, which was to be held in Glide Memorial Church. The first two fiestas were presented at different venues in the city, one in the Mission District and the second in the Haight at the I-Thou. The final presentation, with Sergio and Margaret present, featured many notable musicians and writers, including Michael McClure and Luis Valdez, a former member of the San Francisco Mime Troupe. Valdez had quit the troupe to organize a folk drama unit called Teatro Campesino to aid the striking grape workers trying to organize a union under their leader Cesar Chavez. His appearance at the fiesta was his first performance in San Francisco since he had left the city.

■ ■ ■

The Monday meetings of the Artists' Liberation Front became more and more turbulent and more emotionally exhausting. Fewer and fewer people were in attendance from one meeting to the next. Finally, I stopped going regularly, then not at all. In January 1967, I received a phone call inviting me to a goodbye party for the Front; the organization was disbanding. The party would be a "gathering of the tribes," the caller said, mostly the original members and a "few friends" of the organization. I should have known that the Artists Liberation Front was one of many alternative lifestyle groups being summoned, but it didn't occur to me.

So when I arrived at the Polo Grounds in Golden Gate Park that afternoon of January 14, 1967, I was greeted by an unexpected sight. The "few friends" had turned out to be twenty thousand people, painted, costumed, wearing garishly colored tie-dyed shirts and paisley-patterned blouses and trousers. The police had refused to supply security, and the Hell's Angels, who had become a peaceful presence at many Haight-Ashbury and Artists' Liberation Front events, filled the gap, keeping order where, it turned out, no security force was needed. Jefferson Airplane played rock music, Allen Ginsberg and Lawrence Ferlinghetti read poetry, and Jerry Rubin, Timothy Leary, and others spoke. Food, marijuana, and LSD (which had been outlawed the previous October by the California legislature) were passed around freely, along with food and drink.

I stood on a slope overlooking the Polo Fields with several friends from the Front, and we stared at the masses of people below, a crazy-quilt patchwork of colors. "Well, I guess we did it," one of us finally said. I nodded. What we had tried to do—ignite the minds and souls of the country to new political, social, and cultural possibilities—seemed to be rising like a phoenix out of the ashes of the Artist Liberation Front's demise. The next day the newspapers described the gathering as a "be-in." It was the first one. Woodstock wouldn't happen until two years later.

My involvement in all these activities implies that I was at the center of the social and cultural milieu of those years. But the truth is that I was on the periphery, and I think most people who had anything to do with those explosive times were on the periphery as well. Too much was going on in too many places around the city, and although a lot of the endeavors were merging into collective efforts, most of us were unaware of situations and events that were unfolding around the corners of the streets where we worked.

CHAPTER 20

George Hitchcock and *Kayak*

While all these activities were swirling about me during those San Francisco years, I was working more and more closely with George Hitchcock. Well over six feet tall, with a booming voice and the presence of a Prospero or Oedipus (both parts he had played on stage), Hitchcock was a commanding figure wherever he went. His style was baroque or, less kindly, flamboyant. He reminded me of those bigger-than-life character actors in Hollywood movies, like Wallace Beery and Charles Laughton, or like Vitamin Flintheart, the ostentatiously dressed and extravagantly posturing character in Dick Tracy comic books. Besides his work as a leading actor over the years with the city's Actors' Workshop, Hitchcock was a playwright and novelist before he turned his hand to poetry and editing in the late 1950s.

Hitchcock had come to San Francisco from Oregon in the 1930s and became Kenneth Rexroth's protégé and friend. During the 1930s and 1940s, he had traveled throughout California as a union organizer and had written columns under the alias "Lefty" for *The Western Worker* and *People's Daily World*. Later he taught philosophy at the California Labor School and was chairman of the Independent Socialist Forum in San Francisco. In 1957 he was called before the House Un-American Activities Committee (HUAC) and, in a famous verbal exchange with Frank S. Tavenner, Jr., counsel for the committee, admitted that he did underground work—on plants, because he was a gardener. That statement, and the laughter from the audience in the room that followed it, was heard via radio across the nation and amply illustrates Hitchcock's merry wit and irreverence for all sham and pomposity as did his statement a few minutes later that ". . . this hearing is a big bore and waste of the public's money."

When I began working as his assistant on the Neighborhoods Committee of the Artists' Liberation Front in 1966, he was over fifty years old, had given up his life as an activist, and lived with his wife Eva in a comfortable, rambling, three-story house on Laguna Street, a block from Union.

In 1957, Hitchcock had become poetry editor for the *San Francisco Review*, and when that magazine folded in the early 1960s, he founded *Kayak*, a magazine of poetry. His stint as editor with the *San Francisco Review* had taught him two important lessons—the only way to beat crushing printing costs was to print his journal himself; and to publish the work he liked, he'd have to be the sole arbiter of the contents. Thus, *Kayak*, a vehicle propelled in all respects by one person, was born in 1964.

The style as well as the contents of *Kayak* reflected the man. The magazine was filled with melodramatic engravings and illustrations clipped from nineteenth-century books and magazines. Many of these were usually pasted together as a collage and carried a witty line or two of dialogue or commentary, which ironically commented on the illustration or had some incisive parallel to current events.

The selection of work alternated between surrealist, deep image, or political poems, or all three at once. Hitchcock's rejection slips were florid sentences printed at the bottom of one of his seemingly endless selections of nineteenth-century illustrations. His editorial method was to accept any piece that appealed to him on first reading. The rest he sent back to the would-be con-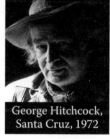 tributor within the week, or, in a typically flamboyant flourish I witnessed several times, he would cast an unacceptable manuscript into the nearest wastebasket. (He would always retrieve the discarded manuscript later and return it to the sender.)

George Hitchcock, Santa Cruz, 1972

Hitchcock's interest in surrealist, imagist, and sensuously surfaced poetry, which gave free rein to the imagination, was what I had been looking for as a home for my work since my first year at Iowa, and I had sent him several batches of poems before we started working together. He rejected all of them.

As his right hand on the Neighborhoods Committee—actually, his gofer—I learned not only a lot about organizing but about the man. His creative ingenuity never ceased to astound me. I would drop over to the house on Liberation Front business while he was printing an issue of the magazine or a book, and he would go about his business while listening to me or instructing me to do one thing or another.

One day I arrived just as he was preparing to do the illustrations for one of the early *Kayak* books. The artist he had contracted for the job had failed to deliver the illustrations, so George, as I stood talking to him, turned away from me, sauntered into the garden, pulled a handful of weeds, and transported them to the photo offset machine; then he scattered them on the glass, putting the resultant photographic plate on his press. Next he loaded different colored inks in the press, and ran the pages of what turned out to be an exquisite floral design in a multitude of swirling reds, greens, oranges and purples. Another time, he gathered a fistful of nuts and bolts and repeated the process with equally stunning, although quite different, results. Literally, it seemed, whatever he touched turned into art.

Even before he began publishing my work, Hitchcock invited me to join the *Kayak* collating parties. These were extraordinary affairs that occurred four times a year when Hitchcock—ever the host and organizer—assembled the finest poets in the Bay Area to put together the magazine at his home. He would load the kitchen table with cold cuts, bread, salads, and cakes, and stock the refrigerator with six-packs of beer and soda. Any poet of note who was passing through the city at the time would be there. W. S. Merwin was there several times, and once David Ignatow appeared, a mild little man wearing thick glasses who was making his first reading tour of the West Coast. He stood all afternoon against one of the living-room walls, while well-wishers and local poets came up to him and paid their respects. When the crowd around him thinned at one point, I went up to him and told him how much *The Gentle Weightlifter* had meant to me during my years in the air force. "You know," he said, "for years I thought my poems were disappearing into the void. But on this trip I've been surprised at the number of people who know my work." His last words were almost whispered, and I saw tears coursing down both his cheeks.

I met many poets at the collating parties who became lifelong friends, among them Robin Magowan, Ray Carver, Jack Marshall, Robert Peterson, Bert Meyers, Lennart Bruce, Robert Peters, and many others. I'm sure Hitchcock had made this meeting of poets, who would form alliances and share ideas one of the purposes of the collating parties. But only one. The main purpose was to put the magazine together and mail it off to its hundreds of subscribers around the world. Many of us would sit around showing each other names and addresses of internationally known poets who subscribed from such faraway places as Europe, India, Thailand, and Australia.

Hitchcock would assign newcomers one of five jobs—collating pages, folding covers, stapling pages and covers together, putting the magazine in envelopes, and addressing and stamping the envelopes. He would have people switch assignments every hour or so, which allowed the happy workers to meet other volunteers as well as not become dazed by production-line boredom and thereby make mistakes.

Starting with the second or third collating party, I attended almost every collating gathering of the magazine—definitely more than anyone else except Hitchcock himself, and Hitchcock would send newcomers to me to instruct them on the assembly process or on how to operate one or the other of the machines.

The magazine was usually collated by 6:00 PM, and all the volunteers were given bundles of magazines to mail in various parts of the city. Sometimes the last of us would go out to dinner or remain and talk. At other times, Hitchcock and one or two of the group would do impromptu dramatic improvisations, to everyone's delight. In time, Hitchcock bought a collating machine that abolished the tiresome circling of the dining room table to collect pages by hand. Soon, other simple machines appeared, all discarded or auctioned from old print shops. In addition to machinery,

Hitchcock managed to find disused rolls of paper that he hauled from factories free of charge most of the time. We made several runs to the factories together, and one day we picked up five or six rolls of a particularly heavy, porous beige paper.

"What's this?" I asked.

"Target paper from the army's shooting range," Hitchcock replied with a smile. "They'll be the pages for the next issue of the magazine," he said.

All in all, *Kayak*, in its design, content, and method of production, reinvigorated small-magazine publishing in the country and elsewhere in the world. Although Hitchcock went more and more to professional typesetters and printing companies as time went on, especially for Kayak books, he proved that literary journals could survive monetarily and at the same time have an exciting look. The magazine was also the only home in the country for a poetry based on all aspects of the image, and Hitchcock's high standards kept each issue's selection vital, compelling, and lively.

In 1967, Hitchcock was invited to Cuba by Fidel Castro to celebrate the eighth anniversary of the Cuban Revolution. He returned with several boxes of Cuban cigars, smuggled into the country for him by the Dutch ambassador, who he had met in Havana. Knowing my mystical pronouncements on cigars (for which he would wryly chide me), he called me up and invited me over for "a smoke." I remember we sat facing each other in his shadowy living room on that sunlit afternoon, puffing contentedly on our cigars, so comfortable together I don't think we said more than two words to one another in an hour. It was one of the best times I had in his presence.

Yes, one of the best times, for with all his talents and know-how, Hitchcock was a hard man to approach personally. I never stopped respecting and looking up to him and feeling a certain kind of affection for him. In many ways he was my teacher. To be candid, he was in many ways the ideal example of the father figure I had been unconsciously looking for all my life. Unlike Justice, whose art was constricting and whose personality was repressed, Hitchcock was expansive, earthy, larger than life, freewheeling, and endlessly inventive. But he was also gruff, impatient, and although he could be charming when he wanted to be, he was easily annoyed and had no tolerance for intimate conversation, anything he considered doctrinaire assumptions, or literary programs. In fact, he refused to be pinned down to any viewpoint or system of beliefs—a strange, if interesting, quality in a person who had been a political activist for years, although he once said that he disapproved of doctrinaire writing because for years as an activist editor he had to read and write it.

At any rate, all my attempts to get close to Hitchcock over the years were met with rebuffs. I don't think he was even aware that I was trying to get close because he was never really that interested in me. If anything, I annoyed him. When I was in his presence for more than half a day, he would become short-tempered with me, and on more than one occasion—to the embarrassment of younger poets present—he would unfairly yell at me for not working or for not keeping on one task or another.

The chief problem, however, was a difference in temperament and, once again, cultural background that, as I've already said, I encountered with many white, Anglo-Saxon American men. It was similar, I felt, to the reactions I would get at times from Jim Houston and others. They represented a world that was laconic and self-protective. They epitomized the self-controlled male who embraced deeds more than words, whereas I had come from the East Coast where Jews, Italians, blacks, and Irish ethnic attitudes were ameliorated into aggressive, intense, highly verbal ways of expressing themselves. My emotional enthusiasms, repartee, and constant machine-gun punning that turned language inside-out were pure Marx Brothers and made the stolid males with whom I came into contact, especially those from the western United States, uncomfortable, and even Hitchcock, for all his flamboyant posturing and verbal wit, in this sense was a Western male to the core. In fact, he was clearly annoyed at my chatter. So what could have been a deep friendship remained an acquaintanceship over the decades to come. Never allowing myself to be vulnerable in his presence, I came to look upon George as a benevolent despot who deigned to publish my work, alternately treating me as a fellow poet and a lowly subject.

Another problem was the differences in our motivations and practices. I was in intense pursuit of meaning and my place in the universe, even in my comic poems, whereas George loosed his considerable poetic talents in extravagant flights of linguistic flourishes. Poetry in many ways was a game to him, and at times he would include in the magazine the amusing, the witty, or the grotesque poem over the truly penetrating one. His own "Villa Thermidor" is a case in point:

> *Villa Thermidor*
>
> He sits in a deckchair reading Colette
> and fanning himself with a pair of
> shoelaces. In the rose garden
>
> giant snails copulate in rhythms
> undulant and infinitely beguiling.
> His ancestors lie snoozing
>
> in the family urns. Fog has lately
> attacked the poinsettias. On the pier
> by the lake there are adenoidal
>
> swellings—the boathouse no doubt
> is ill. Umbrellas are descried gliding
> above the local peaks.
>
> Undulant and infinitely beguiling.
> Next year, says the *Oakland Tribune*,
> snowshoes may be taxed

for their illicit oils. Stingrays
flap in the sand like wounded moths.
Infinite and undulant.

Cocktails are served from five
to seven at the bottom of the pool.

Hitchcock was at his best in short, lyrical nature poems, which usually consisted of a list of closely observed details from the natural world.

Afternoon in the Canyon

The river sings in its alcoves of stone.
I cross its milky water on an old log—
beneath me waterskaters
dance in the mesh of roots.
Tatters of spume cling
to the bare twigs of willows.

The wind goes down.
Bluejays scream in the pines.
The drunken sun enters a dark mountainside,
its hair full of butterflies.
Old men gutting trout
huddle about a smokey fire.

I must fill my pockets with bright stones.

When in the 1970s Hitchcock wrote a series of poems not only in closed verse but in forms for the first time—remember, he had not started writing poetry until the late 1950s— he scoffed at my admiring response to the pieces by saying they were easy to write. I remarked on how effortless the rhymes seemed, how natural the forms—how could they have been easy even for him to execute so professionally? He grinned with satisfaction and confided triumphantly that he had copied the rhymed words and the forms from poems he had found in old anthologies, discarded the rest of the poems, and "filled in" with his own words the lines he had erased. Then he sat back and enjoyed my obvious discomfort at the confession. He was being his most irreverent self, I realized, and I quickly regained my composure, telling him that I had several unpublished villanelles of my own that I would never even consider sending to a magazine. "Why not?" he said, suddenly interested, and smiled again. "Send them to me," he commanded, more amused than serious, and published one of them in the next issue of *Kayak*—one of the two, in fact, I had written for Don Justice in Iowa years before to prove that my subject matter was as reprehensible to him as my free verse.

Finally, the problems between George and I were exacerbated by, I think, his not seeing anything extraordinary in my poetry. But I may be laboring

Shirley Kaufman,
San Francisco,
1972

this point, since he regularly published my work over the years, including my first book.

It was during those first years of getting to know Hitchcock that I had discovered Vasko Popa and had experienced my first uncontrolled outpouring of writing poetry. I was in a small poetry group at the time, which consisted of Shirley Kaufman, Laura Ulewicz, and myself, and was presided over by a fatherly and wise fellow Jew named Larry Fixel, a writer of prose poems, parables, and aphorisms of extraordinary insight and originality. The four of us worked without regard to ego: we just wanted to write the best poems we could, and we listened to each other's perspectives almost fervently. Shirley was the star of the group. She was already a marvelous poet, although she had not yet published her first book. She was a beautiful woman, married with two small daughters, and always coiffed and outfitted as befitted the wife of a successful doctor. In time, she would become quite well-known, fall in love with a professor, move to Israel, travel all over Europe and Asia, and produce a poetry distinctly her own: clear and melodic as well as acutely insightful, whether talking about her family life, the Israeli situation, or her travels. Here is a later poem of hers.

Happy Endings

I want to write stories with happy endings.
I want to write about the good life.
Even if it's somebody else's. Pliny
had a good life here in his villa.
Better than any life in Rome.
Terraces and porticos, a small hippodrome
for riding, hot and cold baths, gravel paths
between boxwood all the way
to Bellagio. And best of all,
one room, remote and quiet,
where he lay in the dark each morning
composing his thoughts.

There's a spider next to Pliny's
left knee, composing his web.
Pliny's nose is broken.
He sits in his carved robes
holding a book in his hand with one finger
missing, watching the lake.
He can barely see the view
From his little stone eyes,
the scrub and the honeysuckle have grown wild
on the cliff before him.

The spider is doing what he knows best.
He spins from the knee to the hand of the statue
as if he were swinging on a kite string
across the whole sky. The late summer air
is thick with insects. It's a good life.
Even if it's somebody else's.

Larry, a contemporary of Hitchcock's, and a fellow activist from the 1930s, was to publish two books under the Kayak Press imprint. Tall and thin, he was a man of slow, measured movements and verbal responses, a man of thought and analysis who eschewed emotional turmoil and relished his role as the group's guiding spirit. His wife, Justine, a psychiatrist and painter, was always welcoming and buoyant. All of the group, as well as Justine, encouraged me to continue my feverish output and provided invaluable critical guidance. One of them must have told Hitchcock what I was doing because one day in the summer of 1968, he called me up and asked to see a manuscript of the new work. The result was the publication of my first book, *Origins*, by Kayak in 1969. I was as surprised by Hitchcock's decision to publish the book as I was by his phone call. But more surprises were to come. I would be dealing with Hitchcock long after I left San Francisco, and I would be considered by many young poets in the future not only a *Kayak* regular but a "*Kayak* poet."

■ ■ ■

If the Artists' Liberation Front dissolved in 1967, my activities in San Francisco continued. I still set up readings with Laura and Steve at the I-Thou and gave readings of my own work in the Haight and around the city.

In either late 1967 or early 1968, the Greek poet Nanos Valaoritis, who had arrived in San Francisco shortly before, and with whom I had become friendly, joined our small poetry group and asked me to take part in a reading against the dictatorship of The Colonels who had seized control of the Greek government in the spring of 1967. The reading was to feature Eleni Kazantzakis, the widow of Niko Kazantzakis, the internationally known Greek writer. Entitled "Freedom or Death," after the title of a Kazantzakis novel, the event was to be a mixture of literature and speeches by writers and Greek politicians in exile. I was already a Grecophile, for reasons I will go into later, and was honored to be included.

It turned out that I was the only non-Greek among the seven speakers, which included Mrs. Kazantzakis. The event took place to a packed audience of hundreds at the old Fugazi Hall in North Beach. The presentations were impassioned, but the audience was quiet, seemingly unresponsive, maybe out of respect for the seriousness of the occasion, until I read my poem. Then they leaped to their feet, applauding and cheering, as did my fellow speakers who were seated on stage behind me. Whatever I read must have been an extraordinarily rabble-rousing piece, but no matter how hard I try to remember what it was or how many times I search through my old poems, I can't recall its name. The reading and my connection with Nanos, which had begun to seem predestined through his earlier meetings with Norman Thomas and Robert Peterson, would eventually lead to my going to Greece.

I was also involved in other antiwar rallies and marched as a veteran against the conflict in Vietnam. On one occasion, I took nine Lick students to Oakland to join the demonstrations that had been going on at the draft center. It was the day the demonstrations turned violent, and I found myself in the middle of the police crack-down, with batons flying, tear gas billowing around us, and bloody demonstrators running in panic. It was a frightening personal experience made more terrifying by my knowledge that I was responsible for the nine teenagers in my charge. I hurried them down one street after another only to find that every possible escape route was blocked by police in anonymous riot gear. Finally, I led the students down a quiet side street and told them to follow me as I ran toward a phalanx of cops and slowed down in front of the armed men who waited like a wall as we approached. I stopped with an open hand in front of the line and began talking, saying something like, "I've got kids here. They're only kids. Let us through." The panic in my voice was evident. Suddenly, one side of the line turned and let us pass. It was a risk that could have ended disastrously, but to this day I feel nothing but gratitude to whoever gave the signal to let us proceed without incident.

■ ■ ■

The media called the summer of 1967 "the Summer of Love," but it was really a time of turbulence and uncertainty, liable to turn violent at any moment. So many issues were coming to a head—social, political, racial—that a simple slogan is inadequate to describe the times. A criminal element, including Charles Manson, had appeared in the Haight. There were several murders purported to be drug related. The atmosphere in the Haight had turned ominous.

The winter of 1968 marked a turning point in my writing. Hitchcock had signed to do my first book, and several of my poems had been selected to appear in the first anthology of new American poetry in more than a decade, *The Young American Poets*. But times in the city were changing.

In April 1968, my daughter Valerie was born after several false labor episodes, and even though I was working full-time at Lick, I could not afford to pay the medical bills. That June, thanks to the intervention of Jim Houston, now a Stegner Fellow at Stanford with his first novel out, I received my MA. When the principal at Lick refused to give me a raise, I knew my days in the city were coming to an end. Then Jim Houston set up an interview for me at Cabrillo College in Santa Cruz County, and my premonitions became reality. Jim and Jeanne had been urging me to move to Santa Cruz ever since Wilma and I had returned from New York four years before. Now we were ready.

Friends in the Haight were ready, too. Every weekend, streams of tourists and weekend hippies in their cars created traffic jams all over the Haight-Ashbury District, as they gawked at the inhabitants. More and more young people arrived in the city in search of drugs and excitement, Most of them had nowhere to stay and wandered aimlessly down Haight, Ashbury, and Masonic streets, looking for an exotic life that NBC or CBS told them they would find in San Francisco. The psychedelic shop had closed more than a year before, with a funeral procession of locals following a black-velvet-covered casket through the Haight, an event many called "the death of the hippie." A number of my friends knew then that the Haight's years of turmoil and creativity were over. Now I knew it too. When the president of Cabrillo College called and offered me a contract to join the English faculty, I consulted with Wilma and agreed to the offer. A month later we reluctantly said goodbye to San Francisco.

BOOK SEVEN

SANTA CRUZ 1

CHAPTER 21

Santa Cruz and Joseph Stroud

In the summer of 1968, Santa Cruz was still a small, rural county hugging the California coast seventy miles south of San Francisco. Its boundaries extended twenty miles inland through a landscape of mountains and redwood forests, while the town of Santa Cruz sat on the northern point of Monterey Bay, which curved in a rough half circle to the city of Monterey on its southern tip, forty miles away.

Most of Santa Cruz's population consisted of farmers, fishermen, shop workers, and retirees. The only industries were the Wrigley gum and Lipton tea factories on the outskirts of the town of Santa Cruz, and the farms, apple storage sheds, and food freezing and canning plants in Watsonville and "south county."

But cosmopolitan changes were already taking place by the time Wilma and I arrived with our two girls. In 1965, the University of California opened its ninth campus on the old Henry Cowell ranchero above the town of Santa Cruz. More important to me, the county had established a community college several years earlier whose administrators and teachers were actively changing the county's political, social, and cultural world. Receptive to new ideas from its rambunctious instructors, the president, Robert Swenson, and the vice president, Floyd Younger, encouraged faculty classroom experimentation as well as participation in community affairs. It was this school, Cabrillo College, with its visionary instructors and dynamic administrators, where I had been hired to teach English.

With Jeanne Houston's help, Wilma and I looked at one house after another, hoping to live by the sea. But shortly before we moved, we found a rental high in the Santa Cruz Mountains. It was part of an undeveloped forty-acre parcel, well off the road, owned by an old couple who lived in a small house at the front of the property. Our house, which had been the main house when the owners were young and raising a family, looked out on a cleared area through which a stream ran beneath a shady acacia tree. The back of the house sat in the shadowy confines of a dense redwood grove. The rest of the property consisted of dirt trails and gravel paths that continued onto thousands of uninhabited acres of county water-table land hidden beneath a dense Redwood forest. There were no fences or boundary markers in the shadowy woods, and I was free to wander wherever I liked in the

uphill-downhill landscape. Occasionally the trees opened on an unexpected upland meadow and led, in
one direction, to an abandoned
quarry. The quarry dramatically fell
more than a thousand feet in three
tiers and resembled, even with its
rusty machinery, the ruins of an
ancient civilization.

After tentatively exploring the
edges of this tree-darkened world, I
plunged deeper and deeper into it,
spending whole days roaming through
it alone, or taking six-year-old Jana or
Wilma with me for short walks. Soon I

Clockwise from top: Wilma, Jana, and
Valerie, Santa Cruz Mountains, 1969

was carrying a light backpack filled with sandwiches and bottles of water on my
jaunts, and after the first poems announced themselves in my head, I added a
spiral notebook to my gear, tied to a belt loop by one of Wilma's old Kotex
belts. The word "announced" is carefully chosen here because I was not writing the poems but hearing them—in many cases fully written—in my head.
The whole process was mysterious and at times frightening, to say the least.
But I gave myself up to whatever was happening to me. Sometimes I would sit
on a lichen-covered, fallen tree trunk and watch the play of light and shadow or
observe the animal life—birds and deer mostly—that would go about their
business around me, unconcerned, after I had remained still for a while. At
other times I would nap and be jolted awake by voices seeming to whisper
from the wind or mutter from the mulch of leaves that carpeted the trails and
hillsides around me. At such times I would swing up the notebook on its elastic
cord and write what I "heard." Am I being fanciful here or giving in to poetic
delusion? Whatever I was experiencing, it was the impetus that accounted for
hundreds of short, Chinese- and haiku-like poems in the next three years, and,
more important, put me intimately in touch with, I still like to think, a mysterious element in my surroundings. Jim Houston defined it as my discovery of
nature, and I'm sure he's correct. I was a city boy, and even though I had
attended schools in the countryside outside of Manhattan, in Santa Cruz I was
living in a closeness with nature I had never experienced before.

As if to increase my newfound identity as nature poet, I turned a one-
room hut close to the house into an office. The hut had been a chicken coop
and contained a potbellied stove and electricity. I moved in a desk, chair,
bed, and carpet, and painted the walls white. Still, I was never able to get rid
of the odor of chicken shit, which was as oppressive as the heat on summer
days and as disturbing as the fat black carpenter bees I encountered every
day on entering the hut. The bees either buzzed half-dead about the room,
looking for a way out, or their corpses lay scattered over the furniture.

In 1971, I chose the best of the poems I had been writing outdoors for the previous three years and arranged them in a sequential order that approximated not only a day-long walk through the mountains but, simultaneously, a trip through a year. I called the manuscript *The Santa Cruz Mountain Poems*. The final versions of the poems revealed that I had continued to purify my notions of language, a process that had begun in the unpunctuated poems of *Origins*, and that I was once more employing Popa's practice of sequencing to a greater degree than in the earlier book. I was not conscious of these concerns during the writing, and the final work was nothing I could have imagined when I began "recording" the forest voices.

■ ■ ■

I quickly adjusted to life at work. Teaching at Cabrillo was exhilarating because I could design my own classes—within the prescribed state regulations of what each class was to accomplish, of course.

That fall I began a poetry series at Cabrillo. At that time, community colleges had special departments called Community Services, whose job was to provide nonclassroom culture for the community. Monthly art shows and foreign films and speakers of state or national prominence were featured in the program. I talked the director of the services to bring poetry into the mix by providing me with a budget to bring poets to campus who had published at least one book.

George Hitchcock was the first poet I chose. He drove from the city, participated in a gathering of four English classes, and gave a reading. He was in fine form, and the response, in attendance and appreciation, was excellent. In the course of his meeting with the classes, he was asked what writing accomplished as far as his well-being was concerned. His answer jolted me. He said he wrote to achieve "heightened consciousness" for as many minutes or hours as he was able to attain it each day. It reminded me of the

In 1970s garb, Santa Cruz, 1974

beginning of a Richard Eberhart poem I had repeated to myself over and over almost daily since I had first read it, "If I could only live at the pitch that is near madness." Hitchcock's quest for heightened consciousness struck me as the precise rendering of that line in two words, and I have used the phrase ever since to explain my pursuit of the creative life.

I took Hitchcock on a tour of Santa Cruz, and he was so impressed by the mountains and the town that he said he would move there within the year. A year later, he managed to get himself a lectureship at the university and purchased a Wagnerian house with a stream running through it high in the mountains among the Redwoods. It was only two miles from my house. For the next several years we were neighbors.

Through Hitchcock and my own contacts, I sent word far and wide about the poetry series, and soon I had more poets requesting readings than I could handle. In addition to old friends and other poets from San Francisco—such as Michael McClure, Shirley Kaufman, Nanos Valaoritis, Larry Fixel, Lennart Bruce, Diane DiPrima, Mary Korte, Jack Marshall, Jack Gilbert, Robert Peterson, Andre Codrescu, Ray Carver, Robert Hass, Gary Soto, Al Young, C. G. Hanzlicek, and James B. Hall—there were poets on tour from all over the country, including Robert Bly, Charles Simic, Galway Kinnell, Allen Ginsberg, John Logan, Robert Peters, Robin Magowan, and a number of others whose names were a veritable roll call of the best American poets of the last half of the twentieth century. All would appear for a pitifully small fee, making Cabrillo part of their itinerary if they were already booked in San Francisco, San Jose, or Monterey.

The following year, I began presenting readings in downtown Santa Cruz after realizing how many first-rate writers and emerging young writers lived in the area. My idea was to have two readers present their work one night a week in a local restaurant. One of the readers would be an established author who would present new work; the other would be a young writer I would select on the basis of work submitted to me. The downtown readings were not restricted to writers who had published books, although all the established writers had. The readings featured fiction writers as well as poets. Among the

Front, left to right: Victor Perera, Peter S. Beagle, James D. Houston, Morton Marcus, William Everson, Anne Steinhardt, James B. Hall, Lou Mathews. *Rear, left to right:* Mason Smith, George Hitchcock, John Deck, Stephen Levine, T. Mike Walker, Nels Hanson, Robert Lundquist. Santa Cruz, 1972.

established writers I had to choose from were Jim Houston, of course, and Peter Beagle, Mary Norbert Korte, Bill Everson, John Deck, Ray Carver, George Hitchcock, James B. Hall, and Victor Perera.

Anyone who read received a meal for two and all the wine or beer they could drink, which was the deal I had worked out with the owners of the three restaurants where the readings were held over the next five years. The readings would start at 9 PM, after the dinner hour, and although they were free to the public, the restaurants, all fine-dining establishments, gained publicity and made money on desserts and drinks with the crowds that packed the premises every week.

It was a time of extraordinary creative energy in Santa Cruz. Handicrafts were thriving, especially in Davenport, a small hamlet in the north end of the county, which had become the virtual center of the ceramics' world in America. Al Johnson was teaching pottery at the university and throwing pots at his Big Creek Pottery studio; and Bruce and Marcia McDougal's pottery school down the road offered courses by world-renowned pottery figures, one of whom, Daniel Rhodes, came to live in the area in the 1980s. Marcia was the housemother, so to speak, to the thirty or so students who attended the six-week course. It wasn't long after I discovered Big Creek and the school that I was visiting both on a regular basis. At Big Creek I spent several afternoons reading poetry and discussing the world with Al while he and his assistants threw pots. Bruce and Marcia became special friends over the years, and I often entertained the students at the school with poetry readings while also cooking gourmet meals for everyone on the premises. On several occasions, I read at the McDougals' Christmas craft show, writing poems on the surfaces of platters, plates, pitchers, and vases. Bruce specially prepared the surfaces of the pots ahead of time, and immediately after I incised my poems with a wooden pencil, we sold the piece to the highest bidder. An hour or two before I began, Bruce made sure to fuel my creative inspiration with cup after cup of mulled wine.

Not only were the energy and camaraderie among the artists extraordinary during those years, but the visitors and local populace supported the artists and craftspeople as well.

JOSEPH STROUD

One of the delightful surprises of my first year at Cabrillo was to discover that Joe Stroud had been hired by the English department too. He was introduced to me as John Logan's protégé when I first met him in John's apartment the night of the party in 1965. We had met several times since then, and he had been a student in Hitchcock's class at San Francisco State in 1967, to which George had invited me to speak as guest poet one day. Cabrillo was Joe's first teaching job, he told me, and he was happy to see a familiar face. We quickly arranged to have offices next to each other, and our devotion to poetry has bonded us in a forty-year friendship. There is no doubt that I was included in the Logan circle because Joe and I were friends. We would go up to the city together or wherever John might be visiting from the East Coast. And there is also no doubt that Joe influenced the poetry I wrote through my years at Cabrillo since we critiqued each other's work continuously—and ruthlessly.

Joseph Stroud, Santa Cruz, 1982

Logan's unerring taste had been particularly incisive in Joe's case. Joe is a master poet whose exquisite language affects all who read or hear his poems. Mostly he writes personal lyrics, which show his sensitivity and Romantic temperament. Tall, good-looking, and athletic, he loves nature, which serves as background to much of his work, and he is given to solitary excursions into the most remote wildernesses.

Joe and I have had a complex relationship down through the years. There are inner conflicts in him I have never been able to plumb. When asked by the editors of such journals as *Choice, Kayak,* and *Ironwood* to submit work, he did. But after I passed on to him the names of magazines and editors, as well as invitations I would receive to submit poems for anthologies, he wouldn't send them work. He claimed that publication was not important to him and that he expected to write only three books in his lifetime. But when he would come across my poems in a journal or anthology, his jaw would harden or he would become openly angry because, I thought, his work was not included. Ironically, of course, I had given him every one of the invitations to those publications a year or so before my work appeared in them. I imagined that his refusal to send out work was because he didn't like being rejected, but he said it was more complicated than that; a big part of it, he insisted, was disgust at the whole poetry scene, with its careerism, scrambling for publication and notice, self-promotion, and egoism. All in all, I have no doubt that if he had submitted work to journals and anthologies, he would have become one of the best-known and most highly respected poets in America.

Joe's personality was equally paradoxical. It seemed to me that he was unconsciously trying to maintain a balance between his father's hearty masculinity and his mother's sensitivity and aesthetic tastes. His dad was a charmer, a lady's man for whom appearance was everything, and he was out and about a good deal of the time. His mother was a reader with a weak heart who spent much of her married life around the household. Joe reflected his parents' dichotomy by being as crude as any fraternity boy one moment and sensitive and compassionate the next, giving vent to sudden tears over the sufferings of both people and animals. Joe had a twin brother who, in my mind, became a metaphor for the conflict. A businessman and

former football star who had played in the Rose Bowl, he couldn't understand Joe's creative impulses, and he became for me a Mr. Hyde to Joe's Dr.
Jekyll. When I told Joe this, he replied that the metaphor was too simple and
added insightfully that as far as he and his brother were concerned, "I don't
think one of us was a monster and the other not." In retrospect I saw the
depth of this statement, for even in his nature poems Joe's gaze is drawn
away from the pastoral to the darkness of primal existence: the two
extremes war with each other and provide much of the dramatic tension in
his poetry. Here's an early poem that illustrates all aspects of that dualism—
as well as his vision of himself as poet—and the rich, almost formal diction
and hushed tone of his early work.

In the House of Silk

When I was a boy
I dreamed in a house of stained-glass wings.
Each morning was a summer of listening.
The soft-tongued birds outside my window.
The opening flowers. I would lie in bed
And watch a breeze rustle the curtains.
I promised myself never to touch the words in my throat,
So my brothers would never know who I was
When we climbed the hills behind our house.

Once I spent a whole day
Crawling through rotted leaves and ferns.
I came upon a clearing
Where the sun laced some white-lipped ivy
And gold pollen eddied like snow
Into the center of a spider's web.
I knelt until I found her
Nestled against a leaf, face sparkling with eyes.
Each skinny leg cramped under her
Like crooked children at suck.

I wanted her to come out of the dark.
So I stabbed my tongue
Through that thin carpet of silk
And drained from the moist threads
The inner gleaming of a spider's heart.
She would not come out.
I think she knew the flesh that tore her home
Had no wings or eyes.
Or perhaps she felt the sudden cries of bees
Swelling in my throat.

That night, my brothers asleep,
I rubbed my sticky fingers beneath the pillow,
And dreamed of women with silk hair,
And those small, needled mouths
That sewed my lips with kisses.

An ardent traveler after 1974, Joe toured the world, fashioning from his journeys poems that were poignant and highly emotional glimpses into the human condition. Like his early work, the poems showed the beauty and suffering of life, in most cases in the lives of the people he encountered as they enacted age-old rituals, suffered through wars and other political abuses, and experienced the joys and sorrows of life.

Below Mount T'ui Koy
Home of the Gods,
Todos Santa Cuchumatan
Guatemalan Highlands

He stumbled all morning through the market,
Drunk and weeping, a young Mayan whose wife
Had died. Whenever he encountered someone he knew,
He'd stop and wail, waving his arms, and try
To embrace them. Most pushed him away,
or ignored him. So he'd stand there like a child,
Forlorn, his face contorted with grief,
Lost among the piles of corn and peppers,
The baskets of bananas, avocados, and oranges,
The turkeys strung upside down, the careful
Pyramids of chicken eggs, the women
In their straw hats and rainbow *huipils*,
The men smoking cornsilk cigarettes,
Meat hanging from the butchers' stalls
(chorizo, goat heads, tripe, black livers),
As everyone talked, laughed, or bartered,
And young boys played soccer in the courtyard,
The Roman priest, like a thin raven, elbowing
His way through the crowds, rain clouds
Swarming from far down the coast, the sun
Shattered among the pines on the high ranges,
And weaving through all of it the sound
Of women who sang over a corpse in an earthen house,
Keening a music like a distant surf breaking
Within the very heart of the mountain.

In the 1990s, Joe simplified his already precise language, and his poems became quieter but even more celebrational than before. Life's tenuousness is more apparent than ever, and Joe's obsession with death, which can be seen even in his earliest poems, is more evident. A later poem about France's Auvergne region recalls his use of foreign places as the basis of a good portion, but certainly not a majority, of his poems. The difference here is that he had not been to the Auverge at the time he wrote the poem but set it up as an ideal, if not a symbolic, oasis in our troubled times.

Auvergne

Oc, Dieu d'amor
Quora me donas jòi, quora m'en ven dolor
—Rambaud de Vaqueiràs

Why should the mindless singing
of the mockingbird high in the avocado tree
so much please me? Or the lure of light
these winter mornings the first days of War? —
as our Century comes down.

I sit on a bench
reading the eight-hundred-year-old poems of a Sufi dervish.
So where is the Beloved Friend? Is it this dog
sleeping at my feet under the shadow of a cow skull
nailed to the fence?

I believe
I no longer believe in the romance of the body.
Once, twenty years ago, in that other country,
in Auvergne, I knelt down inside the fire.
Of my beloved, I remember most her quiet words,
the taste of comice, warm rain in the orchard,
our little happiness inside us. That's not the All
of it. Rumi says, *The price of a kiss from the Beloved*
is your life. What a bargain! But I was a thief,
I did not pay.

Like everybody,
like you, I returned from that country of love
alive. From nights of the Auvergne. The river Lot
with its shade trees in summer, arbors of dusty grapes,
white honey from the blossoms of rosemary,
fields where the dragon sang inside the writhing
mouths of poppies where the black seeds catch fire.

Returned
to the mockingbird, crazed, singing out of season.
To my dog, stretching now, who turns
and shoves her snout over my book, jowls
slobbering on Rumi's ecstatic poem to the Beloved.

What
does she know, this trusting, dumb creature
who forgives me everything? Is *The cure for pain*
in the pain? Grinning, tongue out, tail thrashing,
she knows something is up.

In the next Millennium,
among the nightmares and machines, among time's
indifferent slaughter of our body, there must be poems
to make room of silence, to praise birdsong in winter light,
to sing of Auvergne, the Friend, and the old promises of love.

Joe and I were in competition in several areas, although neither of us acknowledged it at first. I think my numerous publications created one area of conflict, but only because Joe wouldn't submit his work to journals or anthologies. Another was our different personalities. Although he could be gregarious when he wanted to be, Joe was essentially a solitary and loved his privacy. He was also basically passive, whereas I was aggressive.

Our differences found many points of conflict. Joe had been an outstanding basketball player in high school, and we challenged each other to a series of one-on-one games during the first year we worked together. They were cut-throat contests in which Joe, younger, taller, and sharper, would pot-shot me to oblivion for the first half of the game and then run out of steam, after which I'd drive past him left and right, so that each match ended inconclusively.

Joe's lack of stamina showed up in several ways. He tired quickly and seemed to tire of me. I determined that my intensity, as I thought it did with other people, wore on him. After a few hours of my company, he would start to withdraw and his eyes glaze over. My energy level also was a factor, and he was almost always the one to end a night out due to exhaustion.

There were similarities between us too. Like me, Joe was obsessive and continually discovered new outlets for his curiosity. One was pool: for several years he played daily and even purchased his own cue. I had only dabbled in the sport, and he beat me handily. Then, just as suddenly as he had become enthralled with pool, he dropped it. Another outlet was chess. Within a year after discovering it, he was a master and challenged me to a match. I'd never really learned to play and had neither the head nor the patience for the game and told him so. But he thought I was bluffing. I remember the day we finally sat down at his handmade, polished wooden chessboard and he beat me three times in the space of five minutes. He was so embarrassed, he didn't know what to say. Within a few years, as he had with pool, he abandoned chess.

But it was poetry that knotted us together and at the same time provided us with a battlefield for our most bitter arguments. We both loved it beyond reason but in our different ways. For the first several years at Cabrillo, we team-taught creative writing together, sitting on either side of a long table or in the living room of a student's home, critiquing student poems from opposite sides of the room and opposite sides of the critical spectrum. I thought the classes were exhilarating, and so did the students after they realized they were getting two ways of looking at what a poem was and how it worked.

Those classes also brought many of our differences into focus. For one, Joe was offended by my acceptance of a wide range of poetry and poetics, and when I disagreed with him on those matters, he became exasperated. For my part, I saw his canon of what constituted good poetry and good poets as extremely narrow. He defined his position once as a kind of belief in the absolute and sacred coherence between the world and the word, nothing more, nothing less, and an intolerance for anything else. To me that meant he was dealing exclusively with the world around him, a world I saw as one of appearances and reflections of individual perspectives. As I understood the difference, his "absolute and sacred coherence between the world and the word" was my using the word along with the imagination to recreate the world or create it in new ways from different viewpoints, and clashes between us on this notion were inevitable.

It occurred to me more than once that Joe was everything I was not, and, in turn, that I was everything he was not. In many ways, we were each other's alter ego, and the tension that arises from such a relationship would, to the good, keep me from becoming too self-satisfied over the years but would also flare up from time to time in explosive anger on his side or mine.

For the first fifteen years at Cabrillo, Joe and I gave readings together all over California. We also went to Oregon on tour one year, and in 1989, we journeyed to Australia with another colleague to give a series of readings on the East Coast. They were memorable times. But then Joe decided that he no longer wanted to give public readings and, I think, especially not with me. My flamboyant theatrics and clowning offended his sense of the seriousness, or maybe more accurately the sacredness, of poetry. But nothing could separate us, no matter how much we argued or how near we sometimes came to blows. So when I was asked to do the poetry show on the community radio station in 1985, Joe became my partner. Again we were traveling around together, this time interviewing poets, recording readings, and doing special programs on one poet or another. When the Loma Prieta earthquake struck in 1989, Joe wanted to put on a benefit for the downtown bookstores, which had been heavily damaged, and together we put on *The Great Santa Cruz Word Quake Benefit*, enlisting sixty Santa Cruz writers for the daylong event. Poetry had brought us together again, no matter how differently we may have viewed its practice. And I never denied the exceptional work Joe was doing, such as this wonderful little poem, one of hundreds he wrote in the 1990s in a six-line form he invented:

The First Law of Thermodynamics

He was a good ole boy, and when he died his friends carried out
his final wish—the body was cremated and the ashes stuffed
into shotgun shells. They walked through the woods he loved
and fired aimlessly into the trees—he came down everywhere
in a powdery rain, a pollen of ashes that once was the memory
of a boy walking under trees showering him with leaves.

I'm sure Joe viewed our relationship differently than I've recorded, and most of our run-ins we both viewed as comical after the fact. One of the problems was that Joe usually wanted peace and quiet and time to contemplate the world and had to put up with my endless ranting, punning, nonstop chatter, and shenanigans, all of which frazzled his nerves—and most of the time he had to put up with them in a closed car for hours on end.

A typical instance occurred in the early 1980s. Driving back to Santa Cruz from the reading tour we did together in Oregon, Joe wanted to stop for something to eat. We were on Highway 101, an hour or two over the California border, in the midst of the giant redwood forests, no town in sight. I told Joe to wait until we came to a town with a Chinese restaurant.

He looked at me solemnly, with a look of foreboding of what was to come. "I don't care if it's Chinese. I just want something to eat," he said.

"*Chinese* is not the idea," I said with, as usual, complete conviction. "The Chinese restaurants in these small towns are hidden gems. American food, Chinese, they cook both and are the best places. Trust me."

We drove on and on, looking for a Chinese restaurant in one remote village after another, Joe more and more nauseous with hunger, getting more irritated by the mile, and pointing with increased desperation to every diner or fast-food drive-in we passed.

Finally, we found a Chinese restaurant in downtown Ukiah.

"Now you'll see the wait was worth it," I said as we parked.

Joe was almost doubled over as we hurried into the restaurant and ordered several items from the menu which, I was happy to see, came steaming to the table a short time later.

But all the orders were uniformly gray and glutinous with chunks of what looked like boiled alley cat—and all were inedible.

We left without swallowing a mouthful. I think Joe picked up an egg salad sandwich at a diner several blocks away and gobbled it down, staring me in the eye as he chewed with an intensity that resembled a gnashing of teeth.

I didn't say a word for the rest of the trip home.

■ ■ ■

The most serious breach in our relationship occurred in the late 1990s. If my aggressiveness and intensity grated on his nerves, the way I embellished stories and interpreted the world and people in my poetry incensed him. He called it my "spinning" the truth to aggrandize my ego and to prop up the content in my poetry. I didn't agree: I saw my embellishments as one of many ways an artist taps his imagination, and the imagination was the soul of art for me. I also saw it as just another difference in our personalities as well as in our attitudes toward our art. As time went on, my "spinning" became more and more of an issue for Joe, and he began to distrust my motives in writing poetry and to see my poems as a collection of lies. This hurt me greatly because I thought that he of all people, a fellow artist I respected and a friend who I thought understood me and saw through my joviality and bluster, knew me better than that. The day he finished reading one of my poems in the back room of the English Department and shouted that it was a lie, precipitated a separation of three years, during which we didn't talk to each other. Then one night in 2002, he came up to me after a reading at a Santa Cruz bookstore and asked if I had heard about the death of a fellow poet and mutual friend. I told him I had and a moment later we embraced like old comrades-in-arms, which in many ways we were.

At about the time of our rift, Joe began publishing with Copper Canyon, who brought out two of his books by 2005. The books reached the eyes of several major American poets who were publishing with the press, and they wrote to him, telling him of their delight in his work. Finally the recognition Joe never sought had found him.

If my description of Joe seems ambivalent, it's because I have been closer to him than to most people and have therefore seen him in many different situations and moods, and not least because I am trying to explain to myself the nature of my relationship with him. A fitting anecdote to end this section will show my affection for him and, I hope, leave the reader with the impression of Joe I want to be remembered.

In early 2006, Ted Koozer, then Poet Laureate of the United States, awarded Joe the celebrated Witter Bynner Prize, which consisted of $10,000 and a reading of his poems at the Library of Congress. Joe flew off to Washington with his usual trepidations but gave a reading that was well received by the audience. At the reception after the reading, one of his hosts asked if he would be interested in touring the library. I would have accepted the invitation, possibly inquired about restaurants in the area she would recommend, and left it at that. But Joe answered that, yes, he would appreciate a tour, and added, "What I'd really like to see are your archival holdings of Walt Whitman and Emily Dickinson." When he arrived at the library the next afternoon, he found a tour guide waiting for him with a typed itinerary. The guide led him to several underground rare book rooms. In one, he saw a handwritten copy by Robinson Jeffers of his poem "To The Stone Cutters," a letter from Hemingway to Archibald McLeish about Ezra Pound, and, in another basement room, laid out especially for him, a letter from Emily Dickinson, another from Emerson to Whitman, and the early notebooks of Whitman and the first edition of *Leaves of Grass*. Joe was allowed to hold and read through the last two items, and he told me that the experience was one of the most memorable of his life. In fact, he talked about nothing else concerning the trip. So moved was he to be holding the oversized copy of *Leaves of Grass*, which Whitman had printed himself, he said, that he had to quickly return the volume to the curator of the room because tears were welling in his eyes and he was afraid he might stain the pages.

That's the Joe Stroud I prize, who loves poetry as much I do, and who has taught me so much about my own poetry in the forty years of our tumultuous friendship.

Now we see each other all the time and either ignore the sore spots of our relationship or joke about them. But mostly we just enjoy each other's company, eating and talking the nights away and sipping one alcoholic beverage or another while smoking cigars and casually making sure we respect each other's foibles.

CHAPTER 22

Czeslaw Milosz

My first two years in Santa Cruz were highly eventful. In the fall of 1968, I drove to Berkeley to take part in a reading with Ronald Johnson, Dennis Schmitz, and Jack Marshall. The occasion was the publication of the first important anthology of new American poetry in ten years. The anthology consisted of fifty-five poets under forty years of age who the editor, Paul Carroll, deemed the best of the new poets in America, and I was surprised and delighted that he had chosen me to be among them. The anthology was named *The Young American Poets*, and the publisher gave the book a big national publicity campaign, featuring readings by the poets in the sections of the country where they lived.

Since there were twelve poets from Northern California in the anthology, the company had set up three readings in San Francisco and Berkeley, each reading introduced by a well-known older poet in the area. For our reading, the publisher hired Kenneth Rexroth to be master of ceremonies and guide, and the company treated us to a dinner at a restaurant of Rexroth's choice. Rexroth chose a stylish French bistro in Berkeley, fussed over the menu as if we were his children, and ordered several bottles of expensive wine while regaling the four of us with wonderful tales and some highly unorthodox opinions, such as his comment that the anthology was already passé since the poetry of the future would be "off the page," or completely based on performance.

Slightly inebriated, but in an elated mood, the five of us made our way by foot to the campus to find a crowd of three or four hundred waiting for us in Wheeler Hall. I read second, after which there was an intermission and members of the audience crowded around us, clucking their praises at what they had heard. One of their number, a middle-aged man with high cheekbones, pushed ahead of the others and stood quivering in front of me. "You come home with me!" he demanded in a strong Slavic accent. Tears were coursing down his cheeks, and he had obviously been crying for some time.

I didn't know what to say and was as confused as the people around me.

Czeslaw Milosz,
Nobel Prize poet,
Berkeley,
1984

"Come home with me!" he repeated.

"Well, thank you," I finally said, "but—"

"I open special wine for us," he interrupted me.

The crowd around us began to thin.

"I'd like to," I said, "but I have classes tomorrow and a long ride—"

The man straightened, regained his composure, and said, "Oh, you think I am weird," and stalked away, heading for Rexroth, who was talking to several people. The man grabbed Rexroth by the arm and dragged him over to me. "Kenneth, introduce!" he commanded.

"Well, yes," said Rexroth in his most grandiose world-weary manner, as if bored by the man's feverish behavior. "Morton Marcus," he said, "this is Czeslaw Milosz."

I was surprised but immediately understood the man's agitation. I had read a number of poems from my forthcoming book, citing the influence on them of post–World War II East European poetry, especially Polish poetry, and recommended Milosz's anthology *Post-War Polish Poetry* to the audience. I was honored to meet him and grasped his hand warmly.

"Wonderful poetry," he said, referring to my reading. He was still extremely moved. "Now you come home with me."

I refused again, once more citing my ride back to Santa Cruz that night and early classes the next day as my excuse, but we made an appointment for dinner at his house two weeks later.

In 1968, Milosz, who would become the 1980 Nobel Prize laureate, was virtually unknown as a poet in the United States. His reputation here, if he had one, was based on a political volume in which he described the reasons for his defection from Communist Poland in 1951 and another volume, a novel, about the miseries of living under a Communist regime. The first book, *The Captive Mind,* as well as the second, *Seizure of Power,* came out in the 1950s. Milosz had defected in Paris and spent the remainder of the decade there, struggling to support himself and his family. But since 1960, he had quietly taught in the Slavic languages department at Berkeley. Like many other artists living in the United States in political exile, he was renowned in his own country but unknown and ignored here.

Two weeks after the meeting in Wheeler, my wife, our two small daughters, and I pulled up to Milosz's house off Grizzly Peak Boulevard in Berkeley. It was a small house with a steep roof, set in a thicket of trees and foliage, and looked like a cottage out of a Grimm's fairy tale. It was November, so darkness had already descended. Our knock on the thick wooden door was answered by Milosz himself. He was excited to see us but dismayed at first by our arriving with our six- and one-year-olds in tow. I explained that we couldn't afford babysitters, and Milosz, calling to his wife for assistance, good-humoredly found a place for the girls to amuse themselves, and the visit began in the way—I gathered from Milosz's renewed enthusiasm—he imagined it should have started.

He formally introduced us to his wife, Anka, a striking woman with straight white hair and bangs, a sharp nose and a kindly manner, who took the girls to play in the Miloszes' youngest son's room. Then Milosz opened one of the promised bottles of wine, and while Anka and Wilma talked in the kitchen, he hustled me to his study where he told me, with a feverish emphasis I was beginning to suspect was his manner, about the new preface he was writing for the next edition of *Post-War Polish Poetry* that Penguin was bringing out the following year. It was written, he said, with me in mind. He had been impressed by my poetry, but he wanted to warn me—and other young poets—not to overuse sarcastic irony. It was tinged with cynicism, he said. Relying on such irony in your poems, he explained, was tantamount to accepting the horrors perpetrated by governments and individuals, since it implied in its tone and attitude an acceptance of them as the way of the world. At times irony is fine to warn the readers of impending political or social catastrophes, he said, but when the catastrophes occur, the poet has to sing songs of hope and redemption, for that, in the end, should be the primal direction of the human spirit.

He spoke with an orator's vigor, and I was once more beside myself with humility and gratefulness that he would be so moved by my poems that he would write a warning to me and my generation concerning a dangerous path he was afraid we were following. I was so struck by his passionate words that the whole tenor of my work changed from then on. It was as if he had expunged sarcastic irony from my soul.

After he calmed down, all four of us spent a pleasant evening getting to know each other and talking about literature and the world. For the rest of the night, Milosz was not only composed and charming but subdued, and I got the impression that his agitation at the reading and earlier in the evening had to do with the passionate warning he, like a wisdom figure out of some Slavic folktale, had delivered to me in his study.

We visited the Miloszes several times after that, and I remember on one occasion, a month or two after our first meeting, how upset Czeslaw was about the strange death in Thailand of his friend Thomas Merton, the great Catholic contemplative. Milosz was a Roman Catholic at heart, and his continued search for spiritual meaning in a world where moments of transcendent beauty implied a godhead—amid the horrors of history and the dehumanization of science and technology—can be understood in that context.

Certainly Milosz's formidable intellect was fed and honed by a classic European Catholic education, as our conversations revealed early on, but it was his Slavic soul that drew me to him like a magnet. If he embodied the exile's isolation I had felt all my life, he also exemplified the Slavic personality in his passion as well as his intellect. Nowhere are both attitudes more clearly voiced than in his poem "To Robinson Jeffers," where he delineates the difference between the Slavic and Anglo/Nordic temperaments. The poem is also an excellent example of Milosz's methodology—his ruminative, essay-like

approach suffused with an intense sensuousness. Or is it an intense sensuousness suffused with an essay-like approach?

To Robinson Jeffers

If you have not read the Slavic poets
so much the better. There's nothing there
for a Scotch-Irish wanderer to seek. They lived in a childhood
prolonged from age to age. For them, the sun
was a farmer's ruddy face, the moon peeped through a cloud
and the Milky Way gladdened them like a birch-lined road.
They longed for the Kingdom which is always near,
always right at hand. Then, under apple trees
angels in homespun linen will come parting the boughs
and at the white kolkhoz tablecloth
cordiality and affection will feast (falling to the ground at times).

And you are from surf-rattled skerries. From the heaths
where burying a warrior they broke his bones
so he could not haunt the living. From the sea night
which your forefathers pulled over themselves, without a word.
Above your head no face, neither the sun's nor the moon's,
only the throbbing of galaxies, the immutable
violence of new beginnings, of new destruction.

All your life listening to the ocean. Black dinosaurs
wade where a purple zone of phosphorescent weeds
rises and falls on the waves as in a dream. And Agamemnon
sails the boiling deep to the steps of the palace
to have his blood gush onto marble. Till mankind passes
and the pure and stony earth is pounded by the ocean.

Thin-lipped, blue-eyed, without grace or hope,
before God the Terrible, body of the world.
Prayers are not heard. Basalt and granite.
Above them, a bird of prey. The only beauty.

What have I to do with you? From footpaths in the orchards,
from an untaught choir and shimmers of a monstrance,
from flower beds of rue, hills by the rivers, books
in which a zealous Lithuanian announced brotherhood, I come.
Oh, consolations of mortals, futile creeds.

And yet you did not know what I know. The earth teaches
More than does the nakedness of elements. No one with impunity
gives to himself the eyes of a god. So brave, in a void,
you offered sacrifices to demons: there were Wotan and Thor,
the screech of Erinyes in the air, the terror of dogs
when Hekate with her retinue of the dead draws near.

Better to carve suns and moons on the joints of crosses
as was done in my district. To birches and firs
give feminine names. To implore protection
against the mute and treacherous might
than to proclaim, as you did, an inhuman thing.

Although I thought I came to understand Czeslaw in our handful of meetings in 1968 and 1969, I was totally unprepared for the dramatic evening I was to spend with him in the spring of 1970, the subject of Chapter 24.

■ ■ ■

The spring of 1969 began with the publication of my first book, *Origins*. Hitchcock phoned me about the book's arrival from the printer's, and we arranged to have dinner together in San Francisco to celebrate the occasion the following week: he, his wife Eva, Wilma, and I.

Wilma and I arrived to find the door to the Laguna Street house wide open. I had a bottle of champagne in hand and, after calling through the doorway several times, I ventured into the hall. Hitchcock met me after I had taken several steps. He was in a shirt and cardigan sweater and motioned to several cartons in the hallway. "Take the books and go," he said.

"What?"

"Take them and go!" he repeated impatiently.

Clockwise from left: Playing Boltar to Jim Houston's Prince Valiant, novelist Page Stegner as a monk, Santa Cruz, 1969

Wilma had joined me by this time, and after shooting quizzical glances at each other, we took several cartons of books and drove back to Santa Cruz.

A week later, we found out that a few hours before our arrival at Hitchcock's house, Eva had announced that she was leaving George.

George didn't show his vulnerability over the situation when I journeyed to San Francisco for the next two collating parties. For a short time he began to see the sister of Ray Carver's wife, Amy, a young actress, and she and George would engage in some wonderful improvisational skits after the collating was finished and most of the "workers" had gone. I drove up alone for those sessions and would hang around, talking to Ray Carver, his wife Maryann, and other friends, and by 6:00 in the evening we'd all go off for dinner somewhere.

TILLIE OLSON'S LAST DAYS

Besides Hitchcock, I continued my friendships with a handful of people I had met in the Artists' Liberation Front during my San Francisco days. Others I ran into now and then over the years, one of whom was Tillie Olsen. Her youngest daughter, Julie, was a colleague of mine during the years I taught at Cabrillo. Like her mother, she was a committed, eloquent social activist and one of the founders of the school's teachers' union, and I had many dealings with her and her husband, Rob.

Julie would tell me what was happening to her mother, and I'd see Tillie at various times when she came to visit. She was always the same unpretentious, kind woman I'd met that night at the first meeting of the Front, although she had become famous throughout the country as a writer since then and an icon of the women's movement. Her reputation was founded on the short-story volume I'd read in the 1960s, *Tell Me a Riddle*, and two other volumes she published during the 1970s, *Yonnondio* (1974), a novel she had started and abandoned in the 1930s, and *Silences* (1978), a book of essays examining the writer's problem of finding time and circumstances in which to write.

By the start of the new millennium, Tillie's husband Jack had died, she was in her late eighties, and her mental faculties were rapidly deteriorating. She needed care day and night and rarely knew where she was or the content of what she had just read. Julie and one of Tillie's other daughters, Laurie, took turns caring for Tillie on weekends, and in the fall of 2004, Julie told me the following story, one of the most touching accounts of what motivates someone to take up the writing life I have ever heard.

One night, Laurie noticed that the light in Tillie's bedroom had come on again, long after it had been turned off. When she went to investigate, Laurie found Tillie, now a tiny, childlike woman, sitting bent over in bed and weeping.

"I don't want to go to school! I don't want to go to school!" she kept repeating.

Laurie sat down on the bed and assured her mother that she wouldn't have to go to school but asked why she didn't want to go.

"Because the girls will laugh at me and my tattered clothes. Don't they understand that my parents haven't enough money to buy me new dresses?"

Laurie took her mother in her arms to comfort her. But suddenly, with a determined shove, Tillie sat erect and said, "When I grow up I'm going to write a book about why my clothes are so shabby, so other people will understand."

"But you have grown up," said Laurie, "and you have written a book about that. Several books."

"I have?" Tillie replied, her body softening and settling back into the bed-clothes. "Good," she said.

CHAPTER 23

Vasko Popa

In the fall of 1969, Charles Simic, who in the future would win a Pulitzer Prize and become the United States Poet Laureate, called me from the East Coast. Hitchcock had published Simic's first book, *What the Grass Says*, in 1967 and released his second, *Somewhere Among Us a Stone Is Taking Notes*, a month before the phone call. I had read Charlie's poems in *Kayak* and devoured both his books, feeling a visceral kinship with the poems and their maker that I experienced with few other poets. There was a folk-like peasant wisdom at work in the poems that was pure Slav, presented in a deceptively simple, almost offhanded idiomatic American English that took my attention. But it was his imagery that I found spellbinding. It was concise, self-contained, waiting on the page like a spring-loaded trap that grabbed and held the reader's imagination in its grip by showing the ordinary world in new ways.

Vasko Popa, visiting the United States, 1970

Charlie was less enthusiastic about my first book, but the few times we had spoken on the phone, he was friendly and easy to talk with. I don't remember why we communicated. Did I write him an admiring letter? I don't think I did. Nor did I have his address or phone number. Our only relationship existed through our mutual publication in *Kayak* and the inclusion of both our work in *The Young American Poets* anthology.

Now he was calling to inform me that Vasko Popa had been invited to an international poetry symposium to be held in Washington, DC, the following spring. The State Department had asked Charlie to be Popa's host on the East Coast, and he—knowing I had dedicated my first book to Popa and that a long article comparing my poetry and Popa's had been published in the leading literary journal in Yugoslavia—had suggested me as Popa's host on the West Coast. Was I interested?

For the next few months we planned and arranged the tour. After Washington, Popa would have several readings on the East Coast, in the South, and at the new international translation center Paul Engle had set up at the University of Iowa. I would pick Popa up in San Francisco, have him read at

Cabrillo, and, through my connections with Milosz, would provide him with a reading at the University of California at Berkeley, sponsored by the Slavic Languages Department. Milosz, who had never met Popa, was excited at the prospect of meeting him and said he would host a party at his house after the reading.

The week before Popa was to arrive on the West Coast, Charlie called with last-minute instructions. The tour had gone well on the East Coast, and Popa's appearance at the poetry festival in Washington had been a big success, but Charlie wanted to warn me about two things. The first was not to talk about any politically touchy subject with Popa since the State Department interpreter, who was accompanying him, seemed to be trying to bait Popa into making anti-Tito comments. Or so Popa thought. And second—and most important—I was to tell Popa I preferred red wine over white and make sure I had a good supply of red wine on hand, preferably pinot noir.

"What's that about?" I asked.

"Vasko's first impressions of a person are all-important," Charlie said, "and he's decided that people who drink red wine exhibit preferences that show them to be people he can trust."

"Anything else?"

"Yes. The State Department is worried about security. They know Watsonville is populated by Croats, and Popa is not only a Communist, he's a Serb."

"Not to worry. But I'll keep my eyes open," I replied.

I met Popa at the San Francisco airport on a raw, gray day in early spring. He was a big, shambling man, over six-feet-four-inches tall, with jet black hair and sad black eyes. The pain I thought I detected in those eyes was accentuated by the pronounced bags under them. He was wearing a loose-fitting, extremely lightweight brown suit and no topcoat.

The interpreter introduced us, and Popa, staring into my eyes, gripped both my arms and greeted me with a short stream of words in Serbo-Croat, searching my face for the answer.

"Mr. Popa ask, do you like white wine or red wine?"

"Tell him red wine," I answered in the same somber tone in which the question had been asked. When Popa heard my answer, he broke into a smile and hugged me to him.

"Good, good," he said.

Popa walked arm-in-arm with me to the baggage area, making faces and rolling his eyes at the interpreter, who was walking ahead of us. I nodded that I understood the situation, and he was relieved. Vasko spoke only a few words of English and was unhappy that I did not speak French, but we overcame the language barrier in ingenious ways in the days to come and communicated, with difficulty, on the walks in the woods we took without the interpreter's presence.

After I picked up their suitcases, I drove down the coast to Santa Cruz. Popa, the interpreter said, wanted to see the Pacific Ocean, which was fine with me; I had planned to show him the ocean on the drive south to Santa Cruz anyway.

As we drove down the winding coastline, Popa became more and more excited, expostulating wildly.

"Mr. Popa requests we stop near ocean," the interpreter said.

I had been planning that, too, and when we approached one of my favorite beaches, a tidy expanse of sand surrounded by low, worn-down bluffs, I pulled in. "Tell him this is Bean Hollow Beach, called Frijoles Beach in Spanish." Popa repeated the Spanish aloud after the interpreter explained what I had said. I parked on a small rise over the beach, and we piled out of my Volkswagen.

The weather was still gray and raw. Popa ran ahead of us, his brown suit billowing in the sea wind, sprinting from one patch of wild plant life to another, snatching a handful of succulents here and scooping up wildflowers there until he had an armload of flora. Then he marched into the freezing ocean up to his thighs and, casting his bouquet onto the water, proclaimed, said the interpreter, a greeting to the Pacific Ocean on behalf of the Yugoslav people.

We finished our ride with Popa's teeth chattering and the heat in the car on high.

If Popa was flamboyant, he was no clown. He was a highly emotional man who also had the canniness of a showman about him. At times, however, he withdrew into a dark if not painful interior, even in the middle of the parties and gatherings of the many people who wanted to meet him.

We managed to find half a dozen people who spoke French so we could communicate without the help of the interpreter, who was clearly getting on Popa's nerves. They had traveled throughout the country together, and Popa believed the man was a CIA operative who was constantly baiting him, as Charlie had said, into making anti-Tito statements.

Popa and the interpreter stayed in separate rooms in a downtown motel. Every morning I picked them up and took them to my house in the mountains after we had breakfast. Popa was most relaxed in the mountains, playing with Jana, making faces at Valerie, and dancing around with both of them. Once he found a ruby ring on the beach, and later that day at the house he withdrew it carefully from his jacket pocket as if it were a magic amulet and presented it to Jana with great solemnity, vowing to marry her when she grew up. He was charming and a natural ladies' man who flattered and fawned over Wilma. But even then, he often withdrew, it seemed to me, into a place full of ghosts and suffering.

Most of the mornings we worked with the interpreter on the poems Popa would read at Cabrillo and the University of California. He had brought with him Charlie's translations of several sequences—"Games," "Bone to Bone," "The Yawn of Yawns," and "The Little Box." I had "Games" and several loose poems translated by Nijgebauer when I was in San Francisco and had done my own versions from Ann Pennington's translations that had appeared in a Penguin book of Popa's poems the year before. With all these different versions in front of us, and with the interpreter's help, we made new, composite translations, which we read at both readings. The interpreter knew next to nothing about poetry; his translations were accurate but literal and didn't take into account the metaphorical richness and implications that abounded in the poems, which I, to my own amazement, intuited in line after line. Popa warmed to the task, and we drew closer and closer over the days. I pointed out to him Pennington's limitations, which were similar to the interpreter's, but Popa was loyal to her, his first and official English translator. In the end, he insisted I show Charlie our versions, which he thought were the best, telling me that Charlie was preparing several of the sequences for publication. When I went over them with Charlie several years later, he liked them a lot, but, alas, by that time his versions had come out in book form. The composite translations did, however, act as an impetus for Charlie and me to work together on other Popa pieces, notably the sequence "Give Me Back My Little Rags."

Through his interpreter and several French speakers I managed to find at Cabrillo and the university, Popa and I spent the afternoons in conversation. We talked about Europe, the war, his influence on my poetry, and what we were both working on at present. He spoke of his wife, a mathematics professor in Belgrade, who he missed more with each passing day. Certainly part of his brooding silences, I felt, had to do with simple homesickness.

I took Popa to various restaurants, introduced him to colleagues, and had him attend classes where the students looked at him as if he were a strange species of human or a creature from the zoo, mainly because he spoke no English and, when he spoke, the sound of Serbo-Croat struck their ears as a jumble of noises they had never heard before. But Popa's warmth and friendly smile won them over. They knew they were in the presence of an international celebrity and listened intently and courteously to anything he said before the interpreter translated his words.

After each class or gathering of colleagues, we would retire to a restaurant or bar where Popa would drink copious amounts of red wine and sink into a dreamy silence. I got the impression, after a while, that he was performing when he met people, and after the meetings were over he would withdraw in exhaustion, his eyes flooding with inner pain.

I don't mean to romanticize Popa's distracted withdrawals, but I wasn't imagining them. Many times he struggled to talk to me, it seemed, on a personal level, but the language barrier was too great. Then again the inner pain I thought I detected in him could have been physical since he had three ulcers he thought he was controlling by drinking his daily quota of red wine. White wine, he thought, exacerbated his condition. But he said red wine bound the ulcers like a healing potion. Whatever the nature of the pain, I saw him many times gnashing his teeth.

Three days after his arrival, we read at Cabrillo. The interpreter reiterated the State Department's security concerns. I alerted the campus police, but felt the concerns were negligible. Although Santa Cruz's large Slavic population was Croat and Popa was Serbian, I couldn't imagine there would be a problem.

I had reserved the cafeteria in the student union for the reading and had the tables removed and two hundred chairs arranged in rows. I had sent publicity to all the area newspapers, including the San Jose and San Francisco dailies. I had requests for tapes of the reading from several community radio stations in the Bay Area but nervously wondered if my preparations would draw a respectable crowd, especially since both Popa and the interpreter had spoken unhappily about the small turnouts at his other readings. Both of them retold a number of times with great bitterness his last outing at Tulane, in New Orleans, where they had arrived with their hosts to find the auditorium dark and locked and finally read to the host and his wife and the auditorium's janitor.

I needn't have worried. Not only did hundreds of students show up, primed by my colleagues and me, but it seemed all of the Croatian population of Watsonville came as well. The two hundred seats were quickly filled, and students and townspeople stood packed along the walls and in the doorways of the student cafeteria.

The evening was an unprecedented success, and Popa was extremely moved. Before the reading, many of the old Croats from Watsonville came up to him, greeting him in Serbo-Croat, telling him where their families were from in the old country and expressing their delight that he was there, a number of them extending invitations for him to visit them, which we didn't have time to do in Popa's already full schedule. There were so many greetings and introductions that the reading started half an hour later than was scheduled. But everyone was patient, and a festive, expectant mood spread through the crowd as they looked around, recognizing neighbors or classmates and enjoying the atmosphere of international importance that surrounded the event.

I was not about to let the audience's elation deflate. I read the English versions of Popa's poems and introduced him and the nature of his poetry, specifying what each poem was about, how it worked, and what to listen for, and giving a dramatic reading of each one. "Bone to Bone" brought wild laughter and applause after I explained that it was a dialogue between two bones that had been buried for some time, and that each one still maintained the personality of the human to whom it had belonged, one depressed and not too bright and the other optimistic and full of ideas. I also said it was like a dialogue between Estragon and Vladimir in *Waiting for Godot*, and proceeded to read the poem—after Popa's reading of the original in Serbo-Croat—in two different voices. Here's a section from the sequence in the translation I worked out with Vasko.

Before the End

Where shall we go now

Where should we go nowhere
Where else would two bones go

What'll we do there

There waiting for us a long time
There eagerly expecting us
Are no one and his wife nothing

What good are we to them

They are old they are without bones
We'll be like daughters to them

—from the sequence *Bone to Bone*

Vasko and I read several other sequences we had worked on, one of them "Games," which I had been so taken with when I first read Popa's poems in San Francisco several years before. The poems describe, in surreal, parable-like ways, the games we "play" with each other as a species:

Floor Nail

One is the nail another is pliers
The rest are workmen

The pliers grab the nail by the head
With their teeth their arms they grab it
And keep pulling and pulling
Pulling it out of the floor
Usually they just wring its head off
It's hard pulling a nail out of the floor

Then the workmen say
These pliers are lousy
They crush their jaws break their arms
And throw them out the window

Then someone else is a floornail
Another is pliers
The rest are workmen

—from the sequence *Games*

Almost all Popa's poetry is written in sequences of short poems, each poem of a sequence no more than ten to twenty lines long. Every aspect of the poems in the sequences is mathematically related. Each sequence is a sort of surreal epic, and a number of them are cosmic in vision. The individual poems are cerebral, not emotional, philosophical rather than lyrical,

although at times they are composed of all those elements, as the following
example, also read that night, demonstrates.

The Star-Wizard's Legacy

He left behind his words
Lovelier than the world
No one dares look at them

They wait at the corners of time
Bigger than people
Who can pronounce them

They lie on the dumb earth
Heavier than life's bones
Death could not carry them away
As his dowry

No one can lift them
No one can strike them down

Falling stars hide their heads
In the shadows of his words

—from the sequence *The Yawn of Yawns*

At the conclusion of the reading, the audience jumped to its feet, giving
Popa a wild ovation for five minutes. At first he humbly bowed, but as the
applause continued, tears came to his eyes, he put his hand on his heart, and
hung his head in appreciation. When the cheering stopped, fifty or sixty of
the Croats in the audience formed a reception line, each person, teary-eyed,
shaking Popa's hand and saying words of approbation to him in Serbo-
Croat.

The evening had been emotionally overwhelming, and we left with ten people in tow for a restaurant I had arranged to have remain open for an after-
hours snack—and the inevitable red wine. Popa was expansive but depleted.
His arm was continually draped around my shoulders. We had become closer
than ever since the reading had gone better than he had imagined. I had also
taken care of every one of his needs during the three previous days. In fact,
Popa let it be known through the interpreter that I was taking care of him too
well, and he was calling me, with an affectionate smile, "my slave." At the same
time, we had learned to nod and wink to communicate without words, especially in light of the interpreter's supposed troublemaking.

The interpreter was certainly smarmy, and his constant smile had struck
a false note since the meeting at the airport. He would take me aside or
whisper conspiratorially when Popa left the room, hinting at I know not
what, and insinuating that we were Americans and Popa was, when all was
said and done, a Communist, and I should . . . should what? Nothing was
explicitly said, just suggested. The man was irritating, and at an afternoon

cocktail party that included my Cabrillo colleagues, he sat back, nodding and smiling, as if he were picking up bits of information he would file in a report to Washington. Maybe I had seen too many spy films or Popa's paranoia was taking hold of me. But the interpreter's behavior was clearly insinuating and, if nothing else, annoying.

The ten of us settled in at the restaurant. The group included a French professor from the university, an attractive woman, smartly dressed, with neatly coifed straight brown hair that hugged her head in a short haircut. She and Popa flirted harmlessly and kept up a running dialogue in French, which she broke off every few moments to explain in English to the rest of us at the table.

The wine continued to appear, served by one of my students, who was the restaurant's night manager and was keeping the bar open just for us. It was a good restaurant, its wine list excellent, and Popa was enjoying its fine selection of different California pinot noirs, every so often turning to the interpreter, who was muttering to him.

Although he consumed large amounts of wine each day, Popa rarely seemed drunk, but the excitement of the reading and the letdown after it seemed to weaken his constitution, and he was soon inebriated, smiling too broadly. He was also getting more and more annoyed at the interpreter's mutterings, and suddenly he leaped to his feet, reaching into his back pocket, and, taking a card from his wallet, he slapped it on the table, yelling several sentences in Serbo-Croat. The interpreter slunk back in his chair, his face first white, then slowly turning crimson. Still standing, Popa turned to the French professor and said something in French with great vehemence, which she immediately interpreted for us.

"Vasko said he had had enough of this wheedling interpreter and had thrown his Communist party card on the table, telling him to look at it, that he would always be a Communist because the card is signed in blood."

Popa sat down and, in an intense but deliberate voice, explained through the French professor that in the first years of World War II, he had been rounded up with other young Serbs and sent to a concentration camp. Realizing they might well be executed, the entire camp had rushed the wire and escaped, scattering to different parts of Yugoslavia. Popa, like most of the others, went to the mountains and joined Tito, fighting for the partisans until the end of the war.

We sat without speaking at the conclusion of his words, but I thought I had an inkling about at least some of the reasons for Popa's distracted silences. As for the interpreter, his wheedling ways ended abruptly that evening.

CHAPTER 24

Milosz and Popa

Three days later, Popa, the interpreter, and I journeyed to the University of California campus at Berkeley for our reading at the Slavic Languages Department. Milosz had vigorously prepared his colleagues and students for the event, and an audience of several hundred crowded into a small auditorium. Milosz was very excited and, his face flushed, ran from one side of the room to the other, introducing Popa to one person here and another one there, making sure everything was in place for the reading. He had greeted Popa with a warm embrace and kept returning to him, saying several sentences in French before he would rush off again

Vasko and I presented the same bilingual program we had at our first reading and received the same enthusiastic response. Afterward, Milosz hurried us away from well-wishers and told me to drive to his house. When we arrived, we were greeted by what seemed like most of the audience from the reading. Cars lined both sides of the narrow street, and more than a hundred people were jammed inside Milosz's small fairytale-like cottage in the forested hills above Berkeley.

Milosz had arrived before us and, with face still flushed, was moving with Anka from group to group, making sure everyone was taken care of. Several of the students came up to Popa, but most of them spoke neither Serbo-Croat nor French, and, with his interpreter lost somewhere in the crowd, Vasko was soon ensconced alone on a sofa with a glass of red wine in either hand. Now that his responsibilities in California were over, he looked relaxed and pleased, and he stared in glassy-eyed exhaustion at the milling guests. His quiet contentment was disturbed only by Milosz, who would break away from his duties as host to join Vasko and speak to him animatedly in French. I thought I understood Milosz's excitement. He and Vasko had been in the resistance against the Nazi invaders in their separate countries, neither one knowing about the other but both engaged in a common cause. Both had survived, while many of their friends had not, and each had gone on to be an important literary figure not only in his respective country but throughout Europe. It made no difference to Milosz, a staunch opponent of Communism, what Popa's politics were. He and Popa shared a brotherly bond that was welded together by history—and blood.

For the most part, Popa listened to Milosz, smiling and nodding. He seemed comfortable talking to him, and his demeanor radiated affection. I watched the two of them with mounting emotions, pictures fluttering through my mind of haggard refugee faces and bombed-out cities.

The students strolled around the two men or sat in groups on the carpet, and it seemed that Popa and Milosz were encapsulated in a bubble of time none of the guests could understand or were willing to allow themselves to imagine, even though they certainly knew that both men had experienced some of the most traumatic historical events of the century.

The guests, in fact, seemed totally absorbed in their own concerns. Many of them wore white handkerchiefs as armbands which identified them as demonstrators against the government's sending troops into Cambodia. This group was going straight from the party to the staging area of a huge protest march that was to take place the following morning.

Milosz talked to Vasko more vehemently as the evening wore on, darting away to refill his glass or say good night to a departing guest. Soon he was more flushed than ever and slightly drunk. The guests began to leave. Those who stayed were the students wearing white armbands. They stood talking in groups or chatted while seated on the floor. At one point, Milosz, returning from refilling his glass, almost fell over one of the seated figures.

"What do you think you are doing?" he asked the person, a young man in a white shirt who looked at him uncomprehendingly.

"What do you think you are doing with that armband?" Milosz explained, swaying and pointing at the white handkerchief on the young man's arm. The young man looked down at his arm, then up at Milosz.

"We are demonstrating against U.S. involvement in Cambodia."

"And what are you demonstrating *for*?" Milosz retorted.

"For peace and love," replied a girl seated in the group. Milosz swayed some more, saliva flecking his lips, clearly belligerent.

"Love? Love for what?" he asked in a challenging voice.

The party had grown silent and everyone in the room was staring at Milosz and the girl.

Vasko Popa's business card, brought from Belgrade by a mutual friend, 1987.
Illustrations are symbolic icons from his poetic sequences.

"Love for everything and everyone," the girl replied.

"I taught you better than that," Milosz growled. "If you love everything and everyone, you love nothing. Love is selective."

The young man Milosz had first interrogated now came to the girl's rescue. "We demonstrate to stop the injustice going on in Vietnam and now Cambodia," he said.

Milosz's face was crimson.

"Children!" he spat out. "You are children! You know nothing! If you marched in Poland or the Soviet Union, they would shoot you down."

The girl was now incensed and said, "What's wrong with love? It's the only way to stop what is going on. We have to love each other."

"Love, love, love!" mocked Milosz, his voice rising to a shout. "Talk to me about love when they come into your cell one morning, line you all up, and say 'You and you, step forward. It's your time to die—unless any of your friends love you so much they want to take your place.'"

Shocked silence washed over the room. Milosz blinked and swayed, his feet planted angrily. Then he hoisted himself erect and made his way over to Vasko, where, in agitated French, he translated what had just taken place. Vasko listened, nodding and smiling, his eyes half closed, balancing the two half-filled wine glasses on his knees.

The young man in the group Milosz had just harangued snickered and murmured some words to the others who laughed and turned toward Milosz. Other chortles and snickers sprouted around the room. Milosz almost certainly heard them but chose to ignore them and continued talking to Popa. Once more I visualized the two of them encapsulated in a time bubble. In no way could the students fathom the agony as well as the anger that prompted Milosz's words. It was an anger at the memory of millions of dead bodies, an agony felt for all those who had lost their lives in another time and place. At the same time, Milosz seemed incapable of understanding the young people's commitment to their history and the lives they were seeing destroyed around *them*. It was one of those moments filled with tragic irony, the kind of irony Milosz never abandoned in his work—and which is all too poignantly a part of the human condition.

Two days later, Popa and the interpreter left for the East Coast. We said warm goodbyes, and he kissed me on both cheeks, tears in his eyes, murmuring in broken English, "My little slave." We traded addresses, and he commanded me to come to Yugoslavia, where he would have me invited to the annual international poetry festival at Struga.

Over the years we sent notes and good wishes to each other through traveling friends, and finally in 1989 we arranged to meet at his apartment in Belgrade. When I arrived there after spending a week with my second wife's in-laws on the Dalmatian Coast, there was no one home, and downstairs a shopkeeper explained that Popa had broken his leg two weeks

before and was convalescing, of all places, on the Dalmatian Coast. Ironically, I had been within ten miles of where he was staying. I was flying from
Belgrade to Athens, and there was no backtracking allowed on my airline
ticket. On the flight to Athens that night I outlined the following poem,
which not only described my attempt to find Popa in Belgrade, but sought
to analyze and encapsulate his poetry.

Looking for Vasko Popa

Nothing could be less appropriate
than to think of Eliot's winding stair
as I grope my way from landing to landing
in this old apartment house in Belgrade.
The stairs are unlit, and for three floors
I follow a shadowy elevator's iron cage,
shuffling through tumble-down plaster,
newspapers, bottles, and cellophane,
sniffing collapsed oranges and sour wine,
cigarette smoke, oiled machinery, and grime
before I arrive at the old poet's door.

He isn't home. I knock again and listen,
imagining him in a room down a dusty hall,
helpless in a chair, his eyes bulging
as he struggles to work his lips.
Listen, there is only the drone of wind
beneath the door, and again I think of Eliot,
his final silence echoing down his last years
as down a stairwell like this one,
where he saw himself as an old man
still gripping the banister at the bottom step.

Downstairs a plump little shopkeeper,
who speaks no English, grips his thigh
and hops to the right, trying to tell me,
with whistles and grunts, that the poet
broke his leg and has been convalescing
hundreds of miles away, at the seaside.
Images of Eliot rise again: the Fisher King
revitalized, with slashes on his thigh—
imprinted impotence in a hop,
a stutter step, that is one of the meanings

the shopkeeper's pantomime ludicrously implies.
The other is the absence here of a poet's
precise use of words to perfectly describe
the all too apparent imperfection of men.

To think of Eliot at a time like this:
nothing could be less fitting than the dry,
deliberate poetics of the English don
in contrast to the poet I search for here,
a maker of ten-page epics, where bones
don't chirp but comically debate, pliers
with broken jaws, like discarded workmen,
are thrown out of windows, and the combined
sides of triangles, sliding on fiery tracks,
equal human destiny.

       And yet, and yet—
both poets walked among the multitudes
and looked for meaning after major wars,
the Englishman in old books and rusty symbols,
arriving in the end at the arthritic ceremonies
of a doddering church, while this poet,
whose apartment is approached by stumbling
through the rubbish of an age, found meaning
in his native folklore and the fellowship
of mountain fighters defending their land.
All this he compressed into a pristine music,
chimes of sunlight and wind pinging
over an endless line of refugees—
a raised arm, a hammer flying into the air,
an eye peeking from behind a cart.
He made a mythology of this, his people's history:
populations fleeing for their lives,
slaughtering others or those in their ranks,
or flowing through the landscape
on an endless pilgrimage—human parts
seen for an instant and then gone,
as in a crowd we glimpse a shoulder
or the swagger of someone familiar,
or watch a teapot roll from a thicket of legs,
which hands immediately grab, returning it
to the anonymous mass of moving bodies.

He distilled these elements into cosmic yawns
and magic kettles, added the star charts
glinting in the joints of every skeleton,
and made of them all a secondary heaven.
He never abandoned these images of the lost,
now pliers crushing a nail's head,
now pebbles and triangles scurrying
after their gluttonous, comic-book ends,
until he seemed to live in a huge room,
surrounded by clocks and discarded flywheels,
where broken lips and overturned eyeballs—
once the smiles and frightened eyes of dolls—
littered the floor around his easy chair,
and runaway teeth, galloping in cavalry charges
back and forth across the carpet, dashed
headlong into the walls, scattering like dice
before they re-formed their clattering ranks
in readiness for yet another charge.
All the while, the poet did not dare to move,
afraid he might trample his tiny charges or knock over
the miniature kettles and dancing shoes
on the table near his elbow. Nor could he
call out in a voice that might deafen them,
even to answer the pounding down the hall
where someone was knocking on his apartment door.

I never did get to meet Popa again. He died two years later at the age of sixty-nine, just before the break-up of the Yugoslav federation and the wars in Croatia and Bosnia.

I continued to see Milosz on and off, although my trips to the San Francisco Bay Area became more infrequent as the years went on. After he won the Nobel Prize in 1980, Milosz was extraordinarily busy, in demand everywhere, and I felt uncomfortable bothering him. When he came to read at the University of California at Santa Cruz, he asked specifically to see me, and at the party after his reading he asked the host to allow us to talk alone in an unused room. He asked after me, was sorry to hear about my divorce, and told me that Anka was ill. It was a quiet meeting, a father asking after his long-absent son. A few years later, Robert Hass, who had become his reader as well as translator, plucked me out of an audience waiting for Milosz to read in San Jose and told me Czeslaw wanted to see me backstage. There was a brief but warm meeting, and I congratulated Czeslaw on the many honors that had been bestowed on him since I had last seen him.

Our last meeting was at the reception following another reading he gave, again in San Jose. It was 1989, and Milosz was to fly to Poland several days later, his first visit to his homeland, I think, since his defection in Paris in 1951. Anka had died three years before, and Czeslaw had a new female companion who acted as organizer and go-between. When I told her I was an old friend and wanted to say hello, she led me to him. His eyes were rheumy, and he had aged greatly. I said hello and realized he didn't know me. I tried to spark his memory by briefly recalling our first meeting in Wheeler Hall and Popa's reading, but he didn't remember what I was referring to. I smiled warmly, shook his hand, and took my leave. Oh, yes, I was embarrassed and feeling the stares of the people around him. A few moments later, his new companion, who later became his wife, came up to me and said Czeslaw wanted to see me. When I went up to him, he had tears in his eyes and held his arms out to embrace me. "Morton, Morton, of course I remember you," he said. We talked for several minutes and he asked me to write and send my new book to him. I did, and he wrote back the day before he left for Poland. It was good to see me, he said in the letter, and he liked the book, a sequence of poems about my ancestors in Poland and Russia, but he remembered nothing about Popa's reading or his visit to his house.

I have never forgotten Milosz's last comment. The irony in it is too crushing. As an exile in a foreign land and an alien culture, he returned again and again in his poetry and essays to memories of the Poland in which he had grown to manhood—a Poland that had vanished first with the Nazi invasion and then the Communist takeover. In fact, memory is one of the major subjects of Milosz's work, along with spiritual decay and the search for a moral foothold in the ruins of twentieth-century history. That he would not remember meeting such an important fellow poet as Popa, who represented a connection with that vanished world, a meeting that must have been one of the more memorable events of his first decade in an America that ignored him and his country's history and culture, is an irony only the cruelest of gods could have conceived. And I can't help thinking that my rescuing that memory with this remembrance may be the kindest act I could perform for him—and, of course, in its own way, that is an irony too.

CHAPTER 25

1971: Two Traumas

Sometime in 1971, Jeanne Houston's nephew called to ask her what it had been like to be in prison during World War II. Jeanne and her family had always made light of the three-and-a-half years during the war that they had spent at the Manzanar detention center in Southern California—an internment facility that could more accurately be called a concentration camp—because they were of Japanese descent. She had made light of it until that moment, but when her nephew insisted she answer seriously, in her own words, "I started crying, I became hysterical—it was posttraumatic stress that came out of the blue. I didn't know what was happening to me."

Unable to talk about Manzanar or her emotional turmoil concerning it, Jeanne decided to write a family memoir about the experience. But the project was so stressful that she asked Jim for help. By then, she and Jim had been married for fifteen years, but she had never told him about her childhood years in the camp, nor did he, like most other Caucasians, even know what the word "Manzanar" meant, let alone what its function was. Jim was stunned by Jeanne's story and realized immediately that her family's experience at Manzanar was a blatant disregard of constitutional rights by the government and a story every American should know.

Jim and Jeanne Houston, Santa Cruz, 1974

I didn't learn many of those details until two years later. All through 1971, however, Jim told me about how he and Jeanne were collecting information for a book and how it became a healing process for Jeanne's brothers and sisters. I had never seen him so excited and committed to a project, and I listened, fascinated, to his account of the methods he and Jeanne were using to lift the submerged memories from the dark well of her mind.

To write the book, Jim had come up with the idea of using one of the old reel-to-reel tape recorders. He would start each session slowly, asking general questions of Jeanne, both to quell her self-consciousness of the microphone and not to alarm her by having her confront disturbing memories immediately. In this way, he eased her into her confrontations with the past. In the beginning, the interviews were disturbing for her, and she would choke up and even cry. Eventually, she became more comfortable with the process and, under Jim's guidance, told her story and realized the many ramifications her years at Manzanar had on the way she reacted to people and events as she grew to womanhood.

In the end, the sessions acted as a catharsis. By the time the interviews were finished, Jeanne not only felt free of a burden she had not consciously understood she was carrying, but she emerged as a person able to see the world from a wiser, more integrated viewpoint. Jeanne felt so good about the process that she went to her brothers and sisters, who lived in different parts of California, and talked them into telling their memories of Manzanar into the relentlessly whirring tape recorder. In every case, the reactions were the same: initially choked up feelings gave way to an unburdening of long-suppressed memories that was both freeing and healing.

By the end of the year, Jim and Jeanne were searching through the tapes and organizing the material. The result was the book, *Farewell to Manzanar*, published in 1973. It was the first mass-market account of the incarceration of Japanese Americans during the War, the personal story of seven-year-old Jeanne Wakatsuki and her family in the Manzanar internment camp from 1941 to 1944.

The book was a revelation and picked up momentum in sales all across the nation. Over the years, it would become an American classic, selling more than a million copies and would be read by schoolchildren everywhere in the country. Its immediate impact was to inspire other Japanese Americans to come forward and tell their stories, and it influenced young writers of other minority groups to tell their tales of having suffered through racial and ethnic discrimination.

Almost immediately, John Korty, a young film director who was married to a Korean American woman, asked Jim and Jeanne to write a screenplay of the book. Korty's production became a nationally shown television film, featuring prominent Asian American actors and writers, one of whom was Lawson Inada. He had moved to Oregon with Jan, and I hadn't seen him since I left Palo Alto in 1962. His relationship with Jim and Jeanne on the television movie, and their involvement with Asian American culture from then on, was responsible for us getting in touch with each other again and renewing our friendship. We visited back and forth over the ensuing years and gave readings together in both California and Oregon.

Meanwhile, Jim and Jeanne's script for *Farewell to Manzanar* won the newly created Humanitas Award given to screenplays that promoted "those values which most enrich the human person." This helped establish Jeanne's reputation as an editor, writer, and speaker, and Jim as a novelist of national importance and a spokesperson for Cali-

With Lawson Inada, Foothill Writers Conference, Los Altos, 1993

fornia culture and literature. Both their reputations have continued to grow over the years.

■ ■ ■

It was also in 1971 that my marriage to Wilma broke up. I had been having an affair since June of 1970, and by 1971 Wilma asked me to leave the house. The affair was a traumatic experience for both of us and had unexpected consequences.

Being a child of a broken marriage, I'd vowed that when I married, divorce would be out of the question. Marriage, at least to my adolescent mind, meant stability: a family unit that would always remain intact. Never, never would I make my children endure the lack of security I had experienced as a boy.

I had taken my marriage vows seriously, never having engaged in affairs or peccadilloes of any kind. I believed the differences of temperament and both the artistic and emotional clashes between Wilma and I were parts of marriage that we could work out. We had done so for thirteen years when, suddenly, I was the one who was breaking the vows and jeopardizing the marriage. My guilt feelings were overwhelming.

I had not leaped into the affair. It had begun quite innocently with a student who became my assistant in the fall of 1969 and who talked to me about her difficult home life. We discovered a rapport that grew into a friendship over the next nine months. But when it came time to say goodbye in my office at the end of the 1970 spring semester, I found I couldn't and instinctively took the girl in my arms. Her response was immediate and as passionate as my own.

That day I told Wilma what had happened. Reminding me with an amused laugh that she had been half-humorously encouraging me to have an affair for several years, she told me to pursue the incident. I did, and what might have been a brief fling turned into a complex web of responsibilities and obligations on everyone's part. When the girl was kicked out of her house with nothing but the clothes she was wearing, I felt responsible and did all I could to help her establish a new life. Wilma quickly realized the seriousness of the situation, and we tried to keep what was happening from Jana and Valerie as long as we could.

Through it all, I felt responsible for everyone concerned. It was one of the most emotionally trying times of my life—and, I must admit, one of the most exhilarating. I bought my lover a car and found her lodging with Ian and Nan Brown, the two friends I'd met ten years before at Norman Thomas's house in Palo Alto when I'd attended Stanford. I even secured a job for her. As for Jana and Valerie, even after I moved out I was at the house before my daughters awoke each day so they would find me there, as if nothing out of the ordinary were happening. I wrote a number of poems at the time that I hope evoked the turmoil many adults undergo in such situations, which have become all too commonplace. Here's one of the poems.

Two Roads

I live alone above the sea.
Two roads unroll from my door.
One, a highway over mountains,
leads through a forest of creaking trees.
When I'm alone on the road, dry voices
strain like muted trumpets in the trunks,
until the huge trees shudder around me
as if to call me back. Once through,
I am buoyant and begin to sing,
as the sunlight, wet and bland,
bounds through the green leaves.
The house I drive to is sheltered by a hill.
There is laughter there and young hands
fluttering around me like soft white birds,
and a bed to ease me into sleep. And yet,
startled awake, or watching her knit,
I find myself falling backward
down my throat.

The other road
is a steady climb past where I want to go—
so high I think the air will vanish
and leave me weak and clawing
on the slippery walls of my lungs.
The house it leads to is rooted to the ground:

I sniff the evening flowers
and gulp the easy air my children caper in,
while the woman whose body is half my life
watches us play with brimming eyes,
knowing an ache will swell my ribs
and make me go.

Month after month,
I drive through moondrenched forests.
Trees are uprooted, or whirl overhead,
trudging around me with shaggy flanks,
like milling herds who have lost their way.
The blind wind scrapes its fingernails
against the car, and insects,
waltzing through the cool night air,
turn kamikaze on windshield and hood.
Even the moon spins down the sky
and the next day, when it spins up again,
seems surprised to find it's where it was
the night before.

I am most at ease on the road,
and push the gas till I attain a speed
in which I waltz with insects and trees.
We are tireless dancers, awake in the night,
swinging in and out—family, friends,
lovers gone and lovers yet to come,
while the trees shake thunderous thighs
and the moon sews together the skirts of leaves
with a silver thread the sun will unravel.

Did I love the girl? Unequivocally, yes. But love, I was learning, was more than sexual desire and rapport. It arose from psychological obsessions and needs that had gone unacknowledged, unidentified, and unthought-about since I was a boy. Aside from the guilt, I was learning things about myself that had never occurred to me, things which I had avoided thinking about. That realization, in the end, made all the suffering bearable, for I came to see the destruction I had wrought by my actions as also a time of learning for everyone involved.

First, I came to understand that since childhood I had been setting my life up on a set of goals that could not be sustained in the world of men and women. I came to see my marriage to Wilma, and my conception of marriage in general, as a hermetically sealed environment, secure and unchanging, apart from whatever social, political, or natural events might occur.

Second, I had to acknowledge how traumatic my youth had been and what part my mother, in the guise of an unreachable female presence, had played in the formation of my psyche. I was thirty-three in the spring of 1970 and the girl was nineteen. In time, I came to recognize that what she saw in me was the father she wished for—humorous, loving, sensitive, and solicitous to her concerns. Her own father was a cold, deceitful, and cynical womanizer who held her mother in psychological bondage.

Tellingly, the girl was the direct opposite of Wilma in every way: she was blonde, slim, a California beach girl. But, more important, she was understanding, even solicitous, where Wilma was tempestuous, angry, always blaming, and making me feel more and more caught on the roller coaster of her changing moods. Later, I would understand that my attraction to the girl was because she was a picture-perfect WASP, not only blonde and gray-eyed, but a symbol to my Slavic, Semitic, outsider persona of the woman I longed to have love me. What I would learn about her, though, was that she was also deceitful and underhanded, unlike the confrontational, highly emotional people who populated the world I came from.

I also looked at what had attracted me to Wilma. We were both artists, and she held out the possibility of a closed world of creative people working together. But during the thirteen years of our marriage I'd come to recognize that Wilma identified me with the father she alternately loved and hated for his weakness in not standing up to her mother—and that her attitude toward me shifted from day to day and was, to say the least, ambivalent.

1970 to 1972 were years of suffering, especially concerning Jana and Valerie. I could not forgive myself for putting them in the situation in which I'd found myself as a child. I made sure they spent every weekend with me. And to keep my sanity, as I rushed from my new apartment to my girl-friend's apartment and to my family's house, I began to write the series of poems I quoted from above. I collected them in a manuscript called *Toward Certain Divorce*. The manuscript is a book of agonies, one of the most honest things I've ever written. Several of the poems have appeared in magazines and anthologies, but I never published the manuscript as a book.

In the end, I finally found relief from my guilt feelings. It occurred in a therapist's office where Wilma and I had gone for family counseling as a last effort at reconciliation in the spring of 1972. When Wilma, in a challenging, strident manner, demanded the therapist tell us why our relationship wasn't working, he answered that she had been trying to get rid of me for years, first by telling me to go out and have affairs and, second, by encouraging me to continue my relationship with my student. At first angered by the therapist's remarks, Wilma finally acknowledged that they were true.

Like a head under a guillotine, my guilt feelings toward Wilma were sev-
ered in an instant. Here was the ultimate betrayal, a psychological abandonment that uncannily resembled my mother's consigning me to the schools
as a child. All feeling rushed out of me. The world, it seemed, worked in
ways I would never be able to explain.

Only the guilt concerning my children remained, and that I would have
to assuage over the years by loving them and never abandoning them.

Ultimately, I came to regard the break-up as a point of embarkation. I
was leaving the world I had constructed in my head, a Never-Neverland of
fairy-tale permanence where everyone lived happily ever after, and I was
heading toward a world of constant change and endless possibilities, one in
which I couldn't control events or people or feelings, for I finally came to the
most frightening self-realization of all: in my marriage I had become self-
righteous, judgmental, and closed to the world around me—all pitfalls I
should have recognized from my Taoist readings.

Although I didn't quite grasp it as I left the therapist's office, life was
about to become an adventure once more.

BOOK EIGHT

THE 1970s

CHAPTER 26

Leonard Gardner and Gina Berriault

It was during the tumultuous years of the break-up that I became close friends with Leonard Gardner. Leonard was a lean, laconic Californian whose first novel, *Fat City*, became an instant classic when it was published in 1969. I had met him three years before that, when I lived in San Francisco. He was a good friend of Robert Peterson and was at Peterson's house in Marin County the night I first read there along with Robert and several other poets. The people at the party were a loud, hard drinking group. Leonard and his girlfriend, Gina Berriault, battled their way through the crowd in the narrow room to tell me they liked what they had heard. I was flattered. Although I hadn't known of him as a writer at that time, Leonard had a way about him that left you awestruck in his presence. I did know Gina's early work, especially the novels *The Descent*, *The Son*, and *A Conference of Victims*. After that, I saw Leonard and Gina on and off at parties before Peterson moved to New Mexico and I moved to Santa Cruz.

I don't remember how Leonard and I came to meet again, but when we did, I had already read *Fat City* and loved as well as admired it. Leonard's style was spare but evocative and his characters so real they seemed to walk right out of the book. They were people we've known or met or passed on the street, people with dreams that aren't going to happen but who carry a grace and resilience that goes one better than Hemingway's characters much of the time. Leonard's two main characters, young Ernie Munger and older Billy Tully, represented youth and adulthood, but they were as unobtrusively symbolic as the desert Ernie traveled through in one part of the book, a desert that represented the existential universe.

Leonard Gardner, 1969

"Unobtrusive" is the operative word here. The writing and the story are so matter of fact, they seem artless—a trick of many great writers. But the book's honesty and insight about the human condition, as much as

268

the experience of reading the book, have affected more people I know than has any American novel of the last thirty years of the twentieth century, and that speaks to the book's special place in American literature.

It must have been toward the end of 1970 that Leonard and I met again. Leonard was working on the screenplay for *Fat City*, which was to be filmed by John Huston. I had just broken up with Wilma and he had broken up with Gina, and maybe that cemented our relationship. Of course, we shared our love of boxing as well and soon were going to the fights together at Kezar Pavilion and the old Civic Center, and later Joe and I would join him to view Muhammad Ali's closed circuit TV fights at the Cow Palace.

I'd drive up to the city after classes, and Leonard and I, and sometimes mutual friends, would go out to eat and then to the fights. But mostly it was Leonard and me, either going to the fights or sitting around his apartment after going out to dinner, talking about everything under the heavens until the early hours of the morning. Many nights I never got home before dawn and had just enough time to shower and leave for class.

Leonard and I had a routine. I would get to his apartment at 6:00 PM or so, and we'd talk boxing for three hours: the current fight scene, Ali in particular, and crazy speculations, such as "Do you think a fighter loses his punch after he's lost everything else?" "Do you think you would be a better fighter now that you know so much about life as well as what goes on in the ring?" Leonard was still working out at the Newman-Herman Gym in downtown San Francisco and was half serious, but I laughed and pointed out that I was a thirty-three-year-old overweight 200-pound male whose reflexes were gone and who had boxed amateur as a 120-pound teenager.

"But have you lost your punch?" asked Leonard with a grin.

"Only what was in the bowl at the party last night," I quipped, and we would both laugh and continue our chatter.

Our fight banter went on every time and everywhere we met. I remember one evening when Jim Houston came up to us at one of our favorite haunts, the Filipino restaurant the Mabuhay, which was located in the building adjacent to the old International Hotel on the edge of Chinatown. Jim stood with his mouth open for fifteen minutes as we carried on one of our animated, nonstop conversations about a recent boxing match.

But if we were having fun, we were also feinting and verbally jabbing at our real concern, which we began to talk about after the third hour of fight conversation and continued for the rest of the night—and that was discussions about the nature of love and the relationships between men and women.

A year or two later, Leonard and Gina got back together. They had many things in common, not the least of which was a reverence for literature that was almost religious and based on both of them working at the highest levels of the literary art.

Gina was an intense, serious woman. She was thin, beautiful, and dark-haired, and gave the impression of physical fragility. She often hugged herself as if she were cold and spoke quietly and carefully, which gave the impression that her words were never frivolously spoken.

When Leonard and Gina got back together, the three of us continued the friendship. Even after they moved to Marin County, we continued meeting every month or so in the city. I would come up to San Francisco, and we would go out to eat and talk books and writing. One of the topics we continually dwelt on were the peregrinations around New Mexico of our mutual friend Robert Peterson, who by that time had been abandoned by Dorothy and had moved to Albuquerque. Another topic was Ray Carver, another mutual friend, and his changing fortunes. Carver's third book of short stories, *What We Talk About When We Talk About Love*, had come out in 1981, had been reviewed on the front page of the *New York Times*' book-review section, and had launched Ray into celebrity status. We were particularly confused by Ray's paring down a number of the stories we knew in earlier incarnations, especially one of Leonard's favorites, "So Much Water So Close to Home." Later, we learned that Ray had slashed the stories at his editor Gordon Lish's insistence. Over the years that followed, he would either restore the stories to their original form or expand them into new ones.

Gina Berriault,
1970s

Sometimes we were joined by Leonard and Gina's close friend, Clancy Carlile, who quit writing for thirteen years after he had published his first novel and couldn't get anyone to publish his second. Also a country and western singer, he led a tumultuous life and didn't publish his second novel until he was well into middle age, twenty years after his first one. The novel was a medical disaster potboiler called *Spore 7*, and he followed it with a minor masterpiece, *Honky Tonk Man*, which earned him half a million dollars and was filmed by Clint Eastwood. Because his publishers had bungled the publicity on the book, however, it never received the public attention it should have.

As the years went on, Leonard wrote articles on boxing and, because of his classic screenplay for John Huston's film version of *Fat City*, several film scripts. The latter led to his being selected as one of the regular writers for the popular, prize-winning television series *NYPD Blue* in the 1990s. By then we had lost touch, mainly because I got up to the city less and less and Leonard was living much of the time in LA as part of the *NYPD Blue* writing team. Even then we still saw each other at least once a year at one occasion or another, and in 1986, he and Joe acted as best men at my second wedding.

Gina continued to write every day, turning out one brilliant story after another, and one of them, an early story she made into a screenplay called "The Stone Boy," was made into an excellent independent motion picture.

I always thought Gina was complex and shy but at the same time full of inner strength, extraordinary sensitivity, and determination. Even though we were friends, she never took the friendship for granted. Several days after going out with her and Leonard for dinner before I left for Greece, and, in a moment of expansiveness, paying the bill for the three of us as a thank you for a favor they had done me, I received a letter from Gina with a cashier's check for $100. She knew I couldn't afford to pay for the meal, but she also knew I wouldn't accept the money. That's why she put it in a cashier's check—a check that was already cash. She explained in the letter, in a most gracious manner, that she was sending the check so I wouldn't lose face, and concluded that if I wouldn't accept her argument and intended to send the check back, I could get her a present in Greece with the money: a small Minerva's owl statuette for her desk. The statuette cost less than $20, and I hope she glanced at it every now and then with an affectionate smile.

Gina was particularly concerned about her friends and supportive of them. I remember calling Leonard and Gina's apartment after a traumatic night during which I had been cajoled, manipulated, and beseeched by the woman with whom I had had the affair that broke up my marriage: she wanted to get together again. It had been eight years since I had seen her, and she had been married and divorced during that time. Now she was living in Marin County, and I drove up from Santa Cruz, only to be shunned by her once more. The next morning I called Leonard and Gina, and Gina, hearing the misery in my voice, commanded me to come over to the house. She made me breakfast, and she and Leonard commiserated with me the entire morning and afternoon. Gina hovered over me as protectively as a mother, and as the day wore on she became more and more incensed at my ex-lover's behavior, finally declaring she was going to get in touch with her and tell her a thing or two.

Gina was also generous and encouraging. She and Leonard went over Clancy's manuscripts and urged him on in his most unhappy days, and if anyone is responsible for this memoir, it is Gina, who was always coming up with excellent suggestions concerning writing projects and solutions to personal problems. One day, after hearing one of the many stories of my childhood that she had listened to over the years, she pointedly told me to sit down and write my memoirs, and she brought up that suggestion a number of times in the ensuing years.

During those years, Gina was teaching writing at San Francisco State, and North Point Press began to re-release her earlier books. This culminated in Counterpoint publishing her selected short stories, *Women in Their Beds,* in 1996. The book won the National Book Critics' Circle Award and the PEN/Faulkner Award. The stories are brilliant psychological studies of people from all walks of life. They are so perceptive, and her prose so lean and exquisitely turned, that I am amazed she had not been recognized as one of our great writers before then. The reason people are not aware of Gina, even to this day, is that she eschewed publicity.

Unfortunately, just as she began to attract the critical attention she deserved, she was struck down by cancer.

Leonard was also a true friend. Time and again, I saw him go out of his way to help acquaintances. While he was working in Los Angeles as part of the writing team for *NYPD Blue*, he was told that Clancy Carlile had collapsed in Texas. Leonard rushed down to his friend's bedside and stayed with him until just before his death. When I called Clancy's hospital room, Leonard answered. He was on guard, taking care of things, trying to muster Clancy's will to live. And after Clancy died, Leonard proofread the galleys of Clancy's last novel, *Paris Pilgrims*, doing, as he said, "the final things Clancy would have done."

Although he seldom wrote letters to them—a fact Bob Peterson griped about continually—Leonard's friends were important to him. A telling incident concerned my first novel. A mutual friend read it and thought it was good but refused to send the manuscript to his agent because he didn't want to jeopardize his reputation by suggesting a genre novel to him. When Leonard heard about this, he picked up the phone, called the agent in question, and told him he had a "hot" novel for him to look at. Within two weeks the agent had sold the book to a big New York publishing house. Leonard had not read a word of the manuscript, but it was unthinkable to him that any writer would not help a colleague. Such generosity was characteristic. Less dramatic, but equally meaningful to me, he drove more than one hundred miles to celebrate my wedding to my second wife, where, as I've said, he shared best-man chores with Joe.

When Gina died in 1999, Leonard was bereft. It took him more than two years to come out of mourning. I was invited to the small memorial gathering of Gina's friends and, as the years passed, would talk to him on the phone and see him at Christmas and Independence Day, when he came to Santa Cruz to visit his friends, John and Harriet Deck. He also attended all the readings I gave in San Francisco and Berkeley. Leonard's concern for his friends never slackened, as the following example shows.

A few years after Gina's death, another mutual friend, Lennart Bruce, died. Lennart was a Swedish multimillionaire whose board of directors had taken over his fresh fruit and refrigerator companies while he was in Africa, where he had gone to more altruistically than capitalistically develop refrigeration plants in several newly formed African nations.

Lennart was a small, slim, fine-boned man who was as handsome as his wife, and former secretary, Sonja, was beautiful. Kindly, quiet, sophisticated, always friendly and hospitable, he, as well as Sonja, were regarded affectionately by all who knew them. Both had come to America in the late 1960s to talk with the head of International Harvester about setting Lennart up in business once again. But Lennart, a lover of literature all his life, abandoned all thoughts of business when he visited City Lights Bookshop in San Francisco and, on the spot, decided to become the poet he had always wanted to be.

By the early 1970s, Lennart's books were being published by Hitchcock at Kayak Press and Dennis Koran at Cloud Marauder, and he enjoyed a national reputation through the 1980s. I brought him to Cabrillo several times, and both his poetry and personality fascinated the students. But, as inexplicably happens, he was unable to find a publisher in the 1990s and disappeared from the literary scene. All the while, he and Sonja lived modestly on whatever secretarial work she could find. In the end, Lennart was mainly known as a translator of Swedish literature, an enterprise in which he and Sonja collaborated and earned much-needed income.

From the start Lennart's poetry was mostly written in a simple, straightforward English, which enhanced his humorous observations of the world around him. Always interested in the vagaries of consciousness, he would write down his impressions immediately on waking in the morning. Here's one of those poems:

> *Dawn*
>
> There's
> a rustle
>
> in the auricle
> someone
>
> is coming
> down the ear passage
>
> smashing
> the night

His poetry is mainly of two kinds. The first are highly original insights about the minutiae of everyday life that radically shifted ordinary perceptions so the world seemed new, as if just discovered, such as the following:

> *Out Walking*
>
> Ordinarily
> I don't pay much attention
>
> but when I lie down
> on it
>
> I notice, the road
> is out walking too,
>
> an altogether
> different gait,
>
> on its way
> as well

The second kind of poems are tongue-in-cheek narratives of the business and social world in which he had once flourished. His poetry is never bitter about the injustices done him by his business associates but wry observations of the business world. As he said, his life in the business world was "bankrupt," and he had given it up to create "a new individual with another sensitivity potential." It was "a swap of heads."

When Lennart died in 2003, Leonard immediately visited Sonja to console and advise her, and, over time, he searched through Lennart's voluminous manuscripts to make sure "no undiscovered gems [got] stored way." A year later, in 2004, Leonard, the poet Luis Garcia, and I staged a memorial reading of Lennart's work in Berkeley. Leonard was the one who organized the reading.

CHAPTER 27

The Capra Press Affair

I spent Christmas of 1971 in Santa Barbara with the painter Gary Brown. Hitchcock had commissioned Brown to illustrate my first book, *Origins*, in 1969, but it wasn't until September of 1971 that we met. The occasion was the opening of an exhibition of Gary's latest work in the Bay Area. "Got another book for me?" he asked jokingly. He was pleasantly drunk. When I seriously answered that I had, he invited me down to his home in Santa Barbara over Christmas vacation to talk about the project and then disappeared into the clamoring crowd and loud music.

I had no intention of taking him up on his offer, but by mid-December my life was falling apart. Wilma and I were separating, and she had taken Jana and Valerie to her parents' house in Florida for the holidays. At the same time, the affair that had broken up the marriage abruptly ended when the lady in question said goodbye to me. I was feeling guilty and desolate; I definitely didn't want to be alone and remembered Gary's half-serious invitation. I called him up, reminding him of it. He was taken aback at first but then enthusiastically told me to come down. The ride to Santa Barbara was a stormy one, with blustery squalls of rain washing out roads left and right.

What was I doing here, traveling to the house of someone I'd met for five minutes at a drunken art opening?

I took with me the now-completed manuscript of *The Santa Cruz Mountain Poems*. I also brought along a collection of forty poems I had written before and after *Origins* called *Where the Oceans Cover Us*.

Gary and his roommate Dennis had a late supper waiting for me, and although I was exhausted, all three of us formed an instant friendship that has lasted more than thirty years during which Gary and I have done many projects together.

With Gary Brown, Santa Barbara, 1992

The day after I arrived at his house, Gary read *The Santa Cruz Mountain Poems* manuscript and listened to my idea of having illustrations on every page of the book and placing one poem to a page, as if the words were part of a landscape. This would draw the reader into concentrating on each poem, I said, and would provide the illustrator with a display of his work that was as visible as the poetry.

Gary warmed to the idea and called up Graham Macintosh, the great hand-printer who had run White Rabbit Press in Berkeley and had been working at Capra Press in Santa Barbara for the last several years. He came over for a Christmas drink, looked at the manuscript, listened to my plans, and called Noel Young, the senior partner at Capra, who set up a meeting with Gary and me for the next day.

We met Noel at his favorite downtown bar, and immediately he and I took to each other. He was a bon vivant, great storyteller, and lots of fun to be around. I recognized from the start that he drank too much and was further apprised of his character when he explained that Capra stood for Capricorn, the astrological sign under which he was born: like the goat that was Capricorn's emblem, he was a rutting animal.

Although Noel only glanced at my manuscript, within half an hour he was sold on the project. It was clear to me that he could not resist the opportunity to put out what would amount to a book of Gary's work. Gary had done some illustrations gratis for him before, and Gary's reputation as a fine artist was well known in Santa Barbara, where he was an up-and-coming member of the University of California at Santa Barbara Art Department.

Noel and I swapped stories, told outrageous jokes, and generally got to know each other. He invited me to his home and asked if I had any other work ready for publication. I had. In fact, it was the second manuscript I had brought with me, *Where the Oceans Cover Us*. It was comprised of four parts. The first consisted of poems written before the *Origins* outburst of 1967, most of them composed during and after I left Iowa. The second section was a long mystical poem in the voice of an aging cigar maker, the third a ten-poem selection from the series I had been writing about my divorce, and the fourth section was another long poem, an elegy for Kenneth Patchen, the poet whose work had meant so much to me when I was in boot camp and who had died the previous year.

Noel took both manuscripts away with him and arranged for me to come down to Santa Barbara within the month and stay with him and his wife and daughter for the weekend.

Gary, Dennis, and I were excited about the Santa Cruz mountain book. We were slightly dazed that Noel had so quickly and wholeheartedly gotten behind the project, but I was even more stupefied the next morning when Noel called to tell me he wanted to publish *Where the Oceans Cover Us* as well. He said, hoping he was not insulting me, that he liked *Oceans* much more than *The Santa Cruz Mountain Poems* but recognized the latter's merits as a gift book.

I wasn't surprised. *The Santa Cruz Mountain Poems* was a mystical nature book, removed from the conflicts of human relationships, whereas *Oceans* was rooted in the everyday world.

I was elated and couldn't wait to see Noel again. Thus began a year of spending one weekend of every month with Noel in Santa Barbara. Or he would come up to Santa Cruz because, as it turned out, my friends the McDougals were related to him, and all three of us would spend time together at their pottery school on Swanton Road. During that year, Noel sold the print shop to Graham and to his son by his first marriage and set up Capra Press solely as a publishing house.

On my visits, I would eat, Noel would drink, and we would plan. He had started a chapbook series and asked me to suggest writers for the project. I brought him, among others, Jim Houston, Ray Carver, Andre Codrescu, and Peter Beagle. He was especially taken with Jim and Ray's work and became an important stepping-stone in their careers when he published a book of short stories by Jim and two important collections by Ray. A novelist who had abandoned the craft in favor of publishing, Noel had an affinity for fiction writers and a keen eye for the talented ones. I also urged him to publish Joe Stroud's first manuscript, and he brought out Joe's first book, *In the Sleep of Rivers*, the year after he did my books.

Noel and I had become bosom friends by my third visit, and in the lull between one party or another, I wrote descriptions for Capra catalogs or edited what he had sketched to go into them. At that time he had original pieces by Lawrence Durrell and Henry Miller. He also published a book by Bill Everson, who had left the Dominican order and, with his new wife and stepson, had moved to Santa Cruz, where we had become friends.

But peppered throughout those good times were incidents that worried me. Noel was constantly excited by manuscripts he received in the mail, and he made one commitment after another to aspiring poets and fiction writers. He offered to publish books by literally dozens of people that first year, and I couldn't imagine how he could fulfill those promises. In fact, I knew he couldn't. The first time I visited his Buckminster Fuller-inspired geodesic-dome house, he showed me a broadside he had printed by a poet named Carlos Reyes. It was a fine poem that, Noel said, was to be included in a book by Reyes he had planned to put out before he met me but was now delaying to do my two books. Two years later, Reyes' book still had not been published, and it never would be.

I quickly learned that such practices were part of a pattern. Noel would get excited about a manuscript and pledge to publish it, but when he would read an offering by someone else that impressed him, he would put the earlier manuscript on hold. I think that ninety percent of the books he agreed to print never came out. Carlos Reyes' book was one of them. I wish I could ascribe this lapse on his part to intoxication with literature or just intoxication in general, but an interesting addendum to this anecdote is that to my knowledge he never sent a contract to an author until he put the book into galleys.

Another of Noel's questionable practices was that, as far as I know, he almost never paid his authors once he published their work. His ability to find ways not to part with money was one of his singular talents. My first inkling of this aspect of his business dealings occurred six months after I met him. Jim Houston called to say that Noel was bringing out a book of his short stories but had offered him only $250 advance against royalties, and he wondered how much of an advance Noel had given me. The length of my silence must have told Jim more than he wanted to know. Noel had offered me no advance on either of my books. Although I never expected to make money on my poetry, I was perturbed. Not only was he publishing two of my books, but I had written his catalog and brought him a half-dozen first-class writers to publish, including Jim.

I was to learn another of Noel's favorite shenanigans all too soon. If he actually reached the stage where he had signed a contract and begun printing a book, he would inform the writer that he didn't have the funds to bring the book out, and only if the author could come up with the money would he be able to publish the volume. His popular coffee table photography book on the houses of Santa Barbara and Montecito was paid for in this way, each of the homeowners solicited for funds so that Noel could bring the book out.

All these practices became factors that affected both the books we were working on and our friendship in the late summer and early fall of 1972. I had made sure that Noel kept on track with *Where the Oceans Cover Us*. We had decided that *Oceans* would come out before *The Santa Cruz Mountain Poems* because Gary would not have the fifty or so full-page drawings for the "mountain" book finished before September (especially since the originals he was working on were 36 x 22 inches each). Gary had taken a leave without pay from the university that spring in order to work on the drawings and was spending the summer in New England to work on them undisturbed.

When I visited Noel in August, he showed me the preliminary contract for the book. I was to receive 12 percent royalties on every book, but Gary was to get only 1 percent illustrator's fees.

"You can't do this," I said to Noel. "He sacrificed salary as well as time on this project."

Noel shrugged. "He's the illustrator, isn't he?"

"Yes, but this book is as much his work as mine, you know that."

Noel shrugged again.

"Okay," I said, "I want you to give him 5.5 percent of my royalties, so we're both getting an equal 6.5 percent. How do you feel now?"

"Fine," said Noel, as if he couldn't comprehend what I was getting so annoyed about. "If you want to give him your money, that's your business."

I didn't come down to Santa Barbara again until the middle of September when Gary returned from the East Coast with most of the drawings. The three of us arranged to meet at Noel's office for a final conference. At lunch, Gary showed us thirty of the drawings and where he imagined the poems would be placed on them. The drawings were exquisite and his layout ideas were exactly what I had visualized when I first showed him the book the previous Christmas.

Noel admired the drawings, lit a thin cigar, and leaned forward. "We've got problems," he said. "First, the idea of bringing the book out as a fold-out scroll won't work. The Japanese craftsmen don't do a piece this long, and the cost would be prohibitive."

Gary's face showed his disappointment. We had envisioned the book as a giant scroll that would become a continuous landscape when unfolded and either placed on a large surface or attached to a wall. For that reason, Gary had planned to use a single horizon line throughout the drawings. But Gary didn't have time to register his unhappiness before Noel spoke again.

"But the shape of the book is no longer a problem. The fact is, I looked over my finances and I don't have the money to do the book, certainly not the way we planned to do it."

Gary's face clearly showed the shock Noel's statement had caused. My face must have looked the same.

"What do you mean?" I croaked.

"I can't do the book the way we said. The fine-art copy is too expensive, and since that's how I was going to pay for the printing costs of the general market edition, I can't do the book."

Noel was referring to the two ways he had planned to finance the project. First there would be the fine-art edition that would sell to collectors and libraries for $250 to $500 a volume and would be hand-printed and the size of Gary's original drawings. Meanwhile, Noel would print a smaller 11 x 14 version for the general trade edition with the profits from the fine-art edition.

I looked at Gary. He was crestfallen.

"Gary's done a lot of work on this. He took a leave of absence—how come you didn't go over your finances earlier?"

"We're not completely undone. There's still a way we can do it. . . ." Noel said.

Gary and I said nothing.

Noel nodded and continued. "If one of you could raise three or four thousand dollars, I could match that and do both editions."

He sat back and waited.

"And if I could," I said, "what would the investors get?"

"One hundred percent interest on their loans. $6,000 for $3,000. $8,000 for $4,000."

"And you'll do both editions, right?"

Noel nodded, and the conversation was done. Within a week I had raised the money, one half from wealthy friends, the other half from Robert Ludlow, a Santa Cruz lawyer who wanted to promote Santa Cruz's cultural image.

And so *The Santa Cruz Mountain Poems* was published. But the story doesn't end there.

Noel never printed the fine-art edition of the book and used all $4,000 to print the trade edition, and not in color, as we had agreed, but black print with sepia-colored ink for the drawings; and not by hand, but, for the first time in Capra's history, by photo offset. Still, the book sold in the thousands and was continually being reordered by big department stores like Macy's as well as by leading bookstores.

A year later, Ludlow, the lawyer who had generously invested the money, asked a friend of mine if I was a con man. "Why?" I asked, when the friend relayed the statement to me. Because, said the friend, Noel hadn't paid Ludlow a cent. When I called the friends who had put up the rest of the money, they told me they had not been paid either.

I called Noel. He was having a cash-flow problem, he said, but he would pay them in part in the next month. Three months later, they still had not been paid. I drove down to Santa Barbara and appeared unannounced at the Capra office on State Street. Noel was alone. He could see how angry I was but still hemmed and hawed. I grabbed him by the shoulder and practically flung him into the chair behind his desk.

"Your checkbook—where is it? You're going to give my friends everything you owe them—interest and all."

He hurriedly made out two checks and handed them to me. His eyes were darting left and right: I could see he was frightened. As I tucked the checks into my wallet, I said, "I thought we were friends. This was my reputation you were screwing with." And I turned to go, but then I remembered something else. "Come to think of it, you have never sent me a royalty statement on either *The Santa Cruz Mountain Poems* or *Where the Oceans Cover Us*. How many books have you sold?"

He started to protest, but I moved toward him belligerently again. Within five minutes, he had handed me a royalty check for $5,000, and I was driving home.

I repeated this act every six months for the next two years, collecting $3,000 more. By then, Noel and I were barely talking. He had promised to print 3,000 copies of *Where the Oceans Cover Us* but only ran 1,500, promising to reprint the rest when (and if) the first 1,500 sold. I had called him the first of every month for four months, asking how the book was selling, and he would answer that it wasn't selling and would conclude sympathetically, "Unfortunately, poetry, even good poetry, just doesn't sell. You know that."

A week after I called him the fifth time and received the same answer, I strolled into Plaza Books, a bookstore in Santa Cruz owned by a gregarious friend named Hal Morris. Hal swept up to me with a smile and congratulated me.

"What for?" I asked.

"This," he said, holding up a distributor's catalog and tapping a box on the cover entitled *Last Call*. "They've sold the entire run of *Oceans* except for twenty-five copies—and in just five months."

I called Noel immediately. "What's this about?' I asked.

"Oh, yes, I meant to tell you. Everything turned around last week."

I gritted my teeth. "And now you're going to run the remaining 1,500, right?"

"I wish I could, but I've got all my money tied up in the next three books. But soon. Don't worry. Soon."

Where the Oceans Cover Us was never reprinted.

A year or two after I went to Santa Barbara to retrieve my friends' investments, Gary called me. Noel had not paid him a cent for his part in *The Santa Cruz Mountain Poems*, and he needed the money. By then I had made more than $10,000 on the book, which meant Gary was owed the same amount of money.

I drove to Santa Barbara that weekend. My daughters and Gary went with me to Noel's office, and when I began to call Noel every name I could think of, reminding him that Gary had done work for him gratis through the years, and that Gary's 6.5 percent included half "my" share of the royalties. Gary herded the girls out of the office so they wouldn't hear such language.

It was one of the last times I saw Noel. When the Capitola Book Company reprinted *The Santa Cruz Mountain Poems* in 1992, a big book signing was arranged in Santa Barbara "for this new edition of one of Capra's landmark books." By then, Noel had become a town character, an elder statesman of the Santa Barbara art world. He was also a hopeless drunk and, pathetically, still a philanderer. He was to introduce a short reading by me and reminisce about the production of the original book. He, Gary, and I, along with some of his admirers, had dinner together, and Noel and I were civil to each other. But he made me pay for my part of the dinner and disappeared shortly after I began to read.

In the end, dementia or Alzheimer's ravaged him. He was taken care of by loyal friends and idolizing young would-be printers. He died in 2002.

In not one history of the press, done before or after Noel's death, is my name mentioned.

CHAPTER 28

Raymond Carver

One of the most often-used later publicity photos of Raymond Carver shows him seated, leaning forward, hands crossed in front of him, wearing a soft leather flying jacket, eyes peering intently, almost challengingly at the viewer. His hair is mussed but recently razored to fashionably fit his face. He looks like he's just come from a polo match or his fortieth bombing mission over Schweinfurt. He's cool, in control, almost aggressively, intimidatingly self-confident. There are several variations of this photograph, most taken by Marion Ettlinger, but they all insist on the intensity of those eyes, on that self-confidence, and on the hair razored fashionably short and mussed.

The Ray Carver I knew looked nothing like that. He wore ties and rumpled sport jackets and never appeared quite right in them. Not that the jack-

Raymond Carver, Sunnyvale, 1971

ets didn't fit but that he seemed awkward, even uncomfortable wearing them: he held his shoulders too high, away from his body, like adolescent weights, giving the impression that there was an iron bar lashed across his upper back and that his body hung slackly from it. Sometimes it seemed as if that bar was the only thing holding him up. As for his hair, it grew over his ears and sat in uncombed chunks around his head. A nervous, raspy laugh punctuated his sentences, and he had trouble looking people in the eye. The word "youthful" comes to mind and "shy," "bashful," "ingenuous," or "boyish," "eternally boyish." A boy who woke in a nightmare to find himself in an adult's body hemmed in on all sides by sport jackets and snatches of menacing conversation.

As for props, he usually had a glass in one hand and a cigarette in the other. Like the imagined bar across his back, they held him up in their own way, although now I can't help seeing that cigarette as a piece of chalk he used to chart his lifeline on the cosmic blackboard, or as a baton with which he was learning to conduct his own requiem.

■ ■ ■

My relationship with Ray never reached the boozy intimacy he had with others. I knew him from 1967 to 1977, his most notoriously alcoholic period, and even though I can still sit and talk in bars for hours on end, I only drink socially now, and I only drank socially then. For that reason alone it may seem impossible that we were friends at all. Another impediment to our friendship was our personae: Ray, like Jim Houston and George Hitchcock, was an iconic American male through and through; that is, he internalized everything—the pains, the uncertainties, the humiliations, the fears—whereas I gushed them in a torrent of emotions and operatic gestures. Add to this that Ray was a small-town boy, and a small-town boy from the Northwest at that, while I was a city boy from the East Coast, and you've got what seems an almost insurmountable barrier to friendship.

Running counter to the differences, however, were the similarities. Ray and I didn't put on airs; that's what we had most in common. Although I was from New York City, I never pretended to be cool or hip. Ray—and his wife, Maryann, too—were open and generous-spirited from the start. I knew they had no rocks in their hands, and they knew I had none in mine. We never analyzed our friendship or even once questioned why we liked one another: whenever we saw each other we talked, laughed, shared our work, and generally enjoyed one another's company. No matter how many months would go by between meetings, we resumed our friendship where we had left off.

In 1981, Ray sent me a copy of *What We Talk About When We Talk About Love*. In it he had inscribed this dedication: "For Mort, with nothing but love, and admiration." That about says it, although the word "admiration" needs to be explained. I'd like to think it refers to the writing, which truly cemented the friendship, the recognition on both our parts that under the sport coats we were two kids trying to figure out what this life meant, no matter how horrendous the revelations, and that we were both pursuing that goal through a mutually ferocious dedication to words. That commitment was our inseparable bond.

Besides this I was a poet whose work Ray liked, and poets were something special to him. He said toward the end of his life that he would like to be remembered as a poet, and I wish now I had told him more often how good I thought his poetry was. There is a lack of pretentiousness in his poems—in tone and diction—which is unique in contemporary American poetry, and we can all learn from it. It is disarming and therefore makes the implications, ironies, and juxtapositions of images that much more powerful. Ray wrote poetry as if it were written with a small, not a capital, "p", conveying an impression of almost artless naturalness that no other American poet of his generation—and maybe any other generation—has been able to evoke. In his last volume, *A New Path to the Waterfall* (1989), this naturalness reaches its apex, spilling down the page with an appearance of artlessness that resembles

nothing so much as water, which assumes the shapes of every channel it enters
yet remains itself, appearing as swirls, slurs, elongations, and a variety of tex-
tures and colors under the shifts of light and sediments it travels over. At the
same time it continues to be as transparent and ephemeral as breath when you
attempt to lift it in your hands. Here's an example of what I'm talking about:

Happiness

So early it's still almost dark out.
I'm near the window with coffee,
and the usual early morning stuff
that passes for thought.

When I see the boy and his friend
walking up the road
to deliver the newspaper.

They wear caps and sweaters,
and one boy has a bag over his shoulder.
They are so happy
they aren't saying anything, these boys.

I think if they could, they would take
each other's arm.
It's early in the morning,
and they are doing this thing together.

They come on, slowly.
The sky is taking on light,
though the moon still hangs pale over the water.

Such beauty that for a minute
death and ambition, even love,
doesn't enter into this.

Happiness. It comes on
unexpectedly. And goes beyond, really,
any early morning talk about it.

■ ■ ■

Ray always insisted that we knew each other in Iowa, and so did
Maryann, but I don't recall it. And our dates of tenure there don't correspond. Sometimes I think he meant that he knew *of* me from Iowa. Maybe
that was it. As far as I'm concerned we met at a *Kayak* collating party at
Hitchcock's house in San Francisco.

It was in the spring of 1967, I think, that Hitchcock introduced me to Ray
and Maryann, an indulgence to which George's laissez-fair attitude toward
social etiquette usually didn't succumb, despite his desire to have poets
meet each other. Ray said he was an admirer of my poetry from the Iowa
days, and even at the time I wondered if he had asked George to introduce
us. As I have said, I still don't remember Ray from Iowa, and it wouldn't be
until years later that I learned he had been the student of two special and

talented friends of mine, the fiction writer Richard Day at Humboldt State University and the poet Dennis Schmidt at Sacramento State University, both of whom could have exposed Ray to my work. When I learned that, I suspected even more that Ray had asked Hitchcock to introduce us and that he hadn't said he *knew* me from Iowa but rather had *heard* about me there.

Whatever the reason, Ray and I were soon chatting like old friends. There was an openness about Ray and Maryann that could win over anyone. There was nothing morbid or precious about them. They weren't ego-centered or self-absorbed as are so many of the literati I've met. We talked about everything—from literature to sports to politics—and kept talking from one collating party to the next. These were the parties when I would stay late, and Ray, Maryann, and, after George's wife left him, Maryann's sister, Amy, and any odd member of the collating squad still around, would go off to supper together.

At about this time (1969) Hitchcock put out my first book of poems, *Origins*, and a year later he brought out Ray's first book of poems, *Winter Insomnia*. During this period, I knew Ray as a poet. That is what we talked about mostly, and I think the extreme concentration he exercised at times in his prose can be traced to his poetic practices. Gradually he showed me one or two stories, then added others, many in manuscript or in pages stripped from magazines. I was astonished by them, to say the least. As I remember, the first one I saw was "The Student's Wife," and soon after that "Will You Please Be Quiet, Please," and within the next year or two, in the early 1970s, "Fat" and "Neighbors."

What was astonishing, even unique about Ray's stories at that time was not that they engaged everyday American life and went behind the doors of suburban middle-class and blue-collar homes, but that they were scenarios of our worst dreams about the reality of our neighbors' existences, scenarios about the spiritual barrenness at the heart of American life, which, under the surface, the majority of us were living, whether we admitted it or not. Ray had the courage to face this barrenness and the genius to make it come alive on paper.

I sensed that a lot of Ray's writing was autobiographical, either composed of things that had happened to him and Maryann, or things which he feared might. That's why I call them scenarios. He was writing his worst dreams, readying himself for whatever might happen to him and his family, innocent small-town American kids moving through the world like victims in search of an oppressor.

That's why Ray's vaunted realism is so strange, or rather, "unrealistic" in the end and seems to be steeped not in bleakness but in nightmare and approaches the surreal. Especially his poetry. Ray's is a poetry of the threatened. *Winter Insomnia* is propelled by a kind of paranoia, a fear that everyone the speaker encounters means him and his family harm or poses the possibility of it. Menace is everywhere, especially in the poems that deal with the Middle East. It is the paranoia you find in an Alfred Hitchcock film or an Eric Ambler thriller: everyone out there is a threat. This is not realism or super realism; it is, if anything, expressionism, a reality shaped and shadowed by the mind of the artist. That is why I think Ray's poems and stories were so admired by the *Kayak* crowd and why *Winter Insomnia* came out under the Kayak Press imprint.

One more word about the work: Ray knew instinctively about what many of us now know—the unemployment, the fear of homelessness, and the lack of medical security; the terror of being poor or disenfranchised in this land of milk and acid. Intuitively Ray knew what that part of America was all about, and the terror of that knowledge drove him to the bottle and cigarettes, or so I thought then and think to this day.

Now it might seem too simple to name that fear as the reason for Ray's drinking and smoking, but I did. The bottle lip and cigarette tip were nipples on a milk bottle that gave Ray security, pacifiers that let him relax—pacifiers he didn't need any more when he met Tess Gallagher but had needed with Maryann because he and Maryann were both young and he had to grow *through* his fears and *out* of them when he was with her. Which means Tess was the lucky one and Maryann was not. Maybe those notions are too easy. And, again, maybe they're not.

■ ■ ■

After I moved to Santa Cruz, I still journeyed to San Francisco for the *Kayak* collating parties. Within a year, however, Hitchcock moved to Santa Cruz and continued printing *Kayak* magazine and books from his Santa Cruz address. Several years later, George found a new partner, and for him an ideal one. She was Marjorie Simon, a poet who skillfully and lovingly handled his gruffness the rest of his days.

Meanwhile, Ray and Maryann, who had been living in San Jose, moved from there to Sunnyvale, then to Ben Lomond, and in 1972 they bought a house in Cupertino, a suburban town thirty miles south of San Francisco and ten miles north of San Jose. Cupertino was the center of a middle-class residential area, which in the late 1960s and early 1970s served the families of engineers working on defense contracts and soon would be home to the burgeoning computer microchip industry called Silicon Valley. It seemed to me that Ray and Maryann were living the TV version of the American good life, but Ray was drinking too much for things to be going well behind closed doors.

I'm not sure, but I think Ray had not yet lost his advertising job at Science Research Associates and Maryann was teaching high school in Los Altos. Or had he been laid off when she began to teach? What is certain is that something was wrong: either they were living beyond their means or their relationship was crumbling, for soon it was difficult to reach them by phone. I thought the creditors were descending, and any friendly "Hi!" chirping from the receiver could be followed by demands for payment of overdue bills. Was it 1973 or a few years later that Ray's mother or Maryann would answer the phone explaining that the Carvers no longer resided at that address? When I came to visit once, Ray's mother, who didn't know me, insisted I had the wrong house until Ray, who was standing behind an inner door, rescued me.

Sometime during this period, I think in 1971, Ray showed me the manuscript of a new story called "What Is It?" (later renamed "Are These Actual Miles?"), one of the most terrifying pieces he ever wrote. It is about a day in the life of a man burdened with bills whose wife goes off to sell the family car. At different points during the afternoon and evening the man receives calls from his wife who says she is on the verge of making a "great deal" on the car. Finally, in the early hours of the next morning, drunk, she is covertly dropped at home by the car salesman, and the husband stoically puts her to bed. But the salesman returns to place the wife's handbag, which she had left in his car, on the porch. Observing the salesman through the window, the husband wrenches the door open to confront him, but he is unable to say anything to the man, who retreats and drives off behind a nervous spattering of excuses.

The story is filled with a sense of humiliation for both husband and wife, a sense of hopelessness for anyone caught in our socioeconomic treadmill. Few writers anywhere have portrayed economic degradation this nakedly. I was overwhelmed by the story and wondered if it was yet another scenario of Ray's terrors, but I never asked him. Now I assign the story to the category of those chilling pieces of literature which depict the end of an age, such as Ray's beloved Chekhov wrote so relentlessly in plays and stories. The cultures and times are different, but the vision and subject are the same, although Chekhov's vision is not as raw as Ray's.

■ ■ ■

During the early 1970s I was teaching a course I had designed for the University of California Extension called "Writers Off the Page." The class met all day Saturday. In the morning we discussed a novel or book of poems by a contemporary author, and in the afternoon the author met with the class to read aloud, answer questions, and discuss his work.

I asked Ray to be one of the participants and select several stories. He chose "What Is It?" ("Are These Actual Miles?"), "Neighbors," "Fat," and an initiation story he had just finished called "Steelhead Summer" (which appeared renamed and revised, not for the better, as "Nobody Said Anything" in *What We Talk About When We Talk About Love*. The story is about a boy who does combat with a giant fish in the river on the other side of his home town. What makes the story unique is its frame, which comments ironically on the boy's coming of age: at the beginning and end of the story, the boy is witness to his parents arguing. This intrusion of the mundane, drearily unhappy adult world of 1950's America destroys the boy's heroic undertaking, which had charged his imagination by making the everyday world marvelous. All of this was suggested in the original story by medieval quest imagery that paralleled the contemporary images, but the imagery was cut by the time the story reached *What We Talk About When We Talk About Love.*

The class was composed mostly of teachers taking the course for graduate units. Ray's stories excited and horrified them because of their freshness and the way he had directly faced the dark side of American life. The group was filled with admiration and generated the kind of energy you feel when people discover someone in their midst who is going to be a celebrity.

This was the third time I had given the class, and the school administrators had decided to move its location to Palo Alto, fifty miles northeast of Santa Cruz, as an experiment to draw new students. Weather permitting, we would meet for the afternoon sessions under a shady clump of trees in a rolling, open park.

When I met Ray to guide him to our glade, I was surprised by how nervous he was. He was more jumpy than I had ever seen him. I pretended not to notice at first, but as he tremblingly lit one cigarette after another I finally asked what was wrong.

"This is the first time," he said.

"For what?" I replied.

"This is the first time I ever taught a class."

"On your own work?"

"On anything."

It had never occurred to me that Ray hadn't taught before. I tried to calm him, give him confidence, and a few basic pointers—a coach's pep talk. I tried to make him see that he had already introduced himself through his stories, that everyone in the class thought they knew him to the quick because of who they imagined the writer of those stories to be. I don't think that set him at ease in the least.

He was dry-mouthed and twitching as he began the class. But many of the women, seeing his nervousness, gave him maternal encouragement; and the outright admiration of the entire group was so apparent that within fifteen minutes my rhetorical questions and other verbal aides were no longer necessary. Ray's shy, humble manner won everyone over, and he warmed to the serious conversation about his work. I like to think he developed his unassuming, relaxed classroom style because of what happened that day, but the truth is he was just being Ray, and sooner or later he would have realized that simple secret of teaching. As I remember, I invited him to talk to the class for several successive semesters; those, who took the course repeatedly, insisted on it.

One more thing: neither the class nor I could convince Ray that "Steelhead Summer" ("Nobody Said Anything") was a first-rate story. I nagged him about it endlessly over the next several years, and he did finally send it out and get it published in *Sou'Wester*, but he always felt unsure about it. Maybe he thought it was too much like Hemingway's *The Old Man and the Sea*. Maybe he was piqued at himself for writing an initiation story, the kind of tale he had been raised on and knew had become clichéd by the late 1950s. I don't know. But I was happy to see it as the lead story in *Where I'm Calling From*, his selected volume of stories.

■ ■ ■

By 1971, Hitchcock had gotten Ray a teaching assignment at the University of California campus in Santa Cruz. That had to have been accomplished through the man who had hired Hitchcock, the well-known short-story writer James B. Hall, who had been made the provost of the new Creative Arts College on campus, which was called, for lack of a financial donor, College Five. George worked there, and now so did Ray.

While he was at the university, Ray influenced a lot of students, including a number of my former pupils who would tell me how much they loved him as both a teacher and a human being. I, of course, would tell those of my students heading up to the university to be sure and take a class with him. Although he was only working at the university part-time and would soon begin a dizzying travel week teaching at both Santa Cruz and the University of Iowa, a schedule reminiscent of the feverish peregrinations across Siberia of Vasily Sergeich in Chekhov's "In Exile," Ray had the energy to convert U.C. Santa Cruz's literary magazine, *Quarry*, into a publication of national stature, under the name *Quarry West*, by lobbying many of the poets and fiction writers he knew to submit work to it.

It was during his tenure at Santa Cruz that one of the more revealing episodes in my relationship with him took place. As I recall, it was in 1973. Ray had been chosen to host Charles Bukowski, who was to give a reading at the university. When he met Bukowski at the airport, he discovered that the irascible poet had been on a binge for more than a week. I wonder if Ray saw a future image of himself in the creased, pockmarked face of his older contemporary. I know something early on made him decide not to drink glass for glass with Bukowski, and when we met before the reading Ray was completely sober—and worried. He didn't have any idea how Bukowski was going to behave and had quickly realized that the Los Angeles poet operated on both insult and shock.

"Stick close," Ray said to me, "and be sure to come to the party after—please."

Bukowski, on his part, must have taken one look at Ray in his corduroy trousers and rumpled sports jacket and decided to dismiss him as an insipid academic. The reading drew a full audience and was a wild affair. Bukowski punctuated each poem by sucking from a large bottle of gin and tossing raspy insults at the audience—all spoiled middle-class students and prissy professors, as far as he was concerned. The professors grinned condescendingly or left . . . or grinned and then left. But by and large the students were titillated and warmed to this old drunk telling them what little shits they were. I got the impression that Bukowski was delighted in parading his image and that the students were experiencing the taboo excitement of slumming, or being in touch with "real life"—at least for the evening.

Ray wasn't amused by any of it. His worried expression was a mask stuck to his face throughout the reading. As host, he said later, he felt responsible for whatever happened, and I translated this into meaning that he saw his credibility slipping with his superiors at the university with every insult Bukowski growled.

At the party, held in the house of two former students of mine who were currently Ray's students, things got wilder. Only students were present after the first ten minutes. Rock music and pot smoke engulfed the shabby room. Bukowski, drinking everything in sight, muttered, bragged, cursed, and, getting drunker by the minute, grabbed the girls and mashed his whiskery face against theirs or shot his hand to the crotch of their jeans or down their blouses. Several of the girls screamed and ran from the house. A number of the more cerebral students sat back and stared straight ahead, probably stoned. A group of rough town poets watched Bukowski's every move adoringly, as if they were learning how to behave like real poets with Bukowski's every belch or snort. Ray started drinking.

Bukowski blinked when he saw me coming up the stairs. "Allen," he said, "I didn't know you were here. Why doncha recite some lines from 'Howl.'"

I shot back some stupid remark to the effect that "My name isn't Allen. It's Kenneth, Kenneth Patchen."

A malevolent smile lit Bukowski's face, making him look like a sinister pumpkin, as he turned toward Ray. "Hey, Professor, why didntcha tell me that Allen was gonna to be here?" Then he turned back to me and said, "Come on, Allen, give us some 'Howl.'"

My former students were so poor they didn't own a couch, and Bukowski was seated like a malicious Buddha on a mattress set on the living-room floor, stubbing out his cigarettes on the floorboards until one of the students who lived in the apartment stopped him.

Bukowski kept turning to Ray between drinks and grabs, derisively calling him "professor" and treating him like the most menial servant, every once in a while turning to me with that sinister pumpkin face and saying, "Come on, Allen, let's hear it."

I smiled back as malevolently as I could. Bukowski continued drinking. More students ran squealing from the house. Soon Ray, fed up, and by now drunk himself, stalked out. There was no one left but my two former students, Bukowski, and two or three others. Bukowski had not risen from the mattress in several hours. Now, obviously exhausted, he subsided into a stupor, his chin on his chest. "So, Allen," he muttered one more time, "what do you think of this shit?"

At this point Ray clumped up the stairs. Bukowski spied him and raised his head for a moment. "Professor," he said with the last bit of derision he could muster, "Professor . . ."

Ray looked down at him, swaying, but said nothing, his expression caught midway between disgust and pity. But maybe it was neither: Ray was drunker than I'd ever seen him. Something about Bukowski's behavior struck deep inside him, like a pickaxe sinking into the wall of a mine, something he never spoke to me about. My sense of the extremity of Ray's reaction, however, suggests that there was more to it than just disgust or pity. I'm convinced he saw in Bukowski's drinking and behavior intimations of his own future, a sort of Mr. Hyde who would be released by his incessant boozing. On the other hand, this is said with a good deal of hindsight and may be just literary balderdash.

It was a revelatory evening, a historic nonmeeting of two major American writers. For the first time I saw Ray act uncomfortably, feeling responsible for someone else and not knowing how to handle the situation. Bukowski was too much for him: Ray couldn't deal with his continual insults and venomous behavior. But Bukowski was more revealing to me. He showed that the self-image he chose to establish in his poems, an image that limited the poems in both reach and meaning, had taken him over. He had become the mask he chose to face the world wearing. More than this, he was so overwhelmed by this image, and the easy assumptions of others that went with it, that he stereotyped Ray and never realized that he was in the presence of the one artist whose work, on the same subjects and themes, had achieved what he rarely, if ever, could for the very reasons he failed to recognize who Ray was—lack of real interest in others, or compassion.

The upshot of the incident was a nasty poem by Bukowski about the uptight academic host who took care of him in Santa Cruz, and a reply from Ray, the collage-barrage of lines he heard or thought he heard Bukowski speak throughout the evening incorporated into the poem "You Don't Know What Love Is," which can be found in *Fires* and Ray's collected poems.

I've often wondered if Bukowski ever read any of Ray's work and realized that Ray Carver, his "uptight academic" host, was no prissy professor but the author of stories of more depth, passion, and authenticity than he allowed himself to write.

I was to meet up with Bukowski again a year or two later. The occasion was a joint reading he gave with William Stafford. I had known Stafford since the late 1960s; I even visited him at his home on two of my reading tours in Oregon. He was a gentle, kindly man whose poetry and person projected homespun, down-home Americana, and I had always thought of him as a tough-minded West Coast version of Robert Frost. Bill was one of my favorite contemporary American poets, and I attended his readings whenever I got the chance. That's how I wound up at the War Memorial Veterans Building in downtown San Francisco that evening in the early 1970s.

San Francisco State was sponsoring the reading by Stafford and Bukowski, a most unlikely pairing. The theater was packed, and I had to stand in the rear for the entire reading. Half the audience were high school students assigned to hear and do a report on the much acclaimed, award-winning Stafford, and the other half were a rowdy bunch of old time Beats and post-1960s hippies who had come to hear Bukowski.

Stafford read first. As usual, he was humble, self-effacing, undemonstrative, and, as usual, he read from 3 x 5 cards that were scribbled over with revisions—and again as usual his reading was quiet and undramatic, as if your shy uncle had risen to read a letter from an absent relative at the end of Thanksgiving dinner. Bill began and ended his reading praising Bukowski and saying how delighted he was to finally meet him. A smattering of applause greeted his final poem, and several loud yawns.

Then Bukowski was introduced and strode to the lectern, carrying a gallon bottle of gin. He growled at Stafford seated in the front row and muttered something about him under his breath before launching into his reading—or, rather, his performance. He read poems and punctuated them either with verbal swipes at Stafford or by tilting the gin bottle ceilingward and taking loud gulps from it. The crowd loved it. They cheered and whooped and rooted him on while Bill sat quietly in the midst of the mayhem.

I looked around at the people standing near me and caught Kathy Fraser's eye. I hadn't seen her since she had called me a particularly unpleasant name during a rancorous incident at the Marin Writers Conference several years before, an incident I'll talk about later. She edged toward me, an alarmed expression on her face. "What have I done?" she said.

It turned out that she had arranged the reading.

"Don't blame yourself, Kath: it's him," I said, nodding toward Bukowksi who was lifting the gin bottle to his mouth again. "He's a pig."

Kathy looked at me for a second, hesitated, and then all the animosity between us dissolved as she came into my arms to be comforted. I looked over her head at Bukowski doing his shenanigans and felt nothing but revulsion for him and all the loutish poseurs in the audience who wouldn't have known a good poem if they heard one.

After the reading, I went up to Bill Stafford and asked him how he was. "Fine," he said, as if nothing out of the ordinary had happened, and I realized I knew he would have reacted no other way.

■ ■ ■

When I was bringing authors to Noel Young in 1972, well before my arguments with him, Ray was one of the first writers I told him about. I urged him to get in touch with Ray, and urged Ray to get in touch with him. And after Jim Houston joined the Capra fold, he urged the two of them to get together as well.

Nothing happened until the spring of 1972 or 1973, and Jim and I were both involved in it. It was at the annual Swanton Corn Roast, a spring ritual during those years, when all the local craftspeople—potters, weavers, jewelry makers, and leather workers—showed their wares in makeshift stalls set up in the wilds of a rural road north of the coastal hamlet of Davenport. The scenery was the epitome of old California: open farmlands surrounded by woods. The corn roast was held in a meadow hemmed in by redwoods, madrone trees with their sweet potato-colored bark, lime-colored lichen-splotched coast live oaks, and spicy-smelling California bay trees, all tangled together by vines and jumbles of weeds and poison oak still green and succulent from the winter rains.

The corn roast drew people from as far away as San Jose and San Francisco. Hundreds of cars lined the narrow road. The roast was an event, a reason to get into the country for city-dwellers and come away with a pitcher or belt or beaded necklace made by local artisans, not mass-produced by anonymous third-world workers. The roast was a result of the return-to-the-earth movement that gripped the nation in the early 1970s and the creative entrepreneuralism of Al Johnson, who had founded the event.

Noel had come up for the roast, and I was strolling with him past the makeshift kiosks and tables, both of us looking at the displays. Jim Houston was playing bass with a blue-grass band called the Red Mountain Boys, a traditional part of the day's entertainment, and as the banjos caplunketed and the fiddles whined and the guitars thwanged, and Jim plucked baritone sounds of gastric disorder from his phlegmatic bass, Noel and I came upon a tall galoot lying on his side in the grass with his head propped in one hand, listening to the music. Noel remembered that the galoot had a purple wine mustache. I remember that there were several paper cups on the ground nearby.

I turned to Noel and said something like "Remember I told you about a terrific short-story writer you should get a hold of? Well, here he is." Then I spoke to the reclining figure. "How you doing, Ray? Remember that publisher from down south I've been urging you to send stuff to, Noel Young? Well, here he is. Noel, Ray. Ray, Noel."

Now that may sound like one of the great shaggy dog stories of all time, an anti-anecdote, the report of one of the great nonevents in any memoir. But truth to tell, it was a historic meeting. Out of it Noel would eventually publish Ray's short story collection, *The Furious Seasons*, in 1977 and the potpourri of short stories, poems, and essays, *Fires*, in 1983. Capra would become the publishing house where the original and restored versions of some of Ray's best stories would be permanently maintained. That Ray returned to Capra to publish *Fires* after he had become one of the nation's most publicized writers was a symbolic return to the West from the frenetic East, a move he would make physically within two years after the book came out. *Fires* contains the definitive versions of those stories that first appeared in *The Furious Seasons* and that, in two instances, appeared in *What We Talk About When We Talk About Love*, the book that made him famous but that also contained the drastically revised versions I've mentioned before of many previously published stories. In *Fires* Ray re-revised (actually restored) two of the stories that I consider among his best, "Distance" and "So Much Water So Close to Home." For that reason, and its plenteous helping of poems, *Fires* is an important source for understanding Ray's work. We can thank Noel Young for that as well as for the original versions of the stories in *The Furious Seasons*.

■ ■ ■

Ray died too early. Having overcome the booze, he succumbed to lung cancer at the age of fifty, most probably because of his chain smoking. In a letter to an editor who had asked me about my relationship with Ray, I wrote that "I knew him before the fame, before he became a legend, I knew him as he groped his way through the thicket of his problems and I can tell you that even then he was a lovable man who, despite the debts and drinking, I would trust with my life, and for me that is the test of a human being's mettle." A friend, who is a therapist, told me that such values are typical of people abandoned in childhood. Maybe. But loyalty and a good heart go a long way to winning my affections, and Ray had both. Do those words smack of sentimentality too? Probably. I only know that there was a man here who is a hole in the air now, a doorway the wind shuttles through, and that this man left us gifts at great personal expense, a suitcase full of small trick mirrors in which we can see our distorted inner selves.

CHAPTER 29

Charles Simic

In 1970, Charlie Simic and his wife Helen moved to California. He taught for three years at California State University at Hayward, living the first two years close to the campus on the eastern shores of San Francisco Bay. He then moved north, and farther inland, to Santa Rosa, where he leased a house that sat atop a knoll with slanting lawns all around and a commanding view of the neighboring countryside.

When I met Charlie, it was instant friendship. There were qualities I found in him of openness and sweetness—an essential honesty and goodness—that won me over. It was an aura he projected that never lessened over the years, although we met more and more infrequently as the years wore on.

Maybe I'm romanticizing, but I found Charlie, Serbian by birth, a kindred Slavic spirit and never stopped thinking of him as a brother. I felt the same way about his wife Helen, and when the three of us met on the East Coast, in Cambridge, Massachusetts, thirty years later, the same ease and comfort prevailed as it had on our first meeting. My second wife, Donna, Slavic by ancestry, who I'll talk about later, was with me at that later meeting in what seemed like a family reunion with relatives who had seen each other just a few days before.

Not that Charlie and I kept in touch over the years: he was busy and I'm sure had closer literary friends, but the times we saw each other were special. It may have helped, of course, that I was a fan of his work, but I hope it went deeper than that.

We first met at one of Hitchcock's collating parties in the fall of 1970 and talked about Popa's visit earlier that year. Charlie had kept in touch with Vasko and would go

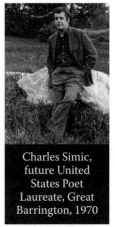

Charles Simic, future United States Poet Laureate, Great Barrington, 1970

to Yugoslavia to visit him and relatives several years later. We also talked about our boyhoods, and I invited Charlie to come down to Santa Cruz to give a reading at Cabrillo and meet my creative-writing class.

The event was not only a huge success, it furthered our friendship when Charlie invited me to visit him. We met several times. These were the years of my break-up with Wilma, and I was happy to accept his invitation the following year to spend a weekend with him and Helen at the hilltop house in Santa Rosa.

Charlie showed me around the house and grounds and challenged me to a game of ping-pong at a table he had set up under a large, shady oak tree. He beat me soundly, and I remembered Alexander Nijgebauer challenging me to a game back in 1967 when he had introduced me to Popa's poetry. Both Nijgebauer and his wife had spent the afternoon taking turns showing me that to the Yugoslavs ping-pong was not a laid-back, friendly way to spend a lazy afternoon. Not only did I lose every game, but I hardly scored a point, and when Nijgebauer's wife allowed me, I'm sure out of feminine compassion, to score a handful of points, Nijgebauer scolded her in no uncertain terms.

Charlie wasn't half as militant as Nijgebauer; he was just a better player than me. But I made a note to avoid playing ping-pong with Yugoslavs in the future. I didn't know then that Yugoslavia was second only to the People's Republic of China in the world ping-pong standings.

We spent the weekend talking about poetry and life, listening to jazz, and eating. The latter was a pastime at which we were equally matched contestants. At that time, Charlie was tall and stout, and I remember Helen's meals were memorable feasts. In preparation for them, and in my honor, Charlie opened a jar of hot peppers he had put up several months before. I was standing at the far side of the large kitchen when he pried open the jar, and almost instantaneously my eyes watered and the room was engulfed in a pungent heat. I coughed, and mucous streamed from my nostrils as it had during tear gas training in the air force years before. Instantaneously, I made another mental note: avoid Yugoslav peppers, as well as ping-pong, in the future.

Eating became a ritual event for Charlie and me. We never met after that weekend without a meal being the center of the meeting, and a certain practice during the meal was inevitably performed. It was more a ritual than a practice and began when Charlie came to Santa Cruz one time while we were working together on shaping some of Charlie's translations of Popa's sequences. He had heard of a French restaurant in Carmel, and we drove down to the restaurant, where we worked on the poems. In the course of the elaborate five-course dinner, Charlie told me a story that became for us the start of the ritual.

Charlie emigrated to the United States when he was eleven years old after spending his childhood in Belgrade during World War II. He and his family were not poor immigrants, since his father, whom Charlie idolized, had continued to work as an electrical engineer for the American firm that had employed him to design telephone systems in Yugoslavia. One day he took Charlie, then twenty, to a fancy dinner at an expensive French restaurant in New York City. He and Charlie were not shabbily dressed but underdressed for the restaurant's clientele, and their waiter was not only a snob but rude: he taunted Charlie's father by sneeringly explaining the menu, assuming he knew neither French nor French cooking and was socially out of place in the exclusive eatery.

Charlie's father, usually flamboyant, was subdued and seemed not to notice. As the meal wore on, Charlie became more and more embarrassed, especially since his father continued to quietly accept the waiter's insulting behavior. It was one of those times when a son realizes his father is not the heroic figure he always imagined him to be. When the waiter presented the bill, however, Charlie's father looked at the statement on the plate before him, ignoring the amount, and quietly said, "We're not finished. We'd like the same meal again, but give the boy what I ordered and serve me what he ordered." The waiter was shocked. Charlie's father, with great poise, refused to acknowledge the man's sputtering. The waiter may or may not have learned to be more prudent with his initial judgments of customers, but Charlie's reaction was one of joy, and his confidence in his father never faltered again.

It was a great tale, especially the way Charlie told it, and we decided then and there, in honor of his dad and all the world's fathers, that we would perform the same act of reordering meals every time we visited a restaurant together.

Charlie moved back to the East Coast in 1973, but whenever we met we would engage in the ritual. In the winter of 1975, I spent two months at the McDowell artists' colony in New Hampshire. Charlie was teaching at the University of New Hampshire by then. He called and told me about a great French restaurant he had discovered, and we arranged to meet.

He drove down to pick me up the day after a huge snowstorm, braving the treacherous roads, and we drove thirty miles to the restaurant. The weather was so bad, we were the only customers. Charlie's taste was impeccable, and we had a sumptuous meal, talking for hours about the new poems we were writing. Charlie was particularly excited about his new work in which, for the first time, he was able to write about his boyhood experiences in Yugoslavia during World War II. The first group of these poems to appear in a book would be published in his 1980 collection, *Classic Ballroom Dances*. They are told as if by a child who is still too young to comprehend the horror about which he is speaking, and they are therefore understated, almost matter of fact, which adds to their emotional impact. A good example of Charlie's approach in them can be seen in the poem, "Prodigy."

When the bill came, Charlie looked at me, smiled, and then looked up at the waiter and said, "We're not finished. We'd like the same dinner again, but reverse the orders." The waiter was open-mouthed and asked Charlie to repeat what he had just said and then scampered off to the kitchen. A few moments later, the chef, who Charlie said had moved to this rural location to escape the craziness of New York City, emerged from the kitchen to see who these two gourmands were. Never, he said, had such a thing happened before.

There were other occasions when we performed the ritual, once at the Oyster Bar in Grand Central Station, but our meetings became more and more infrequent since Charlie rarely came to the West Coast and I almost never visited the East Coast. The few times I did, Charlie was in Europe or I had a limited time in New York City. He did come to San Francisco in the mid-1990s, however. By then, he was a national literary figure, but he didn't come for a reading. He came to show his son, Alexander, where the boy had been born. Helen came, too, and Charlie invited me and one other friend from the Bay Area for a meal at a stylish Italian restaurant. Nicky, his daughter, who I remembered as a little girl, was married, he said, and a political consultant. We spent a long afternoon lunch talking of old friends. Alexander's eyes sparkled at the conversation and about the origin of the ritual. However, we were so full we decided to order more wine instead of another meal. But we were both thinking the same thing, and at one point raised our glasses in silence.

What drew me to Charlie's poetry was its voice as much as its content. Charlie wrote in a style that gave the impression of being an almost offhanded vernacular. It wonderfully underscored his content, allowing him, as it did so many twentieth-century Eastern European poets, to project a wry humor while talking about the most serious subjects. But it was his content, in the end, that intrigued me, since in many ways it mirrored my own. We had the same personal sense of history and of half-drowned ancestors shouting from the bloodstream the old tribal cries for vengeance and love. Both of us shared the same playfulness, the same reliance on the imagination to guide us wherever it would. And both of us saw ourselves, and the rest of humankind, as butts of an unconcerned universe repeating the same joke without a punch line. Many times, unbeknownst to each other, we even wrote about the same subjects, and both of us began writing prose poems at about the same time. There were as many differences between our work as well, not the least of which was that Charlie's poetry suggested deeper meanings and was more accomplished.

Reading a poem by Charlie is like glimpsing, or rather taking a step into, a world beyond this one but parallel to it, a world of half-remembered fragments that are the closest examples of Jung's collective unconscious American poetry has ever touched—it is a poetry that shows, more clearly than any other, the immigrant roots that are buried in our chromosomes and which we have dragged to these shores.

Many times it is not a whole poem but an image that startles in Charlie's work, or a metaphor that skitters along the nerve ends and summons memories of a lost world. There is something not only "right" about the images, something that engenders an immediate instinctive recognition by the reader, but also something animistic about them, as if Charlie is heir to a telluric wisdom that most of us are no longer privy to, if we ever were. Take, for example, this little known poem that Charlie has never included in any of his collections:

The Frost

There's a window in the valley
where the examples
of its fine lacework is displayed.

At dusk, the bare trees set out
like old women on canes and crutches,
to take a close look.

Whether he is writing about urban or rural subjects, Charlie talks about commonplace objects and happenings—rivers, trees, animals; brooms, forks, knives; passing butcher shops, attending weddings, hearing footsteps—which uncannily evoke ghosts of the past, archetypes that resonate in the most ordinary acts. Fear, he wrote in a poem by the same name,

> ... passes from man to man
> Unknowing,
> As one leaf passes its shudder
> To another.
>
> All at once the whole tree is trembling
> And there is no sign of the wind.

In "Ax" he predicts the human race will regress to a state of uncivilized, murderous mayhem because

> These dark prophecies were gathered,
> Unknown to myself, by my body
> Which understands historical probabilities,
> Lacking itself, in its essence, a future.

But if his subject and images are riddles, folktales, and common everyday objects and events, there is always a metaphysical probing at work in his poems that assumes nature, the world in which we live, is a shadowy presence in our lives, a sort of a cosmic jokester who is funnier and all the more terrifying for being a figment of our imaginations and is, in reality, just a proliferating mass of mindless matter. It is as if Charlie realizes that in life the nonexistent jokester's joke may not have a punch line but is definitely a joke on us.

The following poem illustrates several of Charlie's methods and ideas as well as the sense of mystery much of his work evokes.

Return to a Place Lit by a Glass of Milk

Late at night our hands stop working.
They lie open with tracks of animals
Journeying across the fresh snow.
They need no one. Solitude surrounds them.

As they come closer, as they touch,
It is like two small streams
Which upon entering a wide river
Feel the pull of the distant sea.

The sea is a room far back in time
Lit by the headlights of a passing car.
A glass of milk glows on the table.
Only you can reach it for me now.

CHAPTER 30

Robert Bly

Robert Bly read at the Cabrillo Poetry Series several times over the years.

I first came into contact with him when I was at Iowa and he was editing *The Fifties*. As I've already said, *The Fifties* was a groundbreaking literary magazine that took academic poetry to task, presented its canon of important contemporary American poets in a series of long essays, and, most important, introduced in translation poets from around the world whose approach and vision were different from the Anglo-American tradition.

Bly promulgated the work of foreign poets by printing their poems in the magazine and then publishing them in small books with a generic title that began *Twenty Poems of . . .* He translated most of the poems himself or used literal translations by others to make his own versions. Many of the poets were unknown to American readers, and those who were known, like Lorca and Rilke, he provided with fresh, clear translations. The poets included Pablo Neruda, Cesar Vallejo, Kabir, Rumi, Rolf Jacobsen, Rainer Maria Rilke, Tomas Transtromer, Antonio Machado, Juan Ramon Jimenez, Federico Garcia Lorca, Georg Trakl, and Miguel Hernandez.

Kenneth Rexroth recognized the importance of Bly's contribution in this area by saying, "Bly is one of the leaders of a poetic revolution that has turned American literature to the world."

Although all these poets are familiar to readers today, it is generally forgotten that the works of only a few of them were available in English before Bly introduced them to the young poets of the 1950s and 1960s who, as teachers, went on to spread their fame. Neruda, so popular and well-known now in a plethora of translations, was only available in a sanitized, dull translation by Angel Flores, which came out as a New Directions book, and as one of fifteen or so poets in two hard-to-find anthologies of South American poetry, one edited and translated by H. R. Hays and the other by Dudley Fitts.

If Bly is to be remembered for nothing else, his promulgating the work of these poets to both American readers and fledgling American poets will live on as a great achievement. Ironically, years later he commented to me that he may have done more damage than good by introducing his translations,

300

since he was appalled by the lack of music in the new American poetry, much of which, he said, sounded like translations!

My first personal contact with Bly occurred in 1959 when I sent him several poems for *The Fifties*. The poems were all in free verse and in a hardy American vernacular. Bly rejected them with a note that said they sounded too much like Shakespeare. The poems may not have been very good, but that was the strangest rejection I would ever receive. Other poets received similar notes on their returned poems, and soon Bly's rejection slips were famous among poets of my generation for their bizarre comments.

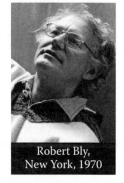

Robert Bly,
New York, 1970

I first met Robert in 1966 when he gave a reading at the University of San Francisco. He was not yet the national figure he would become, nor had he started the Vietnam War resistance readings which the following year would spread his fame. Maybe that was why the reading was held in a classroom attended by no more than twenty people. Bly was over six feet tall and solidly built, and his voice, which sounded like an excited Jimmy Cagney's, kept soaring toward enraptured song. His reading was vigorous. I was moved by his passion as well as the excellence of his presentation and went up to him afterwards. Only two other people joined me. He sat on a desk, chatting with the three of us, and when I told him how moved I was by his reading, he asked my name. When I told him, he said, "So you're Morton Marcus. Everyone across the country has been asking me who you are and what you're really like."

I was shocked and flattered and stammered something like, "Me?" pointing to myself. I couldn't imagine who would know my work. Although my poems had appeared in many magazines, including *Kayak* and several dozen others, my first book had not yet appeared, and the *Young American Poets Anthology* would not come out for another two years.

I was to realize that Bly used such stock statements to flatter poets and others and win their approval and support in the anarchic arena of the mad, dog-eat-dog poetry world—or the literary world in general. We chatted for about fifteen minutes and I left.

My next dealing with Bly came several years later when he wrote a criticism of the first ten issues of *Kayak* magazine at Hitchcock's invitation. Hitchcock, whether he would admit it or not, had modeled *Kayak* after a lot of Bly's ideas, particularly the idea of the deep, surrealistically influenced image. Bly responded to Hitchcock's invitation by taking *Kayak* to task for its lukewarm use of the image and for the preponderance of the word "dark" and other easy adjectives in many of its poems. For most of his critique, as I remember, he chastised Hitchcock for promulgating, if not canonizing, a twelve- to sixteen-line free-verse lyric poem that Bly said was developed in almost all cases in the same four ways.

Hitchcock printed the review, and I wrote a rather long jocular letter in response, which appeared in *Kayak* #13. It began,

> Captain Bly is on the rampage once again, flogging the inno-
> cent, seeking the elusive Christian he loves but is bent on
> destroying, and shouting orders few of us can understand. As
> often happens with the good skipper, his trusty astrolabe
> enables him to find the right direction, but somehow he misses
> port by several thousand miles.

After taking Bly's article to task point by point in the same style, I continued with a direct attack on what I saw as Bly's puritanism:

> The rest of Bly's discourse . . . is as arbitrary as his argument
> on the four parts that make up [the *Kayak* poem]. He is attempt-
> ing to limit an expanding universe, and Ahab found out how dif-
> ficult that was. The metaphor is not so farfetched; Bly has been
> fighting the battle against this whale of a world for years from
> the puritanical posture in which we find Ahab; his moral har-
> poon poised above his head as he thrusts home again and again.
> His attack on James Dickey on moral grounds in the latest issue
> of *The Sixties* is a case in point; the peculiar deletions of erotic
> imagery from the Neruda poems he published as a *Sixties* book
> some years ago, as well as the omission of any of Vallejo's erotic
> poems from a similar *Sixties* collection, are two others.

I ended my letter with a further admonishment:

> It's not surprising, then, that Bly ends his review of *Kayak*
> with a call for pain: the poets published in *Kayak* have not felt
> enough agony, he says; they all need to suffer, to lash their inner
> beings, for out of this suffering poetry is made.
> Well, Captain Bly, I'm afraid I disagree. There is not only pain
> and suffering in this world, but joy and rapture as well. We can
> reach our inner selves that way, too. . . .

Hitchcock said that Bly was not amused by my response, but Robert
never referred to it in any of our future conversations.

■ ■ ■

My second meeting with Bly had less to do with him and more to do with
my old nemesis, Robert Mezey, with whom Bly gave a reading at the University
of California campus in Santa Cruz. It was 1970, and Bly had been touring the
country as organizer of the resistance readings against the Vietnam War. He

had just finished his long antiwar poem, "The Teeth Mother Naked at Last," and he was obviously excited about reading the poem to the three hundred or so people who came to the event. He never got the chance; Mezey made sure of that. Since he had snubbed me in Don Justice's kitchen five years before, Mezey had been hired and fired at Fresno State University and several other colleges and was now appealing to everyone as a martyred performer (or wronged activist) for sympathy (and probably a job).

Bly agreed to share the reading with Mezey at the last moment, and they arranged that they would read in tandem at ten- and fifteen-minute intervals, with Bly starting the reading and returning after Mezey's second set to read "The Teeth Mother" in its entirety. Bly's reading was powerful and his poems well chosen, but Mezey's left the audience cold and Mezey knew it. He strolled to the podium in a flannel shirt with a yellow armband on his sleeve. It was embroidered with a Jewish Star of David, a replica of the armband the Nazis forced the Jews to wear during World War II. When he reached the podium, Mezey pointed to the armband and nodded to the audience as if to say he was a victim of an anti-Semitic Fresno State administration. When each of his poems elicited nothing but silence, Mezey roused audience response by raising his left fist in the defiant black power salute of the time and bellowing, "Power to the people!" or some such slogan that elicited applause and cheers.

I began to seethe at this cheap way of getting response from the crowd.

But my anger reached the stage of molten lava when he returned for his second and supposedly last set and read not for the agreed-upon fifteen minutes but for forty-five minutes. I watched Bly as Mezey droned on. He showed no displeasure, but when he walked to the microphone, he said, "There's no time to read 'The Teeth Mother' complete. I'll just read a section or two."

I was enraged. Mezey had calculatedly abused Bly's generous offer to share the reading. Afterward, there was a party at the house of the provost of the college, James B. Hall. He had organized the reading, and Wilma and I had been invited to the party. I was so angry I didn't want to go, but I wanted to tell Bly how much I liked his presentation and how gentlemanly he had been in handling Mezey's crude behavior. With that in mind, I decided to go to the party and avoid Mezey.

There were several hundred people at Hall's house, which was loud with voices and bright with lights, and I worked my way through the crowd, greeting those I knew, until I was face to face with Bly, who was surrounded by admirers. He remembered me from our first meeting and after I told him how much I liked his new poems and appreciated his political action, I left him to the dozens of people who wanted to speak with him.

I made my way back through the crowd and was just about to leave the large living room when a voice called out, "Mort, Mort." When I turned, there was Mezey, jostling his way through people until he stood smiling in front of me. Before I could respond, he threw his arms around my waist in a bear hug and lifted me off the floor. "Mort, how are you?" I think he said, but it may have been, "Mort, old friend, I hoped I'd see you here," because that was the impression he clearly wanted to convey.

I was startled, but only for a moment. I jerked my arms up and broke his hold, saying, "Get your goddamn hands off me. You're no friend of mine. And what you did tonight was unforgivable."

He looked at me with a confused expression.

"Come on, Robert. You know how you upstaged Bly, and take off that damned armband. You're a disgrace to the millions of the dead."

Mezey was speechless. People turned and stared at us, and Glenna Luschei, who had been a classmate of ours at Iowa, and had come up behind Bob with her husband Martin, said in an aggrieved voice, "Mort, what's wrong? We're all friends from Iowa."

"I was never friends with this bastard, Glenna. Never," I said and left the party.

It was the last time I met Mezey, and Glenna, who lived two hundred miles away and went on to edit Solo Press, never talked to me again.

■ ■ ■

My third meeting with Bly was equally brief and also occurred in a crowd. Larry Fixel was invited with our poetry group to give an extended session, open to a number of other poets, at the new Marin County home of Mark Linenthal, a professor of literature at San Francisco State.

Although I was living in Santa Cruz, I made my way up to the session, which was more a literary gathering of thirty or so professional writers living in San Francisco and Marin County than a work session. Leonard Gardner was there and so was Gina, as was Thomas Sanchez, at that time the talk of San Francisco since he had just sold his first novel, *Rabbit Boss*, for a purported million dollars. Shirley Kaufman and Laura Ulewicz were there as well as was the great Greek poet Nanos Valaoritis, who had joined our group a short time before when he came to teach comparative literature at San Francisco State.

Bly arrived last with a scruffy young man in tow. Bly explained that his companion was a hitchhiker he had picked up on his way to the house and who in the course of their small talk had revealed that he was a poet, so Robert had invited him along. The young man introduced himself as Racing Cloud or some such Native American sobriquet, although he was as white and blond as an Iowa farm boy.

The session came to order with Larry presiding, his gaunt body buried in an oversized easy chair. He explained how we conducted our meetings and asked those present to join in with any work they had brought with them. Since we didn't know many of the people intimately, the gathering became more a series of readings than our usual rigorous critiquing of each other's work.

After Shirley and several others read, Bly suggested that we hear some of his young friend's poems. Racing Cloud stood up and read several pseudo Indian chants. They were embarrassingly bad, but everyone remained respectfully silent—everyone except Thomas Sanchez, whose novel was about the Washoe Indians of the Sierras. After Racing Cloud finished his second piece, Sanchez called out something like, "That's bullshit! Who told you that crap was Indian poetry—was poetry at all?" And he continued to berate the young man in a series of expletives. Racing Cloud looked around for support, clearly hurt and embarrassed.

Bly said nothing. No one did, as Sanchez continued his verbal assault.

I remembered Mezey's similar behavior in the Iowa workshop. I didn't know Sanchez, but he was acting like an arrogant bully, and before I knew what I was doing, I rose to my feet and said in a steely voice, "That's enough."

"Who says so?" said Sanchez.

"I do," I replied. "That was uncalled for."

"I don't think so."

"Shut up!" I said.

"Are you going to make me?" he said, stepping toward me.

"You're damned right I am," I said and moved toward him. He charged me.

Leonard grabbed me and several of the men near Sanchez grabbed him. We glared at each other, straining against the arms that held us.

Bly sat unperturbed, observing the scene, and Larry, clearly startled at the sudden turn of events, seemed to retreat farther into his easy chair, saying nothing.

That was the end of the readings for the day, and shortly afterward people began taking their leave.

Leonard kept close to me until I had calmed down. Sanchez and I left soon after, without trying to patch up our confrontation. I was to meet him several times in the future, once several years later in Santa Barbara at his estate when I was visiting Noel Young, who had become more his court jester than his friend. He told Noel that he wanted to see me and put the Marin County incident behind us, but he really wanted to impress me with his wealth and success and even brazenly flirted with the young woman I had brought to Santa Barbara with me. We never did overcome the incident, but more important neither did Larry who, as leader of the session, many people blamed for not stepping in to stop the altercation. I blamed Bly for setting up the situation and then doing nothing about it once it got out of hand. He should have been sensitive to the gathering and how out of place the young hitchhiker was in such an assembly. At the least, he should have examined the hitchhiker's poems beforehand to spare him the embarrassment that followed. More to the point, I wondered at Bly's insistence that Racing Cloud should read: I was beginning to question my admiration for Bly.

■ ■ ■

My fourth meeting with Bly occurred later that year and created a split between us that has never healed, and which, years later, Bly said he didn't remember. I had been invited to be one of the participants in the Marin Writers' Conference that winter, which was well into the period of my break-up with Wilma. She asked if we could use the time away from Santa Cruz and the kids to go to the conference together and attempt a reconciliation. I agreed, but, as I made clear several times, I planned to read from the sequence of poems I had written about our break-up. At that time I thought they were not only the best poems I had ever written, but the most personally honest and revealing. I told her they were therapeutic for me and may have saved my sanity during the emotional turmoil of the previous year and a half. I also told her that besides being self-questioning meditations, the poems were predominantly love poems to both her and the other woman, and I didn't think she should come to the readings because the poems to the other woman might hurt her. I repeated that warning a number of times on the drive to the conference, but Wilma, always concerned with emotional and psychological revelations of the human psyche in art as well as life, insisted she wanted to attend the readings.

The first day of the conference went smoothly. Though obviously tentative with each other, Wilma and I spent time with mutual friends whom she hadn't seen since we moved to Santa Cruz, and that provided a buffer for our uneasiness. Bly was there and took me aside after the afternoon panel discussion. He said he was looking forward to hearing me read and insisted on picking Wilma and me up at our motel and driving us to the reading that night. Once more, I was surprised and flattered.

The reading took place in an indoor amphitheater on the campus of Marin College and was almost completely full when we arrived. The participants were Robert Creeley, my friend Shirley Kaufman from Larry Fixel's group, and me.

Creeley didn't arrive until Shirley had finished her reading and I had just stepped to the podium after being introduced. The rear doors of the auditorium swung open, and he stumbled and almost fell as he rushed down the stairs and continued past me to disappear on the other side of the stage curtains behind me. He was stoned out of his mind and didn't reappear for the rest of the evening. The murmurs from the audience were an ominous sign I should have recognized. Instead, I announced that I was going to read new poems that had been written more in tears than in ink and proceeded to read from the sequence that eventually would be titled "Toward Certain Divorce." I hadn't read more than three poems when Wilma, who was sitting near Joe, who had come up from Santa Cruz to attend the conference, gasped and began to moan. Soon she was bent double, weeping loudly. Joe, who knew what had been going on for the last year and a half and was highly emotional in such situations, began to weep too, and put his arms around Wilma to comfort her.

I forged on, finishing half an hour later to complete silence from the audience. Only Wilma's sobbing could be heard.

Backstage, Shirley rushed up to me with tears in her eyes and told me to destroy the poems for my children's sake. Kathy Frazer refused to talk to me. Bly had disappeared, and we had to find someone else take us back to the motel to pick up my car.

On the way from the motel to the party afterwards, Wilma, in an eerily calm, matter-of-fact voice, recounted the responses she had received from other poets after the reading. Kathy Fraser told her that I was a macho braggart who was just "waving his cock" on stage. The poet Adrienne Marcus went up to Wilma and commiserated with her, adding as a rather nasty final comment, "My husband would never have done such a thing to me." I was shocked. I thought my fellow poets would understand the suffering the poems recorded of everyone involved in the break-up, and I thought that, though they were personal, the poems expressed universal truths about human relationships.

Kathy Frazer didn't speak to me until the Bukowski-Stafford reading in San Francisco several years later, and Adrienne Marcus never spoke to me again. Shirley, who went through a traumatic divorce of her own within two years, told me that she had reassessed the evening and come to terms with the poems because of her own personal experiences.

At the party, everyone turned away from me, and Bly just nodded. Only the short-story writer James B. Hall and his wife Beth came up to us teary-eyed and embraced us both, saying they had no idea about the collapse of our marriage, and volunteered to help us any way they could. Jim, who was the provost at the University of California at Santa Cruz's Creative Arts College at the time, had employed Wilma as a modern dance instructor the year before.

After fifteen minutes of being shunned by the crowd at the party, we left. In the car, I told Wilma, as I had several times since the reading, that I was sorry the poems had hurt her so much, but I reminded her that I had warned her beforehand about what I was going to read.

Wilma was silent and unnervingly composed, and as we drove away she said, 'I didn't tell you what your precious Robert Bly said to me after the reading.'

"Oh?" I replied.

"He said you were a ruthless son of a bitch for reading those poems with me there, and that it was inexcusable."

I stopped the car and turned to her. Even in the feeble light of the street lamp down the road, I could see the smirk on her face and realized she was enjoying my disgrace. Had she planned the whole thing to humiliate me? Her pleasure certainly suggested it, and I thought so at the time.

In a surge of anger, I started the car, turned around, and raced back to the party. It was winding down, but Bly was still there, seated on a couch, talking with five or six people.

"I want to talk to you," I said to him without a greeting, obviously agitated.
He looked up at me and nodded. "Okay," he said, taking his time to rise.

We went into another room, and I maneuvered him against a wall, standing in front of him with my fists balled. "Did you say I was a ruthless son of a bitch?"

"Yes," he replied calmly, aware of my anger. "I said you were a ruthless son of a bitch in the same way Jim Wright is."

"What do you mean by that?"

"Jim will write about anything, no matter who he hurts. Tonight I realized you were the same way. You should never have read those poems. Not when Wilma was there."

"You think that? I thought you'd understand the agony in those poems and know how hard it was for me to read them."

"That may be, but you should not have read them with Wilma present."

"Should I have read them like a hypocrite, behind her back? I told her not to be there. Told her what I was going to read. But she insisted it was all right."

"That may be, but they were too personal. They were not for public exhibition."

Wilma had come up to us, and Bly put a fatherly arm around her.

"Nothing's too personal," I said. "Anything that deals with life, the dark side or the light, is the poet's subject. Isn't that what Trakl and Rilke and Vallejo and Transtromer, and all those other poets you've translated and praised, believed?"

"That's just the kind of thing Jim would say," Bly replied, still composed and staring me in the eye.

I felt betrayed. "I thought of all people, you would understand," I muttered.

He kept his arm around Wilma, who stood next to him like an ally and eyed me triumphantly.

I didn't know what to say after that. My fists unrolled. I felt foolish. What had I been thinking? Had I come back to challenge him to a fight like a child in a playground, angry at an adult who had told him he couldn't have another candy bar?

I couldn't look Bly in the eye. "Come on," I said to Wilma.

"If either of you would like to talk—" Bly said.

"Let's go," I said to Wilma, and we left.

If I felt like a child, it was only momentarily. As Wilma and I drove back to Santa Cruz in silence, I mulled over the evening's events and realized that Bly had cowed me because, as I surmised standing in front of him at the end of the confrontation, he had betrayed the concept, which I thought we shared, that poetry should plumb the depths of the human soul and show the reader the findings no matter how painful the revelation. As far as I was concerned, he had betrayed the beliefs I had thought he was promulgating in *The Fifties* and *The Sixties* and in the poets he was translating.

Besides my confrontation with Bly, the evening had made me realize several other things. The first was that the San Francisco poetry community, of which I was so proud to be a member, was as staid and prim in their behavior as the most conservative middle-class society. They didn't want to hear poetry that was too raw, too personally agonizing in content.

I kept thinking of Bly's statement that it was not acceptable to read personal poems in the presence of the people who were the subject of the work. It wouldn't be until a month or two later that I realized Bly's poetry did not deal with issues of personal relationships, but rather with perceptions of the psyche and the natural world. That would change when he and his wife divorced and his son was killed in a ski accident years later. For his part, Bly would never again consider me anything but a confessional poet, and in the two or three notes he sent me over the years, he would ask me how I could expose my private life in public and maintain dignity. As if he never received my answer, he asked the same question twenty years later in a short letter that arrived unexpectedly and unprompted by me, and which I answered as I had the first time he asked me the question. I wasn't a confessional poet, I wrote back, and if I used the word "I" in my poems and did write about personal matters, I only made public those experiences I thought were common to all human beings: I was trying to evoke universal experiences and events under the guise of their being personal. I don't think Bly ever accepted my explanation.

As for the incident, I came to realize that I should not have taken Wilma with me to the conference. It was poor judgment on my part, or worse—it was naive, even stupid. I no longer think that Wilma planned the episode. She always acted on whim, on emotionally spontaneous reactions, and I'm sure the poems hurt her. But there's no doubt she enjoyed my embarrassment because of her outburst.

As for the purpose of the weekend, it was the last time we attempted a reconciliation.

■ ■ ■

My next meeting with Bly was less than a year later. He had made San Jose and Pacific Grove (the latter just south of Monterey) a two-stop extension of his annual reading tour of the San Francisco Bay Area. Santa Cruz sat between the two towns, and I asked Bly if he would include Cabrillo on his tour for the pittance of the $75 I could pay him. He generously accepted and gave an inspiring reading. At the party at my apartment afterwards, he offered to look at some of my students' poetry and took the students and their poems one at a time into the bedroom to critique their work.

Bly's energy at that time was prodigious, and although I think he meant to look at the work of only one or two students, he was so impressed with what he was reading he became oblivious to time. I didn't blame him: he was reading work from the best creative-writing class I would ever have the honor of guiding. Bly complimented me on the level at which the students were writing and ended up using one of the students' poems in his *News of the Universe* anthology.

I should have rescued him after an hour or so, but I was living a footloose bachelor's life. I had moved out of the house in the mountains a short while before and was living in a small apartment in the main building of an estate perched on a cliff above the bay while serving as renter and bodyguard for the jovial old woman who owned the property. So I let the party go on and on. By the time Bly emerged bleary-eyed from the bedroom, it was two o'clock in the morning, and he had missed or lost the ride that was to take him back to the San Francisco Peninsula where he was to spend the night.

I volunteered to drive him, and we cruised up the dark empty highways, first along the moonlit ocean and then over the low mountains. We exchanged a few words about my students' work, but soon Bly lapsed into silence, a silence that had nothing to do with our last meeting, which neither of us referred to: he was simply exhausted. However, I had noticed throughout the day that Bly never spoke unless he was answering a question or commenting on something I had just said, a situation I found exasperating in anyone. At our next several meetings, I also became annoyed by this and another trait: when Bly talked to his hosts, no matter who they might be, he asked them to help him solve one problem or another. For instance, he would ask me how I would handle this situation or that, how I would solve a double-booking snafu, or how I would answer an awkward inquiry from someone. He used the same questions with other hosts who entertained him or poets he met at gatherings after his readings. At first I was flattered, as I'm sure they were. But as I saw him ask the same questions of others, I realized it was a social ploy to make his hosts and local poets feel important and by which he ingratiated himself with them.

His reticence to make opening statements or inquiries, on the other hand, made me come to see him as what I term a "conversational counterpuncher," that is, someone who waits for the person he is speaking with to make a statement on which he will then comment. It is much like a boxer who waits for his opponent to throw a punch before he throws one to the place the opponent has left open with his lead. This always gave Bly control of a conversation and, by extension, of the person with whom he was speaking.

I soon came to see Bly as two people, the public man and the private one. No one got to know the private Bly, and the public one was a mask—he cared nothing for the opinions he asked of others. It is interesting to note in this connection that some of the many props he used in his readings and lectures were masks. (Other props included the autoharp and the bouzoukee and his two favorite costumes, a serape and a red satin vest worn over a white shirt clasped at the neck with a string tie, which made him look like a nineteenth-century riverboat gambler.)

I came to view Bly's public appearances more as performances than readings, which was fine since he converted thousands of people who would not otherwise have been aware of poetry into devotees of the art. My problem with Bly had to do with the man when he was offstage. He seemed to have lost his private self somewhere along the way and could only relate to people through his performances.

In the mid-1980s, I asked him to give a benefit reading for the Cabrillo poetry series, which had fallen on hard times because of California budget cutbacks. He accepted when I offered him half of the house revenues. He was at the height of his popularity by then, and I knew that one half of the ticket price would provide funds for two years of my program if Bly was able to draw a sold-out house at the Cabrillo theater, which he did.

Bly arrived at my house before the reading, disheveled and exhausted, having already been on the reading tour for almost a week. He didn't want to speak with anyone or even go to dinner. He had purchased several paper containers of Chinese food, which he ate after taking a nap on my family-room couch. Donna, my new wife, and I acceded to all his wishes. Refreshed, and in his riverboat gambler's costume, he gave a wonderful reading and talk about the mythological underpinnings of fairy tales, especially as they revealed the submerged picture of male identity he had found in his Iron John investigations. It was a subject he was writing about at that time in what would become the *Iron John* book.

While at the house, he asked me to read one or two of my new poems before we left for the reading, and in the course of his presentation, he asked me to read one of the poems on stage. I was surprised but not flattered. I thought he was once more trying to manipulate me as one of the many organizers who had given him a number of readings over the years.

When I drove him to Palo Alto the next day, I decided I would test my theory of Bly as conversational counterpuncher by not saying a word until he did. We drove without talking for the rest of the trip, Bly becoming more and more fidgety. When we arrived at the condominium where he was staying in Palo Alto, he asked to read my latest book. I had sent him a copy six months before, and, as with my other books, he hadn't acknowledged it. His offer was an attempted reconciliation of some kind, I guess, but I was having none of it. With a shrug meant to show lack of concern, I told him I didn't have a copy with me, although I had my book bag in the trunk and he knew it. He also knew he was being rebuffed. The reader might think that Bly was tired and didn't want to talk during the ride to Palo Alto, but, as I've already said, I had noticed his verbal maneuverings several years previous to that trip. And it was several years before this incident that his revealing run-in with Bill Everson occurred, which I talk about in my chapter on Bill.

After we unloaded his valise in front of the condominium, we said a per-
functory goodbye and haven't seen each other since, although we have
exchanged greetings through friends. Other than that he sent me a copy of
his collected essays, *American Poetry*, when it came out in 1990, and in
2004, he sent me his book of antiwar poems concerning Iraq. He even sent a
note out of the blue some time in the 1990s that once more asked me how I
had the temerity to write confessional poetry, which I answered the same
way I had before. Our prose poems have appeared together in magazines
and anthologies and we have written theoretical articles on the form. But
we've never attempted to discuss those ideas or correspond on the subject,
and we probably never will.

■ ■ ■

Of all the chapters in this book, I have found this one the most uncomfortable and in many ways the most difficult to write. A number of times I
even thought about removing it from the manuscript. It was not my intention to attack Bly. I am not envious of his reputation, nor am I a rebellious
acolyte whose father figure has failed him. I did not want to snipe or otherwise poke at his accomplishments. His brilliance and importance for the literature of this country will, I hope, live long after him, and, as far as I'm concerned, he pointed the direction that one way or another American poetry
followed for the last half of the twentieth century.

At the same time, one of the main purposes of my writing these memories is to leave sketches of people I've known that reveal, as accurately as I
remember them, glimpses of their personalities I was privy to in those
moments when they were not in the public eye. Certainly, my own concerns
and issues color my interpretations of those moments, and the reader
should consider what I say in that light. With that in mind, I believe my
intention in this chapter was not to belittle Bly but to provide another perspective from which to see him.

Taking all these points into consideration, the reader, I hope, will understand that Bly's public persona annoyed me because it seem to mask a private self which, when it appeared, not only contradicted his public image
but revealed several character traits I have found hard to tolerate in anyone—manipulation, unwillingness (or inability) to be emotionally present,
and an overriding urge to control—all of which are the distinguishing features of my lifelong adversary, the bully.

CHAPTER 31

Al Young

I kept bumping into the poet and novelist Al Young at one literary event or another in San Francisco during the late 1960s and early 1970s. There were several meetings at readings and parties in the Haight where we chatted and exchanged writer's small talk, and we were two of more than forty poets who read in support of the Native American takeover of Alcatraz in 1969.

In the summer of 1970 Al and I wandered out of a party celebrating the publication of Ray Carver's first book, *Winter Insomnia*. That was before Ray had become a household name as the new Ernest Hemingway. The party was at a rambling, hillside house in Portola Valley, forty miles south of San Francisco, and Al and I stood by our cars, looking at the distant bay lying like smoked glass in the moonlight. We must have talked for an hour about one thing and another, getting to know each other, hardly hearing the music and babble in the house behind us. I know we talked at length about his first book, *Dancing*, and also about mine, *Origins*, both of which had come out the year before. *Dancing* had impressed me quite a bit with its musical voice rhythms. I felt a great kinship with the book, which celebrated the small joys of being alive as a series of "dances" that pictured the persona, who I imagined was Al, as poor and lonely and on his own in the depths of the larger society. One poem depicted him dancing alone in a laundromat. It was a book of youth, full of carefree innocence from which Al's enthusiastic yet quiet wonder at life joyously radiated—a celebratory quality his work has never lost. We ended the conversation vowing to see each other more often.

Our friendship was cemented in San Francisco two years later when he was master of ceremonies at the Kenneth Patchen Memorial Reading at the City Lights Poetry Theater, an event he organized almost single-handedly. He had chosen me, I'm sure, at the suggestion of Miriam Patchen, whom I had met the year before, and who knew how important her husband's work had been to me. I was one of the dozen participants in the reading, which featured Lawrence Ferlinghetti, Gary Snyder, Robert Duncan, Ishmael Reed, and seven others. Al and I, and one or two of the other poets, were verbally badgered by a drunken, drugged-out member of the packed audience who intermittently shouted "I'm the bastard son of Kenneth Patchen! Why aren't I

Al Young, Santa
Cruz, 1996

reading!" and then lapsed into a moody silence, raising
his objections to one poem or another as his stupor or
alcohol-warped perception allowed. Throughout the
evening, Al handled these intrusions with the graceful-
ness of a bullfighter. The upshot of the episode was that
Al and I, two of the heckler's main targets, commiserated
with each other after the reading, our friendship coher-
ing as if we had undergone a baptism of fire together.

By the time of the Patchen reading, Al and I had realized that we had several friends in common. Not only
Ray, but Jim Houston, who had been on a Stegner fellowship with Al at Stanford in 1966, and the novelist Peter
Beagle, who lived a mile or so down the road from me in the Santa Cruz
Mountains and had introduced Jim and Al in 1964. During the early seventies, Al and I saw each other at Jim's house or at Peter's and at the many parties and readings we attended, greeting each other across the room with big
smiles and nods that needed no words. Since then, the friendship has been
an uninterrupted bond of comfort and trust.

■ ■ ■

There is something about Al that inspires good feelings the moment you
meet him. I've observed that phenomenon with everyone he is introduced
to, and I believe that it has to do with how comfortable everyone is in his
presence, which, in turn, has to do with how comfortable Al seems to be
with himself: how relaxed he is in his body, how his voice is a series of
smooth glissandos, and how at ease he is with everyone he talks to.

I've always thought that putting people at ease when you initially meet
them is more than a talent. It's a statement made by your body, an attitude
born of the decision that you will enter a room of strangers or approach the
person coming toward you on the street without fear, suspicion, or resentment. It's the kind of decision made by fools or saints.

I quickly realized that Al was too self-confident and too intelligent to be a
fool and too street smart to be a saint. He was a person who years before
had decided to live life on his own terms by going through the world of war-
ring neighbors, muggers, and hysterical madmen with trust and good will
because, his smile seemed to say, life isn't worth living if you have to do it
any other way.

That attitude is all the more astonishing when you take into account that
Al is an African American, a black man prone to be the target for all the
hatreds, slurs, clichés, and racial violence that these United States are heir
to. Such hatreds are not only directed at blacks by guilt-ridden, frightened
whites, but at whites by humiliated, angry blacks, who were a belligerent

segment of the arts scene in the 1960s and '70s after an emotionally-freeing decade of civil rights actions and the "Black is beautiful" movement.

Many critics and fellow writers have commented on the lack of racial anger and defensiveness in Al's writings. But he looks at it in a different way. "I think it's just a sense of wonder that makes me the way I am," he said to me once. "I have never gotten over the fact that we are here in this event called life, whatever it is, illusory or not. As a kid I used to wonder where it all comes from, where it's all flowing to, what's happened to all the things that happened yesterday, and I've just never gotten over that. And as I learned about people all over the country and all over the world, and met people from different backgrounds, I realized we all have more in common than we have that makes us different from one another. So I made peace with the race issue fairly early."

Who knows what demons and scars lie hidden in the psyche of anyone? What is clear is that you can choose the face you want the world to see and hopefully can become the person you imagine you are. Al chose to be kind, gregarious and generous. I've never seen him act any other way.

A slim, loose-limbed six feet tall, he always talks about being in the moment. "Poetry," he once wrote "keeps teaching me that the only time there is is now"—and maybe that is his secret: he is never remote or conde-scending but fully engaged in whatever he is doing and with whom he is doing it. He isn't "cool" as much as he is "mellow"—relaxed, good-humored, approachable. Or at least that is the image he projects whenever I am in his company.

Unlike most of the men I have written about in this book, Al hasn't sup-pressed his emotions or become self-protective but is open and emotionally present, two traits that appeal to my Slavic soul. In fact, for all his mellow-ness, Al is always getting excited about one thing or another, whether it's music, politics, poetry, computer technology, or the weather. We have long phone conversations about the state of the country and the world in gen-eral, and I remember one day he said, "I'm aware of all the injustices and oppression, and the misuse and disuse of human beings by other human beings, but I like to think that one person operating in a private life, inter-acting with other people, is having an effect on the totality as well."

Although he never ignores the brutalities and tragedies of life, Al's atti-tude of quiet wonder and gregariousness permeates his writing with a clearly optimistic, even cheerful, quality and is traceable, he always said, to his early years in Mississippi before his father moved the family to Detroit. He has told me many times about the closeness of his family and about his grandmother, father, and uncles engaged in "front-porch storytelling." The way his relatives spoke was as fascinating to him as the stories themselves and made him love language.

He particularly remembers his uncle Billy who, he once told me, "as a Pullman porter would meet people and they would tell him their stories and he would memorize what they said and then tell us. His recitations took hours. He would tell each story using the person's voice and point of view and recount major events and scenes. He would even reenact scenes with dialogue and sound effects. So when I write a novel I hear voices, I hear someone telling a story. To go back to voice, I think, is the most important thing in literature."

Al is a great storyteller himself, and when he describes incidents that have happened to him in Berkeley and Palo Alto and in such faraway places as Yugoslavia and India, like Uncle Billy he imitates the characters involved with faultless accents. His ear for speech patterns is pitch perfect, and one of the joys of reading his novels is the dialogues. So I wasn't surprised when he told me one day that his two favorites among his novels are *Sitting Pretty* and *Seduction by Light*, in which he employs first-person narrators who speak with a vernacular immediacy that grabs you by the ears and hauls you into the world of the books.

Not that Al wanted to be a writer all his life, even though he demonstrated a surfeit of literary talents early, learning to read by the age of three and publishing poems, stories, and articles in magazines and local Detroit newspapers while still in his teens. During those formative years, Al was a disc jockey as well as a guitarist and lead singer for a small jazz/folk-song ensemble and wanted to be a musician more than a writer.

His decision to devote himself to writing rather than his other talents came while he was pursuing a career as a musician in New York City. He told me in an interview that "from the age of seventeen to twenty-four I made a partial living singing and playing guitar in coffee houses and clubs, doing other gigs too, such as weddings. What I didn't like about it was the same thing my Dad didn't—the drunks, the smoke, and what happened to his friends, many of whom died very young because of that life. I didn't like to go to the gig and have to put up with people I couldn't stand, obnoxious people. What I always liked about writing was that you could do it anywhere, mail it in, and get an answer back through the mails. I always found that very appealing."

In 1960, Al decided to dedicate his energies to writing. He was twenty-two and moved to the San Francisco Bay Area where he wrote furiously while working as a medical photographer, warehouseman, clerk typist, yard clerk for the Southern Pacific Railroad, interviewer for the California Department of Employment, laboratory aide, and industrial films' narrator. By 1969, he had graduated with honors from the University of California at Berkeley, *Dancing* had come out, and his first novel, *Sitting Pretty*, was about to be published.

After that, he was in demand all over the world as writer, reader, performer, and lecturer. His poetry, fiction, and essays won numerous awards and were translated into a dozen languages as diverse as Swedish, Chinese,

Italian, and Serbo-Croatian. He taught as guest lecturer and writer-in-residence at dozens of universities across the country and toured Asia and Europe a number of times as a visiting writer for the United States government. In 1982 he was given the key to the city of Detroit.

Al is as great a public reader as he is a storyteller. Over the years, he and I have given a number of readings together, and more than once I've witnessed how he mesmerizes audiences. Sometimes he unexpectedly breaks into song in the middle of a poem. His voice is soft and melodious. Once I asked if he had any regrets about giving up music. He answered without hesitation. "Actually, I didn't give up anything, since I always saw writing as music."

The paradox that became increasingly apparent to me as the years passed was that Al, a black man who had found his way to an Olympian vision beyond race, wrote primarily of his racial experience. Such ironies, of course, are unavoidable, since a writer brings the influences and fascinations of his youth to the writing table.

Al writes in a variety of styles, uses closed forms as well as free verse, and his diction can go from formal to vernacular in the space of a word. But in all his poems, there is music, the love of language. Here's a poem in the vernacular that literally sings and amounts to Al's autobiography.

A Little More Traveling Music

A country kid from Mississippi I drew water from the well
& watched our sun set itself down behind the thickets,
hurried from galvanized baths to hear music
over the radio—Colored music, rhythmic & electrifying,
more Black in fact than politics & flint guns.

Mama had a knack for snapping Juicy Fruit gum
& for keeping track of the generations of chilrens
she had raised, reared & no doubt forwarded,
rising thankfully every half past daybreak
to administer duties the poor must look after
if they're to see their way to another day, to eat, to live.

        *   *   *

I lived & upnorth in cities sweltering & froze, got jammed
   up & trafficked
in everybody's sun going down but took up with the moon
as it lit about getting it all down up there where couldn't
   nobody knock it out.

Picking up slowly on the gists of melodies, more noises softened.
I went to school & college too, woke up cold
& went my way finally, classless, reading all, poems,
   some books & listening to heartbeats.

Well on my way to committing the ABC reality,
I still couldn't forget all that motherly music,

those unwatered songs of my babe-in-the-woods days
until, committed to the power of the human voice,
I turned to poetry & singing by choice,
reading everyone always & listening, listening for a silence
      deep enough
to make out the sound of my own background music.

Al is truly a man of belles lettres, one of the few contemporary American writers I would identify by that title. Not the least of his works—actually among his best—is what he calls his "musical memoirs," a series of essays as varied as jazz reviews, record jacket introductions, personal reminiscences of his travels, and thoughts and responses to music and events of all kinds. The memoirs have been collected and published in several volumes over the years, entitled *Bodies and Soul, Kinds of Blue, Things Ain't What They Used to Be*, and *Drowning in the Sea of Love*.

Of all my friends, Al is the most generous. He continually puts me and other writers in touch with people who are looking for judges for literary contests, poets to read or give workshops, and conference faculty members. Several times he invited me to speak to his university classes. He always shares with me whatever contacts come his way, and he is responsible for publishing my ninth book, *Shouting Down the Silence*, when he introduced me to Don Ellis at Creative Arts Books. When my prose-poem collection, *When People Could Fly*, came out in 1997, Al, after reading it, spontaneously penned an enthusiastic review that he published on the *Amazon.com* book site. A few years later, he wrote a laudatory blurb for *Moments Without Names*, my selected prose poems.

In 1997, when he was writer-in-residence for the fall semester at the University of Arkansas at Fayetteville, Al arranged to invite me out for a week of workshops and one-on-one conferences with the graduate poetry students in the creative writing MFA program. It was a wonderful week, but what is most memorable about it for me was how Al—who was frantically busy with his own classes as well as with fulfilling academic social obligations and finalizing a complicated reading tour for himself in different parts of the South—continually went out of his way to make sure I was not only taken care of but wanted for nothing. He even arranged to switch my housing assignment from an out-of-the-way funky motel to the best hotel in Fayetteville.

I have noticed his similar concern for others, no matter who they are, on many occasions. One example of his solicitousness is that he has never forgotten to send a card or phone congratulations to my wife and me on our birthdays and our wedding anniversaries.

I reciprocated, of course, having Al come to my classes in literature and creative writing, and his sessions were always greeted enthusiastically. When I was asked to host a weekly poetry show on the Santa Cruz community radio station, I asked him to be my first guest, knowing it would start my tenure in the best possible light. I was right. I also arranged to have him interviewed by Ray Gonzalez for a long piece entitled "A Lyrical Legacy," which appeared in two issues of *The Bloomsbury Review*.

When I wrote a series of literary profiles for the Metro newspaper chain in the early 1990s, I chose Al to be one of my first subjects. The occasion was the publication of his collected poems, *Heaven*, but the article, which ran over five thousand words, turned out to be a minibiography, complete with an examination of his poems and novels. I focused much of the content of my literary comments on Al's novel *Seduction by Light*, which I still think is the best novel about Hollywood ever written—and that includes Nathaniel West's *The Day of the Locust* and F. Scott Fitzgerald's unfinished *The Last Tycoon*. *Seduction by Light* is an ingeniously conceived, multidimensional, half-comic look at the fringes of the film world as seen through the eyes of an African American housekeeper who for a time was a film starlet and tells her story in a dazzling vernacular.

In the last ten years, Al has been so much in demand he seems to be constantly traveling, and most of our communication has been through endless phone calls from Pennsylvania, North Carolina, Michigan, or any number of places. The subjects are always the same, however: yes, the literary world and what is happening in it, but more important, the political scene and the world situation in general. Al was never an ivory-tower poet: he is someone you brush shoulders with on the street every day. I thought about that aspect of his demeanor and approach to life and literature, as well as the excellence of his work when, in the spring of 2005, he was appointed poet laureate of California. I couldn't think of anyone better suited for the job.

PART

I look upon all mankind as my fellow countrymen.
I embrace a Pole as I do a Frenchman and I prefer the
common bond of humanity above all national ties.

—Michel de Montaigne

BOOK NINE

TRAVELS 1: GREECE

CHAPTER 32

Preparations

My travels to other countries have been instructive in many ways. They've not only woven new sights and sounds into my writing, they've given rise to notions that found their way into my psyche as well. They've also helped formulate some of my core ideas about humanity, history, and the nature of the universe.

Until my first sabbatical from Cabrillo in 1975, I never had the money to engage in what I consider travel, although by then I had done extensive journeying here and there in the United States. As a child I had accompanied my mother to Florida three times and had boarded in schools in Connecticut, New Jersey, and various parts of New York state. As an independent teenager I had hitchhiked with friends to Miami and a number of East Coast states, and in the air force I had flown on free "hops" and TDY assignments all over the Midwest and sundry southern states. As an adult, I had lived in Iowa for three years and driven cross-country several times after I moved to California. So I had seen and had adventures in many sections of the country. But those trips did not fit into my definition of travel, which was enmeshed with notions of foreign climes and history and an exotic aura of otherness.

On my first sabbatical, I finally had the funds and the time to undertake what I regarded as "real" travel, and those travels provided me with a number of small adventures that expanded my concepts of the human condition.

My mother had been urging me to go to Europe and even offered to supplement my modest budget. She thought it was essential for me to see other cultures in order to have a broadened view of life. She needn't have worried. I was eager to embark to foreign places and had worked out an intricate plan for my sabbatical, which would last from January to September. For the first two months of the year, I was accepted to sojourn at the MacDowell Art Colony in New Hampshire, where I not only finished two writing projects but was able to save two months' salary. From there I was to fly from New York to Greece, where I would spend the next six months.

Greece had been my intended destination for years but not because it had been home to Socrates, Plato, and Aristotle, or because, in the vaunted phrase, it was "the cradle of Western civilization." My reasons were more contemporary and, some would say, arcane. Norman Thomas had urged me to go to Greece, as had Bob Peterson. Through them I met and befriended the Greek poet Nanos Valaoritis when he came to live in the Bay area, and he urged me to visit Greece as well.

But my fascination with Greece had begun long before those inducements. The first review I ever wrote was on a book called *Greece and the Great Powers*, and was published in a neighborhood newspaper in 1964, the last time I lived in New York, the same year Norman and Alice Thomas left for their Greek sojourn. The book was about the Greek resistance in World War II and the ill-fated civil war that followed it. Although the volume was practically royalist in its sympathies, it presented a fascinating web of intrigue, deceit at high levels, and charismatic characters, and it described a vivid picture of injustice and international manipulation. The author, Steven X. Xydis, had been a Greek delegate to the United Nations after the war and had access to government documents unavailable to many historians. Four years before I read the book, I had seen Jules Dassin's parable about contemporary Greece, *Never On Sunday*, and, knowing Dassin had been blacklisted from Hollywood, I was alert to the different pictures he and Xydis painted of Greece. I became fascinated with the country's history from these two examples.

Never On Sunday also introduced me to Greek *rembetica*, the music of the Greek waterfronts and cities. Rembetica featured the bouzoukee, a stringed instrument that looked much like a lute, with a long neck and a pear-shaped sounding box that was flat on top and bulbous on bottom, and as far as I was concerned could express the most scintillatingly joyous sounds one moment and the most aggrieved, soul-wrenching ones the next. When I found Greektown on lower Eddy Street in San Francisco, I began collecting Greek phonograph records and attending Greek nightclubs. When I moved to Santa Cruz, my friend Basil Provatakis, the art historian at Cabrillo, and I began taking bouzoukee lessons from a wild Greek American who played at a San Jose Greek supper club.

I was so infatuated with Greek music that I set up a typical taverna evening at the Cabrillo College theater with the great bouzoukee player Johnny "The Seed" Stamitis while he was playing for a few months at my teacher's nightclub. It was a free event that drew more than five hundred students who were dancing in the theater and outside in the quad.

As for my bouzoukee career, Paul, my bouzoukee teacher, got so frustrated with my lack of talent I think he would have broken my cheap bouzoukee over my head if I had continued to work with him longer than I did. Before that happened, however, I realized my inadequacies on the instrument and gracefully took an early retirement to become—as the continued lover of the undertaking at which he has failed is called—an aficionado.

My last session with Paul in many ways tells the story. We met for lessons at the nightclub where Paul played during the afternoons when the club was closed. It was a pretty crass place, large and modern and clean but full of glitter in the walls and ceiling and plaster columns and statues of Greek gods placed strategically around the tables of the dining room. Paul would sit opposite me on the musicians' platform, leaning on his his flower-inlaid, silver-encrusted bouzoukee and shake his head at my junky instrument while he went through the chord changes with me. As usual, he was shaking his head and replaying what he had just shown me, pausing while I fumbled my imitation of his movements, and then he replayed the simple combination yet again for me, becoming more irritated with my lack of progress at each repetition.

It wasn't only my lack of skill that disturbed him; it was my bouzoukee. Bob Peterson had purchased it for me in Greece several years before, but, unbeknownst to him, he had bought an instrument that was more to be shown as a wall decoration than seriously played. As Paul said, because of the construction of the neck, the strings were too high off the fingerboard so when I played, my fingers "were like feet trudging through a marsh."

Finally, Paul stopped playing and said to me, "Enough. Are you practicing on that thing as much as I told you to?"

"I'm practicing two hours a day."

"Yeah, well, I think you need six hours a day, though it won't do you much good on that thing," and he swept the arm of his pick hand to the side in a dismissive gesture.

"Six hours?" I said. "That's the amount of time I devote to poetry each day."

"Poetry? Who gives a crap about poetry! We're talking about bouzoukee."

And so, although we remained on friendly terms for years afterward, Paul and I took leave of each other, he to his art and me to mine—and I to the ranks of bouzoukee aficionados.

I was looking forward to hearing Greek music when I visited Greece, but my plans took a literary turn when I told Nanos Valaoritis I was going there, and he gave me introductions to his friends: composers and poets who had returned to Greece after the banishment of The Colonels in 1974. In fact, his friends had not merely returned from exile; they returned to increased celebrity, several appointed to positions of political power in the Ministry of Culture. Before I left California for the MacDowell Colony, I asked Nanos what I should not miss seeing in Greece. He smiled sagely, his long white hair trailing over his ears and down his shoulders and his walrus-white mustache flowing from either side of his upper lip, and said, "When you get there, wherever you are, look up and down and to the sides. Wherever you look will be eight thousand years of history."

So by my sabbatical in 1975, everything was in place for me to travel to Greece. I would go from the MacDowell Colony to New York, my then girl-friend would fly from California to New York, and the two of us would wing our way to Athens.

Two precipitous events occurred before I left, however. First, on a trip to New York from MacDowell, as if by fate I found a remaindered copy of *The Greek Phoenix* by Joseph Braddock at one of the Marboro Bookstores. The book was a very readable account of the Greek revolt against the Turks in 1821 and was constructed around detailed profiles of some of the most famous heroes of the war. Second, in Santa Cruz I had found Leonard Cottrell's, *The Bull of Minos*, which told the stories of Heinrich Schliemann's discovery of Troy and Mycenae and Sir Arthur Evans' discovery of Knossos, a Minoan city palace on the island of Crete. The book was structured around Cottrell's trip to Greece in 1951.

I read both books with extreme pleasure and determined to find my way to the places they described as well as trace the authors' routes. It is a model for travel I have followed ever since.

CHAPTER 33

Athens and the Peloponnesus

My girlfriend Karen and I flew to Athens in March of 1975. We were to stay there with two friends—Gary Griggs, a geologist at the University of California at Santa Cruz, and his wife, Linda, a weaver—both of whom would orientate us to Greek ways. Gary was in Greece on a Fulbright fellowship to study pollution in relation to the tides in and around Piraeus.

As planned, Gary, Linda, and their two small children met us at the airport and took us to their rented house in the suburb of Kolomaki. They had been in Athens since the previous September, and their advice and suggestions were invaluable. They had also made a number of Greek friends who soon became our friends, and when Karen and I went off on our travels, several times with the Griggs, we stored our luggage at their house.

The morning after we arrived, Karen and I took a local bus into Athens proper. Two of the passengers, whom I took to be an elderly father and his middle-aged son, got into an argument, the old man loudly berating the younger man. The argument rose to a shouting match. The other passengers watched the proceedings with interest, but they were curiously nonplussed, as if they had witnessed such behavior all the time. Karen, a birdlike, petite brunette, quivered with fear. But I felt right at home and reassured her. This was like a dinner with the family at Aunt Bertha's. Here was a people as passionate as my people but unlike most Americans who suppressed their feelings. Just as the altercation between the two men seemed to reach the point of physical violence, both of them fell silent. The argument was over. This was a situation I would come across again and again in Greece—loud and vociferous expostulations followed by calm and peaceful silence.

The bus arrived at Syntagmou Square, with Karen trembling and me elated, and we hadn't walked half a block before we ran into Joe Stroud and his girlfriend Rachel coming in the opposite direction. Joe had taken a full year's sabbatical and had toured Asia during the previous fall and winter. We had made vague plans to rendezvous in Greece but never really firmed them up. Now the four of us greeted one another with hugs and exclamations of disbelief at our chance meeting. For the next two days we explored

Athens together. Then they set off for the remote island of Karpathos in the southern Aegean where they would stay for the next several months.

Athens was a bustling international city with wide avenues radiating from a number of squares like spokes from the central hubs of wheels. It was full of shadowy side streets and lanes where domed Byzantine chapels and churches and classical ruins suddenly appeared like hallucinations. Towering over the busy streets in a dusty haze, the huge sand-colored rock of the Acropolis floated in rarefied silence, as though it were a heavenly city hovering over the earthly city below, a grainy, amber apparition of the beginning and end of all cities.

These glimpses of both earthly and other-worldly presences were everywhere, from the outdoor displays in the flea market where salesmen called out to us, standing in front of shops crowded with coats, sweaters, antique knapsacks, helmets, gas masks, lamps, hardware, and metal pots, to the quiet, timeless, golden sunlight of the Agora, the ruins of the classical marketplace a block away that lay below one side of the Acropolis.

Even in the torrid summer heat that was to come, the city's vibrancy and its energetic inhabitants were exhilarating, made more so by the underlying festiveness I was to experience wherever I traveled in Greece. This almost holiday-like atmosphere was not only because it was spring and the people could spend their days and evenings outdoors with friends in tavernas and cafés after the shut-in winter months, nor because the tourist season was about to begin with its promise of money, but mostly because the repressive, military dictatorship of The Colonels, which had ruled Greece for seven years, had been overthrown the previous summer. It was in protest of their takeover that I had participated in the Freedom or Death reading at Fugazi Hall seven years before, and now freedom as well as prosperity had returned to the country. As if to emphasize this point, wherever we traveled for the next six months, Karen and I seemed to be greeted by the popular composer Mikis Theodorakis, who had returned from exile and was touring the country giving concerts of his work, featuring the well known singers Maria Farandouris and Stelios Kazantzidis. We attended four of the performances in different parts of the country, and in each one a capacity crowd, unable to control its joy, rose to its feet, arms around one another, and, in blissful tears, sang the songs along with the performers.

That was the heady atmosphere I found myself in those first days in Athens. Intoxicated with everything we saw, Karen and I wandered through the city until late at night, exploring side streets and alleys and spending long hours in the Benaki and Byzantine museums on Vasilissus Sofias Avenue. On the second floor of the National Archaeological Museum, we were delighted to find the entire Minoan neighborhood that had been excavated and moved intact from its hiding place under hundreds of feet of volcanic pumice on the island of Santorini, where we would be heading within the month.

My favorite Athens museum, however, was the National Historical Museum, which I discovered by accident. It was on a small, quiet plaza on Stadiou Street, just off busy Amelia Avenue, and looked like a small-town American library. In front was a heroic equestrian statue of the brigand-turned-revolutionary Theodore Kolokotronis who sat astride his stallion with his famous replica of Achilles' feathered helmet clamped on his head. I recognized his visage from Braddock's book and with mounting enthusiasm climbed the staircase behind him through the four-columned entryway.

Inside were rooms filled with glass cases of memorabilia of the 1821 Revolution and walls crammed with larger-than-life-size, richly colored paintings of the revolutionaries and famous battles and events of the war.

As I stood before the portrait of the woman admiral Bouboulina, discoursing about her to Karen, a wizened old man in a brown business suit came up and listened and then continued my description in more detail. He was delighted that I knew about the Revolution and introduced himself in halting but precise English as the curator of the museum. Thus began one of those afternoons a tourist hopes for but rarely finds. The curator, who introduced himself as "Stephen," whisked us from one exhibit to another, prefacing each stop with one of two phrases, either "Now I am going to show you something . . ." or "Now, look here . . ."

He told us that the building was built in 1835 and housed the national parliament from 1875 to 1940, and to illustrate his remark, he unlocked a door in an alcove and ushered us into a dark room. When he snapped on the lights, the room revealed itself to be a large chamber with many plush chairs. He then led us back into the museum proper and, growing more excited at each stop, unlocked other doors, opened trunks and dome-shaped chests, pointed to the contents, or left them out for our inspection. In one room he guided us to a niche housing a metal amphora that contained the heart of Admiral Kanaris. In another room he opened the secret compartments in the elaborate writing desk of Patriarch Gregorios V. All the while, he pointed out blood-splattered or half-burned, tattered flags celebrating one battle or another, and at one point opened an old chest containing a rusty bed, which he removed and unfolded, and on which, he declared, Lord Byron had breathed his last at Missolonghi. When he bid us a warm good-bye two hours later, I was dizzy and exultant. And, I thought to myself, "The trip is just beginning . . ."

But I had more to see in Athens than museums. I also had greetings to deliver from Nanos Valaoritis to various cultural dignitaries. On our third night in Athens, I asked an English-speaking desk clerk in a five-star hotel to dial the phone number of the composer Manos Hajidakis. The clerk laughed, assuring me that one just didn't call such high-ranking people. Did I know that Mr. Hajidakis was Minister of Culture? When I produced Hajidakis' phone number, his attitude changed and he made the call. The great man was excited to hear from me and asked various questions about me and about Nanos's well-being. I met him at his office several days later, where it was apparent he was extraordinarily busy, phones ringing and sub-ordinates sweeping in and out of the office as we drank coffee. "We must have dinner," he said, but he wasn't free for the next few weeks. He had just been appointed and had much to do. He was kind, and it was clear he felt obligated to entertain me but had no opportunity to do so.

I had more luck with the poet and lyricist Nikos Gatsos, whose long sur-realistic poem "Amorgos" remained an influence on younger poets for decades after it was published. Although he had written almost no poetry since, he remained a celebrity for his haunting, Lorca-like folk lyrics that had been set to music by several popular composers, not only Hajidakis, but Mikis Theodorakis as well. Gatsos was a good friend of Odysseus Elytis, and I hoped to meet Elytis through him. When I called, he invited me to a late afternoon coffee and pastry at Zonar's the next day. Zonar's was a fancy restaurant on Amelia Avenue, an avenue that reminded me of Fifth Avenue in New York City. Zonar's served a full complement of food as well as pas-tries and coffee. Here, for years, Nanos had told me, Gatsos held court over painters, poets, and composers every afternoon.

Gatsos, a portly man in his fifties with slicked-back dark hair, wearing a white shirt and tie and expensive slacks, welcomed me and introduced me to his friends. His English was excellent, and I had no trouble interpreting his droll comments and ironic tone of voice. He asked me about American poetry and poets and passed on my words with comments of his own in Greek, which made the seven or eight men at the table snicker. I was more uncomfortable by the minute, an obvious object of ridicule, but I continued to answer his questions with good humor and gave him my latest book before I left. What was I planning to see while I was in Greece, he asked, and when I said the Peloponnesus, he became as serious as an uncle advising his nephew. He was from a small town outside Sparta, he said, and I should not miss visiting Mistra, the abandoned city that had been the capital of the Byzantine Empire in the thirteenth century, when the emperor fled Con-stantinople from the onslaught of the European crusaders. He also told me to visit the Gorge of Samaria on the Island of Crete. It was "a nice stroll" and "a good place for a picnic," he said, an offhand remark that would come to haunt me. As for Elytis, he was out of the country, and Gatsos said he would set up a meeting when Elytis returned.

Each time I returned to Athens, I would spend an afternoon with Gatsos, who was more cordial after that first meeting, having, he said, been impressed by my book and clearly interested in my unorthodox itinerary and method of travel, which was not the way most tourists he had met explored Greece. It helped that I always went where he suggested, and he was eager to hear my impressions each time I returned.

Spending afternoons with Gatsos and wandering around Athens and discovering its secrets was all well and good, but I was eager to start my explorations of the rest of the country.

Of the many adventures I had that first trip to Greece, several stand out as extraordinary for their emotional and mystical resonances. Among other things, they cemented my thoughts on history and humanity in general. And I must start with my first trip from Athens, which I undertook without guidance from Gary and Linda or my newfound friends there.

■†■†■

I was determined to follow Cottrell's path and his method of getting around as he had described it in *The Bull of Minos*. Thus, on my fifth morning in Greece, Karen and I, with backpacks containing a single change of clothes, went to the Peloponnese train station and embarked for Mycenae. The rural landscape was much changed since Cottrell's trip in 1951, and the train chugged for miles through a landscape of refineries and electrical transformers before it reached small towns and dusty forests on one side and the sun-spattered blue waters of the Saronic Gulf on the other, finally depositing us at the small Mycenae station where Cottrell had disembarked at night twenty-four years before.

We arrived early in the afternoon, got off the train with ten others, mostly local farmers or townspeople, women dressed in black and men in work clothes, and asked the way into town.

Almost all tourists took tour buses from Athens to Mycenae as part of package deals, and so we had the road to ourselves for the two-mile walk into the village. A spring breeze was rolling through the tall grasses, and sheep were nibbling or browsing on both sides of the empty road, which was overhung with tall plane trees that dipped and swayed overhead. It was a magical entrance through an arched corridor of welcoming greenery, with bees and buzzing cicadas all around and the sharp scents of thyme and oregano perfuming the air. The goats with their tinkling bells bowed and cavorted in the fields.

Mycenae itself was a nondescript hamlet whose main street was cluttered with cheap trinkets and bric-a-brac for the endless herds of tourists let loose from the buses for half an hour after they visited the

The grand pastoral entrance, Mycenae, Greece, 1975

ruins of Agamemnon's palace on the hill above the village. I wanted to find "La Belle Helene de Menelaus," the inn where Cottrell had spent the night. But when I found it, it was no longer the humble building owned by the proud Greek family that had put Cottrell up but a small, modern hotel with a large dining room and the most powerful flush toilets I had ever encountered. It turned out that the inn had been bought by a German syndicate and was run by several athletically built, middle-aged Teutons who made me recall Cottrell's description of the guest book he encountered there. It had been signed, he noted, by such Nazi elite as Goering, Goebbels, and Himmler, who Cottrell thought "had come to pay tribute to the memory of Heinrich Schliemann." Schliemann was the nineteenth-century German businessman who set the science of archaeology on its ear by discovering the remains of Troy and who then excavated, on the hill above Mycenae, the famous Lion's Gate and vaulted beehive Tholos tomb, which he claimed was the palace of Agamemnon. He also exhumed at Mycenae a treasure of gold burial masks, goblets, and jewelry that had fired the imagination of tourists for eighty years before my trip. He had discovered all this because he believed that the *Iliad* and the *Odyssey* described real people and places.

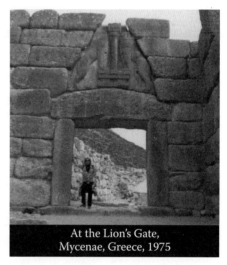

At the Lion's Gate,
Mycenae, Greece, 1975

We spent the afternoon at the site until closing. Then we caught a local bus to Argos, a market town six miles away, where we were caught up in crowds of people shopping and hurrying home. From Argos we took a packed bus on the short ride to Nauflion. I remembered from Braddock's book that Nauflion was the first capital of Greece after the 1821 Revolution. Now it was a rundown old town of narrow streets with two- and three-story buildings that either had shops on the bottom and apartments on top or were still houses of residence with wrought-iron balconies on the second and third floors. We wandered through the town that night, talking or pantomiming to the local people, and stayed at a cheap pension. The next morning we visited the ruins of Tiryns a few miles from town, a jumble of gigantic boulders scattered about or leaning against one another in shady corridors and niches as if placed there by giants playing a game with marbles or rough-hewn building blocks.

We spent the rest of the day and night in Nauflion, wandering about once more, gesturing and trying to talk to the taverna keepers and shop owners

Street in Nauplion, Greece, as it must have appeared in 1827

we'd met the day before. Something was happening I couldn't quite grasp yet. It had started on the train and blossomed at Argos, where I sensed in the crowd the same feelings I had experienced every time I was caught in a New York rush hour as a boy. But I didn't understand what was going on until early the next afternoon when we caught another local bus for our ride to Sparta in the Peloponnesus.

The bus was dilapidated but had been sold out. Not only were there no empty seats, but a number of people had brought folding chairs that they set up in the aisle. Karen and I had to sit in the stairwell of the rear exit. Despite the crowding, the passengers were in a festive mood. As the bus climbed the precipitous mountain roads, they called out and joked from one end of the bus to the other, like neighbors gossiping over a fence.

Karen and I were the only foreigners on the bus and had received curious stares when we climbed aboard. A heavy, middle-aged man and his wife sat on folding chairs above us, and, either in answer to inquiries or because, as it proved, he was the joker of the crowd, the man kept up a running comic description of what we were doing seated on the steps below him. He had good material to work with, because Karen had taken out a packet of multicolored threads and was sewing flower patterns on my backpack, while I was reading a description of the Peloponnesus from a Blue Guide I had bought in Athens.

Soon we were the butt of jokes and counterjokes, and even though the man's wife tried to stop him, he had warmed to his role as chorus and was regaling his fellow passengers in a foghorn voice with one comment after another that elicited laughter from almost everyone.

As he continued his oratory, Karen, who had a wonderful, impish sense of humor and was as aware as I was of what was going on, but, like me, not understanding a word of it, unobtrusively took her needle and, with bright orange thread, sewed the man's pant cuffs together. When he looked down and saw what was happening, he stopped his description in midsentence and began to sputter in obvious shock. His wife looked over and began to howl with laughter and announced to the entire bus what Karen had done. Everyone erupted in laughter, and within moments they were passing us fruit, salami, and wine, and bombarding us with questions in broken English.

At the first rest stop, many of the passengers came up to us, smiling, patted us on the shoulders, and attempted to advise us on one thing and another, offering us more food as well. When they wandered away to the restrooms and a small souvlaki stand near it, we climbed a little hill to stretch our legs, followed by a stocky man in a dark blue suit, white shirt and tie, wearing a fedora. He must have been seventy years old and had a square, expressionless face. The other passengers had given him a wide berth, and he had not taken part in the gleeful proceedings on the bus.

"Hey, you kids," he called in perfect English, his voice deep and gravelly. "Where you from and where you going?"

We told him.

"I'm from Chicago," he offered, his face still expressionless. "Don't mind them. Stick close to me. I think you'll get into Sparta too late tonight. We'll be coming into Tripolis by nightfall, and I'll make sure you're taken care of."

Taken care of? How? Karen and I looked at each other. The man's words could be interpreted in several ways, and his demeanor was more menacing than friendly.

Seeing our discomfort, he continued, as if to reassure us, "I was mayor of Chicago, made my fortune and came home."

But that didn't relieve our anxiety. We both imagined him to be the prototype of the 1930s Chicago gangster and were quietly thankful when the driver called that the rest stop was over and we resumed our respective places on the bus.

The passengers' merriment continued, but I was ruminating on everything that had occurred and was finally able to put my experiences and half-formed impressions of the last two days in order. I was enjoying myself immensely, and I realized that my trip to Greece was not going to be about searching for *laika* music or meeting the cultural elite, but visiting the sights I had set out to see and mixing with the common people, who were eager to find out who Karen and I were and to share with us ideas about the world. This became evident whenever a person we encountered found out I was a teacher, or *daskalos*, who was willing to share their transportation and everyday life. By the time we reached Tripolis several hours later, I was determined that this was the way I would travel and how I would spend my five remaining months in Greece.

But there was still our stone-faced fellow traveler in the fedora. The passengers obviously knew him and were just as obviously avoiding him. He had a presence that commanded attention, however, and after everyone piled out of the bus in Tripolis, I found myself carrying his luggage to a pleasant, well-lit hotel where the entire staff was waiting for him on the steps and addressed him with solemn respect.

As he followed the proprietor into the lobby, he entreated us once more to stay the night, but we told him we were eager to get to Sparta and said good-bye. When we returned to the square, however, we found the bus had left without us and another one wouldn't leave for Sparta until the next day.

We were stranded in Tripolis, which, it was soon clear, was not a tourist destination but a market town for farmers and a transportation center located in the middle of the Peloponnese. As in Argos two evenings before, people were rushing around doing last-minute shopping and heading home. The mostly two-story, squat buildings around us were dilapidated if not in ruins, and we found no places of lodging, so we went back to the hotel where we had left the man in the fedora.

At the front desk we asked the proprietor, who spoke little or no English, if he had a room. But he lifted his chin and shook his head. At that moment the man in the fedora appeared from a stairway and, seeing the situation, spoke a few quiet sentences in Greek. Miraculously, the proprietor remembered he had an empty room. The incident was intriguing, or rather the influence and deportment of our stone-faced friend was. Who was he?

"He'll take care of you," the man said to us, nodding to the proprietor, and left the hotel, still in his jacket and fedora and, we noticed, carrying a large folded paper bag. The room the proprietor showed us was clean and pleasant and cost us far too little. Had our friend arranged the price, too?

We showered and went out to see the town and got something to eat. By the time we set foot in the street again, the town had been transformed. It was after 9 pm, and people were strolling everywhere, not rushing as they had before but ambling back and forth by the hundreds—whole families, young girls and boys in groups of four to six, all greeting each other while going to tavernas or stopping at food stands. Once more we were caught up in a crowd. People eyed us curiously or ignored us as they went about their business in what was clearly an evening promenade, which we observed like spectators at a play.

Then we saw the man in the fedora through the window of what looked like a hardware store. The man behind the counter was handing him blocks of what looked like bills, money which he put in the paper bag that was now unfolded and half full.

At Karen's suggestion, we decided to follow him. He went into one shop or taverna after another, quietly accepting blocks of money that he deposited in the paper bag. After an hour we abandoned our pursuit and got something to eat, caught up in the relaxed, Mardi Gras atmosphere of the town. Both Karen and I were delighted with the whole experience as well as curious about our unsmiling friend.

Next morning we found him in the dining room. He had been waiting for us and asked about what we had done the previous night, ending the conversation by inviting us to his "estate." Again, we looked at each other but decided to continue on to Sparta. Once more I became the old man's porter, carrying his luggage to the bus stop, where we said farewell—and I was left to wonder for years afterward what would have happened if we had accepted his invitation. I no longer found the man menacing, but I'm sure our trip to Greece would have taken a different turn had we gone with him to his home. So much of what we were to do or decide not to do for the rest of our stay in Greece promised such experiences. Possibilities of adventure seemed to present themselves almost daily.

An hour after we said our thank yous and good byes to the old man, we took a bus to Sparta, a surprisingly modern city with wide boulevards and posters everywhere announcing Theodorakis' traveling concert. There were no ruins to be seen. When we visited the small local history museum that afternoon, the English-speaking curator told us why. The ancient Spartans, proud of their military prowess, had built no stone fortresses or palaces since they were confident that invading forces would be stopped before they got near the city.

The following day, we took the two-mile bus trip to Mistra, which Gatsos had insisted I visit. The bus dropped the two of us at the state-run taverna at the bottom of Mount Taigos. We were the only two people there. Opposite was the Lakonia Plain stretching for miles to the west with clusters of olive groves and sprinkled with multicolored wildflowers. Nudged by a spicy spring breeze, we started to climb the mountain along a long, weed-choked stone walkway. This was once the main street of the city and branched off into a maze of other "streets" full of ruins—collapsed walls and rubble. Wildflowers were everywhere on the walkway among the stones—purple, yellow, orange, and the bright blood-red spots of poppies. Bees and butterflies buzzed and floated on the shifting air.

The city was built on the side of the mountain, and a half-dozen churches and monasteries stood at intervals along the way. Several were being restored, and inside were walls covered with peeling Byzantine frescoes in

Ruins of the great palace above the Lakonian Plain, Mistra, the Peloponnesus, Greece, 1975

The main "street" of Mistra, the Peloponnesus, Greece, 1975

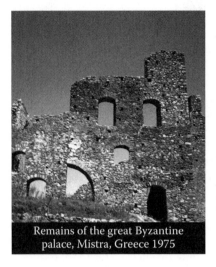

Remains of the great Byzantine palace, Mistra, Greece 1975

Byzantine church, ruins of Mistra, The Peloponnesus, Greece, 1975

many colors, the eyes of saints and other holy figures gouged out or otherwise defaced by the Turks in the Revolution of 1821 when the Turkish forces under Ibrahim Pasha had invaded and burned the almost totally abandoned city to the ground.

It was truly a ghost city, made more ghostly by our being the only people there. Gatsos had told me that Goethe had set the scene where Faust has his love affair with Helena (in Part Two of *Faust*) in Mistra. I could believe it, and my imagination ran wild.

Mistra was the capital of the Byzantine Empire from the thirteenth through the fourteenth centuries, after the crusaders from western Europe had captured Constantinople. At one point it had been home to forty thousand people. Now there were no amenities (no water or toilets), just wind and ruins and wildflowers. Luckily, we had been warned and had brought bread, salami, and water.

We spent eight hours wandering through the city, traipsing through the mammoth stone shell of what had been the royal palace, always climbing, until we reached the ruined fortress on top of Mount Taigos, two thousand feet above the plain, where a handful of Spartan citizens had actually resisted the Turkish siege in 1825.

The city was a labyrinth of walkways shaded by olive and almond trees, ruined churches standing free or partially built into the mountain, and everywhere we strolled we were surrounded by the chirring of the cicadas and the scent of orange blossoms and thyme carried on the breeze. I wanted to spend the rest of my Greek sojourn there. But we had promised Gary and Linda that we would return in a week, and so my first exploration in Greece came to an end, and we returned to Athens the next day on a series of local buses.

The ancient ruins, the bustling crowds in the decaying towns, the comic busride, the man in the fedora, the ghostly remains of Mistra: I have described my first Greek side trip in detail because it was typical of my travels in the country for the next five months. Many of the incidents I would encounter were comic, frustrating, and plainly dangerous at times, but they always involved the people. That first trip also determined the way I would travel for the rest of my life, first reading up on a country's history, traveling by local transportation, staying at secondary accommodations, visiting little-known as well as popular sites, and, later, staying in an area for weeks on end in order to enter the rhythm of life of a place and get to know the people who lived there, who, I found, recognized and appreciated what I was doing and among whom I made both temporary and lifelong friends.

Another result of my day at Mistra was a determination to know more about Byzantine Greece. When I returned to Athens, I bought the two-volume *History of the Byzantine Empire* by A. A. Vasiliev and Romilly Jenkins' *Byzantium: The Imperial Centuries A.D. 610–1074*, which I found in an English-language bookstore. I carried them with me everywhere I went, and read them from cover to cover. Later I would read Steven Runciman's books on Byzantine art and the medieval world of Eastern Europe and David Talbot Rice's books on Byzantine painting. My lifelong fascination with the Orthodox Church began at that time as well and became a passion on another memorable trip, this one to the island of Naxos three weeks after I returned from Mistra.

CHAPTER 34

Naxos

Gary and Linda and the new friends we had met through them had urged us to return to Athens so we could prepare for a holiday trip to the Aegean Islands for Easter. After we returned, I was looking forward to that excursion more than ever. I had never been interested in the Greece of Homer, Plato, and Socrates, and after visiting the Peloponnesus, my attention was focused more and more on medieval Greece and the Greek Revolution of 1821.

The plan was to take a ferry to the island of Paros for a few days and end up on Naxos for Easter, the most important event on the Orthodox calendar. We journeyed to Paros together, but when the others decided to stay there, Karen and I went on to Naxos alone.

I was determined to spend Easter on Naxos, the largest of the Aegean islands, because it was where Nikos Kazantzakis, the Greek novelist and poet, had been educated during his early boyhood. He had written that his schooling there "was the first and perhaps the most decisive leap in my intellectual life." In 1975, Kazantzakis was the most popular Greek writer in America. I had read *Zorba the Greek* and *The Greek Passion*, the latter of which had been made into an enthralling French film, and I had brought along *Freedom or Death* and *Letter from Greco* to read while I was in Greece. Seven years before, I had met Kazantzakis's widow at the reading in San Francisco put on to protest the Colonels' dictatorship. A trip to Naxos was, therefore, a sort of literary pilgrimage. It turned out to be more than that.

Timbered passageway in the upper town, which Kazantzakis must have wandered through as a boy. Naxos, Greece 1975.

After we settled in a pension, we explored the town. On Paros, we had been told that Naxos was not a tourist island, and that was readily apparent. The town, which wound its way up a hill from the harbor and was topped by a medieval Venetian fortress, was dirty and run down, the houses made of rough walls composed of unpainted blocks of stone sloppily splashed with whitewash. Many of the walls were grimy. The streets were, in reality, narrow, paved lanes, and most of the buildings were abandoned or had broken windows. At times, slap-dash whitewashed extensions were joined to unpainted houses of mud-col-ored stacked rock two or three stories high. The lanes twisted in all direc-tions, many overhung with covered passageways whose ceilings were propped with dry gray timbers. Unlike Nauflion and Tripolis, which exuded a well-kept if nineteenth-century decay, the Naxos buildings gave off a crumbling, medieval aura, an impression that was sharpened by the tim-bered underpasses and the chipped heraldic stone-carved Venetian coats of arms that were set above many of the doorways. The old buildings and their extensions were a jumble of several kinds of architecture from different time periods and were made of a hodgepodge of materials, all of which lent the town a surrealistic atmosphere, as if time had been telescoped, one age stacked on top of another, or intruding into each other, so that the inhabi-tants seemed to be living in several epochs at the same time. I soon fancied the past was alive in the present here: at any moment I expected Kazantza-kis to appear in late-nineteenth-century dress or a Venetian nobleman in Renaissance costume to emerge from one of the closed doors.

We wandered out of town at sunset and encountered a macabre scene on a hill overlooking the sea. Several hundred sheep hides, stretched on branches, were propped on one another against two huts. Thousands of flies droned around them. Karen covered her mouth and turned away. I stared at the car-casses, realizing that these were the remains of the lambs that were a tra-ditional part of Easter feasts. On the ferry from Athens, we had seen doz-ens of men carrying lamb carcasses over their shoulders. These carcasses were wrapped in bloody butcher pa-per, and Gary had told us the men were on their way to the islands to cel-ebrate Easter with their families.

Lamb skins drying outside of town, Naxos, Greece. Easter, 1975

We got back to town at nightfall. It was, of course, Good Friday. The streets, which had been moderately busy when we left, were now bustling with jabbering people. By nine o'clock the streets of the lower town were jammed with men and women and excited children, a number of whom were detonating firecrackers. We almost inadvertently joined a throng of several hundred, obviously in a procession, who were wending their way through the narrow lanes.

From the second-story balconies of the houses along the route, young girls threw rose petals on our heads. On the first floor, the windows of the houses were open and the passing crowd stared into the poor but immaculately clean interiors as if they were peering into store window displays. The people inside were mostly old women who squirted the passersby with perfumed water or fanned heavy clouds of incense into the street from brass burners. On the beds and couches behind them, fat "mama" dolls or topless, chocolate-colored Hawai'ian hula dolls, meticulously arranged, grinned at the onlookers. Every once in a while, the old women would greet acquaintances in the crowd who called out to them and then retreat to be part of the display once more.

Excitement grew. Firecrackers were snapping and stuttering everywhere, and the crowd swept us along.

By ten o'clock, we were looking down at the jubilant scene from the second story balcony of a taverna where the burly proprietor had taken us to watch the proceedings, describing what was happening in broken English. The open homes were a tradition, he explained, and he pointed out a white-bearded priest in pink brocaded vestments at the head of the procession we had joined. He was carrying a silver and gold holy book and was followed by a man holding a ten- or twelve-foot flower-wreathed cross. Behind them, several men carried a rose-festooned empty litter. Was the litter waiting for Christ to rise?

I was disoriented. The whole evening reminded me again of the convergence of different time periods I had sensed while wandering through the upper town that afternoon. The people at the head of the procession were serious, religious acolytes, but the boisterous crowd that followed was clearly secular, flirting, gossiping, some singing hymns, others, bits of what sounded like pop songs.

"Look," said the proprietor and pointed to another procession coming in the opposite direction, headed by a rotund patriarch in a dazzling gold miter and golden robes. He was followed by three young priests in black and behind them a man carrying another ten-foot cross edged with sparkling light bulbs, who in turn was trailed by two men carrying a car battery. It was ludicrous and enthralling at the same time, and my heart was beating like a wild bird's, my head pounding as the proprietor told us that both processions were circumventing the town, blessing the streets and buildings. "Don't miss the Easter ceremony tomorrow night at the cathedral," the proprietor said, proudly nodding. "The bishop himself will conduct the mass."

Somehow we got back to our pension. I felt I was in the midst of a ritual that was ancient and modern at the same time. I was feverish and went through the night and the next day as if in a dream.

At 11:45 the next night, Karen and I were in the cathedral, jammed among shoulders and heads. It was close and hot. Suddenly the gates of the sanctuary were flung open, and the bishop appeared in full regalia with a lit candle in his hand, signifying, I guess, that Christ had risen. He carried the candle to three young priests, scolding them about something or other as he lit their unlighted candles with his, and then the four of them lit the candles of the clamoring parishioners who surged forward with unlit candles in their hands as he and the priests battled their way to the crowd outside. There, the bishop mounted a flower-decked platform and proclaimed Christ had risen, as one person after another lighted the candles of those around them. As the bishop continued to speak, the sound of firecrackers spluttered through the commotion, and the people with lit candles scurried to their homes where, the taverna proprietor had told us the night before, they would hold the candles under the arch of their front doorways and wave them so that the smoke would create a black cross on the lintel, a sign that they believed would protect the house against evil spirits for the following year.

Soon the crowd had dispersed, and we turned back to the cathedral. Only several dozen old men and women and their grandchildren were inside. They waited silently for the midnight mass to begin. The bishop reentered the sanctuary and, hidden from sight, called to the priests who responded as if on cue and scurried around the church, swinging incense censers at niches and icons, blessing the building. Was the bishop supposed to be Christ in his tomb? I didn't know, but I felt I was witnessing a ceremony that predated Christianity, a pagan ritual that was restoring order to the world, putting the earth in harmony with the universe.

My two days on Naxos had been an almost mystical experience, a swirl of incidents and impressions: the crowds, the incongruities, the town's jumble of time-spanning architecture—all on an island in the middle of a remote backwater, where I was sure the world was being set right. I staggered out of the church, dragging Karen with me, and stumbled back to the pension, where I fell into bed and a deep sleep until the next morning, Easter Sunday.

I awoke refreshed, buoyant, and light-hearted, thinking I had experienced something profound, something spiritually uplifting—a sense of the unity of human existence through all times and places that transcended the pettiness, greed, and brutality of individuals and joined us to the earth and the earth to the solar system and the solar system to the galaxy and the galaxy to the universe.

But the heady events on Naxos were not over yet. The day before, I had picked up one of many handbills advertising a folk concert in a mountain village, featuring bouzoukee, guitar, and female singer. I had neglected my intention of looking for Greek music the several weeks I had been in Greece, and the Easter Day concert struck me as an ideal outing.

The concert was scheduled for one o'clock, and we took a local bus up to the village fifteen miles away, the engine wheezing up through lush patches of farmland and terraced panoramas to the mountaintop three thousand feet above sea level. The last several miles were nothing but scattered boulders and tough bushes sprouting from gray rock walls. The village, clinging to the mountainside just below the summit, was called Kinidaros and was the last stop on the driver's route. In fact, he lived there and was not scheduled to return to the harbor, a spot of white next to a flat expanse of blue sea in the far distance, until ten o'clock that night.

Kinidaros was small and impoverished, home to no more than several hundred people. We saw no hotels or other amenities, and everything was closed. More worrisome than that, there was no one there except several villagers who looked at us curiously. *Where were the crowds for the concert?* I thought, suddenly aware that Karen and I had been the only passengers on the bus for the last several stops.

There were clumps of cypresses and individual trees here and there, but mostly the village was open to the sun, which baked the whitewashed buildings and the hamlet's two or three streets.

We wandered through the lanes, people leaning out of windows to watch us and calling to neighbors to do the same. A handful of children followed us but kept their distance, staring at us silently when we stopped to rest.

By one o'clock, the village was still deserted and brimming with harsh sunlight. We climbed to a small chapel on an outcrop of rock above the town, close to the summit. It was locked and whipped by a hot wind. By two o'clock, we were back in the village, seated on a stoop below what looked like a bakery, wondering what to do, when a compactly built, unshaven young man wearing a frayed black sports coat came up to us and began talking in broken English. He was carrying a just-skinned bloody sheepskin over one arm, and he held two knives in his left hand. Can he help us? he asked, and shouted for the baker to open his shop and get us some bread. We ate it on the stoop. The unshaven man sat down next to Karen. A slutty-looking redheaded woman came up to us and spoke to the man in Greek, rolling her hips and abdomen suggestively. He ignored her at first, then waved her away. Why were we here, he asked Karen. I handed him the handbill. He took it, his hand caked with dried blood, ignoring me. Oh, the music: it didn't begin until evening. There will be wine and dancing. We must stay. He was addressing all his talk to Karen. An hour passed and he continued on, Karen becoming more and more uncomfortable as the man told us—really her—that we must stay the night. He insisted we stay the night, in fact, and tomorrow he would take her to the quarry to see the ten-foot unfinished statue of the Greek youth that has lain in its marble bed since 700 bce.

"And what about me," I finally asked, with an edge to my voice.

He turned and looked me up and down. "I'll take care of you," he said in a quiet but menacing voice. Karen quivered in alarm. Another hour went by, Karen obviously becoming more and more upset. Finally, the man rose. "I go wash up and meet you at the *cafenion* in one hour," he said, pointing to an café that had opened down the lane. He dropped the handbill in Karen's lap and she stared down at it. By this time I was as alarmed as she was. He could throw me off a cliff or bury me where I'd never be found. No one knew where we were, and we were in the middle of nowhere.

When he left, Karen began to shiver.

"I know you're upset about him," I said.

"I am, but I'm more upset about what's on him," she replied.

"Huh?"

"Look, these were all over him," and she opened the handbill he had dropped into her hands. A tiny bug was inside. "Lice!" she said. "What will we do?"

I shrugged. "Only one thing we can do," I said, rising. "Let's start walking out of here."

We left the village and began walking toward the harbor. It looked incredibly far away. Karen turned to me as if she had the same thought, but we continued walking.

"We've got an hour before he comes looking for us," I said, "and that's a good head start—if he doesn't have a car."

And so began one of the most tense and, in the end, most miraculous hikes of my life. We descended through the switchbacks of naked rock, cicadas ringing like thousands of tiny alarm bells around us and insects whizzing by in the hot, dry wind. We could see cultivated fields like colored handkerchiefs below us, scattered one-story houses with red-tile roofs, trees like puffs of green smoke, and beyond them, far in the distance, the harbor and the cobalt-blue sea stretching toward the horizon. We moved at a fast pace, distancing ourselves as much as we could from the village.

Soon, we were among plane trees and spiraling cypresses and upland farms. The harbor was still far ahead. We passed several farmhouses. From one, a farmer called to us, but we walked on. Half a mile later, another farmer was waiting for us by the side of the road, his decrepit one-story house twenty yards behind him. He was holding a jug of water, which he handed us, and pointed to the harbor. His wife was on the porch behind him and nodded. "*Heratay* (good afternoon)," I said, and drank after Karen did, and "*Karastow* (thank you)," when I handed the jug back to him. We continued to walk.

Soon, children were running up to us from other farmhouses, handing us oranges, peaches, chunks of salami and cheese, bread, and more water. It seemed as if the entire population of the countryside had been alerted to our coming.

Halfway down the mountain, another farmer insisted we rest on his shady porch, where he served us cheese and raki and loaded us down with peaches and apricots when we left.

We continued to descend, aware of the village and its menace receding farther and farther behind us. Soon, it seemed as if every farm along the road was sending someone out to greet us with smiles, fruit, and water, and children appeared from everywhere, skipping after us for several hundred yards, giggling and shouting *"Heratay! Heratay!"* in response to my greetings to them. The late afternoon hike had become a stroll through a carnival of friendly faces, almost as if the people were reassuring us that the incident at Kinidaros was not representative of the island's populace.

By sunset, we were almost at sea level, unable to see the panoramic view to the sea any longer. Tall canebrakes on either side of the road had shut off the view for fifteen minutes or so when a short, thin old man, carrying a briefcase and wearing a double-breasted, brown business suit and maroon tie, walked out of a canebrake by the side of the road and fell into step beside me.

"Good evening," he said in clipped English, as if we knew each other and had been walking along in comradely silence for the past half hour. "Are you enjoying your visit?"

"Yes," I replied in the same comradely fashion, as if his sudden presence was the most natural event.

"Do you mind if I walk along with you?"

"Not at all," I said, and we strolled for several miles, he extolling the wonders of Naxos' history and landscape. When he found out that I was a writer and teacher and had come to Naxos to see where Kazantzakis received his early education, he told me excitedly that he had attended the same school as the writer and invited Karen and me to dinner. Five minutes later, we caught a taxi into town and that night dined with the old man and his friends. They were well dressed and genteel, and the conversation, completely in English, was a delightful potpourri of politics, history, culture, and art, a free exchange of ideas and experiences.

After we said good night, I wondered at the two different experiences of the day. Naxos had been a whirl of impressions, a microcosm of the world. The next day, when Gary and Linda arrived, I told them about everything that had happened, dwelling on the magical hike into town the evening before, an experience that has remained vividly with me for the past thirty years. When I am most depressed about the brutality and selfishness of the human race, the farmers running out to us with food and drink, the children giggling and dancing ahead of us, and the little man with his briefcase and serious conversation about the way of the world, rise to my mind and comfort me.

CHAPTER 35

Crete

O
Of all the events I experienced on my first trip to Greece, my stay on the island of Crete was the most definitive. At the end of May, we left Gary and Linda, who were returning to America, and spent six weeks exploring and wandering everywhere on the western half of the island, both on the north and south coasts. At Heraklion, we went to the historical museum, which had a furnished replica of Kazantzakis' study, and then visited his grave that rests on top of the medieval wall that surrounds the city. The grave is inscribed with the following words:

> I hope for nothing.
> I fear nothing.
> I am free.

From there we inspected Knossos and the other Minoan ruins and went on to the beach at Matala, stayed at Ayia Galini for a few days, then went back to the north coast, toured the city of Chania, hiked through the Gorge of Samaria, and settled in the town of Rethymnon for a month and hiked the gorge again.

In Rethymnon, we made many friends, organized the thousands of English-language books in the town library, and befriended the librarian, who spoke fluent English and introduced us to icon painters, writers, and many townspeople, relatives, and

At Kazantzakis' grave, great wall of Heraklion, Crete, Greece 1975

friends. The month in Rethymnon was a memorable time, and my friendship with the librarian was one of the most intense and rewarding, if one of the most short-lived relationships of my life. But my treks through the Gorge of Samaria were the most exhilarating and spiritually provocative events of my stay there.

We got to the gorge at noon on May 30. Gatsos and other acquaintances we had made in Athens urged us to take the "stroll" and to "bring along a picnic lunch." So we brought bread, eight pieces of salami, oranges, and cheese with us. As for water, "You can drink it from the stream. There's nobody there, and the water is good," we were told in town.

With those offhanded words waltzing through my head, I prepared for a pleasant few hours in the uplands of northwestern Crete and neither inquired about the excursion at our pension in Chania or read about the gorge. So lightly did we take our proposed outing that, on the bus to the gorge, Karen and I swallowed two sugar cubes saturated with LSD, which she had brought into the country in her cosmetic kit. I had never taken LSD before, and I won't deny that the events of that day may have been highly influenced by my state of mind.

As the bus wound several thousand feet up from the coast, I still had no inkling about what lay ahead. The morning was cool and sunny, and we were the only people on the bus and then at the trailhead. We started down the steep, knee-jolting stone staircase called the Xylocol and were soon surrounded by pine and cypress trees, which, every now and then, opened on hazy vistas, yet I was oblivious to the fact that we were not on a stroll but on a hike comparable to trekking through Yosemite's outer regions.

Soon, trees were above and below us. By the time we had descended one or two miles and the path had become earthen and rock-strewn, I was beginning to comprehend my mistake. So steep were the initial two miles that my knees ached.

The magic walking stick, five feet in length. The top half resembled ". . . the head of a goat."

We came to a shaded stream of cold, clear water that tumbled like slurred glass over rocks. The trail continued on the other side. My knees ached so much, I looked around for a walking stick and spotted a five-foot-long cypress branch lying on the ground. When I reached for it, as I recorded in my journal the next day, "it sprang into my hand." I was startled but remembered I had taken the LSD an hour before, and I crossed the stream. However, I also noted that "there was something strange about the branch, and when I looked at it closely, I saw what it was: half of its stippled bark had the coloring and shape of a mountain goat." It looked, in fact, "like the head of a goat that ended halfway down in a little knob like a tufted tail." Beyond the knob, the branch was barkless and curved outward like a naked human leg, ending in a foot, which "was extended delicately like a ballerina's foot on toe."

Still aware of how the branch had seemed to spring into my hand, I was struck with the thought that I didn't know "if I had found the branch or if it had found me," and that "somehow the goat had been cast by a spell into the tree thousands of years ago, grown with it, and now that the tree had fallen, the goat was partially released from the spell and had been waiting for a passing traveler to pick it up." I wasn't to know until weeks later, through research at the library in Rethymnon, that the gorge was the habitat of the rare and seldom seen *cri-cri*, or Cretan mountain goat. Nor was I to know until then that the cypress trees in this part of the gorge were estimated to be three thousand years old, and the little chapel dedicated to St. Nicholas we came upon unexpectedly a moment later, set in a grove of giant

With the magic walking stick, Gorge of Samaria, Crete, 1975

cypresses, was said to be the birthplace of the oracle of Apollo and was once the site of a temple to the goddess Diana Dikta, a holy place.

On that first walk, however, I tried to ignore my musings about the enchanted goat living in my walking stick. But just before we entered the grove, Karen, who had strode ahead, turned to me and laughed. "Who's your friend?" she said.

"What?"

"Your friend," she repeated, gesturing toward me. "You seem to be carrying a goat with the leg of a woman."

A few moments later, Karen found a walking stick of her own. It was much more delicate than mine, a branch shaped like the hands of a clock at twenty to eleven and ending in a perfect goat's foot that pranced in front of her at every step.

Thus began a magical day in what seemed a magical place. We continued the relentless descent. A mile after the grove, we came upon many uprooted trees and stumps in startling shapes and colors on either side of the shadowy, rushing stream. Many of the trees looked like they contained trapped beings with thin arms ending in claws, and faces with mouths open in astonishment or terror that gaped in the center of their trunks. The trees had been tortured by wintry floodwaters into shapes only the imagination could fashion. But these weren't Disneyesque creations or visions from Dante's hell. They were from older concepts, concepts of a nature animated by tree gods and corn goddesses and nether regions that flourished in peoples' minds thousands of years ago.

The tree carcasses, tumbled and piled on top of one another, resembled an elephants' graveyard and went on for half a mile or more, and we were both wary and silent as we passed them. But when the stream broke into sunlight again, we began to frolic and laugh, splashing water on each other, and my walking stick, like an amiable companion, laughed along with us. We crossed and recrossed the stream, the path opening onto panoramic views of mountainsides pocked with caves and backed by distant, snow-covered peaks. Or we found ourselves below cliffs that suddenly loomed above us on both sides, shutting out the daylight, bushes and small pine trees rooted somehow in their sheer rock faces. And growing everywhere along the stone-strewn trail were stands of

Gorge of Samaria, Crete, Greece, 1975

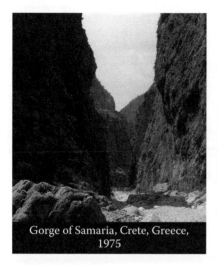

Gorge of Samaria, Crete, Greece, 1975

Ruins of Samaria, Crete, Greece, 1975

pink and white oleanders and small yellow and purple flowers whose names I didn't know.

The only person we saw was a stocky old Cretan in native costume—piratelike black bandana tied around his head, embroidered vest, and jodphur-like dohti. He appeared from around a bend, coming toward us, and trudged past with a stoic nod, like a ghostly inhabitant from another time, reminding us that the gorge was not a playground but a place that had hosted eons of human life with all its sufferings and joys.

We must have wandered off the trail several times, and the hike, which I later learned should have taken five or six hours, went on into sunset and then dusk. We passed a settlement of ruins across a deep river where several people were going about their business, not noticing us, and it was as though we were observing them in a film. I was to find out that this was all that was left of Samaria, the settlement from which the gorge took its name—sainted Maria, holy Mary—which was also the name of the ruins of the small church in its midst, and that it had been abandoned several years before when the gorge was designated a national park. Then who, I thought when I found this out, were the people I saw there?

Nightfall rose around us without our being aware of time passing. Only as darkness enveloped us did we realize we had neither flashlight nor matches—nor did I have any idea how far we were from the end of the gorge. This realization sobered us, and only then did we recognize the efficacy of our walking sticks, whose slender legs, curving outward, thrust their toes forward, as if the sticks were tentatively touching their way several feet in front of us and guiding us away from declivities and sudden drops that would have thrown us twenty to fifty feet onto the rocks below. It seemed that the walking sticks had sprung into our hands hours before with this eventuality in mind, and it turned out that both of us had the same thought, for when we stopped to rest on a boulder, Karen, in a hushed voice, expressed this idea.

Gradually our eyes grew accustomed to the dark, and with my goat-headed stick leading us, we forged on, trudging thigh-deep in a stream before I realized half an hour later that the trail was paralleling us ten feet above.

Night birds shrieked and flapped overhead. Rocks clattered from the gorge walls as if someone or some thing was stalking us. We waded and tramped on and on, and for all the imagined or real dangers, I was thoroughly enjoying myself. Soon, the trail glowed a milky white in front of us, and by eleven o'clock we were exhausted but comfortable, our eyes completely adjusted to the dark. By midnight, the steep walls of the gorge had receded around us, and we were walking on open ground when we saw dark hulking forms ahead of us. As we drew closer, we observed that they were walls, the ruins of buildings, and a rectangle of light was issuing from one of them. A mule or a horse snorted. A dog barked. The shapes of houses appeared around us. We walked through what looked like a patio. I called out "Parakalow! (Please!)" several times, and a door opened and an old woman in black, with an open oil lamp in a metal gravy boat shaped saucer that smelled like lamb fat, waddled out with a barking dog at her side. We asked her for water in Greek, and she hobbled to get us two greasy glassfuls from a sour-smelling cistern outside the door. We asked how far the coast was and where we could find a place to sleep, but she didn't understand us and shrugged. Finally, I pointed to the lamp and extended ten drachmas to her. She gave us the lamp and pointed a direction.

The flame flared in the breeze as we found a dirt road that led over a cobblestone bridge twenty feet above a dry riverbed and past a small, walled chapel. But the road suddenly ended above the river delta, which was filled with acres of boulders.

The lamp had been more trouble than help, since its flame flared wild gothic shadows around us, its glare blinding us at times and destroying the night vision we had developed without it. Just as I was about to complain about this fact, a sudden rush of wind bundled down the gorge like an avalanche and blew out the lamp.

Karen, who had become more and more jittery as the night wore on, began to tremble. She had already been frightened by the night birds' shrieking in the gorge, our tramp through the river when we lost the trail, and our lack of proper clothing, food, and information. The sudden darkness undid her remaining control.

I pointed to the star-filled sky above us to comfort her. I took her hand and led her back to the walled chapel, which I remembered we had passed a few minutes before.

"We can sleep in the chapel," I told her, and I climbed over the four-foot wall, only to find that the chapel was really a graveyard. I climbed back and told her that we would stay where we were, not wanting to alarm her any more than necessary. We lay down on our backs outside the wall, covered ourselves with what clothing we had, and stared up at the stars. I was fearful, too, but at the same time enjoying the adventure. It was not the only nighttime difficulty we had gotten ourselves into in the last two months, but for me it was the most exhilarating, full of mystery and a sense of being close to the earth and its secrets.

I looked at my watch. It was 12:30. We exchanged small talk, but soon, totally exhausted, we fell asleep, still lying on our backs.

At exactly 3 am we both woke with a start and sat up almost involuntarily. A full moon was sliding up above the cliff on our left, outlining the ruins of a fortress on the cliff on our right. There was total silence all around us, as if the Earth was holding its breath. Suddenly, a thrashing wind sprang up and the ground released a spicy fragrance of thyme, oregano, water, and oranges, as if the earth were pushing all its warmth and history from the day before into the sky. We coughed and our eyes watered as the scents ascended around us. It was the most mysterious event I've ever experienced. Several days later I wrote the following poem in less than a minute, and have never revised it.

Once I Woke

Once I woke with a woman in a gorge on the island of Crete
at the moment the moon edged over the cliff above us.
All around, weeds released their spicy scents
as if the earth was exhaling all its worries.

We both sat up at the same instant, as if pushed
from our dreams, as if we were meant to stream
with plant-breath and insect-wings all the way to heaven.
Bits of things rose around us, a heavy dust
seething and hissing.

                    Afterwards, we sat in our bodies,
gazing at one another. And in the silence,
in the clear moonlight, we stared at the stones, the weeds,
and everything else that had been left behind.

The dense, fragrance-packed ascension lasted no more than a minute or two, and we turned to each other without saying a word. I am sure to this day that I had experienced one of the secrets of the earth, and it has provided me with a profound sense of the unity of all things, and the place, however infinitesimal, everything occupies in the universe.

We lay back without a word and soon dozed off. At daylight we woke and trudged back across the bridge, and I returned the lamp along with fifty drachmas to the old woman, who at first didn't want to accept the money and was genuinely concerned about our safety, gesturing that we should have come back and spent the night in her hut.

Then we continued to the coast and caught a small boat to Chora Sfakia and a bus to Chania.

Three weeks later, fully fortified with information and supplies, we hiked the gorge again, wanting to see if the magic we had found there was still evident without our being under the influence of LSD. It wasn't, but the walk was still glorious and the memories of our first visit remained vividly clear, as they do even now, and the incident that happened at 3 am has influenced my thinking to this day. We took along our walking sticks. By then I had painted the facial features on the stick that Karen and I had observed in it, and shellacked the entire branch. Wherever we hiked after that, peasants and shepherds would stop us to admire it.

I had many other adventures in the six months I spent traveling in Greece: trudging a few hundred yards into the pass at Thermopylae; spending several days roaming through the rock monasteries at Meteora, where I staggered for miles along a mountain-goat path, looking for the lost, fabled cave monastery of Hypapanti; exploring the volcanic island of Santorini; and finally settling down for a month on the island of Lesbos. But because the three side trips I have described in such detail included so many aspects of the events in these other places, they are representative of all my Greek experiences.

If Iowa gave me a sense of geologic time, Greece provided me with a sense of human time: generations in multicolored costumes, loving, killing, weeping, and celebrating among facades of different styles of architecture, but remaining inevitably the same—clutching for power and material comforts, or musing on the mystery of the human condition and why we are able to contemplate ourselves and our lives in the midst of the universe's seemingly mindless existence.

■ ■ ■

I would return to Greece three times. The second time, Nanos Valaoritis was there and took me around to his favorite restaurants and introduced me to his friends. I never saw Nikos Gatsos again. He was always out of town when I looked for him at Zonar's, and I settled for leaving messages of greeting with his housekeeper on my visits. He had been delighted with my tales of Naxos and Samaria, and I would have liked to talk with him about the changes in Greece and the world over the years, but it was not to be.

I last visited Greece in 1989, as the final leg of my first trip to Croatia. I wanted to show Donna, my second wife, "my" Greece and renew my relationships with old friends and acquaintances.

Athens had changed in spirit if not in architecture. There was an almost feverish drive for money and an acutely noticeable lack of friendliness. Tourists were everywhere, and even visits to such normally welcoming islands as Aegina were marked by a coldness in the islanders.

But it was in Crete that the change was most evident. The rugged, economically depressed island had found unexpected prosperity, and with it came the destruction of the family unit.

In 1975, families worked together to eke out an existence. By 1989, Greece had become a member of the European Union and was open to European trade and tourism as never before.

In 1975, the only way to fly to destinations inside Greece was to take a flight from Athens on Olympic Airways, the national airlines. In 1989, Europeans could fly directly to the islands from their home countries. Crete was a favorite destination. Planeloads of Scandinavians flew into Heraklion or Chania and were taken by air conditioned buses to dozens of what had been remote locations and were now towns filled with small hotels and large internationally financed resorts.

Rethymnon was no longer a regional market town with a small but pleasant esplanade adjoining the tiny Venetian harbor. Its miles of empty sand beaches had been discovered, and dozens of small hotels and pensions had sprung up alongside them. The esplanade no longer housed a half dozen tavernas and cafenions, but mostly "pizza snack" restaurants and "highball" bars. The town had become a Scandinavian colony.

Along with the prosperity had come the disintegration of the family structure. The villages in the mountains were mostly empty; their inhabitants had moved to the tourist-cluttered coasts, and their children no longer had to work so the family could subsist. Now, a mother gave her children spending money when the father wasn't looking, and the father gave them more money when the mother wasn't looking. As a result, the children became as directionless and bored as American children. They watched TV with its glamorous, excitement-filled images, and bought Vespa motor scooters that they rode full throttle through the streets and countryside at all hours, or they stood by the hundreds outside blaring discotheques, looking for something to do or waiting for something to happen.

My feelings were paradoxical. On the one hand, I was happy for the islanders' prosperity, but on the other, I saw a way of life predicated on honor, integrity, family love, and communal responsibility destroyed as those values had been destroyed in America, and I sensed more had been lost than gained.

I renewed my friendship with the town librarian, who was now the chief librarian of the new, still-being-built University of Crete. He sadly affirmed all I have just written. It was a melancholy visit, which did not impress my wife, and the third day I was in Rethymnon, I sat down on my hotel bed and wept. I have not had the heart to undertake a trip to Greece since then.

All in all, my trips to Greece, especially my first visit, left me with a sense that the old gods of the earth and all the epochs of history are present in our everyday lives, or, to put it another way, that the past is alive in the present. More important, I came to realize that under the high-rises and garish tourist resorts and entertainments resides a reality that unites us with all the things of this world and, despite our frivolities, shows us our place in the universe, if we care to search for it.

BOOK TEN

SANTA CRUZ 2

CHAPTER 36

Community 1

All my travels begin and end in Santa Cruz. Although I had not planned to stay in the area for more than a few years when I arrived, I came to see Santa Cruz as home, a place I had sought all my life. It was not only the beauty of the landscape, with its cold green waters of the bay on one side and the gorges and mountains shaggy with redwood trees on the other, but my growing conviction that the county was a microcosm of human experience that encapsulated the nation as a whole in personal, social, political, and historical events.

If north county was mercantile and essentially entrepreneurial, south county was agricultural. If north county was white, south county was Chinese, Japanese, Filipino, Croatian, and increasingly Mexican. In the 1970s, the county was home to three serial killers and was tagged "the murder capital of the world." Earthquakes and floods made inhabitants aware not only of climate and seasons, but of their vulnerability in the natural world.

At the same time, Santa Cruz and its environs were at the cutting edge of a plethora of human lifestyle experiments, from the takeover by the far-left liberal government of Santa Cruz city, pushed by the university faculty and students, to the presence of "art" movie theaters and excellent bookstores. In addition, many different psychological and social experiments, such as Gestalt therapy, primal-scream practices, and a number of Asian meditation societies as well as other modes of alternative lifestyles not only flourished in the area but in many cases began there.

Years before moving to Santa Cruz, I had been affected by Father Zossima's kneeling on the ground and kissing the earth in reverence in Dostoevsky's *The Brothers Karamazov*, and I vowed that when I found a place where I could imagine doing the same, I would have found a home. Santa Cruz was that place.

In the late 1960s and early 1970s, pensioners, locals, and rural workers predominated as well as artisans, artists, and writers of all kinds. But as the 1970s advanced into the 1980s, property values rose beyond the means of many of these groups. Lawyers and doctors and then computer programmers working "over the hill" in Silicon Valley, forty miles away, bought houses both as residences and rental investments for the vacationers who inundated the county by the tens of thousands every summer. These vacationers included tourists who stopped in Santa Cruz on their way to Monterey and Carmel, or valley people who drove over the hill from San Jose on weekends to lounge on the county's many beaches or promenade along the boardwalk amusement park, the oldest remaining seaside amusement park on the Pacific coast, which sat on a wide beach a mile from downtown Santa Cruz.

The vestiges of history were everywhere. The amusement park, looking for all the world like an 1890s world's fair compound, had been built at the turn of the century to be a "Coney Island of the West." In 1885, the beach in front of the park, which was then the site of several large bathhouses that drew people from far and near, was the location of the first surfing event in the United States: two Hawai'ian princes, attending a military school in San Mateo, discovered Santa Cruz and all summer rode the tumbling waves on long boards they had milled from local redwood logs. Since 1907, the amusement park had loomed above the beach but below a hill where the ornate Victorian mansions of what I imagined were the homes of nineteenth-century robber barons overlooked the tranquil bay. Within a few yards of the amusement park, the city's wharf, where the families of Italian fishermen still controlled the dwindling ocean businesses they had dominated since the early years of the century, tottered creakily a quarter mile into the bay.

Until the 1956 flood, a flourishing Chinatown had existed on the fringes of downtown Santa Cruz along the west bank of the San Lorenzo River, whose waters divided the city of Santa Cruz and rose dangerously during the winter rainy season. And high above the city, the old adobe mission church had been made redundant by an austere puritanical model down the block that was known thereafter by its English name, Holy Cross. The new, spired holy place was a reminder, if not a symbol, of the American takeover of California after the Mexican War, the year before the 1849 gold rush. Distantly, almost erased from memory, the mission church recalled to a sensitive, curious few not only the original Mexican mission that had preceded it and ushered in the beginnings of European settlement in 1791, but the ghostly presence of the Native American world that had existed in the Santa Cruz area for eons before it.

Santa Cruz was a microcosm all right, of both contemporary living, with all its problems, and its history, with its sense of generations of habitation. It was in this setting that my children grew to adulthood, attended local public schools, and mixed with the different communities and their opposing values.

I continued to see my daughters every weekend and watched them grow into beautiful women. Through a series of unforeseen circumstances, Wilma abandoned dance and became a fixture in the theater groups around the City of Santa Cruz that flourished in the 1970s and 1980s. She also became a permanent faculty member of the Cabrillo drama department. She staged one experimental production after another, and the girls were involved in the cultural life of the county through both her dramatic work and my literary endeavors.

Jana, the oldest, was a dresser and theater manager and usher for the Cabrillo Music Festival, which achieved a national reputation, focused at first on the works of Lou Harrison, who had resided in Santa Cruz since the 1950s, and the dancer/choreographer Tandy Beal, whose company called

Jana and Valerie, Santa Cruz, 1988

Santa Cruz home. The festival attracted such notables of the musical world as Aaron Copland, John Cage, Dave Brubeck, and Dennis Russell Davies in the 1970s.

A serious pianist in her early years, Jana abandoned the piano for photography when she was seventeen and went to New York in 1981 to seek her fortune. She apprenticed to two well-known fashion photographers in the city and attended the School of Visual Arts. In 1984, she returned to Santa Cruz to attend the University of California, graduating with honors in social documentation, first doing a portfolio that recorded the living conditions of migrant farm workers in south county, then returning to New York to shoot a book-length study of the culture of the desolated South Bronx for her thesis. In 1986 she returned to New York to pursue her career.

Valerie, five years younger than Jana, became an actress, moved to New York after graduating from Wilma's alma mater, Bennington College, and fruitlessly sought employment in the theater while working as a caterer's assistant. She was soon disillusioned with the lack of opportunity but remained in the city.

In their early years, the girls spent the weekends with me, and we would go to films, local plays, and any Greek festivals we could find in Northern California, driving one hundred miles or more to attend the food and cultural events that celebrated the heritage of Greek communities in Napa County, San Jose, and, several times, in Sacramento.

I also made several trips to Santa Barbara with the girls when I was involved with Noel Young and Capra Press, and once there was a dramatic journey to Hearst Castle during a winter storm, with roads washing out behind us and mudslides slithering down the mountainsides as we passed. For some reason, I had decided to take Route 1 down through Big Sur, and the car was buffeted by fog-laden winds as it veered from one lane to the next, at times sliding dangerously close to the cliff edges above the ocean.

When we arrived at the embarkation station a mile or so below the castle, we found to our disappointment, and the unhappiness of eight other hardy tourists, that all afternoon tours had been cancelled because of the weather. However, the young docents had to make a final trip up to the castle to secure the buildings and pick up their comrades, and after fifteen minutes of haggling, they agreed to take the eleven of us along with them. Once there, they gave us a private tour. We slogged through the water-logged gardens, pools, and staircases, lightning and thunder breaking everywhere around us and sheets of rain soaking us and stinging the windows once we were inside. The electricity had gone out, and we climbed from one floor to another in the shadowy interior, the lightning flashing on the heavy furniture with all the drama of a 1940s movie. At any moment I expected to see Orson Welles descending one of the stairways toward us.

But as usually happened on our outings, the day ended on a comic note early that evening when I put Valerie's bargain brown sandals under our motel room's heater to dry. Within minutes, they were smoking, and by the time I rescued them, the ornamental puffy elephants glued to their tops, which Valerie prized so much, had melted and hardened into two strips of leather stiff as beef jerky. Poor Val: she had nothing else to wear. So I carried her piggy back through the wet, wind-blown streets of Morro Bay to and from the empty restaurant where we had supper, all the while her feet dangling cold and clammy.

Most of our weekends were highlighted by eating at one ethnic restaurant or another, especially a Szechwan restaurant in Santa Cruz, where we regularly spilled whole cups of tea to the manager's consternation, a comic ritual he came to enjoy as much as we did.

I remember such outings with a bitter-sweet nostalgia. While the event was going on, I felt like a good father, and my guilt for leaving the family eased. But the relief lasted only a day or two.

■ ■ ■

Through all of these outings and my daily life, I was becoming more and more involved with the community and began to formulate my idea of communal participation, which I wrote about years later in the following paragraph:

> Making art is a communal act. To communicate, i.e. with others. To move out of the self. To share. In the same way the word "art" comes from "artifice" and "artificial," i.e. to make a semblance of experience, yes, for the joy of the self, but with such care (*craft*) that the joy can be experienced by others: the "community." Ergo: making art is a communal act.

As a result of such thoughts, I concentrated more on community cultural events, turning away from the national scene. I still published in many national journals, but I sent poems out less and less often, concerned more with my classes and local projects. In the 1970s I was the director of Santa Cruz and Monterey counties' Poetry in the Schools program, trained several ex-students to go into the project, and did workshops and residences in Santa Cruz and San Jose high schools. I traveled to San Francisco less and less and read there infrequently. So pronounced was my abandonment of the literary world that in 1980, when I appeared unannounced in two workshops in New York City to say hello to Robert Hass and Charlie Simic, who were running the classes, several of the students, who knew my work, expressed surprise that I was still alive.

SOME STUDENTS

Of the many creative writing students I've had over the years, maybe half a dozen stand out. Chitra Divakaruni, best known as a novelist, is one, and Gregory Hall, a visionary poet in every sense of the word, whose poetry Robert Bly was particularly taken with on one of his visits to Cabrillo, is another. Bly even wrote the introduction for Greg's first book, *Flame People*. Greg has spent most of his adult life in San Jose, California, working as a hospital orderly. He is sweet and skittish, one of the gentle souls of the earth who seems to have been put here like a prophet to record our decadence in fiery poems. Many of his poems are composed of fragments, one-line pictures that form a list of snapshots of our life, as in "It Is the Morning," whose last stanza reads

> It is the morning of departure when the buses
> and the faces that howled in the rain leave at the same time
> a councilman's face peeling from a red brick wall
> a brown snapshot wrinkled in the drawer
> Morning of disease and hypnosis spun on the barber's pole
> and the gray tongue of the barber's wife
> and the hair of those out of luck
> pushed by the broom to the door

At other times, he utters mysterious visions, as if allowing us to glimpse a secret of the earth that was always there, if we would only look at it. The following untitled poem is a good example:

> I love
> the snakes

who hunt at night,
awakened
by the cooling earth
and
who emerge, slick
genital
faces
from the dark
mouth

Yes, Greg's poems are composed of images from beyond our rational, linear view of things. He makes us see the world anew and in so doing asks us, as Rilke said all art should, to change our lives. Here's a complete poem, a meditation that sounds so timeless yet contemporary it could well be uttered by any number of people today, young or old.

All the Women

I

all the women have been taken
down the mountain in small cars
all the men have flown south
in the rainy days
& the birds are singing outside the open morning
door.
counting my blessings, it seems strange
none are within range
of sight or hearing.
perhaps I will stroll in the graveyard today,
with soft grass underfoot,
thankful for the immense silence
that hums in the ground
around the stones.

II

there was a year of hot girls
twisting in nights of sweat & loving,
& lots of wine & music in the valleys.
now I am interested by sunsets,
life seems short enough
without running to catch
another face in the smoke.
distances have increased since i found
theres no place to go.
i don't even write poems anymore,
i move my eyes and hands
i feel the afternoon winds
& see stories of man
in the sticks of the fire

As far as their personalities and work are concerned, Chitra and Greg were exceptional. But the two students who head the list of standouts, first as students and then as long-time friends, are Jeff Tagami and Shirley Ancheta. Born in Watsonville, and childhood sweethearts, they attended Cabrillo together, where they were Joe Stroud's students and tutors before they were mine, so they were set on the best of paths. I did little more than encourage them.

Jeff first came to my attention in a New Journalism class I taught with Joe and another good friend, Kirby Wilkins, when Jeff wrote an article on south county low-riding, at the time a decades-old tradition celebrated by Mexican-American teenagers when the stores stayed open late in downtown Watsonville on Thursday nights. In their souped-up, highly ornamented cars, the low riders would slowly wheel down Main Street, showing off their independence, as well as their disdain, for the dominant white community, as much as they were showing off their cars' garish paint jobs and elaborately decorated interiors. The practice was a social ritual, and Jeff recognized its meaning. In fact, all of Jeff's work reflects such astute social insights.

Jeff and Shirley are not Latinos. They are Filipino Americans and as such are members of one of the most abused minorities in the nation. Luckily Jeff and Shirley's parents were residents of the United States when the two were born. Generally, Filipino men came singly to this country and remained as bachelors to their dying days, sending most of their money home to their families in the Philippines. The Filipinos worked in the canneries, packing sheds, and fields, hard work for which they were poorly paid, and much of the time they were physically abused. Both Jeff and Shirley are acutely aware of the social stigma they inherited, and both have dedicated themselves to eradicating it. As members of the Kearny Street Workshop, a San Francisco collective promoting Asian American and particularly Filipino American art, their writing has influenced the last two generations of Filipino American artists.

Jeff's work surfaced first because when Shirley was nineteen, she was in a horrendous auto accident and had to have a number of operations to save her left arm and shoulder. During the painful years of recovery, she and Jeff were married and most of her time was taken up with raising their two children. By then they were living in San Francisco where they attended San Francisco State University after graduating with BAs from the University of California at Santa Cruz. And it was there in the early 1980s that the Kearny Street Workshop published Jeff's first book of poems, *October Light*. The book brought Jeff national attention and a spotlight on Bill Moyer's panoramic television travelogue of American writing, "The United States of Poetry." *October Light* was an extraordinary book, not only because of Jeff's direct, succinct, and highly evocative style, nor because it was about life in the Filipino community in which he had been brought up, but because it went beyond the depiction of an oppressed people to show the community's enduring joy and love as well as its suffering. Some of the poems are at times tender, at times raucous and vital, and all are so perfectly realized that as a whole the book is a celebration of the life and spirit of all peoples.

Such a vision is a constant struggle for Jeff and Shirley to maintain because they are always aware of Filipino persecution, both in the United States and the Philippines where American foreign policy robbed the Filipino people of their independence more than a century ago in a brutal, unwarranted invasion.

Poets Shirley Ancheta and Jeff Tagami, San Francisco, 1985

I have happy memories of staying at Jeff and Shirley's apartment in the city and dragging them here and there, once to midnight Easter mass at San Francisco's main Russian Orthodox cathedral, an outing I'm sure they both went along with to good-naturedly humor me. But I also remember those times when Jeff would grow apprehensive, sensing danger in situations I had unthinkingly got him into.

One night I took him to dinner with Leonard Gardner, Gina Berriault, and Clancy Carlile, who had read *October Light* and had been so impressed with the book they wanted to meet him. After dinner we went to an Irish bar, whose shadowy walls were decorated with larger-than-life photographs of Irish martyrs. Jeff stopped inside the doorway and stood with his back against the wall. He knew it was not a place Filipinos were welcome, and realizing my error I hustled the group to a more congenial environment. Jeff and Shirley's awareness of their social position was further exacerbated when they moved back to Watsonville and Jeff, despite his literary reputation and qualifications, was denied a full-time teaching position at Cabrillo for almost two decades.

Still, they kept writing. At times their poems were bitter, but mostly they embraced a larger view. Here is one of Jeff's later poems, which talks about John Steinbeck's incipient racism in *Of Mice and Men*. The poem was first published in Bamboo Ridge Press's twenty-fifth anniversary issue.

Message

"But Susy's place is clean and she
got nice chairs. Don't let no goo-
goos in neither."

—John Steinbeck, *Of Mice and Men*

Because George wanted to go to Susy's
where the girls were clean
and he wouldn't have to walk around
bow-legged afterwards

Because Filipinos were allowed into Clara's
though she charged more
and watered down the drinks

Because ranch hands
were "the loneliest people in the world"
and so Filipinos must have been lonelier

Because my father performed his own
circumcision at twenty-one in America
so he wouldn't be different

Because that one Pinoy I heard about
had placed the lit end of a cigar to his penis
so that the cankers might be closed

Because Lennie, the man-child, was impotent
and longed for his own place
though he wasn't the only one chastised

Because for Filipinos
to own a piece of land
was forbidden by Law

Because of what
the Negro stable buck knew about desire
and what Steinbeck didn't

Because every man
had to lie down in his bunk
and think about it

Because Salinas is only seventeen miles away
though most of those Filipinos are dead
or dying, each to his separate dream

And because they were almost left out, unnoticed
like the bleached telephone poles along this road
bearing messages

After their two boys began school, Shirley started writing seriously. She was also working at a number of menial jobs as well as teaching part time so she and Jeff could make ends meet. Whereas Jeff's poetry is generally concerned with Filipino American daily life and history, her poetry is more concerned with women's issues and Filipino folklore and myth and showed a maturity and immediacy from the start. Lately she has been performing her poetry with musicians. She dedicated the following poem to one of the Kearny Street group's founders.

Carabao

*for Al Robles, whose thousands of
carabao appear in his poems*

I have felt them, too.
They come from far, unlighted fields.

They lead us out of city streets
into the sleeping blue of water,
all of us crossing together.
Inside their curved horns, voices
whisper us back from our wanderings.
On Kearny Street, we are far
from the lettuce fields, the cockfights, the blood of the pig.
And still farther, trapped in memory, come
the arrival of workers' boats, of cane fields
waking in the arms of dark men.
I have not always known their tender presence.
In this city cradled by two bridges
the old ones disguised as dog spirits lick
the bowls we leave for the dead.
The wind spins us in this ordinary world until
someone nearly broken with desire
to be lifted to another country in his heart remembers
the feel of the animal's black hair, the slow
but powerful /carabao /walk.
In the dark they chase us into dream,
into wet voices that bathe
in the blue night,
like the blue awakening of fish.

THE NOVEL

Ever since I was in Iowa, I have been an inveterate reader of mysteries and thrillers. I began reading them to relieve the exhaustion of studying or the long hours of writing, when my mind is more focused than at any other time. I soon found that I could only read those thriller novels that were realistic, well plotted and well written, and had fairly complex characters. In other words, I read only genre fiction that approached or crossed the boundary into serious fiction. It was not long before I discovered that a sizeable amount of contemporary genre fiction had greater overall vision than many celebrated contemporary works of "serious" fiction. This was because international intrigue writers used global-affecting events as the basis of their stories, and mystery writers pursued the dark motives that secretly drove their characters and in many cases the individuals who pursued them. Both kinds of stories were set in worlds of inertia and corruption inhabited by politicians, administrators, and petty officials who, by extension, were accurate, insightful reflections of the real world's status quo. Obviously, I found it impossible to read books about such superheroes as James Bond. No, the foreign intrigue writers I read religiously were Eric Ambler, John LeCarre, Charles McCarry, Robert Harris, and Robert Wilson. The mystery writers included Dashiell Hammett, Raymond Chandler, Ross McDonald, Ian Rankin, Michael Connelly, Henning Mankell and Tony Hillerman.

In the spring of 1979, someone, tired of my pronouncements of the excellence of genre fiction, challenged me to write a thriller of my own. I think that's how it happened anyway, although I can't remember who the person was and I may, in actuality, have challenged myself. Whatever the impetus, I attacked the project with gusto. I had enough material from my six-month trip to Greece in 1975 to place the piece in an exotic setting. "What if," I said to myself the first morning I sat down to write, "What if someone I knew from America approached me in Athens and asked me to take a package to Crete for him . . ." It was an old ploy, but within fifteen minutes I had the entire plot of the novel sketched out. I knew that genre fiction was driven by plot, but at this point I set myself a problem I have never abandoned in writing fiction: while the story line may be the main concern of a genre novel, the work must seem as if the characters are caus- ing the various events to happen not only by simple decisions but most often because their personalities, personal interests, or, more simply, their moral failings or strengths dictate those decisions.

The writing was easier than I had imagined. Guided by a rule I had learned from poet and fellow classmate in Iowa, George Keithley, I made sure I wrote at least one page every day (George had pointed out that writ- ing a novel seemed less daunting if you wrote at least a page a day since that meant you would complete 365 pages in a year, and if you wrote two pages a day, you would write 730 pages in the same period).

I followed the same regimen every morning—dressing, exercising, eating at the same time, and reading the last one or two pages I had written the previous day. Then I began to work. I wasn't concerned with style, and strictly forbade myself any polishing or rewriting. I just concentrated on getting the material on paper. As a result, I finished the novel in six weeks, having written it not one but three times.

This was the novel I told Leonard Gardener about when, without looking at a word of it, he called a highly-placed Hollywood agent and urged him to take it on. The agent sold the book, *The Brezhnev Memo*, to Dell/Delacorte, a big New York publishing house, for $20,000.

I immediately started on another, more ambitious novel, telling myself it was important to maintain a rhythm when writing novel-length fiction because if you stopped and looked at what you were attempting, the under- taking would seem too immense in time and effort. The new novel, complet- ed in three months, was better than its predecessor in every way, but Cold War intrigue novels were, by then, no longer on editors' priority lists, and my new agent dissuaded me from sending it to publishers for the time being. The end of the Cold War was less than a decade away, and its eventual demise seemed to bear out the editors' sense of things. Even LeCarre turned from Cold War subjects to the world of terrorism and corporate crime.

With the advance I received from the publisher for *Brezhnev*, I took Jana and Valerie to Europe in the summer of 1980. Jana was sixteen that year and Valerie, twelve. It might be, I thought, the last time we would be able to travel together since the girls were growing up and would soon have their own interests.

By the time I returned to Santa Cruz at the end of the summer, I was ready to begin new writing projects.

PAGES FROM A SCRAPBOOK OF IMMIGRANTS

Writing fiction had taken me away from poetry for a year. At the request of a small publisher, I collected the best of the verse I had written between 1972 and 1979, and he brought it out under the title *Big Winds, Glass Mornings, Shadows Cast by Stars*. The press had no distribution outside of California, and the book went unnoticed by the literary world, garnering only one favorable review by Robert Peters in *Kayak* no. 24. One of the poems in the book, "It Begins Right Here," the longest poem I had ever written, traced my family's journey from Russia to New York and ended with my daughters and me living in California. The poem was written almost as an assignment. Requested by the editor of a local project on immigration, it started out as a simple lyric and grew in length and scope, seemingly of its own volition. I knew it was one of the best poems I had ever written, but I had no idea where it came from.

Other than that, I wrote no poetry between 1979 and 1981, and after finishing the second, ill-fated novel, I found myself in a dry period for eight months, the longest I had gone without writing since I was in high school. My creative impulses were further stifled by the burden of teaching new classes and correcting student papers—a predicament I had sworn years before I would not allow to happen.

To curb the situation, I set up another self-imposed task, an artificial writing regimen in the spring of 1981. I would rise at 6 AM, eat a small breakfast, and write whatever came into my head from 6:30 to 8:00, when I would get ready for my 9 AM class. Further, I would not look at what I had written the previous day, when I had folded over the pages of the pad on which I had written, so I would come fresh to the writing every morning.

At the end of the second week, I realized I was writing about different aspects of the same subjects: my family's immigration to America and my growing up as a second-generation American. Unbeknownst to me, "It Begins Right Here" had been a precursor of the new poems and actually contained in general terms the themes and incidents I was now writing about in detail.

Now understanding what I was about, I continued writing the poems through the summer, and by the fall I had completed the rough draft of *Pages from a Scrapbook of Immigrants.* Not surprisingly, the book turned out to be a sequence. Maybe less surprising in light of the fiction writing I had been doing since 1979, the poems were narrative in approach, although each one concentrated on the lyric moment within a narrative event. I wrote and rewrote the poems for the next seven years. Several times small press publishers showed interest or pledged to bring out the book, and each time the publishing process fell apart, I thoroughly rewrote the manuscript. Finally, Coffeehouse Press published the book in 1988. I was elated and thought for a while that my entire writing career had been a training period that had prepared me to write my family's history. So strong was this notion that I even considered that in writing the book I had fulfilled my purpose as a poet and would never write a poem again.

CHAPTER 37

All Happy Families

Tolstoy wrote, "All happy families are alike, but all unhappy families are unhappy in their own ways." As with most such platitudes, the master's estimation was not accurate; I found over the years that happy families are unhappy in their own ways, just as unhappy families can be happy in theirs.

The spring of 1980 marked the beginning of another important period in my life. It was commonplace in the sexually open 1970s for college teachers to date their students, and I had been in and out of one brief affair after another during that time. I was careful never to let grading or classroom concerns enter my romantic activities, but I was quick to learn that most of the young women I was involved with either were exercising their egos by enticing their teachers into relationships or were looking for father figures against whom they would eventually rebel. In the end, the situation was not a good one for the older man if he wished for a long-term partner, as I did. But students were easier to get to know than women off campus because, as happens in most cases with mature individuals, romance flourishes first and foremost in the workplace where people spend most of their time each day. If I noticed anything else about my affairs, it was that I was attracted to the more intelligent and independent of my students.

By 1980 I had been in a long-time on-again, off-again relationship with the young woman who had traveled to Greece with me. Karen was petite and intriguing, highly intelligent, in many ways gifted, and a wonderfully inventive, humorous companion. But she was also neurotic and unpredictable, and I never knew which one of her three or four personalities I would encounter from one hour to the next, let alone from one day to another. I knew she was seeing other men on the sly. But she had manipulated me into a strange kind of emotional slavery that every month or so I would violently try to break, and in the explosive events that followed, she would become my emotional serf—for a week or two. All in all, it was an unhealthy relationship.

I hope those words do not give the impression that I was a victim or a victimizer. The fact is that until the events I will describe in this chapter, my childhood left me with no conceptions of how I should act in relationships or what I should expect from them. My lack of a father, my mother's disdain for men and her manipulation of them, and my experience of family life with Larry, were not ideal preparations for being a husband and parent. So I grew to adulthood not realizing how those factors determined my choice of partners, and I went from one tumultuous affair to another, performing different roles in each one.

By the start of the spring semester of 1980, I had broken off the relationship with Karen for the tenth time, disgusted with myself for letting it proceed as far as it had. In the next move in the pattern that had emerged, Karen would beg me to take her back, literally groveling for a reconciliation. But the pattern was about to change.

There was a woman in one of my classes that semester who caught my attention the first day of class. She was twenty-six and, I learned, divorced and raising a child. She had returned to school with the intention of eventually graduating from the university and providing herself and her son with a solid economic existence. At the time, the woman, whose name was Donna Mekis, had been working at the nearby University of California as a secretary for eight years.

What I first noticed about Donna was her pulse. She was not, however, cold or aloof: she emanated a sweetness and vulnerability that drew everyone in class to her. This sweetness surrounded her—and I must speak in terms of a prospective suitor here—like an aura, a buoyant light that attracted me immediately. I was also impressed with her determination and her openness toward learning. Soon she was helping the other members of the class, especially when I would divide the students into discussion groups and they would go over each other's drafts and finished papers.

I was strangely comfortable in Donna's presence, and when I would go over her assignments individually with her, as I did with all my students, I experienced a peacefulness I had not known for some time by just talking with her. It was a reaction that was totally different from the tumultuous relationship I had just ended. Still, I didn't approach her on a personal level until well into the semester, fearing she would refuse my advances, and I was content until then to fantasize about having a relationship with her.

On one of the last days of individual conferences before spring break, I arranged to meet with her as the final student, and when the class period was over, I told her I had something personal to ask her and assured her that her grade would in no way be involved in her response to it. I then invited her to dinner. She was shocked and politely refused, informing me that she was in a long-term relationship. We continued to talk for another half hour or so, and when she gathered her books to depart, I told her that if she ever changed her mind to let me know. When she rose, I walked her to the door and watched her stroll down the corridor, a tall, graceful brunette. I sighed, shook my head, and went back to my desk.

Unbeknownst to me, I had upset Donna quite a bit. As she would tell me later, she liked me as a person and as a teacher but never imagined that students dated their instructors. She also thought that I was too old for her to imagine in the role of suitor. But I had opened new possibilities in her mind, and she called one of the women she worked with to tell her of my gentlemanly advance and how easy she found talking with me.

Donna, Santa Cruz, 1980

It so happened that the colleague Donna called knew me. She had been a programmer for several of the classes I had taught at the university. She was also one of Donna's role models, and now she urged her to go out with me. She would find it interesting, a new experience, her colleague said, and as far as my age was concerned, well, she didn't have to marry me. It also turned out that this colleague didn't like Donna's boyfriend.

Donna thought over her response and my offer, then called her boyfriend, with whom she was having problems, and told him she had decided to go out with me. He was angry and immediately broke off with her. The next day, she came to my office and said she would like to accept my offer.

For two weeks the relationship grew quickly and naturally. I met her son, Nicholas, a blond two-year-old who was unusually quiet and watchful in my presence, and I learned that Donna was a third-generation Santa Cruzan whose family was part of the large Croatian community in Watsonville, the agricultural town in the southern part of the county. Her father had married a nurse from Missouri who had come to California during the Second World War, and they had moved to Santa Cruz where he started an auto parts business.

Hearing that she was Croatian, I expounded my theory of Slavic unity, I must admit, to her confusion. I talked about Yugoslavia and showed her my collection of *Yugoslavia Today* magazines. I also learned that she had a number of emotional scars from her first marriage, which had ended so violently that she and her son had to be spirited out of the state for three months to avoid her ex-husband's wrath.

We went to films and dinners, and I introduced her to my friends and colleagues, who were captivated by her ease and friendliness around them, especially in comparison to my old girlfriend's erratic and at times sullen behavior in their presence. At the end of the two weeks, however, Donna abruptly ended the relationship, citing our age difference as insurmountable. I remember picking up my younger daughter Valerie at high school the next day, and when she asked me why I seemed so unhappy, I told her, "I just broke up with a woman I could imagine marrying."

At the end of June, I bumped into one of Donna's friends from class, and she told me that Donna had gone back to her boyfriend and they were engaged to be married. I, meanwhile, had gone back to Karen and the endless rounds of betrayal, revenge, and self-recrimination.

Then in August, Donna called me up. She wanted to meet for lunch. I agreed, and in the course of the meal, she told me that she couldn't stop dreaming about me. As she talked, I thought she had asked to see me in order to indulge her ego by finding out if I was still emotionally involved with her, and I remained aloof and cynical about her motivation throughout the meeting. I had endured such incidents with other women before, and I refused to recognize her "dilemma" as real. I fancied, again cynically, that she was testing me and told her the problem was hers and had nothing to do with me. The lunch ended with a cool good-bye on my part.

That fall, Donna took the second half of the course I was teaching, and we were civil to each other, but no personal communication passed between us. A month into classes I learned from one of her friends that the marriage had been called off. I remember that my heart lurched at the news, but I dared not hope. A month later, Donna called me and said she had ended the relationship with her boyfriend, told me that she had continued to dream about me, and asked if I was still interested in her. I was at her house in fifteen minutes.

We began to see each other with equally serious intentions. But there was a problem. I was still involved with Karen, whom I immediately informed of my attachment to Donna. Thus began a tug-of-war between both women, which, to complete the metaphor emotionally tore all three of us apart.

At that time I had been having conferences with a young therapist named David on an ingenious book he had written called *Prescriptive Metaphors*. It posited the idea that by making up extended metaphors for one's dilemmas, a person could solve them. In many ways, it was an extension of the idea of visualization. But for me, it served to bring one of the primal concerns of poetry into the contemporary, everyday world. I had long thought that the role of the poet as shaman, and poems as shaman chants, in many ways could cure the sick, not by physical remedies but by putting the ill person psychologically in harmony with the universe. Metaphors, I thought, in agreement with Carl Jung, were, in dreams and other instances, expressions of the subconscious, and by interpreting and following their riddle-like messages one could, in psychiatric terms, come into harmony with the self.

David and I had been having long discussions on the topic when my dual relationship with Donna and Karen began, and within a month I asked him for professional help. I could see his interest in the case was more than professional since we had developed a friendship. He asked to see both women separately. Karen, terrified, I'm sure, of what psychological revelations would surface during such an encounter, refused to meet with him. Donna, on the other hand, happily accepted David's invitation.

After several weeks of having me as a patient, and the day after he had talked with Donna, David asked me to his house. This would not be a professional session, he said. He had just a few words to tell me. When I arrived, we took drinks out to the patio and watched the late afternoon sunlight crease the mountains opposite his property. Butterflies drifted through the air.

"You know, Mort," he began, "to survive, people harden their hearts, become jokers, become belligerent; you name it. You certainly had to find ways to survive when you were a child. The trouble is that without recognizing it, we take these methods of survival with us into adulthood when we no longer need them. In your relationships with women, your survival techniques are to push them away in order to bring them close. You desperately want the love your mother never gave you, but at the same time you insist on duplicating the pattern that will drive women away and, in repetition of your childhood, they will therefore abandon you. In most cases you choose women who will oblige you in this cyclical pattern, or women you will be able to force into leaving you by always questioning and testing their affection. From what you have told me, I'd say your old girlfriend fits the model. But Donna is a different story. She brings to you an uncompromising love, a love without strings. Through her, you can break the pattern. You've survived your childhood, and in most cases your survival techniques have worked well. But you're in your forties now, and it's time to let them go. Many people can't do that. Some can. It's up to you."

That was the last word David had to say on the subject. I had long suspected much of what he had said, but he defined the problem in a way that I could finally fully understand. If, however, I could grasp the problem intellectually, emotionally I was far from being able to deal with it. And so for the next six years I went from Karen to Donna and back innumerable times, wrestling with my demons. In the end, I chose Donna who, like Karen, had stayed with me throughout what was an agonizing time for both of them.

Once, in the midst of the turmoil, I asked Donna why she continued to stay with me and put herself through such emotional pain.

"Because I feel safe with you," she replied.

I stared at her questioningly.

"I don't just mean physically safe," she explained. "I mean emotionally safe. That first day in your office, I realized you were not only easy to talk to but were open, direct and honest. I can trust you. I know how hard this has been for you too: you tell me that, and I believe you. I understand what you're working through."

I don't mean to give the impression that Donna accepted the situation without protest. Several times,

With Donna on our wedding day, 1986, Santa Cruz

With friends at my wedding to Donna. *Left to right:* Leonard Gardner, Joe Stroud (my best men), Morton Marcus, Jim and Jeanne Houston, and Al Young.
Santa Cruz, 1906

she ended the relationship. But we were always drawn back together because we continued to find aspects of one another's personality that were difficult for each of us to live without.

Shortly after I made my decision, Donna and I were married, and as David had perceptively predicted, the self-destructive pattern vanished.

During the six tumultuous years of our early relationship, but especially after we were married, I came to know Donna as I did few other people. Her calm and poise had attracted me at first, but I soon learned she was energetic and responsible. She was always moving, investing everything she did with a boundless passion, from her role as mother to her career: from taking care of Nicholas and performing one favor after another for her parents, brothers, sisters, and friends, to her obligations first as an admissions counselor at the University of California and then as transfer director at Cabrillo. And somehow she managed to take care of our home and garden at the same time.

Her energy focused wholeheartedly on anything that engaged her attention. She endlessly prepared for the next day's work and spent much of her free time reading reports or solving work problems. Her work involved helping students transfer from two- to four-year colleges, and I soon realized her commitment to overcoming the bureaucratic barriers that kept students from attending a four-year university reflected a deeper impulse to help others in all phases of life. Her intelligence and diligence led her to create statewide policies on student transfer issues. In later years, her curiosity about her Croatian background led her to a fascination with history and current events, which eventually culminated in her writing a book about her Croatian forbears' immigration to California.

From our first two weeks together, I was struck by her honesty and integrity. They matched my own and led to our communicating our most intimate thoughts from the beginning of the relationship. We still talk endlessly about everything and never tire of each other's company.

If this miniature (and incomplete) portrait paints a picture of a sober, serious person, it is misleading. Donna is lively and outgoing: not only does she enjoy whatever she is doing, she has a healthy sense of humor, and—probably to her discredit—finds my clowning delightful. If we are from opposite sides of the continent and from very different cultures—she was raised in the small town of Santa Cruz in an extremely religious, Roman Catholic family—we agree more than differ on most subjects.

As our years together unfolded, I came to regard Donna more and more as a high-spirited, loving person, committed to helping make people's lives the best they could be. Understand, she is not a do-gooder but someone who is nourished by helping others. The aura of light I had first observed emanating from her I came to see as a metaphor for her outlook and personality, and for twenty years we have enjoyed a partnership that has made both our lives rich in honesty, trust, and humor.

All of this sounds incredibly mawkish, but, as puerile and in the end inadequate as my words may be, I am unable to describe Donna and our relationship in any other way. What I'm trying to say is that we have found what I consider everything the word "love" implies and that I am obviously unable to express. I often think of the story Plato tells in the *Symposium* about the insolent race of creatures who had two faces, four arms and legs, and were round on both sides. In their arrogance they made war on the gods, and Zeus, enraged, hurled his lightning bolts at them, dividing each of them in two so that each part had one face, two arms and legs, and was round on one side only. Then he condemned the divided creatures to seek their other halves throughout the world, in almost all cases never to find them. And that, said Plato, is the nature of love. How wonderful, I have often thought in the last twenty years, that I have found my other half.

■ ■ ■

But all was not perfect. Nick, Donna's son, and I had problems. Although I had always wanted a son, and Jana and Valerie were delighted to have a brother they could fuss over, Nick and I were in a war for his mother's affections. He also had traits, normal for children, which I found difficult to accept. Instead of dealing with them as an adult, however, I became angry or remote—angry because, as kids will, he lied and manipulated, and remote because I didn't feel

I could discipline him or deal with him as a real father should. His own father, who I came to know and like but who had problems of his own, seldom saw him, and when he did make appointments to see Nick, he often failed to show up. I felt compassion for Nick on those occasions, but he always did something to alienate my approaches almost immediately.

On her part, Donna was protective of Nick. She was easily fooled by his manipulations and didn't like my proposals for disciplining him. She also felt guilty that due to work and school she couldn't spend as much time with him as she wished and thought she should, and that made her protectiveness border on possessiveness.

As time went on, we brought Nick to therapists who diagnosed him with ADHD, saying that accounted for his emotional problems, his troubles at school, and even his refusal to do chores around the house. My own diagnosis was that he was spoiled, and I wanted to use stronger disciplinary methods and eventually "tough love." But by then, Donna and I had become polarized over how to raise him. I thought he needed a strong male hand, but she and the therapists disagreed, and I watched Nick grow into a defiant, self-involved young man who was unable or unwilling to fulfill even a medium of familial or personal responsibilities.

Despite all our problems, I loved Nick and believed he had great potential in many areas: he was intelligent, socially adept, and creative. But he was unwilling to work in any area in which he showed interest or talent. That became another raw spot between us. Finally, even Donna saw that something had to be done. It happened when Nick was placed on academic probation after his first semester in college and as a result had to return home. At this point the situation became worse than ever, and after a few months we asked him to leave the house. I write this brief, incomplete history because, after one explosive event ten years later, Nick asked to speak with me. When I agreed, he told me, without rancor, what it was like to grow up with me as a father figure, and his points were so insightful and well thought out, it is worth any parent's time to hear them. It was a necessary and loving thing for Nick to do—to show me our conflict from his perspective and thereby allow me to see the person I seemed to be to others when I donned the parental mask I smugly wore in my domestic role. It was a way I would never have seen myself on my own.

With Nick at a Mekis family gathering, Hollister, 2002

The conversation came about when we were in Croatia in 2005. Nick had just celebrated his twenty-eighth birthday, and he asked to take a walk with me. He had grown into a strapping, good-looking man, with a long face and strong jaw. We strolled by the sun-speckled blue waters of the small town where we were staying. Nick began by saying he didn't want to seem a whiner and knew that the difficulties of his childhood were in no way comparable to mine.

I said nothing, and he continued, "As a kid I felt alone and unappreciated after you guys got married. I wasn't celebrated but felt like a burden to both of you."

The word "celebrated" surprised me, but I remained silent.

He paused, and when I didn't reply, he went on. "I felt you didn't want a kid around, and as for my mom, I was an unpleasant reminder of her marriage to my dad."

I couldn't let that go. "Your mom never felt that way," I said. "She loved you as much as ever. And as for me, I had hoped you would be the son I never had. But I'm not trying to deny your sense of things: if you felt them, they were real, at least to you."

"Look, Mort, you gave my mom a new social life, which excluded me. That's the way it was. Neither one of you paid any attention to me or my friends."

I knew that half of what he said was true. Donna had paid loving attention to him, but as for me. . . . "I'm sorry about not making the house a welcoming place for you and your friends," I said. "But if you have your issues, I have mine, and one of them is that I conceive of my home as a sanctuary after all those years of living in dormitories and having little or no privacy. But you're wrong about your mom: you have always been her primary concern."

I then reminded him of something I had told him years before when I said that children had to forgive their parents and come to terms with their parents' failings or they would remain mental teenagers all their lives. "You know, Nick," I said, "for a long while I've had this idea that almost all children are dissatisfied with their mothers and fathers and envy other children their parents. So children are never happy with the people who conceive them and raise them."

Understand, I was not trying to negate Nick's perceptions but wanted to explain to him, as I saw it, his refusal to function as a member of the family. I went on to say, "You're right: I have never thought of a family as being centered around children, where children were 'celebrated' and the focus of the relationship. To me, a family is a joining of adults whose children partake of their parents' world." The truth was, I had never thought of families being focused on children until he mentioned it. But then, I thought to myself, as we strolled under the shadowy trees, what did I know about family dynamics, being raised as I had?

In the end, each of us recounted those aspects of the other's behavior that most annoyed him, and after we had finished, we embraced and pledged to take one another's concerns seriously and mend our relationship. We have been the best of friends ever since. The conversation affected me in many ways, and I think of it often. Whenever I do, it is always with admiration for Nick's courage in coming to me with his concerns and making me aware of my failings. At the same time, I also think, not inconsequentially, of a similar conversation I had with Jana that I will talk about in future pages.

All in all, my children have taught me a lot about myself.

CHAPTER 38

William Everson

Everything William Everson experienced in this world proved to him that another, holier world existed and that one could see signs, portents, and images of that world everywhere in this one.

Toward the end, he saw angels dancing on the ceiling of his bedroom. There was nothing strange in that, since he was an angel himself, an avenging angel who stalked back and forth from one side of a stage to another in the 1950s and '60s and called himself Brother Antoninus. In those days his lean, clean-shaven face was caught between a sneer of loathing and a grimace of pain. His mouth was full of recrimination, disgust, redemption, and love. His most famous poem, and one he was always asked to recite, was "A Canticle to the Water Birds" and he reminded me in those years of an angry stork, the hemmed skirts of his cowled, white Dominican robes snapping like wings struggling to take flight as he prowled in front of his audiences.

By the time he arrived in Santa Cruz in 1971, Bill had become another kind of angel. He had abandoned his monk's name, robes, and anger and was wearing a smile, a full white beard, a mustard-yellow fringed buckskin jacket, jeans, and a bear-claw necklace—his "new costume," as he called it.

But through all the years I knew him, Bill's vision of his God's handiwork being alive in our world remained as clear as a rain-washed landscape. Every event, even the most trivial, had a metaphorical significance that was symbolic, mythic, and in the end holy, from the death of an elk in the forest to the flight of sea birds along the coast.

William Everson, Santa Cruz, 1972

Bill came to Santa Cruz at the invitation of the university. He had left the monastery two years before when he ran away with a pregnant woman thirty years younger than he, in whom he believed he had failed, years before, to read God's message to save her when she had come to him for advice. Now they were married with a young son, and several times a week Bill would drive from his home in the woods of north county to instruct the University of California students on the craft of hand printing in one course and to talk about the nature of the poet's calling in a series of spontaneous and very personal talks in another.

No one could help but be impressed with Bill's intellectual brilliance and dazzling verbal reasoning or escape the influence of his metaphorical connections that identified his God's presence in our everyday world. Those connections would suddenly be everywhere. Even Bill's name: Everson. Introducing him at a reading once, I took that name apart and reassembled it, describing him as the archetypal *son ever* in search of his father. He growled behind me in response. When I turned, however, I saw that his eyes were twinkling.

But Bill had another side many did not know: a mischievous boy crouched in the prophet's lean body. In the mid-1970s, Bill came to speak to the class on contemporary writers I had put together for the University of California Extension program. This was the same course Ray Carver had spoken to a year earlier. As then, in the morning the students would discuss a book I had assigned the week before, and in the afternoon, the author would visit the classroom to talk about the book and answer questions.

"What did you tell them?" Bill asked me at lunch.

"That you'd probably come on like Isaiah ranting about the end of the world," I answered.

Those eyes twinkled again, but he said nothing. I should have known then, but I was as caught by surprise as the class when Bill proceeded to enchant them with a lamblike gentleness I'd never seen in him before.

"You old fox," I said to him afterward, and he threw back his head, snorted once, and cackled a crescendo of laughter.

Bill and I shared the same birthday. One year we decided to celebrate together at his home in the wilds off Swanton road. This was in 1972, before Parkinson's disease crippled him. Bill was sixty that day. I remember him about to read a poem, standing between two huge redwoods in a shadowy cathedral of trees. When the seventy or so guests had gathered around, he unexpectedly took off his shirt and stood bare-chested in the surrounding greenery. His body was marble-white, translucent, not a gram of fat on it to obscure the sleek muscle groupings beneath the skin. It was, I realized with a start, the same body Michelangelo had given a reclining Adam on the ceiling of the Sistine Chapel, where Adam, his index finger listlessly extended, is about to receive the jolt of life from the touch of his heavenly father.

One night in the early 1980s, Bill, George Hitchcock and I were sitting together in the front row of Santa Cruz's First Congregational church for a reading by Robert Bly. There were several hundred people in the pews. Bly proceeded to berate Western civilization's worship of an authoritarian father figure as its symbol of divinity. Bill squirmed and grunted beside me for five minutes or so before he wrenched himself out of the pew and stalked up the side aisle toward the rear exit. Bly saw him out of the corner of his eye, stopped in midsentence, and called, abashed, "Why, Bill, are you leaving?" to which Bill snapped over his shoulder. "You're damn right I am."

"But Bill—" Bly started to say in confusion.

"For heaven's sake, Robert," Hitchcock interjected, "you've been insulting the man's god and everything he believes in for the past twenty minutes. What did you expect?"

"Oh," said Bly in sudden embarrassed comprehension, "of course."

A year after I published that anecdote as part of a tribute to Bill, Bly published his remembrance of the incident in the Robinson Jeffers Newsletter. Bill, he wrote, "stood up like a shot and was gone." That was it: there were no remarks on either side, and, Bly continues in the article, when members of the audience tried to apologize for Bill's behavior, he told them, "I thought his decisive action was fine. If someone says something you don't agree with and you can't correct it, just leave."

That was not what I remembered, and Bill and I had never talked about the incident. And so our slightly different accounts stood until ten years later, in 2005, when I came across Bill's account of the event in an interview he did with Lee Bartlett in 1988. Bill said he had stomped out of the reading when Bly declared, "Christianity must renounce the doctrine of the one God!" and when Bly asked if he was going, Bill had called, "You better believe it," over his shoulder. Bill's concluding words, however, were most revealing: "I heard many reports that at the time he [Bly] took the whole thing very well. But after a few days he began to steam. I wrote him a letter the next day and sent it along with a book; I told him I'd looked forward to his appearance and that I regretted what happened. Before he got that, though, he wrote me a savage letter saying that if I differed with him I should have stayed to fight. Further, he said that I stood for the Inquisition, that a few hundred years back I would have reported him to the priests and watched him burn at the stake on the plaza in Santa Cruz. So I immediately wrote back and told him that it wasn't my place to dispute with him at his reading and closed by telling him that he'd left me only two options, to leave or to punch him out. And I finished by saying that maybe I made the wrong choice!"

They patched up their differences a year or so later.

Another night, Bill and I were seated together backstage as part of a troupe of poets at a benefit reading. I noticed Bill's left hand was trembling, as if palsied. When I inquired about it, he told me it was a temporary condition, one of the signs of an inner ear infection. I'd had such an infection the previous year and knew that palsy was not one of its symptoms. I insisted Bill go to a doctor friend of mine. A week later, Bill phoned me. "I just wanted to thank you for insisting that I find out I have Parkinson's disease," he said. To this day, I don't know if he was being humorous or bitterly sarcastic, or whether it was just his way of letting me know that the last great struggle of his life had begun.

Bill's life, in many ways, was a series of struggles: one was between his body (which loved women, nature, and Jack Daniel's) and what he perceived to be the demands of his God's spiritual kingdom. In his last years, the struggle was with his disease-twisted body to make it perform as his still dagger-sharp mind wanted it to, so he could shape words with his mouth, write them with his fingers, and embrace those he loved with his arms. His mind remained sharp to the end.

Despite our moments of camaraderie, most of the time Bill and I had difficulty communicating. As in my friendship with Ray Carver and others, Bill and I came from different worlds—he, the hard-bitten Scandinavian from the Central Valley of California; I, the East European Jew from the Atlantic seaboard. He was of the farm; I, of the city. Bill, even in his humor, was tormented, whereas my humor was playful and meaningless, more a verbal babble that celebrated the world around me than a profound utterance. He seemed not to hear my wisecracking, side-of-the-mouth puns, and I got his sly allusions and clever references minutes after he said them.

But most of all, our orientations separated us. In his late thirties, he had adopted the Catholic Church and all its belief systems—its legends, imagery, statues, saints' medals, and rules—and never really abandoned them. His fervor was relentless, almost medieval, and led him to the brotherhood of the monastery. My orientation was also spiritual but was aimed at a Dionysian life force I saw pulsating in every living thing and rooted in this world. Denial of the body's desires propelled Bill's underlying seriousness. Eros propelled my joviality. As far as Bill—another follower of Eros, but at war with that part of his nature—was concerned, my outlook wasn't spiritual at all, and he once referred to it almost sneeringly as my "pursuit of secular vitality."

But beneath these differences, Bill and I shared a bond that was deeper than family, although it was familial in its own way. I'm talking about our belief in the brother- and sisterhood of poets, a family beyond bloodlines, a family based on vision and commitment, which included in its membership all the world's shamans, witch doctors, medicine men, alchemists, prophets, rabbis, mullahs, and priests.

I believe it was that sense of brotherhood that led Bill to the monastery but I think he chose the wrong brotherhood, forgetting poetry's most important element when he donned the cloth—the complete commitment to the Word: the Word as primal source, the Word as utterance made holy, the Word as prayer and hymn, charm and spell, the Word in its power to restore and lead us back to harmony with ourselves and the universe—the Word as healing agent, and the poet as healer. And yet I must question my words even as I write them, remembering that he wrote one of the great religiously inspired poems of English or of any other language in "In All These Acts":

In All These Acts

Cleave the wood and thou shalt find Me, lift the rock and I am there!

—The Gospel According to Thomas

Dawn cried out: the brutal voice of a bird
Flattened the seaglaze. Treading that surf
Hunch-headed fishers toed small agates,
Their delicate legs, iridescent, stilting the ripples.
Suddenly the cloud closed. They heard big wind
Boom back on the cliff, crunch timber over along the ridge.
They shook up their wings, crying; terror flustered their pinions.
Then hemlock, tall, torn by the roots, went crazily down,
The staggering gyrations of splintered kindling.
Flung out of bracken, fleet mule deer bolted;
But the great elk, caught midway between two scissoring logs,
Arched belly-up and died, the snapped spine
Half torn out of his peeled back, his hind legs
Jerking that gasped convulsion, the kick of spasmed life,
Paunch plowed open, purple entrails
Disgorged from the basketwork ribs
Erupting out, splashed sideways, wrapping him,
Gouted in blood, flecked with the brittle sliver of bone.
Frenzied, the terrible head
Thrashed off its antlered fuzz in that rubble
And then fell still, the great tongue
That had bugled in rut, calling the cow-elk up from the glades,
Thrust agonized out, the maimed member
Bloodily stiff in the stone-smashed teeth . . .

                                   Far down below,
The mountain torrent, that once having started
Could never be stopped, scooped up that avalanchial wrack
And strung it along, a riddle of bubble and littered duff
Spun down its thread. At the gorged river mouth
The sea plunged violently in, gasping its potholes
Sucked and panted, answering itself in its spume.
The river, spent at last, beating driftwood up and down
In a frenzy of capitulation, pumped out its life,
Destroying itself in the mother sea,
There where the mammoth sea-grown salmon
Lurk immemorial, roe in their hulls, about to begin.
They will beat that barbarous beauty out
On those high-stacked shallows, those headwater claims,
Back where they were born. Along that upward-racing trek
Time springs through all its loops and flanges,
The many-faced splendor and the music of the leaf,
The copulation of beasts and the watery laughter of drakes,
Too few the grave witnesses, the wakeful, vengeful beauty,
Devolving itself of its whole constraint,
Erupting as it goes.

> In all these acts
> Christ crouches and seethes, pitched forward
> On the crucifying stroke, juvescent, that will spring Him
> Out of the germ, out of the belly of the dying buck,
> Out of the father-phallus and the torn-up root.
> These are the modes of His forth-showing,
> His serene agonization. In the clicking teeth of otters
> Over and over He dies and is born,
> Shaping the weasel's jaw in His leap
> And the staggering rush of the bass.

Bill thought he had failed the Church in the end, and I remember in the fall of 1993, the year before his death, the joy that shone from his disease-wasted body, as if it were a weightless paper lantern, the day after he had received communion for the first time in twenty-five years. But as I said, I think he chose the wrong brotherhood in the monastic life. When the Church assailed him for writing his poems and warned him against the sin of pride, he must have known his mistake.

I believe Bill's love of women was not just the love of Mary as spiritual mother, you see, but an adoration of the life force in all its fleshly succulence. Or it could have been. What he was looking for in his wife Susanna, but in the end did not find in her, was the final turning from spiritual agony in the name of the Father to the celebration of the holiness of the life force in the name of the Mother. Anyway, his words groped toward that realization, like the hands of a blind man touching his way through the dark. And that's where the brother- and sisterhood of poets came in. That's where I came in.

Bill thought of himself as a charismatic poet, one who is divinely called to transmit God's vision to the world. That's why poets comprised a sacred brother- and sisterhood to him. Which explains why he was so generous with his time and counsel to young writers.

Pursuing that line of reasoning: if living poets were sacred, dead poets were saintly. He referred to them once as "those who go before and call us on." In his elegy to his mentor, Robinson Jeffers, he repeats the phrase "the Poet is dead" again and again, like a litany. When I was told of Bill's passing the day he died, I inadvertently murmured, "The poet is dead; long live the poet," and added, "Bill Everson is dead; long live the poet in his words and the man in my memories of him."

CHAPTER 39

Four Poets (Rice, Marshall, Gilbert, and Codrescu)

STAN RICE

One of the poets who took part in the Cabrillo reading series was Stan Rice, at that time the Director of the Poetry Center at San Francisco State University.

To describe Stan as high-strung would be euphemistic. He was of medium height, exceptionally thin, and practically quivered with an inner intensity. When he read his poems, he resembled an angry flame, and he mesmerized his audience with his raw descriptions of a nightmare world that was a verbal equivalent of Hieronymous Bosch's visual one. Not that Stan's words resembled a fire and brimstone preacher's sermon—there was no moralizing in them—but they summoned up a frightening gothic vision of what lay behind the benign façade of daily life. The students were hypnotized by his reading as well as his words.

History: Madness

Smoke beshags
the lemons and olives.
I was not mad.
I have color slides to prove this.
If you see a flayed goat
hanging in a Haitian shack
tell that goat I have a color slide
this side of death; its death.
And that the veins are still violet.
Further: I have evidence
all history is the orange
of blood-stained water.
Here come the lemons from their gallows.
Silk dress, head of spinach, chicken on her bones.
I have this documented.
History: madness: how did they stuff that man's bones
into that jar whose mouth is smaller than his head?

The chalk gasps. And the fish filet
bears the pink imprint of the bones
of the fish that was in it.
You will make a beautiful fossil
because you believe in ideas.
The tapestry was reversed
so that we could see what madness
resembles. If you see that goat tell it
I have a color slide of the metaphor
of its death. I did not suffer madness.
I suffered facts.
And have the bloody photographs to prove it.

Anne and Stan Rice in later years,
New Orleans, 2000

But for all his inner world of demons and strife, Stan was a gentle
person and a great companion. On
one of his visits, Joe, a friend and
former classmate of Stan's at San
Francisco State, took us for a hike in
Nicene Marks Park, a heavily forested ravine that ran several miles in
mid Santa Cruz Cnty. An inveter
ate hiker, explorer, and nature lover,
Joe had found the remains of an old
bridge and wanted to show it to us.

It was winter, the middle of a
rainy season that had been exceptionally stormy. We made our way
through dripping trees and mud, a
misty rain falling around us. When we got to the usually dry streambed in
the center of the park, we found it had become a river fifty yards wide,
hurtling logs and tree stumps down its rushing course.

But Joe wouldn't be dissuaded from his journey, and Stan was willing to
follow him. We watched the torrent for several minutes and then removed
our pants and shoes and socks and waded across the rushing water. In the
middle of the stream, Stan stopped. "Hey, listen," he said. Joe and I paused,
all of us waist deep in the flood. We heard the cataract roar of the water.
"Hear it?" said Stan, pausing until we were listening with him, and then he
continued, "We've got to learn how to spell that sound."

Stan came down to Santa Cruz a handful of times, and on several Sundays visited me in my mountain home with his wife, Anne, and his two children, one of whom, Michelle, was dying of leukemia. Jana and Valerie
played together with the two while Wilma and I visited with Stan and Anne.
We had known Stan and Anne briefly in San Francisco, and it was good to

get to know them better, although it was painful to see the anguish they were going through because of Michelle's condition.

When Michelle died at the age of five in 1972, we heard that Anne had begun drinking heavily. We were sad to hear it, not only because Stan and Anne were nice people and acquaintances, but also because we had heard that many people considered Anne an exceptionally fine fiction writer.

Several years later, of course, Anne published the first of her vampire novels and became a huge financial success. Stan kept teaching at San Francisco State but retired in 1978 to devote all his time to painting and writing poetry, and both Anne and Stan left California to live in New Orleans, Anne's hometown.

On a book tour in the 1990s, Anne came to read in Santa Cruz. I was out of town, but Joe was there and so was my older daughter Jana, then thirty, who had been assigned to cover the event as a photographer. "You might know Jana's dad, Mort Marcus," the bookstore organizer said to Anne.

"Is this little Jana?" said Anne and embraced Jana. She told Jana to stay close to her through the evening, and they struck up a friendship that resulted in Jana's first book, a volume of photographs and interviews with Anne's fans, entitled *In the Shadow of the Vampire*.

But Anne wanted Jana to remain close to her for another reason. After the signing was over, she asked Jana to have me contact Stan and invite him out for a reading. She was worried that Stan was growing inward and remote. She had talked to Joe about her concern before the reading.

Joe and I called Stan separately and told him to come out for an extended visit, but he refused our offer. He had paintings to finish and a full schedule in New York and New Orleans. Maybe he'd come out in a year or so, he said, but it was great hearing from us. Although Stan sounded merely noncommital to me, Joe, who was closer to him, said he was extremely depressed and had told him he was feeling isolated and unknown.

Five years later, in 2002, Stan was diagnosed with brain cancer and died within the month. He was fifty-nine years old.

There is another ending to this story, one that Stan may have found gratifying. I have referred to it before, but it is time to tell it fully now. For several years before Stan's death, Joe and I had not only been feuding but had not been talking to each other. A month after Stan's died, we ran into each other at a bookstore. "You heard about Stan?" Joe asked. I nodded and we stood there, staring at each other. "This is stupid," Joe said. "We don't have much time left, and we've been through too much together." And without a further word, we embraced and have remained the best of friends ever since. Not that we agree with each other on everything, especially poetry. We just respect each other's right to have our own opinions, and, as I wrote before, even to joke about our differences.

JACK MARSHALL

Jack Marshall,
San Francisco,
2002

I met Jack Marshall in 1967. He was the poet whose work followed mine in the *Young American Poets* anthology, and when we met, he was married to Kathy Fraser. If ever a marriage was not meant to be, it was Jack's marriage to Kathy. For the most part he was gentle, kind, and quietly humorous. But he was also reclusive and brooding whereas Kathy was vivacious and sociable, and the marriage brought those differing qualities warringly to the fore. Kathy and Wilma, both young mothers, became friends. I liked Jack immediately and watched him develop over the next few years into one of the best poets in America. Luckily, Allan Kornblum at Coffeehouse Press thought so too and became the publisher of all Jack's later work. By 1970, Kathy and Jack had split up, and Wilma, living in Santa Cruz, almost never saw her after that. But Jack and I grew closer over the years, and though we had our differences, which led to occasional arguments, we were like brothers who squabble but love each other as friends and as family. In our case, the family was the brotherhood and sisterhood of poetry.

Although we met several times before I moved to Santa Cruz, most of our thirty-five years of friendship has occurred since I left San Francisco. This means that we might not see each other for months on end. We've overcome the separation by having long phone conversations and by writing to each other. The conversations are more about poetry than personal matters and are addendums to our sending each other poems and criticizing one another's work. From the beginning, we agreed to be unsparing in our commentaries, and for thirty years we were able to avoid hurting feelings and causing resentments that such continual naked critiquing can easily ignite. This has been made more difficult because we not only write different kinds of poetry but seek different results from our works.

Add to these problems, the fact that Jack, for all his gentleness, can be as irascible and short-tempered as I am, and the difficulties are clear, although Jack's reactions are continually surprising. For example, although a man of uncompromising integrity, he urged me, when I told him about my Bly chapter in this book, to forget it because Bly was like everyone else. People were people, he said: there was no reason for me to be self-righteous. On the other hand, Jack is unforgiving in his attitude toward political corruption.

If I believe that poetry is composed of insights into the human condition, ecstatic flights of spiritual rhapsodizing, and celebrations of life, Jack believes in writing about the current moments of time that are always emerging and departing. As I wrote in my introduction to his long poem, "Chaos Comics," Jack is engaged with

... the endless present, the continuously metamorphosing reality not only around us but which we are in our muscle and blood
as well as in our perceptions. As he explains it, "To make, out of
bits and pieces and seemingly disparate elements, a seamless
flow of musicalized energy which touches, but does not rest for
long, on any firm ground."

But Jack is doing more than that. As I say later in the introduction, "Not
to be lost sight of are the political and social notions interwoven with the
metaphysical and aesthetic aspects of the poem. It is not surprising, therefore, to see the terrorist reappear time and again as a symbol of the ever-
changing and endless present."

At times, Jack wrote, a poem might pursue "a simultaneity of several
meanings at once, sometimes ambiguous and contradictory meanings, as
evidenced by experience ... which provokes a pulse, vibration, tension, possibilities for alternative ways of seeing and sensing. Poetry as precise perception—propelled."

Add to this that he sees the poetic line "as a unit of meaning pushing forward toward a line-break," and a line "moving like a wave, breaking forward
and backward at once, authenticated by the accuracy of sensory data"—and
it can be seen that Jack's poetry demands close attention and thorough
immersion by the reader.

For all Jack's theorizing, what still rises to the surface of his work and
makes it so exceptional is the originality and perfection of his phrasing and
rhythms. Although one would think his poetry might be dispassionate and
analytical, it's personal and passionate and, above all, sensuous, filled with
astonishing images, for when all is said and done, Jack is a poet of Eros. He
can take the latest findings in molecular biology and astrophysics and make
them pulse with the stuff of life.

For me, Jack's poetry is not so much meditative as ecstatic, and I define it
as following a mind at work to the point that the reader becomes the poet
on an odyssey through the psyche as one image ignites another.

Although Jack's far-ranging longer poems are his best work, "Green" illustrates in miniature all the aspects of his poetry as I have discussed it above. In
it, he is reminded of the heat in Africa by an exceptionally hot day in San Francisco.

Green

Heat in the park today, almost an African heat ...
Saw green as something we remember with,
and tonight see miners in Johannesburg just about now

blink, stepping out into broad daylight, as they pile into
trucks

headed for their shanty townships under the shadow
of armored police "hippos"...

While all around others go
full tilt into romance, careers, breakdowns, lawsuits,
I am taking the night

off, time out . . . though so little
am I of my time
it doesn't even notice

I'm missing. Something in me
would rather let the night pass
through; would stroke and play with,

rather than pilot it, because up ahead
or nearby there's a moment
never more

green, more strongly felt
than when the past is dropped,
but now is gripped

by the fatal, fixed attention
of career killers with the fire-
power of gods at their fingertips, who can switch

night into day, day into blinding desert, moon dead,
set on planning war with its two choices: victory
and the unknown.

The way children see
everything, being themselves
unseen, tonight I can be told things

you have not told anyone, since I will not
be here long enough to haunt you
with its revelation.

After weeks besieged by news,
today, over a beer, I heard
someone call the heart

"Beirut of the body." Such poetry
the future has in store! In my notebook
I find: "Don't sink to the bottom,

settling for muck. While you mull
this over, mouthing the words
without having them

swim straight into your bloodstream,
it's just an idea, and life hasn't
grabbed you by the throat yet."

I've championed Jack's poetry, in my small way, more than I have any of the
poets I've known. I've written reviews, introductions, and blurbs to his work.
I've put his name forward to editors who were doing anthologies and had not

heard of him. He has been recognized by others, of course, and won various awards, but he's never achieved the status as poet I thought he should. Every one of my poet friends and acquaintances are impressed with his work, an endorsement I can think of only a handful of other poets sharing.

Not that all his poetry is great, or even good. Jack is constantly writing, many of his poems running for more than three hundred lines. A number of them seem only half done and contain to my ears crude phrasing and confusing if not unclear line endings. And at times, his anger at the social and political events in the country inspires him to write diatribes, tirades, invectives, haranguing the powers that be. His continuing sequence, "The Big Brass Handbook," harbors many of these pieces, which became more strident after George W. Bush became president and Jack's sister died of cancer. From 2000 to 2002, Jack's anger was aimed at Bush and the cosmic prime mover. As a Jew of Iraqi-Syrian descent, and an American with a strong social conscience, his anger at Bush is understandable. As a Jew faced with a world of chance, he believes his Ahab-like wrath should be equally well comprehended. I thought his level of anger, however, hurt his poetry. Not that I disagreed with his stance. It just hurt both the language and the content of his poems at that time.

We had our first big argument over that subject at the beginning of the new millennium. I thought the sheaf of poems he sent me early in 2000 were too full of invective and I warned him about becoming a bitter old man, and he replied by savaging me in no uncertain terms, concentrating on my arrogance and pomposity, about which he was stingingly correct. We didn't talk to each other for two years but picked up our friendship after that as if nothing had happened, thanks to the urging of Larry Fixel and other mutual friends. I wish there was some anecdote I could write about my relationship with Jack, but every one of our meetings and phone conversations are equally intense, jocular and loving. We are comfortable in each other's company and talk poetry and catch each other up on information about our friends and our lives. Uneventful as that may seem, it is the stuff of deep friendship.

JACK GILBERT

Jack Gilbert became a legend with the publication of his first book, the 1962 Yale Younger Poets Award winner, *Views of Jeopardy*. It was a book of precise phrasing, terse, almost epigrammatic personal observations on life and love, rendered, mostly, in short narrative poems charged with acerbic wit and expressed in an easily accessible plain style. The poems were more of the head than of the heart, but they were affecting, even poignant, in their insights into human affairs. And their accessibility can be explained by Jack's statement that the poet must engage the reader with the first level of the poem, since the reader will not be willing to examine the poem deeply if he

Jack Gilbert

hasn't been interested by its surface—a rule I've adopted in my own poems ever since I heard him say this.

I had heard talk of Jack around the Haight and knew that Laura Ulewicz, with whom I had staged readings at the I-Thou Coffee Shop, had been his lover. She had been replaced by Linda Gregg, a startlingly beautiful blonde with a boyish figure, who radiated intensity. Linda and Jack married and left for the Greek islands when the Haight Ashbury years were at their height, their affair adding to Jack's legend. But both had returned separately and gone their individual ways in the early 1970s, she to increased popularity as a poet, and he, several years later, for a short stay to quietly house-sit a friend's basement apartment in San Francisco before departing the country again. Ten years later, he returned to mourn the death of his second wife, a young Japanese sculptor named Michiko, who he considered his soul mate, and who had died of cancer in the mid 1980s. Jack would mourn Michiko for the rest of his life, although his relationship with Linda would surface every now and then in one way or another.

If all this sounds like a tale out of the biography of Byron or Shelley it points up the Romantic side of Jack's nature and explains the tension between the head and the heart that energizes his poetry.

I met Jack through Joe, who had known both Jack and Linda at San Francisco State when Jack would accompany Linda to her classes. Joe idolized Jack's poetry, and examining different aspects of Joe's work with that in mind goes a long way to defining its underlying approach. Jack was enthusiastic about Joe's work as well and performed the role, without meaning to, of spiritual older brother.

I'm sure Jack's friendship with Joe was the reason he was civil to me and accepted my poetry, which he must have hated, without comment. This was a big concession on his part, since he was known for his explosions during other people's readings, when he'd rise from the audience to make devastating comments for all to hear about what he considered the miserable quality of what had just been read.

Jack was a short, bandy-legged man with a large head, pointed nose, and piercing eyes. When he wasn't angered by inferior poetry, he was soft-spoken and friendly and one of the best conversationalists I ever met. Joe, he, and I spent several memorable evenings together, full of mentally stimulating conversation. Jack's conversational technique was to make a provocative and at times outrageous statement that we would then discuss and take in unexpected directions. His comment on the importance of the poem's surface began one such evening. Another was delivered one night as we sat at a table in a Santa Cruz bar and Jack announced that a person can only fall in love three times in a lifetime. Joe listened, mesmerized by Jack's reasoning. I laughed, and as I would do on so many occasions, I chided Jack for the absurdity of his pronouncement. For some reason, Jack never took offense at my challenging his comments, and he responded with the same jocularity as I had to his remark. It was a riotous evening.

The evening had its repercussions, however, when, several months later, Joe walked into my office and asked me where I had been for the past few weeks. I had been engaged in a passionate love affair and told him in my ecstatic state that I was in love again. Joe was incredulous and replied, "That can't be. You've already been in love three times," and left the room. I reminded him of the incident twenty years later. Was he serious? I asked. "I don't remember," he replied with a smile. "I could have been."

Another evening showed me how much Jack let me get away with. Jack was visiting Joe and me in Santa Cruz again, and the three of us had gone to the university to hear Carolyn Forché, who was at the height of her popularity, read her Guatemalan poems. Afterward we retired to a bar where we were joined by Forché and her host, the poet and old friend of mine Lynn Luria-Sukenick, who would die tragically several years later at the age of forty-five.

The meeting began in a friendly enough way, with Forché open and relaxed, but within five minutes Jack was delivering cutting remarks about her, her poetry, and feminism in general. Joe and I looked on helplessly as Jack's remarks became more and more insulting. But he had met his match with two strong women who went on a counter attack like the Furies. The more they answered his insults with insults of their own, the nastier Jack's retorts became. Finally, Lynn looked at me pointedly as if to say, "Are these the kind of friends you have? Aren't you going to do something about this?"

I would have joined in Jack's defense, but he was so wrong-headed at this point, there was no way I could.

"Come on, Jack," I said, "you're way out of line."

Jack made no reply but shot another cutting remark at the two women. They replied in kind, and after another five minutes in which I told Jack to control himself three more times, they got up and left.

Jack never upbraided me for not taking his part, and when we referred to the incident, I always pointed out that he was in the wrong and had insti-gated the blow-up. He never denied it. There's an interesting addendum to this incident: in an interview a year later, Carolyn Forché named Jack as one of her favorite poets.

On the three occasions just mentioned, Jack was in Santa Cruz to give readings at Cabrillo. Joe had invited him, and his readings, as well as his meetings with classes, were inspiring. His warmth and kindness to the stu-dents and faculty members made his behavior of the evening before seem a figment of my imagination.

By then, Jack had published his second book, *Monolithos*, a volume of short narrative poems mainly about his years with Linda in Greece. Although similar in approach and style to *Views of Jeopardy*, the acerbic wit had softened into a tragic ironic tone and added to the dimensions of the poems. I thought the volume was extraordinary.

When Joe and I took over the poetry show on KUSP radio in 1985, we journeyed to San Francisco to record a conversation and reading with Jack. It was a rich evening but overlaid with sorrow, for Michiko had died the previous year. Jack had written a dozen elegiac love poems to her and later that year published them in a chapbook. Almost all of them appeared in his next book, *The Great Fires: Poems 1982 to 1992*. Jack's approach and method in *The Great Fires* were the same as in his previous book. The poems revisited personal events he had previously written about, but now they were infused with a strong sense of compassion. Memory was the dominant concern, but it wasn't accompanied by nostalgia or melancholy; rather, with the sense of celebration for the tiniest experience—a sunset, a trail of ants, a late afternoon walk to the sea. And if his reminiscences were personal, as in his other books, they were never confessional.

His latest book, *Refusing Heaven* (2005), continues the examination of memory in the light of celebration, praising the mistakes we make as part of the process of living. Clearer than ever is Jack's unique praise of life and its vicissitudes: he loves the world as he finds it; there is no attempt to transform it into what he might want it to be. This is an extraordinarily hard-won vision to come to. It also marks Jack as a realist more than a Romantic.

At the same time, Jack's insistence on the necessity of engaging the critical mind is clearly evident, especially in the poem "Halloween." With his old acerbic wit, he pictures Allen Ginsberg, and the rest of the Beat poets, in their last years as

> . . . destroyed
> like the rest of that clan. His remarkable
> talent destroyed. The fine mind grown more
> and more simple. Buddhist chants, impoverishing
> poems.

By the time *Refusing Heaven* was published, Jack had been living on the East Coast for over a decade, and Joe and I have not seen him since he left San Francisco. Would we have learned anything new about him and his writing if he had stayed in San Francisco? I don't think so. His style and approach hasn't changed since *Views of Jeopardy*, and, more telling on a personal level, *Refusing Heaven* was dedicated to Linda and Michiko. The following poem illustrates his style and tone.

A Brief for the Defense

Sorrow everywhere. Slaughter everywhere. If babies
are not starving someplace, they are starving

somewhere else. With flies in their nostrils.
But we enjoy our lives because that's what God wants.
Otherwise the mornings before summer dawn would not
be made so fine. The Bengal tiger would not
be fashioned so miraculously well. The poor women
at the fountain are laughing together between
the suffering they have known and the awfulness
in their future, smiling and laughing while somebody
in the village is very sick. There is laughter
every day in the terrible streets of Calcutta,
and the women laugh in the cages of Bombay.
If we deny our happiness, resist our satisfaction,
we lessen the importance of their deprivation.
We must risk delight. We can do without pleasure,
but not delight. Not enjoyment. We must have
the stubbornness to accept our gladness in the ruthless
furnace of this world. To make injustice the only
measure of our attention is to praise the Devil.
If the locomotive of the Lord runs us down,
we should give thanks that the end had magnitude.
We must admit there will be music despite everything.
We stand at the prow again of a small ship
anchored late at night in the tiny port
looking over to the sleeping island: the waterfront
is three shuttered cafes and one naked light burning.
To hear the faint sound of oars in the silence as a rowboat
comes slowly out and then goes back is truly worth
all the years of sorrow that are to come.

ANDREI CODRESCU

Andrei Codrescu,
New York, 1970

To refer to Andrei Codrescu as a Peck's bad boy rather than an enfant terrible is to miss the evocative power of language—something Andrei would never do. Hennery Peck, a late-nineteenth-century fictional prankster who tormented the small-town Wisconsin authority figures where he lived, is too American, too dated in his shenanigans. "Enfant terrible," a French phrase, suggests a European ambience that is essential when talking about Andrei's personality and sensibility.

Born in Communist Romania in 1946, Andrei immigrated to the United States twenty years later. When I met him in San Francisco in 1972, he was still mastering English and his heavy-tongued syllables emphasized his Slavic background. We were introduced by someone—I don't remember by whom, probably another writer—on the street outside City Lights Bookshop, and with three or four others we went off to a nearby bar.

Andrei was just under average height and his build was slight. But I was initially struck, as I'm sure most people were, by his black hair falling in glinting ringlets to his shoulders and his eyes glowing like black pearls. Along with his moustache, pointed beard, and heavy accent, he was a conspicuous presence even among the costumed multitudes parading San Francisco streets in those days. My first impression was quickly enhanced by his roguish charm and metaphor-laden language.

On meeting him, a friend told me that he thought Andrei was demonic. But from the start I saw him as mischievously comic, a Balkan Till Eulenspiegel, and wonderful company. Andrei is one of the most delightful and certainly one of the most inventive storytellers I ever met. I would listen to him talk for hours. Straight-faced, he would mostly tell about his life and adventures, which I soon realized he was making up as he went along, elaborating and changing his history from one moment to the next. Such identity shape-shifting had fascinated me in his first book, *License to Carry a Gun*, a volume of poems "written by" several different characters. At the time, I hadn't heard of Fernando Pessoa and his four alternate identities and thought Andrei was the first poet to conceive of such an approach. I still hold to that idea, since, unlike Pessoa, Andrei has continued to invent himself and thereby expand his consciousness exponentially. In a section of his latest collection of poems *It Was Today*, he takes on the identities of a Chinese soldier and an imperial courtesan who write poems to each other during the thirteenth-century China.

On one of his visits to Santa Cruz, we spent the evening in a busy bar downtown, and Andrei told me the entire story of his odyssey from Romania through Europe to the United States. In the course of the evening, I kept asking him if the marvelous saga he was telling me was true, and he swore it was, exclaiming, "I wouldn't lie to you, boss." His tongue may have been in his cheek, but his face was, as usual, expressionless. Several years later, I received a request from his assistant to send her my favorite stories that Andrei had told me about himself, since Andrei was preparing his memoirs. I sent several of the stories Andrei had recounted that night in Santa Cruz. When the memoirs, *The Life & Times of an Involuntary Genius*, appeared a year later, not one of the tales was there, and Andrei's odyssey to America did not bear the slightest resemblance to anything he had said. I wasn't surprised.

■ ■ ■

Andrei, who is not just a poet but a novelist, radio commentator, and essayist, is essentially a satirist, and his target is nothing less than the insanity of contemporary life in the United States and around the planet. He is trenchantly insightful, and his language, draped in extravagant metaphors, is always astonishing. It was his language, his words showing things in new and startling ways, that captivated me the night I met him and has won over readers and radio audiences throughout the nation for the past twenty years.

I have often viewed Andrei as a descendant of those eighteenth-century European "adventurers" who were as much con men, swindlers, and fortune hunters as they were ingratiating, witty companions. As a group, they are epitomized by Giacomo Casanova and the self-styled Count Cagliostro. Like his predecessors, Andrei told his stories and performed his seductions with a cool demeanor—with what Casanova and Cagliostro would call sangfroid.

I never really got to know Andrei. He wouldn't allow it. To me, he is a series of impressions that keep changing, protean and uncontainable. He is the mask behind the mask, possibilities giving way to other possibilities. Although a satirist, he is never the clown but the jester, the one whose acerbic comments and penetrating, double-edged jokes show the prince what he has failed to see. He is the magician as magus, his abracadabra the flourish of matter-transforming words. At the same time, he is as much illusionist as shaman, as much mountebank as keeper of the universe's secrets. And yet his verbal sleights of hand never bring to mind that other eighteenth-century figure, Baron Munchausen, for Andrei is not just a garrulous teller of tall tales, but a mordant commentator on our mores and foibles.

It is in these last examples that I most clearly see Andrei's relationship to Casanova and Cagliostro, especially the latter who portrayed himself as a magician and practitioner of the occult, albeit an adherent of white rather than black magic. Such endeavors, even dabblings, were opposed to the worship of Reason, which was the hallmark of eighteenth-century European social and intellectual attitudes. Mystery and imagination were Casanova and Cagliostro's core concerns, and they are Andrei's as well. I was not surprised, therefore, that Andrei's third novel, *Casanova in Bohemia*, is about the great lover's last years, and that Andrei, quite rightly, shows him to be an essayist and thinker of the first order. That description can apply to Andrei as well. His hundreds of NPR radio commentaries are literary gems. Most, of course, are topical, but many are timeless ruminations about human folly and expectations.

All the examples I've used to describe Andrei come from European culture. As I said at the beginning of this piece, Andrei is a representative of European intellectual life. Nor is it by happenstance that I have identified him with eighteenth-century European figures, since the eighteenth century is the great age of European satire, and if Andrei resembles Casanova and Cagliostro, his work shows a marked affinity to Swift's and Voltaire's in both his absurdist imagination and universal vision.

■ ■ ■

My relationship with Andrei was almost totally confined to the four years he lived in San Francisco. I rarely saw him after he moved to Sonoma County, then Paris, and finally Baton Rouge, where he has taught for more than twenty years at Louisiana State University.

During the four years we knew each other, I invited him to read at Cabrillo several times, and we would occasionally meet in the city for lunch or a night out. I believe he enjoyed my company, but I never figured out why he did. It could have been that we were both Slavic and Jewish, but that's only a connection, not a reason for friendship. Other than that, our personalities and attitudes were completely different. From the beginning I thought I must have seemed awfully "square" to him, and my poetry "bourgeois." Imagine my surprise when he told me that he thought I was a great poet, and then went on to write the longest critical piece on one he had written about anyone up to that time. It was called "The Mystic Twang" and was an intriguing examination of my first three books. He was particularly taken with *The Santa Cruz Mountain Poems*, calling them "great American nature songs," and he claimed I was "the kind of priest poet who, like Peguy or Jacob, gets to the light by tearing up the universe in ecstatic dance." Years later, after I hadn't seen him in more than a decade, he spotted me in an audience of several hundred people during one of his readings, and stopped in midsentence to exclaim, "Look: there's Morton Marcus, a great poet."

Was I flattered? Yes. Did I believe him? No. But there was no reason for Andrei to have done any of the things he had for me, and despite my disbelief, it was good to hear he reciprocated my respect and affection. The truth is I was never the free spirit he was, and his spontaneity at times made me blanch. So did his composed demeanor, which I had decided long before I met him was not the way I would or, for that matter, could conduct myself.

The differences between us are obvious. Andrei strolled through the world discarding innumerable identities in his wake, whereas I sought the one or two that would define me and thereby allow me to gain a foothold, at least for a time, on the deck of this ship we call life as it heaved through storm-tossed seas. Up to now I have shied away from using the word "identity," although that is what this narrative of my life is certainly about—the search for an identity, if not a definition, of the self in a world of flux, in a world of fragmentary experiences and shifting moods. It is also an attempt to explain my existence when I know explanations are impossible to establish with any certainty, and further it is the story of my attempt to live a moral life in a universe that seems to be without intrinsic moral values.

In existential terms, Andrei's approach, like Jack Marshall's, was much more sensible. He was, in fact, pursuing Camus' ideal of living in a lifetime as many lives through his imagination as he was able. I admired him for that, even though his search for multiple selves showed me my limitations. But then, I always think it is good to be reminded of one's limitations every once in a while.

■ ■ ■

Andrei held an uncanny attraction for women, which he did everything to enhance. I witnessed several instances of his almost hypnotic powers both in San Francisco and Santa Cruz when women seemed literally captivated by his charms. I use the word "captivated" and "charms" in their original magical senses, as in "to hold one captive in a spell." A charm, of course, is an object believed to be imbued with magical properties in order to bring good luck or ward off evil and is alive and well in the old cliché, "It worked like a charm." Both words come directly out of fairy tales and folklore and in the eyes of the women, I'm sure, went along with the "magical" attraction of Andrei's Romanian background, seductive features, and accent.

And at first glance there *was* something magical about the way women seemed unable to resist Andrei. Certainly what attracted them to him was his aura of fun and play as much as his Slavic accent and cascading hair. But I think there was more to his appeal than that. I think women acted out their most secret fantasies in his presence—and "presence" is the right word here, since Andrei's advances toward women were, for the most part, direct but minimal.

In many ways, I think Andrei was to women an illusory figure they summoned up out of Hollywood notions of Count Dracula, whose sexually mesmerizing persona screen heroines found impossible to deny. Andrei was, therefore, a projection of women's imaginations. Maybe that's why I was not surprised that he seemed bored with his sexual exploits at times, as if he realized the women who obliged him were engaging their own illusions rather than him. It was an irony he was too intelligent and streetwise not to realize.

There is an underlying geometry of mystery and magic in all these suppositions, and I think both fascinated Andrei. I remember how surprised I was at one of his few showings of excitement when he discovered that I shared the same enthusiasm for a little known science fiction film called *Five Million Years to Earth.* The film projected the idea that humans had been programmed by aliens during the early stages of human evolution to become one of two kinds of people, either destructive/militaristic personalities or life-affirming/artistic beings, and that we carried these primal identities in our minds like some kind of Jungian collective unconscious.

■ ■ ■

I was more taken with Andrei's prose than with his poetry. I was excited by his approach in *License to Carry a Gun,* but the poems themselves weren't strong, nor did they cohere into a unity I thought the book was aiming for—and needed. Andrei told me that the publishers had cut half the poems from the book. That explained the lack of unity. But I thought his early poetry in general was too dense, too difficult to understand. Unlike his attitude toward his other work (and, it seemed, life itself), he took poetry too seriously, and I think that inhibited him. However, his later poetry, especially in *It Was Today*, is too simple, his language too fundamental, lacking in those metaphorical extravagances and word usages that make his writing so unforgettable.

It is in his prose that I find Andrei's true literary powers. I remember the delight I experienced when he showed me his early novella "Mr. Teste in America" and later when I read his essays and radio commentaries. By his own admission he has never taken his prose as seriously as his poetry, and maybe for that reason he has been able to exercise a freedom of expression in his prose, a letting go of higher aspirations, which ironically has allowed him to tap his literary strength. I've often said that many of his short prose pieces, mainly the radio commentaries, are some of the best prose poems written by an American, and if I ever edit a prose poem anthology, they will occupy a conspicuous place in it. Andrei's sense of play as well as his verbal pyrotechnics are in ample evidence in the following radio commentary:

The Ultimate Deadline

I'm up against the deadline. Not just one deadline. Several deadlines. If you cross this line, you're dead. It's the line of death. The world's on a deadline: hand up the goods or die. The doomsday clock is working against time. The dead say: our deadline was yesterday. That's the line on the other side. There is still a Party line even if you don't see it. It follows the hemline like the market. The market has a five-o'clock deadline. The bluelines arrived past the deadline and everyone was gone. There were deadlines between the lines. I can read between the lines because I've been up against a thousand deadlines and made it in the nick of time with nary a crease more in my lined forehead.

Looking at my lifeline, the palmist said, you'll live up to here, where the line ends. I looked down from the plane and saw all the neat lines. It's not a country, it's the *Cliff Notes*. The Polish refugee next to me opened the Polish paper: see, it's my byline, he said. Before the revolution you had to wait in line for everything except the newspapers, which were full of meaningless lines. After the revolution you have to wait in line for everything, including the newspapers, which are now full of too many lines. A line is a lie with the lead *n* in its belly. A deadline is a fishing line caught on a root. You have to get to the root of it to meet the deadline. I was ahead of my deadline so I watched "Flatliners," about some serious deadliners with a headliner complex. It's not a linear world, my cosmic adviser told me, but you have to toe the line as if it were. I fired him: gave him a deadline to improve his line. These are the liner notes of a man lying flat on his back on the deadline he isn't going to meet.

As for the power of his insight melded to his prose style, the following two paragraphs from *The Disappearance of the Outside* are eloquent examples. They are commenting on the Romanian folktale about the sheep Mioritza who warns her shepherd that he is to be murdered by envious herdsmen. That tale begins the book-long exploration of being on two sides, outside of time and inside it, in the eternality of the myth as opposed to the reality of everyday life, which Andrei examines in various guises, not the least of which is being on one side of the Iron Curtain or the other in the 1950s. Remembering when he and his friend Ion first heard the tale of Mioritza from "a thousand-year-old shepherd wrapped in a cloak of smoke," Andrei states the political, cultural, and philosophical implications of his two-sided quest:

> Yes, once upon a time there was time for everything. The immensity of time made the borders of childhood as improbable as the world of school that Ion and I knew we had to return to in the fall. Inside the shepherd's story there prevailed an order different from the one in the real world. The journey we undertook with Mioritza was magical and complicated. We were always lost and always home. The images she showed us found homes in us as if there had been holes already there for them to fit in. The stars were already in us. She called them into being by naming them. In the enchanted light of the telling, we were a sieve of possibility: each star streamed through us seamlessly. We were the passageway for stories coming from her world into ours, though it wasn't possible to say which world was which—which was outside, which was inside. If there was an "outside" anywhere, it was the remote one we were expected to return to, the one we were doomed to spend our lives in along with everyone else, the so-called reality of city and school and parents. Nothing seemed more unreal to us than that "reality" while we lived in the inside-outside cosmos of the story . . .

And a short while later, he writes

> Ion stayed in Romania where he is a professor of literature at the University of Cluj, a job that, undoubtedly, offers him many opportunities to footnote the myth of the lovelorn sheep. I have left the country and changed languages but have not stopped telling Mioritza's tale. Ion and I have merely divided the job: he maintained it inside the borders of a modern police state called "Romania," while I kept it outside of them. Our parallel renderings form another border, peculiar to our time, two strands of electrified barbed wire between which lies the no-man's land of politics. Unlike the border drawn by Mioritza's wandering, which is eternal, the border that divides Ion and me is historical. Our stories issue divided from Mioritza's story like the ever-diverging twin spirals of a ram's horns. One of us is inside, the other outside. But which is which?

All in all, Andrei's work continues to grow, becoming more daring and insightful as the years go on. His last two novels are prime examples of this growth and daring. In hindsight, *Messiah* is a frighteningly prescient, visionary novel about the coming of the new millennium, and *Wakefield* is an absurdist picaresque tale of the first rank. It is Andrei, not me, who continues "to get to the light by tearing up the universe in ecstatic dance."

BOOK 11

TRAVELS 2

CHAPTER 40

Stopovers

Throughout the years, my travels confirmed and at times extended my notions of humankind and the cosmos, especially concerning history and culture. Repeatedly I found that I needed the perspective seen from foreign shores to put my experiences in America into some kind of framework. My journeys also reinvigorated my writing and quickened my sense of life.

I call this chapter "Stopovers" because it recalls people, places, and events seen for a instant and then gone, experiences glimpsed by memory that are not destinations but brief stops along the way to them. These are seemingly inconsequential moments that provide continuity by connecting half-finished or incomplete incidents I've already written about. They connect in the same way train tracks connect anonymous stations without whose existence the journey could not continue or be completed. In many ways, these stopovers are concise reminders of friends and events thus far not acknowledged but who cannot be left out of any peregrinations of memory. Like stopovers, people and places will generally be mentioned in a sentence or two. At other times, like the large towns a train unexpectedly passes through on its way to somewhere else, they will spark vignettes or pointed comments that will distinguish them from the anonymity of time's passing landscape. But in all cases, they will draw the years together and, as in all my travels, they will find whatever meaning they hold for me in their connections with history.

■ ■ ■

Besides Greece, I have traveled in a number of foreign countries. In 1978, I went to Germany for the first time at the invitation of the head of Cabrillo's English Department. Bill Grant was not only my boss, but over the years I found him to be a great conversationalist and companion whose friends were educated and urbane and among the most enjoyable people I ever met. As a group, they represented a level of intellectual camaraderie I had hoped to find ever since I was a teenager. After his retirement, Bill found a new vocation as a rose expert and wrote articles on the subject, led garden tours to Europe and Australia, and traveled around the world lecturing, socializing, and charming people wherever he went. In the 1960s and 1970s,

Left to right: Ed and Inge Bower, and Bill Grant, with Waldi perched on the table. Bavaria, Germany, 1979

he vacationed in Germany every summer, gardening and generally helping maintain the small estate of an elderly couple named Ed and Inge Bower, who had befriended him when he was a teenager in Southern California. The Bowers had left Germany for the United States in the 1920s and returned in 1959, and so they were absent from their homeland during the entire Hitler era. They were wonderful people and became good friends of mine, and their home on Lake Amersee, south of Munich, was my jumping off point on my three visits to Germany. On each of those trips, my refusal to set foot in Germany when Dietrich Gerhard had invited me to be his pro- tégé haunted me for all its youthful foolishness. The Germans I encoun- tered were not bestial Nazis, but people as weak, flawed, kind, and inspiring as any others. But like others down through history, many of them had unfortunately succumbed for a time to a mass delusion of superiority to human beings not like themselves in race, nationality, or culture.

Each of my visits to Germany was different in scope and intention. Ini- tially I went alone to get the lay of the land, so to speak, and had several adventures. The most memorable, besides my overall discovery of German culture, was a visit to the Documentation Center on a side trip to Berlin. I had obtained a special pass to the Center from the Hoover Institute and was given a private tour of the facility where the most incriminating Nazi docu- ments were kept, including the complete Nazi Culture Ministry files and 1,200,000 SS personnel records. One of the Culture Ministry files belonged to the great documentary filmmaker Leni Riefenstahl whose affiliations with the Nazis has been a matter of conjecture. Her files left no doubt about her ecstatic endorsement of the Nazi cause. Another file was a request for marriage by Otto Skorzeny, the commander of the famous Condor Regiment. A note attached to his request showed that Hitler and Himmler, head of the SS, were not so strict in their choice of pureblood marriages for SS members. The note from Hitler to Himmler cynically read, "I know he's a mongrel but we need him, so OK his request."

My second trip to Germany was with my daughters, then sixteen and twelve years old, the year I took them to Europe on the advance I received for my first novel. I let the girls choose where they wanted to go. Jana chose Italy and Valerie, Germany, although I'm sure Valerie's choice was made more to please me than out of personal interest. She knew I wanted to show her and her sister Bavaria and that Ed and Inge Bower had invited us to stay at their estate.

The trip gave rise to several events that I remember with the same bittersweet nostalgia as I do the trip to Hearst Castle. One of them turned out to be more amusing than it seemed at first. It occurred at the start of the trip, the day after we landed in Amsterdam. After spending an emotionally turbulent hour at the Anne Frank House, where I was reminded that Jana was virtually the same age as Anne when the Nazis killed her during World War II, we had threaded our way to the Rijksmuseum through a huge protest march against Dutch government social policies. We were looking at "The Night Watch" in a moodily darkened room of the Rembrandt wing, when a sudden commotion—scuffling and yelling—caught our attention. We hurried to the entrance of the wing to find fifteen or twenty people purposefully scurrying about, some forcing open windows, and four or five chaining the glass entrance doors closed. The girls and I seemed to be the only museumgoers in the room.

Jana and Valerie were alarmed, and so was I. They huddled by my side and looked up at me, expecting that I would do something to get them out of the situation. I stood watching the men and women shouting orders to each other in Dutch and soon realized they were part of the protest going on outside.

While I had been figuring this out, half of the group had opened a window, set up a pulley system, and was hauling up bedding and food from the street below. Meanwhile, five policemen in uniform and three men in suits and ties were talking to one of the intruders through the chained glass door.

My alarm had subsided somewhat when I realized none of the intruders were armed. I pointed that out to the girls, and when the police and men in suits had departed, I went up to the person who had been the intruders' spokesman, a squat man in his thirties with thick blond hair combed straight downward on both sides of a part in the middle of his head.

"Excuse me," I said calmly, "are we your hostages?"

He looked at me, perplexed. "What are you doing here?" he asked in a strongly accented English. Then he turned to the man at his side and said something in Dutch, which I surmised would translate as, "I thought you had cleared all the tourists out of here?"

Then he turned to me again, still perplexed. "This is complicated," he said.

"Look," I replied before he could go on, "I've got my daughters here, and they're frightened. I'm sure—

"Don't worry; I'll negotiate something."

And when the police and the men in suits returned, he did, pointing to us as he spoke to them on the other side of the door. A few minutes later, he unchained the door and sent us on our way with a mumbled, "I'm sorry." The men outside stepped back and let us pass. Then, I guess, the two sides resumed negotiations. It was all very civilized and, I couldn't help reflecting, so different from the violent demonstrations against the war in Vietnam I had taken part in ten years before.

From Amsterdam, we took a train to Luxembourg, where I picked up a Renault station wagon I had leased for the trip, and we drove to Germany.

We spent several days with Ed and Inge who, along with Bill, showed us hidden historical sites in the Bavarian countryside. The Bowers were delighted with the girls, and we left their estate reluctantly. On our own, we spent a disturbing afternoon in Dachau, where we watched children playing in the courtyard outside the museum as if the concentration camp was not a memorial but an amusement park, and then drove to Bayreuth, where we spent two days with Dennis Russell Davies, who was conducting *The Flying Dutchman* at the annual Wagner Festival. A gracious host we knew from the Cabrillo Music Festival, Dennis arranged for us to attend a closed rehearsal as his guests and got permission for Jana to play several short pieces on Franz

Jana and Valerie at the old walled city of Rothenberg ob der Tauber, Germany, 1979

Liszt's piano in the Wagner Museum. Then Dennis led us on a tour of Wagner's house. As my fingers brushed the composer's ornate furniture and I looked out the large windows to his private garden, I wryly thought about the irony of visiting this sanctuary of the anti-Semitic maestro who would not have allowed my grandparents to set foot in his private domain a hundred years before.

Next, we drove the back roads of Bavaria, eating and sleeping at local beer halls. We toured all the old towns on the Romantic Road, which brought home to the girls how much Germany resembled the fairy-tale world of the Grimm brothers. We also visited the Chiemsee, a huge lake with two islands, on one of which sat mad King Ludwig's half-built replica of Versailles, and we spent a sunny afternoon at Schloss Linderhof, another of Ludwig's fairy-tale palaces, both of which, like so much built by the king, were celebratory memorials of Wagner's music and vision.

After that we drove over the Alps to Italy and explored the museums, streets, and alleys of Florence and Rome. We also spent several days in Assisi, a medieval hill town that Jana, who was enthralled with its most famous citizen, St. Francis, insisted on seeing. But for all the small adventures we had in Italy, the one that comes to mind again and again occurred as we meandered through the narrow shadowy lanes and over the humped stone bridges of Venice. In Venice, meandering is not as easy as one might think. We were pulled along with crowds from one piazza to another, trying to escape the press of rushing tourists around us, looking for a side street. Suddenly we saw one. The crowd continued in another direction, as we veered off into a shadowy passageway that was more an alley than a street. After several hundred yards, we turned a corner and found ourselves in an empty piazza. A profusion of sunlight lit the plaza like a stage set waiting for the entrance of the actors. The silence was particularly noticeable after the boisterous crowds. We looked at one another other and up at the signs and

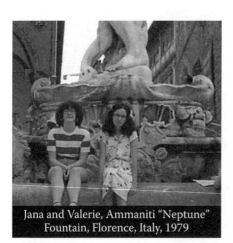

Jana and Valerie, Ammaniti "Neptune" Fountain, Florence, Italy, 1979

realized we had entered the old Jewish section of the city. Around the edges of the plaza were shop fronts and residences with uncurtained windows. Inside were tables and chairs haphazardly positioned and covered with dust. Shafts of sunlight fell on them through the grimy panes. I shivered. It was like looking at a museum display that had nothing to exhibit, just an indication that once there had been a people and a story there. No one knew any longer who the people were nor what their story was. It was a museum of the anonymous dead. Jana and Valerie looked at me uneasily, and I knew they were thinking the same thing. Despite our discomfort, we didn't leave. We went up to one empty building after another and peered in the windows as if paying homage to our ancestors.

The girls and I traveled together for three weeks. In the end, I thought we were closer than we had ever been, and I hoped we had memories to share far into the future.

■ ■ ■

After I bundled the girls onto a plane home in Frankfurt, I drove the station wagon to Aachen, Bruges, Belgium, and, on a car ferry, to Great Britain.

On that second trip, I had been impressed by Rogier Van der Weyden's painting, "Saint Luke Draws a Picture of the Virgin," in Munich's Alte Pinakothek museum. Several weeks later, I was surprised to see the same painting in the Museum de Beaux Arts in Bruges. When I returned to America, I researched the painting and found the "original" was in the Boston Museum of Fine Arts, two others in Luxembourg and Munich, and a fourth, mutilated version in the Hermitage in Leningrad in the Soviet Union. No version was listed as being in Bruges. When I called the curator of the Department of Paintings at the Boston Museum and informed him of my find in Bruges, he huffily said I didn't know what I was talking about. I replied in kind and told him he should at least check my information. Next morning he called back, apologizing profusely. The copy of the painting in Luxembourg had been donated to the Bruges museum, and the Museum of Fine Arts hadn't been informed. "Thank you, thank you," he said. "Whatever we can do for you, we will . . ." He went on to say that, for reasons of security, it was vitally important the museum knew the whereabouts of the other versions of the painting at all times.

Both my visit to the Documentation Center and the discovery of the four versions of the Saint Lukes, along with a number of other incidents I experienced in Germany, found their way into the tour de force novel of intrigue I wrote after *The Brezhnev Memo*. The novel is also an existential narrative of life in the last part of the twentieth century. It is yet to be published.

In 1984, I took my mother to Germany. We stayed at Ed and Inge's. They entertained us royally and were fascinated by my mother. Then I took her on a tour of Bavaria and Austria, showing her palaces and cathedrals and museums and the beauties of the landscape. It was the first time we had traveled together since I was a boy, and she was delighted to be with me and gasped in flamboyant wonderment at all I showed her, although when she returned to New York she told my cousin Carol that "all Morton did was drag me in and out of churches, churches, churches."

■ ■ ■

During the 1980s, I made several trips to England, where I house-sat for my friend, fellow poet and travel writer Robin Magowan. Born into the Fortune 500 family headed by his grandfather, Charles Merrill, a founding partner of the legendary investment firm of Merrill Lynch, Robin spent his early years shuttling between a fabled five-story Manhattan town-house and his

Robin Magowan,
Connecticut, 2007

grandfather's Southampton estate, and he received a classic Ivy League education that would have made Jay Gatsby gasp with envy: Exeter, Harvard, and advanced degrees from Columbia and Yale. Next he taught for several years at the University of California at Berkeley in the tumultuous 1960s, and it was during that time I met him at a *Kayak* collating party.

Magowan's father was Robert Magowan, a poor but ambitious man, who worked his way up in Merrill Lynch and was offered by his father-in-law, as Robin put it, "the choice of running Merrill Lynch, 'the world's greatest money-making machine,' as I remember him calling it, or Safeway." Magowan chose Safeway and built it into the second largest supermarket chain in the United States with, at one time, almost two thousand stores nationwide. He then attempted to pull young Robin and his four brothers into the business in order to continue the family dynasty in his name. But Robin's vivacious mother and her brother, Robin's "Uncle Jimmy," had shown Robin the life of art and culture—and in Robin's case their influence prevailed.

It was a life Uncle Jimmy was well disposed to proselytize, since he was one of the most lauded American poets of the second half of the century: James Merrill, Robin's mentor and in later years cherished friend, who, says Robin, "may have created me out of nothing—the Southampton vacuity, the dreams darting like dragonflies at my boy's feet."

The world Robin Magowan comes from is hard to imagine in America of the new millennium. Such wealth is no longer "practiced." In my youth, it was called "old money" and implied an elegant and highly cultured society. Today's sudden millionaires and their interests are crass in comparison and would have been referred to derogatorily as "nouveau riche" a half century ago. Robin's world is an upper-class world of school neckties and tweed jackets during the day and formal evening attire at night.

Being with Robin is like being back in prep school but with someone who has the same interests as me and who I like as well as respect. Although raised with all the privileges of great wealth, he is unassuming and gentle. Initially our friendship grew out of our love of modern Greek music and culture but soon spread to other areas where we found common ground, especially in poetry and travel. Our meetings are always full of trust and good feeling, although I see him irregularly, since he is always traveling, immersing himself in the ways of different cultures found in such places as

Greece, Haiti, pre-Castro Cuba, Samarkand, Bukhara, the Amazon jungle, and Southeast Asia. But whenever he comes to San Francisco we get together as old friends, either at an out-of-the way ethnic restaurant, his parents' mansion, or at a family wedding. Of course, I also spent time with Robin in London on those trips when I house-sat his three-story town house, and in 2002 he and his new bride Juliet were guests at my younger daughter Valerie's wedding in the Berkshires, which was twenty miles from Robin's new and I think permanent home.

Robin is what I would call a spiritual sensualist and seeks rapture and ecstasy, so it is not surprising that his life has been filled with torrid love affairs, including a character-transforming relationship with Nancy Ling Perry, who, a year after her liaison with him, became the principal architect of the Symbionese Liberation Army, the revolutionary outlaws who kidnapped and brainwashed Patty Hearst and, unbeknownst to the public, had targeted Robin and his father as their next victims before their fatal shootout with police in Los Angeles.

As can be imagined, in his writing Robin seeks to capture the moment in all its sensual aspects. His early work was extraordinarily erotic, and his opulent style more rococo than baroque, a cascade of sensuous images as intoxicating as a dozen incenses swirling through a shadowy flowershop where the flowers lean rapaciously toward the buyer with open mouths and deep throats.

His travel writing and his later writing on birds is filled with acute observations centered around his experiences. His poetry, a quest of pure sensation, is full of sensuous description and is at times composed of fragments: sentences broken into phrases and individual words, creating discordant rhythms as he tears away connectives and normal syntax to grasp (express?) the vocable that will evoke the experience of whatever he is writing about. In "Eye in the Wind," he examines, from several perspectives, the simple act of opening a window. But what at first seems simultaneously rational and sensory, as if he were two people going about the same domestic chore, is revealed to be a subconscious undertaking.

Eye in the Wind

Can the freedom of enactment
wait for the window to be flung open
that wind in its disarray
may circulate more freely?
No, it's a more internal opening
the blue beyond gives
as if picking up a pen
and going to the window
were a discovery of mouth
and glass simultaneously
one hand reaching
under the other's ripening envelope

and walking into the light
alone together calm
one within the other

■ ■ ■

An unforgettable side trip on my first visit to England was a journey to the
Edinburgh Festival with another friend, the historian Bradley Smith, and his
filmmaker wife, Jenny Wilkes. Besides being a colleague at Cabrillo, Brad was
a historian renowned for his findings and interpretations concerning World
War II and the Nazi era, which he published in eleven highly respected

books. It was he who had secured my pass to the Berlin
Documentation Center through the Hoover Institute.
Over the years, we spent a number of high-spirited times
together, in particular several Thanksgivings with his
daughters and mine when we were single fathers. In
addition to his teaching and writing, Brad was a social
activist and had taken leave from Cabrillo to teach at a
black college in the South during the height of the civil
rights movement. Personally, he was irreverent and had
a wry sense of humor. Jenny was highly talented and as
outspoken and rambunctious as Brad. Years later, one of
her short films would be nominated for an Academy
Award. All in all, we were a merry threesome. At Edin-

Brad Smith, Santa
Cruz, 2001

burgh, Jenny had Brad and me pose as filmmakers, and we were included in a
number of insider events. More important, we enjoyed the perks of the
British Film School. From there, the three of us traveled to the Lake District,
where Wordsworth and Coleridge had founded the English Romantic movement, and we continued on to an estate in southern Wales, where we stayed
in a sixteenth-century gamekeeper's cottage with no toilet and only cold running water from a nearby well. The cottage was two miles from any road, and
hidden on the property was a bright, robin's-egg-blue witch's cabin, which
looked as if it was still being lived in although it was tumbled on its side in a
forest ravine. A mile further on was an abandoned country church built on a
druid's circle. The path leading up to the church was part of an old Roman
road, and looking back over the countryside from the church, I could see the
two-thousand-year-old highway slithering over hill and dale into the treeless
distance. These historical secrets were shown to us by the leaseholder of the
cottage, Jenny's friend, the painter and former journalist Robert MacDonald,
who, with his wife Annie, also became good friends.

During this same visit to Britain, an interesting incident occurred with
the well-known poet and playwright Michael McClure. While I was staying
in London, I saw an announcement on TV that McClure was to read on a
segment of a popular TV variety show that was shot in front of a live audience, and since I was alone and feeling homesick, I went to the studio the

night of the performance. I had known Michael well enough in San Francisco to invite him to read at Cabrillo, and so when the overly polite usher led me to my seat and asked if I needed anything else, I told him on a whim to go backstage and tell Michael I was in the audience and wished him good luck.

To my surprise, the usher came back minutes later saying that Michael wanted to see me. I found him in a bare room backstage, striding nervously back and forth. This struck me immediately, since Michael's deportment is the essence of the word "cool," his exquisite good looks usually as expressionless as a Greek statue's.

"Thank God you're here," he said, grabbing my hand. "Allen and Christopher were supposed to be here, but they're not."

Michael was coming from a jamboree of Beat-Generation writers in Holland, and the Allen and Christopher he referred to were Allen Ginsberg and the British poet Christopher Logue.

"I'm going to die out there tonight," he continued. "I hear these English audiences are deadly."

He went on like that for several minutes, and I found myself reassuring him that he was going to be a hit. I meant it. I had seen him on stage at least half a dozen times, and he intuitively knew what to do to win the enthusiasm of the most hostile audience.

I went back to my seat. Michael was preceded by the Charlie Daniels Band, a lively American country music group that was at the height of their international popularity. The audience cheered their performance. As any poet knows, following a musical group with a reading is a difficult assignment. When Michael walked on stage, the audience applauded respectfully, but they were obviously looking forward to the act after him and were preparing themselves to endure his contribution to the evening. Michael decided to read his lion poems, a series of roars and growls, which were greeted with stunned, uncomfortable silence. I thought I could see a sheen of perspiration on Michael's face. He recited another lion roar poem, which was again greeted with silence. Then he turned his back to the audience, straightened his shoulders, turned back to the front of the theater again, and without introduction began to recite the first eleven lines of Chaucer's Canterbury Tales in Middle English. The audience went wild, and from then on Michael could do no wrong.

Afterward, I went out with Michael and several other writers, one of whom was Ginsberg, who I knew slightly and who had arrived shortly before the reading. As we took our places in the pub, and Michael accepted compliments from everyone, he turned to me, his demeanor once more calm and expressionless.

"What did I tell you," I said. He broke into a smile and nodded, while Ginsberg looked from one of us to the other, wondering what we were talking about.

■ ■ ■

Left to right: Bruce and Marcia McDougal, Lisa and Jim Aschbacher, Donna and Morton Marcus, Santa Cruz, 1999

I was accompanied on part of my second trip to England by Donna, who would be my traveling companion thereafter. She knew Brad and Jenny, and Bob took us to stay in the cottage on the estate in Wales for a few days. For my retirement in 1998, Donna took me to Lake Como in Italy. We stayed for three weeks in the town of Bellagio in a room overlooking the lake. Nightly, seemingly for our edification, the lake was bombarded by cannonades of thunder, lightning, and sudden torrential rainstorms. On sunny mornings, tens of thousands of birds chortled madrigals in the trees. We spent our days exploring the decaying nineteenth-century villas, in one of which the Romantic poet Percy Bysche Shelley had stayed, and roamed about the lake and countryside or took picnics to the exotic gardens of the Villa Melzi built two hundred years before by the vice president of the Italian republic and friend of Napoleon Bonaparte. Wherever I went, I seemed to be enveloped by history and was constantly reminded of how past and present entwined in a never-ending continuum.

The same was true in 2001 when Donna and I traveled to France, where my old friends Bruce and Marcia McDougal had bought a converted mill in Burgundy, which had been built during the Napoleonic era. We were accompanied by another couple, Lisa Jensen and Jim Aschbacher. Lisa is a film critic and novelist and Jim, a self-taught artist. All six of us are artists in one way or another, but what had drawn us together several years before our first trip, I think, was that we were three loving couples who brought no marital tensions or doubts to our dinners and conversations and so felt comfortable and open with one another. When we started traveling

With Donna at the McDougal's "Moulin," Burgundy, France, 2005

together, we found that the love each of us bore our mate had created a sense of caring for others that extended to the group, and the friendship between the six of us reached a rare level of camaraderie and trust it still maintains. In the summer of 2005, the six of us, at Jim's request, journeyed from the mill in Burgundy to the medieval city of Bern, Switzerland, for the opening of the Paul Klee museum, and I thought the city as well as the museum were extraordinary finds. In all cases, the present contained acute reminders of the past.

Most of my travels since 1989, however, have been to Croatia (formerly part of Yugoslavia), where Donna's forebears came from, and most of my contemplations have been on the problems in the Balkans, that troubled area rich in traditional folkways and all the pettiness, internecine strife, and ethnic hatreds that go with them, as well as some of the more glorious examples of human compassion and dignity. That Greece is part of the Balkans and that Russia has protectively overseen this area of Slavic inhabitants for several centuries, is no small part of my interest in it. I have come to see the Balkans as the petri dish of humanity where virulent and benign microbes wiggle near, rub against, or ram into one another in a microcosm of the human condition.

CHAPTER 41

Croatia

My seven visits to Croatia brought to completion all the notions I had formulated on my other travels and greatly influenced the content of my writings.

For years George Hitchcock had been urging me to visit Yugoslavia. He was impressed by the physical height, health, and forthrightness of the people. Vasko Popa had urged me to come as well, and, of course, so had Charlie Simic, who was a Serb and had spent his boyhood there, living through the Nazi occupation. But it wasn't until I met Donna that I finally visited the country.

Donna is Croatian on her father's side. He was born in America, but both his parents were from the Konavle Valley on the Dalmatian coast, fifteen miles south of the old walled city of Dubrovnik and ten miles north of the Montenegrin border.

Many of the immigrants from the valley and the area around it had migrated to Watsonville, California, at the turn of the twentieth century, and by the 1920s a large percentage of that agricultural community was composed of "Slav" farmers and apple growers.

The Slavic connection, of course, had been irresistible to me long before I met Donna, and my interest in Yugoslavia had been sparked by my dealings with Popa and Charlie. I had begun collecting the national magazine *Yugoslavia Today* five years before I met Donna, and when I found out she was of Croatian descent, I showed her the magazines and urged her to get interested in her background. Although she had fond memories of her grandparents and various childhood events connected to the Watsonville Croatian community, my efforts were only slightly successful until 1989 when Donna's father proposed we join him on a trip to Dubrovnik with his brother, his brother's daughter, and Donna's mother.

Donna and I had been planning to go to Greece, and Croatia could easily be added to the trip. We would fly from San Francisco to the Dalmatian coast for a week, then fly to Belgrade where we would catch another flight to Athens. I was enthusiastic because such a route would allow me to finally visit Vasko Popa, who lived in Belgrade and had never returned to the

United States after his visit in 1970. I made arrangements with him by letter and phone through a Croatian-speaking friend, and we were off.

Although contemporary Yugoslav politics would soon shock me and the rest of the world with its virulence, my first impression of Croatia was of a land time had forgotten. There was something medieval, ancient, even primordial about the southern Dalmatian coast that seemed to inform everything that took place on it. The terrain was rugged, all rock and mountains. Some of the rock was crumbling sandstone, but mostly it was naked white limestone streaked with rusty brown mineral deposits. Tough, short bushes gripped the ground between the rocks, and the trees were short and gnarled with sharp, dusty foliage. Slim, spiraling cypresses, groves of olive trees, stunted oak, fir, laurel, juniper, bearberry, prickly-leafed holly, and spiky heather clustered together or dotted the fields like clumps of shrubs. But it was the limestone the eye kept coming back to; it was everywhere: steep, treeless mountains of it or sheer cliffs that in places fell a thousand feet to the Adriatic Sea from highways without guard rails that had been hacked from the mountainsides. The limestone was such an integral part of southern Croatian life that it was used for the basic building blocks of the houses and stacked as walls to separate and define ownership of the stony fields. Snarled vines and bunches of many colored flowers jutted from these walls and brightened the landscape's dusty greenness. At times the landscape was softened, especially when seen from a distance, by dense green groves of

Konavle Valley, Croatia, 1989

pine and other conifers that seemed even greener along the coast due to their bordering the startling blue waters of the Adriatic.

If the land seemed from another time, so did the people. They pursued agriculture as they had for hundreds, maybe thousands of years in the rich twenty-mile-long Konavle Valley, and they followed customs and dress whose origins were lost in antiquity. They were a hardy people, tall and healthy, as Hitchcock had said, and it was with them in their stone cottages that I spent my time, for they were Donna's relatives, welcoming and eager to please us as custom and their own friendly nature dictated they should. But it was more than custom that made them treat us so graciously. Andy, Donna's father, had visited them a half-dozen times in the past and over the years had done many favors for them in America, including undertaking money transactions for their benefit, while they remained virtually imprisoned as much by their poverty as by their socialist government. Andy had even acted as godfather for one of their children.

We visited a half-dozen relatives' houses in different communities on that first trip, but the reception, as it would be in the future, was always the same: tearful and happy, the people ushered us onto a patio or into the house where everything was scrubbed clean and settled us at a dining room table where a plate of goat's cheese and a platter of prosciutto sitting next to a bottle of clear grappa and a saucer of dried figs rimmed with pungent bay leaves awaited us. All were grown on the farm, and the welcome and snacks never varied. Only the grappa, distinctively flavored with a variety of grasses and herbs by each family, was different.

Cavtat, south of Dubrovnik, Croatia, 1989

In the beginning, the talk was almost exclusively about family, first catching up on individual stories and then on family genealogy, meticulously going over relationships so they would never be forgotten. Finally, the talk turned to politics, and even then it was hard to reconcile these loving people with the atrocities that had been committed in their name against Serbs, Jews, and gypsies during World War II. In fact, of all the people I've traveled among, the populace of the south Dalmatian coast is the least violent and warlike I've ever met. But the population is 95 percent Roman Catholic, and ingrained in their age-old customs and beliefs are ethnic and religious hatreds which inevitably emerged in the political conversations.

It was June 1989 when we arrived the first time, two years before the fragmenting of the Yugoslav federation, but I knew my history of the area and immediately detected the ethnic tension around me. The Konavle farmers we met complained about the Serbs in Belgrade taking their profits in taxes, and then Slobodan Milosevic delivered a rabble-rousing, pro-Serbian speech in Kosovo on the annual observance of the Serbian kingdom's loss to the Turks on the Field of Blackbirds on June 28, 1389. The speech was well publicized throughout Yugoslavia and Greece, where Donna and I learned of it.

Before then we had gone to Belgrade to visit Vasko, who I had unsuccessfully tried to raise by telephone several times from Croatia in order to cement our plans. When I went to his apartment, as I related before, I learned that he had broken his leg and was convalescing on the coast within ten miles of where I had been staying, but he had no way to reach me since I had no phone number in Croatia.

Since my planned day with Vasko had been cancelled, Donna and I had time to explore Belgrade. We found the apartment building where Charlie Simic had been born and raised, and that led to a poem where, among other things, I was able to voice questions about the way Charlie viewed our relationship, while at the same time affirming our Slavic and poetic brotherhood. I had called him before I left for Croatia to ask if he had a message for Popa and to tell him I wanted to look up the house where he had been born in Belgrade. Charlie was surprised and, it seemed to me, a bit put off by the second part of my request. He couldn't understand why I would want to make such a side trip,

A typical Konavle Valley cottage, hundreds of years old, 1989

whereas it seemed the most natural desire in the world to me. His quizzical response, however, made me question how he saw our friendship, and the poem addresses the multiple reasons why I, or anyone else, would want to make such a visit. The second stanza reads in part

> Perplexed silence channeled
> through the phone wire
> when I told you
> I wanted to visit
> this three story,
> cocoa-colored building.
> Once more you didn't know
> if I were friend,
> idolizing fan,
> or lost Slavic brother
> in need of encouragement
> to continue on.
>
> It's all of those, Charlie.
> And make no mistake,
> this *is* a pilgrimage.
> It is to renew belief,
> revitalize purpose
> that we locate those places
> where journeys meaningful
> to our lives began,
> or paused, or ended . . .
> Its specific detail
> destroys anonymity.
> It is this house, Charlie,
> or your poems.
> —from "Majke Jevrosime #3"

The first stanza of the poem, written later that summer, illustrates the ethnic unrest I sensed in Belgrade. Everyone we encountered seemed impatient, as if waiting for something to happen, and the few people we talked to complained about the Croats having all the money because of their location on the coast, where Tito had put vast sums of state funds into building grandiose hotels to attract foreign visitors.

I was aware by the time of my first visit in 1989 that the Yugoslav economic surge of the 1970s had come to a standstill. Tito had died in 1980, and the government's attempt to repay foreign debts had led to austerity measures that, along with the world economic recession of the 1980s, had been disastrous. One million people were out of work. The jobless rate stood at 20 percent everywhere except in Slovenia and Croatia, and the country's double-digit inflation was out of control, destroying any possibility of savings and, as one commentator put it, "any sense of well-being the growing middle class may have had."

The six-hundred year-old Mekis ancestral home (with new shutters and roof), Croatia, 2006

An equally big factor, however, was that by the end of the 1980s the Soviet Union had loosened its hold over the East European countries it had dominated since the end of World War II. No one could have known of the Soviet collapse that was to come two years after my first visit to Croatia, but the easing of social and political restrictions that had gone on through the 1980s had shown Eastern Europeans the possibilities of democratization, even in Yugoslavia, which had not been under Soviet control.

As the decade moved toward political freedom in Eastern Europe, the targets of prejudice in most East European countries changed. No longer were the pro-Communist regimes castigating the middle classes and the Western capitalist system. Now, friends returning from Eastern Europe told me, in the absence of the government-inspired targets, old ethnic and racial hatreds that had simmered for centuries once more had risen to the surface, a reaction the members of the republics of the Yugoslav federation seemed to long for and which I encountered as I traveled from one ethnic region to another.

I knew that Tito had condemned ethnic conflict and nationalism. He saw them as the two elements that could destroy the Yugoslav experiment, and he had spent his years in power promoting what he called "brotherhood and unity." He can be seen as the arbiter among the ethnic factions of the federation. Tito was a Croat whose partisan forces in World War II were composed of a majority of Serbs. After the war, on the basis of his federalist ideals, he refused to allow the Serbs to take reprisals against the Croats for their atrocities against the Serbian population. In the thirty-five years of his rule, he instituted and carried out various programs to promote unity, and one of the tragedies of the wars of 1991–1999 was the breakup of families composed of Serbs, Croats, and Bosnians who had grown up and embraced his ideas during his tenure as premier by intermarrying.

Do I get ahead of myself? Not really. As we flew out of Belgrade that June night in 1989, I turned to Donna and said, "From what I've seen in Croatia and Serbia, there'll be ethnic war in the next year or two."

Don't misunderstand. If I was sensitive to the ethnic tensions around me, they were a small part of the experience of that first trip. I would never forget the peoples' warmth and friendliness and the country's rugged beauty. Nor would my memories of Donna's loving relatives in their stone farmhouses that had stood for six hundred years lessen over the years, despite the sorrow and bitterness that followed. Donna's father translated for everyone, and tears of joy and much laughter are my overall recollections of that first visit. We also journeyed to many of the famous sites in the surrounding regions, driving to Mostar and its famous eleventh-century arched bridge, and then spent a day in Medjugorje, where since 1981 a handful of Roman Catholic children had continually seen visions of the Virgin Mary. We took Donna's great aunt to see the town, which had become a Catholic pilgrimage site. Every hour, busloads of people arrived at the remote village to be greeted by dozens of hawkers selling cheap tourist trinkets of the supposed visions and of the children. The carnival-like atmosphere in Medjugorje was almost as depressing as the hostility in Mostar where we were eyed with suspicion by the Bosnian inhabitants, who were also selling cheap tourist memorabilia.

If my first trip to Greece had shown me that the old gods of the earth and all the epochs of history were present in our everyday world, Yugoslavia left me with a sense of anxiety of what lay beneath political motivations and a brooding awareness of ethnic chauvinism. When Donna and I returned on our second visit in 1998, again in company with my father-in-law, my fears had been realized. The war in Croatia from 1991 to 1996 had left indelible marks on the landscape and the people. My father-in-law and I drove around the area where we had stayed nine years before, finding devastation and bitterness everywhere. 78 percent of the housing in the region had been destroyed, and bullet holes pocked the limestone walls in one village after another. Roofless ruins were now a part of the landscape, and the statues in the churches had been defaced or destroyed.

More telling was the absence of the Serbs we had met on our first visit, chief among them the man whose house we had rented during our first stay. He had lived in Mlini, a small village ten miles south of Dubrovnik, and had worked as a concierge in the large, modern, state-run hotel on the coast a mile or two below his spacious home. A go-getter in his mid-thirties, he dreamed of material prosperity and was tirelessly working for his wife and two children. When my father-in-law and I drove to the house, we found it had been totally destroyed—not even a wall was standing—and when we went down to the hotel, we found that it was now a bombed-out concrete ruin with wires swinging in the breeze and rubble scattered over its once palatial entrance. We also looked for our former host, but no one seemed to remember who he was or that his house had ever existed. The Serbs and Montenegrins may have invaded and devastated the area, but when the Croats reestablished control, they had eradicated the Serbian presence in their midst.

With Donna in Mostar, Bosnia, 1989

It was during that same visit that I befriended an English-speaking former lieutenant in the Croatian Army, and he arranged a clandestine meeting for me with his old unit commander. We drove to a roadhouse restaurant in what must have been a remote area of Bosnia just across the
Croatian border. Brawny men in camouflage clothing, all with shaved heads
and automatic weapons, lounged outside the single-story stone building.
Inside, I was introduced to the unit's leader, a major. His eyes were the dead-
est I've ever seen, and he talked to me in English for two hours in a rolling
monotone about the Serbian atrocities he had seen and how he and his unit
were avenging them. I thought, but dared not say, that the war had been
over for two years. I listened and heard the hurt and bitterness in the
major's words. As he recounted his acts of vengeance, there was no pleasure
in his face or voice. He was doing what had to be done, his monotone
implied, and his matter-of-fact descriptions conveyed a sense that he was
caught in age-old acts and counteracts, atrocities and reprisals.

The major told me many stories. One of the most chilling and, unfortunately, most typical occurred during the early days of the war when his
hometown was under siege and Croatian Serb citizens had taken to sniping
from their apartments at Croats on the street, a crime that was hard to control since it was difficult to detect where the shots were coming from. One
day a young woman carrying a baby was shot and killed crossing an inter-
section. The bullet had gone through the infant and fatally wounded the
woman. When the major, then newly commissioned, arrived on the scene,
he recognized the woman as a high school classmate.

Typical vegetation in Konavle Valley, Croatia, 2006

As luck would have it, an old man identified the sniper's window in a high-rise apartment house nearby. The major and two enlisted men rushed up to the eleventh floor and broke down the door of the apartment from which the telltale window looked out on the street. Kneeling at the sill, rifle in hand, was the sniper, a Croatian Serb. The major immediately recognized the sniper as a fellow high school classmate who had been on good terms with both him and the dead woman. The major also noticed a high-powered scope on the rifle: the shooting, therefore, was not random—the man had identified the face of the person he purposely shot.

"Don't kill me," the sniper said, dropping the rifle.

"I'm not going to touch you," the major said he answered, "and I'll let you walk away from this totally free when you get to the street. But the only way to get there is through the window."

The man didn't want to jump, so the major "helped him."

"I helped many Serbs out windows during the war," he concluded without irony.

What's typical about this story is the depth of ethnic hatred that emerged again and again during the war—inexplicable cruelty perpetrated by one neighbor against another, which begat equal or greater cruelty from the victims or the ethnic group to which the victims belonged. Vengeance was the order of the day.

I found such anger everywhere. One of the relatives we had visited on our first trip, who had complained about the Serbian-dominated central government's taxes, refused, with a table-slamming fist, to allow the word "Serb" to be used in his presence. He was living in a two-bedroom stone cottage with twelve members of the family. His home, a modern brick structure he and his sons had built with their own hands, had been dynamited by the Yugoslav People's Army to a heap of rubble, and his farm equipment and livestock had been stolen by the Montenegrin militia. Worse, all twelve family members had been forced to live in two rooms of an abandoned hotel for several years during the occupation.

On my third visit, two years later, that same relative had rebuilt his house, and the region had begun to recover. A year later, on our fourth visit, he and other Croatians were trying to put the memories of the war behind them, but the anger seethed everywhere under the surface. I remember one riotous, drunken night around a big table in that new house. We were celebrating a relative's birthday, the completion of the house, and a return to normalcy for the region. As we drank and ate—all the food and wine once more grown by the family on their farm—the relatives began singing old Croatian folk songs with a fierce determination, as if the words were summoning up the reestablishment of ethnic pride and dominance. Besides the old people and the man's children, the guests included cousins from Bosnia who had trekked to Croatia during the war. One, a big, burly man, had enlisted with his brother in the Croatian Army on his arrival. In his first battle, he had seen his brother shot through the head at his side and been splattered with his brains. In another battle, he had lost a leg, and he humped on his synthetic limb in and out of the dining room to the barbecue pit outside. The singing was joyous on the surface but tinged with bitterness and anger. I came away from the evening with an overwhelming sense of loss and irreparable damage.

On subsequent visits, the war receded in conversation, and well-being returned with unexpected swiftness, but ethnic anger remained everywhere I went, like an underground stream waiting to break into the daylight once more.

That impression was put into words by another person I met on my fourth and fifth visits, the United Nations governor of southern Croatia and Montenegro. He told me what was going on beneath the placid surface of everyday life, especially in the province of Kosovo, which at the end of the century had become the focus of Serbian and Albanian strife. The situation seemed hopeless, an ethnic explosion that was waiting to happen all over the former Federation of Yugoslavia.

If I found all of this depressing, a little side trip on my fourth visit put everything into perspective. Donna and I were driven to a graveyard on the high plains of the tallest mountains above the valley by the owner of our pension. He and his family had become our friends on our two previous trips, and he knew I wanted to see a famous tombstone in the small, overgrown cemetery in the hamlet of Brotnice.

There are thousands of these tombstones and sarcophagi in Bosnia, Herzegovina, and parts of Dalmatia and Montenegro, their stone surfaces intricately carved eight hundred to a thousand years ago with scenes of hunting, dancing, and various animals and plants. The inhabitants who made them are long gone, and there is controversy as to who they were. Inscriptions on the stones are also controversial, identified by some as early Cyrillic writing and by others as Glagolitic. As Ivo Andric, the Yugoslav Nobel Prize writer remarked on seeing them in their wild, weed- and lichen-overgrown settings, "This is a land that has lost its history."

The gravestone in Brotnice, Croatia, 2006

The gravestone in the Brotnice cemetery stands five feet high and six feet wide. One side is covered with carvings of deer, a giant bird of prey clutching an animal in its talons, a wolf devouring a lamb, a giant snake slithering to the edge of the stone, and a rider on horseback carrying a bow. On the other side are rows of birds, deer, and humans. Both sides, however, are highlighted by lines of anonymous, skirted dancers, their arms joined, their featureless faces eroded by time. The figures and their meanings have been interpreted in various ways, and I'm no expert on European medieval art. But one night, months after I had returned to the United States, a night when I was particularly depressed by the world situation and the vicious ways people treat one another, I thought about the tombstone and began to write about that tiny cemetery and its landscape so far away and remote from the bustling cities of power and modernity. The result was the prose poem, "Moon and Flower." It is not only one of my favorite poems but one which expresses all I have learned from my travels. The last stanza reads as follows:

> Tonight, quiet, having contemplated all evening the ends of empire—palaces and skyscrapers toppling over the precipice of time—and having been moved to melancholy by the moonlight beyond the window, I thought of the standing stone high in the moonlight of that other place thousands of miles away, and imagined a breeze slipping over the crescent moon and the stone flower and then passing over the skirted figures, who in their place on top of the world, night after night, year after year, their movements open only to the gaze of the blind universe, continue to dance.

PART

We shall not cease from exploration
And the end of all our exploring
Will be to arrive where we started
And know the place for the first time.
—T. S. Eliot

BOOK TWELVE

LOOKING FOR LAMED VOVNIKS

CHAPTER 42

George Ow, Jr.

This book has evolved, at least in part, into a gallery of portraits, recounting incidents at which I was present that reveal character. If certain people have not fared well in my account of them, I did not set out to tarnish their reputations. By far the majority of the portraits paint pictures of integrity, courage, and other beneficent traits—and in almost all of them, I found worthy qualities that have kept in check my increasingly skeptical attitudes about human nature.

There is a beautiful Jewish legend, my favorite story in the vast repository of folklore, that claims the planet continues to exist because there are always at least thirty-six righteous men and women in the world at one time. Because of their essential goodness, God does not destroy the rest of us, his miserable creations. Should the number of these people slip below thirty-six, however, God would eradicate our world in the wink of a star. These just beings, called *lamed vovniks,* feel the collective suffering of humanity and respond to it with acts of benevolence that redeem us all. In almost all cases, the thirty-six are unaware of their sanctity and go about their lives unacknowledged and unknown, enduring the same trials and sufferings we all do. Most of the time, they are poor or destitute and never learn of their importance in the scheme of things, which, because of their humility, they wouldn't believe if they were told of it by a full-winged angel.

I have no doubt been looking for lamed vovniks all my life, not just as father or mother figures, but as people in whom I can see operating those values that I hold to be the only hope of human survival. I have known only a handful of people who I consider meet my criteria for this status, and I am tempted to write about all of them. Certainly I could have included Vasili Karagiannopoulos, a small, wiry, bushy-bearded Greek American restaurant owner whose joy in life is expressed in kindness to everyone around him and is most clearly demonstrated in his obsession with feeding people and, by extension, nourishing the entire community through any charitable cause to which he is asked to contribute. How many meals he gave away for one reason or another are uncountable. But the most telling example of his nurturing goodness was his celebration of the tenth anniversary of his restaurant's opening. After renting a large hall and inviting two hundred of his most loyal customers and friends to the celebration, he personally cooked the crowd a full Greek dinner and danced away the rest of the evening with his grandson in his arms, kissing him endlessly like a pecking rooster.

Another candidate is Alvaro "Yaqui" Lopez, a light heavyweight boxer who lost all five shots at world titles, three of them due to poor and most probably corrupt officiating, yet he never complained and endured his tribulations with a dignity that inspired respect and affection in everyone who met him, including his opponents. But those are public demonstrations of character he shares with a number of other athletes. The courage, humility, and essential goodness he has shown after his retirement are a different matter few people know about. With little money or education, and speaking English with difficulty, he took a job as a garbage man in his hometown of Stockton, California, only to injure his back so severely he had to go on disability for the rest of his life. Without bitterness, however, he continues to spread his good cheer among friends and acquaintances. Most tellingly, he visited his father-in-law, who had also been his manager, every day for years until the old man's death, cleaning his house as well as washing him, giving him insulin injections, making sure he took his medication, and spending hours entertaining him.

Or there is Jim Schwenterley, a small-town theater owner who continually lends his theater free of charge for benefits of all kinds and thinks nothing of it, least of all that he's doing anything out of the ordinary. When the Disney Company leased one of their new cartoon features to him, he sent word to the homeless shelters and orphanages in the area and held several showings of the film free to any children who could attend them. That is a typical example of his almost casual acts of benevolence and illustrative of his overall unassuming kindness.

There are a few other people I could mention, but among the small group who share the principles I deem necessary to be called lamed vovniks, three in particular, described here and in the next two chapters, stand out.

The first is George Ow, Jr., who I met at a bookstore even in Santa Cruze in 1981. George is a second-generation Chinese American whose father came from China to seek his fortune and, through a series of half-comic circumstances, became a millionaire.

George Ow Jr., Santa Cruz, 2006

George, as the oldest son, was sent to UCLA Business School and was quickly given responsibility for both the family business and his extended family's welfare. In Chinese families, the eldest son is responsible for a vast number of obligations and duties, and when he ascends to be head of the family, he becomes advisor, therapist, judge, and chief financial director as well. In George's case, this meant being responsible for parents, brothers, sisters, nieces, nephews, and, it seemed at times, any acquaintances. The pressure is enormous, and George, a slim, good-looking, athletic man (he ran cross-country in high school, and, well into his sixties, still practices yoga and surfs), deals with all these tasks diligently.

But what makes him exceptional in my eyes is not only his diligence in family matters, or his integrity and intelligence, but his deep concern for people and his boundless curiosity. As a boy, George was subject to endless incidents of racial prejudice, but as an adult he has shown no anger or vengeful inclinations. Instead, he meets people of all races with a warm greeting and endless questions about their lives and work.

George's concern for people goes beyond curiosity, however. To him people are not part of an anonymous populace but individuals. So it is not surprising that he gives large sums of money to one cause or another, awarding twenty to thirty scholarships to students at a time, nor that he also supports individuals in their quest for education and a better life. Although everyone shares equally in his philanthropy, he is partial to ethnic and racial minorities and the poor and continually supports people trying to escape lives damaged by alcohol and drugs.

He also gives large sums of money to cultural projects and is a major supporter of many art undertakings in Santa Cruz, from Shakespeare Santa Cruz, an annual festival of the bard's works presented by the University of California, to the Pacific Rim Film Festival, which for decades has brought films to Santa Cruz and filmmakers from cultures and countries existing, geographically, on the shores of the Pacific Ocean. Although I've helped him with many of these endeavors, I'm always surprised to find that he was the main financial support for many organizations and projects I knew nothing about. I remember going to the Chinese Historical Society of America Museum in San Francisco for an exhibit only to find that the Ow Family Properties, as he likes to call his philanthropy, had made such a sizeable donation that a plaque had been placed over the doorway of the main exhibition room. This is another instance where George, a shrewd businessman, demonstrates that he is equally concerned with the way his undertakings will benefit people at large as he is with financial profits.

George and I share a love of books. He is an avid reader and not uncommonly will read three or four books at a time on subjects ranging from literature, history, and business to mystery novels and social studies. Much of our friendship is spent discussing films and books, and we trade books by the hundreds, often buying them for each other.

George always wanted to own a bookstore, so, when a ski shop became vacant in one of his malls during the 1980s, he founded a bookstore, giving his partners the reins to run it and selling it to them to their advantage a decade later.

He also founded a publishing house that specializes in histories of the ethnic groups that have settled in the Monterey Bay area. His first book as publisher was Sandy Lydon's monumental study of the Chinese in Monterey Bay, *Chinese Gold*. But his subjects are not limited to Asian groups. When he heard Donna was writing a history of the Croatians in Watsonville, he offered to publish the volume sight unseen and continues to inquire about its progress.

His support of my work has been unstinting. I felt awkward about his assistance at first because I considered him more a friend than a benefactor, but he would hear none of my excuses and found one way or another to support my books and projects. He has referred to me as his "minister of culture" and his "Tang dynasty poet" and has undertaken almost every art project I suggested to him, from support of indigent writers to dance concerts and avant-garde musical presentations.

I think George understood from the beginning that my promoting art was for the good of artists and, in the end, for the benefit of the community. He recognized my desire to help others as a way of making the world a better place. Many times he has told me that we have our different roles, I as an artist and promoter of artists, and he as a source of financial support for those undertakings.

Although I am essentially an extroverted, emotional talker and he is an introverted, quiet listener, our personalities are similar in many ways. Both of us can be brought to tears by the sufferings of others or by revelations of human compassion and integrity, and we've sat through a number of films together, sniffing quietly at what we were watching. In later years, we have regularly met for breakfast at one restaurant or another, and when I tell him a poignant tale of people I've known or an incident that has just happened, tears spring to his eyes. I've dedicated several poems to him over the years, but none was more personal than the prose poem, "Men Who Cry," which is one of my favorites and was inspired by one such breakfast incident.

Our breakfasts together are almost never prearranged. I'll call him a day in advance, but mostly he calls me on the spur of the moment after he finishes surfing or exercising in yoga class, his two early morning routines. We meet at one of several restaurants in town, either alone, in which case we talk animatedly about books and films, or with the other three members of our breakfast club, in which case we discuss local politics, business, and culture. In the company of the breakfast club, whose members I'll talk about later, George is usually quiet and listens.

In the hubbub of talk around us—amid the mingled scents of coffee, bacon, glazed pastries and the clatter of dishes and clinking silverware—people drop by to say hello to George—old friends from childhood, business acquaintances, and local characters—and George is always delighted to see them. He is never "cordial," a word which suggests detachment, even standoffishness. He is always effusive in his greetings, as outgoing and full of questions with waiters, cashiers, and people he meets for the first time as he is with local politicians and businessmen. Even the mentally challenged postal worker who frequents one of the restaurants we patronize will come up to the table and regale George with his latest accomplishments, which George listens to like a proud cousin.

Strangers are also treated to George's open, friendly response, and I remember a number of times his welcoming smile to people leaning over from another table to add a comment to our expansive conversation. Inevitably, those encounters continue with George asking the speakers' names, where they are from, and conducting a five-minute dialogue with them. By the same token, when we run into someone we know, even if it is a distant acquaintance, George almost always asks them to join us. If the person happens to be someone I know and George doesn't, he will ask the person to join us and then proceed to question the person out of genuine curiosity in order to get to know him or her.

After breakfast, we stroll through town. During the rainy season we may head over to the river to watch the water and tree branches rushing by, or, if we are breakfasting near the bay, we amble down to the wharf and examine the swirling surf flashing in the sunlight or slithering gray and ominous out of the fog. At other times we walk into bookstores and buy each other books. No matter where we are, someone comes up to say hello to one or the other of us.

If the two of us have breakfast in a residential part of town, we meander through the neighborhoods, searching for architecturally interesting houses or following with boyish excitement the course of rushing rivulets that have been diverted underground by drainage pipes but rise unexpectedly in backyards and the middle of streets every now and then, giving us a hint of the marshy, stream-covered landscape the padres encountered when they founded the Santa Cruz mission in 1791.

On all these walks, two things usually occur. First, George engages anyone we come across in conversation, always outgoing and curious about who they are and what they are doing, whether we find them on the levee above the river or puttering in their front yards. But it is the second incident which occurs during our strolls that I find most telling. Whenever we come upon thrown-away candy wrappers, soiled styrene cups, empty cans, or refuse of any kind, George unobtrusively picks it up and carries it with him until he finds a trash can in which to deposit it. It is a small, unconscious act, but it illustrates for me the essence of communal concern. Maybe that's why each time I wander through town with George, I feel I am part of a community that he, through all his efforts, is trying to preserve and enrich.

If the portrait I have drawn of George sounds like an impossible, idealized picture of a saint, then I must conclude that he is just that. It seems he does nothing that is selfish or ego driven, and I can recall dozens of times when his actions astounded people. One example of many similar incidents occurred when a Chinese American documentary filmmaker showed her history of the Chinese in America at the university. Without being asked, George set up a table in the rear of the auditorium and personally sold copies of the videos for her profit.

To George's chagrin, I have introduced him at various events as the last of the Renaissance patrons. He is that, and more, a humanist and a humanitarian who I think of as an example of what human beings can be whenever I am overwhelmed by the stupidity, brutality, and greed of my fellow humans. He is a strong candidate for the title of lamed vovnik.

CHAPTER 43

Lou Harrison:
Of Lou, A Reminiscence Sing

Several days after the local newspapers announced that I had been selected as the 1999 Santa Cruz County Artist of the Year, my doorbell rang. It was a bright, warm morning, and when I opened the door, there was the composer Lou Harrison, a rotund figure silhouetted against a sun-splashed street.

"Ah, you're home," he exclaimed, and with that he turned, scurried down the steps, hurried past the front yard, and crossed the street to where his car was parked.

I stood looking after him. I hadn't had a chance to say hello or tell him how delightful and unexpected it was to see him before he had scampered off. Now, his back toward me, he was rummaging inside the car. When he turned and straightened, he was holding a large green plastic tub in both arms. A sapling with several branches rose like a schooner's mast from its midst. He bustled back across the street with a big smile, while behind him Bill Colvig, his long-time partner, emerged from the car and limped after him. Bill was already quite ill by then, and his slow hobbling gait was painful to watch. But he smiled too, obviously enjoying whatever event Lou had cooked up.

Lou, meanwhile, had arrived at the door and was holding out the green tub. "A laurel for the laureate," he said, and chuckled. "It's a little big to hang around your brows, but a laurel tree it is."

We all laughed—Lou, Bill, Donna, who'd come to the door to see what was going on, and me.

"Come in, come in," I said to Lou and Bill.

"No, no; we're on our way to the city and just wanted to congratulate you," Lou said and, with a wave from Bill, as quickly as they had arrived, they were gone.

Such generosity of spirit and, even more, such thoughtfulness, always accompanied by a robust, joyful energy, are what I remember of that day—and of Lou.

As for the tree, Donna and I planted it that morning, and today it's over fifteen feet high. We named it the Lou Harrison Laurel.

That was Lou Harrison, the man, as I knew him—
generous, humorous, full of play and serious contemplation, endlessly learning, reflecting, and creating. To say
he was a giant among modern American composers
conveys nothing about him. To me he was a joyous force,
a whirlwind of creativity, and, above all, Whitmanesque.
Despite the honored place Walt Whitman's *Leaves of
Grass* occupied in Lou's library and the use Lou made of
Whitman's lines from *Calamus* as lyrics, no one has
made a comparison between Lou and Whitman, but
even in physiognomy and build, Lou resembled Walt.
There was the girth and the beard for one and certainly

Lou Harrison,
Santa Cruz, 1992

Lou's largeness of spirit was like Whitman's as well, and so was his vision.
America was the latest stop in evolution for Walt, and he saw it continuing
onward, enveloping the planet and beyond. Lou's early music was rooted in
America and Europe, and in the latter part of his life went beyond both borders to embrace the world. His breaking out of the confines of Western
thought and music and his unorthodox instrumentations are proof of that.

I became aware of Lou's presence in Santa Cruz just after I moved to the
area. I had known about him as a composer for years. Wilma and I had
owned and treasured several long-playing records of his music since the
early days of our marriage in Iowa. But we had no idea he was living in the
immediate vicinity of our new home.

I had been in Santa Cruz less than a month when the manager of the Catalyst café, a grand dining room that served as a cafeteria and performance
space in the tawdry remains of a Victorian hotel, asked me to read at one of
the café's Sunday evening events and suggested I see what the presentations
were like. "Why don't you come down off the mountain next week and take
a gander at a typical get together. Lou Harrison's going to play some music."

Lou Harrison! What an opportunity. But "play some music"? Had he
become a country-western or rock musician? I arrived the next Sunday to
find a packed room. There were probably 250 people present. I stood in
back and watched Lou and Bill go through a completely unexpected performance that was half-lecture, half-musical demonstration. The topic was
ancient Chinese music, and as Lou explained, his words punctuated with
witty asides, he had acquired the music from a Taiwanese library and translated the Chinese notation into Western notation. He and Bill had also
observed museum models of the ancient instruments and had built their
own versions of them. And then the music began. It was like a blaze of
golden silks, bolts of them unrolling through the darkened dining room.
The crowd was completely still, absorbed in every word, every sound.

As I drove home that night, I thought I was going to enjoy living in Santa
Cruz with such neighbors as Lou and Bill and Jim and Jeannie Houston,

although I was also worried about how my poetry, pitiful in the face of what I had just heard, would be accepted after such an extraordinary presentation by a man who was obviously a genius.

Over the next ten years, I ran into Lou in one place or another, but we only nodded to each other in greeting, and I'm sure he didn't know me. I had more of a relationship, however, with Bill, who I would see in the laundromat or supermarket when I lived in Aptos in the early seventies after my break-up with Wilma. Bill was gregarious and would strike up a conversation with anyone who wanted to talk. He was often alone, tending to one chore or another. He may have been Lou's longtime lover and fellow instrument maker, but he was also Lou's general factotum—shopping, cooking, and doing all the mundane tasks one had to do to keep a household functioning.

My meetings with Bill were few and far between and always by chance. Most of the time we just said hello to one another in passing. But we did have several long conversations. In one, Bill answered my questions about building the Chinese instruments and various percussion pieces. Another time, he talked about hiking in Alaska, and his eyes twinkled under his bushy brows. Bill was bony and shaggy-bearded, and as the years wore on, his bowed legs made walking more and more difficult, but he was always quietly merry and quick to smile with a childlike innocence.

Lou didn't come into the picture until 1984. Before then, Wilma had taken classes from him at San Jose State University and raved about them. I wanted to sign up too, but I never had the time. That is one of the sad facts about artists living in the same area: many times their own artistic projects and daily lives keep them from close association with each other unless they are working in the same medium.

In 1984, when I wrote the script *The Eight Ecstasies of Yaeko Iwasaki: A Legend in Poetry, Dance & Music,* I brazenly wrote Lou and asked him to compose the music for it. He graciously replied from Bali, saying he would have to forego my invitation since he was working on a gamelan piece and had two years of commissions to complete after that.

When he returned, he acknowledged me on several occasions at openings and concerts, and in 1992 when his *Joys and Perplexities*, a book of eighty-eight poems, was published, I invited him to be a guest on my radio show. He accepted, and as a letter he sent me the day after the show made clear, he greatly enjoyed the proceedings, which was more a conversation and poetry reading than an interview. After the show, I invited Lou to lunch, and he accepted my invitation immediately. But one thing and another kept me from following up on my offer. There is no doubt that part of my tentativeness had to do with the fact that I held Lou in awe. He not only composed extraordinary music, he wrote poetry, painted, created his own type fonts, and was a brilliant lecturer, conversationalist, and teacher. And again, as in so many cases with other artists, I didn't want to bother him.

I did, however, send him my verse poem, "Quartet in a Minor Key," when I wrote it a year or two later. The poem is in four parts and dramatizes the relationships that link Robert and Clara Schuman, Brahms, and Brahms' housekeeper. Lou was delighted by the poem and sent me a CD of his work, a practice that would continue for the remainder of his life.

Several more years passed, and we would run into each other occasionally and make small talk. He referred to my poetry on occasion and, I thought, would welcome further contact, which was clear in 1998 when he inscribed a copy of his biography, *Composing a World*, with the following words in his calligraphic handwriting

> for
> our
> marvelous
> poet
> &
> friend
> &
> mentor,
> Mort,
> from
> Lou

Still I didn't pursue a friendship. It was not until I was selected Santa Cruz County Artist of the Year in 1999 that we had more extensive contact, and certainly Lou's bringing me the laurel sapling was the invitation to it. He also made a point of attending my acceptance performance, which consisted of a retrospective poetry reading and talk. Soon after that, we had lunch together and found common interest in such subjects as Chinese culture, the Byzantine Empire and other arcane topics which few in his circle of local musical compatriots shared. Even though I stood in awe of Lou, our conversations were always easy. Unlike Bly and other reticent males, Lou was forthcoming and high-spirited, and our talks were always robust and filled with humor, both qualities I prize in relationships.

Over the years, I learned that Lou possessed other traits I held in high esteem, especially his generosity to his fellow artists. Lou had a healthy ego, but he never hesitated to have friends and artists he respected share the spotlight with him. When Vincent McDermott, composer, gamelan expert, and faculty member at Lewis & Clark College, invited Lou to Portland for a short residency and concert of his work, Lou was delighted but immediately suggested Alan Hovhannes and McDermott present their own works in the concert as well. It was, said Lou's biographers Leta Miller and Fredric Lieberman, "characteristic."

When Lou and I had a second lunch several weeks after the initial one, I was going to propose that he and I collaborate on a suite of poems and music. But by then Bill was quite ill and had been taken to a nursing home. Lou's health was also faltering, and he was preparing to go to San Francisco for an operation. The time was not right for proposals. Instead, I asked his permission to write poems to seven of his shorter pieces, which I would have a dancer choreograph. The piece, as he knew, was to be my entry for an end-of-millennium concert that would feature the work of all past Santa Cruz Artists of the Year, of which Lou had been one of the first. I explained that my approach would be programmatic, but I would try to emulate the rhythms and sounds of his music in language. He was intrigued and accepted my proposal without caveat.

When he saw the finished results at the dress rehearsal, he was over-joyed. Judging by his response, he liked two in particular. The one he appre-ciated most made him jump from his seat in spontaneous applause. It was the most nondramatic and playful of the group, a series of images relent-lessly moved forwarded by puns:

Dance

*(4th Movement
of Lou Harrison's Varied Trio)*

In the dance of life
you've got to woo
the wood in the match
before you light it
and the wavering
shadow of the wave
underneath the wave
in the flame
when you ignite it.
You've got to bet on
the wager that wags
the tale untold
on the shaggy dog
come out of the cold
to warm itself
by the burning logs
roaring in the grate
because from the start
you've got to be so bold
as to woo the fire
dancing in your heart

As an appreciation for what I had done, Lou sent me several more CDs of his work.

To understand what Lou's work meant to me, you have to know something about his music, which from the start was experimental. Born in Portland, Oregon, but raised in the San Francisco Bay area, Lou studied music with such avant-garde composers as Henry Cowell and Arnold Schoenberg and collaborated with John Cage before moving to New York in 1943. There he wrote a music column for the old Herald Tribune, befriended Virgil Thompson, performed his own compositions, and worked tirelessly for an appreciation of the American composer Charles Ives, for whom he is credited with getting long overdue recognition and a Pulitzer Prize.

But it was not until he returned to California in 1953 and settled in Santa Cruz county that he pursued the music that so attracted me in what I call his later period. That was Asian music. In 1961 Lou visited Japan, Taiwan, and Korea, studying the music of each country. Later he became fascinated by the intricacies of Indonesian gamelan music, which extended his knowledge of percussion instrumentation. From the beginning, his music, always on the cutting edge, was highlighted by percussive rhythms punctuating jagged intervals of silence and underlying soaring or staccato string polyphonic melodies.

Interestingly, Lou and I never talked about music during our meetings. I was too musically ignorant, and I'm sure Lou thought (correctly) that I wouldn't understand the complexities of what he was doing in rhythm and polyphony. My musical appreciation was limited to making dramatic or philosophical scenarios of what I heard, and if I was asked to describe what I experienced in Lou's music, I would reply that his sounds aren't abstract, but sensuous, resembling expeditions into the unknown. For me, they are multiple sonorities that twine about each other or soar in different directions. They wend their way through the cosmos, at times spiraling through empty space or surfing down crescendos of silence. At other times, they slide through labyrinthine tunnels of pressure or tip-toe through checkerboard mazes of tinkling threads, suddenly encountering eruptions of nebula or frozen galaxies that shatter as they pass, sprinkling them with luminous shards. Sometimes the sonorities streak by silent clouds of cosmic gas or dark galaxies, which, in their wake, throb like drums or tremble like gongs and cymbals. The sonorities float or hurtle, whirl up on spouts of time but always keep moving, always keep skating, skittering, or riding a tidal ebb and flow, propelled by the life force that pulses in the distance and everywhere around them. And all the while the sonorities are mapping a universe for anyone who wants to follow them.

That was the sense I wanted to get into the seven poems I wrote to Lou's music. It was play, but serious play, play with rhyme and strict accentual and syllabic counts, which approximated Lou's love of closed poetic forms. But my imagery, even the imagery I used in the preceding paragraph to describe his music, points to something else. Let me put it this way: I would not call Lou a humanist or a Renaissance man. Such epithets almost belittle him.

His knowledge and creativity were cosmic. To me he had literally captured—for our hearing—the fabled music of the spheres.

Several months after my dance-poetry piece was performed, Bill died, and Lou successfully underwent his operation. When Bill died, I felt awkward about intruding on Lou's grief and for a while didn't pursue our friendship. Over the next few years, however, we saw each other as often as possible. Lou's exuberance and good humor never flagged, and he was as busy as ever. He found a new companion and spent much of his time in Southern California, where he was building a house literally made of bales of straw. When he was in town, I'd pick him up at his house and we would go to lunch nearby, usually to a gourmet take-out store that had several tables, where our conversations about Byzantium and little known events in medieval and Chinese history continued unabated.

If I ever doubted Lou's respect for my work, I couldn't deny his enthusiastic response to my selected prose poems, *Moments Without Names*, when I sent him a copy shortly after it was published in 2002. In his typewriter calligraphic script, he wrote in a letter

MY DEAR CD ORT
THANK YOU LOTS FOR SENDING ME YOUR WONDROUS
NEW BOOK. I HAVE BEEN READING IT OFTEN, WITH
MOUNTING DELIGHT IN THE EMPIRE OF YOUR MIND, AND
THE FELICITY OF YOUR EXPRESSION. I DON'T SEE HOW YOU
DO IT, BUT THEN I SEE THAT YOU DO DO IT AND AM
DRAWN INTO A KIND OF ENCOMPASSMENT BY YOUR
VOICE. I AM SORRY THAT I DIDN'T HEAR YOUR VOICE AT
THE MARATHON, BUT MUCH HOPE THAT I WILL HEAR YOU
SOON.

LOU

The letter arrived in a small package containing another CD of his work.

All in all, however, I came to regard my contact with Lou as a relationship of missed opportunities, almost all of them because of my timidity. I cherished the moments we spent together and the ease of our conversation and the delight we took in telling each other cryptic anecdotes about artists and peoples from other times and places. But I am aware of something else I haven't been able to put into words until recently: just to know Lou was alive and creating somewhere near me, in the very county where I lived, gave me a sense of balance and well-being on a daily basis. His nearby presence, as to my mind the proximity of a lamed vovnik should, lit up the county every morning like a sun.

As I was listening to his music a few days after his death in 2003, I wrote this short poem:

Listening to Lou Harrison's
Suite for Violin & American Gamelan
Shortly after the Composer's Death

As I listen to Lou Harrison's
"Suite for Violin and American Gamelan,"
a blue jay in the oak tree outside the window
shrieks and shrieks, louder and louder,
the same exclamation over and over again:
"I wrote that! I wrote that! I wrote that!"

CHAPTER 44

Deng Ming-Dao

Of all the people who expanded my notions of humility in the face of the universe's mysteries, and at the same time exemplified the essence of a compassionate human being concerned with the people around him, Deng Ming-Dao is the nonpareil. More than anyone I've known, he comes closest to what I imagine a lamed vovnik to be.

I met him in the spring of 1998. The occasion was interesting but in no way hinted at its eventual importance. At the time, I was teaching a course in Chinese literature and history with a brilliant, antic historian and friend named Sandy Lydon, who invited Deng to talk to the class about Daoism.

Sandy was a great teacher, and a wilder one in the classroom than I was. His humor was infectious and freewheeling, and he delivered his rapid-fire lectures in partial phrases and sentence fragments that the students were expected to complete on their own. He was also a prankster and played constant tricks on his students in order to make them think. In this case, he was eager to dash the students' stereotypical ideas of what a Daoist adept was like, those clichéd notions of mystery and otherworldliness that summon up images of sorcerers and wandering monks in the public's mind.

Sandy introduced Deng, who had published several books on Daoism, as having trained extensively in five ancient Chinese martial arts, which was

Deng Ming-Dao,
San Francisco,
2005

true. However, Deng wasn't an old man with a long white beard who wore flowing silk robes with wide cuffs. He was a slim, forty-four year old who strolled to the podium in an open-collared, button-down shirt and slacks. That was Sandy's joke, but in the end the joke was on me because as the years wore on, I came to see the speaker as an emissary from another world, who stepped effortlessly between that world and ours.

Deng Ming-Dao, it turned out, was a Chinese American book designer by trade, and he didn't lecture the class. He chose a question-and-answer format and replied to the many queries put to him in a relaxed, concise English, enthralling the hundred or so students with his sagacious responses. He spoke for three hours, and almost no one in the lecture hall wanted the evening to end when the class was over at 10 PM. Certainly, George Ow, Jr. who was sitting with us, and Donna and I, were among that number.

Deng's focus was on how Daoism's ages-old philosophy and practices could work in the modern world, and the crowd left the building excited but quiet, deep in thought. Afterward, George took Sandy, Donna, Deng, and me to a Mexican restaurant for a late night snack, and I gave Deng a copy of *The Santa Cruz Mountain Poems*, whose Chinese influence I thought was a suitable token of my appreciation for his visit to the class.

The next morning George hosted a breakfast at a local restaurant to introduce Deng to relatives and friends. As he had been the night before, Deng was gracious and humble and made suitable small talk. At one point, someone at the table, who was familiar with Deng's work, asked him if he was still painting, since he hadn't seen graphic work by him in several years.

"I've set aside my art for the time being," Deng answered. "Now that I have a family, I have to devote myself to providing for them. I'll come back to painting later, when my daughter's grown."

I was struck by the incongruity of this answer in relation to the Daoist ideas Deng had presented to the class the previous evening, and before I considered the possible rudeness of my words, I said, "That's a strange answer from someone who believes that the world is in constant flux and that we cannot put off our plans for a future time."

Everyone greeted these words with silence, and George seemed especially uncomfortable, an impression that was exacerbated when Deng didn't answer immediately and seemed deep in thought.

The breakfast broke up a short time later. Everyone said polite goodbyes, and I sensed that I had once more committed a social gaff. I held back until the last person took his leave, intending to apologize for my remark. But as I was about to speak, Deng turned to me and said, "You were right, of course. What you said in the restaurant is what I tell others all the time but have obviously forgotten to apply to myself in this instance." He paused, then continued. "I read some of the poems in your book last night, and I'd like to write you about them. Would you give me your address?"

I did and took my leave. Deng's words were meant to graciously heal an awkward moment, I thought, but they made me all the more aware of how untoward my remark had been and caused me to reflect on the boorishness of what I considered my Slavic directness in light of Chinese courtesy. I also realized that Deng had parried my apology before I could make it, so that in Chinese terms I saved face and, of course, wound up not apologizing. Such thinking may seem exaggerated, but it was the first of a number of instances in which I was aware of Deng's response to situations before they occurred, instances that not only demonstrated his consideration for other people's feelings but lent him that aura of otherworldliness I mentioned before.

Three days later, I received a letter from Deng. In it he thanked me once again for my comment at breakfast, and he went on to say that when he had looked through *The Santa Cruz Mountain Poems* the night of his talk, he had been surprised to find he had been using poems from the book as models for his own writing for the past twenty-five years without remembering the identity of the author. He would contemplate the poems before he started to write and ask himself, "Why can't I write something as direct as that?" He ended the letter by asking if I would be his teacher.

I was astonished. In the first place, I never expected him to send a letter, but if he did, I was planning not only to ask his forgiveness, but to request that he be *my* teacher. I replied to his letter accordingly, adding that I was more a clown than a teacher and was awed in his presence.

Several weeks later, Donna and I went to San Francisco for some reason and had lunch with Deng. His humility and courtesy were captivating, and, of all things, he seemed delighted by my sense of humor. Of course, this may have been mere politeness on his part, but I like to think he recognized from the outset that I had come to embrace the merry Daoism of Zhuangzi rather that the dour aphorisms of Laozi. More seriously, when I left the table for a moment, he expressed concern about my posture and diet to Donna, as if he was a worried friend. I was touched when she told me, and thus began one of the most treasured friendships of my life.

Deng, as I've called him from then on, is my teacher, my student, and my friend. There is no reticence or self-protective male posturing in him. He has been open and emotionally present from the beginning of our relationship and elicits complete trust from anyone who meets him. Our attachment was immediate, and from the start I have assumed that he understood me as few people have. My buffoonery and irreverent repartee didn't fool him for a moment. Like George Ow, Jr., he recognized the seriousness behind the laughter and my lifelong attempt, as unsuccessful as it was, to live with integrity, loyalty, and honor.

In the course of that first lunch, one of the several subjects he and I discussed was the mystery of his not only knowing my pieces from *The Santa Cruz Mountain Poems* but his using them as models. It was the first of many mysteries that would permeate our relationship with the headiness of jasmine incense.

In fact, "mysteries" is a good word to explain many of the aspects of my dealings with Deng Ming-Dao. For all his outwardly down-to-earth, unassuming, low-key, logical ways, he gives off an aura of things not quite explainable by conventional Western definitions, an aura I termed before as otherworldliness.

One day, a year after I met him, he joined me and an inspired but easily offended poet from the Midwest for lunch in a busy San Francisco dim sum restaurant. As usual, the poet was quiet and watchful, if not wary. But as the meal wore on, I saw his body relax, more evidence, I believe, of the instant trust Deng inspires from even the most cautious people. When Deng excused himself for a moment an hour into the meal, the poet waited until he was gone, then leaned toward me and said in an awed tone, "Who is he?" and went on to explain that he sensed something transcendent about Deng. That confirmed many things about Deng for me. I trusted the poet's instincts in such matters, since his poems are among the most spiritually elevated in American poetry. So impressed was he by Deng that a week later he sent me an email wondering if Deng would consider doing the cover illustration for his next book. That was curious. At no time had I mentioned to him that Deng was a painter. Another mystery.

Many of these "mysteries" would be explained in time, but the explanations were full of coincidences and connections that in themselves were mysterious or at least led to further questions about the limited conceptions we accept in our everyday perceptions of reality.

Daoism, of course, is fraught with mystery. One of the popular notions about Daoist adepts is that they have found the secrets of the universe, and time and again I have read about Daoist wanderers who searched for and supposedly found "the elixir of life," or who experimented with concoctions that could procure immortality. If these anecdotes can be assigned to the clichés Westerners hold about the more esoteric notions of Chinese spiritual practices, they also permeate every cranny of Chinese popular culture and address the more unexplainable aspects of existence.

Such subjects had never been broached by Mei Yi-Pao in my Chinese classes at Iowa. Although Professor Mei had translated one third of the *Daodejing* for the much admired *Columbia Sourcebook of Chinese Civilization*, he was best known for his work on the decidedly un-Daoist philosopher Mozi, where Mei showed himself to be a Western scholar, having adopted Western academic ways.

Deng Ming-Dao usually talks about his mystical beliefs only in his writings. He has had several masters whose teachings he has diligently followed. He wrote about one of them, Kwan Saihung, in an enthralling three-part biography entitled *Chronicles of Tao*. As he described them, his masters were traditionalists, strict disciplinarians who demanded unquestioning obedience as well as commitment. When I began "tutoring" him, my method was more relaxed, not necessarily because I was Western, but because my approach was informal to begin with, and because our relationship was tempered by friendship and a reciprocal student-teacher dynamic in which each of us performed one role or another depending on the circumstances.

My role as teacher crystallized a year after we met. Deng had been contemplating doing a new translation of the *Yijing*, one in which he wanted a Western audience to grasp as much of the book as an educated Chinese person might. That meant his book would not only attempt to communicate the ideas of the *I Ching* but seek to convey the experience of reading it. Over time, he came to the conclusion that he would render his *I Ching* translation in several different sections. In one of them, he decided he would write a poem for each hexagram, based on the hexagram's images, that would evoke the essence of the hexagram's meaning. The only difficulty with this plan was that, except for the aphorisms that appeared at the beginning of each meditation in his book *365 Tao*, he had never written poetry. Would I, perhaps, teach him?

I was taken aback when he came to me with the proposal. But I had so much love and respect for Deng by then that I told him we could try. However, I insisted he get acquainted with Western poetry and suggested several books he should immediately read. That would test how serious he was about the project.

Within a week, he had procured the books and read half of them. He was full of questions about the most basic as well as the most abstruse aspects of poetry. I assigned him several exercises, which he immediately wrote and about which he asked me a number of astute questions concerning philosophical and technical matters. I answered in kind. Next he came down to Santa Cruz, and we spent six hours talking nonstop about various aspects of poetry, during which I laid out twenty or so general "rules" for writing it. After that, we followed a procedure that continued for more than two years: he would mail me his translation and explanation of a hexagram along with the poem he had written to accompany it. I would mark up the poem with corrections, suggestions, and comments that pointed out general poetic issues for which, at times, a particular poem would serve as model. Then I would fax the poem back. Next, Deng, always diligent and punctual, would call me at a prescribed time, and for two or three hours we would go over my comments and his questions in response to them.

Deng became more enthusiastic about our sessions as the project progressed. His questions were so perceptive and his comments so insightful, I couldn't help but be impressed by his intelligence and feel for poetry. But to my amazement, from the start his poetry demonstrated genuine accomplishment.

The sessions became more and more rewarding for me. I was talking about the inner workings of poetry as I had never been able to with my students or for that matter with other poets. Soon I realized that Deng was becoming the repository of everything I knew and had ever thought about concerning the art of poetry: its techniques, various approaches, attitudes toward language and communication, paradoxical ways and means, and, almost more important than all these aspects, its purpose as I saw it.

One day, at the end of an exceptionally long phone lesson filled with one paradoxical notion after another, as well as with the most intricate casuistry, I said to Deng, "You know what's happening in these sessions, don't you?"

"Yes," was all he replied, and I have no doubt he did know, and probably had known long before I recognized the answer to—and maybe even before the formulation of—my question: Deng, through our phone calls and meetings, had become my protégé, the one who would carry on what I had been taught not only by my poetry mentors and professors, such as Dietrich Gerhard and Mei Yi-Pao, but by the voices of my ancestors whose words rippled up from my cells, those murmurings that rise from our chromosomes and direct us to be everything we are. In a word, he was carrying forward my mysticism as well as his own.

It is interesting to note at this point that Deng may have thoroughly known Chinese history and culture, but his knowledge of Western civilization was not nearly as comprehensive, despite his growing up and being educated in California. A good part of our poetry sessions, then, were taken up with my introducing him to various aspects of Western culture, which included my Russian Jewish background and many side talks about Hassidism and one or another little-known episode in Western history. At one point, I bought him the complete essays of Montaigne—one of my favorite writers—at which he marveled, observing that the book read like the writings of a Daoist master, an unorthodox conclusion I had come to years before.

While all this intellectual communication was skittering back and forth through the telephone wires, we would continue to meet every month or so, have lunch or dinner together, and talk about many subjects. Gradually, we began talking about more personal things. But that took time because Deng was generally formal and respectful of me as an older man. I may have considered us equals, but I knew I had to get past the barrier of his politeness if we were to truly become friends. His social graces were so pronounced, I often joked that he was more a Confucian than a Daoist. That light-hearted quip underscored another problem: although Deng enjoyed my jokes and irreverent horseplay, he was essentially a serious person. That, combined with his formal deportment, had to be breached, I thought, if we were to have the kind of friendship I prized but almost never found.

The breakthrough happened in an unexpected way. Deng always signed his letters and emails, "Sincerely." To me, it was an illustration of his overall formality. In the second year of our friendship, I brought this practice up during one of our phone conversations. "My friend, why do you still end your letters with 'Sincerely'? We're beyond that kind of formality."

He was quiet for a moment, then said, "What do you suggest?"

I made believe I was thinking for a moment, but I knew what I was going to say: he had written an essay in which he addressed my age and my combative nature by saying "It was time the old swordsman hung up his sword." Now, as he waited for my suggestion, I said, "I don't know what you're going to do, but from now on I'm signing my letters to you 'The Swaggering Swordsman,' or something like that."

He laughed and signed his next letter "The Solitary Drunkard," and after that regularly changed the adjective with one or another descriptive word that sashayed in front of the inebriated noun at the end of his letters. From that point on, our friendship, more relaxed and jocular, seemed to deepen profoundly.

My trust in Deng was so unquestioning that I asked him to be my literary executor, and he, in turn, introduced Donna and me to his family. His mother was the famous potter and author, Jade Snow Wong, whose autobiography, *Fifth Chinese Daughter*, a straightforward depiction of life in a Chinese American family in the 1920s, '30s, and '40s, became an instant American classic. On the occasion of a retrospective show of her ceramics, which coincided with her eightieth birthday, Deng presented her with an exquisitely designed photography book he had made of her work, as well as a Chinese banquet to which only his immediate family, his mother's closest college friend, and Donna and I were invited. When I told him how honored we were to be included with the family, he replied, "But you are family."

The mystery of how Deng knew my poems from *The Santa Cruz Mountain Poems* was solved the second year of our friendship. Deng's bestselling meditation volume, *365 Tao*, had been used by an Olympic wrestler to build mental strength and concentration. When the wrestler was appointed director of the 1996 U.S. Olympic boxing team, he thought it would be a good idea to have the team read a similar book, and he commissioned Deng to put together a book of interviews of famous sports figures talking about the spiritual side of sports. The project had been put into motion before I met Deng, and by the time he told me about it, he had already interviewed a number of well-known athletes from a variety of sports, but not a single basketball player was among them. I immediately suggested he interview my friend Tom Meschery, the former All-American and NBA basketball star.

Tom Meschery

Tom was not a random choice for the interview. He had brains and an artistic turn of mind. He was a big man in all connotations of the word. Not only did he stand six foot seven, he had huge shoulders and a trim but rugged

Tom Meschery,
Reno, Nevada, 2000

build, with a long face and a lantern jaw. He had played ten years for the Warriors (first in Philadelphia and then in San Francisco) before ending his career with the Seattle Supersonics. For a time after he retired, he had coached in the short-lived American Basketball Association and then was an assistant coach with the Portland Trailblazers, where I met him in the 1970s while I was on a reading tour of the Northwest. Although he had been one of the more aggressive players in the league, known by fans for his combative ways, off the court he was a poet and a gentle, gracious man who took pride in his Russian ancestry. Even though we met only several times a year, we were close enough to consider ourselves Slavic brothers, and Tom had even suggested we take a trip to Russia together with his friend, the famous sports radio announcer Bill King, and our wives.

In the middle of his coaching career, Tom went to Iowa for two years, received an MFA in Creative Writing, and then settled with his wife, the novelist Joanne Meschery, near Lake Tahoe, where I spent several weeks each summer during the 1980s and '90s at my brother- and sister-in-law's ski lodge. That was when Tom and I spent time together. A humorous incident occurred on one of those visits that illustrates the jocular side of his character and the nature of our friendship.

Tom and I always attended one or another of the poetry readings at the Squaw Valley Writers Conference. One year, Dorianne Laux, who I knew from the Foothill Writers Conference, gave a reading at Squaw Valley. Tom liked her poetry but had never met her, and after the reading, Dorianne and her husband, the poet Joe Millar, joined Tom, Donna, and me for drinks at a nearby bar. Dorianne kept staring at Tom. Although she was hip and streetwise, she gave the impression that she had never met a professional athlete, and Tom's size and tranquil demeanor seemed to intrigue her. Possibly to her further surprise, Tom talked knowledgeably and enthusiastically about poetry and as usual was affable and relaxed, slouching comfortably in the low, upholstered bar chair.

The conversation went from topic to topic. Tom wanted to talk about poetry, but Dorianne kept asking him about his career. At one point she stated that she was surprised by his gentleness.

"Don't be fooled," I quipped. "He was one of the roughest, 'baddest' players in the game," and smiled.

Dorianne looked at Tom questioningly, but he sprawled deeper in his chair, said nothing, and answered her look with a beatific smile.

A few minutes later, Dorianne asked how Tom and I came to know each other.

"Mort played ball and was a coach" Tom said, which startled her all the more.

"I didn't know that," she said, turning toward me.

"It was a long time ago, and I was never in Tom's league," I replied. "That was when small men could play. I was a guard: directed the offense and mostly shot from the outside, although I would drive to the basket any time I got the chance—"

"Yeah," Tom cut in, "and if I had caught him underneath the basket I would have swatted him fourteen rows into the crowd with the back of my hand." And he sat back and grinned.

"There," I said in mock anger, pointing to Tom, "that's the real Tom Meschery!"

Dorianne blanched at the sudden change in the conversation, but when she saw our grins, she began to laugh, and all of us joined her.

■ ■ ■

Tom's first book, *Nothing We Lose Can Be Replaced*, came out when he was sixty years old and reads like an autobiography. Divided into three parts, it moves from memories of his upbringing as a Russian immigrant in San Francisco, through a series of anecdotes about his playing days in the NBA, and ends with his career as a high school teacher in Reno, Nevada. Here's a poem from the last section, which shows his empathy and concern for his students:

Suicide

One teacher says she saw it coming
which drives the rest of us by lunch
crazy with guilt, remembering the old
ed. movie, *Cipher In The Snow*.

So we promise ourselves, next period
We'll embrace all our students, even
the wall-eyed one who lurks in the back
drawing obscenities on his desk.

Of course we don't, returning to decorum
with the bell, to Marilyn passing notes,
Harry's runny nose, Carrie's menstrual cramps,
essays overdue, forgotten texts.

In sixth period, one girl by the window starts
to weep, but when I ask her was he her friend
she shakes her head; she never knew him,
but thinks he was her brother's best friend's cousin.

By then, her tears have started a chain reaction.
All around the room, students are crying
the way one can't help humming a certain tune,
or when frightened in the dark, whistling.

■ ■ ■

When I called Tom up about the interview with Deng, he was enthusiastic, and Deng and I met him one evening several weeks later at Bill King's house in Sausalito. We sat at the dining-room table near a large window that overlooked San Francisco Bay, a tape recorder whirring in our midst. It was one of those clear nights when the lights of San Francisco glittered like a cluster of stars in the distant darkness.

The interview included Tom, Deng, King, his wife, and me. Although I had not intended to take part in the proceedings, I thought Tom's humility was causing him to parry Deng's initial questions or evade answering them, and I found myself continually chiding him in an attempt to pin him down for definite answers, something a friend, rather than a respectful, amateur interviewer, could do. My estimate wasn't correct. What I took to be parries and evasions were, in actuality, ideas that were different from mine. I couldn't accept Tom's answers that he had never thought out his game plan in advance nor calculated his moves while he was playing. He played, he said, completely by instinct. This statement brought into question my long-standing belief (and practice) that although sports had its instinctive element, all successful athletes were rational in most aspects of their preparation and play. Years later, Tom elaborated on the kinetic purity of his game: "I think if I had tried to be as rational [as you] I'd never have made it. I remember trying to think through moves, attempting to visualize and to plan. Those were the games I most often wound up on the bench, coach yelling at me where in the hell was my head, so I realized my mistake quickly and went back to pure instinct or maybe as Bill Sharmon put it, 'muscle memory.' Back in the locker room after a game, whenever a player asked me about something I had done, a rebound, a shot, a block, I just stared: the court on which the game had just ended was a total blank."

Toward the end of the interview, Deng asked Tom a few questions about his experiences as a coach, and Tom, pointing to me, answered, "Ask Mort; he was a coach."

Deng looked startled for a moment, then continued the interview. But afterward, as we drove back to the city, he said, "I didn't know you were a basketball coach. Where did you coach?"

"At a high school in the city, called Lick-Wilmerding."

"And what year was that?" he asked.

"I taught English and history at Lick from 1965 to 1968 and coached one year. Why?"

"Because I started as a freshman at Lick in the fall of 1968," he said, and half-turning toward me, he smiled and continued. "You were not meant to be my teacher then, but you were now."

"Come on, pal," I groaned in mock exasperation, shaking my head. "Enough of that."

But once more, as it had so many times before in my relationship with Deng, coincidence touched its toe over the border of mystery, and the sense of everyday reality, for a moment at least, seemed as tenuous as a paper kite snapping in a sunlit gale.

By the time Deng dropped me off at my car, we had figured out that he knew *The Santa Cruz Mountain Poems* because one of his teachers at Lick, most probably Jack Coffey, my friend and fellow teacher there, had his students read some of them before the book came out in 1972, since I had sent Jack dozens of the poems even before they began appearing in literary journals in 1970.

As I drove back to Santa Cruz that night, I mused on my relationship with Deng and on his comment that I had not been meant to be his teacher when he was a student at Lick. He was probably right. He had told me months before that he was a rebellious, angry teenager through his college years, particularly concerned with the racial persecution the Chinese had suffered in this country since the mid-nineteenth century. If he was serious, polite, and respectful now, he had come to this deportment in his later years. Although it's hard to imagine, he might have ignored me, or worse, been disrespectful and incurred my anger, let alone my dislike, if I had been his high school teacher. The time at Lick wasn't right for him to be my student, nor for that matter was it for me. I had a lot to learn about life and poetry then. In fact, we both had a lot of separate growing to do before we could meet in a place where we would recognize that what we were looking for existed in each other. Hadn't I said that about Donna?

I'm sure you are scoffing about this talk of mystery. But such suppositions should not be quickly dismissed. I believe that people bring their realities with them and many times enclose others within the strength of their visions. We accept this about religious and political leaders' ability to create mass hysteria. Neurotic housewives are in this category as well and draw their husbands into their frenzied worlds, in the same way that sadistic husbands intimidate their wives to become mute though not necessarily willing victims. These are examples of the power people's views of reality have over others. In the light of such mundane illustrations, mystics practicing age-old rites that summon up realities other than the tenuous one we live by in our daily lives are not to be ignored.

So, was my meeting Deng Ming-Dao in 1998 another instance of the mystery he brings with him wherever he goes? Yes, but in this case it was a mystery of time and place. Deng and I were different human beings in 1968 than we were thirty years later when Chance, Providence, or the mischievous God of Literature, Wen Chang, playing one of his insufferable but in this case wonderful jokes, brought us together.

BOOK THIRTEEN

THE 1980s AND THE WARTILPA KALIPURNANGKA

CHAPTER 45

The Disappearing World: George Nazar and *The Eight Ecstasies*

Throughout her career as advisor for admissions at the university and then as transfer director at Cabrillo College, Donna had to attend conferences and meetings in the Central Valley and Northern and Southern California. I didn't like the fact that she drove these long distances alone, and I took to accompanying her on days I didn't have classes, and all days after my retirement. The trips became outings on which we shared the driving and could spend hours talking and just being together.

One of her regular destinations was Sacramento, and while she attended to her duties, I roamed downtown or spent the afternoon with Denny Schmitz, with whom I had read all those years ago at the Young American Poets reading in Berkeley, the night I had met Milosz. A former student of John Logan's and a mentor of Ray Carver, Denny has never gottten the recognition he deserves. From the beginning, I thought he was one of the best and most original poets in the nation. He is a quiet, humble man who loves basketball and played several hours a day well into his sixties. His poems not only demonstrate his individual style but his singular thought patterns that reveal through image and metaphor what is really going on in

Dennis Schmitz, Sacramento, California, 1998

the poem, as if the speaker is at first unaware of what he is talking about. So in "Abbot's Cove" the speaker, while jogging, stops to observe the roiling tide, but the images of his description transform the scene (and by extension the world) into a vision of chaos in which for a moment the speaker's belief system teeters and leads him to thoughts of suicide. In the end, he continues his "workout," a phrase that by the last line is fraught with several meanings, one of which suggests that his morning's confrontation is much like Thomas Aquinas's contemplations of the most difficult metaphysical questions, questions that have as much to do with the relations between men and women as humans and nature.

Abbot's Lagoon

The storm's still everywhere I step,
affectionate as a lover who touches you

with pliers at the periphery
of the ego, little wavelets, like blisters.

The lagoon's surface is folded
in labial wind-stirrings; a few birds twitch

in & out of the water onto the sand
that's the color of a rainblasted trenchcoat.

Then, at the edge of the ocean,
I study three minutes (I time myself

to know when to wade in) the loose
mound in the backwash that's flexing

& bobbing in the ocean's insomnia.
Is it the suicide you always promise in the storm

against yourself, or just more kelp
torqued around its own embrace, loving

any sort of afterlife, self-tangled like all
of us, oozing the bottom's root-grease

into the water around it? Glad to be puzzled
I step back, turn from all the evidence

& trot into another morning's workout.

Another regular destination was Fresno, where Phil Levine lives and taught. Phil is not only a great American poet, he is a poet whose work strikes me at an almost visceral level. I've often said I would have been happy to have written like him. He taught at Fresno State College for more than thirty years and turned out dozens of the finest poets of the last third of the twentieth century, such as Gary Soto, Larry Levis, and my old friend Lawson Inada, among many others. The results of Levine's teaching are a startling accomplishment that matched and maybe surpassed in numbers and quality John Logan's record as poetry mentor.

Phil was always out of town when I visited, but I saw his old friend and mine from Iowa once or twice, the equally excellent poet Peter Everwine. Mostly, however, I spend the afternoon with another fine poet who taught at Fresno State, Chuck Hanzlicek, and his wife Dianne, whose bird-filled backyard was an aviary of sunlit fluttering song. Chuck's poems, which he publishes under the name C. G. Hanzlicek, are tight, laconic, and direct.

C.G. Hanzlicek,
Fresno, 2000

They display a variety of moods as he confronts his Czech American ancestry and the world at large from his "cave of air." Here's a poem to his daughter that shows his tenderness and the characteristic varied tones he projects so masterfully and that imbue his poetry with its individual voice.

Egg

I'm scrambling an egg for my daughter.
"Why are you always whistling?" she asks.
"Because I'm happy."
And it's true,
Though it stuns me to say it aloud;
There was a time when I wouldn't
Have seen it as my future.
It's partly a matter
Of who is there to eat the egg:
The self fallen out of love with itself
Through the tedium of familiarity,
Or this little self,
So curious, so hungry,
Who emerged from the woman I love,
A woman who loves me in a way
I've come to think I deserve,
Now that it arrives from outside me,
Everything changes, we're told,
And now the changes are everywhere:
The house with its morning light
That fills me like a revelation,
The yard with its trees
That cast a bit more shade each summer,
The love of a woman
That both is and isn't confounding,
And the love
Of this clamor of questions at my waist.
Clamor of questions,
You clamor of answers,
Here's your egg.

When none of my Fresno acquaintances were available, I explored different parts of the city, which was filled with neighborhoods of Mexicans, African Americans, Japanese, Filipinos, and, since the end of the Vietnam War, a large population of Hmong people. Mostly, I'd wander through shops and seek an authentic ethnic restaurant for lunch. The largest and oldest ethnic group in the city was the Armenians, whose residence had been celebrated in the 1930s and 1940s by the American writer William Saroyan. Many an afternoon I sought an Armenian lunch of lamb and dolmas, so much like the Greek cuisine I relished.

One day I found myself driving in a run-down section of Olive Avenue. I passed an abandoned theater and a number of empty shop fronts when, with a sideways glance, I discovered a tobacco shop called *Tabatiere*. I parked the car and entered the store. It was a long, narrow room. At one end were plates and ceramic knickknacks and on the other, jars of tobacco, pipes, cigars, and smoking utensils. Overlooking the avenue, a plate glass window ran the length of the shop. A gnomelike, wizened old man, no more than five feet tall, nodded to me from behind the counter of the dishes section and came up to me when I made my way to the tobacco area.

The old man stood at my elbow as I inspected the dozen or so large jars filled with pipe tobacco and labeled with such intriguing names as "Almondine," "Honey," "Bohemia," "My Favorite," "Golden Radiator," and "Playboy: The Best of the Best." I turned to him and nodded, and after a few moments he plucked at my shirtsleeve, lifted his chin toward the window, and led me over to it. Without an introduction, he looked out on the sunny street and said, "I look out on the street and watch what is happening there with one eye, but what do I look at with my other eye?"

He had an impish smile on his face. I smiled back and without hesitation said, "With the other eye, you look inside yourself for the truth."

"I knew it! I knew it!" he replied, clapping his hands and shuffling his feet in imitation of a jig. "Come, come," he beckoned, plucking at my sleeve again and leading me back to the jars of tobacco, choosing one and opening it for me.

"I don't have a pipe with me," I said. He replaced the jar and led me excitedly to the counter, saying, "If one ear hears the traffic noise, the other ear hears . . . ?"

"The music of the spheres," I answered.

"Ah!" He was beside himself with joy.

There was some cake, cheese, and what looked like dried beef on the counter and he offered me some.

"So, who are you? What are you doing here?" he asked.

"I've come to see you," I replied, enjoying the game.

He waved away my answer: the game was over.

I told him I was a teacher and a poet, and that sent him into more paroxysms of joy—waving arms and fluttering hands. And when I finished, he told me his name was George Nazar and he was one of the Armenians of Fresno. But, mind you, he had not always been from here. No, don't think that, young man. He had been part of an illustrious family of Armenian tobacco growers and merchants living in Egypt where the family had flourished for generations. But government interference and the upheaval of the Second World War had destroyed his fortune and sent him and his wife and daughter wandering the planet. There was no possibility of going to Armenia after the Turks had massacred most of the Armenian population and where he had only distant family to begin with, so he had sought a new home, finally coming to Fresno, where he found a lively Armenian community to his liking.

"What brought you to Fresno, of all places?" I asked.

He had read the work of William Saroyan in the 1930s when he was a young man and had slowly but, he now thought, inevitably made his way around the world to the community Saroyan so lovingly depicted in his work. The first day he was in the city, he had met Saroyan and they had become instant friends.

"You see that chair? Every day, he would sit there and we'd drink and smoke the afternoon away." He shook his head, and his eyes blinked. "He's been dead for ten years now, and I count the days."

Then he shook himself from his growing reverie, smiled, and asked again why I was in Fresno. I told him, and we began to talk about pipes and the intricacies of blending tobaccos. He'd create a special mixture for me to suit my personal tastes, he said. All the tobaccos in the shop were the finest grade and his mixtures were like no one else's. I took samples and promised to send him my books, which I did when I got home.

For the next four years I saw George every six months or so, and we'd spend the afternoon talking about Armenian history and customs and current politics and inevitably about the human condition. But mostly we would talk poetry, for literature was George's passion. He would have me read aloud poems from my books that he particularly liked or would ask me to read new poems, and he would loudly declaim Armenian poetry in both the original language and in translation, explaining what he correctly supposed were references and nuances I didn't understand.

These afternoons were delightful. I met his wife, who crept about the store at times and seemed to affectionately tolerate her excitable husband's antics, and on the second visit I brought Donna to meet them both. On a number of visits, I urged Chuck Hanzlicek and Dianne to meet Nazar, but they weren't much interested, nor was Peter Everwine, the one time I mentioned George to him.

No, George Nazar was my own discovery and my private delight, as, I imagined, I was his. Friends and customers dropped in the store, but when I was there, I was the center of his attention.

George's enthusiasm for life and art outdistanced my own. I often imagined him scurrying around that narrow, shadowy shop, brimming with energy, like Vulcan stoking the furnace of the universe so it would continue to roar, or like Loki mumbling some mischievous prank he was about to play on humankind—a prank that would wake us from our stupor, quicken each of our heartbeats, and charge our lives with meaning. In many ways I saw in George Nazar the old man I hoped to be, brimming with passion, curiosity, and a hunger for life.

For four years, we wrote letters to one another, even talked by phone once or twice. But mostly, we visited in his shop and seemed to reinvigorate each other with energy we could take to our separate worlds—he to his friends, customers, wife, and daughter, and me to my writing, classes, friends, and family.

Then on my visit to Fresno during the winter rainy season in 1986, George announced that he was going on vacation to Hawai'i because his wife had become quite ill and he wanted to take her to a sunny climate. A few months after he returned from that sojourn, she died. A month later, George closed the shop, and on my last visit, extolled his latest enthusiasm—the Hawai'ian Islands, where he had stayed in a condominium. Now his plans were to buy a condominium on Maui or Kaua'i and spend his last years in his newfound tropical paradise.

Our last meeting was in his shop, with its empty display cases and bare tables. He read his favorite Armenian poems to me, packed his books away, and sent me off with half a dozen five-pound bundles of pipe tobacco. There were tears in his eyes as we parted, but I also recognized that his determination to leave Fresno and his enthusiasm for his new home were ways of dealing with the loss of his wife of sixty years. He didn't expect to live much longer, he said, but he would die among many-colored, perfumed flowers, choruses of brightly plumed birds, a lawn-green sea, and a genial, happy people. What more could one ask for after a full life?

A few weeks later I received several packages from him that I imagined he had mailed just before he left for the islands. They contained several signed copies of books to him from Saroyan, a first edition of *My Name Is Aram*, and an envelope and stamp honoring Saroyan's contribution to American culture. I understood that I was now the guardian of them and the life they depicted, as I was also the repository of George's past. Although I had asked George to send me his new address when he got settled, there was only his Fresno address on the packages, and as if to confirm my suspicion that I was part of a life he had left behind, I never heard from him again.

■ ■ ■

Poetry audiences waned in Santa Cruz in the 1980s, since poetry was no longer fashionable. The two literary bright spots of the decade were the arrivals and residences of Robert Sward and Robert Peterson. Sward was returning to the United States after a ten-year hiatus in Canada. I had been drawn to his anarchically humorous poems since I had read them in Iowa, where he had been a student several years before me—and where his free-spirited verse had not been appreciated by the staid powers that be. It was good to finally get to know him, the author of this classic poem:

Robert Sward,
Santa Cruz, 2004

Uncle Dog: The Poet at 9

I did not want to be old Mr.
Garbage man, but uncle dog
Who rode sitting beside him.

Uncle dog had always looked
To me to be truck-strong
Wise-eyed, a cur-like Ford

Of a dog. I did not want
To be Mr. Garbage man because

All he had was cans to do.

Uncle dog sat there me-beside-him
Emptying nothing. Barely even
Looking from garbage side to side:

Like rich people in the backseats
Of chauffeur-cars, only shaggy
In an unwagging tall-scrawny way.

Uncle dog belonged any just where
He sat, but old Mr. Garbage man
Had to stop at every single can.

I thought. I did not want to be Mr.
Everybody calls them that first.
A dog is said, Dog! Or by name.

I would rather be called Rover
Than Mr. And sit like a tough
Smart mongrel beside a garbage man.

Uncle dog always went to places
Unconcerned, without no hurry.
Independent like some leashless

Loaf friendship without scavenger
Can-picking dogs. And with a bitch
At every other can. And meat:

His for the barking. Oh, I wanted
To be uncle dog—sharp, high fox-
Eared, cur-Ford truck-faced

With his pick of the bones.
A doing, truckman's dog
And not a simple child-dog

Nor friend to man, but an uncle
Travelling, and to himself—
And a bitch at every second can.

I hadn't seen Bob Peterson, who had moved to New Mexico, since our San Francisco days in the late 1960s, and it was delightful to be able to hang out with him again and his old friends, the novelist John Deck and his wife Harriet, who I had befriended since moving to Santa Cruz.

THE EIGHT ECSTASIES OF YAEKO IWASAKI

Poetry audiences may have waned, but poetry was far from extinct. In the mid-1980s I received a phone call from Sara Wilbourne, who asked me to write a dance idea for her. Sara was one of the lead dancers for the Tandy Beal Dance Company, a national drama/dance organization presided over by the dynamic, multitalented Beal, whose equally talented husband, the composer Jon Scoville, often provided experimental music to accompany her productions. Sara had attended one of Tandy's workshops at the University of Utah, and Tandy asked her to join the company.

Sara was a superb dancer technically and, as I was to learn, a brilliant choreographer. Her mind was both creative and analytical, and she was able to verbalize her ideas—three traits not always present in excellent dancers. She was also to teach me an important lesson about life and art.

I had never met Sara. She called me out of the blue with her request, which was purposely vague. She wanted me to create a dance for her in any way I was moved to do so: a script, a dance drama, a narrative sketch, a poem, a tableau, an image—anything that she could expand imaginatively through movement.

"Do you have any images in mind?" I asked.

She had seen a Buddhist graveyard in Japan, she replied after a few moments. It was a collection of crooked stelae, seemingly arranged haphazardly and crowded together. "There's no hurry, and you don't have to use that image either. It's just haunted me, that's all," she said, and after giving me her phone number, she hung up.

I was intrigued. Wilma and I had talked about doing poetry and dance projects together, but we never had the time or wherewithal to do more than hold a few desultory talks about it. Sara's image of a Japanese cemetery nagged at me.

"Something I've read somewhere, something I've read," I kept repeating to myself all that day and the next. Then I remembered. Several years before, I had read Philip Kapleau's *The Three Pillars of Zen* and was taken by his account of the experiences of a young Japanese woman named Yaeko Iwasaki. Yeako had undergone all the steps of Zen Buddhist enlightenment in five days, after practicing zazen meditation for five years with Sogaku Harada, or Harada-roshi (Harada, the teacher). What makes Yaeko's story memorable is that during those five days she recorded her experiences in eight letters she sent to Harada, urging him to come to her during this tumultuous time. Harada received the letters and wrote extensive commentaries in the margins, but before he could travel to her side, she died. What complicates this tale of spiritual fervor is the knowledge that Yaeko had been bedridden for years with tuberculosis and was dying during the five days of her transcendent experience. In other words, there is a possibility that her enlightenment was at least partially the result of a series of paroxysms brought about by the dying process. Still, her letters and the roshi's commentaries make up an extraordinarily detailed, step-by-step documentation of spiritual illumination.

Whatever the reason for Yaeko's enlightenment, the story had marvelous dramatic possibilities. But something had disturbed me when I read the account the first time; and when I reread it now, I remembered what it was: Yaeko's letters and Harada's comments were bland, emotionless, and conveyed none of the intensity such an extreme situation, I thought, should engender. Certainly, I wouldn't have written such dull, impassive prose if I were either Yaeko or Harada.

I actually experienced a pinch of anger as I mulled over those thoughts. My writer's sensibility had been tweaked, as had my most un-Zen-like Slavic soul. Did I dare, I thought, rewrite the letters as I thought they should read? The answer was there before I finished the thought. Already I saw Harada standing in a Japanese cemetery, thinking about Yaeko. He would introduce the subject and the story as a sort of one-man Greek chorus, and the body of the piece would be a dialogue between Yaeko's letters and Harada's commentaries.

I set to work writing the piece. Harada's opening scene—which provided the piece's dramatic setting—I created from scratch. Then I took the few concrete images I found in the letters and commentaries, as well as the moods and tones of voice I thought would reflect the emotions Yaeko and Harada were undergoing, and wrote entirely new material. In fact, many of the ideas, as well as images, were not Buddhist at all but expressed my own maturing vision of the world and the place humans occupy in the universe.

Within a week I completed the first draft, which included a made-up epilogue that matched the prologue, and two weeks later I called Sara and told her I had a rough "scenario" for her to look at.

She was surprised by my call and dumbfounded when I handed her the thirty pages of what amounted to a script. She immediately realized the potential of the piece but also recognized that such a production would run more than an hour—an expanse of time that would mean a prodigious amount of choreography. But after she read the manuscript and heard my ideas on how it could be performed, she accepted the challenge. I had conceived of the performance centered around two actors, one male and the other female, who would read the letters and commentaries as if they were having a running dialogue. Sara immediately transformed the piece by having the dialogue take place offstage, while onstage the dancers would "dance" the mood changes and words, but not as mime. Would I mind that? she asked. Not in the least, I replied: she could do whatever she wanted with the script; that was what collaboration was all about, I said: the artists' egos had to be left at the door, so to speak, and the project at hand had to be the focus of everyone concerned.

We set about signing up a crew and a composer. I quickly found out that Sara was no dreamy aesthete but a highly intelligent, well-organized artist who got things done on a practical basis as she created highly original and imaginatively choreographed work. We worked hand in foot together.

But who would be the composer? she asked. I suggested Lou Harrison, which amazed her, and I sent a letter off to him. He was in Bali at the time and, as I've already written, he wrote back two weeks later, saying the project intrigued him, but he would be away for the rest of the year and had to finish two major commissions in the next two years.

By the time I received Lou's reply, Sara had signed a lighting expert and gotten together a troupe of four dancers besides herself, one of whom, the person who would dance the role of Harada, had been taking lessons with her for the past eight months. His name was Erik Stern. The piece, which I had named *The Eight Ecstasies of Yaeko Iwasaki*, would be his first major role in what would be a stellar dance career.

The endless meetings had begun. They were delightful and energizing for everyone involved. Everyone was enthusiastic about the project and had automatically drowned their egos in a sea of creativity. It didn't take more than three meetings for me to realize that I was working with a group of world-class theater people.

At the initial brainstorming sessions, the members of the group came forward with their wildest creative ideas, assuming whatever they suggested would be impossible to implement due to budget constraints. In the past, costs had always limited their creative conceptions. I was so impressed by the ideas everyone was coming up with, however, that I urged them to try to stick with their most experimental notions and draw up a "dream" budget. They did, and over the next three months Sara and I secured enough money to present *The Eight Ecstasies* in accordance with everyone's initial ideas.

We also secured a theater in downtown Santa Cruz that sat 250 people. But instead of using the stage, we set up a rectangular platform in the middle of the auditorium as the performing area, and put 150 chairs around it. The platform would be covered with rough silk, and Ronn Reinberg, the lighting designer, would shoot his lights from above the platform through the same kinds of silk. This would give the platform an otherworldly glow.

As time went on, we began to conceive of setting up the entire theater as an otherworldly environment: the theater lights would be lowered when the audience entered, but the platform would be lighted and surrounded by hundreds of stones and rocks reminiscent of the Ryoanji temple rock garden in Kyoto. The dancers, in costume, would usher the audience to their seats while serene Japanese string music played in the background. During intermission, the same dancers would serve green tea in Japanese tea bowls. For the latter, I enlisted my friends Bruce and Marcia McDougal, who, with friends of their own, enthusiastically made and contributed two hundred tea bowls.

As for the performers, the two actors would stand in the back of the theater, hidden from the audience, their disembodied voices reciting my transformed versions of the letters and commentaries, while Sara and the dancers performed on one half of the rectangular platform and Erik on the other. At no time would either group onstage invade the other's space—and Sara and Erik would perform their duets no closer than fifteen feet from each other. Meanwhile, the musicians would perform the music from the theater's unlit stage.

All this planning and preparation came together with astonishing quickness. Our one problem—and it was a major one—was finding someone to compose the music.

That Lou Harrison would not be able to do the music was a letdown. But everyone acknowledged that getting him had been a pipe dream, and we turned our thoughts to a practical search for a composer who could handle such a project.

Our first interview was with Gene Lewis, a musician and performer many of the crew had worked with before. Gene would be easy to work with and was a person willing to suspend his ego: he would easily fit in with the group, they said. I was leery, knowing that the music would be all-important and doubting we could find another local artist whose caliber of work and creativity could match the quality of the people I was working with. When Gene showed up for the interview, my doubts increased.

Gene was nice enough, even delightful. He had a twinkle in his eye and a wonderful smile. He was small and thin and looked like a leprechaun, an impression that was solidified by a nervous energy that made me picture him as hopping from one project to another. But he knew nothing about Japanese music and had never even heard it before. We played him cuts from long-playing records of taiko and kotsumi drums, the thirteen-string koto zither and shakuhachi flute, and he listened politely. I was less enthusiastic than ever about him. But the rest of the group, handing him the records and a copy of the script, told him to go home and see what he could come up with.

A week later, Gene showed up carrying what looked like wooden crates and assorted junk from a lumberyard. He had known nothing about the instruments on the records we had given him, but he was so intrigued by the project and what he had heard that he had built six or seven instruments that echoed the sounds the Japanese instruments made. He played us several samples from a sketch of the score he proposed to write.

I sat listening to all this with what must have been the most astonished expression my face ever registered. We had found our composer, and I had learned to expand my notions of suitability. Gene's final score was more than I could have wished for, and as another marvelous member of the crew, he energetically arranged to get an extraordinary trio of local musicians to play for the performances.

All we needed was a director to guide and coordinate what had now become an extravaganza. Sara, a wise and knowing theater person, had insisted on this addition and came up with Marcia Taylor, who had just returned from Europe where for ten years she had coordinated productions for MGM. I insisted on being her assistant director, wanting to keep a wary eye on the script. But for no reason: Marcia understood every nuance of it, and she guided the entire production with faultless acumen.

I have gone into the making of *The Eight Ecstasies of Yaeko Iwasaki* in such detail because it was the most extraordinary and satisfying collaboration of my creative life. In the end, twenty-one people made up the group, and we got along like the proverbial family, each of us igniting the creative ideas of the others.

The news of the production ran like wildfire through the county, and everyone, from businesses to arts organizations, contributed money and goods to the project. We opened to an unheard of amount of publicity in the local press and even had our notices carried in San Francisco by both

The creative powers behind *The Eight Ecstasies. From front:* Gene Lewis, Marcia Taylor, Ronn Reinberg, Sara Wilbourne, Diane Neri, Morton Marcus. Santa Cruz, 1984

Sara Wilbourne as Yaeko,
Santa Cruz, 1984

the *Examiner* and the *Chronicle*. As a result, we sold out all our performances. The reviews were euphoric and appeared in newspapers as far away as San Francisco. At the final performance, several hundred people tried to storm the theater, and we promised to do a second three-week run the following spring when the theater would once more be available. I had never been so happy. By the following spring, I was in the midst of shooting my television history of film and easily persuaded my partner and director, Stuart Roe, head of TV production for De Anza and Foothill Colleges, to shoot a performance of *The Eight Ecstasies* for posterity at the school's state-of-the-art TV studio. But it was not to be. By the time we had rung down the final curtain, most of the dancers and production crew had commitments in other cities and states.

The project and its aftermath defined a truth I already knew—that world-class, dedicated artists of all media who would never be recognized lived in Santa Cruz and communities like it throughout the nation and certainly throughout the world.

But I was crestfallen that we were unable to have a record of what we had created. Seeing this, Sara and Marcia took me aside and taught me a lesson that was, it seemed to me, something I should have known from my Daoist studies and especially from the tale of Yaeko's tragic enlightenment. They explained that in the performing arts everything is ephemeral, and the artists had to let each project fade into the ether. As a writer, I always tried to grasp the moment and make it permanent by bringing it alive in the writing. But they knew better than I ever would that nothing lasts.

A decade after we closed the show, Gene Lewis contracted a rare form of cancer and died, smiling and joyous to the end, and the rest of the crew were scattered throughout the country, each of them with their own triumphs and failures, joys and miseries. We saw each other less and less, although Sara and I did other, smaller productions that incorporated poetry and dance. Once she joined me at a writers' conference where we both taught a workshop in movement and words, and another time I joined her in a similar project during a dance conference weekend.

I recognize that even this description of the production is an attempt to secure the memory of *The Eight Ecstasies* from the relentless movement of time, but all that remains of it is an exquisite, hand-printed broadside of my poem of Harada's reply to Yaeko's fifth letter. No, that's not true: several hundred copies of the show's program, which unfolds to a 17 x 22 inch poster of the entire script, a sequence of poems that I have never published, resides in a carton in my garage as a sobering reminder that nothing is permanent in this world.

> Out of innumerable shadows
> the Spirit that is One rises like a moon.
> What is that Spirit if not you, me, everyone?
>
> With each breath of ordinary air,
> we repeat, *I am holy, I am I, I am selfless I—*
> as if breathing is as much a spiritual
> as a physical act,
> and each breath an involuntary hymn.
>
> —from *The Eight Ecstasies of Yaeko Iwasaki*

CHAPTER 46

The Earthquake of 1989, Kirby Wilkins, and Other Odds and Ends of the 1980s

Weather disasters remind us not only of our mortality but of how small we are in the scheme of things. Normal Santa Cruz weather conditions provide gentle reminders of both truths annually, but the 1980s were particularly harsh, especially 1989.

First there was the flood of 1982. A windless rain fell from the sky in thick ropes for more than twenty-four hours. Rivers poured over their banks, highways were washed out, and houses tobogganed down mudslides in the mountains. The county was isolated for days without electricity or amenities, and a number of people died.

But the earthquake of 1989 provided the most forceful example of nature's power. It was a warm, sunny October afternoon. I was sitting in my back yard, entertaining the poet Diane Wakowski, who was to read at Cabrillo that night. Diane, her driver, Donna, and I were getting to know each other over wine and snacks when, without warning, the ground trembled beneath us, a thunderous crack startled the air as though two gigantic, invisible hands had caught us like flies between them as they clapped together, and the earth began to heave and hump in waves, as if it was a carpet under which a huge prehistoric beast had suddenly awoken and was speedily slithering past us toward the conclusion of a cataclysmic nightmare we hadn't known we were dreaming.

All of us instinctively dove to the ground. The yard is open, except for a few small fruit trees and a giant redwood whose branches cover half its space. Before I headed for the grass I involuntarily glanced at the redwood. It shook as if it were having an epileptic fit, showering dust and leaf bits everywhere around us, but it held its place.

The aftershocks continued for days, and the human tragedies the quake caused have been well-documented. But two things stand out for me. One was Jim Houston's comment a week later as we stood staring at the rubble downtown. He said in a quiet, almost reverential voice, as if he was still con-templating what he was about to say, "If you can't trust the earth beneath your feet, what can you trust?"

My other memory involves an irony I cannot avoid telling. A native Cali-fornian, Diane Wakowski had moved to Michigan years before 1989 to, among other things, "avoid the big one," the mythical earthquake that is always in the back of every Californian's mind, with its vision of the state breaking off from the continent like a piece of cake and sinking beneath the green waters of the Pacific Ocean.

The quake, therefore, forced Diane to face one of her worst fears, and as people so often do in such circumstances, she quickly adjusted to the situa-tion. I'm sure that, like all of us she was shaken up, but she remained calm, and, after seeing how our neighbors were doing, we spent the night in the yard, talking quietly, clearly not wanting to alarm one another. In fact the night took on the aspect of a camping trip with friends, except when Diane's driver and I made forays into the darkened house for mattresses, blankets, and food, and we had to carefully pick our way through overturned book-cases, broken glass, and the rest of the chaos inside.

One of the upshots of the earthquake was the earthquake benefit read-ing. Joe was so upset by the devastation the earthquake had visited on the downtown Santa Cruz bookshops that he wanted to gather all the Santa Cruz writers together in a daylong reading to raise money to help the stores recover and show the writers' solidarity with them. He asked me to join him in organizing the event, and we enlisted more than sixty local writers to read at the Santa Cruz High School auditorium. Joe named the afternoon- and evening-long event *The Great Santa Cruz Word Quake Benefit*.

The earthquake accounted for losses of all kinds to the community. A few months after it, George Hitchcock and Marjorie left Santa Cruz for Oregon.

EL ANDAR

An enterprise that arose just before the earthquake was the newspaper, *El Andar*. At the end of the 1980s, a talented ex-student of mine named Jorge Chino founded the bilingual newspaper in Watsonville. Working with a small core group of fellow students from the university, he struggled to promote news of the Hispanic community and Hispanic culture. A month after the earthquake he asked for my aid, and I had a number of restaurant owners I knew in Santa Cruz donate food to a fiesta of music and poetry on Main Street in Watsonville.

The fiesta was held in the large patio of a Hispanic mall named La Man-zana that had been built a year or so before by Manuel Santana, the popular restaurant owner and painter who had been active in county political and cultural events since the early 1960s. Manuel donated food and whatever else was needed with his usual generosity. It was a wonderful event attended by hundreds throughout the day and night and was made more significant because the earthquake had devastated Watsonville and many people who attended the fiesta were still living in tents in the parks. I was one of the few Anglo readers, and a few days later Jorge asked me to be on the editorial board of the newspaper.

For four years Jorge struggled to get steady financial backing for *El Andar*. A fascinating prose stylist, he gave up writing to pursue promoting the paper. It was a social mission he felt compelled to embrace with all his energy. Then in 1993, he and his friends decided to convert the newspaper into a slick national magazine and published essays, interviews, and fiction by the best Latino writers in Central and South America. It also featured political exposés. The magazine was physically and intellectually impressive. By this time Jorge had moved *El Andar's* offices to Santa Cruz, and the old editorial board had long since been replaced, but I remained in close contact with him. To raise money he put on several annual bilingual readings in honor of the seventeenth-century Mexican nun poet Sor Juana Inés de la Cruz at Holy Cross church in Santa Cruz, filling the several-hundred-seat nave with an enthusiastic audience of Anglos and Hispanics. The events featured music and mostly local Hispanic writers, although Gary Soto came down from the Bay Area, and Francisco Alarcon and Elba Sanchez, then working at the university, both readers at the first fiesta in 1989, were always on the programs. Of the two or three Anglos who took part each year, Adrienne Rich and I were always invited.

The magazine, ever impressive in its writing and layout, limped along for another seven years, always in need of funds. Then it suspended publication. As for Jorge, I haven't seen him for some time and hope he has rediscovered the power that his own rich writing can bring to the world he so desperately wanted to inform and change.

HOW I BECAME A FILM HISTORIAN

The year before *The Eight Ecstasies* was produced, I was approached by several senior colleagues from the English Department who asked me to take over the Film History class at Cabrillo while its regular instructor was on sabbatical. They knew I was a film buff, and they wanted to keep the class in the college schedule while the regular instructor was gone because of the revenue it brought to the school through the numbers of students who enrolled in it, numbers that in the last several years had been falling. Although I protested that I wasn't qualified, I allowed myself to be persuaded into accepting the assignment and spent the summer of 1983 learning film history and film techniques.

It was soon clear that the amount of study involved in being even minimally prepared to teach the class was enormous, and I called a meeting of the people who had asked me to do the course, telling them that the commitment required would have to be repaid by a guarantee that I would teach the class on a regular basis, along with the original instructor. They assented, and I threw myself into learning everything I could about film, as well as viewing every "great" film from the past I could find. I literally gorged myself on films and film information twenty-four hours a day. There was nothing new about my pursuing a project in this obsessive way. I had been choosing topics and throwing myself into learning everything about them with the same intensity for decades. It was the way I made sure I kept learning, and it can be traced all the way back to my reading every book in the Irving School library when I was fourteen, and later, during my air force years, when I devoured books for Dietrich Gerhard's class on the French Revolution at Washington University.

As a former history instructor, I was enthralled to find out how the history of film paralleled and embraced world history for the past hundred years and noted the relevance of national cinemas to their respective countries' histories, ideals, and social customs. I took courses at the local University of California campus, attended lectures, and read, read, read about, and saw, saw, saw films, films, films.

I had thought film critics and film historians were generally idlers and dreamers: those who refuse to look at life and take refuge from it in the darkened theaters of their imaginations. But I quickly came to realize that the opposite is true, since films can act literally as mirrors we either hold up to the world outside the theater to see how they conform to our notions of how we would like the world to be, or how they can reveal the banality and frivolity of their own world view in contrast to the real one. Either way, the serious viewer is engaged in assessing the world when he watches a film.

The class I taught in the fall of 1983 was enormously successful. Enrollment jumped to over 150 students and, through word of mouth, approached 200 students the following fall. That just spurred me on in my cinema studies.

Soon I was teaching the course every semester, and during the fall of 1984 I was approached by Stuart Roe to audition to be part of a television history of film being produced by the Bay Area Television Consortium. The consortium was looking for an on-camera host who would also write the series. Stuart and I hit it off immediately. He was both director and producer for the project, and when I told him my ideas for the structure and presentation of the entire series, he asked me to put my ideas together in a mini version for the audition tape. The result was that I won the assignment, and over the next several years Stuart and I shot sixteen half-hour tapes, which ran through the entire history of film until the 1950s. I wrote a thousand-page book to accompany the tapes. Everything was moving along smoothly until the fall of 1988 when the budget for the Bay Area Television Consortium was suspended and the powers that be told us to turn over what we had done and abandon the project. Instead, Stuart and I bought the project by forfeiting the money the area office had originally contracted us for.

We never finished the series, but Stuart and I used the tapes in our classes at Cabrillo and Foothill Colleges, and the series was shown on half a dozen California and Oregon television stations in its truncated form over the next ten years and is still shown occasionally.

The project had made me delve into film history with even greater intensity than before, and I emerged from the experience with enough knowledge of cinema technique and history to write articles and monographs on all aspects of film. From 1985 to the present, at least half my time has been spent dealing with film in one way or another—as film reviewer, film critic, film festival steering committee member, and cohost of a television film-review program that at one time had a possible audience of more than 2,500,000 people throughout the San Francisco Bay Area. Ironically, more people in Santa Cruz County know me as a film critic than as a poet.

I was engaged in a number of other local activities during the 1980s as well. I was asked to take over a weekly hour-long radio program entitled "The Poetry Show" on the Santa Cruz community radio station in 1986, which I cohosted with Joe. Although presented under several titles with various cohosts over the years, the show is the longest continuously running poetry show on American radio, and although Joe retired from the program in 1995 and various people have taken his place, at the time of this writing I remain as cohost, interviewing poets and reading the work of poets past and present.

It was also during this period that I undertook the writing of a series of literary profiles for the *Metro* newspaper chain, in-depth portraits of such writers as Ray Carver, Chitra Divakaruni, Li-Young Lee, Vern Rutsala, Al Young, Lawson Inada, and Adrienne Rich. All this outside activity, as well as keeping up with my regular classes, meant that my literary output was curtailed, a situation I already alluded to in how and why I came to write *Pages from a Scrapbook of Immigrants*, which finally appeared in 1988.

THE READING TOURS OF THE NORTHWEST

As if I was not busy enough, I gave frequent readings of my poetry at colleges, bookstores and coffeehouses in San Francisco and the Bay Area, became a permanent faculty member of the Foothill Writers' Conference, and continued to make what turned out to be more than half a dozen tours of Oregon and Washington. The tours began in the 1970s and were planned to coincide with the publication of each of my books. It was on these tours that I renewed my friendship with Lawson Inada and Vern Rutsala.

The preparation and route of the trip were almost ritualistic. I would pack the trunk of my car with cartons of new and old books and drive up Highway 5, through the Central Valley, past Redding, and over the state line into Oregon. Crossing the state line was like going into another world because the first fifteen miles or so on either side of the border were a windswept wasteland of blown newspapers, bed springs, candy wrappers, beer cans, and whatnot overseen by snow-shouldered Mount Shasta in the distance. That introduction made travel through Oregon proper like entering Paradise, since the landscape became more lush with green foliage and trees the farther north I went.

I would stop first at Ashland, always months after the famous Shakespeare season was over, and do a reading and several classes for Lawson at Southern Oregon University. After Ashland, I would continue north giving five to ten readings wherever they were scheduled for me by the Mount Hood organizers under Sandra Williams's direction, and I would finally end up in Portland, where I'd give three or four readings and workshops in the area and stay most of the time with Vern and Joan Rutsala. Sometimes I would have readings in Washington, but by the time I arrived in Portland I would have sold most of the books I had brought with me. Not only were audiences large in the 1970s, 1980s, and early 1990s, but I usually sold over 150 books by the time the tour was over. By the early years of the new millennium, those audiences were still strong, but students were no longer buying books, and on my last tour in 2002, I sold only two books and realized our culture had drastically changed.

STEPHEN KESSLER

In many ways, Stephen Kessler represents the intelligent, dedicated artist and organizer at the grassroots regional level who has kept literature and independent thinking on all topics alive in the United States in the second half of the twentieth century. I first came into contact with Stephen in 1967 when he accepted the first prose poem I ever wrote for publication. At that time, he was a student at Bard College in New York and editor of their literary magazine, *The Lampeter Muse*. The following year we met face to face almost by accident on a street in downtown Santa Cruz. I forget who introduced us, or why.

Stephen Kessler,
Santa Cruz, 1988

Small, slim, and good-looking, Stephen's cool, deliberate demeanor belies a vigorous, intelligent mind. Aided by a small trust fund, he has directed his energies over the years to the arts, social causes, and culture in general. He settled in Santa Cruz, founded a small publishing company called Alcatraz, brought out a thick, well-designed annual and several books under its

imprint, and when the best of the two weekly alternative newspapers folded
in 1986, he picked up where it left off, and as publisher and editor, founded
a new and better weekly he named *The Sun*. For three years he directed the
paper's fortunes, wrote dozens of smart editorials on a variety of subjects in
various experimental styles, and had to close the business mainly because of
the 1989 earthquake. When the community radio station, KUSP, was looking for new hosts of the poetry show, he and our mutual friend Gary Young
took it over for several years, and he then suggested to the management that
I replace him.

Stephen's entrepreneurial side surfaced in other ways too. In the early
1980s, he staged several readings featuring dozens of poets, one against
nuclear proliferation called "Bombs Away," and another a celebration of
multicultural literature. The events drew hundreds of people. From time to
time, he and I joined forces on several projects. Together, we provided seed
money to the organizer of the third Santa Cruz Poetry Festival, and when
Stephen convinced Allen Ginsberg to come to town in the early 1980s to
read at the Kuumbwa Jazz Center, he asked me to read with him. I think his
invitation had less to do with his estimate of my poetry than with his
shrewd belief that my reading style might ignite Ginsberg's energy. It did,
and he gave electrifying readings at both shows. In fact, they were the best
readings I ever heard Ginsberg give.

After the earthquake in 1989, Stephen left Santa Cruz for New York City
and a few years later settled in Gualala, California, the same town where I
had lived all those years ago when I taught at Point Arena. There, in 1999,
he founded *The Redwood Coast Review* in partnership with the Coast Community Library. The publication is a sophisticated book review in tabloid
format with excellent, in-depth essays on literature and culture.

While he was engaged in all these undertakings, Stephen wrote his own
poetry, and by the early years of the new millennium, he had published six
books of his poems, which are marked by great vitality and edged with
social commentary and memories of his Los Angeles youth. But for the
most part Stephen's reputation rests on his translations for which he has
won many awards. At this writing he has published ten books of poetry and
fiction translations from the Spanish, including works by Fernando Alegría,
Julio Cortázar, Ariel Dorfman, Luis Cernuda, and Nobel laureates Vicente
Aleixandre and Pablo Neruda.

Here is one of his Los Angeles poems:

I Live Just Over There

Those rows of magnolias on either side of the dark
street where I walked some nights in late spring
had the smell of a young man's thought,
not philosophy but
the brooding musings of a boy beginning to lose
his adolescence and looking for some reason,

some light burning in one of the neighborhood houses
where someone was reading a book who understood,
someone he could imagine talking to
who knew more than his father was letting on,
that his distressed mother could ever begin to think
because she was more entangled in herself
than even he, the young man, was caught in his
inner drama, walking those quiet, carefully tended
streets where now and again a police car
cruised past and sometimes stopped
so the cop could inquire what he was doing
out on foot this time of night,
but how could he answer "Thinking" or
"Trying to invent philosophy" when all he was
was barely beyond a boy, a gloomy truant too timid
to run away from home or burn it down
to give his folks something to think about,
too shy even to sneak into yards to spy
on women as they slipped out of their skirts,
and so replied "I live just over there"
and was left to walk on, alone,
drunk on the scent of philosophy trees,
thinking.

KIRBY WILKINS AND THE LOST FATHER

Kirby Wilkins is as close a friend as Joe Stroud, and together the three of us have been on-again, off-again buddies for over thirty-nine years. At first, Kirby and I were leery of each other. It was the old problem I have talked about before: the fast-talking, wisecracking East Coast city slicker who loved the comforts of civilization and home, and the reticent Westerner who loved travel and the solitary, outdoor life. Kirby, when I met him, was the most unmistakable, and complex, example I ever met of the "Western man," as I have defined the term in this book. But as I
was to learn, that persona was a mask that covered a vulnerable, haunted man who was searching for something many men do and which for years I refused to acknowledge as part of my own pursuit of self-understanding—the coming to terms with an absent father and the pain and lack of guidance that absence caused.

Kirby Wilkins,
Santa Cruz, 1990

It was Joe who brought us together, and through most of the years that followed, Kirby and I looked ironically at each other's personalities. There was no doubt Kirby didn't trust me, and I thought his respect for and friendships with mainly taciturn men was a sort of misplaced romanticism. To me, the people he chose to hang around refused to examine, let alone know, their own feelings, and by and large I didn't trust *them*.

Another problem was that Kirby almost never asked a question, requested a favor, or made a statement directly. He hinted or led up to whatever he was after in roundabout ways, a trait that may have been part of his detached persona but rankled me. I was direct: I wanted no misinterpretations in any of my dealings with people. I found his indirect ways exasperating as, I'm sure, he found my blunt, head-on manner uncomfortable if not plainly disingenuous and rude. Yet in the end, he would be responsible for my acknowledging an essential lack in my life that I had refused to think about since I was a teenager.

Don't misunderstand. Kirby is no somber introvert. Outwardly, he is quiet, good-humored, and unpretentious and carries his slim, six-foot, two-inch frame with ease. He has movie-star good looks, but what people first notice about him is his smile. With his full head of hair, triangular face moving from a wide forehead to a pointed cleft chin, and that smile, he called to mind Robert Mitchum—the slim, young Mitchum who starred in *Out of the Past* and *Where Danger Lives* in the late 1940s. Amused and detached in the early years of our relationship, Kirby's smile was that of an observer or a gentle cynic and at times stretched into a smirk.

But if Mitchum's smile evoked a sullen weariness, Kirby's smile was always on the edge of breaking into a boyish grin. His smile was good-natured. The Mardi Gras of human life paraded by—with its hysterics, horrors, and celebrations—and Kirby watched it pass with that smile, with those lidded eyes. His was an expression of amusement.

Yes, Kirby and I were different, yet there was also no doubt that our differences accounted for a curiosity about one another, if not a respect, which brought us close.

Of course, there were similarities too. Kirby is a fellow scribbler, a fiction writer of great talent. Over the years he has published two excellent novels and an insightful, beautifully crafted book of short stories. He was also an English Department colleague at Cabrillo and a legendary teacher adored by his students. But whereas I was full of passion and answers to my students' academic questions, he was quiet and easy-going in the classroom, cleverly guiding and encouraging his students to find answers on their own. Everyone—fellow teachers, students, and administrators—loved him and his pleasant, relaxed manner. But Kirby's agreeable ways, in those early years, were edged with a caustic self-righteous wit that periodically leaped to the surface, especially when he had drunk a few beers.

Born in 1936 to an alcoholic father and a reticent mother who later became an alcoholic, Kirby spent his first eleven years in the sagebrush and dry arroyos of the desert country on the outskirts of Reno, Nevada, and in the parched Sierra Nevada mountains above them. This, and landscapes like them, is where the characters in his fiction return again and again to regain orientation, if not to be spiritually reinvigorated—and to search for the father figure Kirby lost when he was eleven and his parents separated.

As a result of the separation, Kirby lost not only his father but his boyhood landscape because he and his mother moved to Menlo Park on the peninsula of San Francisco Bay. However, he never forgot those early years among what my East Coast imagination summoned up from his stories as shattered homesteads, ghost towns, and abandoned gold mines that to me are the remnants of western Americana and to Kirby is a loss of primal space and light. They are also the source of confusion and lack of direction in regard to his father that has plagued his adult years.

Kirby became interested in writing when he attended Stanford University in the early 1950s. He worked his way through school by operating early, room-size computers at Lockheed—an important contribution to his later thoughts on physics and technology. After graduating in 1958, he embarked on his first trip. With his new bride he traveled to New Zealand where he worked as a stevedore and construction worker and wrote for a local newspaper. A year later, he was back in the United States, pursuing a master's degree in Creative Writing at San Francisco State and once again working at Lockheed, where a career in computer technology seemed assured. But life was curiously aimless and stagnant—and worse, he found he was unable to write. At his wife's suggestion he went on to get a teaching credential at San Jose State and a year later found himself teaching high school in Sonora, near the region in the Sierras where he had spent his early boyhood. It was then that he mapped the Sierras as his symbolic territory, eventually identifying it as the country of the lost father in his writing, a site of sacrifice and redemption.

When Kirby's wife left him a year later, he went on a two-year odyssey through Asia and Europe, stopping in Japan for six months, where he taught English and took karate lessons. Over the ensuing years, he would travel for long periods to India, Pakistan, Japan, Alaska, and Greece, and several other third-world countries. To Kirby, travel is not tourism but a transforming experience that also provides the settings for his novels and stories—not as exotic backdrops, but as places where the day-to-day struggle to survive is always apparent and where, like Joe when he travels, Kirby attempts to live as a member of the community. He likes best, he told me, "those places where people live at the edge of life and death," which gives him an intense sense of being "plunged into the stream of pure life" from which he feels alienated in his daily existence in America.

It was that sensibility, so torturously thought out and deeply felt, that won me over. We may have been different, but his intelligence and complex view of things made me see that he was much more than the two-dimensional, cut-out figure I first thought him to be, as were, I thought with a sudden uncomfortable realization, the other men I had labeled with the epithet "Western men."

There were, of course, more similarities between us than the ones already mentioned, especially ones concerning travel and our observations about the rootless, spiritually empty ways of American society, similarities Joe also shared. So we formed a merry trio, teaching together, chiding one another, spending late afternoons and evenings talking about politics and literature, and going to parties with our colleagues, spouses, and girlfriends, which included Kirby's second wife, Anita—a fellow poet and Cabrillo colleague—and later Donna.

Meanwhile, Kirby's travels not only provided backdrops for his work, but ideas and plots as well. Many of these elements are present in his book of short stories, *Vanishing*, which appeared in 1984. Of the eleven stories, seven are set in the desert landscape outside Reno or in the small towns that dot the Sierras, his lost world, which I came to realize was similar to my view of the New York City of my boyhood. Many of the stories are about unsatisfied young or older people looking for guidance they haven't received from adults who are as confused and lost as they are, and although his stories are set by and large in the American West, I was surprised to find how personally I responded to them.

Kirby's search for a lost father was clearly apparent in his first novel, *King Season*, which was published in 1985. The book is based on his experiences as a member of a king-crab fishing crew in Alaska and tells the story of Lee Redfield, a well-educated writer who takes a job on a fishing boat. One of the crew is a violent old fisherman named Cody who identifies with the old Wild West. Cody is losing his mind and becomes a strange kind of failed guru to the young writer. In many ways Lee's story is Kirby's and his attempt, he readily admits, to get out of himself and into direct, spontaneous contact with the world around him. When Lee recalls his timid father in Nevada, he is not only contrasting him with Cody, but Kirby is talking about his own father and the landscape from which he was separated before he was a teenager. As Kirby told me, "A dominant theme throughout my work is of males being absent, which represents inadequate guidance." It was a comment I wouldn't forget, although I didn't realize until a long time afterward that this obsessive theme was an essential component of my own concerns.

In his second and most recently published novel, *Quantum Web*, which came out in 1990, all of Kirby's travels and themes are brought together, from his sojourns in Nepal and India to his work on early computers and his interest in physics. The book is cast as both a spy novel and an adventure tale but is actually a serious exploration of where humankind finds itself at the end of the last millennium. As the book opens, a Berkeley physicist named Jack Malloy kills a man near the Tibetan border. Later, leading a motley band of travelers that includes CIA and KGB agents, Malloy is compelled to return to the killing site in order to understand the factors behind the incident. Close at hand is a detachment of Chinese Communist soldiers searching for Malloy and his group as well as a mysterious old holy man

Left to right: Robert Sward, Kirby Wilkins, Al Young, and poet Anita Wilkins, Santa Cruz, 1990s

dying in a cave. The novel is marvelous, and the scenes with the holy man in the cave contain extraordinary writing. The holy man, needless to say, is the ultimate guru—the ultimate father figure.

As far as I was concerned, the stuff of Kirby's fiction pierced his mask of cynical detachment to show the person who struggled beneath it. More important, I couldn't forget the brief scene in *King Season* when Lee, crewing in Alaska, remembers his father in Nevada. Years later I recognized how I had emotionally shut out my own father, denying his existence, and I'm sure the scene in *King Season*, and another similar but more detailed scene in his unpublished novel of Nevada, *Lucky Dog*, both of which recurred in my thoughts at odd moments for the next decade, were important influences in making me acknowledge my own search to find a father figure and in seeing how effete and detached, for all my experiences and emotional nature, my own life had been.

By the time I recognized the resentment and pain my own father's absence had caused me, the scenes in both books had merged in my imagination to the picture of a man in shirtsleeves and knee-high riding boots standing in a desert. A dust-filled wind swirls behind him, suffusing the scene with a sepia hue. In that haze I can make out the ruins of a ghost town and in the hills beyond it the entrance to several abandoned mines. The man just stands there, expressionless, staring at me as at a camera from a distance that is no more than ten yards away but is absolute and unapproachable.

In my childhood and adult years, I had seen my father only twice for a total of little more than half an hour. Other than those moments, he had never tried to contact me, either by letter or phone. And when he didn't reply to the invitation I had sent him to my bar mitzvah, I jettisoned my longings for a paternal relationship: I literally erased my father from my mind. The only male guidance throughout my boyhood and youth, therefore, were Leo's brotherly solicitude, Larry's warped example, and Richard Martin's nine-month tutelage when I was a freshman at the Irving School.

In reality, I had guided myself to manhood with whatever notions I picked up from my schoolmates, books, films, and American popular culture in general. I would think of the scenes from *King Season* and *Lucky Dog* when I saw a film about older, strong men serving as clichéd examples to young men, and tears would inexplicably course down my face, even when the film was a comedy. But the reasons for my tears did not occur to me until I was almost sixty years old. And then it was too late. After the recognition, when I would sit alone late at night, the same rhetorical questions would shoot up from somewhere inside me: What kind of a father could I have been to Jana and Valerie? What kind of guidance could I have given Nick? By the time I had come to these thoughts, all three children were grown, and all I could do was come to terms with my own shortcomings and how I had ignored this important element of my existence.

For all our differences, that unacknowledged similarity, even though I wouldn't recognize it for years, may have been the basis of my friendship with Kirby. When Donna and I started going together seriously, we spent a lot of time with Kirby and Anita at their "ranch" in Watsonville, and the four of us would take long walks along the roads nearby and then go to dinner. They were evenings filled with laughter and far-ranging conversations, and Kirby and I became closer than ever. Several times I took Kirby up to San Francisco and introduced him to Leonard and Gina, who were quite taken with him. He, in turn, took me up to Sonora to visit friends and tromp through "his" hills. On one occasion we went camping in the Sierras, where our superficial differences came to the fore if for no other reason than my ineptness in the wilds was painfully evident.

Our basic personality differences, however, came swarming to the surface in the 1990s, and now that I think of it, they had to do with our changed professional roles. Kirby became head of the English Department in the mid-1990s, and I was president of the school's union. The once-united English Department had become fragmented over new school policies and, more important, pedagogical issues. It was a difficult time to be head of the department, and Kirby expected his friends, especially those among the old guard, to help him keep at least a semblance of order. Since becoming head of the union, I had grown accustomed to bulling my way through difficulties and getting quick compliances to my requests, and as time went on I was more and more concerned with the problems in the department. Kirby, as a good leader should, wanted patience and compromise. But I wanted an immediate end to what I saw as a worsening situation. I talked to him about it in private several times, and when no changes occurred, I became outspo-

ken in my views during department meetings. Soon Kirby and I were darting sarcastic comments at each other in public. I even accused him of being
an inept leader. I'm sure he thought I had betrayed him both as a friend and
as a colleague. Things went from bad to worse until we could no longer talk
to each other without trading insults, a situation that continued after both
of us retired.

Even before these events came to a head on campus, Kirby's life had
taken several dramatic turns. He and Anita had divorced, and he had
remarried and left the county to live in the house in which he had been
raised in Menlo Park. Finally, his new wife had given birth to his first child, a
boy they named Jake. But the birth had been a tragic one: Jake had emerged
from the birth canal with the umbilical cord wrapped around his neck, and
by the time the doctor untangled him he had lost so much oxygen he had
developed extensive brain damage. The doctor called his condition "cerebral palsy," which meant Jake would never be able to speak, walk, or control
his body. Several years later, Kirby's new marriage fell apart. He was sixty-
three years old at the time, and since then he has dedicated himself to raising Jake, who he has loved maybe more than anyone else. Jake has become
the center of Kirby's life. In a way, the boy who had lost his father, and the
male guidance that went with it, has become the father he longed to have.

It was Joe who brought Kirby and me back together. He had been suggesting a reconciliation meeting for several months and invited me over to
his house one sunny, summer afternoon in 2006 when Kirby was visiting
him. We drank and smoked in Joe's back yard, a sort of English country cottage garden, complete with wandering chickens, panting dog, and rows of
flowers and vegetables in a rustic but well-kept environment. Seated at an
outdoor wooden table, at first Kirby and I talked tentatively about one thing
and another, but soon we pushed aside the difficulties and hurt feelings of
the past, and the three of us were the old friends we had been years before.
No, not quite; the three of us have changed, and we value our friendship too
much to let petty, superficial differences get in the way of being together.
Kirby's change is visible. Even nearing seventy, he is still a good-looking
man, but the Mitchum smile is now devoid of its smirk, and his silences are
not so much those of a cynical observer as an empathetic contemplative.
The self-righteousness, it seems to me, has given way to compassion and a
tragic vision of the human condition.

For all our differences, in the end, Kirby and I were searching for the
same thing. In a way, we were brothers on a quest that was archetypal if not
biblical. My revelation of what we shared came much later than his. It was
on a night in 2001 as I was listening to a recording of the tenor Jossi Bjorling
and I suddenly recognized that Bjorling bore an uncanny resemblance to
my father, both in build and looks. Tears streamed down my cheeks when I
realized that I had substituted Bjorling's vibrant face, his mouth releasing
passionate, rhapsodic song, for my father's immobile features. My father's

With Kirby Wilkins and Joe Stroud in the Santa Cruz mountains. Spring, 2007

face, like his identity was anonymous, a mask I had never been able to penetrate. As I listened to Björling sing, I came to acknowledge that my father was one of life's mysteries I would never solve, like the identity of the person whose features were stamped on the gold burial mask Schliemann had dug from the bowels of time at Mycenae and of whom the poet George Seferis wrote, "Under the mask, a void." He was the expressionless man I had pictured in Kirby's novels, standing in a desert landscape among the ruins of a bygone age. I had realized that before. Now I knew I would never know the character of the man who stood before me in that timeless desert of my imagination, a man who neither beckoned me to come closer nor waved me away. He was nobody, a stranger: someone I didn't know who had never cared to know me.

Though officially out of print, all of Kirby Wilkins's books are available through Amazon.com.

■ ■ ■

On the day I was to send the final draft of this memoir to the publisher—which coincidentally was also the fifth anniversary of my mother's death—Jana, who had been searching for information about my father for years, found a member of the Marcus clan on the Internet. He was a retired professor of Education and Social Studies named Stanley Rothstein, the son of my father's sister Sophie, which made him my first cousin. When Jana, Donna, and I called him, he was delighted to hear from us. He immediately accepted our identity because we knew too much not to be who we said we were. Did he know my father Max, I asked? Did he!

With humor and energy, he told us story after story about my father. Max, he claimed, was "the legend of the Marcus family." As my mother had told me, Max had made several fortunes, lost them all, and wound up driving a cab in New York City. But there was more. Each fortune was in excess of ten million dollars, Stanley said, and each one Max gambled away. No wonder, I mused, that we had servants, a nanny, a chauffeur, and a fancy Cord automobile during the Depression.

As a person, Stanley continued, Max was charismatic: when he wanted to, he had a roguish charm, loved music (he was an exceptional self-taught pianist), had irrepressible energy, an infectious sense of humor, and was generally "fun to be with." In addition, he always took care of his family, setting up each of his siblings in business and paying for medical bills and anything else that might come up for them when the need arose. On the other hand, he was a compulsive gambler, and despite being successful and one of the best designers and cutters in the women's undergarment trade, he swindled, cheated, and conned everyone with whom he dealt in the business world. Because of his behavior, Stanley said, Max was "hated" by his colleagues in the industry.

Stanley remembers his mother asking Max to find him a job that might start his career, as Max had done with his brothers and sisters. Max was at the height of his second fortune and was delighted to provide help for Stanley who he told to come to his office in Manhattan. It was 1945, the last year of World War II, and Stanley was sixteen years old. When he arrived, he was told that Max was in a conference in his luxurious inner office, and he was asked to wait in an adjacent room crowded with twenty-four desks and a bulletin board that occupied one entire wall. Stanley was alone in the room, left to stare at the untended desks and the bulletin board, the latter of which he soon realized contained what seemed the names and miscellaneous information about every major racetrack in the nation. For three days, Max kept Stanley waiting. At the end of each day, Max's secretary told Stanley, to his exasperation, to return the next day. On the third day, a bored and fuming Stanley, just to have something to do, decided to rummage through the untended desks. When he opened the drawer of the first one, he was stunned to find that it was stuffed with money. So were all the other desks. It seems that Max had made his latest fortune in the black market, and since this was during the war, he couldn't deposit the illegal cash in a bank. Stanley left the office and had nothing to do with Max for a number of years.

It turned out that Frank Erickson, one of New York's most notorious bookies, would visit Max several times a week and haul away drawerfuls of the money in valises and bet the sums on various races and sports events for Max. In this way, as well as through cards and dice, Max eventually gambled away his second fortune. Soon after Max lost all his money, the IRS discovered his black market activities and he spent three years in the New York State Penitentiary at

Dannemora on tax evasion charges. Never again would he achieve financial success, and within a decade or two he was working as a New York City cab driver.

In the early 1970s, Max called Stanley on the phone. He explained that he was in his seventies, knew he was going to die soon, and wanted to leave his nephew a legacy. By then Max was penniless—or was he? "What could the legacy be?" Stanley wondered on his way to see him. Max's legacy, it turned out, were words for Stanley's ears only: a sure way to untold wealth; namely, an unbeatable system for winning any dice game Stanley might enter.

"He was a remarkable bastard," Stanley concluded. I had to agree, especially when Stanley told me that Max's son by his first wife, my half-brother Walter, although a talented pianist like his father, became a hustler and small-time con man who wound up as a "five-time loser" in the California prison system. I have to think that the example Max set for Walter influenced the way he turned out, and as I listened to Stanley I wondered how Max would have influenced me. In the end, I was glad Max had decided to have nothing to do with my life, especially my childhood. As Kirby would have put it, what kind of male guidance could Max have given me?

Donna reacted differently to Stanley's stories. She thought Max and all my family, as well as all the first generation of immigrants like them, were "larger than life characters." In their own way, and then through their children, she said, they had helped build the America that rose to prosperity and world dominance after World War II. In the end, I had to agree with her—but I was still glad that Max had decided to have nothing to do with me.

Jana's response was even more far-reaching. She was affected by Stanley's description of Max's father William, our mutual grandfather, a man he described as ethical and loving and someone who lit up any room he entered "like sunshine," but none of whose children, alas, were like him. She wrote, "I picture him deserting the Russian army in 1905 and traveling against arctic winds across Siberia and back to Kiev to retrieve his family and take them out of Russia to a new world. The choice this one man made changed so many people's lives . . . as did all the immigrants back then." How true. Had William not chosen as he did, neither Jana, Stanley nor I would probably be here today.

CHAPTER 47

Tahiti and Australia

Of all the events of the late 1980s, one stands out for its extravagance and unexpected aftermath. I still call it "the Australian adventure" and its wild conclusion, "The Wartilpa Kalipurnangka."

In the fall of 1988, Kirby's wife Anita was invited by a friend to come to Australia for a poetry reading tour. She immediately asked Joe and me to join her. The three of us were friends who also respected each other's work. I thought Anita's poems were excellent, and several were favorites of mine. Although he wouldn't be able to go on the tour, Kirby was as excited at the prospect of the trip as Anita, Joe, and I were. Years before he had introduced us to the person who had sent Anita the invitation, an old friend of his from Sonora named Dave Purdy. A charismatic theater director, bon vivant, and boisterous companion, Dave had been commissioned to direct several plays in Sydney in 1988, and he wholeheartedly embraced Anita's request to include Joe and me on the trip.

Within a month, Anita, Joe, and I were sent an itinerary for a three-week tour of Australia's east coast, which included my giving several talks at the two government sponsored schools for film and drama, the Australian Film Television and Radio School (the AFTRS) and The National Theatre Drama School. But we were at a loss as to how we could accept the invitation. First, the tour was to take place in March of 1989 when the three of us would be immersed in a full complement of classes at Cabrillo, and second, the cost of the flight was $2,000 for each of us. Our Australian hosts would provide room and board and a small stipend when we arrived, but that would not be nearly enough to cover our air fares.

Our English Department colleagues generously volunteered to take our classes while we were gone, but the price of the travel tickets was still prohibitive. We sat around for days, trying to figure out how we could pay for the trip, but we couldn't come up with a solution. It looked as if we would have to refuse the invitation.

It was in that frame of mind that the three of us sat in my office one afternoon, staring gloomily at the floor. "Well, there's only one thing to do," I said. "Let's ask the school to pay for our tickets."

Joe and Anita looked up for an explanation.

"We'll go to the president and ask him to pay for our flight," I explained.

As far as Joe was concerned, it was another one of my outlandish ideas, and this time he was going to have none of it. He threw up his hands and looked at me as he had many times before—as if I were his idiot half brother. It was the fundamental difference in our personalities surfacing again. Many times I thought that my aggressiveness seemed like crass huckstering to him, and on my part, I looked at his passivity with exasperation.

"As my mother always said," I continued, "'If you don't ask, you don't get'—all the president can do is refuse. Or accept."

Joe slapped the desk, dismissing the idea with a wave of his hand as if he were batting away a mosquito.

Joe's attitude, as it had many times before, made me determined to go through with my idea, no matter how ridiculous it seemed, if for no other reason than to prove him wrong.

I turned to Anita. At first she seemed as shocked as Joe at my proposal, but soon her features relaxed.

"What do you say, Anita?"

She smiled, and both of us went off to the president's office.

The president welcomed us, and without hesitation accepted the request. I prefaced my appeal by pointing out what an honor our tour would be for the school, which I would make sure was mentioned in all press releases everywhere we traveled.

When we returned to my office, Joe shook his head and smiled in incomprehension, and the three of us put the final touches on our plans.

The following March we flew to Australia. Before before we arrived there, however, we had an unexpected side adventure. The flight to Australia was such a great distance from San Francisco that the plane, an Air France jumbo jet, had to land in Tahiti to refuel. But when we landed, the pilots and crew went on strike and everyone on board found themselves stranded. However, the Air France management put everyone up in hotels and gave them meal coupons at local restaurants. So for three days, Joe, Anita, and I were unexpectedly on vacation in the heart of Polynesia, almost every Western European and American's dream of paradise.

The three of us rented a Jeep and drove around the island, visiting the Gauguin Museum and other sights. As we drove from one place to another I was struck by several connections and began writing a long poem composed of what turned out to be eight short sections. I called it "Marooned." Using the mutiny on the *Bounty* as the underlying metaphor, I explored different aspects of Tahitian history in relation to the world and my own personal impressions of landing there as I had. I also played with three recurring images: Edith Piaf's great classic song "La Vie en Rose," the French colonial presence in Tahiti, and Bobby McFerrin's hit song at the time, "Don't Worry, Be Happy." I used those images to explore the romanticized vision Westerners had of Tahiti and the reality of poverty and desolation I saw all around me. I also depicted the island metaphorically as the planet adrift in the sea of interstellar space, much like Bligh set adrift in a long boat on the open sea by the mutineers, and, in a way, the *Bounty* itself when it set sail for Pitcairn Island. The microcosm inherent in those images allowed me to look at the human condition as we approached the new millennium, which was only eleven years away.

But none of my ideas or my treatment of the subject was cut and dried. As so many before me, I was enthralled by the island, both by its beauty and its squalidness, and hearing Piaf and McFerrin singing on the radio in their different languages from different times and different perspectives, as well as the situation that I found myself in, were all jumbled together and made me write at a feverish pitch.

I never published the poem, which never came together satisfactorily. But several stanzas from it will, if nothing else, give a sense of this place that since its discovery by Captain Cook in 1769 has intoxicated the Western imagination.

Besides the *Bounty* connection, my first impression of Pape'ete, the capital of Tahiti, was the immediate spark for the poem. I tried to capture its mythical beauty and contrasting shabbiness in the following stanzas:

> Marooned on this island
> bobbing in the South Pacific,
> here at the end of the twentieth century
> on a castaway planet
> carrying its bounty of the past
> into a future we can no longer imagine,
> I stroll through the streets of Pape'ete
> among the island natives,
> all bulk and smooth brown skin,
> and hear on a car radio
> my countryman, Bobby McFerrin,
> a black African marooned all his life
> in Oakland, California,
> singing, "Don't worry, be happy,"
> as, like crowded cattle,
> mud-spattered, stumbling to market,
> trucks lurch and stall,
> their doors ripped off, paint
> rusting at the edges.
>
> The buildings on the street
> are mostly concrete,

> a wet-looking gray,
> three- and four-stories high,
> slabs half-painted, wires dangling
> like metal vines in the air.
> But everyone seems happy,
> at least contented,
> and certainly not worried.

On the outskirts of the town, I experienced an overwhelming sense of being an outsider, as if I was entering a place beyond my comprehension.

> On the outskirts of town,
> surrounded by palm trees and flowers
> and imperious chickens,
> small square bungalows
> are marooned behind wire-mesh fences
> spotted with hibiscus.
> The yards are shadowy and cool,
> yet unexpectedly remote,
> their inhabitants as out of reach
> as photographs in *National Geographic*.

The beauty of the countryside, however, was astonishing, and I could see how Tahiti had been considered paradise by the early explorers.

> Beyond town, the island
> is still a dream of paradise,
> the air heavy, a swoon of perfumes.
> The fragile scent of frangipani
> swoops from the trees, its wide white flowers
> set among the leaves as if in the hair
> of green-headed Polynesian gods.
> Whiffs of gardenia, breezes
> doused with jasmine,
> and from the foliage along the road,
> red bursts of hibiscus, bougainvillea,
> and the vaginal-colored stalks
> of ginger plants.

I was especially struck by the beautiful colors of sunset and what they did to the mountains. This impression touched off what became the poem's all important rose imagery when I heard the recording of Edith Piaf singing

"La Vie en Rose" on a radio in the bar of the hotel in which I was staying. I made this connection between the two:

> Above all this, clouds bloat and shift
> across the green-carpeted mountains.
> At dusk, the clouds redden,
> tinting the landscape pink.
> The mountains, the entire island,
> for an instant are a flower,
> a rose in the sea, so otherworldly
> that this Tahiti just might be
> as Bougainville—happy, not worried—
> surmised: a second paradise.

But the lie is put to the wonders of paradise by the extract of a letter I saw at the Gauguin Museum, and in the following stanza I pictured the throngs of people who still look at Gauguin's paintings in European museums and imagine the paradise he portrayed with his beautiful women in brightly colored clothes. Then I reversed the mood at the end of the stanza with the quote from Gauguin's letter. I begin by stating the fact that almost all of the paintings in the island's museum are reproductions of the originals:

> Most of the paintings are reproductions
> tracing his career, the originals
> in European museums
> where viewers by the millions
> see his mud-brown or banana-yellow
> solid Tahitian virgins
> wearing red sarongs or orange muumuus
> in green jungle clearings,
> and dream of the paradise
> he thought Tahiti would be
> but ended by writing: "Insane but sad
> this cruel trip to Tahiti.
> I see nothing but death
> to deliver me from all this."

The poem, over-ambitious and clumsy in treatment, is a reminder of an extraordinary three days in which my conception of past and present, as well as the conflict between Western clichéd notions of paradise and the way we forcibly try to make traditional peoples and the natural world conform to them, revealed their somber realities.

Three days later, the powers that be at Air France arranged to fly the three of us to Australia on Qantas Airways.

■ ■ ■

We were met at the Sydney Airport by our hosts, Bill Marshall-Stoneking and Nigel Roberts, and whisked off to a reading, since we had already lost two days of scheduled appearances by the delay in Tahiti.

For the next three weeks we were rushed from pubs to college campuses to studios and ateliers, giving readings, meeting, talking, and exchanging ideas with visual and literary artists. Among the writers we met were such bastions of Australian poetry as John Millet and Les Murray and rising younger poets and fiction writers like Alan Wearne, Peter Skryznecki, Terry Gilmore, Pi-o, and Rudi Krausmann.

Billy and Nigel put us up in a traveling friend's tiny, one-bedroom apartment, complete with kitchenette and living room, that overlooked Sydney harbor. Anita slept in the bedroom, and Joe and I took turns sleeping on the living-room couch or on the floor beside it. I was fifty-three years old at the time, but the tour felt like a youthful adventure to me, much like my first trip to Greece.

The three of us did whatever we were asked to do, happily participating in any event planned for us and enthusiastically taking part in discussions and debates with Billy, Nigel, and their friends.

Our hosts, it turned out, were the leading performance poets in Australia, and Joe and I engaged them in spirited conversations on the limitations of performance poetry. Joe's position and mine was that performance poetry was more concerned with performance than language. Based on what we were seeing, we told them that props and costumes were at times more in evidence than the performance poets' attention to words, and the words themselves in the best poets we saw in action were many times (except in the case of the amazing Pi-o) simple and direct, since they had to be fully understood and to "work" dramatically on a single hearing. Therefore, by definition, performance poetry's language lacked nuances and layering that poetry on the page, which the reader could return to again and again, was able to achieve. In short, poetry on the page could continually produce waves of emotional and intellectual resonances that performance poetry, by its very nature as a one-time, live art form, rarely, if ever, could.

In addition, Billy and Nigel were enamored with the Beats and outlaw art of all kinds, and Joe and I soon realized we were seeing a very narrow segment of Australia's poetry and art scene.

Overall, however, I found great vitality everywhere we went, which included north to Newcastle, south to Canberra, and east to the Blue Mountains and the beginning of the outback. Typical of the direct lack of effete or false good manners was the wiry guy who came up to me in a pub near the racetrack in Sydney just before I was about to read. He held a pint glass of beer in either hand like six-shooters and said, with jaw thrust forward, "I'm here to hear what you've got, Yank," and stared me in the eye as if whether I lived or died depended on how good my poetry was. But when I smiled, he broke into a big grin and nodded good-naturedly. However, he didn't offer me one of the beers.

The drives into the outback and along the coast were through landscapes that can only be described as primordial, as if I had gone back to the Stone Age. As in Tahiti, but with greater immediacy, I was acutely aware of how far away I was from the lands and people on the rest of the planet.

My talk at the The National Theatre Drama School went well. So did my first two lectures at the Australian Film Television and Radio School. But my third lecture was a disaster, as I found out later. After my second talk, some of the students asked me to speak about my impression of current Australian film, which I thought had been the most exciting cinema in the world for the past fifteen years. I had seen more than sixteen Australian films, and impetuously gave my theories concerning the influences on Australian film and how it followed the traditions of post-World War II British film and BBC TV as its main sources. I was wrong, as my further studies would prove. But worse, I had not realized the antipathy in Australia to things British or the Australians' national inferiority complex, which became evident after I had been in the country for two weeks.

Other than that, the three weeks were exciting and revitalizing for the three of us. The night before we left, Billy and Nigel threw a raucous farewell party for us with a number of the people we had met. The party took place in the tiny apartment our hosts had found for us, and as the crowd departed, Anita, Joe, and I felt contented and brimming with good feelings for a job well done. But our hosts weren't finished with us. They had more far-reaching plans, which, after the last guests had left, they shared with us. In order to give a sense of our hosts and the place we were staying, I will quote from an article I wrote two years later about that night.

> When I first heard about the *Wartilpa Kalipurnangka*, I was sitting with two other American poets, Anita Wilkins and Joe Stroud, in an apartment overlooking Sydney Harbor on a sultry March night in 1989.
>
> It was the end of the Australian summer, the temperature was 70 degrees at 11 PM, and the air was thick as honey. Anita, Joe and I were chatting with poets Billy Marshall-Stoneking and Nigel Roberts, our hosts for a reading tour of the Sydney area.
>
> Billy and Nigel had become as close as brothers to us. Billy is a fine prose writer and playwright and one of the most popular performance poets in Australia. Tall and loose limbed, with an

untrainable blaze of red hair and scruffy beard, he is one of those extraordinary people whose enthusiasm inspires trust and affection in everyone.

From 1979 to 1984, Billy had lived among the Pintupi Aborigines of the central desert and so endeared himself to them that they considered him one of their own. Since returning to Sydney, Billy had produced three documentary films about the Pintupi and set up several visits for Pintupi sand painters to show their work in the white cultural centers of the east Australian coast.

Billy had us over at the urging of Dave Purdy, a stage director and mutual friend who had traveled to Sydney to put on several plays and to lecture on American drama. Dave had left for England by the time we arrived, but his influence lingered.

Billy was talking about Dave and the Pintupi now. "You know, this doesn't have to end here. Dave and I have drawn up plans for a Wartilpa Kalipurnangka, a walkabout tour of California, a sort of traveling show demonstrating a 30,000-year continuance of Australian performance art."

Observing our growing interest, he continued. "Nigel and I will bring over some of the black fellas who live in the bush to chant their songlines and do communal sand paintings. We'll bring over my films as well and do some performance poetry, which arises from the Aboriginal chanting. This will shed some light on Aboriginal culture, in which many western artists and thinkers are finding their notions of art, their attitudes towards the land, even their assumptions about the nature of reality, challenged and changed.

"I want to highlight how contemporary Australian poetry has been affected by the traditions and knowledge of the first Australians and show how the ways of all traditional peoples who venerate and still live on the land can influence us whites for the better."

By the time Billy finished, his eyes were radiant behind his round, wire-rimmed glasses. I caught some of his excitement, but I didn't know what to say. I stared at Joe and Anita, and they stared at me. The silence was as thick as the yellow air in the room.

Nigel broke the silence. He is more than ten years older than Billy, in his fifties, and has been termed "the grand old man of Balmain [the Haight Ashbury of Sydney] poetry," and is one of the founders of the Australian performance poetry movement. Although short and chunky, he moves and speaks with a deliberate self-possession and poise that can only be termed continental. He helped organize the first major exhibition of Aborigine sand paintings in Sydney in 1981.

"You see, mate," he said, "we've got something with real vitality here that has endless possibilities. We bring the aborigines not only to perform but to meet with Native Americans, and both groups sit down together and talk about the way they do things. That interaction is a first, a dream, important for them and maybe for us all."

I could hear the hammering in my chest as I looked out the window. What was I feeling? What did Joe and Anita think about all this? The lights from passing boats sprinkled the black surface of the harbor, and I thought, as I had so often in the past three weeks under that strange, southern hemisphere sky, that I couldn't tell the difference between the stars and the lights on the water. Everything was new, strange, upside-down—everything was possible. Billy and Nigel seemed to be waiting for us to say something.

"Great!" I heard Anita, Joe, and I exclaim almost simultaneously, as I continued to stare at the sparklings in the harbor. "Let's do it."

Afterward, as we flew back to the United States, Anita, Joe, and I realized the enormity of what we had agreed to. But we were so grateful to our hosts and so enthusiastic about all we had seen and done in Australia that we knew we were going to do the best we could to arrange what amounted to be an expedition party of six Australians to America.

CHAPTER 48

The Wartilpa Kalipurnangka

For two years we planned, cajoled, and raised funds among cultural organizations, government bureaus, and private sources for the Wartilpa Kalipurnangka, or what became known as "The Walkabout Tour of California and the Southwest." Billy and Nigel took care of everything at their end, which included bringing along a part-Aborigine Tasmanian woman poet named Terry Whitebeach, a film director, and two Aborigine sand painters from the Pintupi tribe of the central desert of Australia, whom Billy had known from his days at Papunya Station ("station" being the Australian term for our "reservation").

At the last minute, one of the Aborigines had a heart attack, and the other one, his mate and blood brother, refused to leave his side. Billy secured the services of two other Pintupi tribesmen he found in Alice Springs to take their place. Their inclusion would cause unexpected difficulties. The first problem was that they had no passports, and it would be hard to secure passports for them since they, being tribal Aborigines living on tribal lands, had no birth certificates. We got around this by explaining the problem to Senator Leon Panetta, who persuaded his contacts in the Australian diplomatic corps of the importance of the cultural exchange.

The second problem was that Billy, rushed by the last-minute change of plans, had failed to inform the two of the purpose of the tour and what was expected of them. As far as the two Aborigines were concerned, they were going to perform tribal chants and ceremonies, exhibit their paintings, create paintings with different groups, and get a chance to paint and sell their work wherever they went. No one foresaw the problems this would create.

The plan was for the Australians to give performances that started with chants and dances by the Aborigines, followed by readings and performances by Terry, Billy, and Nigel. During the day, the two Aborigines, Paddy Carrol Tjungurrayi and his blood brother, Dinny Nolan Tjampitjinpa, both well-known aboriginal painters, would hold group-painting sessions and paint their own paintings, which they would sell for $800 to $1,000 each.

The paintings, which for thousands of years had been sand and rock paintings of Pintupi creation myths called "dream time paintings," had been made into transportable art pieces in 1971, when Geoffrey Barden, a Caucasian art teacher at Papunya, had shown the tribesmen how to put the images on canvas and masonite boards with acrylic paint, thus starting a lucrative art genre that by the 1980s had a worldwide market.

The problems started immediately with Terry Whitebeach, a pretty but high-strung young woman who arrived a week before the rest of the group. Terry was a wonderful person, but except for several brief visits to Australia, she had never been out of Tasmania, and America was a major cultural shock for her. Going into a supermarket was an overwhelming experience. She was undone by the numerous choice of goods, the noise, and the numbers of cars on the streets, the trucks, gadgets, and number of people she encountered. She reacted with a series of hysterical crying fits, angry outbursts, and long periods of catatonic silence. Joe and I, and especially Anita, who Terry stayed with, took turns comforting and soothing her until the rest of the group arrived. But she never fully acclimated to her new surroundings and was prone to volatile fits at the most unexpected times.

Billy was little better and in many ways more difficult. He was an American, born in Florida, raised and educated in California, who had emigrated to Australia in 1971 to avoid the draft during the height of the Vietnam War. This was the first time he had returned to the States in twenty years, and the changes he found had an affect on him similar to the ones they had on Terry. We also came to see various sides of his personality we had not experienced in Australia. He was secretive, backbiting, and had his own, never-articulated agenda for making the trip. His aggressive good nature soon impressed me as the mask of a hustler who was out to secure whatever material gains he could get for himself. He belittled the film director and berated Nigel behind his back and continually disrupted the tour in one way or another, making things difficult for everyone. As leader of the Australians and handler of the two Aborigines, he was responsible for what became the nightmare atmosphere of the tour.

It was to be expected that Dinny and Paddy would suffer more culture shock than any of the other Australians, but the two Aborigines maintained, at least for the first month, their dignity and composure, looking to Billy for guidance in all matters. Realizing this, Billy made demands for himself in their name.

Nigel, on the other hand, tried to keep everything together. Billy insisted that Nigel was a drunken fool, warned us to be wary of him, and told us he was a drug addict to boot. But we observed Nigel taking care of the Aborigines, securing materials, setting up the painting sessions, and trying to calm everyone down when things got out of hand. He did all this in addition to reciting his own poetry, which in many cases was the most popular part of the performances.

Dinny and Paddy suffered culture shock in many ways. The food they received during their week in Sonora sickened them. It was 1990s American finger food, health food. They wanted and needed lots of proteins: steaks, chops, as well as potatoes and other starches. They also needed to be around open fires, as if fire were an elixir to them. The first morning they came to my house, the following incident occurred, which I put here as a verbal photograph. It's from my long prose poem, "Fire."

> The two old men, both Aborigines, emanated a chalky pallor from beneath their black skins. Might they trouble me for a fire? they asked, nodding to the fireplace in the living room. It had been five days since they'd arrived in America on a cultural exchange, and in all that time, they explained, they "hadn't had a single blaze." Ten minutes later they sat cross-legged on the tiny hearth, muttering to each other and leaning toward the flaming logs, their backs to me and the other guests at the breakfast table. When they rose half an hour later, their pallor was gone and they came to the table all smiles and quiet charm. "Fire's their spiritual oxygen," the interpreter said. "They haven't been in a house with a fireplace since they arrived, and they'd been feeling so ill they'd contemplated building a fire on their last host's lawn."

The two Aborigines were inseparable. They would go everywhere and do everything together. They were what we would call blood brothers but had quite different personalities. Both were middle-aged. Paddy, the older of the two, was thin and gaunt-faced and an elder of the tribe. Though friendly, he was quiet, taciturn, even reticent, and was constantly observing and mulling over everything around him. Dinny was plump and jovial, outgoing, and liked the ladies, a proclivity he showed whenever the American custom of hugging was practiced, a custom he was soon exercising on his own. He was carefree and open to any escapade. Paddy kept a close eye on him.

It was in this highly-charged, emotional climate that the Australians began the tour. Before they came to Santa Cruz they presented a week of performances at Dave Purdy's theater in Sonora. Then they had a number of painting sessions and performances at De Anza College in the San Francisco Bay Area, and a week at Cabrillo. From there, they did a week at a repertory theater in San Francisco, drawing huge crowds—and bad feelings behind the scenes from their hosts everywhere they appeared because of Billy's demands and shenanigans. Then they returned to Santa Cruz.

While the Australians were in Santa Cruz, we put them up in a four-star hotel. On the afternoons when they were free of obligations or had finished them, the group would congregate in Joe's back yard or mine where we would eat, drink, plan upcoming events, and the Aborigines would paint commissioned paintings. I commissioned them to do two paintings for me.

Joe Stroud looking on with Dinny Nolan Tjampitjinpa as Paddy Carrol Tjungurrayi puts the finishing touches on Dinny's "Spring In The Desert." Santa Cruz, 1991.

Dinny enthusiastically set to work on a large colorful canvas depicting a corroborree, or ceremony, celebrating spring in the desert. To this day, it hangs on the wall alongside my bed and never fails to lift my spirits. Paddy was less enthusiastic, and painted a rough, non-descript work of little merit.

But don't misunderstand: Paddy's desultory response to my request may have been more a lack of inspiration than anything else. Both men were always friendly and Dinny, a boon companion. On the day they painted my commissions they announced that they were making Joe and I honorary members of the tribe. Dinny went on to describe the corroborree they would make in our honor when we visited them in the outback: they would catch and kill a kangaroo and bury it unskinned in a pit of hot coals they would cover with bushes and sand. The skin would fall off the carcass when they dug it up, Dinny said, leaving the meat savory and succulent, seasoned by the desert brush. Then they would give Joe and me the best pieces as honored guests.

■ ■ ■

After the Australians had performed for three weeks in the San Francisco Bay Area, Anita, Joe, and I accompanied them to New Mexico and Arizona for a week of what had been planned as the most important part of the tour: the Aborigines and the Australians meeting with the Pueblo, Navajo, and Hopi tribes. We drove to the Southwest in two vehicles, one a van for Billy, Paddy, Dinny, Nigel, Terry, and the director with his camera equipment. Anita, Joe, and I led the way in a separate car in which the Australians, one at a time, would join us at different points along the way. Thanks to the generous help of the poet Jimmy Santiago Baca, who I had met briefly once and called on for help in planning the Wartilpa in the Southwest, I had set up more than half a dozen meetings and performances in New Mexico and Arizona.

Our first performance was in New Mexico, and on the first afternoon we arrived in Santa Fe, all of us ambled downtown to see the sights. Passing one of the many art galleries, we saw a large painting by Paddy in the window. It had a price tag of $10,000. "He probably sold it in Alice Springs for $250," Billy growled. Paddy, as usual, said nothing and strolled on.

The first night in Santa Fe, the group presented a concert in the Museum of New Mexico to a sellout crowd. Afterward, we had a party at an Indian women's college dorm where Paddy and Dinny were being put up. We met various members of the Native American and arts communities, and then Anita, Joe, Billy, Terry, Nigel, and I were housed at an expensive estate in the mountains overlooking the city, leaving Dinny and Paddy alone with the film director, since it was Easter break and the dormitory was empty.

I strongly suspect we were quartered separately from Dinny and Paddy, who had been living with us up to then on an equal basis, out of some restrictive racial bias on the part of our hosts. Whatever the reason, the separation had disastrous consequences.

As I remember, the film director was supposed to keep an eye on Dinny and Paddy and make sure they were all right, but he became involved with a young lady at the party and went off with her. Left alone, the two Aborigines wandered through the empty dormitory and discovered six or seven cases of beer stacked in one of the rooms. By the time we returned to pick the Aborigines up the next morning, they were unconscious on the floor of the room, surrounded by three or four dozen empty beer cans. They had drunk all but one of the cases.

Sick does not describe their condition. Poisoned is more like it. They vomited and sweated, swayed and fell, slumped and moaned as we showered them and tried to sober them up before our next hosts arrived to pick us up. A group of Pueblo Indians were going to give us a tour of a sacred mesa and had scheduled an evening get-together in which everyone in the Pueblo and surrounding lands would exchange songs and dances with the Aborigines, and a veritable banquet of Native American cuisine would be enjoyed by all.

When the delegation arrived, however, Paddy and Dinny were sicker than ever, but they and everyone else insisted that the plans for the day should go forward. Everyone was sure the Aborigines would be better by noon. With that anthem on our lips and in our minds, we piled Paddy and Dinny into the Pueblos' van and drove off to the sacred mesa.

Before we arrived, both Aborigines had vomited all over themselves, silently regurgitating, it seemed, everything they'd ever eaten. The Pueblos, wonderful, gentle people, and extraordinary hosts, said nothing and continued the tour as if nothing had happened, as unobtrusively as possible cleaning the van and their two guests as best they could. They seemed fixated on not humiliating Paddy and Dinny and on saving face for them at all costs.

The Pueblos' task was a heroic one, especially since the visit to the sacred mesa, this particular Pueblo group's original home site, was approached by a winding dirt road and a climb of a thousand feet along a narrow path to the ruins on top. All of us took turns guiding and holding Paddy and Dinny in place, afraid they might slip and fall to the flatlands below.

Somehow they tottered and staggered to the windswept top of the mesa, where they sunk to their knees and continued to vomit.

By now we were getting worried, but the Pueblos said their women would remedy the alcohol's poisons. So we descended as cautiously as we had climbed up, bundled Paddy and Dinny back into the van, where they were sick to their stomachs once again, and drove to the pueblo. Through it all, the two Aborigines had not said a word, and I think they were barely conscious.

By the time we reached the pueblo, preparations for the evening meal and jamboree were well underway, and more and more Pueblos from outlying areas were arriving with food in hand and some with native dress over their arms.

The Pueblo remedies, however, didn't work, and by the time the festivities began, Dinny and Paddy, woozy and disoriented, were sitting on the steps of the main meeting building, chalk white. But again, the Pueblos refused to let them lose face, and women, children, and burly men welcomed them and tended them as if they were family members with pneumonia or some illness other than alcohol poisoning. Unfortunately, a good part of the tending had to do with offering the two men plates of food, which set off further misery for them since Paddy and Dinny, as if realizing the graciousness of their hosts, politely tasted every morsel on the paper plates handed them.

By sundown, more than a hundred Pueblos had arrived. They built and ignited a huge bonfire in a clearing surrounded by squat buildings and began singing and dancing for their shaky guests, who in turn, from some internal sense of obligation or pride, reciprocated with wobbly motions and mumbled songs of their own.

By the time we left the pueblo under a star-spattered sky four hours later, the temperature had dropped 30 degrees, and we took a shivering Paddy and Dinny back to Santa Fe, hoping they would feel better the next day, when a Navajo medicine man was to pick us up early in the morning. He was to drive us to the Navajo nation for what had been set up as the highlight of the tour, a three-day exchange of customs concerning sand painting and its attendant rituals.

But when the Navajo representatives arrived the next day, Dinny and Paddy were still woozy and sick to their stomachs. We drove the 150 miles or so from Santa Fe to Shiprock with the two barely uttering a word and sitting in the van in a catatonic state.

The medicine man who picked us up, a young, taciturn, not overly-friendly thirty-year-old, led the caravan to his house, which was in sight of the holy mountain of Shiprock. No sooner had we pulled into his driveway then he invited Dinny and Paddy to enter a sweat lodge with him. This was a great honor to which the rest of us were not invited, and would have done the two Aborigines a world of good medicinally, but they refused the invitation. Not only were they too sick, they were wary of what seemed to them going underground in the windowless sod hogan, which looked more like a mound than a building. Their refusal was an enormous insult to Navajo custom, and bad blood immediately sprang up between the Navajos and our group. It was also clear that the Navajos were not as forgiving nor as concerned with the Aborigines' saving face as the gentle Pueblos had been.

To make matters worse, Paddy and Dinny refused to eat or stay at the medicine man's house, a ramshackle clapboard affair that reeked of poverty. In fact, they had refused to leave the van after Billy had reconnoitered the house and said they wanted to stay at a motel in town. Or so Billy, their handler and go-between, told us. It was clear to everyone, including the Navajos, that Billy was the one who wanted to stay at a motel and was telling us his desires as if they were Paddy and Dinny's.

Billy would hear no argument, and disregarding our objections, he drove off with the two Aborigines in the van. The rest of us were left to patch things up with our hosts, who had killed and cooked a sheep in our honor and invited various members of the local Navajo community to come over that evening. It was an awkward situation all around, and the Navajos were visibly angry as they drove us into the desert that afternoon to visit Shiprock and entertained us grudgingly that evening.

The medicine man was able to get word to most of the people he had invited for the evening not to come. The rest of us tried to be as friendly and accommodating as we could, bedding down in sleeping bags in various nooks of his house, along with his wife, children, and other relations.

The next day Billy and the two Aborigines returned at noon, several hours after the now belligerent medicine man, smoldering with anger, had scheduled several meetings to occur. We did the tour of a local Navajo school, but Billy and his two charges left for the motel once again in the late afternoon. Paddy and Dinny were still the worse for wear and were more reticent than ever to take part in any of the events that had been prepared for them.

Once more we retired to our nooks and sleeping bags, but the food and hospitality of our hosts were meager and sullenly offered.

The next day the entire group left for Rough Rock, the spiritual center of the Navajo nation, where we were to meet with the most holy of the Navajo medicine men, of whom our host was an acolyte. This time Billy and the two Aborigines returned on time, and we drove through the breezy, sunny morning in a caravan led by our host to the Navajo capital a hundred miles away. By this time, no one was talking to anyone. Terry had had several more emotional outbursts during the trip, and the dissension was not confined to the Navajos but within our own group. Everyone was seething, trying to fulfill a schedule that no one wanted to follow any longer. Everyone was tired from four weeks on the road, and the Australians were furious with Billy. Billy, for his part, was belligerent and seemed to be nearing a mental breakdown. Anita, Joe, and I, as go-betweens and organizers of the tour, were disgusted and could do little to alleviate the damage. Nigel did everything possible to save the situation, but it seemed hopeless.

We drove the hundred miles or so in silence through a beautiful but desolate landscape of grotesque, wind-sculpted, red stone formations twisting up from the desert floor. We stopped two or three times to reconnoiter and check on the other vehicles, and once everyone piled out of the cars to look across a rolling vista at the Canyon de Chelly trembling in the distant heat. No one said much even there. Everyone was apprehensive about the meeting at Rough Rock. And for good reason.

We turned off U.S. 191, and drove for twenty miles along the empty landscape of Navajo Route 59 to Rough Rock. A welcoming party met us in the sun-drenched parking area, headed by a short, thickset, middle-aged man wearing what seemed to be a uniform-like tan Stetson hat with matching slacks and short-sleeved shirt. The rest of his outfit consisted of spit-shined black brogans, a string tie fastened by a large turquoise stone, and a turquoise studded belt. He was recording our arrival on a camcorder.

"Who's the clown with the camcorder?" someone in the group muttered as we piled out of our vehicles.

"I think it's our most high holy man," someone else replied.

"Well, the high holy man forgot to take the cover off his camera lens," the first speaker said.

The thick-set man was indeed the holy man. He walked toward us with a smile, introduced himself, and led us to the largest building in the enclave, a concrete edifice that was a giant replica of a hogan. Due to its size and material, it looked like a space age geodesic dome. Inside were various offices and recreational and museum areas, all leading to an amphitheater that occupied almost one half of the building's sloping interior.

We were late, the medicine man explained, so proceedings had to begin immediately. Lunch would be served in the compound's dining room after the morning session.

A crowd of fifty or so Navajos were seated on the amphitheater benches, and the holy man sat us several rows above them and strode to the podium at the bottom of the space. He introduced us to the crowd and explained that a number of the audience were medicine men he had trained; they had come from all parts of the Navajo nation for the day's events. He then launched into a well-organized talk about Navajo history and customs, emphasizing the role of sand painting in Navajo ritual and beliefs, illustrating his words by referring to a large pad of butcher paper, which sat on an easel by his side. He would fold over the pages of the pad as he spoke. Each page illustrated with drawings or graphs what he was saying. Wherever we had gone in Navajo country, this same talking aid had been used.

Throughout the talk, the holy man energetically and clearly directed his words at Paddy and Dinny, asking them to respond and tell how their tribal customs and beliefs were similar or different to the ones he was describing. But all his questions were greeted with silence by the two Aborigines.

By now, Dinny and Paddy, although still queasy, were over the effects of their Santa Fe drinking orgy, and their silence, which was not only rude but increasingly hostile, it seemed to me, was inexplicable. I was standing with Joe in the rear of the theater and could see Paddy's posture growing more rigid with each of the medicine man's questions. Several times he turned to Dinny and muttered a word or two, but other than that, both men sat stiff and motionless.

Standing a few feet away from me, four middle-aged white men in short-sleeved white shirts, who had been introduced as representatives of the Indian Commission of the Department of the Interior, were observing the proceedings. As the holy man continued to talk and Paddy and Dinny refused to respond to his questions, they began to whisper to one another. At the same time, the holy man's acolytes and the rest of the audience were twisting on the benches and murmuring irritably. The tension in the theater became so palpable, I wandered away to relieve the quickening of my pulse and hopefully alleviate the sweat that had broken out all over my body.

There was a glass counter in the hall beyond the doorless theater. It contained various Navajo tourist artifacts and books for sale. A number of the books were on special display and as I scanned them I realized they were written by the speaker. All of them had a photograph of him with a short biography on the back cover. With growing alarm, I read that he had been a radio repairman in the military during the Korean War and had returned to New Mexico where, while training to become a medicine man, he worked as a tribal policeman and then a state trooper and was winner of the New Mexico and Arizona Peacemaker Marksman's contest for several years running. Clearly, he had a sensibility that was divided between the ways of his tribesmen and the ways of the white man, and he may have adopted, I feared, the mindset of the white policeman and therefore could become violent at the Aborigines' reticence.

I went back in the theater, grabbed Joe's arm, and led him to the book display, showing him the back cover biography and whispering that the situation could get uglier than it already was. By the time we returned to the theater, the event had begun to unravel: Paddy and Dinny continued to sit in stony silence, the holy man was sweating, and his tone was no longer friendly, the audience had grown belligerent, and the white Department of Interior Indian officials were whispering vociferously among themselves. Finally, one of the white officials stepped forward and called out to the speaker, "I think we've gone as far with the talk as we can go. Why don't you wind it up now, Joe," he said with a firmness that brooked no argument.

It was a humiliating moment for the holy man: in front of his acolytes, the white officials had shown in a most undiplomatic way that the Department of Indian Affairs was in charge of the event, not him. If the moment was embarrassing for the holy man, it was also evident that he, frustrated by Dinny and Paddy's refusal to take part in the proceedings, was now furious. He flipped the pages of the butcher paper over and left the podium, climbing to the rear of the theater where Joe and I were now standing with Billy, quizzing him about the Aborigines' behavior.

Before Billy could answer us, the holy man came up to him and said, "On what street corner did you pick up those drunken black bastards!"

Billy exploded, "That's it!" he said, and stalked over to Paddy and Dinny, who were still seated on the benches. He said a few words to them and announced that the three of them were leaving. Then he and the two Aborigines tromped to the van in the parking lot below the concrete hogan, climbed in, and refused to return.

The twenty or so acolytes surrounded the holy man, clearly waiting for instructions. He was enraged. The white officials tried to calm everyone, and Nigel, Anita, Joe, I, and the rest of our group tried to maintain our poise. Several of us went to the van and remonstrated with Billy. The rest of us talked to the holy man and the white officials and agreed to attend the luncheon and see what would transpire in the next hour or so.

We walked in silence to the dining room without Billy and the Aborigines and ate in hostile, isolated groups. Things had gone too far to be repaired. Everyone had been insulted, and matters were not helped by our host at Shiprock, who then, and maybe by phone a day or two before, told his friends the insults he had suffered from Billy and the Aborigines for the last several days. Meanwhile, nothing our group said to Billy, Paddy, or Dinny would make them leave the van in the now sun-baked parking lot.

Finally, the afternoon events were cancelled, and we prepared to leave for our next stop, a Hopi mesa thirty or forty miles away.

By 1:30 we were packing up our camera equipment and loading our vehicles, saying good-bye to the white officials and several stony-faced Navajos, when the holy man, followed by his troupe of acolytes, appeared.

For the past several hours, I had been steeling myself for the first outbreak of violence, and I knew that this was the moment I had been dreading for the past few days.

But the holy man strode right by me, stopped at the open van, and humbly began talking to the two Aborigines. "I'm sorry," he began. "What I said was unforgivable. But let us not leave on bad terms. I bless your journey and wish you the best. Join me in our farewell custom."

And with that, he opened a cloth pouch, reached inside, and withdrew a pinch of powdered sage, which he brought to his forehead, intoning some words in Navajo, and threw to the wind. He then extended the pouch to the Aborigines in the van. Paddy refused to look at him, and the holy man stood there, almost beseechingly, his hand with the pouch held in front of him. A minute passed, then another. Everyone was waiting, not moving. I couldn't believe Paddy's inflexibility. Dinny began to fidget and finally, just as the tension became unbearable, he reached forward, took the pouch, and imitated the holy man's gestures.

That broke the tension, and everyone, except Paddy, bid one another good-bye, and with much waving and calls of thanks and farewell, we piled into the vehicles and departed.

Half an hour later, we stopped at a ramshackle diner on Highway 191 and all of us crowded around Paddy and Dinny, asking what had come over them at Rough Rock. It was at this point that Billy told us that, in his haste to get substitutes for the original Aborigines, he had neglected to tell Paddy and Dinny what was expected of them on the tour. As far as they were concerned, they were coming to America to make lots of money. They were not told that they were expected to share the beliefs behind their paintings and ceremonies with Native Americans. Billy explained that Paddy, as an elder of his tribe, had been shocked to find out that the holy man had wanted to exchange information on rituals and customs that were taboo for Aborigines to talk about with outsiders. Paddy would never have agreed to come on the tour, Billy said, if he had known this was one of the requirements. That explained Paddy's increasing silence and hostility since he had come to Rough Rock. Once more, Billy was to blame for the difficulties. His desire to make the walkabout tour happen had almost resulted in an international incident.

The Southwest tour had been scheduled to coincide with spring break. After the Navajo meeting, Anita, Joe, and I had to get back to Cabrillo for the resumption of classes. The Australians were on their way to visit the Hopis and continue on to do several days of classes and performances at the University of California at San Diego under the guidance of the well-known poet and folkways scholar Jerome Rothenberg, whose concerns with the relationship between "primitive" and modern poetry were legend.

We took our leave, telling the Australians we would see them in Santa Cruz in five days. Then we drove home with a feeling more of relief than ill will, although we were none too happy about the tour, and we talked all the way back about the personal interactions and individual difficulties that had arisen among the Australians during the previous four weeks, which culminated with the dangerous situation at Rough Rock. We kept coming back to Billy as the cause of most of the problems.

Five days later the Australians were back in Santa Cruz, all of them healthy and in high spirits. The Hopis had been as kind and hospitable as the Pueblos, diplomatically avoided taboo subjects in their exchanges and events with the Aborigines, and the events planned by Rothenberg at the University of California at San Diego had drawn enthusiastic crowds.

We threw several farewell parties for the Australians. At the Pacific Rim Film Festival, Billy showed his two short films on Nosepeg, the legendary Pintupi elder who became an Australian cultural icon and who was befriended by Billy during his three years at Papunya.

Paddy and Dinny had fulfilled their reason for coming on the tour: they were weighed down with the thousands of dollars they had made, and proceeded to spend all of it their final week in Santa Cruz. They had us drive them to every secondhand thrift shop in the county—Goodwill, the Salvation Army shops, and St. Vincent de Paul's—where they bought all the men's, women's, and children's clothing they could find, as well as eighty valises to pack them in. Billy explained that the two men would go home and host a giant corroboree, a gathering of relations and fellow tribesmen, and among a plentitude of food they provided and giant bonfires, they would tell about their adventures in America and give away all the clothes they had bought in what amounted to an Aborigine potlatch.

All of the strife and bitterness of the past seven weeks were forgotten as we drove the Australians to the San Francisco Airport. But when we arrived at the Qantas ticket counter with the eighty suitcases, the Aborigines had to pay an exorbitant amount of money to ship their treasure trove home. Both men happily paid the fee with what money they had left and said farewell among tears and promises to see each other again when we returned to Australia, at which time both men would hold the corroboree they had promised in our honor. That trip never happened.

I heard from Billy several times over the next few years and, after giving him a tongue-lashing over his behavior, hunted down books and other material for him about the Russian film director Sergei Eisenstein, whose visit to Mexico Billy was turning into a play. I ran up a bill of $350 in phone calls and books, which he never repaid. Our relationship became more and more strained and finally came to an end when he visited the United States five years later. His play about Ezra Pound, *Sixteen Words for Water*, had become a hit in Sydney and London, and he had broken up with his wife and decided to leave Australia, which he told me on his arrival had become "too small" for him. His talents needed an international audience, he said. I couldn't believe his arrogance and vanity and told him so. He looked at me with disdain and flew off to Italy, only to return to Australia a year later when he realized, I'm sure, that the world didn't share his opinion of himself. While in Europe, he wrote several articles on writers he had known and events he had organized, dismissing me in one paragraph as a poet bereft of talent and focusing on my prose poetry, which he considered so much artless drivel. At last report, he was on the permanent faculty of the National Film School as a screenwriting instructor and was working as an editor on the side.

Nigel visited the United States several times in the next few years, and Joe and I spent two pleasant evenings with him in San Francisco. He retired from the middle school at which he taught and still lives in the Balmain section of Sydney, but we haven't heard from him in some time now. Anita received several letters from Terry and answered them enthusiastically, but they haven't corresponded in years. Paddy and Dinny continued to live and paint at Papunya Station, where Dinny still resides. Paddy died in 2000.

All in all, the Wartilpa introduced thousands of Americans to Australian culture, and that has to be considered worth the effort. The personal and vituperous internecine difficulties among the Australians that went on behind the scenes have faded with time. When Joe and I talk about the tour now, we inevitably grow silent with our own thoughts, and smile.

BOOK FOURTEEN

SLOUCHING TOWARD THE NEW MILLENNIUM: THE 1990s

CHAPTER 49

Community 2 and the Mentor Found

The work I did to bring about the Wartilpa and produce *The Eight Ecstasies* reflect my ideas on art and community. All my writing, teaching, and organizing artistic events over the years have been based on my belief that art is not a solitary act of self-expression for its own sake but an undertaking for the edification of the entire community. I have followed that notion as a guiding principle for all my public actions, in everything I have done, even in the writing of this memoir.

From the start, I never considered that art was created for art's sake, that, more specifically, the poet as priest, prophet, and shaman—which I believe to be the poet's role—is in any way elevated above or separated from anyone else in the human community. Poetry is a job like any other, a labor of head, heart, and words, just as muscle and planning are used for other undertakings that ultimately benefit not only the self but society.

I follow Wordworth's dictum that a poet is "nothing different in kind from other men but only in degree . . . by a greater promptness to think and feel," and that he has "a greater power in expressing such thoughts and feelings." And Wordsworth adds, significantly for me, that these thoughts and feelings are expressed "in the common language of men."

I had no difficulty with the apparent contradiction in those statements, which imply that the poet is like other men but different from them, because I see myself as just one human being among others, different from them only in that my occupation as poet is different. I have a job, an expertise, in the same way a shoemaker, a steel worker, a carpenter, or a scientist has one, and all our efforts benefit society—that is, the community at large—in different ways.

These ideas have guided my teaching from the beginning. In 1972, I wrote for the *Journal of English Teaching Techniques* that

> . . . what readers experience and half-create in the poem is the primal vision they have forgotten, or which society, with its moral and economic needs, has trained out of them. Thus, at first, the

poem acts as a tool of recognition, enabling readers to see who and where they are as social beings, and who and where they are as individuals. In the first, they are members of a social group. In the second, they are evolving, spiritual entities.

Therefore, the poem allows us to rediscover our spiritual selves: its function is to put us in touch with our feelings, or, in a deeper sense, to reveal to us once again "the primal vision"—the psychic and physical goals of both the human race and life itself, which are indelibly stained on our chromosomes.

By the 1990s, these notions had made me question the efficacies of the personal lyric, the most common type of poem being produced in American poetry, which explores feeling states and impressions and looks at poetry as a form of self-expression, even therapy, and I wrote:

> We've gone too far with the personal lyric. If as a society we are too self-indulgent, in our literature we've become too self-absorbed. The way we pamper and preen ourselves and whine over the slightest trespasses against us, as if they were deformed infants, has, in many ways, deformed us. In pursuit of the personal, we've turned away from our place in the larger worlds of society, the nation, the planet, and history, and we're trapped in the household of our petty self-concerns and domestic relationships.

I went on to say:

> The attempt to speak to the human condition must replace our puling about our individual lots. The guideline I've always used in my work is that when speaking about myself, I make sure that my conclusions reflect the interests of all humanity, or, in other words, that they move from individual to universal concerns.

I was addressing those ideas in particular to language poets and the plethora of memoirs that were flooding the market and creative writing classes at the time. In the language poets I found the pursuit of a private utterance that was intrinsically solipsistic, the antithesis of what I thought poetry should be.

On the other hand, I also made clear that "my poetry and prose are easy to understand and extremely vivid because of their direct everyday language and use of imagery. However, the difficulty for the reader is that my poetry does not reflect the world as they ordinarily see it."

And I continued:

> In my poetry, reality is used as a façade to reveal scenes cho-
> sen from everyday life transformed by fantasy, folklore, and myth
> into a dream world which reveals the inner life of things . . . I am
> not a realistic writer. Verisimilitude is not my concern. My
> poetry evokes an inner world reflecting the outer one in
> metaphor and simile. I guess that makes me an expressionist by
> definition.

All of these conceptions can be applied to teaching, where I understood that my task was to make students acutely aware of the world around them and to think critically about it. As these ideas were coalescing in the early 1990s, two events occurred that had a profound effect on the way I conducted my public pursuits for the remainder of the decade.

Since the late 1970s, I had attempted to get in touch with those people who had influenced me in my various undertakings over the years. I wanted to thank them, to show them that I appreciated the time and patience they had given me. Jarvis Thurston, Dietrich Gerhard, and Mei Yi-Pao were dead. But I phoned Don Justice to thank him for instilling in me an unrelenting rational questioning of every aspect of a poem. Our talk was friendly, but, unfortunately, he was skeptical about the intent of my call. I couldn't locate Richard Popkin, and my original mentor, Richard Martin, who had introduced me to reading and the world of culture in general, was nowhere to be found, although I had sought his whereabouts for more than twenty years.

One day, my phone rang. I picked it up and said, "Hello."

"Is this Morton Marcus?"

"It is."

"Are you the Morton Marcus who had an article on poetry in the *Metro* this week?"

"The same," I said, preparing myself for the inevitable complaint, angry disagreement, or inquiry if I would read the speaker's manuscript. But instead, the voice said, "Do you remember maybe forty years ago at a place called the Irving School—"

My heart lurched. "Yes!" I said.

"—a teacher named Richard Martin?"

"You're not!"

"I am."

"I'll be damned! I've been looking for you for years."

"You have?"

"Where are you?"

"Here."

"Here?"

"Penelope and I are staying with a colleague of yours in the Santa Cruz Mountains."

"Penelope? You married her?"

"And have two grown children."

"How long are you out here? We must get together," I blurted.

"That's why I'm calling—"

"I've been looking for you for years. I even called Goodman up in 1970, but I think he thought I was a crank and said he didn't know where you were."

"I've been wondering what became of you, too."

"Really?" I said. "I thought I was a thorn in your side, and you were really more interested in such polite achievers as Van, Van, what was his name—Snow."

"No. It was you. You were the one with the potential, for all your rough ways."

"I'll be damned!"

"That's possible, maybe even probable, but before then, the people I'm staying with have invited you to dinner so we can get together."

Two days later, Donna and I drove to the address Martin had given me. My palms were sweaty on the steering wheel. The drive took us up Empire Grade, the same road I traveled day after day when I lived in the mountains twenty years before, and I had the impression that I was traveling back in time, first to the mountains where I had lived my last years with Wilma, Jana, and Valerie, and had written *The Santa Cruz Mountain Poems*, and then all the way back to my freshman year at the Irving School when I was fourteen and Martin's student.

The impression stayed with me after we arrived at the house. Martin had hardly changed in the forty years since I'd last seen him. He was still painfully thin, and Penelope was still tall and bony. They were graying, but other than that, they were the same.

The meeting was delightful. Martin, and especially Penelope, were happy to meet Donna, and I was not only friends with the colleague they were staying with but her admiring associate in a school project I will talk about in a few pages.

It turned out that Penelope and my colleague, whose name is Nancy Andreasen, had been roommates at college and were such close friends they visited each other every year or so. All of these connections were amusing if not astonishing coincidences for everyone concerned.

We talked and talked, spinning the connecting threads among all six of us tighter and tighter into a garment of mutual concerns and activities—politics, social action, the arts.

Penelope had become a psychotherapist in New Jersey, where she and Martin had raised their children on a small plot of land that had chickens and one or two other domesticated animals and on which they grew their vegetables.

"And you?" I asked Martin toward the end of the evening. "What have you been doing all these years? I've looked you up in publishers' lists and composers archives but couldn't find anything."

"I stayed home with the kids."

"Did you teach?"

"Irving was enough of the teaching life for me," he said.

"What about writing, and your music?"

He shook his head. "I tended my garden and took care of the chickens."

I wanted to say something like, "That's it? You didn't do anything with all your talents?" But I didn't.

"No," he continued, "Penelope has been the family breadwinner."

"And mother and housewife, too," Penelope added.

I sat back without saying a word but caught my colleague, Nancy's eye. She nodded knowingly.

I had been overjoyed hearing from Martin and had looked forward to seeing him and hearing about the things he had accomplished during the last forty years, but I was surprised by his revelations. Penelope was as buoyant and lively as ever, and as the evening wore on, her accomplishments became the topic of conversation. She was charming. It was clear she still adored Martin, had the same outgoing, innocent nature that had made her so appealing all those years before, and had engaged in the hurly-burly of life. On the other hand Martin's year at Irving, it seemed, had been the high point of his professional and possibly personal life. Penelope had provided for him and the family with what must have been an extraordinary outpouring of energy.

As I took my leave that night, I gave Martin a handful of my books. He was eager to read my work, to see what kind of artist his teaching had engendered. But as I drove home, I was confused and uncomfortable. The man who had changed my life, had given it a direction to an even greater extent than Leo had, had shut away his talents and lived his life, it sounded to me, puttering about on his wife's good graces and energy. It also seemed, and this may sound harsh and priggish, that he was, by his own proud admission, an idler. No, I refused to believe it.

Several days later, he called me, and we arranged to have lunch in town before he and Penelope and Nancy and her husband came over to my house for dinner. At lunch he launched into a brutal, dismissive critique of my poetry. He said it was too personal, too surrealistic, had little to do with the world. I sat listening to him drone on, realizing he knew little about the changes that had taken place in American poetry since the 1950s. At the same time, I silently questioned his charge that my work had nothing to do with the world when he, by his own admission, had long before retired from it. What annoyed me was not that he disliked my writing but that he could sit in judgment of me when he had done nothing with his own talents, while I, at least, was developing mine, as pitiful as they may have been. I listened to him in silence, but he seemed to be oblivious to my annoyance and the hypocrisy of his position. It seemed to me that he had chosen to fill his life with self-indulgent trivia, content to sip tea and watch the sun rise and set for forty years of days and nights, during which his wife and the larger society had taken care of his wants as if he were a potentate.

Those thoughts proved to be more accurate than I imagined when several days later he suffered a heart attack and was rushed to a local hospital. It turned out that he had no medical insurance, and as the bills mounted up over the weeks, he seemed unconcerned about them. I visited him in the hospital a number of times and then at Nancy's house where he convalesced for six weeks. He thought no more about this intrusion on Nancy and her husband than he did of his medical bills. As he made clear by his lack of concern and actual words, he thought that everyone—friends and the state—should take care of him; that, in fact, he was entitled to be served by everyone concerned. If I was appalled by his attitude, Nancy was clearly angry, but she couldn't see turning him out of her house.

When he finally left, weeks after he was actually well enough to do so, I was happy to see him go. I don't know how the entire visit affected Nancy's friendship with Penelope, but I was disillusioned by the entire experience.

I came to see Penelope as a wonderful person who had grown intellectually with the years but who had remained emotionally subservient to the image of the man I had known, or thought I had known, when I was fourteen. She deserved more.

As for me, I recalled my drive up the mountain to my initial meeting with Martin two months before when I thought I was traveling into the past. I now realized that I had been traveling from the past into the present.

Would it have been better for me never to have found the mentor I idolized when I was a boy? No. I could never and would never denigrate Martin's effect on my life. But becoming reacquainted with him was another lesson about the way of the world and the many ways humans engaged in living their lives. Above all else, it showed me that many times even those who have the most to offer choose to squander their talents and refuse to contribute to the community.

■ ■ ■

Such realizations were continually on my mind at this time and may have made my estimates of Martin more severe than they should have been. If my contributions to society had been mainly through my writing, teaching, collaborating, and programming artistic events as an individual, they had taken a new turn several years before Martin had so propitiously shown up.

I had almost always come forward in my criticism of things I thought unjust. Since I was a boy, I had followed Leo's chant to "fear not, and do right." I had defended victims against bullies, refused to go along with racial slurs or racially discriminating actions, protested injustices in the military, and demonstrated against government foreign policy in Southeast Asia as well as against city politics in San Francisco. When I settled down in Santa Cruz, however, my attention and time were mainly taken up with events in my workplace, Cabrillo College.

For a long time the few criticisms I had were solitary and far between. The second year I was at Cabrillo, I went into the vice president's office to personally argue against his decision to increase class size. Although he reversed his decision, my complaint, which was calm and reasonably argued, was not the reason he changed his mind. Rather, it was a joint effort in a brilliantly composed paper submitted to him by my colleagues in the English Department.

Ten years later, I once more protested, on my own, a decision by the administration to fire more than twenty faculty members due to cuts in the budget. The academic senate had amassed more than 170 instructors to march behind its president, the previously mentioned Sandy Lydon, who delivered an impassioned speech and clever alternate plan that the board later adopted. But I had decided to come on my own—the only faculty member to do so—and deliver my own alternate plan.

By then I was a well-known figure in the community and an even better-known figure on campus, so the board, several of whom I knew socially, graciously welcomed my words—until they heard them. I pointed out that the cuts the administration had proposed were aimed only at faculty and support staff (secretaries, clerks, and technical and maintenance workers). There had been no cuts included for administrators. I spoke about the unfairness of this plan and went on to cite Plato's Academy in which there were only teachers and students, ending my brief presentation with the proposal that all the cuts should come from the administrators, since they were the least important part of a college's educational mission.

The board and my 170 fellow teachers standing behind me listened to my words in stunned silence. Was I joking? My delivery had been too passionate not to be taken seriously. Was I, then, insane? A few laughs and several cheers broke the tension, and the board chairman thanked me for my words, but the members of the administration stared at me with humorless faces.

In the ensuing years I took part in various campus committees where I proposed various changes and addenda to existing policy. But in the early 1990s an event occurred that changed my approach to public service.

The new president of the college proposed that an unexpected and much needed windfall of state money be used to install a school-wide computer system and buy several new campus police cars. I was appalled. So was the rest of the faculty, many of whom rallied behind the school's new union to protest the action.

I was particularly incensed because I had seen the wooden ventilating slats in classroom windows, as well as desks, blackboards, and other equipment fall into disrepair over the previous decade due to stringent budget cuts. Many of the classrooms only had half their overhead lights working, and the campus itself, once a collection of mission-style buildings surrounded by tubs of flowers and other blooming flora, had become a desolate collection of concrete brick buildings with broken shingled roofs. I, along with many other faculty members, had brought the situation to the president's attention, but he ignored our concerns.

I decided to go to the board as a private citizen, speaking to them in the opening segment of their monthly meeting, which was devoted to comments from the public. I delivered an angry attack on the president, once more pointing out the importance of the teaching mission over self-aggrandizing administrative planning and received enthusiastic applause from members of the audience when I finished.

The board accepted my recommendation, ruling that the money should be used for school repairs. The president was furious. He was an autocrat of the first order, and no one had stood up to him before then. But more important, the officers of the union came to me the next day and asked if they could print my speech in the union newspaper. They further recruited me to join the union executive council, pointing out that my reputation and visibility among the faculty, which had grown exponentially larger over the decade since I'd made my Plato speech, would be a huge asset to the organization. I consented to both, having been an advocate of union solidarity for years and harboring enormous respect for the core group who had founded and led the union in its formative years, which included Tillie Olsen's daughter, Julie Olsen Edwards, and her husband Rob.

I was trained by the local leaders and sent to the statewide union leadership school. Within a month I was made grievance officer, and within a year I was voted vice president of the Cabrillo chapter of the union, serving under the same Nancy Andreasen who had been Penelope Martin's roommate at college. And a year after that, when Nancy retired, I was voted union president.

In that position, I was engaged in one committee after another, protecting contract agreements, overturning self-serving administrative proposals, saving dozens of jobs, instituting new policies, and acting as watchdog for teachers' rights—all the while continuing to teach classes.

I was also assigned an assistant by the state AFT (our parent union), and with her I worked determinedly to increase the instructors' salary, which was the second lowest in the state, and which, after six years of strategizing and implementing, we were able to raise to match the top fifteen salary schedules among California community colleges. My passion and my persuasive powers, whose strengths I had first discovered all those years before in the air force, allowed me to eliminate a number of unfair workplace problems as well, and my commitment took me beyond the campus to work with the county labor union and take part in the AFT's statewide think tanks. I also insisted that my union work closely with SEIU, our sister union on campus, because we had the same goals and would both be stronger if we aided one another. After my term was over as president, I continued to be a member of the executive council and served as vice president until I retired.

Never had I been so happy. Never had I been able to accomplish so directly so much for my fellow humans as I had in my union work. When I retired from Cabrillo in 1998, I felt a satisfaction with my teaching and school-wide activities that I had never imagined possible. All in all, I recognized in my union participation and my standing up for my underrepresented colleagues another aspect of my lifelong fight against bullies and an expression of Leo's dictum, once again, to "fear not, and do right."

But my undertakings in the 1990s were more far-reaching than my work at Cabrillo. Although on the periphery, over the years I had taken part in various community projects involving the arts or political and environmental issues. In a small way, I also aided in the purchase of the Del Mar Theater, the old "dream palace" movie house downtown, by the City of Santa Cruz.

A lot of these community projects after 1990 had to do with my membership in a remarkable breakfast club that formed around George Ow, Jr. All of the members admired him greatly and had become friends with him and over time with each other. "Diversity," one of the most popular catchwords of the 1990s, perfectly described the group: George was Chinese American; Sandy Lydon, my old colleague from Cabrillo, was Irish American; Tony Hill was African American; Geoffrey Dunn was Italian-Irish American; and I was Russian-Jewish American. George called us his United Nations.

But the diversity went deeper than race and ethnicity. Each of us represented different attitudes and perceptions, but we were joined together by our desire to help our fellow citizens and by our camaraderie. George, of course, was well-known for his beneficent support of the poor.

Sandy was a local historian who, aside from his teaching, worked with most of the ethnic groups in the area to promote their history and bring an understanding of them to each other and the county in general through his books, newspaper articles, and extremely popular off-campus talks, which always drew hundreds of people.

Tony Hill was a social activist who worked with local government on behalf of minority groups and kept the county residents generally aware of the deeper, often hidden, aspects of racism in their midst. He also had a one-man business that specialized in conflict resolution, and he would be invited to large and small corporations to give workshops and settle disputes among management and labor on issues as far ranging as gender, race, and workplace discord.

Geoffrey Dunn was a brilliant documentary filmmaker, investigative reporter, local historian, and political insider who had deep roots in the Italian fishing community and, even though he was by far the youngest of us, brought astonishing practical savvy in a variety of areas to the group.

With the Breakfast Club. *Front, left to right:* Tony Hill and George Ow, Jr. *Rear, left to right:* Morton Marcus, Jeff Dunn, and Sandy Lydon.

I brought my arts connection and union perspective.

Besides all that, the five of us were honored to be in each other's company and relished our times together. We were always joking and ribbing one another unmercifully while we formulated community projects. So popular were our breakfasts that local and state politicians, as well as those seeking help with their ventures, would ask to join us for our weekly get-togethers.

But that wasn't all. I was also involved in another project. In 1988 I had become a member of the steering committee for the Pacific Rim Film Festival and continued to work energetically through the 1990s with the rest of the steering committee members—which included Jeff Dunn, Jim and Jeanne Houston and their daughter Cori—to annually stage this unique event. The festival had been founded by George Ow, Jr. and Jim and Jeanne to show films that promoted understanding of the many different peoples living around the rim of the Pacific Ocean. Every year we presented five days of films, in many cases with the filmmakers on hand, and all events were free of charge to the public.

ROBERT HERSHON

If my rediscovery of Richard Martin had proven less than gratifying, my finding Robert Hershon was not. I had been delighted by his poetry since the early 1970s and had taken courage in pursuing the comic in poetry because of the wit and wisdom I found in his work and that of several others. I had never gotten in touch with Hershon because I didn't know where he was, and over the years I had read less and less of his work. In fact, I had assumed he was no longer writing or had died. What impressed me most about his work

Robert Hershon,
New York City,
2005

was that it was urban in setting and New Yorkese in flavor and language, and if it was antic, there was an underlying thoughtfulness, expressed in a contemplative, even judicious tone, that I didn't find in my other favorite comic poets, such as Jack Anderson and Russell Edson. Robert was not a satirist; he was an intelligent, observant, insightful "man on the street" with a comic view of life. His comedy, therefore, was rarely bitter, cutting, sarcastic, or cynical. It was humane and sadly cognizant of human foibles and follies.

In 1995, I found out from another humane comic poet, my old friend Robert Peterson, that Hershon was very much alive and writing voluminously at the top of his form. Peterson had been looking for a publisher for his latest manuscript and had come upon Hanging Loose Press in his quest The editors at Hanging Loose enthusiastically agreed to bring out what proved to be his last book, *All the Time in the World*. The day the press accepted his manuscript, he called me and told me of his good fortune and about his dealings with the group of five editors who ran the press, among whom was Robert Hershon. I immediately wrote Hershon, and over the next several years published a number of poems in *Hanging Loose* magazine. That phase of the relationship culminated in 1997, when Hanging Loose brought out my book of prose poems, *When People Could Fly*. By then I had gotten to know Robert and had met him when he came to Santa Cruz to read at the university with another Hanging Loose poet, the extraordinary Native American poet and novelist Sherman Alexie. Hershon was all I imagined him to be. He was warm, humane, and judicious, and my experience working with him and the other editors was among my happiest dealings with publishers. I have continued to publish in *Hanging Loose* magazine without letup in the new millennium, and although Robert lives across the continent and we rarely see each other, I have considered him a friend since we first corresponded. And his poetry? It is as strong and wise today as it ever was. Here's an example of it:

Calls from the Outside

Celeste called work to leave a message
for Nathan. "Tell him Celeste called.
Tell him *something happened*"

And that became a famous phone message
and part of the folklore
finally working its way into a byword at the
shop and it came to designate a
call from anyone's spouse or
companion Hey Richie, line six—
something
And there was an amused pride in
having invented such a good piece of
workplace slang, so specialized and so secret
and so site-specific

but before long Nat was gone and then
one by one nearly everybody else
so today the slang is as good as ever
but completely forgotten or unknown
to the present staff

So we see that for slang to survive
we require a body of speakers
initiated in its use
large enough to provide continuity
and with a core of permanence

This must be why the linguists
invented prisons, as language laboratories
so that the whole country can imitate
the speech of young black men but
never actually have to see them, so white
golfers can cry *You the man*
and little blond girls can shout
You go, girl

CHAPTER 50

My Mother's Last Days

The end of the 1990s was marked by a number of personal and public events.

On the personal side, my relationship with Jana went through several turnabouts. After the European trip in 1979, when she was seventeen years old, we had grown apart. I watched her change into someone I didn't recognize. Her sweetness and sensitivity were replaced by a hard-edged rebelliousness. She shaved half her head, dyed different sections of her hair blue and pink, and adopted punk fashions.

After she moved back to New York for a second time in 1986, our estrangement grew if for no other reason than the physical distance between us, and her life took its own direction. Continuing her interest in subcultures, but always as a curious observer rather than a participant, she was drawn to the punk nightclub scene in the East Village. As she had done with her South Bronx portfolio, she made a book-length photo study of what she saw called

Brother and sisters: Valerie, Nick, and Jana. Santa Cruz, 2003.

Midnight in Manhattan, which she had started on her first stay in New York in the early 1980s.

But by day she was locked in a drab, underpaying job whose demands, she said, "drained the life out of me," and eventually brought on an ulcer. Shortly after that she developed strep throat, which turned into rheumatic fever, and in 1992 her illnesses forced her to come home.

On her return to Santa Cruz, we were at odds much of the time. She felt I cared nothing about her life—that I had rejected her as a person. Finally, in much the same way Nick would ask to talk with me years later, she requested I attend a therapy session with her, during which the therapist pointed out that I was unwilling to accept the fact that Jana had become a woman. I was clinging to my memories of her as the little girl who would ask me how the world worked on our many long drives to and from Santa Barbara and other places, while Valerie slept in the back seat and on-coming headlights lit up Jana's enraptured face as she listened to my explanations.

The therapist explained to Jana that my telling her I couldn't solve her problems when she called me from New York was not a rejection of her, but an acknowledgement that she was an adult, a realization, the therapist was quick to add, that I was unwilling to accept in other areas. After several meetings most of our problems were solved, and thereafter we considered each other adults as well as father and daughter.

Jana has remained in Santa Cruz and gone on to produce photographic work of originality and social value in a series of projects dealing with American subcultures. One of the projects became, as I've written in earlier pages, her first published book, a collection of interviews and photographs of Anne Rice fans and the vampire culture surrounding her, entitled *In the Shadow of the Vampire.* Jana also won several Best Photo awards in nationally prominent photographic magazines, and in 2005 received an MFA in photography from San Jose State University. Her thesis, a study of transgenderism called *Transfigurations,* became an award-winning exhibition that was shown in a number of galleries in San Francisco, New York, and elsewhere. She continues to work as a freelance photographer, and for

With Donna and my grandson Zachary, Union City, New Jersey, 2004.

years was the official photographer and marketing director for Cabrillo Stage, a
large-scale professional musical theater company.

Valerie, meanwhile, stayed on the East Coast, holding a series of menial
jobs looking for work as an actress. Slowly, her interest turned to costume
design, and nine years after she graduated from Bennington, she applied to
the prestigious graduate program in Costume Design in NYU's Tisch School
of the Arts, from which she graduated in 2001 with an MFA. She continues
to work as a costume designer in New York and has been the main designer
for Broadway shows such as *Tuesdays with Morrie*. In 2002, she married
Steve Ramshur, a director with whom she had shared an office at NYU. In
2004 she gave birth to a boy, my first grandchild, Zachary Marcus Ramshur.
And in 2006, she was one of five costume designers nominated for the year's
best costume design for an off-Broadway play. Although she lives across the
continent, we remain close. I never have had the same kind of talks with her I
had with Jana and Nick. And I hope there is no need for one.

My feelings about both girls growing up was the subject of another of my
favorite poems, which I wrote several years after my therapy meetings with
Jana and which followed a discussion on the subject with Donna.

My Daughters, Grown

1.

I have returned numberless times
to that room where my daughters slept
when they were seven and two
and I heard the slender wings
of their breathing climb
and hover above their heads,
a slow flexing in that house
they haven't lived in for twenty years.

It is a father's journey undertaken
again and again to watch over and protect
in the night, while the wind
roars outside and the stars'
blue fires burn like sapphires
around that house of memory.

2.

Grown now, both live lost and alone
in the small high rooms of tall buildings

in separate cities far away, and each night
I lumber toward those cities
but get no farther than that room
they slept in so long ago. Exhausted,
I loosen the straps of my knapsack
and set it aside like another body
at their bedsides, watching them
as they were when I wished
what a father does for his daughters,
a jumble of longings I could never
put into words and knew even then
were impossible.

                              So is it any wonder
that I cannot tell them by phone
what I wish for them, or at least
say something that will ease
the hurt and confusion in their words,
as sirens and horns and random shouts
enter the windows behind them
and wrestle with their voices
over the wire?

                    3.

                              My wife,
who has similar problems with her father,
says I always imagine my daughters
as little girls asleep in that ancient room,
and only when I portray them as women
will we be able to converse in a manner
that will satisfy us all. She' s right,
I'm sure, but she's not a father.

Last night I visited that room again,
but it rolled and pitched, the house
no longer a house but a ship plunging
through the night, transporting
a cargo of children all in my care
to an unknown destination. I stood
on the deck, knowing there was
no wheelhouse behind me and no rudder,
and all I could do was pray for them all,

while, like a celestial liner,
the ship slid through the night,
its hull scarred and scraped
by the hot sapphire of the stars.

Nick has lived on his own since the mid-1990s and graduated with a degree in film production from the University of California. He struggled for several years, trying to find suitable employment, but he seems to have found peace with a woman he has been with for a number of years now and who was with him when we had our talk in Croatia.

The most important personal event of the 1990s, however, was my mother's decision to move to California. She was eighty-eight years old in 1995 when she agreed, at my urging, to come out. She admitted that she was tired of fighting the daily difficulties of city living and was more and more

With my mother after she moved to California, Monterey, 1998.

worried about falling on the city's icy streets in winter and enduring the unbearable East Coast heat in summer.

Donna took it upon herself to research retirement homes from San Jose to Monterey, scheduling visits for my mother at half a dozen places in which she thought my mother might consider residing. Meanwhile, my mother sold her lease and auctioned off paintings and antiques she had bought or retained from her marriages, especially her last one, which had been to the great-nephew of Theodor Herzl. By the time she came to the places Donna had suggested, she knew she could financially handle her stay in California, no matter how long it would be.

To Wilma and any other woman she met with whom I'd had a relationship, my mother had been cruel and insulting. On my first trip with Donna to New York, she actually had driven Donna out of the house, a not-uncommon situation that had occurred several times with Wilma when we were married. When my mother would visit my house and provoke such situations, I almost always ended them by telling her to go to hell, kicking her out of the house, and not speaking to her for one or two years at a time. Such had been the pattern of our relationship since my air force days. As can be imagined, my relationship with my mother was as prickly as hers was with my girlfriends, a situation that I go into in some detail in the mother poems in Pages from a Scrapbook of Immigrants.

In social situations, on the other hand, my mother captivated anyone who met her. She was beautiful, vivacious, and charismatic, even in old age. But that captivating personality masked an angry, narcissistic, brutal human being, as anyone who got to know her soon found out. Still, I was her son, her only child, and I felt responsible for her in her last years.

I wanted her to choose a retirement home in Santa Cruz, but she chose one in Monterey, a posh building with elevators and large mirrors and paintings covering the cherry-wood, white-wainscoted walls, a building, as the reader may have guessed, that resembled the upscale New York apartment building she had grown used to. As she said to me bluntly one day, "I want to die at a good address." But there was another reason. She didn't want to be a burden on Donna and me, which she thought she would be if she chose a retirement home in Santa Cruz. "You'll feel you have to see me all the time if I'm that near you," she said. Such was the paradoxical nature of this chameleon-like creature I had never gotten to know or understand but called mother.

She wound up her affairs in New York and moved to California in 1995, but not before she alienated the entire family, insulting and lambasting Leo, Carol, and their children. She was saying good-bye to the life she knew the only way she knew how—by divorce.

But shortly after she moved into her one-bedroom apartment in Monterey, it was apparent that she had left a number of other things in New York. Her anger and bitterness abruptly ceased; she became more humorous than ever and great company.

If she had moved to Monterey not to interfere with my life, she made it necessary for me to drive there two or three times a week. On those occasions, she would take Donna and me to lunch or dinner, and the three of us would go on short drives or visit various tourist spots like the Carmel Mission. She also stayed over at the house in Santa Cruz several times a month.

Soon her attitude toward Donna began to change. I watched her staring at Donna, and noted how relaxed her body became after the first day. She would talk to her more and more on any number of subjects and ask her advice, and within months the bad feeling between them was forgotten. She finally saw in Donna the extraordinary person I did. In fact, my mother became Donna's strongest advocate, taking her side in any disagreement and telling me how lucky I was to have her. More astonishing than that, my mother shared confidences with Donna she had shared with no on else, confidences that put her in an uncharacteristically vulnerable position. Once, when they were alone in the car, my mother asked Donna if she thought that a person would be cold buried underground, and when Donna, realizing what my mother was really asking, answered with a tender, "I don't think so," my mother timidly asked, "Would you come and visit me and tell me what was going on with the children?" I believe Donna became possibly the only person my mother ever trusted and loved.

My mother was also delighted with Donna's family, who always invited her to family functions. My mother- and father-in-law, as well as Donna's brothers and sisters, were delighted by her in return. They loved her humor and energy.

It didn't take me long to see that my mother was a much more complex person than I had thought her to be. She had accomplished admirable things for a barefoot six-year-old who had arrived in this country in steerage in 1914. She had become cultured, despite a lack of education, and had managed to travel to Europe half a dozen times. She loved music and had been a season ticket holder at the Metropolitan Opera. She had tried to live her life as fully as possible, knowing that the way she had chosen to climb the social ladder, through good looks and sexual promises, was a dangerous course that would bring her to grief at the hands of the greedy, the grasping, and the powerful people with whom she associated.

Because of her continued good humor I also came to understand that her spitefulness and nasty ways were a defense against the tough life she had experienced in New York and had allowed her to survive since she was a child, and I was all the more amazed and grateful that she had left that aspect of her personality behind her.

As time went on, she became more and more frail, and I had to spend more time taking care of her, seeing that her daily needs were met by paying her bills, getting her to doctors' offices, shopping for her, and doing any number of errands and chores. Finally, she turned all her money and private papers over to me. It was an astonishing act of trust by a person who had spent her life trusting no one. She was—there is no other way of saying this— enjoying herself, looking forward to her outings with Donna and me, although I did many of the weekday visits on my own. For our part, Donna and I looked forward to spending time with her. We were a trio of friends. More and more I caught my mother staring at me as she had at Donna. She was studying me, sizing me up. As her physical frailness turned into chronic illnesses, we spent more and more time together—and she studied me more and more.

I knew she hated men and had used them for her own purposes throughout her life. I may have been her son, but I had never been part of her life—and I was a man. It was easy for me to see how Donna had found a place in her affections: my mother always had female friends and was more forthcoming with them than with the men she was manipulating, and, when all was said and done, I was a member of that hated gender.

It was totally unexpected, then, when, one day after I had taken her to the doctor's and was sitting at her small dining room table doing her monthly bills, she began to nod and grunt as if she had come to a decision. She had been sitting on the couch she used as a bed and had been staring at me again, her head shaking slightly with palsy. When she had gotten my attention, she said in what I can only term a tone of disbelief, "You're a real mensch, aren't you."

It was a statement, not a question. I sat in shock, the pen poised above the bill I was paying, and tears immediately welled in my eyes. It was the biggest compliment one can receive from a Yiddish speaker, and it was a term I had never heard my mother use to describe anyone: it was a sacred word no one, in her eyes, deserved. *Mensch* in Yiddish is a person who has admirable characteristics such as fortitude and firmness of purpose, one who is fundamentally decent and good, full of integrity and honor, takes responsibility for others' welfare, and has a sense of right conduct: in short, someone of noble character.

When my mother addressed me with that word, I knew she had come to love me, not as the son she had abandoned, but as the middle-aged man she had known since she moved to California. At the same time, I realized that I had come to know and love her, too.

Throughout her stay in California, my mother would ask me every once in a while if she had been a good mother, and I would answer her honestly that she had been, but I'm sure she didn't know the reason for my answer. Yes, she had abandoned me, sent me to the schools those endless years of my childhood and youth, and when I was five, turned me out of the house to face the janitor's son and his gang. But those trials had made me independent at an early age. I had quickly learned to take care of myself. More important, since I had no mother and father and no home life, I was able to see the world without the inhibiting values and perceptions most children grow up with and must put aside, usually with great difficulty, before they can become independent beings.

When my mother died in January 2002, I felt no remorse or guilt, nor did I feel resentment. In the less than seven years she had been in California, we had built a relationship most parents and children do not achieve in a lifetime.

The end came suddenly. My mother had been taken to the hospital with a minor heart attack, but at ninety-four she was too weak to overcome the physical stress. Within a few days she lapsed into a coma. I would sit by the side of her bed reading a book or watching her. The day before she died, she seemed to swim out of her unconsciousness for a moment. She looked at me and smiled. "My little bubbie," she said contentedly, and closed her eyes again. Those were the last words she spoke.

Interestingly, Donna brings my mother up in conversation at least twice a month. She misses her. She still considers her the most frightening person she ever met, but she just as freely admits she was also one of the most fascinating—and that she loved her.

A year after my mother's death, I wrote this curious little prose poem, one of a group concerning her life.

> When my mother died, I felt no remorse. She was 94 and I had taken good care of her for the last seven years of her life. At all the doctors' offices, the nurses loved me, said I was one of the few who looked after their parents. "She's lucky to have a son like you." They didn't know she'd sent me to boarding schools when I was three and visited me only once or twice a year. This paragraph is not about the disparity of how my mother and I looked after each other, but the uneasiness I've felt more and more since her death. I keep waiting for the phone to ring, or remember something I forgot to tell her, or wonder if she's all right.
>
> —from "My Mother was a Beautiful Woman"

CHAPTER 51

The Prose Poem

Among the many things that happened during the 1990s, my writing took an unexpected and efficacious turn.

I had become mildly interested in the prose poem when I came upon Richard Ellman's *Selected Writings of Henri Michaux* in the San Francisco Public Library in 1966. I tried my hand at several prose poems but desultorily, only half interested in the form during the ensuing years. My interest sharpened when I read W. S. Merwin's *The Miner's Pale Children* in 1970 and intensified in 1976 when I discovered Michael Benedikt's invaluable anthology of international practitioners of the genre, *The Prose Poem*. A year later, a young publisher asked me for a short manuscript, and I found I had twenty or so of my prose experiments that I thought suitable for publication. The result was *The Armies Encamped in the Fields Beyond the Unfinished Avenues*, with brilliant ink drawings by Futzi Nutzle, at that time a featured artist in *Rolling Stone*. The book came out in 1977 to no distribution and no interest.

Although I did not realize it at the time, the narrative impulse coursing through the prose poem had begun as a stream in my fiction writing between 1979 and 1980 and continued like an underground river in *Pages from a Scrapbook of Immigrants* to emerge into the sunlight like Coleridge's sacred river in "a mighty fountain" in 1992.

The immediate inspiration for my undertaking new prose poems was a book of prose poems and parables by my old friend Larry Fixel, entitled *Truth, War and the Dream Game*. It was a selection of Larry's best work written over the preceding twenty-four years. At that time, I was writing the long feature articles about poets and writers I have mentioned before for the weekly San Francisco Bay Area newspaper *Metro*, and I persuaded the editor to let me write a three-thousand-word article on the book. It was really a labor of love, since Larry, of course, had been the encouraging director of the small poetry group I was part of during the 1960s and early '70s.

There is no doubt that my writing such a detailed piece forced me to look at the ramifications of the prose poem and the parable I had been unwilling or too lazy to see before. Many of the elements, I discovered, allowed me to verbalize my own practices and concerns and to recognize directions I had either half developed or hadn't pursued.

Larry's engagement with the parable made me acknowledge not just the narrative impulse in my work, but my reliance on storytelling. It further made me aware of the symbolic subtext I saw in the simplest everyday incidents, subtexts that assumed mythic if not archetypal proportions. As I said about Larry in the article, "Fixel's parables belong to a tradition that includes Kafka, Borges, Italo Calvino, Henri Michaux, and even Herman Melville. In their hands, the parable can parade as an imitation of everyday reality, but it is really made of the stuff of dreams, of the unconscious, of myth." I went on to say, "Fixel describes the parable in its modern guise as a narrative that provides 'a devastating illumination of a world split between psyche, spirit and material concerns [and is] especially suited to convey the distilled essences of a fragmented world.' Essentially, the parable, as Fixel uses it, challenges our assumptions while, paradoxically, it evokes universal meanings." I went on to describe this situation as follows: "As we wish for and never get in newspaper accounts, Fixel's tales go beyond the surface description of events to their possible meanings. Fixel makes the reader aware of the significance of the words used to describe the happenings. These words become metaphors and symbols that lead us to a deeper and unexpected examination of the subject under discussion."

These thoughts made me realize that my work had veered toward the parable since I had first put pen to paper all those years ago in high school. But as if I were driving a car, I had willingly, although unconsciously, brought my work back from a side road to the main highway—that is, to the main and therefore restricting thoroughfare of American poetry.

At the same time, I realized that the freedom I thought I had achieved when I abandoned closed verse and adopted free verse was an illusion because if closed verse had determined my phrasing, the way I got from one line to the next and even the structure of my poems—all of which, I came to realize, I had almost unconsciously learned from my readings of the old masters—then free verse, while giving me a latitude that made my voice more lively, still restricted my structures by the way I advanced from one line to the next. However, when I gave up the line in writing the prose poem, I experienced new ways of seeing and saying.

As I said in an interview in the *Bloomsbury Review* several years later, what I had come to realize was that the line had inhibited my thinking process since my choice of words and sense of structure (in terms of word choice, syntax, and overall development of the poem) was determined as much by the line as by the way I conceived of moving from one thought, image, or metaphor to another and how, in the end, I structured the entire poem. In other words, I found content was as much determined by my using or not using the line as free verse had been in releasing me from the tried and true ways of getting from one line to another in closed verse. Thus, in writing the prose poem, I had not only gotten rid of "the tyranny of the line," I had also gotten rid of the baggage I had not realized came with it.

At the same time, the chains fell away from my imagination, and ultimately my greatest discovery in writing the prose poem was its ability to free the imagination. To me this freeing has everything to do with my vision as a poet, since I seek the level below consciousness from which to speak. As I said in the *Bloomsbury* interview, "My world is composed of funhouse-mirror distortions of reality, dream visions rooted in metaphor and symbol, which for me evoke a more resonant picture of the world than everyday realism does."

Looked at another way, my choice to abandon the line allowed me to pursue an unshackled phrase as my basic unit of rhythm, which at times extended to thirteen and even fifteen beats before a caesura, something that would be prohibitive in a verse poem. In a prose poem I could pursue "a sweep of words," as I wrote in *The Prose Poem: An International Journal*, "that in its unfolding opens unexpected vistas of content by releasing my imagination from conventional modes of thought, which the line and other poetic devices, it seems, unconsciously dictate."

However, I also observed that I employed all the techniques of poetry, such as figurative language, assonance, consonance, and even internal as well as what can only be called "end-sentence" rhyme to drive my rhythms and energize my prose poems.

The result of all this thinking and verbalizing was that several months after I wrote the Fixel article, I experienced an eruption of writing even more explosive than during the period in which I created *Origins* or *Pages from a Scrapbook of Immigrants*.

The pieces seemed new, fresh, and exploited language, image, and idea as I never had before. My imagination constantly surprised me. I let my flights of fancy carry me along, not understanding what I was writing at first, but trusting the energy that was propelling my words forward. Many times I discovered that the fantastic situations and outlandish images I'd put on paper were the beginnings of extended metaphors or parables that themselves, in the end, were metaphors.

I had read Coleridge's definition of the imagination and the fancy, and abided by his pronouncements, but now the fancy was no longer a dirty word. As I said in an interview with Robert Sward that was published in *Caesura* magazine in 2003, "To me, the fancy is a plaything, which can be taken in hand and elevated to the level of the imagination—that is, it can be forced to be more than itself."

However, I pointed out that there were pitfalls in this thinking that the poet should be wary of since the fancy would allow his or her imagination free range and "weirdness for weirdness' sake is not acceptable, nor is the poet's indulging his or her facility for invention unless it is being used for specific purposes in a poem. The imagination's 'genuine' images and metaphors are the only route to vision, to the momentary glimpse we can get of the essential order of things, which is what the creative act allows the poet (or artist of any medium) to apprehend and through him or her the reader (or audience) to experience." The last part of that statement, which is really talking about structuring and craft, is what I take to be Coleridge's notion that in the end the imagination is more genuine, more solid than the fancy because it is also an organizing agent.

That wasn't all. By relentlessly following images that popped into my head, I soon came to believe that any idea or image that is manifested in the brain is not accidental and should be developed seriously by the writer.

While all these elements were surging to the fore of my work, humor, more antic than ever, gushed up, spreading in garish colors over the poems. As I said in the *Bloomsbury Review* interview

> My predilections for the comic extend to my favorite authors: Rabelais, Cervantes, Stern, Swift, Aristophanes, Zhuangzi, the Rumi of the *Mathnawi,* and the folk hero Nasrudin. I'm drawn to the holy fools, the cosmic clowns, idiot savants, not just for their boisterous, fun-loving, and at times scathingly sardonic attitudes toward humanity and the bumbling ways of the universe, but because they upset our habitual ways of seeing the world, show us new perspectives by presenting us with the unexpected, and destroy our comfortable expectations and conventional values so we will once again encounter the world in fresh ways, renewed.

It is interesting to note that most of the writers I listed in that quotation speak in parables and extended metaphors.

In the interview with Sward, I talked about one of the ways the preceding statements allowed me to develop a poem. I started by saying that many times I begin a poem by imagining a voice speaking, a particular voice that is talking to me or which I'm overhearing, a voice whose rhythm and tone I let guide the method and structure of what I'm writing. I go on to say that images and metaphors present themselves in my psyche but that their appearances are unplanned and unexpected, and it is my task to pursue their meanings by following their development, which many times consists of grappling with their changes in shape and direction. Along with the notions of pursuing and wrestling with the images, and after reiterating that the poet should never consider such images to be trivial or "accidental," I concluded by describing somewhat fancifully my scenario for writing the poem by comparing my pursuit of the images and metaphors

> . . . to riding bareback on a runaway horse, and what I had to do to survive was grab its mane with my hands, grip its flanks with my legs and hold on for dear life as it took me wherever it would. . . . To complicate the matter—and the metaphor—the metaphoric horse I was riding might at any moment change shape under me,

as if I were riding not a horse but some shape-shifting, Proteus-like beast on the road to oblivion . . . and that the imagination in this case is not so much "imagery" as "imaging," that is, it is not a noun but a transitive verb, an action, an act of becoming, the core of creativity. It propels the images and metaphors out of nothing-ness into being. So, as I ride the shape-shifting beast, I pronounce (intone?) both its twists and turns and the twists and turns of its route. When the beast finally collapses in exhaustion, I sift through and polish my memories of the ride and from them shape a verbal map from this formerly uncharted landscape, a structure the reader can follow for whatever reason he chooses. And that's the poem.

PETER JOHNSON

The prose poems I wrote took many forms. Some were outlandish satires of travel books, historical monographs, saints' tales. I wrote on an enor-mous range of subjects, as Jack Marshall said, "literally constructing an entire universe."

I showed the prose pieces I was working on to Larry Fixel and Jack. Both were enthusiastic and urged me to continue. Larry, more the networker than ever, put me in touch with a press in England that was soliciting prose poems for an Anglo American prose poem anthology entitled *A Curious Architecture*. They took three of the new pieces. Larry also urged me to send the new poems to Peter Johnson, who had just started a journal called *The Prose Poem: An International Journal*. Peter, a fine prose poet himself, so appreciated what I was doing, he included new prose poems by me in every succeeding issue of the journal, asked me to do a long review of Rus-sell Edson's selected prose poems, *The Tunnel*, wrote an appreciation of my work that appeared in the journal, and made me an advisory editor for the magazine. He also invited me for a three-day visit to Providence College, the university at which he taught.

As a result of my visit to Providence, Peter and I became friends. Often frustrated by lack of concern or cooperation from his college's administration, he tire-lessly devoted unending hours to editing the journal, which, after several issues, was responsible, I have no doubt, for creating a prose poem renaissance throughout the country. Peter introduced the work of many new poets in the magazine and encouraged a variety of approaches to the prose poem as well as printed reviews of most of the new prose poem books that appeared in the 1990s. Certainly, he reawakened the literary world to

Peter Johnson, Providence, Rhode Island, 2005

the important, iconoclastic work of Russell Edson and, I also have no doubt, renewed interest in my work.

By the time exhaustion forced him to suspend the magazine's publication, national interest in the prose poem was in full swing. His final act as editor was to cull the best work of the journal's seven annual issues in what became an influential anthology, *The Best of the Prose Poem*.

Besides his excellence as an editor, Peter was writing some of the best prose poems in the country. Starting with the short, paragraph-long prose poems he collected in his first book, *Pretty Happy*, he graduated to writing book-length, one-paragraph prose-poem sequences. His second book, *Miracles & Mortifications*, was composed of two of those sequences and won the prestigious James Laughlin Prize of the Academy of American Poets. Another two sequences, entitled *Eduardo and 'I,'* appeared in 2006. All the sequences share a similar persona narrating his adventures, which are not so much descriptions of events as fragments sifting through a mind bombarded with thoughts, impressions, and musings about his being as an individual and as a representative of the male sex. The simultaneous evocation of the personal and the archetypal is effortless, and the word play extraordinary. Johnson's method is to mix a cacophony of phrases and sentence fragments coming from different directions and pushed forward by puns, jokes and arcane allusions in a blizzard of darkly humorous tones marked by hilarity, fears, self-questionings, and alternate poses as the speaker flounders between imagining himself as victim and victimizer.

In the first sequence of *Miracles & Mortifications*, "Travels with Gigi," the speaker journeys to various exotic tourist destinations with the enigmatic Gigi, who soon becomes the mysterious female figure that haunts the male psyche and is more a figment of the protagonist's imagination than she is a real person. In "Travels with Oedipus," the second of *Miracles & Mortifications'* sequences, a similar persona, maybe even the same as in the first sequence, travels to various places through time with his son to visit great male figures from history. Again a kaleidoscopic exploration of male identity, the sequence becomes an examination of father and son relationships, full of pop, punk, and other contemporary fragments and allusions, set against its historical background.

As this brief analysis of Peter Johnson's work demonstrates, the prose poem can be of complex and far-reaching literary and thereby cultural importance in the hands of a master. All in all, Johnson is confronting the uncertainties and contradictions that have become increasingly apparent to each of us in the global village of this millennium's technological age.

Here's an early poem, the title piece from his first book. Although it has none of the complexity of the later poems, it gives a strong sense of Johnson's sensibility.

Pretty Happy

I have no siblings who've killed themselves, a few breakdowns here and there, my son sometimes talking back to me, but, in general, I'm pretty happy. And if the basement leaks, and the fuses fart out when the coffee machine comes on, and if the pastor beats us up with the same old parables, and raccoons overturn the garbage cans and ham it up at 2 o'clock in the morning while some punk is cutting the wires on my car stereo, I can still say, I'm pretty happy.

Pretty happy! Pretty happy! I whisper to my wife at midnight, waking to another night noise, reaching for the baseball bat I keep hidden under our bed.

MIKE CATALANO AND GERALD FLEMING

Besides *Hanging Loose* and several other literary journals, including Peter's *The Prose Poem: An International Journal* and *The Denver Quarterly*, two individuals were important boosters of my new prose poems. Like Stephen Kessler, both of them show the commitment, energy, and self-sacrifice at the grassroots level that have been the reason most of the arts in this country have flourished, and they should be recognized for their efforts. In the early 1970s, another of their number, an accountant named Neil Lehrman, copublisher of Dryad Press, moved to San Francisco from Washington, DC and championed my poetry, devoting the thirteenth issue of *Dryad* magazine entirely to my work. In return I had introduced him to John Logan, Joe Stroud, and Noel Young at Capra Press, who he worked with to bring out a book of John's. I also taught him how to make poached eggs by cracking the eggs into an open pan of boiling water, an art he never mastered. Neal and I became friends, but when *Dryad* folded a few years later, which such enterprises sadly and inevitably do, he and I lost touch.

Mike Catalano, an ex-student of mine, was one of the two people who promoted my work in the 1990s. Mike had moved to Alabama where he raised a daughter on his own and for several years spent a good portion of his meager salary earned at various odd jobs to edit and publish a very small, poorly produced literary magazine called *Melting Trees*. Indefatigable in his commitment to poetry, he sought established poets as well as hunted for new talent to fill his pages. He not only published my new prose poems but ran an interview with me. More important, he was the go-between who reintroduced me to Tom Meschery, who he also admired and whose work he promoted; and on a trip to Santa Cruz, he snatched up what would be one of the most popular of my new prose poems, "My Father's Hobby," from a sheaf of writings I was going to throw out. Unfortunately, diabetes and other pressures curtailed Mike's publishing endeavors in the late 1990s, although he continues to write.

A person with a grander vision, and luckily more lasting health as well as energy, is Gerald Fleming. For years a teacher in the San Francisco school system, Jerry put away a portion of his salary to edit and publish a handsome, beautifully produced literary magazine called *Barnabe Mountain*

Review. The journal, which from the start was planned to come out in only five issues between 1995 and 2000, was an annual. Jerry had conceived of it as a platform to publish those writers he thought weren't getting enough national attention. Along the way, he solicited work in national magazines and discovered many new writers. All five volumes can be found in The Bancroft Library at UC Berkeley.

A selfless, self-effacing poet himself, Jerry championed Jack Marshall's work as well as mine, and as a colleague and friend soon entered the small group that included Larry Fixel and his wife Justine, Jack and his wife Naomi, and Carl Rakosi. Jerry's devotion to people as well as literature is unstinting. So is his humor. Vacationing in Prague, he sent me a postcard supposedly written in broken English by a Czech who claimed to be a feverish fan of my work, and for months I tried to find out who this poor, misguided soul could be.

Gerald Fleming, Lagunitas, California, 2005.

For a time, it looked as if I had gotten Jerry's first book published by Creative Arts Books, but then the company failed. The book, *Swimmer Climbing onto Shore*, finally came out in 2005 when Jerry was sixty. A prose poet as well as verse poet, his work is different in both genres, since he is given to parable-like fantasy in his prose poems and to realistic, straightforward personal lyrics in his verse. In "The Daily Spanking, Child Next Door," his identification with his subject, whether an incident or person he is intensely observing, both hallmarks of his approach, are joined by evocatively rhythmic language that attempts to suggest the child's terror through precise external description.

The Daily Spanking, Child Next Door

First the crying is a jagged graph,
direct response to pain: One. Two. Three.
Four. Five, but the final number never
known. When the blows stop,
it hollows—a long voweled moan, chant
of a child lost in a public place. Then a cry
almost private: gathered, guttural,
having to do more with rage than loss of love,
aimed at whatever force put him here—with her.
Then, at the end, a sound I first mistook for doves.

RAY GONZALEZ

Another poet I met at this time was Ray Gonzalez, whose poems are shaman-like chants with extraordinary twists and turns of unexpected language. Along with Ray's many verse books are the prose poem volumes *Turtle Pictures,* a mixed verse and prose poem book; *Humans Crying Daisies*; and *The Religion of Hands: Prose Poems and Flash Fictions.* I read *Turtle Pictures* when it first came out. I was so taken with the scope of the book that I went to Monterey when Gonzalez came to read on the West Coast and introduced myself to him after his presentation. We chatted, and I asked him if he had free time in the next day or two to come to Santa Cruz. He was wary, even reticent, two traits he often shows to those he doesn't know, but he brightened when I told him I wanted to interview him for my radio show. He was still leery the next day before we taped the show, but our rapport, and I guess my questions and comments, so appealed to him that we became close friends after that. The following year, he came to read in Santa Cruz and stayed at my house. We strolled around the bay and the wharf. I drove him from reading to reading and then to San Francisco, and all the while we gossiped and complained to each other and told stories about poets we both knew and those we didn't. I introduced him to Gary Young and cemented a relationship between Ray and Peter Johnson, who asked Ray to read at Providence the next year. By this time Ray had read my poetry and must have been taken with it, because he conducted the long interview with me for *The Bloomsbury Review* and published a number of my best verse and prose poems in his journal *Luna.*

We continue our friendship with periods if intense e-mailing back and forth and get angry at each other when one or the other of us doesn't write. It is an interesting relationship.

Certainly the one constant is our respect for each other's work. To me, Ray is an absolute original. He has taken Latino American poetry to another level. Before him, Chicano literature, which had surfaced throughout the 1970s to become a major component of American literature in the 1980s and 1990s, had been concerned with describing life in the barrio and in any Latino American community. The work of Gary Soto, another acquaintance, comes to mind, and Ana Castillo. Their work introduces and humanizes to the dominant Anglo population what life is like in the Latino American communities. And that is one of the groundbreaking endeavors any minority group's artists, especially writers, have to accomplish. That's what Jeanne Houston did in *Farewell to Manzanar* and Lawson did in his Fresno and internment camp poems.

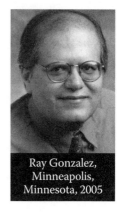

Ray Gonzalez, Minneapolis, Minnesota, 2005

Ray takes those social concerns and shows the mythic and cosmic resonances humming inside them. He writes about the personal, cultural, and historical concerns of Mexican Americans living on the Texas border but transforms those concerns, or, better, interweaves them into the warp and woof of a timeless visionary universe. Reading his work, at times, I get the impression that a shaman's spirit has gained control of Ray's psyche and is speaking through him. As I wrote in a blurb for one of his books: "Ray Gonzalez continues his exploration of personal and cultural identity. Ghosts, totemic animals, and magical objects emerge from the day-to-day settings in the Southwest to transform the ordinary into the marvelous. Like a contemporary Yaqui shaman, Gonzalez metamorphoses the natural world into a landscape where wonder is palpable and the past refuses to be buried . . . ."

Here are two prose poems that illustrate many of the themes I mentioned above. They are not the most complex or hermetically visionary pieces of his work, but they do supply the reader with a way into Gonzalez's prose and verse poems. The first shows the pull he feels between his place in the present world and the past, the tensions in him created by his sense of the vanished cultures he comes from and the contemporary one he lives in.

Acoma, New Mexico

I wanted to go to Acoma, but the pueblo was way up in the sky. I wanted to climb the cliff road, but the people said stay away. I did not deserve the silence of great heights. I wanted to be a tourist, but my feet said I was born in the desert. I wanted to go to Acoma, but the painting in the postcard held me back, the marked path of invasion erased long ago. I wanted to go up there, but stayed away for years, my brown skin refusing to turn darker in the desert sun, my rough Spanish changing gradually to a miserable croaking, the sound of someone destroyed by not being able to climb the ancient roads and alight to a level of the burning star left flaming there by Coronado and his men 500 years ago, fourteen of the conquistadors thrown off the cliffs when they reached the top, the people waving their arms at the falling bodies, watching the rocks take apart the first animals who tried to sing the same songs the people knew by heart.

The second poem provides a glimpse of his oracular and visionary impulses:

The Bird of Dreams

It was huge and hovered mightily, with a blue and red head. I couldn't see its wings, thought of a giant hummingbird. The bird came out of the gray sun to trace the lines on the face of a strange god before flying into view, suspended over me, letting me know the sun would turn back to yellow upon the tapping of the bell, the start of the music, the moment I opened my eyes to see the wing of color was the extended arm I was told about before I was born.

Ray is also a fiction writer and essayist of high repute and has had books out in both genres. He is an editor as well and has put together a dozen anthologies of Latino and Anglo literature, most recently an important collection of twenty-four very different prose poets that showcases the many approaches to the prose poem with a generous sampling from each poet's work. My friend Gary Young is in it, so is Peter, and so am I. The volume, entitled *No Boundaries*, appeared in 2004.

GARY YOUNG

I have a more long-standing relationship with Gary Young than I do with Ray Gonzalez. Gary has lived in Santa Cruz since his student days at the university in the 1970s. An artist and fine printer (he had been Bill Everson's student), Gary is kind, personal, highly intelligent, and a boon companion. We have read together on many occasions, have been on panels at various literary conferences, and when we were both published by Creative Arts Books in the early years of the new millennium, we traveled as a team to read at various bookstores in Northern California.

Gary Young, Santa Cruz, 2004

For all that, Gary and I have never developed the same kind of intimacy Joe Stroud and I have, probably because Gary is occupied with any number of responsibilities. He had come of age at a time when jobs for artists and perspective teachers were scarce, and he is always off trying to make ends meet one way or another from one year to the next. Family responsibilities are also an important part of his life. Married for a second time in his fifties, he found himself the father of two boys a decade apart in age. Since he bought George Hitchcock's original house high in the Santa Cruz mountains, he is continually driving the boys to events in town and takes his paternal role so seriously that he volunteered to be the coach for his eldest son's little-league baseball team.

Added to the stress of Gary's life is the shadow of his own mortality, which haunts him daily. In his late twenties, he developed melanoma. By the year 2000, the melanoma had recurred a number of times, and he had undergone twenty operations. Finally, he volunteered to test a new drug that would increase his immune system, but the drug had the opposite result. All through these trials, he never complained, although at times his arm would go numb, his fingers wouldn't work, and he experienced extreme nausea and other debilitating physical effects.

His physical condition is a good starting point for discussing his poetry because it reveals the basis of his vision and can be seen clearly at work in one of the many untitled prose poems that make up his award-winning trilogy of book-length prose poem sequences pointedly titled, *No Other Life*:

The doctor says, I don't like this, shakes his head, and leaves. I can hear him in the next room. He's found something in the X-ray, and when he comes back he waits for me to ask, what's wrong. Outside, the warm air buoys a perfume of roses, asphalt and ether. Is this the world I just left? Under the knife a dozen times, I always come back stunned by what I've missed: that date palm obscured by the branches of a cedar, the letters on a handmade sign; a child's cough, my fears, how much I love this life.

Gary's poems are celebrations. As he looks at the most minute aspect of life around him, he is always aware that he may die at any moment. Thus, every moment is wondrous. His poems look at the ugliness and tawdriness of existence as well, at the many ways we treat and mistreat each other as a species. He flinches from nothing. His is a poetry that ranges over the entire spectrum of experience, as *No Other Life* amply demonstrates.

Gary once told me he couldn't invent incidents or characters, that the incidents in all his poems had actually happened. That means his poems, with all their bustling characters and events, are largely autobiographical or ruminations about stories he has been told, heard on newscasts, or read in newspapers. Such knowledge makes *No Other Life* an inspiration. The tender, loving poems about nature, his children, and family, as well as his reflections about the larger world, make that volume for me one of the premier books of poetry of the last thirty years. It is literally the history of the last fourth of the twentieth century as one man experienced it. At the same time, the experiences he records are timeless reflections of the human condition.

Not surprisingly, *No Other Life*, despite being published by a small West Coast press, won the coveted William Carlos Williams Award for 2002 and

Reading with Gary Young at The Main Library, San Francisco, 2003

was reprinted in 2005. The book is not only notable for its far-ranging content but for its contribution to the prose poem form. Young condenses the poems to three- and four sentence pieces that work much like haiku. Their succinctness and highly evocative language bring whole scenes and incidents vividly to life in one or two words, which is the very core of the poetic craft. The rhythms of his sentences, moving together or in counterpoint, as well as his various tones of voice, are further demonstrations of his mastery of the poet's art.

Here are several very different examples of his prose poems, all untitled, from *No Other Life:*

She took my two hands in hers, pressed and caressed them as if she were bathing me. I held hers as mine were held, stroked her knuckles, her palms, then realized the finger I lightly traced was my own. How strange to find I could show myself such tenderness.

* * *

The baby grabs at sunshine by the window. He has walked across the room just to touch the air, and laughs each time he reaches for the light. He wants to hold it. He can't.

* * *

Two girls were struck by lightning at the harbor mouth. An orange flame lifted them up and laid them down again. Their thin suits had been melted away. It's a miracle they survived. It's a miracle they were ever born at all.

* * *

In New Jersey a couple pulled a man from his car, shot him, and locked him in a box to die. They'd had a plan, but their plan fell through. They were captured, and the woman claimed she had been forced; she had never wanted to do it. When she testified against her husband, someone shouted, what do you think of your wife now? And he turned, and said, I love her. The stories I must tell myself about myself seem even more pitiful repeated in the history of others.

* * *

VERN RUTSALA

An older poet who wrote several award-winning volumes of prose poems was my old friend from Iowa, Vern Rutsala. I would see him every year or two when I went on my reading tours of the Northwest. He lived in Portland, Oregon, and would always schedule a reading and several workshops for me at the college where he taught, Lewis & Clark. He and Joan's hospitality was always overwhelming, and we would visit for days, sometimes Lawson joining us, all of us talking nonstop. The Iowa days were a

Vern Rutsala,
Portland, Oregon,
1990

glue that held us together, but our continued pursuit of poetry was the true cement: we relished each other's growth as writers. In the main, our discussions were serious and mostly concerned the state of the world and U.S. politics, but laughter was also an unvarying part of our conversations: we would rib each other unmercifully and were always comfortable in each other's company, especially Joan whose droll sense of humor always led us in our evenings of wild repartee.

Vern and Joan liked to sit in their living room, drinking and smoking and talking with friends well into the night. Vern could be close-mouthed, but as the beer flowed and he knew he was with people he could trust, he was open and joined the fray, matching and often topping our bon mots as the evening wore on.

From the day I met Vern in Iowa, I followed his lead in the direction of my poetry, since I found my concerns with American speech rhythms vigorously developed in his work. He pursued an American idiom in his poems with an eloquence that was enhanced by precise phrasing and imagery from the everyday world. This made the poems accessible to a wide, nonpoetry reading audience.

If in Iowa Vern had written poems from the viewpoint of a removed observer, after he had moved back to Portland in the 1970s, his work became more personal, especially when he began to write about his early years among the Finnish-American population of McCall, Idaho, of which his family was a part. He wrote about the dreams, confusions, and hard economic conditions that beset the people in portraits of family members, neighbors, and childhood friends. He also described events that had uprooted his family, who served as a microcosm for an entire generation of the poor living through the Great Depression. It should be clear to anyone that my concept for *Pages from a Scrapbook of Immigrants* is based on his approach to his Idaho poems.

Vern's remembrances of his early years led him to a fascination with the process of memory itself, and in the last twenty years of the century and in the opening years of the new millennium, he combined his social criticism and interest in memory with contemplations of American history and culture in an ever-broadening vision of the nation as it was and, by implication, what it could be .

Vern writes in both closed and free verse and has published several books of award-winning prose poems. The prose poems are of particular interest because they show a side of him that is full of humor and wry commentary as he encounters everyday objects. Here are two examples.

Salt and Pepper

Monogamous as wolves they move through life together, rarely separated. To humor their feeling for fidelity we have developed the habit of asking for them together, knowing that they keenly feel any separation, however brief. Though salt is our favorite, a relative really, we never indicate this in order to spare pepper's volatile but delicate feelings.

Telephone

Like the rattlesnake it has the decency to make a noise before it strikes though it is, of course, capable of emitting far more venom than any snake.

Whenever I discuss with other poets who they think are in the front rank of contemporary American poets, Vern's name is always mentioned. But although he has been a recipient of many awards, he has never achieved the recognition or status I, or they, thought he deserved. Even the publication of his *Selected Poems* in 1992 passed without comment in the national press, a situation I have never understood, since that volume bore out what every lover of American poetry knew: Vern never wrote a bad poem, either technically or thematically, and his poems were easy for anyone to understand.

Finally, in 2005, his book, *The Moment's Equation*, was named one of the five finalists for the National Book Award.

■ ■ ■

During the time I visited Vern and got to know the younger prose poets and their work, I published many of the new pieces I was working on in various literary journals. In what seemed quick succession, Hanging Loose Press, directed by Bob Hershon and several longstanding cohorts, began printing a number of my prose poems in their magazine and brought out a book of seventy-two of them in 1997 under the title *When People Could Fly*. New Rivers Press included two of my pieces in its definitive anthology of North American prose poetry, *The Party Train*, and one of the editors, Robert Alexander, who, I found out, had included a discussion of *The Armies Encamped* in his PhD thesis years before, asked to do a book of my selected prose poems two years later. That book, which came out with White Pine Press in 2002, is *Moments Without Names* and includes thirty-five of the pieces from *When People Could Fly* and *Armies* and sixty-five new prose poems. A new book of prose poems, *Pursuing the Dream Bone*, was published by Quale Press in 2007.

Long forgotten was my notion that I had written my last poem with the end of *Pages from a Scrapbook of Immigrants*. Ever since embarking on the prose poem, I have felt like a moth who has risen from its cocoon to find itself a radiant butterfly, although, to tell the truth, I still write as many verse poems as I do prose poems.

CHAPTER 52

Travels 3:
Prague in the New Millennium,
or the Deceptions of Tourism

First impressions are often deceptive. This is especially true of cities whose sponsors show us their best sides, beautifying with paint and lights historic buildings and monuments in whose company tourists pay handsomely for the privilege of spending a few hours or days. But the cosmetic treatment many times hides a physiognomy pockmarked and scarred by history, and we wander happily through picturesque streets, attended by smiling salespeople in quaint shops, unaware of the painful memories beneath the facades.

This fact was brought home to me in Prague as in no other city. It was a discovery that was all the more significant because if New York is the lost city of my youth, Prague has become the ideal city of my adulthood, and all the more so because of its dark history, which, if one looks for it, is everywhere to be found. As I made my way from one festive square to another or discovered a shadowy alleyway lit by an iron-caged lantern embedded halfway up a palace wall, I simultaneously experienced the gaiety of the present and the ghosts of bygone centuries in a way that I never did on Naxos and Crete.

Prague has become both my ideal and favorite city not because of the cobblestone streets or the four- and five-story buildings with their ornate Renaissance and Baroque facades, or because of the corridor from the old town square that winds its way across The Vltava river over Charles Bridge and up to Hradcany castle—a route almost always crowded with thousands of tourists in spring and summer—but because I feel a comfort there, a sense of belonging, which initially, I'm sure, had to do with my projection of my family's past as I imagined it was lived in similar cities in Russia and Lithuania hundreds of years ago.

On my first visit in 2002, I was able to maintain these romantic notions for a few days, most probably because Donna and I found it easy to avoid the tourists doggedly trudging back and forth from the castle. We also kept away from the noisy café-, hotel-, and department store-cluttered area around upper Narodni Street and Wenceslas Square and were lucky enough to find a quiet pension on the other side of the river in Mala Strana, an area that fans out under the castle and once had been crowded with monasteries, churches, and palaces, which, over time, had been emptied or made into foreign embassies and museums, and their grounds into public parks.

The pension further encouraged my early romantic illusions. It was a five-hundred-year-old lime-green, red-tile-roofed, three-story house that at one time had been the domicile of the famous German family of Baroque architects, Christoph and his son Kilian Ignaz Dientzenhofer, who in the early 1700s had designed some of the city's most famous landmarks, among them Mala Strana's St. Nicholas Church and the Loreta.

The pension backed onto Kampa Park, which, in turn, ended at the river, across whose wide blue expanse sat the tourist-filled precincts of old and new town. The rear of the pension featured a narrow garden that was separated from the park by a diversion of the river, a steep moat-like waterway we could hear rushing past at all hours. Birdsong and breeze-song brushed through the leaves and branches of tall trees, and the shrubs and ivy on the walls fluttered like the yellow butterflies that slipped about from morning till night.

All these factors, as well as the pension's location—five minutes from Charles Bridge and ten minutes from the castle in one direction and old town in the other—made it a welcome, almost pastoral retreat in the middle

Early morning on the Charles Bridge, Prague 2006

of the city, and even though my idealized picture of Prague had changed early on that first visit, we decided to return to the pension when Richard Katrovas, the ebullient director of the Prague Summer Program, contracted me to teach a poetry composition class in the summer of 2006.

In fact, I insisted on staying there on that second visit. Dreamy, ambiguous reveries nudged aside my hardheaded knowledge of facts as I imagined walking each morning to my classes at the fourteenth-century Karlova Universitat, fifteen minutes from the pension on the other side of Charles Bridge. My walk would begin, I imagined, just as the city was waking up, with the government gardeners hosing the flowerbeds and shrubs and clerks opening shop doors. That fantasy worked out as I had planned, and for the length of the class I didn't feel like a tourist but a working member of the city. Soon waiters in cafés and restaurants were nodding to me as I made my daily stroll from the pension to the university and back.

My earlier inclination to romanticize the city seemed to be taking hold of me again, a situation that was augmented by my faculty colleagues and students at the university, a merry, congenial group. They had spent several weeks in Prague before I arrived, had acclimated themselves to the city' ways, and were extremely friendly. I met a number of extraordinary writers, many of whose work I had enjoyed for years, such as the poets Richard Jackson and Michael Waters. Also present were the novelists Mary Morris and Robert Eversz and the playwright Lisa Dillman. But of all of my colleagues, Donna and I were most taken with Patricia Hampl, and soon the three of us were meeting for dinner or late-night snacks at one historically famous café or another—in one, where Kafka had been a nightly visitor, and in another, where Havel and his friends had planned the Velvet Revolution that would eventually topple the Communist regime.

When we weren't socializing with Patricia and our other colleagues, Donna and I were out and about, exploring the city and its sights. Classes were over at a little after noon, and we would take a tram to one part of the city or another and walk for hours, discovering cul-de-sacs, hidden parks, or small, shaded plazas where the old buildings, many of them flaking and empty, enclosed the palpable remains of a world hundreds of years old. I seem to be romanticizing again, but truth to tell, Prague is the best walking city I have ever visited. Since it had not been bombed in the wars of the twentieth century and has maintained its physical integrity through many religious and political conflicts over the past six hundred years, the city sits in the middle of Europe like an island of the past, still ushering generations of citizens through its narrow, shadowy streets below the spires and towers that have marked its skyline for centuries.

But as we wandered from one section of the city to another, I was always aware that there were two Pragues, since I knew enough Czech history before my first visit to appreciate that the picturesque streets and parks were crowded with century after century of ghosts—maimed, mutilated,

The view from my classroom: Hradcany Castle, Prague, 2006

martyred ghosts who fought for religious and political goals that vanished almost as quickly as they were achieved. And as we strolled from street to street on my first visit, I noticed that the city was dotted with monuments to those conflicts, from Vysehrad—the fortress where the mythical world of the Czechs began over a thousand years ago and which is now a peaceful park looking down from its heights on the river—to the gardens, churches, outbuildings, and several miles of grounds of Hradcany Castle, which towers over the city from its high hill and still serves as the site of the nation's parliament.

The markers of the Czechs' sad history are everywhere in the city if one chooses to notice them, and the onslaught of tourism since 1989 has not caused the government tourist agency to hide the many memorials that dot the streets and squares, a number of them statues or anonymous sites identifiable by small tinfoil wreaths tied with blue and red ribbons or a handful of flowers. The memorials indicate oppression that goes back a millennium but becomes an ominous presence for me in the sixteenth century. Let me explain.

Before the sixteenth century, the Czechs—called Bohmens in German or Bohemians in English—were ruled by native monarchs of the Premyslid dynasty as first dukes and then kings of Bohemia. But in 1526, the "king of Bohemia" title and the lands under its sway became appendages of the Austrian Habsburg dynasty when the Habsburg Emperor Ferdinand I agreed to accept the heirless Bohemian throne under the condition that its title and holdings would become part of the Habsburg crown from that point on. The overall effect of Ferdinand's pact made Czech lands little more than a province of what was the Habsburg Empire, which, generally speaking, ruled central Europe from its capital in Vienna from medieval times to the end of World War I.

Ferdinand's deal is for me one of the most significant facts of Czech history—and the one I choose to highlight out of all the dynastic and politically complex changes in Czech life—because, as I see it, it is the root of Czech sorrows for the 370 years that followed.

The Habsburgs brought with them the German language, which over time became the official language of Bohemia and was responsible for virtually erasing the Czech tongue. The Habsburgs were also Holy Roman emperors, which meant they were charged by the Vatican with defending the Roman Catholic Church. This last fact becomes vitally important to Czech history because more than a hundred years before Martin Luther began the Protestant reformation—and a hundred years before Ferdinand added the Bohemian throne to his kingdom—a gentle priest by the name of Jan Hus led a rebellious religious reform movement in Bohemia that was embraced by much of the Bohemian nobility and the general populace. However, two hundred years later, in the Thirty Years War (1618–1648), the Catholic Counter-Reformation, led by the Habsburgs, viciously put down Hus's by then entrenched, centuries-old movement. So brutal was the conflict that it has been estimated that two-thirds of the country's population lost their lives, and Prague's population was reduced by half.

After the war, the Habsburgs gave loyal Catholic nobles from all over Europe the Bohemian nobilities' palaces and lands. They also brought in German-speaking artisans and professionals—among them Christoph Dientzenhofer and his family—who eventually gained control of the country's infrastructure. At the same time, they outlawed all forms of Protestantism and imported a number of Catholic religious orders who built the monasteries and churches that still dominate Prague's architecture and skyline (and which draw most of the tourists to the city). These orders, led by the Jesuits, were given the responsibility of directing all aspects of education, learning, and culture in the country. It was at this point that the German language took precedence over Czech. Whereas German immigrants had always been welcomed in Bohemia, after the end of the Thirty Years War they became ascendant in Czech life.

Visiting Prague's Klementinum, with its five-million-volume baroque library, I was not surprised to learn that it was part of a Jesuit college established in 1556, which, with the exception of Hradcany Castle, would become the largest single property in the city by 1706. I was also aware of the bitter irony of the library's being thrown open to public use in the 1750s, ironic because all the volumes were in Latin, German, and other European languages, but not in Czech, a fact the guide chose to exclude from his witty commentary on the library's history.

It would not be until the rise of nationalism throughout Europe in the second half of the nineteenth century that the Czech language would be virtually rediscovered by Czech philologists who found it being spoken in the hinterlands by farmers and their families. And it was not until the end of World War I and the collapse of the Habsburg monarchy that the Czechoslovak Republic, a democratic government, was founded. But Czech independence was short-lived. Twenty years after the republic was established, Hitler marched in and ruled with Nazi viciousness until the end of World War II. His pretext for taking over the country was, ironically again, the predominance of German speakers to whom he was "returning" their "rightful" land.

After the war, the second Czech Republic was put in place only to be taken over a few years later by the Communists under Soviet Russian control. They ruled almost as oppressively as the Nazis and Habsburgs until 1989 when a spontaneous uprising of the long-suffering populace brought about the current Third Republic, and Prague—described by the few people I knew who had visited it during the Communist years as a gray, miserable place populated by downtrodden people trudging from street to street— bloomed like a flower, full of color and gaiety.

This is not accurate history. It is selective, if not biased; at best, it is an attempt to capture an attitude rather than encapsulate facts. I have chosen these scattered dates and events, while ignoring others, to suit my interpretations because I wanted to present my sense of the Czech experience for the last five hundred years, knowing that almost all the tourists who have made Prague one of the world's favorite vacation destinations since 1989 have little idea of the story that underlies the atmospheric, picturesque streets through which they plod. More than that, Prague's history has made me come to terms once again with the ironies and changes wrought by time on a people and a place and has made me look with foreboding at what the world—with its religious, political, economic and environmental problems—can become in a matter of weeks or months.

While I was in Prague in 2006, Israel attacked Lebanon, and the Arabic Islamic countries found more common cause in their distrust, if not hatred, of Israel and the West. At the same time, the heat of global warming was on everyone's mind as temperatures in the United States and Europe rose to record-breaking heights. And again, I was forced to contemplate change, the world's constant flux, which my readings of Laozi and Zhuangzi insisted I should keep continuously in mind. I thought of their writings daily as I climbed the wide staircase to my class in the Philosophy and Arts building of Karlova University. Outside the building's doors is one of those small, beribboned, tinfoil wreaths, in this case dedicated to a student named Jan Palach who, in 1968, burned himself to death in protest of Communist oppression. The building is not far from Charles Bridge, and the memorial, if it's noticed at all by passing tourists, is nothing more to most of them than a colorful decoration curiously placed on the dirty brown wall of a block-long anonymous building, signifying nothing.

At the Vltava River with the Charles Bridge in the background. Prague, 2006.

How could that simple, ignored memorial so affect me, I wondered at first? I knew the answer had something to do with the overlapping of the current atmosphere of joy and prosperity with the bloody epochs of the past, including many aspects of Prague's history I have not mentioned, such as the existence of the city's Jewish population, which from one century to another had endured persecution and calamity in their ghetto. But why had my knowledge and acknowledgment of those events made Prague my ideal as well as favorite city? In fact, how could they?

The answer lies in the seemingly contradictory aspects I have just mentioned. What so captivates me about Prague is knowing what I do of both its suffering and gaiety. Even the superficial charm the tourists experience strolling through its winding streets have made Prague the city I rank above all others, since it is a city where I am always aware of the mask it wears for tourists and the anguished face that hides beneath it. It is the city where I was able to strike through the mask and, always aware of its two identities, hold both personas clearly in mind.

As I wandered from street to street, I experienced, as I had on Naxos, the merging of past and present. But in Prague, the overlapping of epochs had become that much more real for being so clearly delineated. In time, the city became a microcosm of human history for me. I felt in its streets not like an observer in a museum but a participant in an ongoing story, carrying into the future the hopes and longings of all those who had suffered, died, or endured political and religious oppression, as if Czech heritage was the heritage of people everywhere, and each step I took became a recognition and therefore a memorial for those who could no longer tread what remained of the planet's cobblestone streets, nor could look with hope or foreboding at their children's possible futures.

CHAPTER 53

An End and a Beginning

And so I come to the end of my book. I have told all the stories that I think have shaped my life and thought. There may be others I have forgotten and will remember later. And there will probably be new events in the future I may deem worth telling—I have long thought that even in old age a man should be open to change. But for now I have come to an end, except for a few last episodes, a handful of remembrances that will serve as a final gathering of incidents and a summing up.

■ ■ ■

On the professional side of my life, the 1990s were a busy, gratifying time. My intense engagement with the prose poem yielded renewed interest in my work, the publication of two books, and representation in four prose poem anthologies by the first years of the new millennium. My verse poems had also continued to garner recognition, although more and more infrequently, which wasn't surprising since I had written mostly prose poems during the 1990s and had gotten into the habit of sending poetry to magazines less and less often than in the 1960s and '70s. Still, by the end of the 1990s my poems had appeared in eighty anthologies in the United States, Europe, and Australia. The small amount of work I had done in verse became clear to me when Don Ellis at Creative Arts Book Company wanted to do a book of them, and I could put together a collection of only forty-eight poems, which he released in 2002 under the title *Shouting Down the Silence: Verse Poems, 1988 to 2001*. In many ways, the subtitle was a misnomer since at least half of the poems had been written during the seven years I was writing and rewriting *Pages from a Scrapbook of Immigrants* but were independent of that project in style and content.

With Jim Houston, Santa Cruz, 2000

Alan Cheuse, 2007

In the 1990s I continued hosting my poetry radio show, remained an active member of the Pacific Rim Film Festival steering committee, and pursued my teaching as a permanent faculty member of the Foothill Writers' Conference. It was at the conference, which I did each year with Jim and Jeanne Houston and Al Young, that I met many other first-class writers. Among them was Alan Cheuse, who journeyed from the East Coast to spend his summers in Santa Cruz. Jim introduced me to him, and I team-taught a workshop with him at the conference. Best known for his book reviews on NPR radio, Alan also writes novels and short stories, which impressed me on several levels. One of his books, *Fall from Heaven*, is a nonfiction account of traveling with his son to Russia in the 1990s to follow his father's route out of that country in the 1920s. In alternate chapters, Alan tells about his relationship with his son and describes his father's odyssey to America, as well as the old man's early years as a Soviet fighter pilot in the little-known ethnic conflicts along the Soviet Union's southern borders. The book is a classic of travel writing, a wonderful adventure tale, and an exploration of father son relationships over three generations in the rapidly changing world of the twentieth century.

Alan's first novel, *The Grandmothers' Club*, also impressed me with its wonderful dialogues and atmosphere of New York Jewish life that reminded me of my childhood and now is an all-but-vanished part of American history. I got to hear Alan's new short stories at the conference every year. They were more far-ranging in content than the semiautobiographical books I just mentioned, and they grappled with the social changes in the South and Midwest as well as with the changing value systems of the younger generations. Some of the stories are collected in the books *The Tennessee Waltz and Other Stories* and *Lost and Old Rivers*. They add a dimension to his work that makes me look forward to anything he writes and led me to read his collected essays, *Listening to the Page*, which appeared in 2001.

ADRIENNE RICH

Another writer I came to know in the 1990s was the legendary poet Adrienne Rich, who had moved to Santa Cruz from the East Coast for medical reasons in the late 1980s. I was introduced to her by Phil Levine and immediately invited her onto a special two-hour radio show I arranged in her honor.

I had been impressed with Adrienne's work since the 1950s when she won the Yale Younger Poets Award with *A Change of World,* and I read her second book, *The Diamond Cutters,* over and over again when I was in the air force. Then I had watched her emerge as a socially and politically committed leader of the women's movement in the 1970s.

I found her to be a person of uncompromising beliefs, intolerant of small talk, with a mind and vocabulary as sharp as a guillotine. To say that we couldn't find common ground is an understatement. But my admiration for her was boundless. In the 1990s she continued to write relentlessly, viewing American sexual and national politics with a rigorous insight, despite living in constant pain from crippling arthritis, which had wrenched her body into permanently contorted postures.

I think part of the problem between Adrienne and me was that her mind was quicker to grasp the ramifications of things and on all counts was more brilliant than mine. That was apparent in our conversations, including my two-hour radio interview with her. Those traits also gave our discussions an air of counterpunching that I had experienced with Robert Bly and which always made me uncomfortable. She would correct or expand anything I said with comments of greater insight.

At first, Adrienne was pleasant and, what I have to term, tolerant of me. But when I did a long review of her work in connection with her visionary and I think best book, *An Atlas of the Difficult World,* the pleasantness came to an end.

As I have mentioned before, I wrote a series of long literary profiles of contemporary writers in the 1990s for the *Metro* newspaper chain, and it was natural that I would write one on Adrienne when *An Atlas* appeared in 1991. My view was laudatory of her and the book, but among my comments, I questioned several "postcard poems"—short pieces addressed to particular women, a kind of poem that Adrienne had written in earlier books. I stated that they were not up to the ambitious achievements of the book's two long poems and they would only be of interest to the women they addressed and possibly to women in general. When Adrienne read the profile, she shot me a short note that said, in no uncertain terms, I should have known better than to suggest her poems were written only for women. I saw a literary battle looming in any response I might give, and I certainly didn't want to engage a poet of such stature, who I admired so much, in a battle I could never win and didn't particularly want to fight, so I wrote back simply:

> Adrienne,
> I stand corrected.
> Mort

Several years went by, during which we had no contact. Then in 1995, Adrienne won the Santa Cruz County Artist of the Year Award. For her obligatory acceptance performance, she chose to do a program showcasing local poets of color, several of whom, including Jeff Tagami and Shirley Ancheta, had been my students. It was a wonderful social gesture, devoid of ego. A month before the performance, she sent me a short note, asking me to be one of the two masters of ceremonies for the event and to read two of my poems as well.

I was flattered and touched, but my pugnacious nature made me send her a reply in which I accepted her invitation because, I said, the program she chose for her performance was an admirable gesture, and I saw in her invitation to me an extended olive branch. Several days later, I received a carton containing three jars of olives and a short note from her thanking me for agreeing to appear on the program. As Donna succinctly remarked, "That's classy." I couldn't agree more.

Adrienne and I have seen each other on and off since then, and Donna and I had her and her partner to dinner at the house. We're always friendly and always equally concerned about the world situation and particularly about the increasingly destructive path we find American politics has taken. But since the mid-1990s, her excruciating physical condition has kept her housebound a good deal of the time.

GREG KEITH

Greg Keith, Santa Cruz, 1998

I met Greg Keith in Oregon in the early 1970s. I was in Ashland for a reading at Southern Oregon University, and my host, my old friend Lawson Inada, introduced Greg as his best poetry student. Several years later, Greg showed up in Santa Cruz and began working as a computer programmer in Silicon Valley.

Tall and easy-going, he was always affable and good company, although we didn't have much contact until one night in 1990 when I attended a local reading by him. I was astonished by what I heard and asked to see a manuscript of his work. I thought the manuscript was marvelous, something old and new at the same time: I had never read anything like it and gave him the names of several editors. We continued to see each other off and on, and in the late 1990s, I heard he had cancer of the right cheek which soon progressed to his right eye socket. By then he desperately wanted to publish a book of his poems before he died, and he phoned to ask if I would write an introduction for it, which I eagerly agreed to do. The book, *Life Near 310 Kelvin*, which came out in 1998, a few months after his death, is his legacy. The last time I saw him was at the pre-publication party he threw for friends and colleagues, and he seemed at peace. He was barely fifty-three years old when he died.

His wife, Susan, loyally brought the book forward as best she could, but without wide distribution the task was impossible. This sketch is a remembrance and an advertisement for Greg's work.

The book is worth the reader's search and should not be forgotten. *Life Near 310 Kelvin* is a collection of sixty-three poems and a CD of Greg reading thirty-four of them. What makes Greg's poetry so exceptional is his point of reference. His language is a masterful, seemingly easy vernacular, and his insight into human nature is acute. But it is his imagery and the way he develops his arguments that make his work unique. Both are enmeshed in the language and vision of science, especially physics, zoology, and microbiology, which he uses as naturally as everyday speech because he thought about and saw the world in terms of science. His vocabulary expresses his sensibility. But that sensibility is not remote or esoteric; it is concerned with common experiences we all share and is expressed with great immediacy. The poems usually take place in a dramatic setting, which makes them all the more immediate. Essentially a love poet, Greg employs scientific metaphors in many instances that remind me of John Donne's metaphysical conceits. But his topics are far-ranging, and many of his poems have overtones of social and political meanings set against a metaphysical vision. Here are his words of wisdom for the young.

Another Note to the Young

Change accumulates. My body, still tall, slows,
thickens. One thing that happens, love takes hold
and acts, somehow like gravity, by curving
space around the body's tiny masses.

Well, my electrons don't care. They do as they must,
just as if they existed. Light, too, shines as it has to.
Doorknobs get harder against a careless hip, the bruise broader.

Of vertebrates, only tortoises routinely live longer, some whales.

Love doesn't care if you're ready or handsome or old
or crippled or smart or rich or not. It's like the busy
whispering when space embraces time, that whiff of
bodies emerging from covers, each breathing in
the other's face; conspiracy. Not long, but deep and wide.
The feel of time changes over time. I mentioned the body,
surprise. More surprise, almost, than you can handle.
I never used to cry so much, so quickly.

I've learned to push a table under the hanging lamp.
My irises pale toward green, but I'd still say brown eyes.

I've seen grasses set wild root and bloom in red
gritty brick in San Francisco last week and twenty
years ago in stone cracks of Chapultepec Palace.

Life's not what we think. It's what the body does. Surprise.

■ ■ ■

In 1998, I retired from my teaching position at Cabrillo and was able to devote full time to writing. The highlight of the 1990s, however, was my being selected the Santa Cruz County Artist of the Year for 1999. I was only the third poet, along with Adrienne Rich and Bill Everson, to receive the award. With my concerns for community and for all the literary and cultural work I had done in the county as teacher and organizer over the years, I was flattered and satisfied. As my final gesture of the year, I said good-bye to the old millennium and welcomed the new one by organizing a New Year's Eve extravaganza that showcased the work of all the previous fifteen Artists of the Year.

Also in 1999, I began my stint as cohost of a television film review show called "Cinema Scene," which I continue to do at this writing. That same year I was asked to lead a twice-monthly discussion group at the Nick-elodeon Theater in Santa Cruz, which also continues to this day.

As Artist of the Year, I was asked to deliver the commencement address to the 1999 graduating class of Santa Cruz High School. I spoke to an audience of several thousand people who attended the event at the Cabrillo College football stadium. In the address, I presented in general terms the fundamental lessons of my life. At the insistence of a number of people who had attended the graduation, the major daily newspaper in town published the entire address a week later.

SANTA CRUZ POETRY IN THE 1990s

Although the national poetry craze of the 1970s waned in the 1980s and generally disappeared in the 1990s, many Santa Cruz poets kept writing. In fact, the poetry scene remained viable, blossoming toward the end of the 1990s when Dennis Morton, a poetry aficionado and former businessman, along with Len Anderson, a former physicist and excellent poet in his own right, and several others reinvigorated a tired reading series under the title *Poetry Santa Cruz*. Morton's creative ideas and businessman's acumen not only rejuvenated the county's public readings, they attracted a number of young, upcoming poets from around the nation to journey to Santa Cruz because Dennis, who took over for Joe as my co-host on the Poetry Show, could promise them an hour-long radio program as well as an audience of fifty or more for a reading, which by 1990 standards was large.

Many of the members of that audience were long-time local poets who received national acclaim during the late nineties and early years of the new millennium. Already established poets like Joe Stroud, Robert Sward, and Gary Young, were joined by Ellen Bass, whose book, *Mules of Love,* won the Lambda Award in 2005, David Swanger, whose *Wayne's College of Beauty,* won the 2005 John Ciardi Prize, and Charles Atkinson, whose first book,

The Only Cure I Know, won the American Book Series Award in 1991, and who since then has gone on to win more than half a dozen national prizes for individual poems.

With Joe Stroud on his 50th Birthday, Santa Cruz, 1993

Many of the poets, like Joe, Robert, Gary, David and Chuck were college instructors, but others, like Ellen, Patrice Vecchione, and Maude Meehan, taught inspirational private writing workshops, which were never without eager participants. For years, Vecchione conducted special creative writing classes in Santa Cruz and Monterey primary schools as well as edited a number of anthologies for teenagers through Henry Holt and Company. Her own first book of poems, *Territory of Wind,* came out in 1998, and was followed in 2001 by her brilliant how-to book, *Writing and the Spiritual Life,* which was as much a volume of philosophy and vision as it was an instruction manual. For a time she was my co-host on the Poetry Show after Joe left the program.

I was friendly with all these poets, as they were with me. But I was not close enough to any of them to elicit more than an acknowledgment of them here. But the work of one them, Nathaniel Mackey, another Santa Cruz poet and distant acquaintance, seems so important I cannot leave him with just a passing mention.

Nate has been a professor at the University of California at Santa Cruz since 1979. During that time, he has kept a low profile as poet in the county, but nationally he has long been well known and respected. He is the editor of *Hambone* magazine and a Chancellor of the Academy of American Poets. As a poet, he writes long, interconnected poems about the contemporary world which are shot through with figures and tales from Caribbean and African folklore and mythology. In fact, he borrows from those aesthetic traditions, as well as the rhythms of Jazz, to fashion his own distinctive postmodern voice and syntax. His cultural and aesthetic perspectives effectively entwine African and Caribbean folklore with the Greek and northern European myths which have dominated Western literature. By combining these disparate texts through allusions and other correspondences, Nate creates an intertextuality he calls "discrepant engagement," which inject his poems with an aura all their own.

Nathaniel Mackey, Santa Cruz, 2006

For the last twenty years, Nate has been writing a long serial poem called *Songs of The Adomboulou* based on the mythology of the Dogon tribe of West Africa. The Adomboulou are spirits who wander the world, half-formed humans who have failed to evolve into complete beings. In Nate's poetry, they are a central metaphor for all people, and their wanderings comprise a history of the world as they traverse the cities and landscapes of the earth in different time periods. The Adomboulou, through puns and other wordplay, are archetypal yet specific, and their identities continually shift from one guise to another, so that at one time they may be slaves wrenched from their African homes to wander in foreign lands during the years of The Middle Passage, and in another Sephardic Jews expelled from Spain in The Expulsion of 1492.

Each of the spirits is composed of two parts, male and female, flesh and spirit, dreamer and dreamt, and together the two parts yearn for a Utopian stasis. But everything is fluid and ever-changing, especially history, which emerges and regresses and is viewed as not progressive but circular. Thus at the end of *Splay Anthem*, his last book, which concludes with "The Song of Andomboulou: 60," the United States (called Nub) is destroyed, leaving a desert landscape of material debris, but there is a sense of rebirth about to happen in the last lines as history once more begins to turn back on itself.

In creating his ambitious vision of the human condition, Nate pursues a sensuous, experimental language, taking his direction from Charles Olson's open-field theories of composition, the poems of Robert Duncan, and from, among others, the jazz experiments of Don Cherry and John Coltrane.

It is difficult to convey the overall richness and power of Nate's poems, but here is his description, through the eyes and words of an Adomboulou narrator, of rush hour in Los Angeles. It is the first part of a poem that was published in the aforementioned *Splay Anthem*, which won the 2006 National Book Award.

> It was a freeway overpass we
> were on, a overpass east of
> La Brea. There we stood watching
> cars pass under us, desert
>   flutes gargling wind at
>   our
> backs, an overpass we stood
>   on
> looking west . . . What there
> was wasn't music but music was
> there. Where it came from
> was nowhere, we heard it
>   nonetheless, not hearing
>   it
> before put us there . . . So we
>   thought

but wrongly thought, wrong to have
   thought we could. There we stood
atop the world looking out at
   the world. L.A. it now was we
                   were in . . .

   Inside each car someone bore the
world away, each a fleeting guest
      whose going we lamented, kin we
could've sworn we saw . . . It was
   a bridge over the river of
             souls
     we were on. Lower than we thought
     we stood, we stood looking, eyes
     all but shut by glare . . . It was
a river never stepped into less
than twice. A river of light, it
            was
a river of lies we were told, the
     biggest we'd outrun river's end . . .
   Where we stood was a ledge beneath
   in-between feet. Elegiac traffic
           ran
endlessly away. Our one resort, it
          said,
     was a lie . . . A glittering rung it was
we took it we stood on, strung light
filled with grit lit by sunset, soon
to be remembered rush. It was twilight,
                the
    river was headlights and taillights,
   flowing both ways
at once

—from *Song of The Adomboulou: 48*

■ ■ ■

BERT MEYERS AND *IN A DYBBUK'S RAINCOAT*

I have always advocated artists helping one another unselfishly, believing that the arts should be made available to as many people as possible. That is the reason I organized readings and festivals and undertook my job as cohost of the poetry radio show. It is also the reason I came to coedit the collected poems of Bert Meyers with his son Daniel. How that happened is a minor saga all its own.

I was neither a close friend of Bert's nor one of his many students, just an admiring fellow poet and, in Bert's last days, a warm acquaintance. Bert was a handsome man with chiseled movie-star good looks—a sharply angular

Bert Myers, Los
Angeles, 1978

face topped by a shock of butter-colored hair—which, along with a forceful personality and an ever-present tan, lent him an undeniable magnetism. Both of us had books out from Kayak Press, as well as continual representation in the pages of *Kayak* magazine, and we first met at a *Kayak* collating party at George Hitchcock's house in Santa Cruz in 1975. That year Bert had moved to the Bay Area from Southern California, where he'd spent most of his adult life. He had to leave Los Angeles, he said, because he was suffering from emphysema, and the smog would be fatal for him. We chatted and enjoyed each other's company and saw each other on and off a dozen times or so afterward, until his untimely death in 1979 at the age of fifty-one.

I flatter myself when I say there was a deep rapport between Bert and me, and I say this not only because our meetings were cordial and filled with intense conversations about the nature of poetry, but because Bert's widow Odette, who corresponded with me either by mail or phone concerning Bert's work at least several times each year after his death, told me so.

Like so many other poets of the 1960s and '70s, I had been enormously impressed by Bert's poems for their brightness and delicacy. They were built like tiny precision engines fueled by his mesmerizing images and subtle rhythms. In poem after poem, using the simplest language, he *showed* the world anew, making the reader *see* it in fresh ways. As far as I was concerned, his stripping away rhetoric in favor of an at times metaphysical and always socially engaged poetry, a poetry which was expressed almost completely through images, had gone several steps beyond the much lauded work of James Wright. No poet has more succinctly and disturbingly described Los Angeles as he does in "L.A.," when he writes

> The world's largest ash-tray . . .

Three examples of Bert's poems will show why Denise Levertov wrote that he was "one of the best poets of our time." The first shows the apparent simplicity of his work, but really reveals his ability to condense while using the most commonplace language. It demonstrates the poignancy and insight found in many of his poems.

> *The Old*
>
> Their children are gone;
> almost everyone
> they loved and half
> of what they understood,
> has disappeared.
>
> But the door's still open,
> the porch light's on;

a little wind at night
and they hear footsteps
when a few leaves fall.

The second example shows Bert's image-making powers. He is the poet of minutiae who focuses on ordinary objects and events with startling results.

Sunflowers

No one spoke to the sunflowers,
those antique microphones
in the vacant lot.
So they hung their heads
and, slowly, fell apart.

Or he could render a landscape (usually a cityscape) with equal ease:

Daybreak

Birds drip from the trees.
The moon's a little goat
over there on the hill;
dawn, as blue as her milk,
fills the sky's tin pail.

The air's so cold a gas station
glitters in an ice-cube.
The freeways hum like a pipe
when the water's on.
Streetlights turn off their dew.

The sun climbs down from a roof,
stops by a house and strikes
its long match on a wall,
takes out a ring of brass keys
and opens every door.

■ ■ ■

Odette's devotion to Bert's work after his death was similar to Muriel Patchen's to Kenneth's. A poet, teacher, and prose writer herself, Odette never stopped lobbying publishers and fellow poets on Bert's behalf, wanting to keep his voice and vision from fading away like Keats's dryad "into the forest dim."

Bert had put together a selection of what he considered his best poems shortly before he died, and it was that manuscript that Odette carried like a sacred text into the future. Many well-known poets and well-wishers promised to boost the volume and get it published. One of them kept the manuscript for seventeen years, continually assuring Odette that he would get the book into print. But for one reason or another, all his efforts came to nothing.

In 1997, Odette called me in desperation. She had just learned she had cancer and didn't know how long she would live. She had finally taken Bert's manuscript back from the poet who had held it for seventeen years, and she wondered if I knew of anyone who might want to publish it. By then, I was working with several different publishers who were handling my work, and I thought there was a chance that I could do what others hadn't. But after several years of mixed signals and lost manuscripts on the publishers' parts, my efforts, like the others, came to nothing.

In the first year of the new millennium, Odette and I were thinking of publishing the "Selected" privately, with all work done gratis by Deng Ming-Dao. Before any of that effort went beyond the preliminary stages, however, Odette died, leaving copies of the manuscript and attendant papers with me.

Less than a year later I began my association with Don Ellis at Creative Arts Book Company, who had signed to do one of my books. I showed him Bert's manuscript, and he was so impressed he offered to do Bert's collected poems. I had all of Bert's books and could easily have put the collected works together, but I thought at that point I should get in touch with Bert's daughter and son, Anat and Daniel, who I hadn't seen since they were children. Daniel, who lived in Paris, was handling his father's literary estate and was excited about a substantial portion of his father's work finally finding its way into print.

Within the month, Daniel and Anat put Bert's collected poems on disk, and several months later he came to the United States, where, rummaging through his mother's storage facility, he found his father's notebooks, journals, and half-written poems, some from when Bert was a teenager. We sifted through the material and selected several articles written about Bert's poetry, some journal entries and letters Bert wrote about poetry, and put together a collected poems which, in reality, was a Bert Meyers reader, using Bert's title for the manuscript he had left with Odette before his death, *In a Dybbuk's Raincoat*.

But in 2003, the year before the book was to be published, Creative Arts sank into bankruptcy and dragged Bert's manuscript with it into oblivion. Several years later, however, *In a Dybbuk's Raincoat* finally found a publisher, thanks to several of Bert's old friends, and in 2007 it rolled from the University of New Mexico Press. It had taken twenty-eight years after Bert's death to get the volume into print.

During the years we worked together, Daniel's commitment to following the project through to completion was unwavering. At times his energy had about it an almost biblical aura of the son fulfilling his parents' final wishes as a sacred duty. In many ways being part of his and Odette's devotion was as rewarding for me as seeing *In a Dybbuk's Raincoat* on bookstore shelves.

■ ■ ■

On the night of June 19, 2007, I found myself on stage at Carnegie Hall in New York City, bowing to a capacity audience who had been cheering in a raucous standing ovation for the past ten minutes. How I came to be standing before them is still a bit bewildering, but in many ways it was the logical conclusion to a series of events that began two years before when the Latvian Canadian composer Imant Raminsh, who had been commissioned to write a piece of music for chorus and orchestra by three Monterey Bay music groups, chose three of my poems to be included in the work.

The commission had been arranged by John Anderson, director of Ensemble Monterey Chamber Orchestra, and his wife Cheryl Anderson, a former colleague of mine at Cabrillo and director of at least three choral groups in the area. Both she and John are energetic, world-class musicians, and Cheryl has conducted her choral groups in some of Europe's most famous musical venues. With the contract for the commission signed, Cheryl set to work collecting poems for Raminsh to read and was advised by Cabrillo librarian, Topsy Smalley, to include several of my books in the mix. That was how my poems were chosen, along with works by E.E. Cummings and Wendell Berry, to be included in the song cycle for large chorus and full orchestra entitled "The Peace of Wild Things."

Until the piece was written, I had nothing to do with the project. But when Cheryl went into rehearsal in late 2005, she asked me to attend several sessions to answer the chorus's questions about various aspects of Cummings and Berry's poems as well as my own. I had talked to one or two of Cheryl's classes while I was teaching, and I was happy to oblige her now,

With Donna, Cheryl Anderson, Imant Raminsh, and John Anderson,
New York, 2007

With Cheryl Anderson and conductor
Lynn Trapp, New York, 2007

especially since the subject was not only poetry but included my poetry. The questions from the chorus members, each of whom was completely committed to the project, were serious, challenging and demanding. In a word, the chorus wanted to understand every nuance of the words they were singing. The result was my attendance at a number of rehearsals for two to three hours at a time—and what, other than *The Eight Ecstasies*, became for me the most rewarding collaboration of my career.

Cheryl and John recognized the level to which I had become part of the project and generously included me in all aspects of the weeklong premiere festivities in the spring of 2006. Imant flew down from Canada to attend the performances, and he and I hit it off immediately. We became a comic duo, introducing the work before each performance and playing off each other during a series of radio interviews. In the space of those seven days, Cheryl, John, Imant, Donna and I became a quintet of fast friends.

Even before the premiere week was over, Cheryl announced that she had been contracted to conduct "The Peace of Wild Things" the following year at Carnegie Hall. Again, I attended rehearsals, lecturing and answering questions for what was now a chorus of 190 singers. By the time of the performance in New York I had thoroughly bonded with the group. Once again, Imant flew down from Canada, and the five of us met in the city with the same warm feelings we had established the year before. The Chorus's performance was flawless as Imant, sitting next to me in the fifth row, exclaimed. Cheryl, always inspired and inspiring, was at the top of her form, and the conclusion of "The Peace of Wild Things" was greeted by a fifteen minute standing ovation, during which Cheryl beckoned Imant and me to come on stage. And that was how I came to be bowing before a cheering audience at Carnegie Hall on June 19, 2007.

The Carnegie Hall event is not typical of my experiences in the new millennium. Aside from brief trips to Croatia, Prague, France and Switzerland, my life has been taken up with local affairs. I continue to conduct my radio and television programs, my Saturday discussion groups at the local art theater, and I do my duties as a member of the steering committee for The Pacific Rim Film Festival. I also write a bi-weekly column and occasional film reviews for the local daily newspaper, and in 2004 I published a long article on the effects of the new technology on our culture. I have also curated several film programs at museums. A far as my literary endeavors are concerned, I've written a novel and published three volumes of poetry since 2000, and I continue to work at writing conferences and to appear on panels addressing political, social and cultural matters. In 2007 I received a Gail Rich Award in recognition of my contributions to the cultural life of Santa Cruz, and Quale Press published a new collection of my prose poems entitled *Pursuing The Dream Bone.*

My friends say I'm busier now than when I was teaching. I smile at that, knowing I'm just trying, as much as I can each day, "to live at that pitch which is near madness." At the same time,

> Every day I talk with neighbors, tradesmen, cashiers and friends I've known for years, some of them my students from decades ago. I call to my wife from the front door and she answers. The children have been gone for years, but the neighbor's cats lounge in the back yard, and every spring doves roost in the planter boxes on the front porch and stay all summer. Alone at night in the room upstairs, I read Montaigne, Twain, Zhuangzi, Rumi and Chekhov, listen to music, and watch the stars. Tell me, has anyone been luckier or had a richer life?

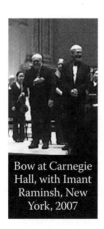

Bow at Carnegie Hall, with Imant Raminsh, New York, 2007

Epilogue

This is no century for old men, to misquote W.B. Yeats who believed less than a hundred years ago that the human race had entered a state of cyclical decline and cultural desolation.

The rapidity with which the American dream has come apart in the few short years of the new millennium is a situation my friends and I struggled to avert but never imagined could have occurred so quickly. As ugly as things got in the twentieth century, the American dream kept us hopeful. I'm not talking about our grandparents' dreams of gold in the streets, but of freedom to live as one wanted, guided by the stipulation that one respected and protected other people's rights to live and believe as they wanted, and to ensure that everyone was taken care of physically and mentally to the best of our abilities as individuals and as a nation among other nations. It was what I had learned so many years ago—Benjamin Franklin's enlightened self-interest, which was also the great idea of union solidarity: in protecting others, one protected oneself. So I had worked as a poet, believing that through my language I could make my fellow humans experience that sense of life which vitally hummed beneath the mask of things. So I had worked as a teacher, believing that education would, through knowledge and rigorous thinking, make my students aware of the blunders as well as the victories of the human experiments of the past and strive to make things socially, economically, and politically viable for all people in the future.

But more and more I found myself mumbling another poet's lines like a mantra that I ended with my own words: "America was promises," Archibald MacLeish said, and I added, "promises that have never been kept and were being extinguished one by one like lights in a mansion."

I have been one of the luckiest human beings in the history of the world, as have most of the American members of my generation. By and large, we have been able to live the lives we have wanted while enjoying material comfort and personal freedom. The rest of the world has not been so fortunate, nor have a number of racial and ethnic groups in my country. But the promises of America were always there as a possibility to aim for, as they had been for my immigrant forebears.

Now I see those possibilities, the hope of those promises, shrinking around me daily. In the 1990's, factories, whole mill towns, were shut down and working-class jobs sent by the tens of thousands to third-world countries where labor was cheaper, or the jobs were given to immigrants here at the lowest possible wages. In the early years of the new millennium, middle-class jobs were outsourced to foreign places as well. Now freedoms are being legislated away by the handful, politicians seem more corrupt than ever, corporations control more and more of our lives, and the rich get richer and the poor not only get poorer, but, having nothing to look forward to except continually borrowing in order to subsist, cling to a shriveling credit line—if they can afford one—as if it were a lifeline. At the same time, under the bombardment of corporate advertising, the nation's vaunted physical comforts and well-being have given rise to a mindless, glitzy materialism at the expense of culture in general, and I fear too many of us have become either greedy and unthinking beings or frightened zealots who distrust change of any sort and preach a culture-destroying, puritanical approach to life that in the end will destroy the very values they seek to protect.

Most sorrowful of all, our materialistic way of life has led many of our children to think that the world has been created to provide them with one material comfort after another. All too frequently, they are oblivious to the world and their responsibilities in it. The past, the world at large, the concerns and problems of the people on the rest of the planet are often of no interest to them. For me such attitudes are the unmistakable signs of cultural decline and possibly the end of civilization as we know it.

But even as I write these words, I remind myself of other young people and adults of all ages—several of whom I have written about in this book—who continue to strive to make this planet a better place for everyone, and I know that for all my gloomy talk of the end of an age I still believe in the benevolent impulses they represent.

Things are bad, but, I remind myself, things have always been bad. History is a series of crises, of endings or approaching endings that gave way to new beginnings. The world is in constant flux, constantly in the grip of yin-yang imbalances, and the Dao that cannot be named see-saws back and forth. I know that, but I always seem to forget it, always have to remind myself that we can throw up our hands or we can continue on, doing the best we can.

Certainly those values and hopes, however battered by experience, are what my writing has been all about. In the poem "Goodbye To The Twentieth Century," I personify the departing century as an old woman, the mother of us all, whose house transforms into a museum where the hopes of all past centuries reside.

Goodbye to the Twentieth Century

Goodbye, Mother. Don't feel guilty. You didn't let us down; we let you down. You existed only for us, and we responded to your pampering and protectiveness by destroying almost everything that came within our grasp. And now with few regrets, most of us turn our back on you and leave you behind.

You had such hopes, such ambitions for us, and we disappointed you. Now you sit, a palsied old woman hunched on the corner of the kitchen, hardly more than a large shadow hovering on the wall, watching us, it must seem, celebrating your death, behaving like children concerned only with the party ahead, as we continually glance at the door on the day we finally leave home.

Don't be despondent. At the stroke of midnight, the house won't become a pumpkin rotting in a field. The instant the tower clock rolls twelve, the house will transform into a museum, which will carry in its depth the mementos and bric-a-brac of the century, like those children's rooms that mothers keep exactly as they were before the children left home for good.

And what a museum it will be—large enough to house biplanes with canvas wings, zeppelins and B-17s, jet fighters and rockets, and a complete collection of antique cars. Entire wings of the museum will be devoted to fashions in clothes and hairdos, and others to all sorts of weaponry. Exhibition halls will be dedicated to toys and games, portrait galleries to photographs of prime ministers and athletes and movie stars, and room after room to instruments of torture and to dioramas of plaster animals posed among exotic trees, all now extinct. Many of the exhibits will be painful reminders, to be sure—but at least some of your children and grandchildren will come to visit on weekends and rainy days.

And of those visitors, some, perhaps, will be curious, and stroll thoughtfully from room to room, and maybe, just maybe, they will find the chamber that sits in the center of the museum, surrounded by all the other rooms and connecting halls, like a throne room in the middle of a maze. You know the room, the one that glows in the darkness and is filled with display cases stretching into the shadows on all sides. Each case contains not butterflies but dreams in many shapes and hues, iridescent pinks and golds and blues that retain their brilliance and seem to wait in breathless slumber, as if they would take wing at the slightest prodding, flying from those glass cases that every hundred years are transported from the depths of one museum to another.

There is another poem, one of my favorites, that talks not so much in terms of hope but of renewal, the constant possibility of spiritual as well as physical renewal that I believe the world and art will always provide for us. The poem is entitled "The Library," and fittingly, I think, it ends this book.

■ ■ ■

Personally, I have said my goodbyes and hopefully left no emotional scars on anyone who has known me. Well, almost anyone. I have recognized at least a few of my faults, and those who have read this book thus far I'm sure have recognized many others. But in the end I am left with my work and the values it espouses. And what, in a nutshell, are those values, you ask? They are contained in the words of the commencement speech I gave in 1999, and which seem to be more pertinent now than they were then, and which I leave you with here.

The 1999 Santa Cruz High School Commencement Address

I want to thank *you*, the senior class of Santa Cruz High School, for inviting me to speak at your graduation. I'm especially honored because this is the last such ceremony at your school in the twentieth century, the end of the current millennium. However, for you, every one of you, today, June 10th, 1999, is not an ending but a beginning, a launching forth on your own, in many ways leaving your parents waving goodbye to you from a receding shore.

Because of my constant sense of your future in the new millennium and my existence in the old one, this talk has been difficult for me to prepare. I was born in the 1930s and graduated from high school into a now-forgotten war in the early 1950s. So my life has been spent grappling with the events and dilemmas of *this* century, the one your future is pulling away from. Let me put the problem as I saw it this way: for you, the future is a gleaming starship called *Enterprise* that is streaking where no man has gone before. For me at your age, the future was a propellor-driven airliner, and for my mother it was the leaking cattle boat on which she arrived in America as a little girl in 1914.

Do you understand my problem? I kept asking myself, "What can I, so much a representative of the ideas and traumas of *this* century, possibly tell you that you'd want to hear, or that would be relevant to your lives in the *next* century?"

After weeks of trying to solve this problem, I finally realized that all I could talk to you about today were the guidelines I've discovered for myself among this century's bric-a-brac, guidelines that have made my life meaningful and will hopefully touch some part of your imaginations.

One thing I knew early on: I was *not* going to talk to you about money. I'm not going to talk about your achieving material success aboard the starship *Private Enterprise*. You've heard, and are hearing about, that subject from all sides, I'm sure. Not that I have anything against money or material success. In fact, I wish every one of you careers and jobs that will allow you and yours to live sumptuous, comfortable lives. I sincerely do. But you see, very little of what has made my life worthwhile has had to do with money in the end. Luckily, I earned a livable salary as a teacher, but it was *being* a teacher, not earning the money for being one, that was worthwhile for me. And what was worthwhile was—well, let me tell you a story . . .

In June 1975, almost a quarter of a century ago, I found myself in Greece, Athens to be exact, ready to embark the next day on a ship to the island of Crete, where I'd been dreaming of going for years, because Crete is the site of one of the most intriguing of lost worlds, the world of the Minoans, who built vast stone palace-cities, with indoor plumbing and rainbow-colored murals on all the walls, at about the same time the Egyptians were erecting the grandest of their pyramids. You still don't hear much about the Minoans because their civilization wasn't unearthed until 1905, and the stipulation made to the Cretan people for his work by Sir Arthur Evans, the man who spent his life digging the Minoans' greatest city out of a hillside, was that their art treasures must never leave the island. Suffice it to say, many archaelogists believe that Crete is the lost continent of Atlantis.

So that's what I was thinking about that warm evening in Athens as I strolled along a street near Syntagmou Square, when suddenly I heard my name being called: "Mr. Marcus! Mr. Marcus! Awesome!"

And I turned to see two of my former students, boyfriend and girlfriend, who together had taken an English class from me that winter at Cabrillo. They were energetic, bright kids who had stumbled on me half a planet away from Santa Cruz, in a country not only where a different language was spoken but where all the street signs were written in a different alphabet. In other words, they were in a situation where anyone from home, even a teacher, is a welcome sight.

I greeted them with a big hello, took them to a pastry shop on the Square, and quickly found out that they'd just arrived and would be taking the ferry to Crete three days after me. I was surprised and delighted. "So you're going to see the ruins," I said.

They stared at me blankly.

"The Minoan ruins," I elaborated.

Still staring at me, the boy slowly shook his head, as if he had just realized the person he was talking to had sunstroke. "Nooo," he said uncertainly, "we're going there for the beaches. We've heard that Crete has the best beaches in Greece."

"Beaches?" I said incredulously. "You've come halfway around the world from the beaches of Santa Cruz just to go to the beaches in Greece?" And I launched into a tale of gold and jewels and massive stone palaces lifted three stories high on bright red columns—the history of the Minoans and their world—that went on for hours over dinner at a cheap taverna I knew, and then with the three of us trudging (rather tipsily, as I remember) below the hill of the Acropolis lit that night not only by floodlights but by a full moon rising over the temple ruins high above us.

The couple staggered away finally at about 2:00 in the morning, and the last I remember of them as they turned to go were their flashing eyes.

I never saw them again, but when I got back to Cabrillo that fall there was a postcard from Crete waiting in my mailbox. It was from them, with a picture of the island's most famous Minoan excavation on one side, and their names and one word on the other: *Awesome!*

I've long considered that "Awesome!" one of the best teacher evaluations I ever received, and its meaning, as I see it, is what I want to impart to you today.

That "Awesome!" let me know that the Crete my two ex-students found was different from the one they had originally sought. Even after our evening together, they could have gone to a Crete that was beaches and five-star hotels, but what the "Awesome!" said to me was that they had found an island and a people with traditions and a meaningful existence beyond what they had known; that they had connected their lives with the centuries—no, millenniums—of human endeavor called history that has brought us as a species to where we are now.

As I prepared this talk, all these thoughts tumbled through my mind, and I realized that the new millennium and this old century are connected, as everyone here—young, old, middle-aged; parents and children—are connected. If you will permit a poet his metaphors as silly as they may sound at first, we're all like body surfers riding the same cresting wave of Time into the future. Because that's how we travel in the end: not in cattle-boats, airliners, or starships named *Enterprise* this-or-that, but in our bodies, surfing our lives.

And so I decided to say to you today what I said to my two students a quarter of a century ago: learn and continue learning. Try to be as aware, sensitive, thinking, and feeling as you can every moment. In fact, be quiveringly alive to every instant of your existence, for whether you're rich or poor, everything around you is as laden with as many wonders as the vanished world of Crete or the legends of lost Atlantises.

That's how I've tried to spend my days. Oh, yes, I've had to work. But as often as I could I've filled my hours with ideas—with a passion for life, with news of who we as a species are and have been, and with an awareness of who I am as an inhabitant of the planet. Those pursuits have made my life worth living. And that is the simple message I not only have to tell you today, but which I urge you to use as a guideline for your lives.

But I want to go further than that. I also want to urge you to take up some kind of creative activity to go along with that endless learning—music, dance, painting, drama, writing—so you can express your responses to this great march of Time because 1) creating is a scintillating way to discover for yourself what you are thinking and feeling about the world, and 2) the creative act provides the greatest high you will ever know. Drugs be damned, as far as I'm concerned, not because they're illegal, but because they keep you from being aware, sharp, in control of your faculties, and able to hone them to a pitch where every dust mote floating through a sun-drenched window vibrates like an instrument in a symphony orchestra.

So experience the world as fully as you can, but realize there are dangers in such a pursuit, dangers that I think we as a society and a nation have fallen into, whether we pursue an existence of material comfort or the kind of personal awarenesss I have been talking about. You see, we can become so alive to every nuance of our changing moods, can feed so much on our whims and desires, can become so self-absorbed, that the world we experience becomes nothing more than a giant supermarket in which we constantly cry, "I want, I want, I want," and we forget that we live on this planet not only with plants and animals, air and water, but with other people—family, neighbors, fellow citizens, and fellow human beings all over the world.

There is another dangerous area of self-absorption I want to touch on, one that I was a victim of for years, and that is the nursing of self-pity, harboring resentments—in many cases for good reasons—against parents, siblings, and friends. I'm not telling you to forgive the wrongs done you. I just found I was getting bogged down in my resentments for things others had done to me when I was twelve years old. I wasn't growing, and one day I realized I was on my way to being a mental teenager all my life. From that day, being mature for me has meant getting beyond my childhood angers and resentments. Yes, I'd try to make my parents and friends understand how they had made me unhappy, but if they couldn't or wouldn't comprehend what I was saying, I'd reason that the problem was theirs, not mine, and I'd put it behind me, and go on my way.

Over the years I found several ways to avoid the dangers of self-involvement. Let me share the most important one with you. It's simple, actually: I realized I wasn't alone. This came about because by sharpening my sensibilities, I couldn't feel fully alive, no matter how aware or personally in tune with myself I was, unless I was also entering the lives of others through compassion and imagination. I had to be involved in making the world as livable for my fellow human beings as it was for me. And it went beyond that. Part of going to Crete for me, and I hope what I passed on to my two students, was a passion for learning by being open to the experiences of other lives and other ways of doing things. In my case creating—or recreating in art—allowed me to approach the lives of others as closely as I could.

Continually learning, using your imagination and compassion, and making the world ever new and full of joy for yourself and others—those have been the guidelines of my life, and I hope you may find them suitable or at least thought-provoking for your own lives in the next millennium.

That's all I have to say. But before I go, I'd like to do a little experiment, one that may seem a bit unorthodox for a commencement address. I'd like you to look at your lives from a different perspective. For this experiment, I don't want you to look toward the future; I want you to look toward the past.... Ready? ... Close your eyes.... Take a deep breath. Go on.... Good. Now imagine you are old. June 10, 1999 has long been a faded memory. It's the year 2050. Your children are grown, you're retired, most of you are almost seventy years old, and you're looking back on your lives much as I'm looking back on my life now. "Was my life successful?" you'll ask yourself. How will you answer that question? What are the guidelines you'll use to measure such a success?

Let me end my talk by telling you the conclusions *I've* come to on this question. First, I hope you'll be able to say, as I hope I can, that you'll leave this planet a little better than you found it; that you'll leave it with a minimum of regrets and guilt feelings because you've tried to keep the planet flourishing in a number of ways, not because you're environmentally or politically correct, but because you've realized this planet—its plants and animals, its winds and waves, and its human inhabitants—is your home.

And I hope you'll be able to look back on your lives with the satisfaction of knowing that you haven't compromised your ideals of right and wrong, or that you've compromised them on the fewest occasions—and at none of those times did you intentionally hurt another human being—because you've realized that more than anything else you've learned in this life, it is vitally important to be able to live with yourself if you want to be free of guilt and regrets, and that possibility becomes harder to accomplish the more you compromise your ideals.

As for hurting other human beings, sacrificing their feelings or their lives for your ambitions or desires or material comforts, ridiculing them for their religion, race, or ethnicity, or keeping them from living a life as good as yours—those are the hardest compromises to live with or forgive yourself for—not because you're a "do-gooder" or think you *should* help your fellow humans, but because you recognize that every person on this planet is your relative and deserves the chances you've had for a good life. For only when you acknowledge that all the people on earth are your brothers and sisters, and that you've worked in your own small way for them to lead the same life you have, will you be able to say, "I have lived a successful life!"

The Library

When I die I will be a book on a shelf in the library, and this notion doesn't bother me. I look forward to leaning against Melville and Montaigne, and I can't wait to stand in the ranks shoulder to shoulder with Rabelais, Sterne, and Twain, laughing with them and pausing now and again to listen entranced to sonorous Willie S.

Think of it: Cervantes and his knight proclaim the difficulties of chivalry a dozen rows above me, while next to them Chekhov sighs among his landowners and peasants and shakes his head. Just below them, Dostoyevsky rants about salvation and guilt, while on the shelf over mine, Li Bo, intoning words of reverence, raises a wine cup to the moon, and, dozens of rows farther down, Whitman, enraptured by it all, bellows his exaltation.

What more can one wish for than to be buried in such a mausoleum, where my friends and I will live forever, better prepared for eternity than a pharaoh in his tomb, since the words in books will provide us with all the earthly goods we'll need to live a luxurious afterlife.

Meanwhile, here, now, the words in books plant trees, launch rivers through forests and plains, and build cities crowded with skyscrapers and tenements. But what if the world, I often wonder, is only a ball of light we populate with phantoms of the mind and flickering longings of the heart? Then this edifice of books I choose to be my crypt exists only in my head and will not outlast the moment of my death. Not even a vacant lot, littered with fluttering pages and toppled walls, will remain.

That possibility doesn't disturb me: I've assumed from the start that the library continually disappears, as if, like an enchanted castle, it is under a spell from which it can be resurrected only when a boy or girl, man or woman, finds and steps inside its hidden entrance—that secret door which is always close at hand, yet, until we recognize it, we think is nothing more than the cover of a book.

Photo Credits

Every effort has been made to locate the photographers and get their permission to use their photographs in this volume.

SHIRLEY ANCHETA: Photo of Shirley Ancheta and Jeff Tagami, p. 365. Courtesy of Shirley Ancheta and Jeff Tagami.

MARYANN CARVER BORK: Photo of Raymond Carver, p. 282. Courtesy of Maryann Carver Bork.

DAN COYRO: Photos of Morton Marcus, pgs. xiii, 580. © Dan Coyro 1988.

DENG MING-DAO: Photo of Mort Marcus and Gary Young, p. 544. © Deng Ming-Dao.

LEONARD GARDNER: Photo of Gina Berriault, p. 270. © Leonard Gardner.

WILLIAM GRANT: Photo of Donna Mekis, p. 373. © William Grant.

GARY GRIGGS: Photo of Santa Cruz writers, p. 227. © Gary Griggs.

DIANNE HANZLICEK: Photo of C.G. Hanzlicek, p. 459. © Dianne Hanzlicek.

DANIEL HARPER: Photos of Joseph Stroud, p. 229; Kirby Wilkins, p. 479. Photos © Daniel Harper.

DAVID HARSANY: Photo of Lou Harrison, p. 439. © David Harsany.

JULIA JACOBSON: Photo of Stephen Kessler, p. 477. © Julia Jacobson.

NORMAN LEZIN: Photos of James D, Houston, p. 164; Jeanne and James D. Houston, p. 259. © Norman Lezin.

ALICE LOGAN: Photo of John Logan, p. 191. Courtesy of Alice Logan.

GERARD MALANGA: Photos of George Hitchcock, p. 213; Andrei Codrescu, p. 397; Charles Simic, p. 295; and Robert Bly, p. 301. © Gerard Malanga.

MORTON MARCUS: Photos of Greece, pgs. 324–356; Jana and Valerie Marcus, pgs. 409, 410; Joseph Stroud and Aborigine painters, p. 501. © Morton Marcus.

MORTON MARCUS AND DONNA MEKIS: Photos of Croatia, pgs. 548-554. © Morton Marcus and Donna Mekis.

JANA MARCUS: Photos of Al Young, 314; wedding photos of Donna Mekis and Morton Marcus, pgs 375, 376; William Grant, Ed and Inge Bower, p. 407; Stan and Ann Rice, p. 388; Breakfast Club, p. 521; Jim Houston and Morton Marcus, p. 555; Joe Stroud and Morton Marcus, p. 561. © Jana Marcus.

VALERIE MARCUS: Photo of Donna Mekis, Morton Marcus, and Zachary Marcus Ramshur, p. 525. © Valerie Marcus.

BOB McCLURG: Photo of Leonard Gardner, p. 268. © Bob McClurg.

DAVID McGUIRE: Photos of Morton Marcus and Donna Mekis, p. iii; Bradley Smith, p. 414. © by David McGuire.

DONNA MEKIS: Photos of Gary Brown and Morton Marcus, p. 275; Nick Galli and Morton Marcus, p. 378; Joseph Stroud, Kirby Wilkins, and Morton Marcus, p. 528; Valerie and Jana Marcus, and Nick Galli, p. 524; Rae and Morton Marcus, p. 528; Prague, pgs. 548-554. © Donna Mekis.

DANIEL MEYERS: Photo of Bert Meyers, p. 564.

N.Y. DAILY NEWS: Front page of *The New York Daily News,* p. 12. Courtesy of *The N. Y. Daily News.* © *The N. Y. Daily News.*

MARY-JO O'SHEA: Photo of Lewis Turco, p. 136. © Mary-Jo O'Shea.

ROBERT PETERSON ESTATE: Photo of Robert Peterson, p. 201. Courtesy of the estate of Robert Peterson.

ELIOT ROCHOZ ROBERTS: Photo of Mort Marcus, Clemens Starck, Joseph Stroud, and Gary Young, p. 203. © Eliot Rocholz Roberts.

STEVE RAMSHUR: Carnegie Hall photos, pgs. 568, 569. © Steve Ramshur.

VERN RUTSALA: Photos of Vern Rutsala, pgs. 106, 516. Courtesy of Vern Rutsala.

PAUL SCHRAUB: Photos of Lawson Inada, p. 137; Jana and Valerie Marcus, p. 360; the crew of *The Eight Ecstasies of Yaeko Iwasaki* and Sara Wilbourne, pgs. 469, 470; Greg Keith, p. 558; Nathaniel Mackey, p. 561. Photos © Paul Schraub.

NAOMI SCHWARTZ: Photo of Jack Marshall, p. 390. © Naomi Schwartz.

MARTIN SMITH: Photo of Morton Marcus, p. 226. © Martin Smith.

THOMAS VICTOR: Photo of Czeslaw Milosz, p. 237. © Thomas Victor.

GARY WEBER: Photo of Clemens Starck, p. 202. © Gary Weber.

PEGGY YOUNG: Photo of Gary Young, p. 453. © Peggy Young.

PHOTOGRAPHERS UNKNOWN: Donald Justice, p. 131; Shirley Kaufman, p. 218; Vasko Popa, p. 244; William Everson, p. 381; Jack Gilbert, p. 394; George Ow, Jr., p. 433; Tom Mescher, p. 452; Dennis Schmitz, p. 458.

Poem Permissions

Every effort has been made to get permission from publishers and/or poets for the use of the poems in this volume.

SHIRLEY ANCHETA: "Carabao" by Shirley Ancheta. Used by permission of Shirley Ancheta.

LENNART BRUCE: "Dawn" ("December 19") and "Out Walking" ("December 20") by Lennart Bruce from *The Mullioned Window* by Lennart Bruce. Kayak Book. Copyright 1970 by Lennart Bruce. Used by permission of Sonja Bruce.

RAYMOND CARVER: "Happiness" and the excerpt from "In 2020" by Raymond Carver from *All of Us* by Raymond Carver. Albert A. Knopf. Copyright 1998 by Raymond Carver. Used by permission of Albert A. Knopf.

ANDREI CODRESCU: "Deadline" by Andrei Codrescu from

Zombification by Andrei Codrescu. Picador USA. Copyright 1994 by Andrei Codrescu. Used by permission of Picador USA. Excerpts from *Disappearance of The Outside* by Andrei Codrescu. Addison Wesley. Copyright 1990 by Andrei Codrescu. Used by permission of Addison Wesley.

WILLIAM EVERSON: "In All These Years" by William Everson from *The Veritable Years* by William Everson. Black Sparrow Press. Copyright 1978 William Everson. Used by permission of Black Sparrow Press. Everson's memory of the Robert Bly incident is from "The Talking Poetry Interview" reprinted from Lee Bartlett's *Talking Poetry: Conversations in the Workshop with Contemporary Poets,* University of New Mexico Press. Copyright Lee Bartlett. Used by permission of The University of New Mexico Press.

GERALD FLEMING: "The Daily Spanking, The Child Next Door" by Gerald Fleming from *Swimmer Climbing Onto Shore* by Gerald Fleming. Sixteen Rivers Press. Copyright 2005 by Gerald Fleming. Used by permission of Sixteen Rivers Press.

JACK GILBERT: "A Brief For The Defense" and the excerpt from "Halloween" by Jack Gilbert from *Refusing Heaven* by Jack Gilbert. Albert A. Knopf. Copyright 2005 by Jack Gilbert. Used by permission of Albert A. Knopf.

RAY GONZALEZ: "The Bird of Dreams" by Ray Gonzalez from *Human Crying Daisies: Prose Poems* by Ray Gonzalez. Red Hen Press. Copyright 2003 by Ray Gonzalez. Used by permission of Red Hen Press. "Acoma, New Mexico" by Ray Gonzalez from *The Religion of Hands: Prose Poems and Flash Fictions* by Ray Gonzalez. University of Arizona Press. Copyright 2005 by Ray Gonzalez. Used by Permission of The University of Arizona Press.

GREGORY HALL: "All The Women," "I Love/The Snakes" and the excerpt from "It Is Morning" by Gregory Hall from *Flame People* by Greory Hall. Green House Press. Copyright 1977 by Gregory Hall. Used by permission of Gregory Hall.

Mountain by Joseph Stroud. Copper Canyon Press. Copyright 1994 by Joseph Stroud. Used by permission of Copper Canyon Press.

ROBERT SWARD: "Uncle Dog: The Poet at 9" by Robert Sward from *Half A Life's History* by Robert Sward. Coffee House Press. Copyright 1995 by Robert Sward. Used by Permission of Coffee House Press.

JEFF TAGAMI: "Message" by Jeff Tagami from *Bamboo Ridge Press 25ᵗʰ Anniversary Issue*. Used by permission of Jeff Tagami.

LEWIS TURCO: "Burning The News" by Lewis Turco from *The Shifting Web: New and Selected Poems* by Lewis Turco. University of Arkansas Press. Copyright 1989 by Lewis Turco. Used by permission of the University of Arkansas Press.

Al YOUNG: "A Little More Traveling Music" by Al Young from *Heaven: Collected Poems: 1956-1990* by Al Young. Creative Arts Book Company. Copyright 1990 by Al Young. Used by permission of Al Young.

GARY YOUNG: "The Doctor Says." "She Took My Two Hands In Hers, "The Baby Grabs At Sunshine," "Two Girl Were Struck By Lightning," and "In New Jersey" by Gary Young from *No Other Life* by Gary Young. Hey Day Press. Copyright 2005 by Gary Young. Used by permission of Hey Day Press.

About the Author

Morton Marcus is the author of ten volumes of poetry and one novel, including *The Santa Cruz Mountain Poems, Pages from a Scrapbook of Immigrants,* and recently, *Moments Without Names: New & Selected Prose Poems,* and *Shouting Down the Silence: Verse Poems 1988–2001.* In 2007, he published a new volume of prose poems, *Pursuing the Dream Bone.* He has had more than 450 poems published in literary journals, his work has been selected to appear in over 85 anthologies, and he has read his poems and taught creative writing workshops at universities throughout the nation and Europe. Marcus taught English and film at Cabrillo College for 30 years before his retirement in 1998. In 1999, he was selected to be Santa Cruz County Artist of the Year, and in 2007 he was a recipient of a Gail Rich Award for his contributions to Santa Cruz culture. For 22 years, Marcus has been the co-host of *The Poetry Show,* the longest running poetry radio program in the nation. A film historian and critic as well as poet, his reviews appear regularly in West Coast newspapers, and for the past nine years he has been the co-host of a television film review show called *Cinema Scene,* which broadcasts in the San Francisco Bay area and is podcast internationally at cinemascene.org. For more than eighteen years he has served on the steering committee of the Pacific Rim Film Festival, and he has taken part in panel discussions on literature and film at the John Steinbeck Center. His website is **www.mortonmarcus.com**.